FINANCIAL MODELING

Simon Benninga

with a section on Visual Basic for Applications
by Benjamin Czaczkes

SECOND EDITION

The MIT Press
Cambridge, Massachusetts
London, England

Second Printing, 2001

This book was set in Times Roman by Omegatype Typography, Inc. and was printed and bound
in the United States of America.

Library of Congress Cataloging-in-Publication Data

Benninga, Simon,
    Financial modeling / Simon Benninga ; with a section on
  Visual Basic for Applications by Benjamin Czaczkes.—2nd ed.
        p.   cm.
  Includes bibliographical references and index.
  ISBN 0-262-02482-9
      1. Finance—Mathematical models.   2. Excel—Finance applications.
  3. Microsoft Visual Basic for applications.   I. Czaczkes, Benjamin.
  II. Title.
  HG173 .B46   2000
  332.01'5118—dc21   00-035473

To our parents: Helen and Noach Benninga, Esther and Alfred Czaczkes

Contents

Preface

The purpose of this book remains to provide a "cookbook" for implementing common financial models in Excel. This edition has been expanded by six additional chapters, covering financial calculations, cost of capital, value at risk (VaR), real options, early exercise boundaries, and term-structure modeling. There is also an additional technical chapter containing a potpourri of Excel hints.

I am indebted to a number of people (in addition to those mentioned in the previous preface) for help and suggestions: Andrew A. Adamovich, Yoni Aziz, Roman Weissman Bermann, Michael Giacomo Bertolino, Enrico Camerini, Roy Carson, John Carson, Philippe Charlier, Michael J. Clarke, Beni Daniel, Moacyr Dutra, Hector Tassinari Eldridge, Shlomy Elias, Raz Gilad, Nir Gluzman, Doron Greenberg, Hitoshi Hibino, Foo Siat Hong, Russell W. Judson, Rick Labs, Allen Lee, Paul Legerer, Guoli Li, Moti Marcus, Jackie Rosner, Steve Rubin, Dvir Sabah, Roger Shelor, Maja Sliwinski, Bob Taggart, Maurry Tamarkin, Sandra van Balen, Ubbo Wiersema, Khurshid Zaynutdinov, and Eric Zivot. I also want to thank my editors, who again have been a great help: Nancy Lombardi, Peter Reinhart, Victoria Richardson, and Terry Vaughn.

As always I welcome suggestions and comments.

Simon Benninga
http://finance.wharton.upenn.edu/~benninga
benninga@post.tau.ac.il

Preface to the First Edition

Like its predecessor *Numerical Techniques in Finance,* this book presents some important financial models and shows how they can be solved numerically and/or simulated using Excel. In this sense this is a finance "cookbook"; like any cookbook, it gives recipes with a list of ingredients and instructions for making and baking. As any cook knows, a recipe is just a starting point; having followed the recipe a number of times, you can think of your own variations and make the results suit your tastes and needs.

Financial Modeling covers standard financial models in the areas of corporate finance, financial statement simulation, portfolio problems, options, portfolio insurance, duration, and immunization. Clear and concise explanations are provided in each case for the implementation of the models using Excel. Very little theory is offered except where necessary to understand the numerical implementations.

While Excel is often inappropriate for high-level, industrial-strength calculations (portfolios are an example), it is an excellent tool for understanding the computational intricacies involved in financial modeling. It is often the case that the fullest understanding of the models comes by calculating them, and Excel is one of the most accessible and powerful tools available for this purpose.

Along the way a lot of students, colleagues, and friends (these are nonexclusive categories) have helped me with advice and comments. In particular I would like to thank Olivier Blechner, Miryam Brand, Elizabeth Caulk, John Caulk, Benjamin Czaczkes, John Ferrari, John P. Flagler, Kunihiko Higashi, Julia Hynes, Don Keim, Anthony Kim, Ken Kunimoto, Philippe Nore, Nir Sharabi, Mark Thaler, Terry Vaughn, and Xiaoge Zhou.

Finally, my thanks go to a wonderful set of editors: Nancy Lombardi, Peter Reinhart, Victoria Richardson, and Terry Vaughn.

I   Corporate Finance Models

The six chapters that open *Financial Modeling* cover some problems in corporate finance that are highly numerically intensive. Chapters 1 and 2 are a review of some finance basics. Chapter 1 is an introduction to basic financial calculations using Excel. Almost all of the applications discussed center on variations of the discounted-cash-flow method. The cost of capital, discussed in Chapter 2, is the rate at which corporate cash flows are discounted to arrive at enterprise value. Calculating this rate is not trivial and involves a combination of some theoretical models and numerical computation.

Chapter 3 shows how to build pro forma models, which simulate the corporate income statement and balance sheets. Pro forma models are at the heart of many corporate finance applications, including business plans, credit analyses, and valuations. The models require a mixture of finance, accounting, and Excel. In Chapter 4 we use pro forma models to do a valuation of a firm; the simple example we develop is typical of an exercise that accompanies many merger and acquisition valuations.

Chapters 5 and 6 discuss the financial analysis of leasing. In Chapter 5 we concentrate on the basic lease/purchase decision using the equivalent-loan method. An appendix to Chapter 5 discusses some tax and accounting considerations relating to leases. Chapter 6 discusses the financial analysis of leveraged lease arrangements, including a discussion of the multiple-phases method of Statement 13 of the Financial Accounting Standards Board (FASB 13). The multiple-phases-method rate of return is a hybrid internal rate of return (IRR), and Excel can easily be used to calculate this return.

1 Basic Financial Calculations

1.1 Introduction

This chapter aims to give you some finance basics and their Excel implementation. If you have had a good introductory course in finance, most of the topics will probably be superfluous.

This chapter covers the following:

- Net present value (NPV)
- Internal rate of return (IRR)
- Future value
- Pension and accumulation problems
- Continuously compounded interest

Almost all financial problems center on finding the *value today* of a series of *cash receipts over time.* The cash receipts (or cash flows, as we will call them) may be certain or uncertain. In this chapter we analyze the values of nonrisky cash flows—future receipts that we will receive with absolute certainty.

The basic concept to which we will return over and over is the concept of *opportunity cost.* Opportunity cost is the return that would be required of an investment to make it a viable alternative to other, similar, investments.[1] As illustrated in this chapter, when we calculate the net present value, we use the investment's opportunity cost as a discount rate. When we calculate the internal rate of return, we compare the calculated return to the investment's opportunity cost to judge its value.

1.2 Present Value (PV) and Net Present Value (NPV)

Both concepts, present value and net present value, are related to the value *today* of a set of future anticipated cash flows. As an example, suppose we are

---

1. In the financial literature you will find many synonyms for *opportunity cost,* among them *discount rate, cost of capital,* and *interest rate.* When it is applied to risky cash flows (as in the next chapter), we will sometimes call the opportunity cost the risk-adjusted discount rate (RADR) or the weighted average cost of capital (WACC).

valuing an investment that promises $100 per year at the end of this and the next four years. We suppose that there is no doubt that this series of five payments of $100 each will actually be paid. If a bank would pay us an annual interest rate of 10 percent on a five-year deposit, then this 10 percent is the investment's opportunity cost, the alternative benchmark return to which we want to compare the investment. We may calculate the value of the investment by discounting its cash flows using this opportunity cost as a discount rate:

	A	B	C	D
2	Discount rate	10%		
3	Present value	$379.08	<-- =NPV(B2,B7:B11)	
4				
5		Cash		
6	Year	flow		
7	1	100		
8	2	100		
9	3	100		
10	4	100		
11	5	100		

The *present value* (PV) of $379.08 is the value today of the investment.

Suppose this investment was being sold for $400. Clearly it would not be worth its purchase price, since—given the alternative return (discount rate) of 10 percent—the investment is worth only $379.08. The *net present value* (NPV) is the applicable concept here. Denoting by *r* the discount rate applicable to the investment, the NPV is calculated as follows:

$$NPV = CF_0 + \sum_{t=1}^{N} \frac{CF_t}{(1 + r)^t}$$

where CF_t is the investment's cash flow at time t and CF_0 is today's cash flow:

	F	G	H	I	J
2	Discount rate	10%			
3	Net present value	-20.92	<-- =G7+NPV(G2,G8:G12)		
4					
5		Cash			
6	Year	flow			
7	0	-400			
8	1	100			
9	2	100			
10	3	100			
11	4	100			
12	5	100			

A Note about Nomenclature

Excel's language about discounted cash flows differs somewhat from the standard finance nomenclature. Excel uses the letters NPV to denote the present value (*not* the net present value) of a series of cash flows.

To calculate the finance *net present value* of a series of cash flows using Excel, we have to calculate the *present value* of the future cash flows (using the Excel **NPV** function) and subtract from this present value the time-zero cash flow. (This is often the cost of the asset in question.)

1.3   The Internal Rate of Return (IRR) and Loan Tables

We continue with the same example. Suppose that we indeed paid $400.00 for this series of cash flows. The *internal rate of return* (IRR) is defined as the compound rate of return r that makes the NPV equal to zero:

$$CF_0 + \sum_{t=1}^{N} \frac{CF_t}{(1+r)^t} = 0$$

Excel's function **IRR** will solve this problem; note that the IRR includes as arguments *all* of the cash flows of the investment, including the first (in this case negative) cash flow of -400:

	A	B	C	D
15	IRR	7.931%	<-- =IRR(B19:B24)	
16	NPV	-20.92		
17		Cash		
18	Year	flow		
19	0	-400		
20	1	100		
21	2	100		
22	3	100		
23	4	100		
24	5	100		

The IRR is the compound *rate of return paid by the investment.* To understand this point fully, it helps to make the following table:

	E	F	G	H	I	J	K
15	LOAN TABLE			Division of payment			
16				between interest			
17	=-B19	Principal	Payment	and return of principal			
18		at beginning	at end				
19	year	of year	of year	Interest	Principal		
20	1	400.00	100	31.72	68.28	=G20-H20	
21	2	331.72	100	26.31	73.69		
22	3	258.03	100	20.46	79.54		
23	4	178.50	100	14.16	85.84		
24	5	92.65	100	7.35	92.65		
25							
26	=F20-I20		=$B$15*F20				
27							

The *loan table* divides each of the payments made by the asset into an interest component and a return-of-principal component. The interest component at the end of each year is the IRR times the principal balance at the beginning of that year. Notice that the principal at the beginning of the last year ($92.65 in the example) exactly equals the return of principal at the end of that year.

We can actually use the loan table to find the internal rate of return. Consider an investment costing $1,000 today that pays off at the end of years 1, 2, ..., 5.

As the following loan table shows, the IRR of this investment is larger than 15 percent:

	A	B	C	D	E	F	G
2	Cost	1000					
3	IRR?	15.00%					
4							
5							
6	**LOAN TABLE**			**Division of payment**			
7				**between interest**			
8	=B2	**Principal**	**Payment**	**and return of principal**			
9		**at beginning**	**at end**				
10	**Year**	**of year**	**of year**	**Interest**	**Principal**		
11	1	1000.00	300	150.00	150.00		=C11-D11
12	2	850.00	200	127.50	72.50		
13	3	777.50	150	116.63	33.38		
14	4	744.13	600	111.62	488.38		
15	5	255.74	900	38.36	861.64		
16	6	-605.89					
17	=B11-E11		=$B$3*B11				
18							

Note that we have added an extra cell (B16) to this example. If the interest rate in cell B3 is indeed the IRR, then cell B16 should be 0. We can now use Excel's **Goal Seek** (found on the **Tools** menu) to calculate the IRR:

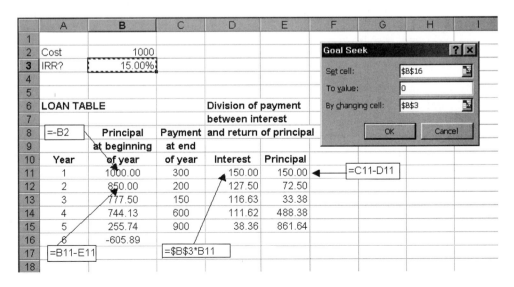

You can see the result in the following display:

	A	B	C	D	E	F	G
2	Cost	1000					
3	IRR?	24.44%					
4							
5							
6	LOAN TABLE			Division of payment			
7				between interest			
8	=-B2	Principal	Payment	and return of principal			
9		at beginning	at end				
10	Year	of year	of year	Interest	Principal		
11	1	1000.00	300	244.36	55.64		=C11-D11
12	2	944.36	200	230.76	-30.76		
13	3	975.13	150	238.28	-88.28		
14	4	1063.41	600	259.86	340.14		
15	5	723.26	900	176.74	723.26		
16	6	0.00					
17	=B11-E11		=$B$3*B11				
18							

Of course, we could have simplified life by just using the **IRR** function:

	A	B	C	D
22	Year	Cash flow		
23	0	-1000		
24	1	300		
25	2	200		
26	3	150		
27	4	600		
28	5	900		
29				
30	IRR	24.44%	<-- =IRR(B23:B28)	

1.4 Multiple Internal Rates of Return

Sometimes a series of cash flows has more than one IRR. In the next example we can tell that the cash flows in cells B8:B13 have two IRRs, since the NPV graph crosses the *x*-axis twice.

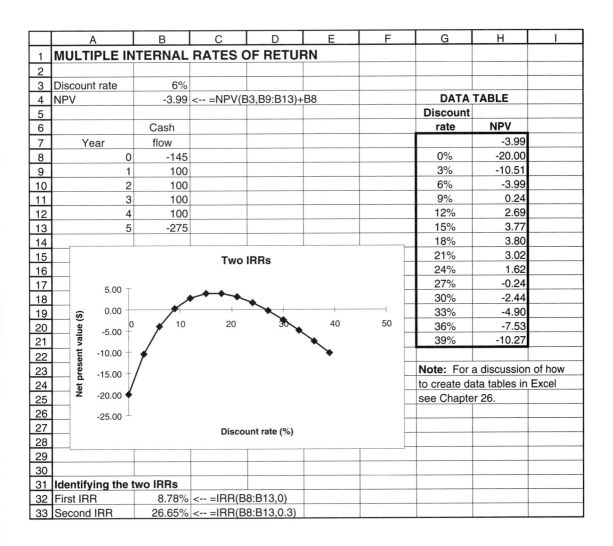

	A	B	C	D	E	F	G	H	I
1	**MULTIPLE INTERNAL RATES OF RETURN**								
2									
3	Discount rate	6%							
4	NPV	-3.99	<-- =NPV(B3,B9:B13)+B8				**DATA TABLE**		
5							**Discount**		
6		Cash					**rate**	**NPV**	
7	Year	flow						-3.99	
8	0	-145					0%	-20.00	
9	1	100					3%	-10.51	
10	2	100					6%	-3.99	
11	3	100					9%	0.24	
12	4	100					12%	2.69	
13	5	-275					15%	3.77	
14							18%	3.80	
15							21%	3.02	
16							24%	1.62	
17							27%	-0.24	
18							30%	-2.44	
19							33%	-4.90	
20							36%	-7.53	
21							39%	-10.27	
22									
23							**Note:** For a discussion of how		
24							to create data tables in Excel		
25							see Chapter 26.		
26									
27									
28									
29									
30									
31	**Identifying the two IRRs**								
32	First IRR	8.78%	<-- =IRR(B8:B13,0)						
33	Second IRR	26.65%	<-- =IRR(B8:B13,0.3)						

Excel's **IRR** function allows us to add an extra argument that will help us find both IRRs. Instead of writing IRR(B8:B13), we write IRR(B8:B13,guess). The argument **guess** is a starting point for the algorithm which Excel uses to find the IRR; by adjusting the **guess,** we can identify both the IRRs. Cells B32 and B33 give an illustration.

There are two things we should note about this procedure.

1. The argument **guess** merely has to be close to the IRR; it is not unique. For example by setting the guesses equal to 0.1 and 0.5, we will still get the same IRRs:

	A	B	C	D
31	**Identifying the two IRRs**			
32	First IRR	8.78%	<-- =IRR(B8:B13,0.1)	
33	Second IRR	26.65%	<-- =IRR(B8:B13,0.5)	
34				

2. In order to identify the number and the approximate value of the IRRs, it helps greatly to graph the NPV of the investment as a function of various discount rates (as we have already done). The internal rates of return are then the points where the graph crosses the *x*-axis, and the approximate location of these points should be used as the guesses in the IRR function.[2]

From a purely technical point of view, a set of cash flows can have multiple IRRs only if it has at least two changes of sign. Many "typical" cash flows have only one change of sign. Consider, for example, the cash flows from purchasing a bond having a 10 percent coupon, a face value of $1,000, and eight more years to maturity. If the current market price of the bond is $800, then the stream of cash flows changes signs only once (from negative in year 0 to positive in years 1–8). Thus there is only one IRR:

	A	B	C	D	E	F	G	H	I	J	K	L
1	**BOND CASH FLOWS**											
2												
3	Year	Cash flow				Data table: Effect of		Table header				
4	0	-800				discount rate on NPV		=NPV(F5,B5:B12)+B4				
5	1	100					1000.00					
6	2	100				0%	1000.00		NPV of Bond Cash Flows			
7	3	100				2%	786.04					
8	4	100				4%	603.96					
9	5	100				6%	448.39					
10	6	100				8%	314.93					
11	7	100				10%	200.00					
12	8	1100				12%	100.65					
13						14%	14.45					
14	IRR	14.36%	<-- =IRR(B4:B12)			16%	-60.62					
15						18%	-126.21					
16						20%	-183.72					
17												
18												

1.5   Flat Payment Schedules

Another problem: You take a loan for $10,000 at an interest rate of 7 percent per year. The bank wants you to make a series of payments that will pay off the loan and the interest over six years. We can use Excel's **PMT** function to determine how much should each annual payment be:

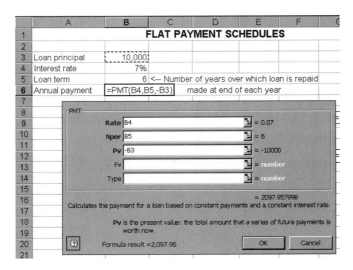

	A	B	C	D	E	F	G
1			FLAT PAYMENT SCHEDULES				
2							
3	Loan principal	10,000					
4	Interest rate	7%					
5	Loan term	6	<-- Number of years over which loan is repaid				
6	Annual payment	=PMT(B4,B5,-B3)	made at end of each year				
7							

PMT

Rate	B4	= 0.07
Nper	B5	= 6
Pv	-B3	= -10000
Fv		= number
Type		= number

= 2097.957998

Calculates the payment for a loan based on constant payments and a constant interest rate.

Pv is the present value: the total amount that a series of future payments is worth now.

Formula result = 2,097.96   OK   Cancel

Notice that we have put "PV"—Excel's nomenclature for the initial loan principal—with a minus sign. Otherwise Excel returns a negative payment (a minor irritant).

You can confirm that this answer is correct by creating a loan table:

	A	B	C	D	E	F	G	H
1			FLAT PAYMENT SCHEDULES					
2								
3	Loan principal	10,000						
4	Interest rate	7%						
5	Loan term	6	<-- Number of years over which loan is repaid					
6	Annual payment	2,097.96	<-- To be made at end of each year					
7								
8			Principal at	Payment	Split payment into:		=$B$4*C11	
9		Year	beginning	at end of		Return of		
10			of year	year	Interest	principal		
11		1	10,000.00	2,097.96	700.00	1,397.96		
12		2	8,602.04	2,097.96	602.14	1,495.82	=D11-E11	
13		3	7,106.23	2,097.96	497.44	1,600.52		
14		4	5,505.70	2,097.96	385.40	1,712.56		
15		5	3,793.15	2,097.96	265.52	1,832.44		
16		6	1,960.71	2,097.96	137.25	1,960.71		

=C11-F11

1.6   Future Values and Applications

We start with a triviality. Suppose you deposit $1,000 in an account, leaving it there for 10 years. Suppose the account draws annual interest of 10 percent. How much will you have at the end of 10 years? The answer, as shown in the following spreadsheet, is $2,593.74.

	A	B	C	D	E	F
1		SIMPLE FUTURE VALUE				
2						
3	Interest	10%				
4						
5	Year	Account	Interest	Total in		
6		balance	earned	account		
7		beg. year	during year	end of year		
8	0	1,000.00	100.00	1,100.00	<-- =C8+B8	
9	1	1,100.00	110.00	1,210.00		
10	2	1,210.00	121.00	1,331.00	=$B$3*B8	
11	3	1,331.00	133.10	1,464.10		
12	4	1,464.10	146.41	1,610.51		
13	5	1,610.51	161.05	1,771.56		
14	6	1,771.56	177.16	1,948.72		
15	7	1,948.72	194.87	2,143.59		
16	8	2,143.59	214.36	2,357.95		
17	9	2,357.95	235.79	2,593.74		
18	10	2,593.74				
19				=D8		
20						
21	A simpler way		2593.74	<-- =1000*(1+B3)^10		

As cell C21 shows, you don't need all these complicated calculations: The *future value* of $1,000 in 10 years at 10 percent per year is given by

$$FV = 1,000 * (1 + 10\%)^{10} = 2,593.74$$

Now consider the following, slightly more complicated, problem: Again, you intend to open a savings account. Your initial deposit of $1,000 this year will be followed by a similar deposit at the beginning of years 1, 2, ..., 9. If the account earns 10 percent per year, how much will you have in the account at the start of year 10?

This problem is easily modeled in Excel:

	A	B	C	D	E	F	G
			FUTURE VALUE WITH ANNUAL DEPOSITS				
3	Interest	10%					
4							
5	Year	Account	Deposit at	Interest	Total in		
6		balance	beginning	earned	account		
7		beg. year	of year	during year	end of year		
8	0	0.00	1,000	100.00	1,100.00	<-- =D8+C8+B8	
9	1	1,100.00	1,000	210.00	2,310.00		
10	2	2,310.00	1,000	331.00	3,641.00	=$B$3*(C8+B8)	
11	3	3,641.00	1,000	464.10	5,105.10		
12	4	5,105.10	1,000	610.51	6,715.61		
13	5	6,715.61	1,000	771.56	8,487.17		
14	6	8,487.17	1,000	948.72	10,435.89		
15	7	10,435.89	1,000	1,143.59	12,579.48		
16	8	12,579.48	1,000	1,357.95	14,937.42		
17	9	14,937.42	1,000	1,593.74	17,531.17		
18	10	17,531.17					
19			=E8				
20							
21		Future value			$17,531.17	<-- =FV(B3,A18,-1000,,1)	

Thus the answer is that we will have $17,531.17 in the account at the beginning of year 10. This same answer can be represented as a formula that sums the future values of each deposit.

$$\text{Total at beginning of year 10} = 1,000 * (1 + 10\%)^{10} + 1,000 * (1 + 10\%)^{9}$$
$$+ \cdots + 1,000 * (1 + 10\%)^{1}$$
$$= \sum_{t=1}^{10} 1,000 * (1 + 10\%)^{t}$$

An Excel Function   Note from cell D21 that Excel has a function **FV** that gives this sum. The dialog box brought up by **FV** is the following:

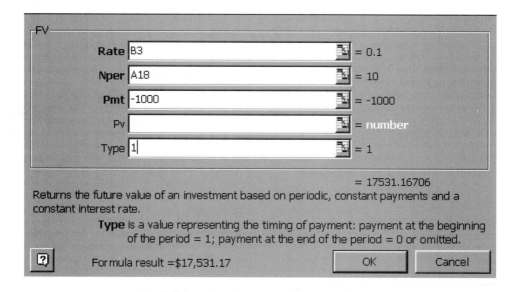

We note three things about this function:

1. For positive deposits FV returns a negative number. There is an explanation for why this function is programmed in this way, but basically this outcome is an irritant. To avoid negative numbers, we have put the **Pmt** in as −1,000.

2. The line **Pv** in the dialog box refers to a situation where the account has some initial value other than 0 when the series of deposits is made. In this example, this line has been left blank, indicating that the initial account value is zero.

3. As noted in the picture, "Type" (either 1 or 0) refers to whether the deposit is made at the beginning or the end of each period.

1.7 A Pension Problem—Complicating the Future Value Problem

A typical exercise follows. You are 55 years old and intend to retire at age 60. To make your retirement easier, you intend to start a retirement account.

- At the beginning of each of years 0, 1, 2, ..., 4 (i.e., starting today and for each of the next four years), you intend to make a deposit into the retirement account. You think that the account will earn 8 percent per year.

- After retirement at age 60, you anticipate living eight more years.[3] During each of these years you want to withdraw $30,000 from your retirement account. Of course, account balances will continue to earn 8 percent.

How much should you deposit annually in the account? The following spreadsheet fragment shows how easily you can go wrong in this kind of problem—in this case, you've calculated that in order to provide $30,000 per year for eight years, you need to contribute $240,000/5 = $48,000 in each of the first five years. As the spreadsheet shows, you'll end up with a lot of money at the end of eight years! (The reason—you've ignored the powerful effects of compound interest. If you set the interest rate in the spreadsheet equal to 0 percent, you'll see that you're right.)

	A	B	C	D	E	F	G	H
1				A RETIREMENT PROBLEM				
2								
3	Interest	8%						
4	Annual deposit	48,000						
5	Annual retirement withdrawal	30,000				=$B$3*(D10+C10)		
6								
7			Year	Account	Deposit	Interest	Total in	
8				balance	at beginning	earned	account	
9				beg. year	of year	during year	end of year	
10			0	0.00	48,000	3,840.00	51,840.00	<-- =E10+D10+C10
11			1	51,840.00	48,000	7,987.20	107,827.20	
12			2	107,827.20	48,000	12,466.18	168,293.38	
13			3	168,293.38	48,000	17,303.47	233,596.85	
14			4	233,596.85	48,000	22,527.75	304,124.59	
15			5	304,124.59	-30,000	21,929.97	296,054.56	
16			6	296,054.56	-30,000	21,284.36	287,338.93	
17			7	287,338.93	-30,000	20,587.11	277,926.04	
18			8	277,926.04	-30,000	19,834.08	267,760.12	
19			9	267,760.12	-30,000	19,020.81	256,780.93	
20			10	256,780.93	-30,000	18,142.47	244,923.41	
21			11	244,923.41	-30,000	17,193.87	232,117.28	
22			12	232,117.28	-30,000	16,169.38	218,286.66	

---

3. Of course you're going to live much longer! And I wish you good health! The dimensions of this problem have been chosen to make it fit nicely on a page.

There are two ways to solve this problem. The first involves Excel's Solver. This can be found on the Tools menu.[4]

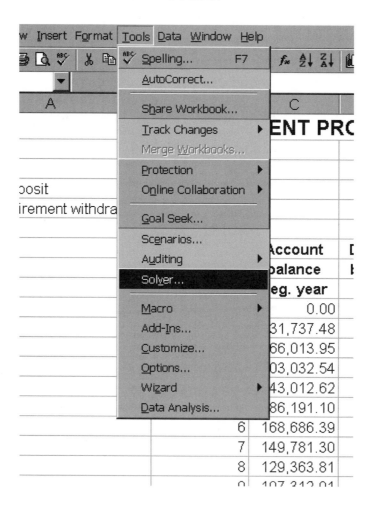

---

4.   If the Solver does not appear on the Tools menu, then you have to load it. Go **Tools|Add-Ins** and click **Solver Add-In** on the list of programs. Note that you could also use the **Goal Seek** tool to solve this problem. For simple problems such as this one, there is not much difference between the Solver and Goal Seek; the one (not inconsiderable) advantage of the Solver is that it remembers its previous arguments, so that if you bring it up again on the same spreadsheet, you can see what you did in the previous iteration. In later chapters we will illustrate problems that cannot be solved by Goal Seek and where the use of the Solver is a necessity.

Clicking on the **Solver** makes a dialog box appear; here we've filled it in:

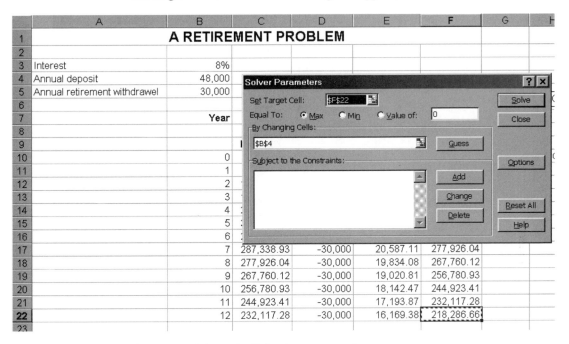

If we now click on the **Solve** box, we get the answer:

	A	B	C	D	E	F	G	H
1				A RETIREMENT PROBLEM				
2								
3	Interest	8%						
4	Annual deposit	29,387						
5	Annual retirement withdrawel	30,000						
6							=$B$3*(D10+C10)	
7		Year	Account	Deposit	Interest	Total in		
8			balance	at beginning	earned	account		
9			beg. year	of year	during year	end of year		
10		0	0.00	29,387	2,350.92	31,737.48	<-- =E10+D10+C10	
11		1	31,737.48	29,387	4,889.92	66,013.95		
12		2	66,013.95	29,387	7,632.04	103,032.54		
13		3	103,032.54	29,387	10,593.53	143,012.62		
14		4	143,012.62	29,387	13,791.93	186,191.10		
15		5	186,191.10	-30,000	12,495.29	168,686.39		
16		6	168,686.39	-30,000	11,094.91	149,781.30		
17		7	149,781.30	-30,000	9,582.50	129,363.81		
18		8	129,363.81	-30,000	7,949.10	107,312.91		
19		9	107,312.91	-30,000	6,185.03	83,497.94		
20		10	83,497.94	-30,000	4,279.84	57,777.78		
21		11	57,777.78	-30,000	2,222.22	30,000.00		
22		12	30,000.00	-30,000	0.00	0.00		

1.7.1   Solving the Retirement Problem Using Financial Formulas

We can develop an even more intelligent solution to the problem if we understand the discounting process. The present value of the whole series of payments, discounted at 8 percent, must be zero.

$$\sum_{t=0}^{4} \frac{\text{Initial deposit}}{(1.08)^t} - \sum_{t=5}^{12} \frac{30{,}000}{(1.08)^t} = 0$$

$$\Rightarrow \text{Initial deposit} = \left[\sum_{t=5}^{12} \frac{30{,}000}{(1.08)^t} \right] \bigg/ \left[\sum_{t=0}^{4} \frac{1}{(1.08)^t} \right]$$

Both the numerator on the right-hand side as $\displaystyle\sum_{t=5}^{12} \frac{30{,}000}{(1.08)^t} = \frac{1}{(1.08)^4} \sum_{t=1}^{8} \frac{30{,}000}{(1.08)^t}$
and the denominator $\displaystyle\sum_{t=0}^{4} \frac{1}{(1.08)^t}$ can be calculated using Excel's **PV** function:

	A	B	C	D	E
24	Numerator	126,718.54	<-- =1/(1+B3)^4*PV(B3,8,-30,000)		
25	Denominator	4.31	<-- =PV(B3,5,-1,,1)		
26	Annual deposit	29,386.55	<-- =B24/B25		

1.8   Continuous Compounding

Suppose you deposit $1,000 in a bank account that pays 5 percent per year. At the end of the year you will have $1{,}000 * (1.05) = \$1{,}050$. Now suppose that the bank pays you 2.5 percent interest twice a year. After six months you'll have $1,025, and after one year you will have $1{,}000 * \left(1 + \dfrac{0.05}{2}\right)^2 = \$1{,}050.625$.

By this logic, if you get paid interest n times per year, your accretion at the end of the year will be $\$1{,}000 * \left(1 + \dfrac{0.05}{n}\right)^n$. As n increases, this amount gets larger, converging (rather quickly, as you will soon see) to $e^{0.05}$, which in Excel is written as the function **Exp.** When n is infinite, we refer to this process as *continuous compounding* .

(By typing **Exp(1)** in a spreadsheet cell, you can see that $e = 2.7182818285....$)

As you can see in the next display, \$1,000 continuously compounded for one year at 5 percent grows to $\$1,000 * e^{0.05} = \$1,051.271$ at the end of the year. Continuously compounded for t years, it will grow to $\$1,000 * e^{0.05*t}$.

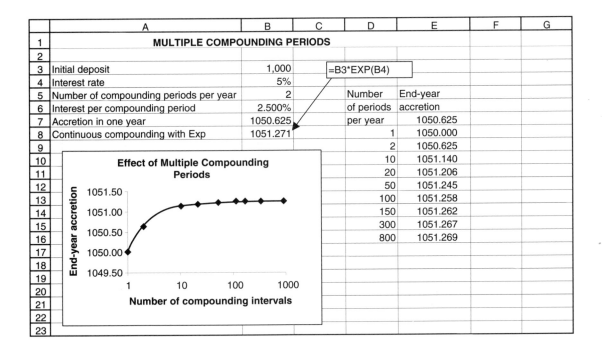

	A	B	C	D	E	F	G
1	MULTIPLE COMPOUNDING PERIODS						
2							
3	Initial deposit	1,000		=B3*EXP(B4)			
4	Interest rate	5%					
5	Number of compounding periods per year	2		Number	End-year		
6	Interest per compounding period	2.500%		of periods	accretion		
7	Accretion in one year	1050.625		per year	1050.625		
8	Continuous compounding with Exp	1051.271		1	1050.000		
9				2	1050.625		
10				10	1051.140		
11				20	1051.206		
12				50	1051.245		
13				100	1051.258		
14				150	1051.262		
15				300	1051.267		
16				800	1051.269		

Effect of Multiple Compounding Periods

1.8.1   A Technical Note on the Graph

The graph is an Excel XY (Scatter) chart; the x-axis in the chart has been set to be in logarithmic scale. This emphasizes the compounding process. The following picture shows the graph's x-axis marked and the relevant dialog box (right-click after marking the axis and go to **Format Axis**).

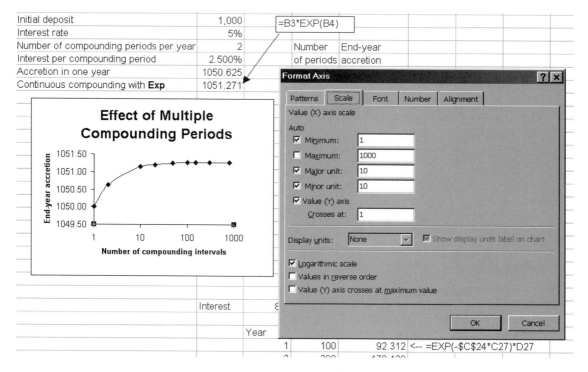

1.8.2   Back to Finance—Continuous Discounting

If the accretion factor for continuous compounding at interest r over t years is e^{rt}, then the discount factor for the same period is e^{-rt}. Thus a cash flow C_t occurring in year t and discounted at continuously compounded rate r will be worth $C_t e^{-rt}$ today, as illustrated here.

	B	C	D	E	F	G	H
24	Interest	8%					
25				Continuously			
26		Year	Cash flow	discounted PV			
27		1	100	92.3116	<-- =EXP(-$C$24*C27)*D27		
28		2	200	170.4288			
29		3	300	235.9884			
30		4	350	254.1522			
31		5	400	268.1280			
32							
33		Present value		1021.0089	<-- =SUM(E27:E31)		

1.8.3   Calculating the Continuously Compounded Return from Price Data

Suppose at time 0 you had $1,000 in the bank and suppose that one year later you had $1,200. What was your percentage return? Although the answer may appear obvious, it actually depends on the compounding method. If the bank paid interest only once a year, then the return would be 20 percent:

$$\frac{1,200}{1,000} - 1 = 20 \text{ percent}$$

However, if the bank paid interest twice a year, you would need to solve the following equation to calculate the return:

$$1,000 * \left(1 + \frac{r}{2}\right)^2 = 1,200 \Rightarrow r = \left(\frac{1,200}{1,000}\right)^{1/2} - 1 = 9.5445 \text{ percent}$$

The annual percentage return when interest is paid twice a year is therefore $2 * 9.5445$ percent $= 19.089$ percent.

In general, if there are n compounding periods per year, you have to solve $r = \left(\frac{1,200}{1,000}\right)^{1/n} - 1$ and then multiply the result appropriately. If n is very large, this solution converges to $r = \ln\left(\frac{1,200}{1,000}\right) = 18.2322$ percent:

	A	B	C	D	E	F	G	H	I
37	Initial deposit	1,000					**Annual rate with**		
38	End-of-year value	1,200					**n compounding periods**		
39	Number of compounding periods	2							
40	Implied annual interest rate	19.089%	<-- =((B38/B37)^(1/B39)-1)*B39					19.089%	<-- =B40
41							1	20.000%	
42	Continuous return	18.232%	<-- =LN(B38/B37)				2	19.089%	
43							4	18.654%	
44							8	18.442%	
45							20	18.316%	
46							50	18.265%	
47							100	18.249%	

1.8.4   Why Use Continuous Compounding?

All of this may seem somewhat esoteric. However, continuous compounding and discounting are often used in financial calculations. In this book, continuous compounding is used to calculate portfolio returns (Chapters 7–12) and in practically all of the options calculations (Chapters 13–19).

There's another reason to use continuous compounding—its ease of calculation. Suppose, for example, that your $1,000 grew to $1,500 in one year and nine months. What's the annualized rate of return? The easiest—and most consistent—way to answer this question is to calculate the continuously compounded annual return. Since one year and nine months equals 1.75 years, this return is

$$1{,}000 * \exp\left[r * 1.75\right] = 1{,}500 \Rightarrow r = \frac{1}{1.75} \ln\left[\frac{1{,}500}{1{,}000}\right] = 23.1694 \text{ percent}$$

Exercises

1.   You are offered an asset costing $600 that has cash flows of $100 at the end of each of the next 10 years.

  a. If the appropriate discount rate for the asset is 8 percent, should you purchase it?

  b. What is the IRR of the asset?

2.   You just took a $10,000, five-year loan. Payments at the end of each year are flat (equal in every year) at an interest rate of 15 percent. Calculate the appropriate loan table, showing the breakdown in each year between principal and interest.

3.   You are offered an investment with the following conditions:

  • The cost of the investment is 1,000.

  • The investment pays out a sum X at the end of the first year; this payout grows at the rate of 10 percent per year for 11 years.

  If your discount rate is 15 percent, calculate the smallest X that would entice you to purchase the asset. For example, as you can see in the following display, $X = \$100$ is too small—the NPV is negative.

	A	B	C	D
2	Discount rate	15%		
3	Initial payment	100		
4	NPV	-226.52		
5				
6	Year			
7	0	-1000.00		
8	1	100.00	<-- =B3	
9	2	110.00	<-- =B8*1.1	
10	3	121.00	<-- =B9*1.1	
11	4	133.10		
12	5	146.41		
13	6	161.05		
14	7	177.16		
15	8	194.87		
16	9	214.36		
17	10	235.79		
18	11	259.37		

4.   The following cash-flow pattern has two IRRs. Use Excel to draw a graph of the NPV of these cash flows as a function of the discount rate. Then use the IRR function to identify the two IRRs. Would you invest in this project if the opportunity cost were 20 percent?

	A	B
5	Year	Cash flow
6	0	-500
7	1	600
8	2	300
9	3	300
10	4	200
11	5	-1000

5.   In this exercise we solve iteratively for the internal rate of return. Consider an investment that costs 800 and has cash flows of 300, 200, 150, 122, 133 in years 1–5 (see cells A8:B13 in the following spreadsheet). Setting up the loan table shows that 10 percent is greater than the IRR (because the return of principal at the end of year 5 is less than the principal at the beginning of the year).

	A	B	C	D	E	F	G	H	I	J
2				IRR?	10.00%					
3										
4				LOAN TABLE			Division of payment			
5							between interest			
6					Principal	Payment and return of principal				
7	Year			=-B8	at beginning	at end				
8	0	-800		year	of year	of year	Interest	Principal	=F9-G9	
9	1	300		1	800.00	300	80.00	220.00		
10	2	200		2	580.00	200	58.00	142.00		
11	3	150		3	438.00	150	43.80	106.20		
12	4	122		4	331.80	122	33.18	88.82		
13	5	133		5	242.98	133	24.30	108.70		
14										
15				=E9-H9		=$E$2*E9				
16										

Setting the **IRR?** cell equal to 3 percent shows that 3 percent is less than the IRR, since the return of principal at the end of year 5 is greater than the principal at the beginning of year 5.

By changing the **IRR?** cell, find the internal rate of return of the investment.

	D	E	F	G	H	I	J
2	IRR?	3.00%					
3							
4	LOAN TABLE			Division of payment			
5				between interest			
6		Principal	Payment	and return of principal			
7	=-B8	at beginning	at end				
8	year	of year	of year	Interest	Principal	=F9-G9	
9	1	800.00	300	24.00	276.00		
10	2	524.00	200	15.72	184.28		
11	3	339.72	150	10.19	139.81		
12	4	199.91	122	6.00	116.00		
13	5	83.91	133	2.52	130.48		
14	6	-46.57					
15	=E9-H9		=$E$2*E9				

6. An alternative definition of the IRR is the rate that makes the principal at the beginning of year 6 equal to zero.[5] This is shown in the preceding printout, in which cell E14 gives the principal at the beginning of year 6. Using the **Goal Seek** function of Excel, find this rate (we illustrate how the screen should look).

	A	B	C	D	E	F	G	H	I	J
1										
2				IRR?	3.00%					
3										
4				LOAD TABLE			Goal Seek		? X	
5										
6				=-B8	Principal	Payment	Set cell:	$E$14		
7	Year				at beginning	at end	To value:	0		
8	0	-800		year	of year	of year	By changing cell:	$E$2		
9	1	300		1	800.00	300	OK	Cancel		
10	2	200		2	524.00	200				
11	3	150		3	339.72	150				
12	4	122		4	199.91	122	6.00	116.00		
13	5	133		5	83.91	133	2.52	130.48		
14				6	-46.57					
15				=E9-H9		=$E$2*E9				
16										
17										

(Of course, you should check your calculations by using the Excel **IRR** function.)

7. Calculate the flat annual payment required to pay off a five-year loan of $100,000 bearing an interest rate of 13 percent.

8. You have just taken a car loan of $15,000. The loan is for 48 months at an annual interest rate of 15 percent (which the bank translates to a monthly rate of 15 percent/12 = 1.25 percent). The 48 payments (to be made at the end of each of the next 48 months) are all equal.

   a. Calculate the monthly payment on the loan.

   b. In a loan table, calculate, for each month, the principal remaining on the loan at the beginning of the month and the split of that month's payment between interest and repayment of principal.

   c. Show that the principal at the beginning of each month is the present value of the remaining loan payments at the loan interest rate (use the **PV** function).

9. You are considering buying a car from a local auto dealer. The dealer offers you one of two payment options:

   • You can pay $30,000 cash.

   • The "deferred payment plan": You can pay the dealer $5,000 cash today and a payment of $1,050 at the end of each of the next 30 months.

---

5. In general, of course, the IRR is the rate of return that makes the principal in the year *following* the last payment equal to zero.

As an alternative to the dealer financing, you have approached a local bank, which is willing to give you a car loan of $25,000 at the rate of 1.25 percent per month.

a. Assuming that 1.25 percent is the opportunity cost, calculate the present value of all the payments on the dealer's deferred payment plan.

b. What is the effective interest rate being charged by the dealer? Do this calculation by preparing a spreadsheet like this (only part of the spreadsheet is shown—you have to do this calculation for all 30 months):

	C	D	E	F
14			**Payment under**	
15		**Cash car**	**deferred payment**	
16	**Month**	**payment**	**plan**	**Difference**
17	0	30,000	5,000	25,000
18	1	0	1,050	-1,050
19	2	0	1,050	-1,050
20	3	0	1,050	-1,050
21	4	0	1,050	-1,050
22	5	0	1,050	-1,050
23	6	0	1,050	-1,050

Now calculate the IRR of the numbers in column F; this is the monthly *effective interest rate* on the deferred payment plan.

10. You are considering a savings plan that calls for a deposit of $15,000 at the end of each of the next five years. If the plan offers an interest rate of 10 percent, how much will you accumulate at the end of year 5?

Do this calculation by completing the following spreadsheet. This spreadsheet does the calculation twice—once using the **FV** function and once using a simple table that shows the accumulation at the beginning of each year.

	A	B	C	D	E	F	G	H
						Accumulation	**Payment**	**Interest**
3	Annual payment	15,000				**at beginning**	**at end**	**on beg. year**
4	Interest rate	10%			Year	**of year**	**of year**	**accumulation**
5	Number of years	5			1	0	15,000	0.00
6	Total value	$91,576.50	<-- =FV(B4,B5,-B3,,0)		2	15,000	15,000	1,500.00
7					3	31,500		
8					4			
9					5			
10					6			
11								

11. Redo the calculation of exercise 10, this time assuming that you make five deposits at the *beginning* of this year and the following four years. How much will you accumulate by the end of year 5?

12. A mutual fund has been advertising that, had you deposited $250 per month in the fund for the last 10 years, you would now have accumulated $85,000. Assuming that these deposits were made at the beginning of each month for a period of 120 months, calculate the effective annual return fund investors got.

Hint: Set up the following spreadsheet, and then use **Goal Seek**

	A	B	C	D
3	Monthly payment	250		
4	Number of months	120		
5				
6	Effective monthly return?			
7	Accumulation		<-- =FV(B6,B4,-B3,,1)	

The effective annual return can then be calculated in one of two ways:

1. $(1 + \text{Monthly return})^{12} - 1$: This is the compound annual return, which is preferable, since it makes allowance for the reinvestment of each month's earnings.

2. $12 * \text{Monthly return}$: This method is often used by banks.

13. You have just turned 35, and you intend to start saving for your retirement. Once you retire in 30 years (when you turn 65), you would like to have an income of $100,000 per year for the next 20 years. Calculate how much you would have to save between now and age 65 in order to finance your retirement income. Make the following assumptions:

- All savings draw compound interest of 10 percent per year.
- You make the first payment today and the last payment on the day you turn 64 (30 payments).
- You make the first withdrawal when you turn 65 and the last withdrawal when you turn 84 (20 payments).

14. You have $25,000 in the bank, in a savings account that draws 5 percent interest. Your business needs $25,000, and you are considering two options: (a) Use the money in your savings account or (b) borrow the money from the bank at 6 percent, leaving the money in your savings account.

Your financial analyst suggests that solution (b) is better. His logic: The sum of the interest paid on the 6 percent loan is lower than the interest earned at the same time on the $25,000 deposit. His calculations are illustrated in the following spreadsheet. Show that this logic is wrong. (If you think about it, it couldn't be preferable to take a 6 percent loan when you are getting 5 percent interest from the bank. However, the explanation for this may not be trivial.)

	A	B	C	D	E
1		Financial analysts' calculations			
2					
3	Interest earned	5%			
4	Interest paid	6%			
5	Initial deposit	25,000			
6				=PMT($B$4,2,-$B$5)	
7		THE 6% LOAN			
8	Year	Principal	Payment	Of which	
9		beginning	at end of	interest	Repayment
10		of year	year	paid	of principal
11	1	25,000.00	13,635.92	1,500.00	12,135.92
12	2	12,864.08	13,635.92	771.84	12,864.08
13		Total interest paid		2,271.84	
14					
15		Savings Account			
16	Year	In savings	End-year	In account	
17		account	interest	at end of	
18		at beginning year	earned	year	
19	1	25,000.00	1,250.00	26,250.00	
20	2	26,250.00	1,312.50	27,562.50	
21		Interest earned	2,562.50		

2   Calculating the Cost of Capital

2.1   Introduction

The most widely used valuation method for firms is the discounted cash flow (DCF) method. In the next two chapters we show how to use integrated accounting-based financial models for the firm to calculate the firm's free cash flows. Discounting these cash flows at an appropriately risk-adjusted discount rate will give us the value of the firm.

In this chapter we discuss how to calculate the firm's cost of capital, the discount rate applied to future cash flows. We consider two models for calculating the cost of equity, the discount rate applied to equity cash flows:

• The Gordon model calculates the cost of equity based on the anticipated dividends of the firm.

• The capital asset pricing model (CAPM) calculates the cost of equity based on the correlation between the firm's equity returns and the returns of a large, diversified, market portfolio. As we will see, the CAPM can also be used to calculate the cost of the firm's debt.

The other component of the cost of capital is the cost of debt, the anticipated future cost of the firm's borrowing. We illustrate three models to calculate the cost of debt.

We use all of these models to calculate the weighted average cost of capital (WACC), the appropriate discount rate for valuation of firm cash flows. Throughout this chapter we apply our techniques to calculating the cost of capital for Abbott Laboratories.

A Terminological Note   As noted in the previous chapter, "cost of capital" is a synonym for the "appropriate discount rate" to be applied to a series of cash flows. In finance, "appropriate" is most often a synonym for "risk-adjusted." Hence, another name for the cost of capital is the "risk-adjusted discount rate" (RADR).

2.2   The Gordon Dividend Model

The Gordon dividend model[1] derives the cost of equity from the following deceptively simple statement:

---

1. This model is named after M. J. Gordon, who first published this formula in a paper entitled "Dividends, Earnings and Stock Prices," *Review of Economics and Statistics* 41 (May 1959), pp. 99–105.

The value of a share is the present value of the future anticipated dividend stream from the share, where the future anticipated dividends are discounted at the appropriate risk-adjusted cost of equity.

Consider, for example, the case of a stock whose dividends are anticipated to grow at 10 percent per year. If next year's anticipated dividend is $3 per share, then the value of the stock today, P_0, is given by

$$P_0 = \frac{3}{1 + r_E} + \frac{3 * (1.10)}{(1 + r_E)^2} + \frac{3 * (1.10)^2}{(1 + r_E)^3} + \frac{3 * (1.10)^3}{(1 + r_E)^4}$$

The formula in cell B6 of the following spreadsheet discounts 67 years of dividends (not all for which are shown):

	A	B	C	D
1	**Share value and anticipated dividends**			
2				
3	Year 1 anticipated dividend	3		
4	Growth rate of dividends	10%		
5	Cost of equity	15%		
6	Share value	56.95	<-- =NPV(B5,C10:C76)	
7				
8			**Anticipated**	
9		**Year**	**dividend**	
10		1	3.00	<-- =B3
11		2	3.30	<-- =C10*(1+$B$4)
12		3	3.63	<-- =C11*(1+$B$4)
13		4	3.99	
14		5	4.39	
15		6	4.83	
16		7	5.31	
17		8	5.85	
18		9	6.43	
19		10	7.07	
20		11	7.78	
21		12	8.56	
22		13	9.42	

Notice that our "solution" is really only an approximation. We've simply taken the NPV for a *very long* series of dividends, whereas the actual problem in the equation relates to an *infinite series* of dividends. To do this infinite-series calculation, we need to resort to some manipulation of the formula. We rewrite the formula using D_1 to denote the next period anticipated dividend and using g to denote the anticipated growth rate of dividends:

$$P_0 = \frac{D_1}{1 + r_E} + \frac{D_1 * (1 + g)}{(1 + r_E)^2} + + \frac{D_1 * (1 + g)^2}{(1 + r_E)^3} + \frac{D_1 * (1 + g)^3}{(1 + r_E)^4}$$

$$= \sum_{t=1}^{\infty} \frac{D_1 * (1 + g)^{t-1}}{(1 + r_E)^t} = \frac{D_1}{r_E - g}, \text{ provided } |g| < r_E$$

The last equality, $P_0 = \dfrac{D_1}{r_E - g}$, was derived by the Swiss mathematician Leonhard Euler (1707–83), and its derivation (which we won't give here) is a staple of high-school algebra classes. Note the proviso at the end: In order for the infinite sum on the first line of the formula to have a finite solution, the growth rates of the dividends must be less than the discount rate. We can use this formula in our spreadsheet:

	A	B	C	D	E	F
3	Year 1 anticipated dividend	3				
4	Growth rate of dividends	10%				
5	Cost of equity	15%				
6	Share value	56.95	<-- =NPV(B5,C9:C75)		Share value using formula	60.00
7						
8			**Anticipated**			=B3/(B5-B4)
9		**Year**	**dividend**			

So—if the dividend to be paid one year from now is anticipated to be $3, and if this dividend is expected to grow by 10 percent per year, and if the correct discount rate is 15 percent, then the value of the share should be $60. We can fix the technical problem by redefining the formula, as in the following spreadsheet:

	A	B	C	D	E	F	G
3	Year 1 anticipated dividend		3				
4	Growth rate of dividends		18%				
5	Cost of equity		15%				
6	Share value	Formula doesn't work		<-- =IF(B5<B4, "Formula doesn't work", B3/(B5-B4))			

2.2.1 "Supernormal Growth" and the Gordon Model

Notice that if the condition $|g| < r_E$ is violated, the formula $P_0 = D_1/(r_E - g)$ gives a negative answer. However, this does not mean that the value of the share is negative; rather it means that the basic condition has been violated. In finance examples, violations of $|g| < r_E$ usually occur for very fast-growing firms, in which—at least for short periods of time—we anticipate very high growth rates, so that $g > r_E$. In this case the original dividend discount formula shows that P_0 will have an infinite value. Since this result is clearly unreasonable (remember that we are valuing a security), it probably means either (1) that the long-term growth rate is less than the discount rate r_E, or (2) that the discount rate r_E is too low.

The following spreadsheet illustrates an initial, very high, growth rate that ultimately slows to a lower rate. We consider a firm whose current dividend is $8 per share. The firm's dividend is expected to grow at 35 percent for the next five years, after which the growth rate will slow down to 8 percent per year. The cost of equity, the discount rate for all of the dividends, is 18 percent:

	A	B	C	D	E	F	G	H	I
1	THE GORDON MODEL WITH 2 GROWTH RATES								
2									
3	Current dividend	8.00		Dividend valuation					
4	Growth rate g₁, years 1-5 ("supernormal")	35%		PV of years 1-5	60.99	<-- =NPV(B6,B9:B13)			
5	Growth rate g₂, years 6 - ∞	8%		PV of years 6 - ∞	169.35	<-- =B13*(1+B5)/(B6-B5)/(1+B6)^5			
6	Cost of equity	18%		Share value	230.33	<-- =SUM(E4:E5)			
7									
8		Year							
9		1	10.80	<-- =B3*(1+$B$4)					
10		2	14.58	<-- =B9*(1+$B$4)					
11		3	19.68	<-- =B10*(1+$B$4)					
12		4	26.57	<-- =B11*(1+$B$4)					
13		5	35.87	<-- =B12*(1+$B$4)					
14		6	38.74	<-- =B13*(1+$B$5)					
15		7	41.84	<-- =B14*(1+$B$5)					
16		8	45.19						
17		9	48.80						
18		10	52.71						
19		11	56.92						
20		12	61.48						

To calculate the value of the firm's share, we first discount the dividends for years 1–5. Cell E4 shows that these five future dividends are worth $60.99. Now look at years 6–∞. Denote the long-term growth rate by g_2 (in our example this is 8 percent). At time 0, the discounted dividend stream from years 6–∞ looks like:

$$\frac{Div_5(1 + g_2)}{(1 + r_E)^6} + \frac{Div_5(1 + g_2)^2}{(1 + r_E)^7} + \frac{Div_5(1 + g_2)^3}{(1 + r_E)^8}$$

$$= \sum_{t=6}^{\infty} \frac{Div_5 * (1 + g_2)^{t-5}}{(1 + r_E)^t}$$

$$= \frac{1}{(1 + r_E)^5} \sum_{t=1}^{\infty} \frac{Div_5 * (1 + g_2)^t}{(1 + r_E)^t}$$

This last expression is basically the Gordon model discounted over five years.

$$\frac{1}{(1 + r_E)^5} \sum_{t=1}^{\infty} \frac{\text{Div}_5 * (1 + g_2)^t}{(1 + r_E)^t} = \frac{1}{(1 + r_E)^5} \frac{\text{Div}_5 * (1 + g_2)^t}{r_E - g_2}$$

As shown in the spreadsheet, the value of the share is estimated at 230.33.

2.2.2   Back to the Gordon Model with Constant Growth Rates

Now we return to the Gordon model with a single growth rate. Since in this model $P_0 = D_1/(r_E - g)$, we can rearrange the formula to give us the cost of equity r_E:

$$r_E = \frac{\text{Next period anticipated dividend}}{\text{Current stock price}} + \text{Anticipated dividend growth rate}$$

$$= \frac{D_1}{P_0} + g$$

Often we assume that the $D_1 = D_0(1 + g)$, where D_0 is the last dividend the firm has paid; in this case the Gordon model is written

$$r_E = \frac{D_0(1 + g)}{P_0} + g$$

2.3   Calculating the Cost of Equity for Abbott Laboratories Using the Gordon Model

In the following spreadsheet you can see the dividend history of Abbott Laboratories from 1988 to 1998. The compound growth rate of Abbott's dividends over the period is 14.87 percent (and the five-year growth rate is 12.03 percent). Abbott's stock price at the end of 1998 was $49. Applying the Gordon formula gives (cells J22 and J23) Abbott's cost of equity as 16.28 percent or 13.4 percent depending on which growth rate we use.

2.3.1   Choosing the Growth Rate in the Gordon Model

The growth rate g in the Gordon formula is the *anticipated* rate of dividend growth, which is not necessarily the historical growth rate of dividend. Thus the "correct" growth rate is a judgment call—it depends on your expectations of what the company can and will pay out in dividends in the future.[2] In the case of Abbott Labs, we might decide that the five-year growth rate is more representative of future anticipated dividend growth than the 10-year rate. In this case, the cost of equity would be 13.40 percent instead of 16.28 percent. (Based on a more extensive analysis of Abbott, you might decide that the historical rate of Abbott's dividend growth has no relevance for its *future* dividend growth rate. This is one of the hard decisions that analysts have to make!)

	A	B	C	D	E	F
1	ABBOTT DIVIDEND HISTORY					
2						
3	1988	0.15				
4	1989	0.17	13.33%	<-- =B4/B3-1		
5	1990	0.21	23.53%	<-- =B5/B4-1		
6	1991	0.25	19.05%			
7	1992	0.30	20.00%			
8	1993	0.34	13.33%			
9	1994	0.38	11.76%			
10	1995	0.42	10.53%			
11	1996	0.48	14.29%			
12	1997	0.54	12.50%			
13	1998	0.60	11.11%			
14	Compound growth, 10 yr.		14.87%	<-- =(B13/B3)^(1/10)-1		
15	Compound growth, 5 yr.		12.03%	<-- =(B13/B8)^(1/5)-1		
16						
17	Gordon model					
18	P_0		49.00	<-- Ending 1998 share price		
19	D_0		0.60	<-- 1998 dividend		
20	r_E					
21	10-yr. growth		16.28%	<-- =B19*(1+C14)/B18+C14		
22	5-yr. growth		13.40%	<-- =B19*(1+C15)/B18+C15		

---

2. The pro forma financial statements discussed in the next chapter can sometimes help in this matter. By anticipating future sales growth and capital needs for the company, we can perhaps predict the company's future dividend.

2.4 Capital Asset Pricing Model

The capital asset pricing model (CAPM) is the other viable alternative to the Gordon model for calculating the cost of capital. The CAPM derives the firm's cost of capital from its covariance with the market return.[3] In the following table we show part of a 10-year price and return history for Abbott Labs and the S&P 500 index (the actual β calculation was done with 10 years of data—see the spreadsheet on the book CD-ROM).

	A	B	C	D	E	F	G
		SP500				**Abbot Labs (ABT)**	
1							
2							
3		**Closing**	**Monthly**			**Closing**	**Monthly**
4	**Date**	**price**	**return**		**Date**	**price**	**return**
5	Dec-88	277.72			Dec-88	4.8182	
6	Jan-89	297.47	7.11%		Jan-89	4.9369	2.46%
7	Feb-89	288.86	-2.89%		Feb-89	5.1510	4.34%
8	Mar-89	294.87	2.08%		Mar-89	5.5162	7.09%
9	Apr-89	309.64	5.01%		Apr-89	5.6023	1.56%
10	May-89	320.52	3.51%		May-89	6.0079	7.24%
11	Jun-89	317.98	-0.79%		Jun-89	5.8812	-2.11%
12	Jul-89	346.08	8.84%		Jul-89	6.7062	14.03%
13	Aug-89	351.45	1.55%		Aug-89	6.4512	-3.80%
14	Sep-89	349.15	-0.65%		Sep-89	6.5022	0.79%
15	Oct-89	340.36	-2.52%		Oct-89	6.6903	2.89%
16	Nov-89	345.99	1.65%		Nov-89	7.1005	6.13%
17	Dec-89	353.40	2.14%		Dec-89	6.9723	-1.81%
18	Jan-90	329.08	-6.88%		Jan-90	6.6989	-3.92%
19	Feb-90	331.89	0.85%		Feb-90	6.6087	-1.35%
20	Mar-90	339.94	2.43%		Mar-90	6.7762	2.53%
21	Apr-90	330.80	-2.69%		Apr-90	6.9225	2.16%

Abbott's *beta*, β_{Abbott}, shows the sensitivity of its stock return to the market return. It is calculated by the following formula:

$$\beta_{Abbott} = \frac{\text{Covariance(SP500 returns, Abbott returns)}}{\text{Variance(SP500 returns)}}$$

In cell J5 of the spreadsheet fragment in section 2.5.1 we show that Abbott's β is 0.8055.

---

3.   The CAPM is discussed in detail in Chapters 7–11. At this point we outline the application of the model to finding the cost of capital without entering into the theory.

Another way of calculating the β is to graph the S&P 500 returns on the *x*-axis and to graph the Abbott stock returns on the *y*-axis and then use the Excel **Trendline** function to calculate the regression equation:

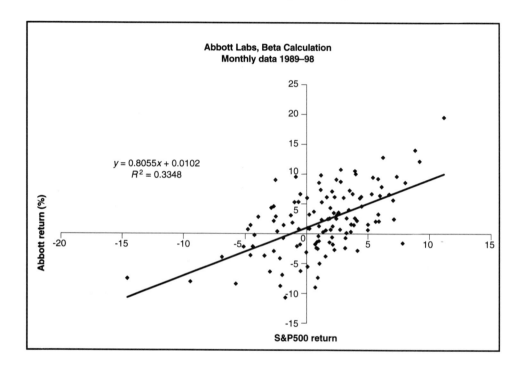

The *regression equation* in the graph shows the best linear function that explains the Abbott's returns (the *y* in the equation) in terms of the S&P 500 returns (the *x* on the right-hand side of the equation).[4] The regression equation shows that, during 1997, a 1 percent increase or decrease in the S&P 500 return led to a 0.8055 percent increase or decrease in Abbott's return. The $R^2 = 0.3348$ says that about 33 percent of the variation in Abbott's returns was explained by the variation in the S&P 500 returns.[5]

---

4. The use of Excel's **Trendline** function—used to calculate the regression equation—is further explained in Chapter 29.

5. An R^2 of 33 percent may seem low, but in the CAPM literature this is actually quite a respectable number. It says that roughly 33 percent of the variation in Abbott's returns is explicable by the variation in the S&P 500 return. The rest of the variability in the Abbott returns can be diversified away by including Abbott's shares in a diversified portfolio of shares.

2.5   Using the Security Market Line (SML) to Calculate Abbott's Cost of Equity

In the capital asset pricing model, the security market line (SML) is used to calculate the risk-adjusted cost of capital. In this section we consider two SML formulations. The difference between these two methods has to do with the way taxes are incorporated into the cost of capital equation.

2.5.1   Method 1: The Classic SML

The classic CAPM formula uses a security market line (SML) equation that ignores taxes.

$$\text{Cost of equity} = r_f + \beta [E(r_M) - r_f]$$

Here r_f is the risk-free rate of return in the economy and $E(R_M)$ is the expected rate of return on the market. The choice of values for the SML parameters is often problematic. A common approach is to choose

- r_f equal to the risk-free interest rate in the economy (for example, the yield on Treasury bills).

- $E(r_M) - r_f$ equal to the historic average of the "market risk premium," defined as the average return of a broad-based market portfolio minus the risk-free rate.

The following spreadsheet fragment illustrates this approach.

	I	J	K	L	M	N
3	**CAPM cost of equity calculations**					
4						
5	Abbott's beta	0.8055	<-- =COVAR(C5:C124,G5:G124)/VARP(C5:C124)			
6						
7	**Classical CAPM cost of equity**					
8	Risk premium	8.40%	<-- E(r_M)-r_f			
9	Risk-free rate	4.40%	<-- Treasury bill rate, end 1998			
10	r_E, the cost of equity	11.17%	<-- =J9+J5*J8			

2.5.2   Method 2: The Benninga-Sarig Tax-Adjusted SML

The classic CAPM approach makes no allowance for taxation. Benninga-Sarig (1997) show that the SML has to be adjusted for the marginal corporate tax rate in the economy. Denoting the corporate tax rate by T_C, the Benninga-Sarig tax-adjusted SML is

Cost of equity $= r_f(1 - T_C) + \beta[E(r_M) - r_f(1 - T_C)]$

This formula can be applied by an adaptation of the previous approach:

- r_f is equal to the risk-free interest rate in the economy (in this case, the yield on Treasury bills).
- $E(r_M) - r_f(1 - T_C) = [E(r_M) - r_f] + T_C r_f$, which is equal to the historic average of the market risk premium plus $T_C r_f$.

For Abbott Labs, the Benninga-Sarig approach gives a slightly lower cost of equity:

	I	J	K	L	M	N
12	**Benninga-Sarig tax-adjusted CAPM**					
13	Risk premium	8.40%	<-- E(r_M)-r_f			
14	Risk-free rate	4.40%	<-- Treasury bill rate, end 1998			
15	Corporate tax	40%				
16	Tax-adjusted SML slope	10.16%	<-- =J13+J15*J14 = E(r_M)-r_f*(1-T_C)			
17	r_E, the cost of equity	10.82%	<-- =J14*(1-J15)+J5*J16			

2.5.3   Calculating the Expected Return on the Market, $E(r_M)$:
Using the Gordon Model

The 8.40 percent figure for $E(r_M) - r_f$ approximates the historic market risk premium in the United States for 1926–1994. On the one hand, historic averages are appropriate if we think that the future anticipated rates of return will correspond to the historic average. On the other hand, we may want to take current market data to calculate directly the future anticipated market yield.

As Benninga and Sarig show, the Gordon model gives us an approach for doing so.[6] Recall that the model says that the cost of equity r_E is given by

$$r_E = \frac{D_0(1 + g)}{P_0} + g$$

---

6.   A fuller exposition of this model can be found in Chapter 8 of *Corporate Finance: A Valuation Approach* by Simon Benninga and Oded Sarig (McGraw-Hill, 1997).

Rewriting this formula, assuming that the firm pays out a constant proportion a of its earnings as dividends, indicating by EPS_0 the current earnings per share, and interpreting g to be the earnings growth of the firm:

$$r_E = \frac{a * EPS_0(1 + g)}{P_0} + g = \frac{a * (1 + g)}{P_0/EPS_0} + g$$

The term on the right-hand side of this equation P_0/EPS_0 is the price-earnings ratio of the firm. This formula ties the cost of equity to currently observable market parameters. Here is an implementation for calculating Abbott's cost of equity:

	A	B	C	D	E	F	G
1	IN THIS SPREADSHEET WE USE THE P/E MODEL TO CALCULATE THE EXPECTED MARKET RETURN						
2	AND THEN COMBINE THIS WITH ABBOTT'S BETA TO CALCULATE ITS COST OF EQUITY						
3							
4	Expected market return using the P/E model						
5	Market dividend-payout ratio	40%	<-- Reasonable estimate				
6	Median market price-earnings ratio	25	<-- Approximate for end-1998				
7	Anticipated median earnings growth	7%	<-- Analysts' estimate?				
8	E(r_M) using P/E model	8.71%	<-- =B5*(1+B7)/B6+B7				
9							
10	CAPM cost of equity calculations						
11	Abbott's beta	0.8055	<-- From previous calculation				
12							
13	Classical CAPM cost of equity						
14	Risk-free rate	4.40%	<-- Treasury bill rate, end 1998				
15	Risk premium, E(r_M) - r_f	4.31%	<-- =B8-B14				
16	r_E, the cost of equity	7.87%	<-- =B14+B11*B15				
17							
18	Benninga-Sarig tax-adjusted CAPM						
19	Risk-free rate	4.40%	<-- Treasury bill rate, end 1998				
20	Corporate tax, T_C	40%	<-- Approximate U.S. marginal corporate tax rate				
21	Tax-adjusted risk premium, E(r_M) - r_f*(1-T_C)	6.07%	<-- =B8-B19*(1-B20)				
22	r_E, the cost of equity	7.53%	<-- =B19*(1-B20)+B11*B21				

2.6   Calculating the Cost of Debt

Thus far we have calculated the cost of equity for the Abbott Labs. We now want to calculate the cost of the firm's debt. In principle, this is the marginal cost to the firm (before corporate taxes) of borrowing an additional dollar. In practice the cost of debt often turns out to be more difficult to calculate than the cost of equity. There are at least four ways of calculating the firm's cost of debt. We will state them briefly and then go on to illustrate the application of three of the methods to Abbott Labs. The first two methods are easy to apply and, although they may not be theoretically perfect, they are often used in practice.

• As a practical matter, the cost of debt can often be approximated by taking the *average cost* of the firm's existing debt. Although this method is the easiest to use, it confuses *past costs* with the *future anticipated* cost of debt that we actually want to measure.

• We can use the yield of similar-risk corporate securities. If a company is rated A and has mostly medium-term debt, then we can use the average yield on medium-term, A-rated debt as the firm's cost of debt. Note that this method is somewhat problematic because the yield on a bond is its *promised return,* whereas the cost of debt is the *expected return* on a firm's debt. Since there is usually a risk of default, the promised return is generally higher than the expected return.

Both these methods are relatively easy to apply. In many cases problems or errors that are encountered in these methods are not critical.[7] As a matter of theory, however, both these methods fail to make proper risk adjustments for the cost of the firm's debt. The next two methods make risk adjustments but are harder to apply:

• The CAPM can be applied to the cost of capital by estimating the β of the firm's debt. We can then estimate the firm's cost of debt by using the security market line (SML). This approach is, in principle, similar to the process applied to the firm's equity, although—as we will show—the actual application requires many shortcuts and fuzzinesses.

• We can use a model that estimates the cost of debt from data about the firm's bond prices, the estimated probabilities of default, and the estimated payoffs to bondholders in case of default. This method requires a lot of work and is mathematically nontrivial; we postpone its discussion until Chapter 23. For cost of capital calculations it would be used in practice only if the firm we are analyzing has significant amounts of risky debt.

2.7   Calculating Abbott's Cost of Debt

We now apply the first three of these methods to calculate the cost of debt for Abbott Labs.

---

7. Calculating the cost of capital requires a large number of assumptions and does not necessarily give a precise answer. Thus cost of capital estimation is not a *science,* it is an *art.* Users of cost of capital estimates should always do a sensitivity analysis around the numbers calculated. Given the data on the company you are analyzing, some sloppiness in the cost of capital calculations (with its accompanying savings in time) may be expedient.

2.7.1   Method 1: Abbott's Average Cost of Debt

The average cost of Abbott Lab's debt in 1998 can be calculated from the financial statements as 5.49 percent:

	A	B	C	D
1	**Abbott's Average Cost of Debt**			
2				
3	(All figures in million $)	End-1998	End-1997	
4	Long-term debt	1,339.7	938	
5	Short-term debt and current portion of long-term debt	1,759.1	1,781.4	
6	Total debt	3,098.8	2,719.4	
7				
8	1998 interest expense	159.8		
9	Interest as percentage of average 1997-1998 debt	5.49%	<-- =B8/AVERAGE(B6:C6)	

Note that we include all of Abbott's debt (short term and long term), but that we exclude all other current liability items in the balance sheet.

2.7.2   Method 2: The Rating-Adjusted Yield on Abbott Labs' Debt

At the end of 1998, Abbott was rated AA1. The average maturity of this debt was about five years. At the end of 1998 the yield to maturity of five-year AA1 debt was about 5.25 percent (see the following Bloomberg picture). The second method uses this number as the cost of debt.

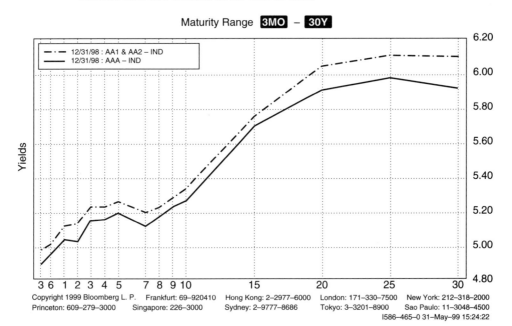

Maturity Range **3MO** – **30Y**

Copyright 1999 Bloomberg L. P.   Frankfurt: 69–920410   Hong Kong: 2–2977–6000   London: 171–330–7500   New York: 212–318–2000
Princeton: 609–279–3000   Singapore: 226–3000   Sydney: 2–9777–8686   Tokyo: 3–3201–8900   Sao Paulo: 11–3048–4500
I586–465–0 31–May–99 15:24:22

2.7.3   Method 3: Applying the CAPM to Calculate the Cost of Abbott Labs' Debt

In principle we should be doing here the same as we did for Abbott's stock, namely, calculating the debt beta, $\beta_{\text{debt}}^{\text{Abbott}} = \dfrac{\text{Cov}(r_{\text{debt}}^{\text{Abbott}}, r_M)}{\text{Var}(r_M)}$, where $r_{\text{debt}}^{\text{Abbott}}$ is the return on Abbott's debt and r_M is the return on some market index (typically, the S&P 500). When we try to apply this formula, things get very complicated: Firms typically have many bond issues, and these issues—if traded at all (much corporate debt consists of private placements)—are typically traded infrequently. Compared to stock data, bond return data are thus hard to get and may be inaccurate.

In practice the β of corporate debt relates to two factors:

1. The maturity of the debt. The longer the term of a firm's debt, the more risky it is.

2. The default risk of the debt. The greater the default risk, the greater is the debt β.

For many corporate debt issues, the first factor is more important than the second. For a relatively highly rated company like Abbott, this factor is dominant.

A good rule of thumb for estimating the firm's debt β is the following (these numbers—very crude estimates—are justified somewhat in the appendix to this chapter):

Term	Riskiness	Bond Beta
Very short	Low	0
Short (1–3 years)	Low	0.1
Medium (3–10 years)	Intermediate	0.35
Long (> 10 years)	Low	0.6
Long (> 10 years)	Intermediate	0.8

Abbott Labs is a low-risk company. Its average debt maturity is on the low side of the medium-term debt. We can thus plug its debt β as $\beta_{\text{debt}} = 0.15$. As in the case of the CAPM calculations for equity, there are two models with which to calculate the cost of debt. The classic CAPM formulation is that the cost of debt is calculated using the following security market line (SML):

$$r_D = \text{Cost of debt} = r_f + \beta_{\text{debt}}\left[E(r_M) - r_f\right]$$

The Benninga-Sarig tax-adjusted cost of debt SML for debt is

$$r_D = \text{Cost of debt} = r_f + \beta_{\text{debt}}\left[E(r_M) - r_f(1 - T_C)\right]$$

The following spreadsheet fragment illustrates both calculations:

	A	B	C	D	E
12	**CAPM cost of debt calculations**				
13	Abbott's debt beta	0.15			
14					
15	**Classical CAPM cost of equity**				
16	Risk premium	8.40%	<-- E(r$_M$)-r$_f$		
17	Risk-free rate	4.40%	<-- Treasury bill rate, end 1998		
18	r$_D$, the cost of debt	5.660%	<-- =B17+B13*B16		
19					
20	**Benninga-Sarig tax-adjusted CAPM**				
21	Risk premium	8.40%	<-- E(r$_M$)-r$_f$		
22	Risk-free rate	4.40%	<-- Treasury bill rate, end 1998		
23	Corporate tax	40%			
24	Tax-adjusted SML slope	10.16%	<-- =B21+B23*B22 = E(r$_M$)-r$_f$*(1-T$_C$)		
25	r$_D$, the cost of debt	5.92%	<-- =B22+B13*B24		

2.8   Weighted Average Cost of Capital (WACC)

The preceding examples for the Gordon dividend model and the CAPM derive the cost of equity, the risk-adjusted discount rate that should be applied to the firm's equity payouts to shareholders. The discount rate that should be applied to the firm's free cash flows—the cash flows of the firm as a whole—is called the weighted average cost of capital (WACC). The WACC is a weighted average of the cost of equity and the cost of debt.

$$WACC = \frac{E}{E + D}r_E + \frac{D}{E + D}r_D(1 - T_C)$$

where E is the market value of the firm's equity, D is the market value of the firm's debt, and T_C is the corporate tax rate.

In the next spreadsheet we calculate Abbott's WACC for the case where the cost of debt is calculated by Method 1 but where we use both the Gordon model and the CAPM for the cost of equity:

	A	B	C	D	E
1	**CALCULATING ABBOTT'S WACC**				
2					
3	**Calculation of end-1998 market value of equity**				
4	Number of shares, end 1998	1,516,063,000			
5	Share price, end 1998	49.00			
6	Market value of equity, end 1998, $billion	74.29			
7					
8	**End-1998 value of debt (book value of debt assumed = market value)**				
9	Long-term debt	1,339,694,000			
10	Short-term debt and current portion of long-term debt	1,759,076,000			
11	Total debt	3,098,770,000			
12	Less cash and cash equivalents	308,230,000			
13	Less investment securities	75,087,000			
14	Net debt, $billion	2.72			
15					
16	Cost of debt	5.49%			
17					
18	Enterprise value = equity + debt, $billion	77.00	<-- =B14+B6		
19	Equity (%)	0.96	<-- =B6/B18		
20	Debt (%)	0.04	<-- =1-B19		
21					
22	Abbott's marginal tax rate	40%			
23					
24	**COST OF CAPITAL CALCULATIONS**				
25					
26	**Using Gordon model**				
27	Cost of equity	13.40%			
28	WACC	13.05%	<-- =B19*B27+B20*(1-B22)*B16		
29					
30	**Using the CAPM**				
31	Cost of equity (Benninga-Sarig tax-adjusted SML)	10.82%			
32	WACC	10.56%	<-- =B19*B31+B20*(1-B22)*B16		

2.9   When the Models Don't Work

All models have problems, and nothing is perfect.[8] In this section we discuss some of the potential problems with the Gordon model and with the capital asset pricing model.

2.9.1   Problems with the Gordon Model

Obviously the Gordon model doesn't work if a firm doesn't pay dividends and appears to have no intention—in the immediate future—of paying dividends.[9]

---

8. "Happiness is the maximum agreement of reality and desire."—Stalin.

9. Firms cannot intend *never* to pay dividends, because such an intention would rationally mean that the value of the shares is zero.

But even for dividend-paying firms, it may be difficult to apply the model. Particularly problematic, in many cases, is the extraction of the future dividend payout rate from past dividends.

Consider, for example, the dividend history of Ford Motor Company in the years 1989–98:

	A	B	C	D	E
1	**FORD MOTOR CO. DIVIDEND HISTORY, 1989–1998**				
2					
3	**Year**	**Dividend**			
4	1989	3.00			
5	1990	3.00			
6	1991	1.95			
7	1992	1.60			
8	1993	1.60			
9	1994	1.33			
10	1995	1.23			
11	1996	1.46			
12	1997	1.64			
13	1998	22.81			
14	Growth rate, 1989–1997	−7.27%	<-- =(B12/B4)^(1/8)−1		
15	Growth rate, 1989–1998	25.28%	<-- =(B13/B4)^(1/9)−1		

The problem here is easily identifiable: Ford, whose dividends were in steady decline until 1997, paid a cash dividend of $21.09 in 1998, in addition to its regular quarterly dividends (which summed to $1.72 in 1998). If we use past history to predict the future, any inclusion of the extraordinary cash dividend will cause us to overestimate the future dividend growth. Excluding the $21.09 dividend, however, also does not reflect the actual situation.

It appears that the 10-year history of Ford's dividends is not, perhaps, the best guide to its future dividend payout. There are several solutions for those wishing to use the Gordon model:

• If we exclude the extraordinary dividend of $21.09 in 1998, then the dividend growth over the four years ending in 1998 is a respectable 6.64 percent. If Ford's anticipated future dividend growth is estimated to be this rate, then—given its end-1998 stock price of $58.69—the Gordon-model cost of equity is 9.77 percent.

	A	B	C	D	E
18	**FORD'S DIVIDENDS EXCLUDING THE 1998 $21.09 DIVIDEND**				
19	**Year**	**Dividend**			
20	1989	3.00			
21	1990	3.00			
22	1991	1.95			
23	1992	1.60			
24	1993	1.60			
25	1994	1.33			
26	1995	1.23			
27	1996	1.46			
28	1997	1.64			
29	1998	1.72			
30	Growth rate, 1994-1998	6.64%	<-- =(B29/B25)^(1/4)-1		
31	Ford's stock price, end-1998	58.69			
32	Gordon cost of equity	9.77%	<-- =B29*(1+B30)/B31+B30		

- A second alternative to finding Ford's cost of capital is to predict its future dividends by doing a full-blown financial model for the company. Such models—illustrated in the succeeding two chapters—are often used by analysts. Though they are complicated and time-consuming to build, they take into account all of the firm's productive and financial activities. Potentially they are, therefore, a more accurate predictor of the dividend.

2.9.2 Problems with the CAPM

In the following spreadsheet fragment you will find the return of the S&P 500 and Big City Bagels (notice that the spreadsheet fragment skips from row 8 to row 35—some of the rows of the data have been hidden). Immediately after the spreadsheet is a graph that shows the calculation of Big City's β, which is computed to be -0.6408.

	A	B	C	D	E	F	G
2	**S&P 500 Index**				**Big City Bagels (BIGC)**		
3		**Closing**				**Closing**	
4	**Date**	**price**			**Date**	**price**	
5	May-96	669.12			May-96	46.25	
6	Jun-96	670.63	0.23%		Jun-96	38.75	-16.22%
7	Jul-96	639.95	-4.57%		Jul-96	50.00	29.03%
8	Aug-96	651.99	1.88%		Aug-96	45.63	-8.75%
35	Nov-98	1163.63	5.91%		Nov-98	0.38	50.00%
36	Dec-98	1229.23	5.64%		Dec-98	0.25	-33.33%
37	Jan-99	1279.64	4.10%		Jan-99	0.38	50.00%
38	Feb-99	1238.33	-3.23%		Feb-99	1.06	183.33%
39	Mar-99	1286.37	3.88%		Mar-99	0.97	-8.82%
40	Return sigma (monthly)		4.91%				43.81%
41	Return sigma (annual)		17.02%				151.75%
42							
43	=STDEV(C6:C39)				=SQRT(12)*C40		

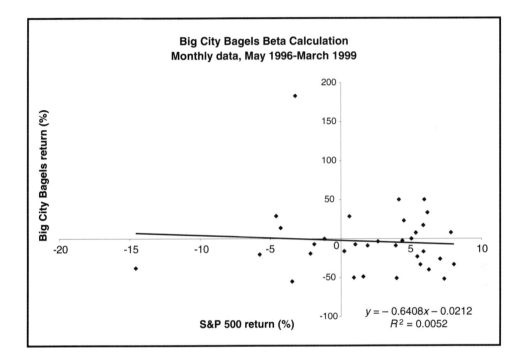

Big City Bagel's stock is clearly risky—the annualized standard deviation of its returns is 152 percent as compared to about 17 percent for the S&P 500 over the same period. However, the β of Big City Bagels is -0.6408, indicating that Big City has—in a portfolio context—*negative risk*. Were this conclusion true, it would mean that adding Big City to a portfolio would lower the portfolio variance enough to justify a below-risk-free return for Big City. While this statement might be true for some stocks, it is hard to believe that—in the long run—the β of Big City is indeed negative.[10]

The R^2 of the regression between Big City's returns and the S&P 500 is extraordinarily low, 0.0052, meaning that the S&P 500 simply doesn't explain any of the variation in Big City returns. For statistics mavens: The situation is actually worse—the standard error of the slope estimate is 1.57, which is 2.5 times larger than the slope itself (meaning that the slope estimate is not statistically significantly different from zero).

What are we to make of this situation? How should we calculate the cost of capital for Big City? There are several alternatives.

---

10. A more plausible explanation is that—for the period covered—Big City's return has *nothing whatsoever* to do with the market return.

• We could assume that the Big City β is -0.6408. Depending on which version of the CAPM you use, this would give Big City's cost of equity as follows:

	I	J	K	L	M	N
3	**CAPM cost of equity calculations**					
4						
5	Big City's beta	-0.6408	<-- =COVAR(C5:C38,G5:G38)/VARP(C5:C38)			
6						
7	**Classical CAPM cost of equity**					
8	Risk premium	8.40%	<-- E(r_M)-r_f			
9	Risk-free rate	4.40%	<-- Treasury bill rate, end 1998			
10	r_E, the cost of equity	-0.98%	<-- =J9+J5*J8			
11						
12	**Benninga-Sarig tax-adjusted CAPM**					
13	Risk premium	8.40%	<-- E(r_M)-r_f			
14	Risk-free rate	4.40%	<-- Treasury bill rate, end 1998			
15	Corporate tax	40%				
16	Tax-adjusted SML slope	10.16%	<-- =J13+J15*J14 = E(r_M)-r_f*(1-T_C)			
17	r_E, the cost of equity	-3.87%	<-- =J14*(1-J15)+J5*J16			

• We could assume that the β of Big City is in fact zero. Given the standard deviation of the β estimate for Big City, the β is not statistically different from zero, so that this assumption makes sense. We can conclude that all of Big City's risk is diversifiable and that the correct cost of equity for Big City is the riskless rate of interest.

• We could assume that the covariance (or lack thereof) between Big City and the S&P 500 is not indicative of their future correlation. This assumption would eventually lead us to conclude that Big City's risk is comparable to that of similar companies. A small study of the βs of snack food companies shows their βs to be well over 1: New World Coffee has a β of 1.15, Pepsico has a β of 1.42, and Starbucks has a β of 1.84. Thus we might conclude that the β of Big City (in the sense of its *future* correlation with the market) would be somewhere between 1.15 and 1.84.

2.10   Conclusion

In this chapter we have illustrated in detail the application of two models for calculating the cost of equity: the Gordon dividend model and the CAPM. We have also considered three of the four practicable models for calculating the cost of debt. Because the application of these models includes many judgment calls, our advice is to

• Always use several models to calculate the cost of capital.

• If you have time, try to calculate the cost of capital not only for the firm you are analyzing, but also for other firms in the same industry.

• From your analysis try to pick out a *consensus* estimate of the cost of capital. Don't hesitate to exclude numbers (such as Big City's negative cost of equity) that strike you as unreasonable.

In sum, the calculation of the cost of capital is not just a mechanistic exercise!

Exercises

1. ABC Corp. has a stock price $P_0 = 50$. The firm has just paid a dividend of $3 per share, and knowledgable shareholders think that this dividend will grow by a rate of 5% per year. Use the Gordon dividend model to calculate the cost of equity of ABC.

2. Unheardof, Inc. has just paid a dividend of $5 per share. This dividend is anticipated to increase at a rate of 15% per year. If the cost of equity for Unheardof is 25%, what should be the market value of a share of the company?

3. Dismal.com is a producer of depressing Internet products. The company is not currently paying dividends, but its chief financial officer thinks that starting in 3 years it can pay a dividend of $15 per share, and that this dividend will grow by 20% per year. Assuming that the cost of equity of Dismal.com is 35%, value a share based on the discounted dividends.

4. Consider the following dividend and price data for Chrysler Corporation:

	A	B	C	D
1	CHRYSLER CORPORATION (C)			
2		Year-end	Dividend	
3		stock	per	
4	Year	price	share	
5	1986		0.40	
6	1987		0.50	
7	1988		0.50	
8	1989		0.60	
9	1990		0.60	
10	1991		0.30	
11	1992		0.30	
12	1993		0.33	
13	1994		0.45	
14	1995		1.00	
15	1996	35.00	1.40	

Use the Gordon model to calculate Chrysler's cost of equity in 1996.

5.   On the spreadsheet associated with this chapter you will find the following monthly data for IBM's stock price and the S&P 500 index during 1998:

	A	B	C
1	**S&P 500 AND IBM**		
2			
3		**S&P 500**	**IBM**
4		**index**	**price ($)**
5	Jan-97	786.16	78.32
6	Feb-97	790.82	71.77
7	Mar-97	757.12	68.52
8	Apr-97	801.34	80.13
9	May-97	848.28	86.37
10	Jun-97	885.14	90.12
11	Jul-97	954.31	105.59
12	Aug-97	899.47	101.23
13	Sep-97	947.28	105.84
14	Oct-97	914.62	98.35
15	Nov-97	955.40	109.34
16	Dec-97	970.43	104.47

a. Use these data to calculate IBM's β.

b. Suppose that at the end of 1997, the risk-free rate was 5.50 percent. Assuming that the market risk premium, $E(r_m) - r_f = 8$ percent and that the corporate tax rate $T_C = 40$ percent, calculate IBM's cost of equity using both the classic CAPM security market line and Benninga-Sarig's tax-adjusted security market line.

c. At the end of 1997, IBM had 969,015,351 shares outstanding and had $39.9 billion of debt. Assuming that IBM's cost of debt is 6.10 percent, use your calculations for the cost of equity in part b to arrive at two estimates of IBM's weighted average cost of capital.

6.   A firm has a current stock price of $50 and has just paid a dividend of $5 per share.

a. Assuming that investors in the firm anticipate a dividend growth rate of 10 percent, what is the firm's cost of equity?

b. Draw a graph showing the relation between the cost of equity and the anticipated dividend growth rate.

7.   Exercise on supernormal growth: ABC Corporation has just paid a dividend of $3 per share. You—an experienced analyst—feel quite sure that the growth rate of the company's dividends over the next 10 years will be 15 percent per year. After 10 years you think that the company's dividend growth rate will slow to the industry average, which is about 5 percent per year. If the cost of equity for ABC is 12 percent, what is the value today of one share of the company?

8.   Consider a company that has $\beta_{equity} = 1.5$ and $\beta_{debt} = 0.4$. Suppose that the risk-free rate of interest is 6 percent, the expected return on the market $E(r_m)$ is 15 percent and the corporate tax rate is 40 percent. If the company has 40 percent equity and 60 percent debt in its

capital structure, calculate its weighted average cost of capital using both the classic CAPM and the Benninga-Sarig tax-adjusted CAPM.

9. You are considering buying the bonds of a very risky company. A bond with a $100 face value, a one-year maturity, and a coupon rate of 22% is selling for $95. You consider the probability that the company will actually survive to pay off the bond 80%. With 20% probability, you think that the company will default, in which case you think that you will be able to recover $40. What is the expected return on the bond?

10. It is January 1, 1997. Normal America, Inc. (NA) has paid a year-end dividend in each of the last 10 years, as shown by the following table.

	A	B	C	D	E	F	G
1	**NORMAL AMERICA, INC.**						
2							
3		Dec. 31	Dec. 15				
4		stock	dividend				SP 500
5	year	price	per share				return
6	1986	33.00					
7	1987	30.69	2.50			1987	4.7%
8	1988	35.38	2.50			1988	16.2%
9	1989	42.25	3.00			1989	31.4%
10	1990	34.38	3.00			1990	-3.3%
11	1991	36.25	1.60			1991	30.2%
12	1992	32.25	1.40			1992	7.4%
13	1993	43.00	0.80			1993	9.9%
14	1994	42.13	0.80			1994	1.2%
15	1995	52.88	1.10			1995	37.4%
16	1996	55.75	1.60			1996	22.9%

Calculate NA's β with respect to the SP500.

Appendix 1: A Rule of Thumb for Calculating Debt Betas

Vanguard is a large manager of mutual funds. Among its funds is the Vanguard Index 500 fund, which tracks the S&P 500 portfolio. The company also has numerous bond funds. The following table shows the β of these bond funds derived by calculating the

$$\frac{\text{Cov}(\text{return}_{SP500}, \text{return}_{\text{bond fund}})}{\text{Var}(\text{return}_{SP500})}$$

for each fund. When we do this calculation for a number of Vanguard funds, we get the following results.

Regressing the β on the bond fund average maturity gives:

$$\beta_{\text{fund}} = 0.1313 + 0.0118 * \text{maturity}, R^2 = 0.56$$

The rules of thumb for debt betas in the chapter are based on this regression.

	A	B	C	D	E	F	G	H	I	J	K	L	M
1	BETAS FOR SELECTED VANGUARD FUNDS												
2	Note: The source is Vanguard's Web site—http://majestic4.vanguard.com												
3	This isnot meant to be a scientific study!												
4													
5	Year	Vanguard				High-			PA Insured		Insured		Long-term
6	ended	Index 500	Short-term	Short-term	Short-term	yield		Total	long-term	High-yield	long-term	Long-term	U.S.
7	December 31	portfolio	federal	corporate	treasury	corporate	GNMA	bond index	tax-exempt	tax-exempt	tax-exempt	tax-exempt	treasury
8	1999	21.07%	2.07%	3.30%	1.85%	2.55%	0.78%	-0.76%	-2.66%	-3.38%	-2.91%	-3.53%	-8.66%
9	1998	28.62%	5.94%	6.57%	7.36%	5.62%	7.14%	8.58%	6.19%	6.45%	6.13%	6.02%	13.05%
10	1997	33.19%	6.46%	6.95%	6.39%	11.91%	9.47%	9.44%	8.25%	9.24%	8.65%	9.29%	13.90%
11	1996	22.88%	4.78%	4.79%	4.39%	9.54%	5.24%	3.58%	4.33%	4.46%	4.02%	4.41%	-1.25%
12	1995	37.45%	12.26%	12.74%	12.11%	19.15%	17.04%	18.18%	16.45%	18.13%	18.60%	18.72%	30.11%
13	1994	1.18%	0.94%	-0.08%	-0.58%	-1.71%	-0.95%	-2.66%	-4.54%	-5.06%	-5.58%	-5.75%	-7.03%
14	1993	9.89%	7.00%	7.07%	6.41%	18.24%	5.90%	9.68%	12.74%	12.66%	13.09%	13.45%	16.79%
15	1992	7.42%	6.19%	7.20%	6.75%	14.24%	6.85%	7.14%	10.17%	9.88%	9.17%	9.30%	7.40%
16	1991	30.22%	12.24%	13.08%	6.75%	29.01%	16.77%	15.25%	12.20%	14.75%	12.49%	13.50%	17.43%
17	1990	-3.32%	9.31%	9.23%	3.08%	-5.85%	10.32%	8.65%	6.92%	4.92%	7.04%	6.82%	5.78%
18	1989	31.36%	11.34%	11.45%		1.89%	14.77%	13.64%	10.56%	11.07%	10.60%	11.54%	17.93%
19	1988	16.22%	5.73%	6.95%		13.55%	8.81%	7.35%	11.95%	13.81%	12.79%	12.24%	9.15%
20	1987	4.71%	0.00%	4.46%		2.65%	2.15%	1.14%	-1.26%	-1.57%	0.12%	-1.14%	-2.93%
21	1986	18.06%		11.42%		16.86%	11.69%	-0.21%	7.52%	19.67%	18.62%	19.38%	7.22%
22	1985	31.23%		14.90%		21.99%	20.68%			21.65%	19.35%	20.77%	
23	1984	6.21%		14.22%		7.86%	14.03%			9.70%	2.19%	8.55%	
24	1983	21.30%				15.09%	9.65%			10.38%		9.50%	
25	1982	21.00%					31.56%			35.89%		38.56%	
26	1981	-5.20%					4.78%			-8.77%		-11.15%	
27	1980	31.90%					-6.61%			-11.43%		-16.00%	
28													
29	Beta wrt S&P 500	1.0000	0.1609	0.1267	0.1815	0.3507	0.1833	0.2647	0.2110	0.3034	0.2854	0.2931	0.4847
30	Average maturity		2.9	2.4	2.8	7	8.4	9	12.5	14.1	14.5	14.8	19.7

The regression results can be seen in the following graph:

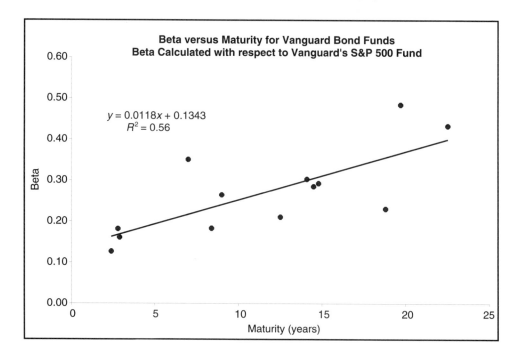

Beta versus Maturity for Vanguard Bond Funds
Beta Calculated with respect to Vanguard's S&P 500 Fund

$y = 0.0118x + 0.1343$
$R^2 = 0.56$

Appendix 2: Why Is β Such a Good Measure of Risk? Portfolio β versus Individual Stock β

Although β may not be a very good measure of the riskiness of an individual stock, the average β is a very good measure of the riskiness of a diversified portfolio. This point is illustrated in this appendix. However, before we fire into the illustration, we want to stress the meaning of the first sentence:

If portfolio β is a good measure of portfolio risk, then—for holders of diversified portfolios (and these include most investors)—the individual-share β is a good measure of the risk of a share, *when this share is ultimately held in a diversified portfolio.*

To illustrate, consider the following graph, which gives the βs of 23 shares.[11] As you can see, the R^2 for the individual regressions are not high (the highest R^2 is 35 percent and the lowest is close to zero). The average R^2 for the 23 stocks is 16.05 percent, and the average β is 0.944.

Betas (connected line) and *R*-Squares (dots)

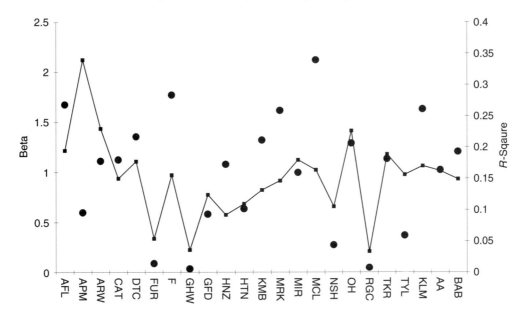

---

11. β is calculated against return data for the S&P 500 for monthly return data from July 1994 through June 1999.

When we combine the 23 shares into an equally weighted portfolio, the portfolio β is 0.944, which is equal to the average beta of the component securities.[12] However, the portfolio's $R^2 = 61.44$ percent, which is much larger than average R^2 of the component securities. For a large, well-diversified portfolio, the portfolio R^2 approaches 1.

The meaning of this number is that—when we invest in large diversified portfolios—almost all of the risk is due to the individual assets' βs.

Appendix 3: Getting Data from the Internet

All of the data used in this chapter were retrieved from the Internet. This appendix provides a brief description of how they were obtained. Keep in mind that, since the Internet is a very lively place, some of the technical details and addresses may have changed by the time you read this book.

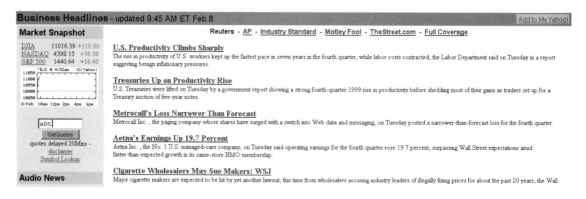

1. By going to the Yahoo business news page (http://dailynews.yahoo.com/headlines/business/) you can indicate in the **Get Quotes** window the ticker symbol of the company you want to look up. In the following picture, I have asked for information on **abt,** the symbol for Abbott Laboratories.

---

12.   This equality will always hold: Suppose we take n securities whose βs are $\beta_1, \beta_2, ..., \beta_n$. Now suppose we take a portfolio in which the weight of each security is $x_1, x_2, ..., x_n$, where $\sum_{i=1}^{n} x_i = 1$. Then the portfolio β will be equal to the weighted average of the individual security βs: $\beta_{\text{portfolio}} = \sum_{i=1}^{n} x_i \beta_i$.

2. Clicking on the **Get Quotes** box gives you the company's latest stock quote.

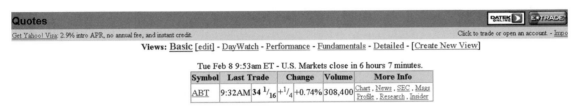

3. Clicking on **Profile** (in the box labeled **More Info**) gives a page of basic financial information about the company, including its β.

Statistics at a Glance -- NYSE:ABT				As of 3-Feb-2000
Price and Volume		**Per-Share Data**		**Management Effectiveness**
52-Week Low on 25-Jan-2000	$29.375	Book Value (mrq*)	$4.38	Return on Assets (ttm)	18.32%
Recent Price	$33.25	Earnings (ttm)	$1.58	Return on Equity (ttm)	39.21%
52-Week High on 13-Apr-1999	$53.313	Earnings (mrq)	$0.43	**Financial Strength**
Beta	0.86	Sales (ttm)	$8.52	Current Ratio (mrq*)	1.36
Daily Volume (3-month avg)	5.45M	Cash (mrq*)	$0.41	Debt/Equity (mrq*)	0.33
Daily Volume (10-day avg)	6.47M	**Valuation Ratios**		Total Cash (mrq)	$630.2M
Stock Performance		Price/Book (mrq*)	7.59	**Short Interest** As of 10-Jan-2000
		Price/Earnings (ttm)	21.00	Shares Short	10.0M
		Price/Sales (ttm)	3.90	Percent of Float	0.7%
		Income Statements		Shares Short (Prior Month)	47.7M
		Sales (ttm)	$13.1B	Short Ratio	1.71
		EBITDA (ttm*)	$3.97B	Daily Volume	5.86M
52-Week Change	-27.1%	Income available to common (ttm)	$2.44B	
52-Week Change relative to S&P500	-36.1%	**Profitability**		
Share-Related Items		Profit Margin (ttm)	18.6%	
Market Capitalization	$50.6B	Operating Margin (ttm)	24.2%	
Shares Outstanding	1.52B	**Fiscal Year**		
Float	1.39B	Fiscal Year Ends	Dec 31	
Dividends & Splits		Most recent quarter (fully updated)	30-Sep-1999	
Annual Dividend (indicated)	$0.68	Most recent quarter (flash earnings)	31-Dec-1999	
Dividend Yield	2.04%			
Last Split: 2 for 1 on 1-June-1998				

See Profile Help for a description of each item above; **M** = millions; **B** = billions; **mrq** = most-recent quarter; **ttm** = trailing twelve months; (as of 31-Dec-1999, except **mrq*/ttm*** items as of 30-Sep-1999)

Note that the β for Abbott is not the same as the one calculated in the chapter. There are two reasons for this difference: First, the chapter uses return data that include dividends, whereas the calculation on Yahoo excludes dividends.

Second, the time horizon is different—the Yahoo calculation uses five years of data, whereas the calculations in the chapter are based on 10 years.

Note also that the page can direct you to much more information about Abbott. The company's Web site has all its financial statements in downloadable form.

4. To get downloadable price information on Abbott Labs in Yahoo, click on **Chart** in the **Basic Info** box. You will then see a page like the following:

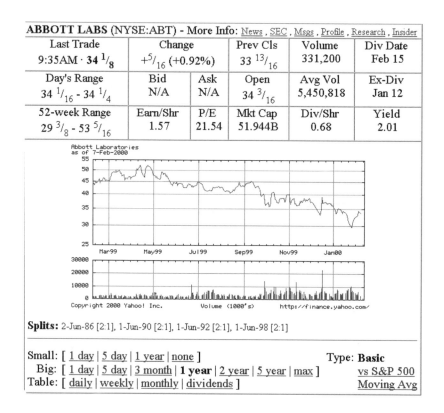

ABBOTT LABS (NYSE:ABT) - More Info: News , SEC , Msgs , Profile , Research , Insider					
Last Trade	Change		Prev Cls	Volume	Div Date
9:35AM · **34 $^1/_8$**	+$^5/_{16}$ (+0.92%)		33 $^{13}/_{16}$	331,200	Feb 15
Day's Range	Bid	Ask	Open	Avg Vol	Ex-Div
34 $^1/_{16}$ - 34 $^1/_4$	N/A	N/A	34 $^3/_{16}$	5,450,818	Jan 12
52-week Range	Earn/Shr	P/E	Mkt Cap	Div/Shr	Yield
29 $^3/_8$ - 53 $^5/_{16}$	1.57	21.54	51.944B	0.68	2.01

Splits: 2-Jun-86 [2:1], 1-Jun-90 [2:1], 1-Jun-92 [2:1], 1-Jun-98 [2:1]

Small: [1 day | 5 day | 1 year | none]   Type: **Basic**
 Big: [1 day | 5 day | 3 month | **1 year** | 2 year | 5 year | max]   vs S&P 500
Table: [daily | weekly | monthly | dividends]   Moving Avg

5. Clicking on **Table** and choosing the appropriate time interval (here we chose **monthly**) gives you the following:

More Info: <u>Quote</u> | <u>Chart</u> | <u>News</u> | <u>Profile</u> | <u>Research</u> | <u>SEC</u> | <u>Msgs</u> | <u>Insider</u>

Historical Quotes

	Month	Day	Year	
Start Date:	Dec ▾	01	97	○ Daily
End Date:	Jan ▾	31	99	○ Weekly
				● Monthly
				○ Dividends

Ticker Symbol: abt

Get Historical Data

Date	Open	High	Low	Close	Volume	Adj. Close*
Jan 99	49.3125	50	44.9375	**46.4375**	2,204,800	45.6808
Jan 99	$0.15 Cash Dividend					
Dec 98	48	49.75	47.50	49	1,846,700	48.0463
Nov 98	47.25	49.8125	46.6875	48	1,679,600	47.0658
Oct 98	42.50	47.8125	40.875	47	2,144,200	46.0852
Oct 98	$0.15 Cash Dividend					
Sep 98	38.75	44.3125	36.625	**43.4375**	2,866,800	42.4433
Aug 98	41.375	42.9375	37	**38.50**	2,526,000	37.6188
Jul 98	41.25	43	40.6875	**41.625**	1,654,500	40.6723
Jul 98	$0.15 Cash Dividend					
Jun 98	37	42.1875	36.375	41	1,967,700	39.9246
Jun 98	2:1 Stock Split (before market open)					
May 98	73.1875	75.1875	72.125	**74.1875**	794,900	36.1208
Apr 98	76.125	76.4375	71	**73.125**	1,527,300	35.6035
Apr 98	$0.30 Cash Dividend					
Mar 98	74.625	75.5625	74.50	**75.3125**	1,074,300	36.5245
Feb 98	71.5625	75	71.125	**74.8125**	1,324,800	36.282
Jan 98	65.625	72	65.0625	**70.8125**	1,351,000	34.3421
Jan 98	$0.27 Cash Dividend					
Dec 97	66.9375	67.50	65.375	**65.50**	920,100	31.6424

Download Spreadsheet Format

Clicking on **Download Spreadsheet Format** gives the data (already adjusted for dividends and splits) in a **csv** file that can be opened with Excel. Note that you can change the **Start Date** and the **End Date** for the data.

Final Note   Ticker symbols for two indexes commonly used: **^SPX** (S&P 500), **^DJI** (the Dow-Jones 30 Industrials).

3 Financial Statement Modeling

3.1 Overview

The usefulness of financial-statement projections for corporate financial management is undisputed. Such projections, termed *pro forma financial statements,* are the bread and butter of much corporate financial analysis. In this and the next chapter we will focus of the use of pro formas for valuing the firm and its component securities, but pro formas also form the basis for many credit analyses; by examining pro forma financial statements we can predict how much financing a firm will need in future years. We can play the usual "what if" games of simulation models, and we can use pro formas to ask what strains on the firm may be caused by changes in financial and sales parameters.

In this chapter we present a variety of financial models. All the models are sales driven, in that they assume that many of the balance-sheet and income-statement items are directly or indirectly related to sales. The mathematical structure of solving the models involves finding the solution to a set of simultaneous linear equations predicting both the balance sheets and the income statements for the coming years. However, the user of a spreadsheet need never worry about the solution of the model; the fact that spreadsheets can solve—by iteration—the financial relations of the model means that we only have to worry about correctly stating the relevant accounting relations in our Excel model.[1]

3.2 How Financial Models Work: Theory and an Initial Example

Almost all financial-statement models are *sales driven;* this term means that as many as possible of the most important financial statement variables are assumed to be functions of the sales level of the firm. For example, accounts receivable may be taken to be a direct percentage of the sales of the firm. A slightly more complicated example might postulate that the fixed assets (or some other account) are a step function of the level of sales:

$$\text{Fixed assets} = \begin{cases} a \text{ if sales} < A \\ b \text{ if } A \leq \text{sales} < B \end{cases}$$

etc.

---

1. The mathematics of balance sheet spreadsheets involve an iterative method for solving simultaneous equations known as the Gauss-Seidel method. Although you do not need to know this method to understand the contents of this chapter, it may be interesting to know that Gauss-Seidel can be implemented directly in Excel. For details, see Chapter 28.

In order to solve a financial-planning model, we must distinguish between those financial-statement items that are functional relationships of sales and perhaps of other financial-statement items and those items that involve policy decisions. The asset side of the balance sheet is usually assumed to be dependent only on functional relationships. The current liabilities may also be taken to involve functional relationships only, leaving the mix between long-term debt and equity as a policy decision.

A simple example is the following. We wish to predict the financial statements for a firm whose current balance sheet and income statement are as follows:

	A	B
14	**Year**	**0**
15	**Income statement**	
16	Sales	1,000
17	Costs of goods sold	(500)
18	Interest payments on debt	(32)
19	Interest earned on cash and marketable securities	6
20	Depreciation	(100)
21	Profit before tax	374
22	Taxes	(150)
23	Profit after tax	225
24	Dividends	(90)
25	Retained earnings	135
26		
27	**Balance sheet**	
28	Cash and marketable securities	80
29	Current assets	150
30	Fixed assets	
31	At cost	1,070
32	Depreciation	(300)
33	Net fixed assets	770
34	**Total assets**	1,000
35		
36	**Current liabilities**	80
37	Debt	320
38	Stock	450
39	Accumulated retained earnings	150
40	**Total liabilities and equity**	1,000

The current (year 0) level of sales is 1,000. The firm expects its sales to grow at a rate of 10 percent per year. In addition, the firm anticipates the following financial-statement relations.

Current assets:	Assumed to be 15 percent of end-of-year sales
Current liabilities:	Assumed to be 8 percent of end-of-year sales
Net fixed assets:	77 percent of end-of year sales
Depreciation:	10 percent of the average value of assets on the books during the year
Fixed assets at cost:	Sum of net fixed assets plus accumulated depreciation
Debt:	The firm neither repays any existing debt nor borrows any more money over the five-year horizon of the pro formas.
Cash and marketable securities:	This is the balance sheet *plug* (see explanation that follows). Average balances of cash and marketable securities are assumed to earn 8 percent interest.

3.2.1 The "Plug"

Perhaps the most important financial policy variable in the financial statement modeling is the "plug": deciding which balance-sheet item will "close" the model. As an example, consider the balance sheet of our first pro forma model:

Assets	Liabilities and Equity
Cash and marketable securities	Current liabilities
Current assets	Debt
Fixed assets	Equity
Fixed assets at cost	Stock (paid in capital)
– Accumulated depreciation	Accumulated retained earnings
Net fixed assets	
Total assets	Total liabilities and equity

In this balance sheet we assume that that cash and marketable securities will be the plug. This assumption has two meanings:

1. The *mechanical* meaning of the plug: Formally, we define

$$\text{Cash and marketable securities} = \text{Total liabilities and equity} - \text{Current assets} - \text{Net fixed assets}$$

By using this definition, we guarantee that assets and liabilities will always be equal.

2. The *financial* meaning of the plug: By defining the plug to be cash and marketable securities, we are also making a statement about how the firm finances itself. In our next model, for example, the firm sells no additional stock, does

not pay back any of its existing debt, and does not raise any more debt. This definition means that all incremental financing (if needed) for the firm will come from the cash and marketable securities account; it also means that if the firm has additional cash, it will go into this account.[2]

3.2.2 Projecting Next Year's Balance Sheet and Income Statement

We have already given the financial statement for year zero. We now project the financial statement for year one:

	A	B	C	D	E	F
1	**SETTING UP THE FINANCIAL STATEMENT MODEL**					
2						
3	Sales growth	10%				
4	Current assets/Sales	15%				
5	Current liabilities/Sales	8%				
6	Net fixed assets/Sales	77%				
7	Costs of goods sold/Sales	50%				
8	Depreciation rate	10%				
9	Interest rate on debt	10.00%				
10	Interest paid on cash and marketable securities	8.00%				
11	Tax rate	40%				
12	Dividend payout ratio	40%				
13						
14	**Year**	**0**	**1**			
15	**Income statement**					
16	Sales	1,000	1,100	<-- =B16*(1+$B$3)		
17	Costs of goods sold	(500)	(550)	<-- =-C16*$B$7		
18	Interest payments on debt	(32)	(32)	<-- =-$B$9*(B37+C37)/2		
19	Interest earned on cash and marketable securities	6	9	<-- =$B$10*(B28+C28)/2		
20	Depreciation	(100)	(117)	<-- =-$B$8*(C31+B31)/2		
21	Profit before tax	374	410	<-- =SUM(C16:C20)		
22	Taxes	(150)	(164)	<-- =-C21*$B$11		
23	Profit after tax	225	246	<-- =C22+C21		
24	Dividends	(90)	(98)	<-- =-$B$12*C23		
25	Retained earnings	135	148	<-- =C24+C23		
26						
27	**Balance sheet**					
28	Cash and marketable securities	80	144	<-- =C40-C29-C33		
29	Current assets	150	165	<-- =C16*$B$4		
30	Fixed assets					
31	At cost	1,070	1,264	<-- =C33-C32		
32	Depreciation	(300)	(417)	<-- =B32-$B$8*(C31+B31)/2		
33	Net fixed assets	770	847	<-- =C16*$B$6		
34	**Total assets**	1,000	1,156	<-- =C33+C29+C28		
35						
36	Current liabilities	80	88	<-- =C16*$B$5		
37	Debt	320	320	<-- =B37		
38	Stock	450	450	<-- =B38		
39	Accumulated retained earnings	150	298	<-- =B39+C25		
40	**Total liabilities and equity**	1,000	1,156	<-- =SUM(C36:C39)		

---

2. The cash and marketable securities account can be viewed as a kind of "negative debt." We will return to this point later when we use the pro forma model to value the firm.

The formulas are mostly obvious. (The dollar signs—indicating that when the formulas are copied, the cell references to the model parameters should not change—are very important! If you fail to put them in, the model will not copy correctly when you project years 2 and beyond.) Model parameters are in bold-face in the following list:

Income Statement Equations

- Sales = Initial sales $*$ $(1 + $ **Sales growth**$)^{year}$
- Costs of goods sold = Sales $*$ **Costs of goods sold/Sales**

The assumption is that the only expenses related to sales are costs of goods sold. Most companies also book an expense item called selling, general, and administrative expenses (SG&A). The changes you would have to make to accommodate this item are obvious (see an exercise at the end of this chapter).

- Interest payments on debt = **Interest rate on debt** $*$ Average debt over the year

This formula allows us to accommodate changes in the model for repayment of debt, as well as rollover of debt at different interest rates. Note that in the current version of the model, debt stays constant; but in other versions of the model to be discussed later debt will vary over time.

- Interest earned on cash and marketable securities = **Interest rate on cash** $*$ Average cash and marketable securities over the year
- Depreciation = **Depreciation rate** $*$ Average fixed assets at cost over the year

This calculation assumes that all new fixed assets are purchased during the year. We also assume that there is no disposal of fixed assets.

- Profit before taxes = Sales $-$ Costs of goods sold $-$ Interest payments on debt $+$ Interest earned on cash and marketable securities $-$ Depreciation
- Taxes = **Tax rate** $*$ Profit before taxes
- Profit after taxes = Profit before taxes $-$ Taxes
- Dividends = **Dividend payout ratio** $*$ Profit after taxes

The firm is assumed to pay out a fixed percentage of its profits as dividends. An alternative would be to assume that the firm has a target for its dividends per share.

- Retained earnings = Profit after taxes $-$ Dividends

Balance Sheet Equations

- Cash and marketable securities = Total liabilities − Current assets − Net fixed assets

  As explained earlier, this formula means that cash and marketable securities are the balance sheet plug.

- Current assets = **Current Assets/Sales** ∗ Sales

- Net fixed assets = **Net fixed assets/Sales** ∗ Sales

- Accumulated depreciation = Previous year's accumulated depreciation + **Depreciation rate** ∗ Average fixed assets at cost over the year.

- Fixed assets at cost = Net fixed assets + Accumulated depreciation

  Note that this model does not distinguish between plant property and equipment (PP&E) and other fixed assets such as land.

- Current liabilities = **Current liabilities/Sales** ∗ Sales

- Debt is assumed to be unchanged. An alternative model, which we will explore later, assumes that debt is the balance-sheet plug.

- Stock doesn't change (the company is assumed to issue no new stock).

- Accumulated retained earnings = Previous year's accumulated retained earnings + Current year's additions to retained earnings

---

Financial statement models in Excel always involve cells that are mutually dependent. As a result, the solution of the model depends on the ability of Excel to solve circular references. To make sure your spreadsheet recalculates, you have to go to the **Tools|Options|Calculation** box and click **Iteration.** If you open a spreadsheet that involves iteration, and if this box is not clicked, you will see the following Excel error message:

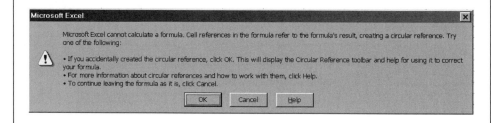

Depending on where you are in Excel when you open the file with the circular references, you may get a slightly different version of this message. Whatever message you see, get out of it and go to **Tools|Options|Calculation|Iteration.** In this dialog box click the box labeled **Iteration:**

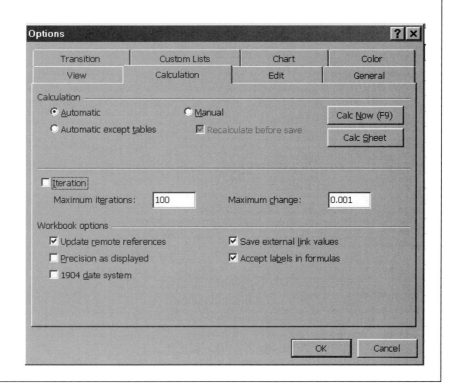

3.2.3   Extending the Model to Years 2 and Beyond

Now that you have the model set up, you can extend it by copying the columns.

	A	B	C	D	E	F	G
1	FIRST FINANCIAL MODEL						
2							
3	Sales growth	10%					
4	Current assets/Sales	15%					
5	Current liabilities/Sales	8%					
6	Net fixed assets/Sales	77%					
7	Costs of goods sold/Sales	50%					
8	Depreciation rate	10%					
9	Interest rate on debt	10.00%					
10	Interest paid on cash and marketable securities	8.00%					
11	Tax rate	40%					
12	Dividend payout ratio	40%					
13							
14	Year	0	1	2	3	4	5
15	Income statement						
16	Sales	1,000	1,100	1,210	1,331	1,464	1,611
17	Costs of goods sold	(500)	(550)	(605)	(666)	(732)	(805)
18	Interest payments on debt	(32)	(32)	(32)	(32)	(32)	(32)
19	Interest earned on cash and marketable securities	6	9	14	20	26	33
20	Depreciation	(100)	(117)	(137)	(161)	(189)	(220)
21	Profit before tax	374	410	450	492	538	587
22	Taxes	(150)	(164)	(180)	(197)	(215)	(235)
23	Profit after tax	225	246	270	295	323	352
24	Dividends	(90)	(98)	(108)	(118)	(129)	(141)
25	Retained earnings	135	148	162	177	194	211
26							
27	Balance sheet						
28	Cash and marketable securities	80	144	213	289	371	459
29	Current assets	150	165	182	200	220	242
30	Fixed assets						
31	At cost	1,070	1,264	1,486	1,740	2,031	2,364
32	Depreciation	(300)	(417)	(554)	(715)	(904)	(1,124)
33	Net fixed assets	770	847	932	1,025	1,127	1,240
34	Total assets	1,000	1,156	1,326	1,513	1,718	1,941
35							
36	Current liabilities	80	88	97	106	117	129
37	Debt	320	320	320	320	320	320
38	Stock	450	450	450	450	450	450
39	Accumulated retained earnings	150	298	460	637	830	1,042
40	Total liabilities and equity	1,000	1,156	1,326	1,513	1,718	1,941

Note that the most common mistake to make in the transition between the two-columned financial model and this one is the failure to mark the model parameters with dollar signs. If you commit this error, you will get zeros in places where there should be numbers.

3.3   Free Cash Flow (FCF): Measuring the Cash Produced by the Business

Now that we have the model, we can use it to make financial predictions. The most important calculation for valuation purposes is the *free cash flow* (FCF). FCF—the cash produced by a business without taking into account the way the business is financed—is the best measure of the cash produced by a business.[3] The easiest way to define the free cash flow is as follows:

Defining the Free Cash Flow

Profit after taxes	This is the basic measure of the profitability of the business, but it is an accounting measure that includes financing flows (such as interest), as well as noncash expenses such as depreciation. Profit after taxes does not account for either changes in the firm's working capital or purchases of new fixed assets, both of which can be important cash drains on the firm.
+ Depreciation	This noncash expense is added back to the profit after tax.
+ After-tax interest payments (net)	FCF is an attempt to measure the cash produced by the business activity of the firm. To neutralize the effect of interest payments on the firm's profits, we • Add back the after-tax cost of interest on debt (*after-tax* since interest payments are tax deductible). • Subtract out the after-tax interest payments on cash and marketable securities.
− Increase in current assets	When the firm's sales increase, more investment is needed in inventories, accounts receivable, etc. This increase in current assets is not an expense for tax purposes (and is therefore ignored in the profit after taxes), but it is a cash drain on the company.
+ Increase in current liabilities	An increase in the sales often causes an increase in financing related to sales (such as accounts payable or taxes payable). This increase in current liabilities—when related to sales—provides cash to the firm. Since it is directly related to sales, we include this cash in the free cash flow calculations.
− Increase in fixed assets at cost	An increase in fixed assets (the long-term productive assets of the company) is a use of cash, which reduces the firm's free cash flow.

Here is the calculation for our firm:

	A	B	C	D	E	F	G
43	Year	0	1	2	3	4	5
44	**Free cash flow calculation**						
45	Profit after tax		246	270	295	323	352
46	Add back depreciation		117	137	161	189	220
47	Subtract increase in current assets		(15)	(17)	(18)	(20)	(22)
48	Add back increase in current liabilities		8	9	10	11	12
49	Subtract increase in fixed assets at cost		(194)	(222)	(254)	(291)	(333)
50	Add back after-tax interest on debt		19	19	19	19	19
51	Subtract after-tax interest on cash & mkt. securities		(5)	(9)	(12)	(16)	(20)
52	**Free cash flow**		176	188	201	214	228

---

3. Extensive discussions of free cash flow and its uses in a valuation context can be found in books by Benninga and Sarig (1997) and Copeland, Koller, and Murrin (1996).

3.3.1   Reconciling the Cash Balances

The free-cash-flow calculation is different from the "consolidated statement of cash flows" that is a part of every accounting statement (an example of such a statement for Abbott Labs follows). The purpose of the accounting statement of cash flows is to explain the increase in the cash accounts in the balance sheet as a function of the cash flows from the firm's operating, investing, and financing activities.

Consolidated Statement of Cash Flows—Abbott Labs

		Year ended December 31	
(dollars in thousands)	1998	1997	1996
Cash Flow from (Used in) Operating Activities:			
Net earnings	$2,333,231	$2,094,462	$1,882,033
Adjustments to reconcile net earnings to net cash from operating activities—Depreciation and amortization	784,243	727,754	686,085
Exchange (gains) losses, net	(14,176)	31,005	(3,419)
Investing and financing (gains) losses, net	90,798	113,999	57,224
Trade receivables	(143,470)	(222,427)	(163,621)
Inventories	(111,649)	(98,964)	(125,726)
Prepaid expenses and other assets	(239,533)	(491,769)	(303,766)
Trade accounts payable and other liabilities	178,979	485,407	342,407
Income taxes payable	(145,522)	(10,700)	10,845
Net Cash from Operating Activities	2,732,901	2,628,767	2,382,062
Cash Flow from (Used in) Investing Activities:			
Acquisition of International Murex in 1998, Sanofi's parenteral products businesses in 1997, and MediSense in 1996, net of cash acquired	(249,177)	(200,475)	(830,559)
Acquisitions of property, equipment and other businesses	(990,619)	(1,007,296)	(949,028)
Purchases of investment securities	(278,002)	(25,115)	(312,535)
Proceeds from sales of investment securities	78,898	43,424	117,783
Other	18,034	(8,209)	19,098
Net Cash Used in Investing Activities	(1,420,866)	(1,197,671)	(1,955,241)
Cash Flow from (Used in) Financing Activities:			
Proceeds from (repayments of) commercial paper, net	42,000	402,000	317,000
Proceeds from issuance of long-term debt	400,000	—	500,000
Other borrowing transactions, net	(59,499)	16,085	18,037

Consolidated Statement of Cash Flows—Abbott Labs *(continued)*

(dollars in thousands)	Year ended December 31		
	1998	1997	1996
Purchases of common shares	(875,407)	(1,054,512)	(808,816)
Proceeds from stock options exercised	150,881	137,482	109,638
Dividends paid	(891,661)	(809,554)	(728,147)
Net Cash Used in Financing Activities	(1,233,686)	(1,308,499)	(592,288)
Effect of exchange rate changes on cash and cash equivalents	(143)	(2,782)	(5,521)
Net Increase (Decrease) in Cash and Cash Equivalents	78,206	119,815	(170,988)
Cash and Cash Equivalents, Beginning of Year	230,024	110,209	281,197
Cash and Cash Equivalents, End of Year	$308,230	$230,024	$110,209
Supplemental Cash Flow Information:			
Income taxes paid	$1,060,479	$922,242	$801,107
Interest paid	153,875	132,645	89,509

In the next example, we treat the cash and marketable securities account as if it were solely a cash account; we then derive the increase in this account through a consolidated statement of cash flows:

	A	B	C	D	E	F	G
55	**RECONCILING THE CASH BALANCES**						
56	**Cash flow from operating activities**						
57	Profit after tax		246	270	295	323	352
58	Add back depreciation		117	137	161	189	220
59	Adjust for changes in net working capital:						
60	Subtract increase in current assets		(15)	(17)	(18)	(20)	(22)
61	Add back increase in current liabilities		8	9	10	11	12
62	Net cash from operating activities		356	400	448	502	562
63							
64	**Cash flow from investing activities**						
65	Acquisitions of fixed assets–capital expenditures		(194)	(222)	(254)	(291)	(333)
66	Purchases of investment securities		0	0	0	0	0
67	Proceeds from sales of investment securities		0	0	0	0	0
68	Net cash used in investing activities		(194)	(222)	(254)	(291)	(333)
69							
70	**Cash flow from financing activities**						
71	Net proceeds from borrowing activities		0	0	0	0	0
72	Net proceeds from stock issues, repurchases		0	0	0	0	0
73	Dividends paid		(98)	(108)	(118)	(129)	(141)
74	Net cash from financing activities		(98)	(108)	(118)	(129)	(141)
75							
76	Net increase in cash and cash equivalents	=C74+C68+C62 ➤	64	70	76	82	88
77	Check: changes in cash and mkt. securities	➤	64	70	76	82	88
78		=C28-B28					
79							

Line 77 checks that the changes in the cash accounts derived through the consolidated statement of cash flows match those derived in the financial model (which uses cash as a plug).

3.4   Using the FCF to Value the Firm and Its Equity

The *enterprise value* of the firm is defined to be the value of the firm's debt, convertible securities, and equity. In financial theory, the enterprise value is the present value of the firm's future anticipated cash flows.

We can use the FCF projections and a cost of capital to determine the enterprise value of the firm. Suppose we have determined that the firm's weighted average cost of capital (WACC) is 20 percent (recall that the calculation of the WACC was discussed in Chapter 2). Then the *enterprise value* of the firm is the discounted value of the firm's projected FCFs plus its terminal value:

$$\text{Enterprise value} = \frac{FCF_1}{(1 + WACC)^1} + \frac{FCF_2}{(1 + WACC)^2} + \dots$$

$$+ \frac{FCF_5}{(1 + WACC)^5} + \frac{\text{Year-5 terminal value}}{(1 + WACC)^5}$$

In this formula, the year-5 terminal value is a proxy for the present value of all FCFs from year 6 onward.[4]

Here's an example that uses our projections:

	A	B	C	D	E	F	G	H	I	J
55	**Valuing the firm**									
56	Weighted average cost of capital	20%								
57										
58	Year	0	1	2	3	4	5			
59	FCF		176	188	201	214	228			
60	Terminal value						2,511	<-- =G59*(1+B3)/(B56-B3)		
61	Total		176	188	201	214	2,740			
62										
63	NPV of row 61	1,598	<-- =NPV(B56,C61:G61)							
64	Add in initial (year 0) cash and mkt. securities	80								
65	Enterprise value	1,678								
66	Subtract out value of firm's debt today	-320								
67	Equity value	1,358								

---

4.   We don't actually project these cash flows. Instead, as you will see in a moment, we determine the terminal value based on year-5 FCF.

3.5   Some Notes on the Valuation Procedure

3.5.1   Terminal Value

In determining the terminal value we used a version of the Gordon model described in Chapter 2. We have assumed that—after the year-5 projection horizon—the cash flows will grow at a rate equal to the sales growth of 10 percent. This assumption gives the terminal value as

$$\text{Terminal value at end of year 5} = \sum_{t=1}^{\infty} \frac{FCF_{t+5}}{(1 + WACC)^t} = \sum_{t=1}^{\infty} \frac{FCF_5 * (1 + \text{growth})}{(1 + WACC)^t}$$

$$= \frac{FCF_5 * (1 + \text{growth})}{WACC - \text{growth}}$$

The last equality is derived in a manner similar to the dividend valuation of shares (the Gordon model) discussed in Chapter 2.

There are other ways of calculating the terminal value. All of the following are common variations that can be implemented in the framework of our model (see end-of-chapter exercises):

- Terminal value = Year-5 book value of debt + Equity.
This calculation assumes that the book value correctly predicts the market value.

- Terminal value = (Enterprise market/book multiple) * (Year-5 book value of debt + Equity)

- Terminal value = P/E ratio * Year-5 profits + Year-5 book value of debt

- Terminal value = EBITDA ratio * Year-5 anticipated EBITDA
(EBITDA = Earnings before interest, taxes, depreciation, and amortization.)

3.5.1.1   The Treatment of Cash and Marketable Securities in the Valuation

Note that we have added the initial cash balances back to the present value of the projected FCFs to get the enterprise value. This procedure assumes the following:

- Year-0 balances of cash and marketable securities are not needed to produce the FCFs in subsequent years.

- Year-0 balances of cash and marketable securities are "surpluses" that could be drawn down or paid out to shareholders without affecting the future economic performance of the firm.

A wholly equivalent assumption sometimes made by investment bankers and equity analysts is to assume that initial cash balances are *negative debt*. If you made this assumption, you would value the equity in the following way:

	A	B	C	D
69	**Cash and Marketable Securities as Negative Debt**			
70	NPV of row 61 = enterprise value	1,598		
71	Net year 0 debt	-240	<-- =-B37+B28	
72	Equity value	1,358		

3.5.2   Half-Year Discounting

While the NPV formula assumes that all cash flows occur at the end of the year, it is more logical to assume that they occur smoothly throughout the year. For discounting purposes, we should therefore discount cash flows as if, on average, they occur in the middle of the year. Thus the enterprise value is more logically calculated as follows:

$$
\text{Enterprise value} = \frac{FCF_1}{(1 + WACC)^{0.5}} + \frac{FCF_2}{(1 + WACC)^{1.5}} + \ldots
$$

$$
+ \frac{FCF_5}{(1 + WACC)^{4.5}} + \frac{\text{Year-5 terminal value}}{(1 + WACC)^{4..5}}
$$

$$
= \left[\frac{FCF_1}{(1 + WACC)^1} + \frac{FCF_2}{(1 + WACC)^2} + \ldots \right.
$$

$$
\left. + \frac{FCF_5}{(1 + WACC)^5} + \frac{\text{Year-5 terminal value}}{(1 + WACC)^5} \right]
$$

$$
* (1 + WACC)^{0.5}
$$

Incorporating this half-year discounting into our value calculations gives

	A	B	C	D	E	F	G	H	I	J
75	**Valuing the Firm–Using Half-Year Discounting**									
76	Weighted average cost of capital	20%								
77										
78	Year	0	1	2	3	4	5			
79	FCF		176	188	201	214	228			
80	Terminal value						2,511	<-- =G72*(1+B3)/(B69-B3)		
81	Total		176	188	201	214	2,740			
82										
83	NPV of row 81	1,750	<-- =NPV(B76,C81:G81)*(1+B76)^0.5							
84	Add in initial (year 0) cash and mkt. securities	80								
85	Enterprise value	1,830								
86	Subtract out value of firm's debt today	-320								
87	Equity value	1,510								

3.6   Sensitivity Analysis

As in any Excel model, we can perform extensive sensitivity analysis on our valuation. Taking the last case as our base case, we can ask, for example, what is the effect of the sales growth rate on the equity value of the firm?

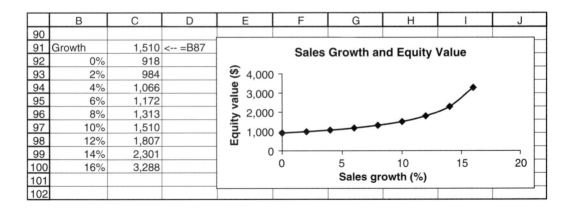

	B	C	D	E	F	G	H	I	J
90									
91	Growth	1,510	<-- =B87						
92	0%	918							
93	2%	984							
94	4%	1,066							
95	6%	1,172							
96	8%	1,313							
97	10%	1,510							
98	12%	1,807							
99	14%	2,301							
100	16%	3,288							
101									
102									

Cells B91:C100 contain a data table (see Chapter 26 if you are unsure of how to construct these tables). As you might expect, the higher the sales growth, the higher the equity value of the firm.

Another variation is to calculate the effect on equity valuation of both the sales growth and the WACC. Here, however, you have to be careful: Examining the terminal value equation

$$\text{Terminal value} = \frac{FCF_5 * (1 + \text{growth})}{WACC - \text{growth}}$$

will show you that this calculation only makes sense if the WACC is greater than the growth rate.[5] To overcome this problem we define the data table cell B107 (this is the calculation on which the data table does its sensitivity analysis) in the following way:

	A	B	C	D	E	F	G	H	I	J	K
104											
105	=IF(B76<=B3,"nmf",B87)										
106			WACC								
107		1,510.41	10%	12%	14%	16%	18%	20%	22%	24%	26%
108		0%	1,924.40	1,590.09	1,350.72	1,170.74	1,030.36	917.73	825.31	748.05	682.47
109	Growth rate of sales	2%	2,333.27	1,848.81	1,525.20	1,293.54	1,119.39	983.59	874.66	785.29	710.60
110		4%	3,014.72	2,236.89	1,769.46	1,457.28	1,233.85	1,065.90	934.97	829.97	743.84
111		6%	4,377.63	2,883.69	2,135.86	1,686.52	1,386.46	1,171.74	1,010.37	884.58	783.72
112		8%	8,466.36	4,177.29	2,746.52	2,030.37	1,600.12	1,312.85	1,107.30	952.85	832.48
113		10%	nmf	8,058.09	3,967.84	2,603.47	1,920.62	1,510.41	1,236.55	1,040.62	893.42
114		12%	nmf	nmf	7,631.79	3,749.65	2,454.77	1,806.75	1,417.49	1,157.65	971.77
115		14%	nmf	nmf	nmf	7,188.21	3,523.08	2,300.64	1,688.91	1,321.49	1,076.24
116		16%	nmf	nmf	nmf	nmf	6,728.01	3,288.44	2,141.28	1,567.25	1,222.50

3.7 Debt as a Plug

In the models that we have shown so far, cash and marketable securities were the plug and debt was a constant. However, for some values of the model parameters, you can get *negative* cash and marketable securities. Consider the following example, which is still the same model, but—as indicated on the spreadsheet itself—with some different parameter values.

---

5. If the growth rate is greater than the WACC, then the terminal value is equal to $\sum_{t=1}^{\infty} \frac{FCF_5 * (1 + \text{growth})^t}{(1 + WACC)^t}$. This problem was also discussed in Chapter 2 in the context of the Gordon dividend model.

	A	B	C	D	E	F	G
3	Sales growth	20%	<-- Increased from 10%				
4	Current assets/Sales	20%	<-- Increased from 15%				
5	Current liabilities/Sales	8%					
6	Net fixed assets/Sales	80%	<-- Increased from 77%				
7	Costs of goods sold/Sales	50%					
8	Depreciation rate	10%					
9	Interest rate on debt	10.00%					
10	Interest paid on cash and marketable securities	8.00%					
11	Tax rate	40%					
12	Dividend payout ratio	50%	<-- Increased from 40%				
13							
14	**Year**	0	1	2	3	4	5
15	**Income statement**						
16	Sales	1,000	1,200	1,440	1,728	2,074	2,488
17	Costs of goods sold	(500)	(600)	(720)	(864)	(1,037)	(1,244)
18	Interest payments on debt	(40)	(40)	(40)	(40)	(40)	(40)
19	Interest earned on cash and marketable securities	6	4	(0)	(6)	(13)	(21)
20	Depreciation	(100)	(124)	(156)	(194)	(242)	(299)
21	Profit before tax	366	440	524	624	742	884
22	Taxes	(147)	(176)	(210)	(249)	(297)	(354)
23	Profit after tax	220	264	314	374	445	530
24	Dividends	(110)	(132)	(157)	(187)	(223)	(265)
25	Retained earnings	110	132	157	187	223	265
26							
27	**Balance sheet**						
28	Cash and marketable securities	80	28	(36)	(113)	(209)	(325)
29	Current assets	200	240	288	346	415	498
30	Fixed assets						
31	At cost	1,100	1,384	1,732	2,157	2,675	3,306
32	Depreciation	(300)	(424)	(580)	(774)	(1,016)	(1,315)
33	Net fixed assets	800	960	1,152	1,382	1,659	1,991
34	**Total assets**	1,080	1,228	1,404	1,615	1,865	2,163
35							
36	Current liabilities	80	96	115	138	166	199
37	Debt	400	400	400	400	400	400
38	Stock	450	450	450	450	450	450
39	Accumulated retained earnings	150	282	439	626	849	1,114
40	**Total liabilities and equity**	1,080	1,228	1,404	1,615	1,865	2,163

Given these changes, the cash and marketable securities account (line 28) turns negative by year 2, a result which is obviously illogical. However, the economic meaning of these negative numbers is clear: Given the increased sales growth, increased current-asset and fixed-asset requirements, and increased dividend payouts, the firm needs more financing.[6]

What we want is a model which recognizes that

- Cash cannot be less than zero.

- When the firm needs additional financing, it *borrows* money.

---

6.   If you examine the model as it now stands, you will see that it implicitly assumes that this extra financing comes at the cost of the cash and marketable securities. If we consider this account a kind of checking account with interest, then the model implicitly assumes that the firm can finance overdrafts from this account at the same rate of interest as it is being paid on the account.

Here is the model:

	A	B	C	D	E	F	G	H	I	J	K
1		**NO NEGATIVE CASH**									
2											
3	Sales growth	20%	<-- Increased from 10%								
4	Current assets/Sales	20%	<-- Increased from 15%								
5	Current liabilities/Sales	8%									
6	Net fixed assets/Sales	80%	<-- Increased from 77%								
7	Costs of goods sold/Sales	50%									
8	Depreciation rate	10%									
9	Interest rate on debt	10.00%									
10	Interest paid on cash and marketable securities	8.00%									
11	Tax rate	40%									
12	Dividend payout ratio	50%	<-- Increased from 40%								
13											
14	Year	0	1	2	3	4	5				
15	**Income statement**										
16	Sales	1,000	1,200	1,440	1,728	2,074	2,488				
17	Costs of goods sold	(500)	(600)	(720)	(864)	(1,037)	(1,244)				
18	Interest payments on debt	(40)	(40)	(42)	(47)	(56)	(67)				
19	Interest earned on cash and marketable securities	6	4	1	-	-	-				
20	Depreciation	(100)	(124)	(156)	(194)	(242)	(299)				
21	Profit before tax	366	440	524	622	739	878				
22	Taxes	(147)	(176)	(209)	(249)	(296)	(351)				
23	Profit after tax	220	264	314	373	443	527				
24	Dividends	(110)	(132)	(157)	(187)	(222)	(263)				
25	Retained earnings	110	132	157	187	222	263				
26											
27	**Balance sheet**										
28	Cash and marketable securities	80	28	-	-	-	-	<-- =G40-G29-G33			
29	Current assets	200	240	288	346	415	498				
30	Fixed assets										
31	At cost	1,100	1,384	1,732	2,157	2,675	3,306				
32	Depreciation	(300)	(424)	(580)	(774)	(1,016)	(1,315)				
33	Net fixed assets	800	960	1,152	1,382	1,659	1,991				
34	**Total assets**	1,080	1,228	1,440	1,728	2,074	2,488				
35											
36	Current liabilities	80	96	115	138	166	199				
37	Debt	400	400	436	514	610	728	<-- =MAX(G29+G33-G36-G38-G39,F37)			
38	Stock	450	450	450	450	450	450				
39	Accumulated retained earnings	150	282	439	626	847	1,111				
40	**Total liabilities and equity**	1,080	1,228	1,440	1,728	2,074	2,488				

The equations for cash (line 28) and debt (line 37) are indicated for the year-5 entries. What they do in accounting terms is the following:

Cash and marketable securities remains the plug in the model.

The debt on the balance sheet conforms to the following test

- Current assets + Net fixed assets > Current liabilities + *Last year's debt* + Stock + Accumulated retained earnings

If this relation holds, then there is no need to increase debt, and, in fact, the firm has to have positive cash and marketable securities as a balancing item. The fact that we have made cash the plug will take care of this concern.

- Current assets + Net fixed assets < Current liabilities + *Last year's debt* + Stock + Accumulated retained earnings

In this case, even if cash and marketable securities are equal to 0, we need to increase debt balances in order to finance the firm's productive activities.

- In Excel programming terms, this formula becomes (for year 5, but each previous year has the same type of equation) Max(G29+G33-G36-G38-G39,F37).

As shown in the exercises to this chapter, the model can easily accommodate a situation in which there are minimum cash balances.

3.8   Incorporating a Target Debt/Equity Ratio into a Pro Forma

Another change we might want to make in our model relates to the plug. Suppose that the firm has a target ratio of debt to equity: In each of the years 1–5 it wants debt and equity on the balance sheet to conform to a certain ratio. This situation is illustrated in the following example:

	A	B	C	D	E	F	G	H	I	J
1	**TARGET DEBT-EQUITY RATIO**									
2										
3	Sales growth	10%								
4	Current assets/Sales	15%								
5	Current liabilities/Sales	8%								
6	Net fixed assets/Sales	77%								
7	Costs of goods sold/Sales	50%								
8	Depreciation rate	10%								
9	Interest rate on debt	10.00%								
10	Interest paid on cash and marketable securities	8.00%								
11	Tax rate	40%								
12	Dividend payout ratio	60%								
13										
14	**Year**	0	1	2	3	4	5			
15	**Income statement**									
16	Sales	1,000	1,100	1,210	1,331	1,464	1,611			
17	Costs of goods sold	(500)	(550)	(605)	(666)	(732)	(805)			
18	Interest payments on debt	(32)	(30)	(29)	(28)	(29)	(32)			
19	Interest earned on cash and marketable securities	6	6	6	6	6	6			
20	Depreciation	(100)	(117)	(137)	(161)	(189)	(220)			
21	Profit before tax	374	409	445	483	521	560			
22	Taxes	(150)	(164)	(178)	(193)	(208)	(224)			
23	Profit after tax	225	246	267	290	313	336			
24	Dividends	(135)	(147)	(160)	(174)	(188)	(202)			
25	Retained earnings	90	98	107	116	125	134			
26										
27	**Balance sheet**									
28	Cash and marketable securities	80	80	80	80	80	80			
29	Current assets	150	165	182	200	220	242			
30	Fixed assets									
31	At cost	1,070	1,264	1,486	1,740	2,031	2,364			
32	Depreciation	(300)	(417)	(554)	(715)	(904)	(1,124)			
33	Net fixed assets	770	847	932	1,025	1,127	1,240			
34	**Total assets**	1,000	1,092	1,193	1,305	1,427	1,562			
35										
36	Current liabilities	80	88	97	106	117	129			
37	Debt	320	287	284	276	302	331	<-- =G42*(G38+G39)		
38	Stock	450	469	457	451	412	372	<-- =G34-G36-G37-G39		
39	Accumulated retained earnings	150	248	355	471	596	730			
40	**Total liabilities and equity**	1,000	1,092	1,193	1,305	1,427	1,562			
41										
42	**Target debt-equity ratio**	0.53	0.40	0.35	0.30	0.30	0.30			

Initial (year 0) debt/equity ratio: =B37/(B38+B39)

Line 42 of the spreadsheet shows the target debt/equity ratio in each of years 1–5. The firm wants to lower its current debt/equity ratio of 53 percent to 30 percent over the next two years. The relevant changes to the equations of our initial model are the following:

- Debt = Target debt/equity ratio * (Stock + Retained earnings)
- Stock = Total assets − Current liabilities − Debt − Accumulated retained earnings

Note that the firm will issue new debt in years 4 and 5; in year 1 the stock account grows (indicating that new equity is issued), whereas in subsequent years stock decreases (indicating a repurchase of equity).

3.9   Project Finance: Debt Repayment Schedules

Here is another use for pro forma modeling: In a typical case of so-called "project finance," the firm borrows money in order to finance a project. The borrowing often comes with strings attached:

- The firm is not allowed to pay any dividends until the debt is paid off.
- The firm is not allowed to issue any new equity.
- The firm must pay back the debt over a specified period.

The following simplified example uses a variation of the version of our basic model with cash balances. A new firm or project is set up; in year 0,

- The firm has assets of 2,200, which are financed with 100 of current liabilities, 1,100 of equity, and 1,000 of debt.
- The debt must be paid off in equal installments of principal over the next five years. Until the debt is paid off, the firm is not allowed to pay dividends (if there is extra cash, it will go into a cash and marketable securities account).

	A	B	C	D	E	F	G
1	**PROJECT FINANCE**						
2							
3	Sales growth	15%					
4	Current assets/Sales	15%					
5	Current liabilities/Sales	8%					
6	Costs of goods sold/Sales	45%					
7	Depreciation rate	10%					
8	Interest rate on debt	10.00%					
9	Interest paid on cash and marketable securities	8.00%					
10	Tax rate	40%					
11	Dividend payout ratio	0%	<-- No dividends until all the debt is paid off				
12							
13	Year	0	1	2	3	4	5
14	**Income statement**						
15	Sales		1,150	1,323	1,521	1,749	2,011
16	Costs of goods sold		(518)	(595)	(684)	(787)	(905)
17	Interest payments on debt		(90)	(70)	(50)	(30)	(10)
18	Interest earned on cash and marketable securities		1	3	9	21	40
19	Depreciation		(211)	(233)	(257)	(284)	(314)
20	Profit before tax		333	428	539	669	822
21	Taxes		(133)	(171)	(216)	(268)	(329)
22	Profit after tax		200	257	323	401	493
23	Dividends		-	-	-	-	-
24	Retained earnings		200	257	323	401	493
25							
26	**Balance sheet**						
27	Cash and marketable securities	the plug: =C39-C28-C32	-	19	64	173	359	633
28	Current assets	200	173	198	228	262	302
29	Fixed assets						
30	At cost	2,000	2,211	2,443	2,700	2,985	3,299
31	Depreciation =B31-$B$7*(C30+B30)/2	-	(211)	(443)	(700)	(985)	(1,299)
32	Net fixed assets	2,000	2,000	2,000	2,000	2,000	2,000
33	**Total assets**	2,200	2,192	2,262	2,401	2,621	2,935
34							
35	Current liabilities	100	92	106	122	140	161
36	Debt	1,000	800	600	400	200	-
37	Stock	1,100	1,100	1,100	1,100	1,100	1,100
38	Accumulated retained earnings =B36-$B$36/5	-	200	456	780	1,181	1,674
39	**Total liabilities and equity**	2,200	2,192	2,262	2,401	2,621	2,935

The debt repayment terms are incorporated into the model by simply specifying the debt balances at the end of each year. Since the firm is assumed to
issue no new equity (in accordance with the covenants on the lending), it follows that the model's plug cannot be on the liabilities side of the balance sheet.
In our model the plug is the cash and marketable securities account.

The model incorporates one other assumption often made about fixed assets: It assumes that the *net* fixed assets stay constant over the life of the project. As you can see from looking at lines 30–32, this assumption means that the fixed assets at cost grow each year by the increase in asset depreciation. It also means that in there is no net cash flow from depreciation:

	A	B	C	D	E	F	G
42	**FREE CASH FLOW CALCULATION**						
43	**Year**	0	1	2	3	4	5
44	Profit after tax		200	257	323	401	493
45	Add back depreciation		211	233	257	284	314
46	Subtract increase in current assets		28	(26)	(30)	(34)	(39)
47	Add back increase in current liabilities		(8)	14	16	18	21
48	Subtract increase in fixed assets at cost		(211)	(233)	(257)	(284)	(314)
49	Add back after-tax interest on debt		90	70	50	30	10
50	Subtract after-tax interest on cash & mkt. securities		(1)	(3)	(9)	(21)	(40)
51	**Free cash flow**		308	311	350	394	445
52	Note that the cash flow generated by						
53	depreciation equals the increase in fixed						
54	assets at cost.						
55							

In this example the firm has no problem in making its debt principal repayments. As credit analysts, we might be interested in how the firm's ability to meet its payments is affected by the various parameter values. In the following example we have increased the ratio of cost of goods sold to sales. With the new parameter values, the firm can no longer meet its debt repayments in years 1–3. This fact can be seen in the pro forma: In years 1–3 the balances of cash and marketable securities are negative, indicating that—in order to make the repayment of the loan principal—the firm had to borrow money.[7]

---

7. From the point of view of corporate finance, positive balances of cash are like *negative balances* of debt. Thus, when the cash is negative, it is equivalent to the firm having borrowed money.

	A	B	C	D	E	F	G
1		**PROJECT FINANCE**					
2							
3	Sales growth	15%					
4	Current assets/Sales	15%					
5	Current liabilities/Sales	8%					
6	Costs of goods sold/Sales	55%					
7	Depreciation rate	10%					
8	Interest rate on debt	10.00%					
9	Interest paid on cash and marketable securities	8.00%					
10	Tax rate	40%					
11	Dividend payout ratio	0%	<-- No dividends until all the debt is paid off				
12							
13	**Year**	0	1	2	3	4	5
14	**Income statement**						
15	Sales		1,150	1,323	1,521	1,749	2,011
16	Costs of goods sold		(633)	(727)	(836)	(962)	(1,106)
17	Interest payments on debt		(90)	(70)	(50)	(30)	(10)
18	Interest earned on cash and marketable securities		(2)	(6)	(7)	(4)	4
19	Depreciation		(211)	(233)	(257)	(284)	(314)
20	Profit before tax		215	287	370	469	585
21	Taxes		(86)	(115)	(148)	(187)	(234)
22	Profit after tax		129	172	222	281	351
23	Dividends		-	-	-	-	-
24	Retained earnings		129	172	222	281	351
25							
26	**Balance sheet**	the plug:					
27	Cash and marketable securities	=C39-C28-C32	-	(52)	(92)	(83)	(18)	114
28	Current assets		200	173	198	228	262	302
29	Fixed assets							
30	At cost		2,000	2,211	2,443	2,700	2,985	3,299
31	Depreciation	=B31-$B$7*(C30+B30)/2	-	(211)	(443)	(700)	(985)	(1,299)
32	Net fixed assets		2,000	2,000	2,000	2,000	2,000	2,000
33	**Total assets**		2,200	2,121	2,107	2,145	2,244	2,416
34							
35	Current liabilities		100	92	106	122	140	161
36	Debt		1,000	800	600	400	200	-
37	Stock		1,100	1,100	1,100	1,100	1,100	1,100
38	Accumulated retained earnings	=B36-$B$36/5	-	129	301	523	804	1,155
39	**Total liabilities and equity**		2,200	2,121	2,107	2,145	2,244	2,416

3.9.1   Calculating the Return on Equity

Equity owners in the project have to pay 1,100 in year 0. During years 1–4 they get no payoffs, but in year 5 they own the company. Suppose that the book value of the assets accurately reflects the market value. Then at the end of year 5 in the previous example the equity in the firm is worth Stock + Accumulated retained earnings = 2,255. The expected return on the equity investment (ROE) is calculated as follows:

	A	B	C	D	E	F	G	H	I
57	**RETURN ON EQUITY (ROE)**								
58	**Year**	0	1	2	3	4	5		
59	Equity cash flow	-1,100	-	-	-	-	2,255	<-- =G23+G37+G38	
60	RETURN ON EQUITY (ROE)	15.44%	<-- =IRR(B59:G59)						

It is interesting to note that this equity return increases as the equity invest-ment decreases.[8] Consider the case where the firm initially borrows 1,500 and the equity owners invest 600:

	A	B	C	D	E	F	G	H	I
57	RETURN ON EQUITY (ROE)								
58	Year	0	1	2	3	4	5		
59	Equity cash flow	-600	-	-	-	-	1,602	<-- =G23+G37+G38	
60	RETURN ON EQUITY (ROE)	21.70%	<-- =IRR(B59:G59)						

As the following data table and graph show, the less the initial equity invest-ment, the greater the equity return:

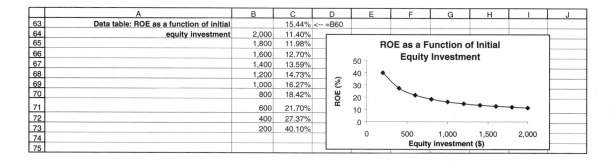

	A	B	C	D	E	F	G	H	I	J
63	Data table: ROE as a function of initial		15.44%	<-- =B60						
64	equity investment	2,000	11.40%							
65		1,800	11.98%							
66		1,600	12.70%							
67		1,400	13.59%							
68		1,200	14.73%							
69		1,000	16.27%							
70		800	18.42%							
71		600	21.70%							
72		400	27.37%							
73		200	40.10%							
74										
75										

3.10   Conclusion

Pro forma modeling is one of the basic skills of corporate financial analysis. Remember that financial modeling is a devious combination of finance, the im-plementation of accounting rules, and spreadsheet skills. In order to be useful, financial models must match the situation at hand, but they must also be simple enough so that the user can easily understand *why* the results happen (be they valuations, creditworthiness, or simply commonsense predictions of how a firm or project might look several years down the road).

---

8. Interesting but not surprising: As the equity investment goes down, the project becomes more leveraged and hence more risky for the equity investors. The increased return should compen-sate the equity holders for this extra risk. The really interesting question (not answered here) is whether the increased return is in fact a compensation for the riskiness.

Exercises

1. Here's a basic exercise that will help you understand what's going on in the modeling of financial statements. Replicate the models in sections 3.2, 3.7, and 3.8. That is, enter the correct formulas for the cells and see that you get the same results as the book. (This turns out to be more of an exercise in accounting than in finance. If you're like many financial modelers, you'll see that there are some aspects of accounting that you've forgotten!)

2. The model of section 3.2 includes cost of goods sold but not selling, general, and administrative (SG&A) expenses. Suppose that the firm has $200 of these expenses each year, irrespective of the level of sales.

   a. Change the model to accommodate this new assumption. Show the resulting profit and loss statements, balance sheets, free cash flows, and valuation.

   b. Create a data table in which you show the sensitivity of the equity value to the level of SG&A. Let SG&A vary from 0 to $500 per year.

3. Suppose that in the model of section 3.2 the fixed assets *at cost* for years 1–5 are 100 percent of sales (in the current model, it is *net* fixed assets that are a function of sales). Change the model accordingly. Show the resulting profit and loss statements, balance sheets, and free cash flows for years 1–5. (Assume that in year 0, the fixed assets accounts are as shown in section 3.2. Note that since year 0 is given—it is the current situation of the firm, whereas years 1–5 are the predictions for the future—there is no need for the year-0 ratios to conform to the predicted ratios for years 1–5.)

4. Referring again to the model of section 3.2, suppose that the fixed assets at cost follow the following step function:

$$\text{Fixed assets} \atop \text{at cost} = \begin{cases} 100\% * \text{Sales} & \text{if Sales} \le 1{,}200 \\ 1{,}200 + 90\% * (\text{Sales} - 1{,}200) & 1{,}200 < \text{Sales} \le 1{,}400 \\ 1{,}380 + 80\% * (\text{Sales} - 1{,}400) & \text{Sales} > 1{,}400 \end{cases}$$

   Incorporate this function into the model.

5. Consider the model in section 3.7 (where debt is the plug).

   a. Suppose that the firm has 1,000 shares and that it decides to pay, in year 1, a dividend per share of 15 cents. In addition, suppose that it wants this dividend per share to grow in subsequent years by 12 percent per year. Incorporate these changes into the pro forma model.

   b. Do a sensitivity analysis in which you show the effect on the debt/equity ratio of the annual growth rate of dividends. Vary this rate from 0 percent to 18 percent, in steps of 2 percent. For this exercise, define debt as net debt (i.e., debt minus cash and marketable securities).

6. In the model of section 3.7, assume that the firm needs to have minimum cash balances of 25 at end of each year. Introduce this constraint into the model.

7. In the valuation exercise of section 3.4, the terminal value is calculated using a Gordon dividend model on the cash flows. Replace this terminal value by the year-5 book value of debt plus equity. In making this change, you are essentially assuming that the book value correctly predicts the market value.

8. Repeat exercise 7, but this time replace the terminal value by an EBITDA ratio times year-5 anticipated EBITDA. Show a graph of the *equity value* of the firm as a function of the assumed year-5 EBITDA ratio, varying this ratio from 6 to 14.

9.   In the project finance pro forma of section 3.9 it is assumed that the firm pays off its initial
      debt of 1,000 in equal installments of principal over five years. Change this assumption and
      assume instead that the firm pays off its debt in equal payments of interest and principal
      over five years. Hint: You have to use the **PMT** function to find the annual payments; then
      set up a loan table (as in Chapter 1) to split the annual payments into an interest and repay-
      ment of principal.

10.   This problem introduces the concept of "sustainable dividends": The firm whose financials
      are illustrated following wishes to maintain cash balances of 80 over the next 5 years. It also
      desires to issue neither additional stock nor make any changes in its current level of debt.
      This means that dividends are the plug in the balance sheet. Model this situation. Note that
      for some parameter levels you may get "negative dividends," indicating that there is no sus-
      tainable level of dividends.

	A	B	C	D	E	F	G
1	**SUSTAINABLE DIVIDENDS–Template**						
2							
3	Sales growth	10%					
4	Current assets/Sales	15%					
5	Current liabilities/Sales	8%					
6	Net fixed assets/Sales	77%					
7	Costs of goods sold/Sales	50%					
8	Depreciation rate	10%					
9	Interest rate on debt	10.00%					
10	Interest paid on cash and marketable securities	8.00%					
11	Tax rate	40%					
12							
13	**Year**	0	1	2	3	4	5
14	**Income statement**						
15	Sales	1,000					
16	Costs of goods sold	(500)					
17	Interest payments on debt	(32)					
18	Interest earned on cash and marketable securities	6					
19	Depreciation	(100)					
20	Profit before tax	374					
21	Taxes	(150)					
22	Profit after tax	225					
23	Dividends	(90)					
24	Retained earnings	135					
25							
26	**Balance sheet**						
27	Cash and marketable securities	80	80	80	80	80	80
28	Current assets	150					
29	Fixed assets						
30	At cost	1,070					
31	Depreciation	(300)					
32	Net fixed assets	770					
33	**Total assets**	1,000					
34							
35	Current liabilities	80					
36	Debt	320	320	320	320	320	320
37	Stock	450	450	450	450	450	450
38	Accumulated retained earnings	150					
39	**Total liabilities and equity**	1,000					

Appendix 1: Calculating the Free Cash Flows When There Are Negative Profits

We start off with a simple example. A firm that has no depreciation, no changes in net working capital, and no capital expenditures has the following profits in two successive years:

	A	B	C
2	**PROFIT AND LOSS WITH CARRYFORWARD**		
3	**Year**	**1**	**2**
4	Earnings before interest and taxes (EBIT)	-100	400
5	Interest	-50	-80
6	Profit before tax	-150	320
7	Loss carryforward	0	-150
8	Taxable income	-150	170
9	Taxes (30%)	0	-51
10	Profit after tax	-150	119

Recall that the FCF is the amount of cash generated by the firm under the assumption that it has no debt. Thus, to calculate the FCFs of the firm, we calculate the profit and loss statement that it would have had (including tax carryforwards) if it had no interest payments:

	A	B	C
13	**FCF WITH NO DEBT**		
14	**Year**	**1**	**2**
15	Earnings before interest and taxes (EBIT)	-100	400
16	Interest	0	0
17	Profit before tax	-100	400
18	Loss carryforward	0	-100
19	Taxable income	-100	300
20	Taxes (30%)	0	-90
21	Profit after tax	-100	210
22	Add back tax-loss carryforward	0	100
23	Free cash flow (FCF)	-100	310

The loss carryforward is added back to the profit after tax because it is a *non-cash* charge against earnings (like depreciation). We can also do this calculation directly from the profit and loss statement. However, we have to recognize that the tax-loss carryforward includes an element of the interest charges, which needs to be netted out:

	A	B	C	D
26	**CALCULATING FCF FROM PROFIT AND LOSS STATEMENT**			
27	**Year**	**1**	**2**	
28	EBIT	-100	400	
29	Interest	-50	-80	
30	Profit before tax	-150	320	
31	Loss carryforward	0	-150	
32	Taxable income	-150	170	
33	Taxes (30%)	0	-51	
34	Profit after tax	-150	119	
35				
36	**FCF Calculation**			
37	Profit after tax	-150	119	
38	Add back loss carryforward	0	150	
39	Add back interest, net of tax	35	56	
40	Subtract interest tax shield on carryforward	0	-15	
41	Free cash flow (FCF)	-115	310	

Appendix 2: Accelerated Depreciation in Pro Forma Models[9]

The models in the chapter all use straight-line depreciation. However, they can be adjusted to accommodate accelerated depreciation (whether this adjustment is worth the effort is another question that is discussed at the end of this appendix).

As an example, consider a company that depreciates all of its assets using the five-year accelerated cost recovery system (ACRS) depreciation schedule that is part of the 1986 Tax Reduction Act in the United States.[10] Under this schedule, the depreciation rates for an asset are as shown in the following table.

---

9. This appendix contains an advanced topic that can be skipped on first reading.

10. For more information about the ACRS depreciation schedules, you are referred to standard U.S. finance texts, such as Brealey and Myres (1996, chapter 6).

	A	B	C	D
74	**Depreciation Table–Five-year Asset Life**			
75		**Depreciation**	**Cumulative**	
76	**Year**	**rate**	**depreciation**	
77	1	20%	20%	
78	2	32%	52%	
79	3	19.20%	71%	
80	4	11.52%	83%	
81	5	11.52%	94%	
82	6	5.76%	100%	
83	7	0%	100%	

(Note that the "five-year" depreciation schedule actually depreciates the asset over six years.)

The following spreadsheet fragment shows the fixed-asset schedule over the next five years:

	A	B	C	D	E	F	G
55	**DEPRECIATION CALCULATION--year 0 assets assumed three years old**						
56	Sales growth	10%					
57	Net fixed assets/Sales	77%					
58	Sales	1,000	1,100	1,210	1,331	1,464	1,611
59							
60	**Year**	**0**	**1**	**2**	**3**	**4**	**5**
61	Fixed assets at cost, end of year	2,674	3,155	3,838	4,536	5,290	5,815
62	Accumulated depreciation	(1,904)	(2,308)	(2,907)	(3,511)	(4,162)	(4,575)
63	Net fixed assets required, end of year	770	847	932	1,025	1,127	1,240
64							
65	New assets acquired during year		481	683	698	754	526
66							
67	Accumulated depreciation calculation						
68	Accumulated depreciation, end of previous year		1,904	2,308	2,907	3,511	4,162
69	Depreciation of year 0 assets		308	308	154	0	0
70	Depreciation of assets acquired year 1		96	154	92	55	55
71	Depreciation of assets acquired year 2			137	219	131	79
72	Depreciation of assets acquired year 3				140	223	134
73	Depreciation of assets acquired year 4					241	145
74	Depreciation of assets acquired year 5						168
75	**Accumulated depreciation**	1,904	2,308	2,907	3,511	4,162	4,575

Here's an explanation of this schedule:

• In each of the years, the ratio of net fixed assets to sales is assumed to be 77 percent. With anticipated sales as in row 58, the required net fixed assets are given in row 63.

- At date 0, the firm's assets are assumed to be three years old. Therefore, the cumulative depreciation on the assets is 71 percent of their initial value (0.71 ∗ 2,674 = 1,904).

- The cumulative depreciation in years 1–5 is calculated by summing the annual depreciation on each set of assets using the **VLookup** function (for a description of this function, see Chapter 29):

	A	B	C	D	E	F	G	H	I
68	Accumulated depreciation, end of previous year		1,904	2,308	2,907	3,511	4,162		
69	Depreciation of year 0 assets		308	308	154	0	0		
70	Depreciation of assets acquired year 1		96	154	92	55	55		
71	Depreciation of assets acquired year 2			137	219	131	79		
72	Depreciation of assets acquired y =VLOOKUP(3+C$60,$A$81:$B$87,2)*$B$61				140	223	134		
73	Depreciation of assets acquired year 4					241	145		
74	Depreciation of assets acquired year 5						168		
75	**Accumulated depreciation**		1,904	2,308	2,907	3,511	4,162	4,575	
76									
77					=VLOOKUP(C$60,$A$81:$B$87,2)*$C$65				
78	**Depreciation table--5-year asset life**								
79		Depr.	Cumulative						
80	Year	rate	depreciation		=VLOOKUP(D$60-1,$A$81:$B$87,2)*$D$65				
81		1	20%	20%					
82		2	32%	52%	=VLOOKUP(E$60-2,$A$81:$B$87,2)*$E$65				
83		3	19.20%	71%					
84		4	11.52%	83%					
85		5	11.52%	94%					
86		6	5.76%	100%					
87		7	0%	100%					

- The results from the cumulative depreciation calculated in the previous screen are then referenced in row 62. The fixed assets at cost are calculated in row 61:

	A	B	C
58	Sales	1,000	1,100
59	=C63-C62		
60	**Year** =-C75	0	1
61	Assets in place, end of year	2,674	3,155
62	Accumulated depreciation	(1,904)	(2,308)
63	Net fixed assets required, end of year	770	847

Is This Worth It?

As you can see, writing pro forma models to account for accelerated depreciation is a fairly big mess! Modeling accelerated depreciation requires additional assumptions about the schedule in use for the assets (i.e., are assets depreciated on a three-year, five-year, seven-year, ... schedule?). It also requires the modeler to make assumptions about the average age of existing assets; in the present example, we have assumed that assets are all depreciated on a five-year schedule and that existing assets in place at date 0 are three years old. Accelerated depreciation also requires separate depreciation schedules for assets acquired in each year.

As a financial analyst, you have to ask yourself whether this is worth the effort. In our opinion the detailed analysis of accelerated depreciation is worthwhile only in cases where the firm has large amounts of fixed assets that generate significantly large accretions to the fixed asset base (meaning that the cash-flow effect of doing an accelerated-fixed-asset calculation versus a straight-line calculation is large).

4   Using Financial Statement Models for Valuation

4.1   Overview

In this chapter we use the pro forma models developed in Chapter 3 to perform a corporate valuation. The valuation is typical of those done in many analyses of mergers and acquisitions (though far simpler).

A valuation of a company requires the consideration of many complex issues:

- Building a pro forma model for the company to be valued.
- Calculating the relevant free cash flows.
- Calculating the cost of capital for the free cash flows.
- Determining the *terminal value* of the firm.
- Properly discounting the free cash flows.
- Sensitivity analysis on the results.
- A bold combination of finance, accounting, and common sense!

These are a lot of issues for one small chapter of a book on financial modeling![1] Nevertheless, we discuss each issue briefly in this chapter and show how to implement them. We illustrate most of the issues through the valuations of a fictitious company, Farmers Bagels.

4.2   Farmers Bagels—Some Background

Farmers Bagels, started at the beginning of 1995, has become the successful operator of a large chain of bagel stores. In each store customers can buy not only bagged bagels for home consumption, but also bagel sandwiches and coffee.

At the beginning of 1997, shortly after the publication of Farmers' 1996 results, Buyout, Inc., a large diversified food products firm, became interested in buying the equity of Farmers. Buyout hired a group of financial analysts to help it value Farmers and determine a price range for the equity of the company.

The analysts started by looking at Farmers' financial statements for the two years of its existence:

---

1.   A fuller discussion of these issues requires a whole book. The reader is (immodestly) referred to *Corporate Finance: A Valuation Approach,* by Simon Benninga and Oded Sarig (New York: McGraw-Hill, 1997).

	A	B	C
1	**FARMERS BAGELS, INC.**		
2	Financial results for first two years of existence		
3			
4		**1995**	**1996**
5	**Current assets**		
6	Cash and cash equivalents	2,016,245	3,023,989
7	Accounts receivable	1,278,771	4,194,238
8	Inventory	185,314	759,104
9	Prepaid expenses and other current assets	392,116	1,006,169
10			
11	**Property and equipment**		
12	At cost	4,000,000	13,030,853
13	Less accumulated depreciation	(400,000)	(1,703,085)
14	Net property and equipment	3,600,000	11,327,768
15			
16	**Total assets**	7,472,446	20,311,268
17			
18			
19	**Current liabilities**		
20	Accounts payable and accrued expenses	906,648	3,271,271
21	Income taxes payable	157,935	423,486
22	Other current liabilities	52,910	151,189
23			
24	Long-term debt	846,058	8,597,874
25			
26	**Stockholders' equity**		
27	Common stock	4,610,999	4,610,999
28	Retained earnings	897,896	3,256,449
29	**Total liabilities and equity**	7,472,446	20,311,268
30			
31			
32	**Income statement**	**1995**	**1996**
33	**Sales**		
34	Product sales	6,076,345	18,977,564
35	Other income	131,326	176,111
36	**Total sales**	6,207,671	19,153,675
37			
38	**Operating expenses**		
39	Cost of products sold	(2,461,470)	(7,839,481)
40	Depreciation	(400,000)	(1,303,085)
41	Selling, general, and administrative expenses	(1,866,614)	(6,045,369)
42	Interest expense	(50,763)	(84,606)
43	Interest income	100,812	171,362
44	Earnings before income taxes	1,529,636	4,052,496
45	Provision for income taxes	(631,740)	(1,693,943)
46	Profit after taxes	897,896	2,358,553

The analysts performed an analysis of Farmers' financial ratios. Here are some relevant ratios.

	A	B	C
1	**FARMERS BAGELS, INC.**		
2	**Ratio Analysis**		
3			
4		**1995**	**1996**
5	**Current assets**		
6	Accounts receivable	20.6%	21.9%
7	Inventory	3.0%	4.0%
8	Prepaid expenses and other current assets	6.3%	5.3%
9			
10	New property and equipment at cost, % of new sales	64.4%	69.8%
11			
12	**Current liabilities**		
13	Accounts payable and accrued expenses	14.6%	17.1%
14	Income taxes payable (as % of income tax)	25.0%	25.0%
15	Other current liabilities	0.9%	0.8%
16			
17	**Operating expenses**		
18	Cost of products sold	39.7%	40.9%
19	Selling, general, and administrative expenses	30.1%	31.6%
20	Provision for income taxes (as % of earnings before taxes)	41.3%	41.8%

4.3   Building a Financial Model

The analysts used the ratios derived in the preceding section (and some additional information that they gleaned from conversations with Farmers and Buyout) to build a financial model from which to predict the future financial performance of Farmers. To build such a model, they had to make a lot of assumptions:

Model Assumptions

• Drop the distinction between product sales and other income, and predict only total sales. The consultants decided that they could not predict other income with any degree of accuracy. Their predictions for Farmers' sales are as follows:

	B	C
2	**FARMERS BAGELS**	
3	**PROJECTED SALES**	
4		**projected**
5	**year**	**sales**
6	1997	28,048,500
7	1998	42,021,000
8	1999	55,993,500
9	2000	69,966,000
10	2001	83,938,500

The analysts were wary of predicting sales past 2001; as a result, we will have a *terminal value* problem, which is discussed in section 4.5.

• Cost of products sold will be 40 percent of sales.

• Selling, general, and administrative expenses will drop by 1 percent per year, from 32 percent of sales in 1996 to 28 percent of sales in 2001.

• Interest expenses on debt will be 12 percent of average debt balances throughout the year, and interest income will be 6 percent of average balances of cash and cash equivalents throughout the year.

• Farmers Bagels' income tax rate will be 41.5 percent of its income.

• The consultants felt that a "cash cushion" would be needed for Farmers, though the size of this cushion could decrease as the firm grew. They predicted that cash and cash equivalents would be a declining proportion of sales:

	A	B	C	D	E	F	G
17	Year	1996	1997	1998	1999	2000	2001
18	Cash and cash equivalents as proportion of sales		20%	15%	10%	10%	10%

• Accounts receivable will remain at 22 percent of sales.

• Inventory will be rise to 5 percent of sales over the next two years and remain there.

• Prepaid expenses will drop to 5 percent of sales.

• Property and equipment at cost will drop from 70 percent of incremental sales in 1996 to 40 percent of incremental sales in 2001. The consultants explained that this decrease would result from greater efficiency in producing bagels.

• Depreciation will be straight line at 10 percent of property at cost.

• Accounts payable and accrued expenses will rise by 1 percent per year until they reach 20 percent.

• Income tax payable will remain at 25 percent of taxes owed for each year. This item represents the portion of the current year's taxes that will actually be paid in the following year.

• Other current liabilities will be 1 percent of sales.

• Farmers will pay no dividends during the next five years and will raise no new equity. Therefore, debt is the "plug" in the model.

The model with results from these assumptions and predictions is given as follows.

	A	B	C	D	E	F	G
13	**FARMERS BAGELS: INITIAL PRO FORMA MODEL**						
14							
15	Predicted financial statement ratios: All ratios are a percentage of sales unless otherwise stated.						
16							
17	**Year**	**1996**	**1997**	**1998**	**1999**	**2000**	**2001**
18	Cash and cash equivalents as proportion of sales		20%	15%	10%	10%	10%
19	Accounts receivable		22%				
20	Inventory		4.5%	5.0%	5.0%	5.0%	5.0%
21	Prepaid expenses and other current assets		5%				
22							
23	Property and equipment at cost, as percent of incremental sales	70%	65%	58%	51%	44%	40%
24	Depreciation		10%				
25							
26	Accounts payable and accrued expenses		17%	18%	19%	20%	20%
27	Income taxes payable (as percent of income tax)		25%				
28	Other current liabilities		1%				
29							
30	Interest expense		12%				
31	Interest income		6%				
32	Cost of products sold		40%				
33	Selling, general, and administrative expenses		32%	31%	30%	29%	28%
34	Provision for income taxes (as percent of earnings before taxes)		41.5%				
35							
36		**1996**	**1997**	**1998**	**1999**	**2000**	**2001**
37	**Income statement**						
38	**Total sales**	18,977,564	28,048,500	42,021,000	55,993,500	69,966,000	83,938,500
39							
40	**Operating expenses**						
41	Cost of products sold		(11,219,400)	(16,808,400)	(22,397,400)	(27,986,400)	(33,575,400)
42	Depreciation		(1,892,696)	(2,703,101)	(3,415,699)	(4,030,489)	(4,589,389)
43	Selling, general, and administrative expenses		(8,975,520)	(13,026,510)	(16,798,050)	(20,290,140)	(23,502,780)
44	Interest expense		(1,325,198)	(1,782,358)	(1,756,823)	(1,216,577)	(278,387)
45	Interest income		259,011	357,386	357,075	377,879	461,714
46	Earnings before income taxes		4,894,697	8,058,017	11,982,604	16,820,273	22,454,258
47	Provision for income taxes		(2,031,299)	(3,344,077)	(4,972,781)	(6,980,413)	(9,318,517)
48	**Profit after taxes**		**2,863,397**	**4,713,940**	**7,009,823**	**9,839,860**	**13,135,741**
49							
50	**Balance sheet**						
51	**Current assets**						
52	Cash and cash equivalents	3,023,989	5,609,700	6,303,150	5,599,350	6,996,600	8,393,850
53	Accounts receivable	4,194,238	6,170,670	9,244,620	12,318,570	15,392,520	18,466,470
54	Inventory	759,104	1,262,183	2,101,050	2,799,675	3,498,300	4,196,925
55	Prepaid expenses and other current assets	1,006,169	1,402,425	2,101,050	2,799,675	3,498,300	4,196,925
56	**Total current assets**	8,983,500	14,444,978	19,749,870	23,517,270	29,385,720	35,254,170
57							
58	**Property and equipment**						
59	At cost	13,030,853	18,926,962	27,031,012	34,156,987	40,304,887	45,893,887
60	Less accumulated depreciation	(1,703,085)	(3,595,782)	(6,298,883)	(9,714,581)	(13,745,070)	(18,334,459)
61	Net property and equipment	11,327,768	15,331,180	20,732,129	24,442,405	26,559,817	27,559,428
62							
63	**Total assets**	20,311,268	29,776,158	40,481,999	47,959,675	55,945,537	62,813,598
64							
65							
66	**Current liabilities**						
67	Accounts payable and accrued expenses	3,271,271	4,768,245	7,563,780	10,638,765	13,993,200	16,787,700
68	Income taxes payable	423,486	507,825	836,019	1,243,195	1,745,103	2,329,629
69	Other current liabilities	151,189	280,485	420,210	559,935	699,660	839,385
70	**Total current liabilities**	3,845,946	5,556,555	8,820,009	12,441,895	16,437,963	19,956,714
71							
72	Long-term debt	8,597,874	13,488,758	16,217,205	13,063,172	7,213,105	(2,573,325)
73							
74	**Stockholders' equity**						
75	Common stock	4,610,999	4,610,999	4,610,999	4,610,999	4,610,999	4,610,999
76	Retained earnings	3,256,449	6,119,846	10,833,786	17,843,609	27,683,469	40,819,210
77	**Total liabilities and equity**	20,311,268	29,776,158	40,481,999	47,959,675	55,945,537	62,813,598

4.3.1   Negative Debt

Notice that in the pro forma statements, the long-term debt balance in 2001 is projected to be negative. The model's construction explains why this result occurs: Since debt is the model "plug," when the firm produces enough cash, the debt balances will all be paid off, and the amount of debt needed to balance the liabilities against the assets will be negative. This outcome is not aesthetic (balance sheet debt is almost invariably a positive entry), although in principle there is nothing wrong with this procedure: Negative debt simply represents positive amounts of cash for the firm. In our model this projection is somewhat more problematic, not only because the interest on debt (12 percent) is greater than the interest earned on cash (6 percent), but also because Farmers wants to have a certain minimal amount of cash on hand. However, the solution to this problem follows the lines laid down in section 3.7. The implementation involves the following logic:

• Farmers Bagels wants to have a certain minimum ratio of cash to sales on hand. If the total value of this minimum cash balance *plus* all other assets is greater than current liabilities plus equity, then Farmers needs debt.

• If, on the other hand,

[Cash ratio] ∗ Sales + Accounts receivable + Inventory + Prepaid expenses + Net property and equipment − Current liabilities − Common stock − Retained earnings < 0

then debt is set at 0. In this case

Total liabilities and equity > Accounts receivable + Inventory + Prepaid expenses + Net property and equipment

The difference between the two sides of this inequality is the cash account (which will exceed the minimum desired cash balances).

   This procedure produces the following pro forma financial statements.

	A	B	C	D	E	F	G
1	FARMERS BAGELS: PRO FORMA MODEL WITHOUT NEGATIVE DEBT						
2							
3	Predicted Financial Statement Ratios: All ratios as percent of sales unless otherwise						
4							
5		1996	1997	1998	1999	2000	2001
6	Cash and cash equivalents		20%	15%	10%	10%	10%
7	Accounts receivable		22%				
8	Inventory		4.5%	5.0%	5.0%	5.0%	5.0%
9	Prepaid expenses and other current assets		5%				
10							
11	Property and equipment at cost, as percent of incremental sales	70%	65%	58%	51%	44%	40%
12	Depreciation		10%				
13							
14	Accounts payable and accrued expenses		17%	18%	19%	20%	20%
15	Income taxes payable (as percent of income tax)		25%				
16	Other current liabilities		1%				
17							
18	Interest expense		12%				
19	Interest income		6%				
20	Cost of products sold		40%				
21	Selling, general and administrative expenses		32%	31%	30%	29%	28%
22	Provision for income taxes (as percent of earnings before taxes)		41.5%				
23							
24							
25	**Income statement**						
26	Total sales	18,977,564	28,048,500	42,021,000	55,993,500	69,966,000	83,938,500
27							
28	Operating expenses						
29	Cost of products sold		(11,219,400)	(16,808,400)	(22,397,400)	(27,986,400)	(33,575,400)
30	Depreciation		(1,892,696)	(2,703,101)	(3,415,699)	(4,030,489)	(4,589,389)
31	Selling, general, and administrative expenses		(8,975,520)	(13,026,510)	(16,798,050)	(20,290,140)	(23,502,780)
32	Interest expense		(1,325,198)	(1,782,358)	(1,756,823)	(1,216,577)	(432,786)
33	Interest income		259,011	357,386	357,075	377,879	537,284
34	Earnings before income taxes		4,894,697	8,058,017	11,982,604	16,820,273	22,375,429
35	Provision for income taxes		(2,031,299)	(3,344,077)	(4,972,781)	(6,980,413)	(9,285,803)
36	**Profit after taxes**		**2,863,397**	**4,713,940**	**7,009,823**	**9,839,860**	**13,089,626**
37							
38	**Balance sheet**						
39	Current assets						
40	Cash and cash equivalents	3,023,989	5,609,700	6,303,150	5,599,350	6,996,600	10,912,882
41	Accounts receivable	4,194,238	6,170,670	9,244,620	12,318,570	15,392,520	18,466,470
42	Inventory	759,104	1,262,183	2,101,050	2,799,675	3,498,300	4,196,925
43	Prepaid expenses and other current assets	1,006,169	1,402,425	2,101,050	2,799,675	3,498,300	4,196,925
44	Total current assets	8,983,500	14,444,978	19,749,870	23,517,270	29,385,720	37,773,202
45							
46	Property and equipment						
47	At cost	13,030,853	18,926,962	27,031,012	34,156,987	40,304,887	45,893,887
48	Less accumulated depreciation	(1,703,085)	(3,595,782)	(6,298,883)	(9,714,581)	(13,745,070)	(18,334,459)
49	Net property and equipment	11,327,768	15,331,180	20,732,129	24,442,405	26,559,817	27,559,428
50							
51	Total assets	20,311,268	29,776,158	40,481,999	47,959,675	55,945,537	65,332,630
52							
53							
54	Current liabilities						
55	Accounts payable and accrued expenses	3,271,271	4,768,245	7,563,780	10,638,765	13,993,200	16,787,700
56	Income taxes payable	423,486	507,825	836,019	1,243,195	1,745,103	2,321,451
57	Other current liabilities	151,189	280,485	420,210	559,935	699,660	839,385
58	Total current liabilities	3,845,946	5,556,555	8,820,009	12,441,895	16,437,963	19,948,536
59							
60	Long-term debt	8,597,874	13,488,758	16,217,205	13,063,172	7,213,105	-
61							
62	Stockholders' equity						
63	Common stock	4,610,999	4,610,999	4,610,999	4,610,999	4,610,999	4,610,999
64	Retained earnings	3,256,449	6,119,846	10,833,786	17,843,609	27,683,469	40,773,095
65	Total liabilities and equity	20,311,268	29,776,158	40,481,999	47,959,675	55,945,537	65,332,630

4.4   Deriving the Free Cash Flows (FCF) for Farmers Bagels

As explained in section 3.3, free cash flow (FCF) is a concept that refers to the *cash produced by the business activities of the firm.* Another way of viewing the FCF is that it is the amount of cash that the firm would produce if it had no financial assets whatsoever—no debt and no cash or marketable securities.

The formal definition is the following:

Calculation of the Free Cash Flow

Profit after taxes (PAT)

Add back depreciation

Add back interest paid, net of taxes

Subtract out interest earned, net of taxes

Subtract increase in current assets except for cash and cash equivalents

Add increase in current liabilities

Subtract new fixed assets purchased (subtract change in fixed assets at cost)

A firm's FCF is often negative, even if it has positive profits. This tends to be true especially during periods of quick growth, when large amounts of new assets are needed to provide the basis from which to make new sales. It was certainly true for Farmers during the first two years of its existence:

	A	B	C	D
50	**FARMERS BAGELS: FREE CASH FLOWS FOR 1995-1996**			
51				
52		**1995**	**1996**	
53	Profit after taxes	897,896	2,358,553	
54	Add back depreciation	400,000	1,303,085	
55	Add back interest expenses, net of taxes	29,798	49,241	
56	Subtract interest costs, net of taxes	(59,177)	(99,733)	
57	Subtract increase in current assets	(1,856,201)	(5,959,511)	
58	Add back increase in current liabilities	1,117,493	2,728,453	
59	Subtract increase in property and equipment at cost	(4,000,000)	(9,030,853)	
60	**Free Cash Flow**	(3,470,191)	(8,650,766)	

During its first two years of existence, Farmers Bagels produced healthy profits, but much financing was needed for increases in net working capital (defined as the difference between current assets and current liabilities) and for the purchase of new fixed assets. Until the growth of Farmers' sales moderates, or until the company gets larger, we can expect this trend to continue.

The following table shows the projected free cash flows for Farmers Bagels in the next five years:

	A	B	C	D	E	F	G
68	**Projected Free Cash Flow, 1997-2001**		**1997**	**1998**	**1999**	**2000**	**2001**
69	Profit after taxes		2,863,397	4,713,940	7,009,823	9,839,860	13,089,626
70	Add back depreciation		1,892,696	2,703,101	3,415,699	4,030,489	4,589,389
71	Add back interest expenses, net of taxes		775,241	1,042,679	1,027,741	711,697	253,180
72	Subtract interest costs, net of taxes		(151,521)	(209,071)	(208,889)	(221,059)	(314,311)
73	Subtract increase in current assets, except cash		(2,875,767)	(4,611,443)	(4,471,200)	(4,471,200)	(4,471,200)
74	Add back increase in current liabilities		1,710,609	3,263,454	3,621,886	3,996,068	3,510,572
75	Subtract increase in property and equipment at cost		(5,896,108)	(8,104,050)	(7,125,975)	(6,147,900)	(5,589,000)
76	**Free cash flow**		(1,681,453)	(1,201,388)	3,269,085	7,737,955	11,068,256

Only in 1999 was Farmers projected to produce its first positive cash flows.

4.5 Calculating Farmers' Weighted Average Cost of Capital

In order to value Farmers Bagels, we calculate its weighted average cost of capital, defined as

$$WACC = r_E \frac{E}{E+D} + r_D(1-T_C)\frac{D}{E+D}$$

where r_E is the firm's cost of equity, r_D is its cost of debt, T_C is its marginal corporate tax rate, and D and E refer to the market values of Farmers' equity and debt, respectively. Cost of capital calculations tend to have a lot of "noise": The cost of capital for an individual firm may be affected by random factors that are not necessarily relevant for the future. To avoid this problem, we calculate the average cost of capital for firms in the bagel industry, using the capital asset pricing model (CAPM). As the next spreadsheet shows, the average asset β for firms in Farmers' industry is 1.56, and the industry-average WACC is 20.43 percent:

	A	B	C	D	E	F	G	H	I
93	**CALCULATION OF WACC**								
94	Market risk premium	8.40%							
95	Risk-free rate	6%							
96	Marginal corp. tax rate	40%							
97									
98		**Market**		**Equity**	**Cost of**	**Marginal**	**Cost of**		**Asset**
99		**Equity**	**Debt**	**Beta**	**Debt**	**Tax Rate**	**Equity**	**WACC**	**Beta**
100	Firm 1	10,000,000	3,000,000	1.5	6.80%	35.0%	19.80%	16.25%	1.17
101	Firm 2	123,000,000	50,000,000	2.1	7.30%	40.0%	26.28%	19.95%	1.51
102	Firm 3	15,826,000	0	1.9	6.50%	38.0%	24.12%	24.12%	1.90
103	Firm 4	38,000,000	45,000,000	3.2	12.20%	35.0%	38.16%	21.77%	1.68
104	Farmers Bagels	37,500,000	8,597,874	1.8	12.00%	41.5%	23.04%	20.05%	1.52
105									
106							Average	20.43%	1.56

We use the industry average WACC to value Farmers:

	A	B	C	D	E
79	**FARMERS BAGELS–VALUATION USING INDUSTRY-AVERAGE WACC**				
80	Cost of capital	20.43%			
81	Growth of free cash flows after 2001	5.00%			
82					
83	Present value of free cash flows, 1997-2001	8,444,910	<-- =NPV(B80,C76:G 76)*(1+B80)^0.5		
84	Terminal value, after 2001	32,632,731	<-- =G76*(1+B81)/(B80-B81)/(1+B80)^ 4.5		
85	Enterprise value = PV of discounted FCFs + Terminal	41,077,640	<-- =SUM (B83:B84)		
86	Value of debt at end 1996	8,597,874	<-- =B60		
87	Value of equity	32,479,766	<-- =B85- B86		
88					
89	Number of shares of Farmers	5,000,000			
90	Value per share	6.50			

The present value of the 1997–2001 FCFs assumes that—on average—the cash flows occur in midyear; as discussed in section 3.5.2, it is therefore necessary to multiply the Excel present-value formula by $(1 + WACC)^{0.5}$. This adjustment is incorporated in cell B87. When the terminal value proxies for the present value of all the FCFs beyond the prediction horizon, the same adjustment has to be made (cell B88):

$$\text{Terminal value} = \left\{ \frac{FCF_{2001} * (1 + g)}{WACC - g} \right\} (1 + WACC)^{0.5}$$

where g is the terminal growth rate.

4.6   Sensitivity Analysis

The valuation calculations offer many opportunities for sensitivity analysis, which are easy to implement using Excel. Here we build a two-dimensional data table to calculate the value of Farmers as a function of the WACC and the terminal growth rate:

	A	B	C	D	E
77					
78					
79	**FARMERS BAGELS--VALUATION USING INDUSTRY-AVERAGE WACC**				
80	Cost of capital	20.43%			
81	Growth of free cash flows after 2001	5.00%	Table		? ✕
82					
83	Present value of free cash flows, 1997-2001	8,444,910	<-- Row input cell:	$B$80	
84	Terminal value, after 2001	32,632,731	<-- Column input cell:	$B$81	
85	Enterprise value = PV of discounted FCFs + Terminal	41,077,640	<--		
86	Value of debt at end 1996	8,597,874	<--	OK	Cancel
87	Value of equity	32,479,766	<--=B85-B86		
88					
89	Number of shares of Farmers	5,000,000			
90	Value per share	6.50			

Here's the resulting data table:

	A	B	C	D	E	F	G	H	I
108	**SENSITIVITY ANALYSIS: SHARE PRICE AS FUNCTION OF TERMINAL SALES GROWTH AND WACC**								
109		=B90	WACC						
110		6.50	15%	17%	19%	21%	23%	25%	27%
111	**Terminal sales growth**	0%	8.23	6.63	5.39	4.40	3.60	2.95	2.40
112		2%	9.62	7.63	6.14	4.97	4.05	3.30	2.68
113		4%	11.52	8.94	7.08	5.68	4.59	3.72	3.01
114		6%	14.26	10.73	8.32	6.57	5.25	4.23	3.41
115		8%	18.57	13.31	10.00	7.73	6.09	4.85	3.89
116		10%	26.33	17.37	12.43	9.32	7.19	5.65	4.49

Another sensitivity analysis can be done be using different proxies for the terminal value of Farmers:

	A	B	C	D	E
119	**SENSITIVITY ANALYSIS ON PROXIES FOR TERMINAL VALUE**				
120	**Using the Market/Book ratio**				
121	Present value of free cash flows, 1997–2001	8,444,910	<-- =B83		
122	Industry average market/book ratio	1.5			
123	End-year 2001 market value of equity + debt	45,384,094	<-- =G60+G63+G64		
124	Projected value of equity + debt, year-end 2001	68,076,141	<-- =B123*B122		
125	End-year 2001 cash balances	10,912,882	<-- =G40		
126	Projected terminal value	78,989,023	<-- =B125+B124		
127	WACC	20.43%	<-- =B80		
128	Enterprise value	39,627,806	<-- =B121+B126/(1+B127)^5		
129					
130	**Using the P/E ratio**				
131	Present value of Free Cash Flows, 1997–2001	8,444,910	<-- =B121		
132	Industry average Price/Earnings ratio	8			
133	Year-end 2001 earnings	13,089,626	<-- =G36		
134	Projected equity value, end 2001	104,717,010	<-- =B132*B133		
135	Year-end 2001 debt	-	<-- =G60		
136	Year-end 2001 cash balances	10,912,882	<-- =G40		
137	Projected terminal value	115,629,892	<-- =B136+B135+B134		
138	WACC	20.43%	<-- =B127		
139	Enterprise value	54,092,707	<-- =B131+B137/(1+B138)^5		

4.7   Conclusion

A pro forma model is an extremely useful tool for projecting cash flows and for building an integrated framework in which to value the firm. However, you should not be misled by the welter of numbers into thinking that the resulting valuation is precise and immutable: The model builder uses an artistic mixture of financial theory, accounting structure, and educated guesses to value the firm.

Exercises

1. In the valuation model of section 4.5 for Farmers Bagels, build data tables that show the sensitivity of

    a. The value of Farmers' equity to changes in the ratio of accounts receivable to sales.

    b. The value of Farmers' equity to changes in the income tax rate.

2. The valuation model in section 4.5 assumes that increments to fixed assets at cost are a decreasing function of sales. Change the model and assume that *net* fixed assets are a constant function of sales.

3. Extend the model in section 4.5 past 2001. Show that if Farmers will continue not to pay dividends, there will be a large buildup of cash and cash equivalents. "Fix" this problem by assuming that starting in 2002, Farmers will start to pay a fixed proportion of its profits in dividends.

4. Do a sensitivity analysis of the section 4.6 valuation using the market/book (M/B) ratio. Vary the M/B ratio from 0.8 to 2.

5. Do a sensitivity analysis of the section 4.6 valuation using the price/earnings (P/E) ratio, varying this ratio from 4 to 20.

6. Suppose that the average EBITDA ratio for the bagel industry is 8. Use this EBITDA ratio to value Farmers Bagels' shares.

5 The Financial Analysis of Leasing

5.1 Introduction

A lease is a contractual arrangement by which the owner of an asset (the *lessor*) rents the assets to a *lessee*. In this chapter we analyze leases, starting from the viewpoint of the lessee. The leases analyzed in this chapter are long-term leases, in which the asset spends most of its useful life with the lessee. In economic terms the leases we consider in this chapter are considered by the lessees as alternatives to purchasing an asset.[1]

In the example that follows we consider a company that is faced with the choice of either purchasing or leasing a piece of equipment. We assume that the operating inflows and outflows from the equipment are not affected by its ownership—irrespective of how the asset is held (whether owned or leased) the owner/lessee will have the same sales and must bear the responsibility for maintaining the equipment. In the words of Statement 13 of the Financial Accounting Standards Board, the lease we are considering is one that "transfers substantially all of the benefits and risks incident to the ownership of property" to the lessor.

The analysis in this chapter concentrates exclusively on the *cash flows* from the lease. It is assumed that the lessor pays taxes on the income from the lease rentals and gets a tax shield on the depreciation of the asset, and that the lessee can claim the rent as an expense. The analysis implicitly assumes that the tax authorities treat the lessor as the owner of the asset and the lessee as the user. As is explained in the appendix to this chapter, this assumption is not trivial. In addition to the cash-flow issues of leasing there are heavy accounting issues, which are also touched on briefly in the appendix.

5.2 A Simple Example

The essence of our analysis can be understood from the following simple example: A company has decided to acquire the use of a machine costing $540,000. If purchased, the machine will be depreciated on a straight-line basis to a residual value of zero. The machine's estimated life is six years, and the company's tax rate T_C is 38 percent.

---

1. Thus the analysis of this chapter fits many long-term equipment leases, but not short-term leasing (car rentals, for example).

The company's alternative to purchasing the machine is to lease it for six years. A lessor has offered to lease the machine to the company for $130,000 annually, with the first payment to be made today and with five additional payments to be made at the start of each of the next five years.

One way of analyzing this problem (a misleading way, as it turns out) is to compare the present values of the cash flows to the company of leasing and of buying the asset. The company feels that the lease payment and the tax shield from depreciation are riskless. Suppose, furthermore, that the risk-free rate is 12 percent. On the basis of the following calculation, the company should lease the asset.[2]

$$\text{NPV (leasing)} = \sum_{t=0}^{5} \frac{(1 - T_C) * \text{Lease rental}}{(1 + 12\%)^t}$$

$$= \sum_{t=0}^{5} \frac{(1 - T_C) * 130,000}{(1 + 12\%)^t} = 371,145$$

$$\text{NPV (buying)} = \text{Asset cost} - \text{PV(tax shields on depreciation)}$$

$$= 540,000 - \sum_{t=1}^{6} \frac{0.38 * 90,000}{(1 + 12\%)^t} = 399,390$$

This analysis suggests that leasing the asset is preferable to buying it. However, it is misleading because it ignores the fact that leasing is very much like buying the asset with a loan. The financial risks are thus different when we compare a lease (implicitly a purchase with loan financing) against a straightforward purchase without loan financing. If the company is willing to lease the asset, then perhaps it should also be willing to borrow money to buy the asset. This borrowing will change the cash-flow patterns and could also produce tax benefits. Hence, our leasing decision could change if we were to take the loan potential into account.

In the following section we present a method of analyzing leases that deals with this problem by imagining what kind of loan would produce cash flows (and hence financial risks) equivalent to those produced by the lease. This method of lease analysis is called the *equivalent-loan method.*

---

2. At this point we assume that the residual value of the asset at the end of its life is zero. In section 5.5 we drop this assumption.

5.3   Leasing and Firm Financing: The Equivalent-Loan Method

The idea behind the equivalent-loan method is to devise a hypothetical loan that is somehow equivalent to the lease.[3] It then becomes easy to see whether the lease or the purchase of an asset is preferable.

The easiest way to understand the equivalent loan method is with an example. We return to the previous example:

	A	B	C	D	E	F	G	H
1			EQUIVALENT LOAN METHOD					
2								
3	Asset cost	540,000						
4	Interest rate	12%						
5	Lease rental payment	130,000						
6	Annual depreciation	90,000						
7	Tax rate	38%						
8								
9	Year	0	1	2	3	4	5	6
10								
11	**After-tax cash flows from leasing**							
12	After-tax lease rental	-80,600	-80,600	-80,600	-80,600	-80,600	-80,600	
13								
14	**After-tax cash flows from buying the asset**							
15	Asset cost	-540,000						
16	Depreciation tax shield		34,200	34,200	34,200	34,200	34,200	34,200
17	Net cash from buying	-540,000	34,200	34,200	34,200	34,200	34,200	34,200
18								
19	**Differential cash flow**							
20	Lease minus buy	459,400	-114,800	-114,800	-114,800	-114,800	-114,800	-34,200
21								
22	IRR of differential cash flow	9.60%						
23								
24	Decision??	Buy	<-- =IF(B22<(1-B7)*B4,"lease","buy")					

Rows 3–7 give the parameters of the problem. The spreadsheet then compares two *after-tax* cash flows, that of the lease and that of the buy. Note that we write outflows with a minus sign and inflows (such as the tax shield from the depreciation) with a plus sign.

- The cash flow from leasing the asset is (1 − Tax rate) * Lease payment in each of years 0–5.

- The cash flow from buying the asset is the asset cost in year 0 (an outflow, hence positive) and the tax shield on the asset's depreciation, Tax rate * Depreciation, in years 1–6 (an inflow, hence written here with a negative sign).

---

3. This method is due to Myers, Dill, and Bautista (1976). A somewhat more accessible explanation can be found in Levy and Sarnat (1979).

Line 20 of the spreadsheet shows the *differential cash flow* between the lease and the buy decision. This line shows that leasing the asset, instead of buying it, results in

- A cash inflow of $459,400 in year 0. This inflow is the *cash saved at time 0* by the lease.
- A cash outflow of $114,800 in years 1–5 and an outflow of $34,200 in year 6. This outflow corresponds to the *marginal after-tax cost of the lease versus the buy* in these years. This marginal cost has two components: the after-tax lease payment ($80,600) and the fact that when we lease we do not get the tax shield on the asset's depreciation ($34,200).

Thus leasing instead of purchasing the asset is like getting a loan of $459,400 with after-tax repayments of $114,800 in years 1–5 and an after-tax repayment of $34,200 in year 6. The lease, in other words, can be viewed as an alternative method of financing the asset. *In order to compare the lease to the buy, we should compare the cost of this financing with the cost of alternative financing.* The internal rate of return of line 22—9.60 percent—gives us the cost of the financing implicit in the lease; this is larger than the after-tax cost of firm borrowing, since in this case (where the firm's tax rate is 38 percent and its borrowing cost is 12 percent), this cost is 7.44 percent. Thus our conclusion: Buying is preferable to leasing.

5.3.1 Why We Decided Against the Lease

Not everyone is fully convinced by the preceding argument. We therefore present an alternative argument in this subsection. We show that if the firm can borrow at 12 percent, it can borrow *more money* with the *same schedule of after-tax repayments* as that which resulted from the lease versus the buy. This hypothetical loan is shown in the following table:

	J	K	L	M	N	O	P
2		Principal	Loan	Of which		After-tax	
3		at beginning	payment,		Repayment	loan	
4	Year	of year	end of year	Interest	of principal	repayment	
5	1	487,443	137,027	58,493	78,534	114,800	114,800
6	2	408,909	133,446	49,069	84,377	114,800	114,800
7	3	324,532	129,599	38,944	90,655	114,800	114,800
8	4	233,877	125,465	28,065	97,400	114,800	114,800
9	5	136,478	121,023	16,377	104,646	114,800	114,800
10	6	31,832	35,652	3,820	31,832	34,200	34,200

The table (a version of the loan tables discussed in Chapter 1) shows the principal of a hypothetical bank loan bearing a 12 percent interest rate. At the beginning of year 0 (i.e., at the time when the firm either purchases or leases the asset), for example, the firm borrows $487,443 from the bank. At the end of the year, the firm repays $137,027 to the bank, of which $58,493 is interest (since $58,493 = 12 percent * 487,443) and the remainder, $78,534, is repayment of principal. The net, after-tax, repayment in year 1—assuming full tax deductibility of the interest payment—is (1 − 38 percent) * 58,493 + 78,534 = 114,800, which is, of course, the same after-tax differential cash flow calculated in our original spreadsheet.

Payments in subsequent years are calculated similarly to the illustration in the preceding paragraph. At the beginning of year 6, there is still $31,832 of principal outstanding; this is fully paid off at the end of the year with an after-tax payment of $34,200.

The point of this example? If the firm is considering leasing the asset in order to get the financing of $459,400 that the lease gives, it should instead borrow $487,443 from the bank at 12 percent; it can repay this larger loan with the same after-tax cash flows as are implicit in the lease. The bottom line: Purchasing is still preferable to leasing the asset.

The loan table was constructed in the following way:

• The principal at the beginning of each of years 1–6 is the present value of the lease-versus-buy outflows, discounted at (1 − 38 percent) * 12 percent. Thus, for example,

$$487{,}443 = \sum_{t=1}^{5} \frac{114{,}800}{\left[1 + (1 - 0.38) * 0.12\right]^1} + \frac{34{,}200}{\left[1 + (1 - 0.38) * 0.12\right]^6}$$

$$408{,}909 = \sum_{t=1}^{4} \frac{114{,}800}{\left[1 + (1 - 0.38) * 0.12\right]^1} + \frac{34{,}200}{\left[1 + (1 - 0.38) * 0.12\right]^5}$$

$$\vdots$$

$$31{,}832 = \frac{34{,}200}{\left[1 + (1 - 0.38) * 0.12\right]}$$

Once the principal at the start of each year is known, it is an easy matter to construct the rest of the columns.

Interest = 12 percent $*$ Principal, beginning of year

Total payment = Interest in year t + Repayment of principal in year t

After-tax payment, year t = $(1 - $ Tax rate$) *$ Interest + Repayment of principal

5.4   The Lessor's Problem: Calculating the Highest Acceptable Lease Rental

The lessor's problem is the opposite of that of the lessee:

• The lessee has to decide whether—given a rental rate on the leased asset—it is preferable to buy the asset or lease it.

• The lessor has to decide what *minimum rental rate* justifies the purchase of the asset in order to lease it out.

One way of solving the lessor's problem is to turn the preceding analysis around. We use the Excel Goal Seek (**Tools|Goal Seek**) to get $121,047 as the lessor's minimum acceptable rental:

	A	B	C	D	E	F	G	H
1	CALCULATING THE HIGHEST ACCEPTABLE LEASE PAYMENT							
2								
3	Asset cost	540,000						
4	Interest rate	12%						
5	Lease rental payment	121,047	<-- Computed with either Goal Seek or Solver					
6	Annual depreciation	90,000						
7	Tax rate	38%						
8	After-tax interest rate	7.44%						
9								
10	Year	0	1	2	3	4	5	6
11								
12	**After-tax cash flows from leasing**							
13	After-tax lease rental	-75,049	-75,049	-75,049	-75,049	-75,049	-75,049	
14								
15	**After-tax cash flows from buying the asset**							
16	Asset cost	-540,000						
17	Depreciation tax shield		34,200	34,200	34,200	34,200	34,200	34,200
18	Net cash flow from buying	-540,000	34,200	34,200	34,200	34,200	34,200	34,200
19								
20	**Differential cash flow**							
21	Lease minus buy	464,951	-109,249	-109,249	-109,249	-109,249	-109,249	-34,200
22								
23	IRR of differential cash flow	7.44%	<-- =IRR(B21:H21,0)					

Here's what the Goal Seek settings look like:

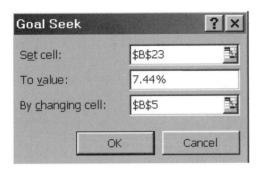

If you're using Solver to do this problem, it would look like:

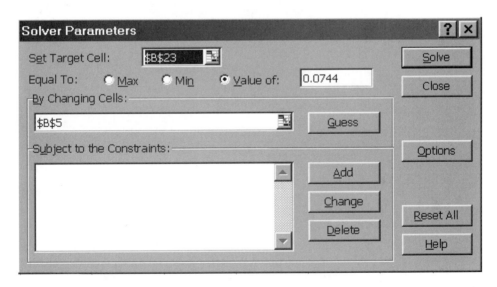

The symmetry between the lessee's problem and the lessor's problem suggests that if the lessee wants to lease, it will not be profitable for the lessor to purchase the asset in order to lease it out. In some cases, however, it may be that depreciation schedules and differences in tax rates between the lessee and the lessor make it profitable for both to enter into a leasing arrangement. An example is given in the exercises for this chapter.

Some Peculiarities of the Excel **Solver** and Excel **Goal Seek**

1. Neither of these (otherwise wonderful) Excel tools will accept a formula in the box that specifies the target. Thus—in the present example—we would have liked to write the formula **=(1-B7)*B4** in the **To value** box of **Goal Seek.** But that technique won't work: We have to specify a numerical value (in this case, the after-tax interest rate).

2. You may have to fiddle with **Tools|Options|Calculation** in order to specify enough accuracy to get cell B23 to be exactly 7.44 percent. If you do not get an acceptable answer, set a higher value for the option **Maximum change.**

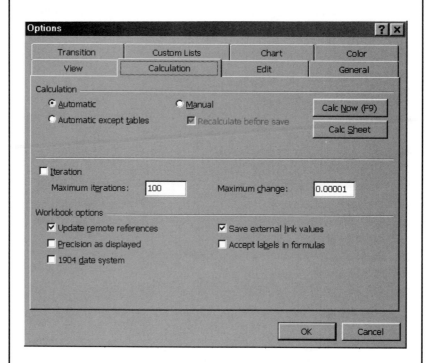

3. **Goal Seek** does not remember its settings between accesses. Therefore, you will have to reenter the data each time. (**Solver,** on the other hand, does remember its settings.)

5.5   Asset Residual Value and Other Considerations

In the example, we have ignored the residual value of the asset—its anticipated market value at the end of the lease term. In a mechanical sense, it is easy to include the residual value in the calculations (but you have to be careful—see the warning after the next numerical example). Suppose, for example, you think that the asset will have a market value of $100,000 in year 7; assuming that this value is fully taxed (after all, we've depreciated the asset to zero value over the first six years), the after-tax residual value will be $(1 - \text{Tax rate}) * \$100,000 = \$62,000$.

	A	B	C	D	E	F	G	H	I
1			RESIDUAL VALUES IN LEASE ANALYSIS						
2									
3	Asset cost	540,000							
4	Interest rate	12%							
5	Lease rental payment	121,048							
6	Annual depreciation	90,000	Asset fully depreciated over six years						
7	Tax rate	38%							
8	Residual value	100,000	Anticipated to be realized in year 7; fully taxed						
9									
10	Year	0	1	2	3	4	5	6	7
11									
12	**After-tax cash flows from leasing**								
13	After-tax lease rental	-75,050	-75,050	-75,050	-75,050	-75,050	-75,050		
14									
15	**After-tax cash flows from buying the asset**								
16	Asset cost	-540,000							
17	Depreciation tax shield		34,200	34,200	34,200	34,200	34,200	34,200	
18	After-tax residual								62,000
19	Net cash flow from buying	-540,000	34,200	34,200	34,200	34,200	34,200	34,200	62,000
20									
21	**Differential cash flow**								
22	Lease minus buy	464,950	-109,250	-109,250	-109,250	-109,250	-109,250	-34,200	-62,000
23									
24	IRR of differential cash flow	10.02%	<-- =IRR(B22:I22,0)						
25									
26	Decision??	Buy	<-- =IF(B24<(1-B7)*B4,"lease","buy"						

Not surprisingly, the possibility of realizing an extra cash flow from asset ownership makes the lease even less attractive than before (you can see this difference by noting that the return rate in cell B24, the IRR of the differential cash flows, has increased from 9.60 percent in our original example to 10.02 percent).

Be a bit careful here, however; the spreadsheet treats the residual value as if it has the same certainty of realization as the depreciation tax shields and the lease rentals. This assumption can be far from the truth! There is no good practical solution to this problem; an ad hoc way of dealing with it might be to reduce the $100,000 by a factor that expresses the uncertainty about its realization. The finance technical jargon for this is "certainty-equivalence factor," and you can find it referenced in any basic finance text.[4] The last spreadsheet snapshot in this chapter assumes that you've decided that the certainty-equivalence factor for the residual value is 0.7:

	A	B	C	D	E	F	G	H	I	J	K
1	RESIDUAL VALUES IN LEASE ANALYSIS–Certainty equivalence factor										
2											
3	Asset cost	540,000									
4	Interest rate	12%									
5	Lease rental payment	121,048									
6	Annual depreciation	90,000	Asset fully depreciated over six years								
7	Tax rate	38%									
8	Residual value	100,000	Anticipated to be realized in year 7; fully taxed								
9	CE factor	0.7	Certainty-equivalence factor								
10											
11	Year	0	1	2	3	4	5	6	7		
12											
13	After-tax cash flows from leasing										
14	After-tax lease rental	-75,050	-75,050	-75,050	-75,050	-75,050	-75,050				
15											
16	After-tax cash flows from buying the asset										
17	Asset cost	-540,000									
18	Depreciation tax shield		34,200	34,200	34,200	34,200	34,200	34,200			
19	After-tax residual								43,400	<-- =(1-B7)*B8*B9	
20	Net cash flow from buying	-540,000	34,200	34,200	34,200	34,200	34,200	34,200	43,400		
21											
22	Differential cash flow										
23	Lease minus buy	464,950	-109,250	-109,250	-109,250	-109,250	-109,250	-34,200	-43,400		
24											
25	IRR of differential cash flow	9.30%	<-- =IRR(B23:I23,0)								
26											
27	Decision??	Buy	<-- =IF(B25<(1-B7)*B4,"lease","buy")								

Exercises

1.   Your company is considering either purchasing or leasing an asset that costs $1,000,000. The asset, if purchased, will be depreciated on a straight-line basis over six years to a zero residual value. A leasing company is willing to lease the asset for $300,000 per year; the first payment on the lease is due at the time the lease is undertaken (i.e., year 0), and the remaining five payments are due at the beginning of years 1–5. Your company has a tax rate $T_C = 40$ percent and can borrow at 10 percent from its bank.

---

4.   For further references on certainty equivalents, see Brealey and Myers (1996, p. 225). However, note that neither this work nor the present text (nor anyone else) can tell you precisely how to calculate the certainty-equivalence factor. It depends on your attitudes toward risk.

     a. Should your company lease or purchase the asset?

     b. What is the maximum lease payment it will agree to pay?

2. ABC Corporation is considering leasing an asset from XYZ Corporation. Here are the relevant facts:

Asset cost	$1,000,000
Depreciation schedule	Year 1: 20%
	Year 2: 32%
	Year 3: 19.20%
	Year 4: 11.52%
	Year 5: 11.52%
	Year 6: 5.76%
Lease term	6 years
Lease payment	$200,000 per year, at the beginning of years 0, 1, ..., 5
Asset residual value	Zero
Tax rates	ABC: $T_C = 0\%$ (ABC has tax-loss carryforwards that prevent it from utilizing any additional tax shields)
	XYZ: $T_C = 40\%$

Show that it will be advantageous both for ABC to lease the asset and for XYZ to purchase the asset in order to lease it out to ABC.

3. Continuing with the same example: Find the *maximum rental* that ABC will pay and the *minimum rental* that XYZ will accept.

4. Perform a sensitivity analysis (using **DataTable**, see Chapter 26) on the certainty-equivalence factor in section 5.5, showing how the IRR of the differential cash flows varies with the CE factor.

Appendix: The Tax and Accounting Treatment of Leases

This chapter discusses the case where the lessor retains the tax benefits of ownership; that is, the lessor is able to take the depreciation on the leased asset, and the lessee deducts the lease payments from his income as an expense. In order for these things to happen, it is critical that the Internal Revenue Service be willing to recognize the lease as a *true lease*.

Although the specific IRS rules change from time to time, the principle underlying the rules remains that the lessor should be accorded the benefits of ownership only if he bears some of the economic risks of ownership. This principle has led the IRS to develop a series of tests to determine whether or not the lessor has transferred essentially all of the ownership risks to the lessee. If this is the case, the IRS treats the "lease" arrangement as a sale of the asset by the "lessor" to the "lessee." If the ownership risks have not all been transferred to the lessee, then the lease is a true lease, and the analysis of the chapter holds.

Revenue Ruling 55–540 sets out seven conditions under which a transaction will be found to be a sale rather than a lease for tax purposes:

• Portions of the rental payments are specifically applicable to an equity interest to be acquired by the lessee.

• The lessee will acquire title upon payment of a stated amount of rentals.

• A substantial proportion of the asset's purchase price is paid in rentals in a relatively short period of time from the inception of the lease.

• The rental payments exceed a "fair" rental value.

• There is a bargain-purchase option; the option price is nominal in relation to the fair market value of the asset at the time when the option can be exercised.

• Some part of the payments is designated as interest.

• The lease may be renewed at nominal rentals over the useful life of the asset.

In addition to these conditions, Revenue Ruling 55–541 deals with the relation of the lease term to the useful life of the asset. The ruling would seem to suggest that the transaction will be classified as a conditional sale and not as a lease if the useful life of the asset is not in excess of the lease term.

One lease packager states that the IRS will generally classify a lease as a true lease if all of the following criteria are met:

• The estimated fair market value of the leased asset at the end of the lease term will equal at least 20 percent of the original cost of the leased property.

• The lease term does not exceed 80 percent of the estimated useful life of the asset.

• There is no bargain-purchase option.

• The lessor's equity in the leased asset is at least 20 percent.

The Accounting Treatment of Leases

Accountants have found leases troublesome. Before the advent of Financial Accounting Standards Board Statement 13 (FASB 13) in 1976, it was common for firms to leave leases off their balance sheets altogether, and to record the fact that some assets were leased only in footnotes to the financial statement.

This practice created an asymmetry between the accounting treatment of a lease and the accounting treatment of a purchase of an asset with debt. Since the economic similarity between these two transactions is great, this asymmetric treatment is illogical.

FASB 13 attempts to solve this problem. The statement is long and complex, and it is beyond the purview of this book to fully present the statement's solutions. We will sketch here the solution to the problem as outlined in FASB 13; the next chapter deals with FASB 13's treatment of the leveraged leases.

The basic idea behind the FASB 13 treatment of leases is that *in some cases* the lessee should record a leased asset on his balance sheet, *even though legally the asset belongs to another party*. The cases in which this should happen are those in which the economic substance of the lease transaction (as opposed to the legal fiction) is that the lessee effectively owns the asset. An example would be a 10-year noncancelable lease of an automobile. By the time the car is returned to the lessor, it is likely to be practically worthless; hence, FASB 13 would require the lessee to record the asset on his balance sheet.

Formally, FASB 13 requires the lessee to put the lease on his balance sheet (the terminology is that in this case the lease is a *capital lease*) if one of four criteria applies:

1. The lease transfers ownership of the property to the lessee at the end of the lease term.

2. The lease contains a bargain-purchase option, which allows the lessee to purchase the leased asset at a very low price at the end of the lease term.

3. The lease term exceeds 75 percent of the life of the asset.

4. The present value of the lease payments (at the lessee's incremental borrowing rate) exceeds 90 percent of the asset's fair value.

If a lease is a capital lease under the FASB 13 rules, then the lessee records the capital lease as an asset and records a corresponding liability on his balance sheet. The asset is then depreciated, and the liability is amortized, over the lease term. It is as if the asset in question has been bought with 100 percent loan financing.

What does the lessor do if the lessee has to record the lease on his balance sheet? If the lessee has (in an accounting sense) bought the asset with 100 percent loan financing, then the lessor must have (in the same sense) sold the asset with 100 percent loan financing. This is the essence of the FASB 13 treatment of the lessor.

Reconciling the Tax and Accounting Treatments of Leases

The tax treatment and the accounting treatment of leases are very similar in spirit. It is therefore logical to expect that whenever a lease is classified under the FASB 13 rules as a capital lease, it should be classified by the IRS as a sale. If the world were a rational place, lessees would put leases on their books only if the IRS decided to treat leases as sales.

However, the world is a funny place. It turns out to be fairly simple to keep a lease off the lessee's balance sheet, have the IRS treat it as a true lease, and still have all the parties involved feel as if they had transferred all of the economic benefits of ownership from the lessor to the lessee. See the references for further reading.

6 The Financial Analysis of Leveraged Leases

6.1 Introduction

In a *leveraged lease* the lessor finances the purchase of the asset to be leased with debt. From the point of view of the lessee, there is no difference in the analysis of a leveraged or a nonleveraged lease. From the lessor's point of view, however, the cash flows of a leveraged lease present some interesting problems.

At least six parties are typically involved in a leveraged lease: the lessee, the equity partners in the lease, the lenders to the equity partners, an owner trustee, an indenture trustee, and the manufacturer of the asset. In most cases, a seventh party is also involved: a lease packager (a broker or leasing company). The following figure illustrates the arrangements among the six parties of a typical leveraged lease.

LEVERAGED LEASING

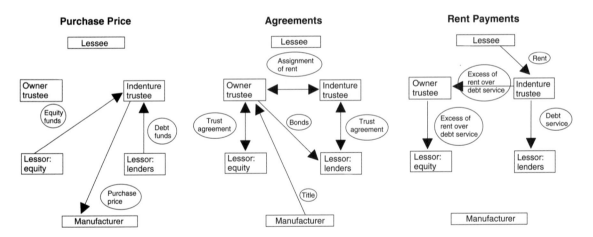

The two major problems related to the analysis of leveraged leases are these:

1. *The straightforward financial analysis of the lease from the point of view of the lessor.* This concerns the calculation of the cash flows obtained by the lessor, and a computation of these cash flows' net present value (NPV) or internal rate of return (IRR).

2. *The accounting analysis of the lease.* Accountants use a method called the *multiple phases method* (MPM) to calculate a rate of return on leveraged

leases. The MPM rate of return is different from the internal rate of return (IRR). In an ordinary financial context this difference should be of no concern, since the efficient-markets hypothesis tells us that only cash flows matter. However, in a less than efficient world, people tend to get very concerned about how things look on their financial statements. Since the accounting rate of return on the lease is difficult to compute, we will use Excel to calculate it; then we will analyze the results.

6.2   An Example

We can explore these issues by considering an example, roughly based on an example given in Appendix E of FASB 13, the accounting profession's magnum opus on accounting for leases.

A leasing company is considering the purchase of an asset whose cost is $1,000,000. The asset will be purchased with $200,000 of the company's equity and with $800,000 of debt. The interest on the debt is 10 percent, so that the annual payment of interest and principal over the 15-year term of the debt is $105,179.[1]

The company will lease the asset out for $110,000 per year, payable at the end of each year. The lease term is 15 years. The asset will be depreciated over a period of eight years, using the standard IRS depreciation schedule for assets with a seven-year life.[2] The depreciation schedule for such assets is as follows:

Year	Depreciation %
1	14.28
2	24.49
3	17.49
4	12.5
5	8.92
6	8.92
7	8.92
8	4.48

---

1. Using Excel: **=PMT(10%,15,-800,000)** gives 105,179.

2. Refer to Ross, Westerfield, and Jaffee (1996), table 7.3 (p. 171). Note that by IRS rules, an asset depreciated over a seven-year life has eight years of depreciation deductions, since it is assumed that the asset is purchased in midyear.

Because the asset will be fully depreciated at the time it is sold (year 16), the whole anticipated residual value ($300,000) will be taxable. The company's tax rate is 40 percent.

These facts are summarized in the following spreadsheet, which also derives the lessor's cash flows.

	A	B	C	D	E	F	G	H	I
1			**BASIC LEVERAGED LEASE EXAMPLE**						
2									
3	Cost of asset	1,000,000							
4	Lease term	15							
5	Residual value	300,000							
6	Equity	200,000							
7	Debt	800,000	15-year term loan, equal payments of interest and principal						
8	Interest	10%							
9	Annual debt payment	105,179							
10	Annual rent received	110,000							
11	Tax rate	40%							
12									
13					Principal			Repayment	
14		Equity	Rental or		at start	Loan		of	Cash
15	Year	invested	salvage	Depreciation	of year	payment	Interest	principal	flow
16		-200,000							-200,000
17	1		110,000	142,800	800,000	105,179	80,000	25,179	49,941
18	2		110,000	244,900	774,821	105,179	77,482	27,697	89,774
19	3		110,000	174,900	747,124	105,179	74,712	30,467	60,666
20	4		110,000	125,000	716,657	105,179	71,666	33,513	39,487
21	5		110,000	89,200	683,144	105,179	68,314	36,865	23,827
22	6		110,000	89,200	646,280	105,179	64,628	40,551	22,352
23	7		110,000	89,200	605,728	105,179	60,573	44,606	20,730
24	8		110,000	44,800	561,122	105,179	56,112	49,067	1,186
25	9		110,000		512,056	105,179	51,206	53,973	-18,697
26	10		110,000		458,082	105,179	45,808	59,371	-20,856
27	11		110,000		398,711	105,179	39,871	65,308	-23,231
28	12		110,000		333,403	105,179	33,340	71,839	-25,843
29	13		110,000		261,565	105,179	26,156	79,023	-28,716
30	14		110,000		182,542	105,179	18,254	86,925	-31,877
31	15		110,000		95,617	105,179	9,562	95,617	-35,354
32	16		300,000						180,000
33									
34								IRR of cash flows	12.46%

The last column gives the cash flow to the equity owners of the asset. A typical year's cash flow for the equity owner is calculated as follows:

$$\text{Cash flow}(t) = (1 - \text{Tax})\text{Rent} + \text{Tax} * \text{Depreciation}(t) - (1 - \text{Tax})\text{Interest}(t) - \text{Principal repayment}(t)$$

The explanation is as follows:

Item	Explanation
$+ (1 - \text{Tax}) * \text{Rent}$	Equity owners get the rental from the asset, net of any taxes.
$+ \text{Tax} * \text{Depreciation}$	Equity owners get the tax shield from the depreciation of the asset.
$- (1 - \text{Tax}) * \text{Interest}$	The interest on the debt is tax deductible.
$-$ Repayment of debt principal	Repayment of debt principal is not tax deductible.
$+ (1 - \text{Tax})$ $* \text{Residual value}$	This item only occurs in the last year; the residual is usually fully taxed, since the depreciation has been taken on the whole value of the asset.
Cash flow$(t) =$ $(1 - \text{Tax})\text{Rent}$ $+ \text{Tax} * \text{Depreciation}(t)$ $- (1 - \text{Tax})\text{Interest}(t)$ $-$ Principal repayment(t)	The cash flow in a typical year (excluding the residual).

The cash flows of the typical long-lived leveraged lease are usually positive at the beginning of the lease term, and then decline over time, turning positive again at the end, when the residual value is received. There are three reasons for this phenomenon:

1. The cash flow that stems from depreciation typically ends or falls off rapidly before the end of the lease term. The more accelerated the depreciation method, the larger will be the depreciation allowances (and hence the larger the depreciation tax shields) at the beginning of the asset's life.

2. In the later years of the lease, the portion of the annual debt payments devoted to interest (tax deductible) falls, while the portion of the annual debt payments that constitutes a repayment of principal (not tax deductible) rises.

3. Finally, of course, we anticipated a large cash flow from the realization of the asset's residual value at the end of the lease term.

Cash Flows from Leveraged Lease

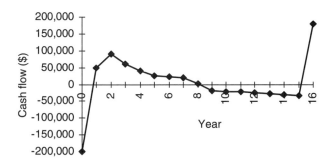

6.3   Analyzing the Cash Flows by NPV or IRR

What do we make of these cash flows? One way of viewing the cash flows (probably the best, at least in theory) is to take their net present value (NPV) at some appropriate risk-adjusted discount rate. If we analyze the cash-flow components, we see that the primary riskiness stems from three sources:

1. The lessee may default on the rental.

2. Tax rates can change, affecting the tax shields from depreciation and the cash flow from the interest payments.

3. The residual value is highly uncertain.

The following graph shows the NPV of the cash flows at various interest rates:

**NPV of Leveraged Lease Cash Flows
at Various Interest Rates**

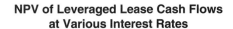
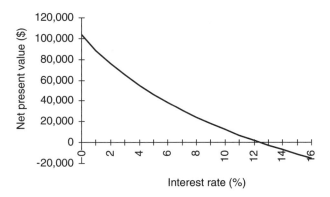

Note that since the cash flows are *after-tax,* the relevant basis for comparison is an after-tax interest rate. For example, suppose the lessor feels highly certain about all the cash flows and therefore wants to compare the cash flows to his loan rate of 10 percent. Then, since the lessor's tax rate is 40 percent, the appropriate discount rate for comparison is $(1 - 40 \text{ percent}) * 10 \text{ percent} = 6 \text{ percent}$; at this rate the lease cash flows have an NPV of $38,068.

Lessors are often uncomfortable with net present value. They prefer internal rate of return as a measure of the acceptability of the lease. Since the cash flows of the lease have two changes in sign, it is—in principle—possible that they have two IRRs. Since the IRR is the interest rate for which the NPV graph crosses the *x*-axis, we can use Excel to determine graphically how many IRRs there are. The following graph shows that for a very large range of reasonable interest rates, there is only one IRR:

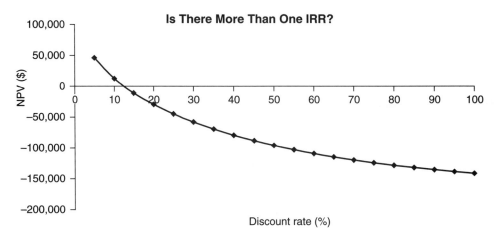

We are thus safe in using **IRR(cash flows,0)** to determine that the internal rate of return of the lease cash flows is 12.46 percent.

6.4   What Does the IRR Mean?

Asking what the IRR means is relevant both to an economic understanding of the meaning of the internal rate of return and to the discussion in the next section of the accounting determination of the income from a leveraged lease. To illustrate the complexities, we stray for a moment from our original example to study a much simpler example. Consider an investment of $100,000 that has positive cash flows only for the next five years.

	B	C	D	E
4	**Year**	**Cash**		
5		**flow**		
6	0	-100,000		
7	1	31,000		
8	2	22,000		
9	3	16,000		
10	4	22,000		
11	5	35,000		
12				
13	IRR	8.097%	<-- =IRR(C6:C11,0)	

What is the meaning of the IRR of 8.097 percent? If we think of the initial investment of $100,000 as a loan to the project, then each cash flow is attributable to

1. Interest on the "loan principal" outstanding at the beginning of the period,

2. Repayment of this "principal."

Of course, at the end of the five years, all of the principal must be repaid. *The IRR is the "rate of interest" that exactly repays the "loan," with its "interest payments," over the life of the project.* We can see this point in the following table, which attributes each cash flow to either "income" on the "investment outstanding at the beginning of the period" or to the "repayment of the investment":

	G	H	I	J	K
1		**CASH-FLOW ATTRIBUTION TABLE**			
2					
3		**Investment**		**Attribution of cash flow**	
4	**Year**	**at beginning**	**Cash**		**Repayment**
5		**of period**	**flow**	**Income**	**of investment**
6	1	100,000	31,000	8,097	22,903
7	2	77,097	22,000	6,242	15,758
8	3	61,339	16,000	4,966	11,034
9	4	50,305	22,000	4,073	17,927
10	5	32,378	35,000	2,622	32,378

In each period, we first "charge" the investment at the beginning of the period with an "interest charge," which is the IRR. The remaining cash flow is attributed to the repayment of the investment. Thus, for example:

Investment at beginning of period 1 (i.e., the initial investment)	100,000
Cash flow for period	31,000
8.10% ∗ Investment at beginning of period	8,097
Cash flow available for repayment of investment	22,903
Investment at beginning of period 2 = Investment at beginning of previous period − Cash flow available for repayment in period 1	100,000 − 22,903 = 77,097

Note the last line in our cash-flow attribution table: At the beginning of year 5, we still have $32,378 of investment left; the cash flow of $35,000 for year 5 suffices exactly to pay the income of $2,622 on this investment and to repay the investment itself. At the beginning of year 6, there is no investment left! (This result, of course, is not a miracle—it's the way we calculated the internal rate of return.)

6.4.1 Back to the Leveraged Lease Example

We now apply this same logic to the cash flows of the leveraged lease.

	C	D	E	F	G
1	**ATTRIBUTION OF LEVERAGED-LEASE CASH FLOWS**				
2	**TO INCOME AND REPAYMENT OF INVESTMENT**				
3					
4	IRR		12.46%	<-- =IRR(E9:E25)	
5					
6			Investment		Attribution of cash flow	
7		Year	at beginning	Cash		Repayment
8			of period	flow	Income	of investment
9		0		-200,000		
10		1	200,000	49,941	24,913	25,028
11		2	174,972	89,774	21,796	67,978
12		3	106,994	60,666	13,328	47,338
13		4	59,656	39,487	7,431	32,056
14		5	27,600	23,827	3,438	20,389
15		6	7,212	22,352	898	21,454
16		7	-14,242	20,730	-1,774	22,504
17		8	-36,746	1,186	-4,577	5,763
18		9	-42,510	-18,697	-5,295	-13,401
19		10	-29,108	-20,856	-3,626	-17,230
20		11	-11,878	-23,231	-1,480	-21,751
21		12	9,873	-25,843	1,230	-27,073
22		13	36,945	-28,716	4,602	-33,319
23		14	70,264	-31,877	8,753	-40,630
24		15	110,894	-35,354	13,814	-49,168
25		16	160,062	180,000	19,938	160,062

Note that—as in our simple example—the IRR of 12.46 percent successfully attributes income in such a way that the whole of the investment is accounted for at the end of the project's life (after 16 years, for the case of the leveraged lease). However, note that there are some unusual features of the table: five of the income figures are negative, as are seven of the "repayment of investment" terms. There are two ways to understand these features:

• In "mechanical" terms, the only way to make the table work is to have some negative income numbers. This interpretation, though true, is not very interesting.

• In economic terms, the negative income figures mean that in some years the project is not worth holding onto, but that it cannot be given away. As an example consider the lessor's position at the beginning of year 9. *Seven years* of negative cash flows lie ahead. Only in eight years, in year 16, will the lessor again see a positive cash flow from the lease. A rational lessor would like to give away the lease contract at this point; the present value of the cash flows at the beginning of year 9 at a 10 percent discount rate is –$39,333 (and this includes the realization of the residual value at the end of year 16!). But of course no rational investor would take over the contract at the beginning of year 9 *unless she were paid to do so,* or unless her discount rate were negative. It is this fact—that the lessor would have to pay someone to take the contract off her hands in year 9—that makes us attribute negative income to the project at this point.[3] In economic terms the lease at this point is worse than valueless; it is a burden.

As we shall see in the next section, the negative income of leveraged leases causes the accounting profession a considerable headache.

6.5 Accounting for Leveraged Leases: The "Multiple-Phases Method"

Financial Accounting Standards Board Statement 13 (FASB 13) mandates that the lessor in a leveraged lease allocate the cash flow from the lease between income and investment. The logical way to do so would be to use the IRR of the lease's cash flows in the way illustrated in the preceding section. But here the promulgators of FASB 13 apparently ran up against the troublesome facet of

---

3. Negative income attribution in fact starts in year 7, showing that already at this point the project has negative economic value.

human nature that hates to record a loss even if it is economically warranted. (The implausibility of the method for leveraged leases mandated in the statement is explained only by the assumption that lessors did not want, under any circumstances, to record economic losses that stemmed from the leases.)

The method that was devised to avoid the reporting of negative income is sometimes termed the multiple-phases method (MPM). A better term might have been "bastardized IRR method."

The fact that a somewhat silly method of recognizing income is used shouldn't bother us, since foolishness is rampant in this world. However, the complexity and the opaqueness of the method have lent it respectability. (There must be a lesson in this!) A little debunking, in the form of an explanation, is in order.

Suppose we let the multiple-phases rate of return Q (short for *quirky*) be defined as follows:

Year	MPM	Explanation
1	The lessor's investment in the lease at the beginning of year 1 is equal to her initial investment in the lease's equity. In our example, Investment(1) = \$200,000	This is the same as the calculation of the IRR.
t	The lessor's accounting income from the lease at the end of year t is $$\begin{cases} Q * \text{Investment}\,(1) & \text{if this number} > 0 \\ 0 & \text{otherwise} \end{cases}$$	If income is positive, MPM follows the attribution of income and investment of the standard IRR method. Otherwise, income is set to zero.
t	The lessor's investment in the lease at the beginning of any year $t > 1$ is defined as $\text{Investment}\,(t) = \text{Investment}\,(t-1)$ $- [\text{Cash flow}\,(t-1) - \text{Income}\,(t-1)]$	Follows IRR method
Last year	Cash flow(last year) = Investment(last year) $* (1 + Q)$	Similar to IRR method.

6.5.1   Calculating the Multiple-Phases-Method Rate of Return

To calculate the MPM Rate Q, we first set up a spreadsheet similar to the one we used to illustrate the IRR in section 6.4. The one difference is that we have extended the years to include year 17 (one year after the project ends). A solution Q should give a zero investment at the beginning of year 17. The following, for example, is *not* a solution for Q.

	C	D	E	F	G
1			**MPM METHOD:**		
2		**ATTRIBUTION OF LEVERAGED-LEASE CASH FLOWS**			
3		**TO INCOME AND REPAYMENT OF INVESTMENT**			
4					
5	Q	12.00%			
6					
7		Investment		**Attribution of cash flow**	
8	Year	at beginning	Cash		Repayment
9		of period	flow	Income	of investment
10	1	200,000	49,941	24,000	25,941
11	2	174,059	89,774	20,887	68,887
12	3	105,172	60,666	12,621	48,045
13	4	57,127	39,487	6,855	32,632
14	5	24,495	23,827	2,939	20,887
15	6	3,608	22,352	433	21,919
16	7	-18,312	20,730	0	20,730
17	8	-39,042	1,186	0	1,186
18	9	-40,228	-18,697	0	-18,697
19	10	-21,531	-20,856	0	-20,856
20	11	-675	-23,231	0	-23,231
21	12	22,556	-25,843	2,707	-28,550
22	13	51,105	-28,716	6,133	-34,849
23	14	85,954	-31,877	10,314	-42,192
24	15	128,146	-35,354	15,378	-50,732
25	16	178,878	180,000	21,465	158,535
26	17	20,343			

All the formulas in this table are the same as in the case of the IRR, with the exception of the formulas in the income column. For example, the income in year 1 has the following formula:

=IF($D$5*D10>0,$D$5*D10,0)

Using the Excel Solver, we find the solution for *Q*. The solver (**Tools|Solver**) dialog box looks like this:

The **target cell** $D$26 is the investment at the beginning of year 17; since this is one year after the project ends, this investment should be zero. When this method is applied in our case, the solution is as follows:

	C	D	E	F	G
1		**MPM METHOD:**			
2		**ATTRIBUTION OF LEVERAGED-LEASE CASH FLOWS**			
3		**TO INCOME AND REPAYMENT OF INVESTMENT**			
4					
5	Q	10.91%			
6					
7		Investment		**Attribution of cash flow**	
8	**Year**	at beginning	**Cash**		**Repayment**
9		of period	flow	**Income**	of investment
10	1	200,000	49,941	21,822	28,119
11	2	171,881	89,774	18,754	71,019
12	3	100,862	60,666	11,005	49,661
13	4	51,201	39,487	5,587	33,901
14	5	17,301	23,827	1,888	21,939
15	6	-4,638	22,352	0	22,352
16	7	-26,990	20,730	0	20,730
17	8	-47,721	1,186	0	1,186
18	9	-48,906	-18,697	0	-18,697
19	10	-30,210	-20,856	0	-20,856
20	11	-9,354	-23,231	0	-23,231
21	12	13,877	-25,843	1,514	-27,357
22	13	41,234	-28,716	4,499	-33,216
23	14	74,449	-31,877	8,123	-40,001
24	15	114,450	-35,354	12,488	-47,842
25	16	162,292	180,000	17,708	162,292
26	17	0			

6.6   Comparing the MPM Rate of Return with the IRR

The MPM rate of return is widely used in the leveraged-leasing industry. How does it compare with the IRR?

• In general, the MPM rate of return is less than or equal to the IRR. The two will be equal if all the lease's cash flows are positive. Otherwise the MPM rate of return is less than the IRR.

• If the MPM rate of return is less than the IRR, then at some point the IRR will attribute negative income to the lease, whereas the MPM will attribute zero income to the lease.

Graphically, for the specific example of this chapter, we have

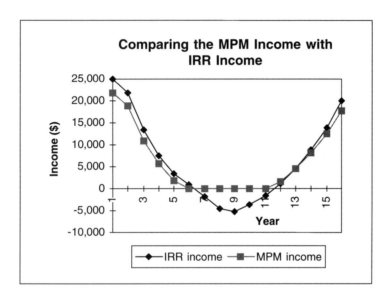

Exercises

1.   Reconsider the leveraged-leasing example in this chapter. Show that if depreciation is straight line over 15 years, then the MPM rate of return is equal to the IRR. Explain.

2.   In the leveraged-lease example of section 6.6, find the lowest lease rental so that the MPM is equal to the IRR (assume the original depreciation schedule).

II Portfolio Models

Modern portfolio theory, which has its origins in the work of Harry Markowitz, John Lintner, Jan Mossin, and William Sharpe, represents one of the great advances in finance. Chapters 7–12 implement some of the ideas of these researchers and show you how to compute the standard portfolio problems in finance. In these chapters we make intensive use of Excel's matrix functions and data tables (see Chapters 26 and 27).

Chapter 7 reviews the basic mechanics of portfolio calculation. Starting with price data, we calculate asset and portfolio returns. While the bulk of the chapter deals with the simple two-asset portfolio problem, the general case is discussed in sections 7.3 and 7.4.

In Chapter 8 we show how to use return data to calculate the variance-covariance matrix. Excel's matrix-handling capabilities make it easy to do this calculation. Chapter 9 discusses both the theory and the mechanics of the calculation of efficient portfolios when there are no restrictions on short sales. Using Excel's matrix functions we can calculate two efficient portfolios, which can then be used to plot the whole efficient frontier.

In Chapter 10 we replicate a simple test of the capital asset pricing model (CAPM). We use some market data to derive the security market line (SML). We then relate the results to Roll's criticism of these tests. Excel makes it easy to do the regression analysis required for these tests. (Regressions are discussed in Chapter 29.)

The preceding chapters have assumed that portfolio optimizers could sell securities short. In Chapter 11 we show how to use Excel's **Solver** to compute efficient portfolios when short sales are not allowed. Finally, Chapter 12 is an introduction to value-at-risk (VaR) techniques in a portfolio context.

7.1 Overview

In this chapter we review the basic mechanics of portfolio calculations. We start with a simple example of two assets, showing how to derive the return distributions from historical price data. We then discuss the general case of N assets; for this case it becomes convenient to use matrix notation and exploit Excel's matrix-handling capabilities.

It is useful before going on to review some basic notation: Each asset i (they may be shares, bonds, real estate, or whatever, although our numerical examples here will be confined to shares) is characterized by several statistics: $E(r_i)$, the expected return on asset i; $\text{Var}(r_i)$, the variance of asset i's return; and $\text{Cov}(r_i, r_j)$, the covariance of asset i's and asset j's returns. In our applications, it will often be convenient to write $\text{Cov}(r_i, r_j)$, as σ_{ij} and $\text{Var}(r_i)$ as σ_{ii} (instead of σ_i^2, as usual). Since the covariance of an asset's returns with itself, $\text{Cov}(r_i, r_i)$, is in fact the variance of the asset's returns, this notation is not only economical but also logical.

7.2 A Simple Two-Asset Example

Suppose we have monthly price data for 12 months on two shares: one of Stock A and one of Stock B. The data look like this:

	A	B	C
1		**Stock prices**	
2	**Month**	**Stock A**	**Stock B**
3	0	25.00	45.00
4	1	24.12	44.85
5	2	23.37	46.88
6	3	24.75	45.25
7	4	26.62	50.87
8	5	26.50	53.25
9	6	28.00	53.25
10	7	28.88	62.75
11	8	29.75	65.50
12	9	31.38	66.87
13	10	36.25	78.50
14	11	37.13	78.00
15	12	36.88	68.23

These data give the closing price at the end of each month for each stock. The month-0 price is the initial price of the stock (i.e., the closing price at the end of the month preceding month 1). We wish to calculate the relevant return statistics for each stock.

First we calculate the *monthly return* for each stock. This is the percentage return that would be earned by an investor who bought the stock at the end of a particular month $t - 1$ and sold it at the end of the following month. For month t and Stock A, the monthly return r_{At} is defined as

$$r_{At} = \ln\left(\frac{P_{At}}{P_{A,t-1}}\right)$$

We note two things about this return calculation: First, we are using the continuously compounded return on the stock. An alternative would have been to use the discrete return, $P_{At}/P_{A,t-1} - 1$. Appendix 2 at the end of this chapter discusses the reasons for our choice of the continuously compounded return. Second, we are calculating the price return of the stock. Had the stock paid a dividend in month t, the total return would have been

$$r_{At} = \ln\left(\frac{P_{At} + Div_t}{P_{A,t-1}}\right)$$

In the examples that follow, we ignore dividends.

The return calculation is easily done in Excel. Setting up the proper formulas gives

	A	B	C	D	E	F	G	H
18		**CALCULATING THE RETURNS**						
19		**Stock A**			**Stock B**			
20	**Month**	**Price**	**Return**		**Price**	**Return**		
21	0	25.00			45.00			
22	1	24.12	-3.58%		44.85	-0.33%		
23	2	23.37	-3.16%		46.88	4.43%	<-- =LN(E23/E22)	
24	3	24.75	5.74%		45.25	-3.54%		
25	4	26.62	7.28%		50.87	11.71%		
26	5	26.50	-0.45%		53.25	4.57%		
27	6	28.00	5.51%		53.25	0.00%		
28	7	28.88	3.09%		62.75	16.42%		
29	8	29.75	2.97%		65.50	4.29%		
30	9	31.38	5.33%		66.87	2.07%		
31	10	36.25	14.43%		78.50	16.03%		
32	11	37.13	2.40%		78.00	-0.64%		
33	12	36.88	-0.68%		68.23	-13.38%		

We now make a heroic assumption: We assume that the return data for the 12 months represent the distribution of the returns for the coming month. We thus assume that the past gives us some information about the way returns will behave in the future. This assumption allows us to assume that the average of the historic data represents the *expected monthly return* from each stock. It also allows us to assume that we may learn from the historic data what is the variance of the future returns. Using the **Average( )**, **Varp( )**, and **Stdevp( )** functions in Excel, we calculate the statistics for the return distribution:

	A	B	C	D	E	F	G	H	I
35	Monthly mean		3.24%			3.47%	<-- =AVERAGE(F22:F33)		
36	Monthly variance		0.23%			0.65%	<-- =VARP(F22:F33)		
37	Monthly stand. dev.		4.78%			8.03%	<-- =STDEVP(F22:F33)		
38									
39	Annual mean		38.88%			41.62%	<-- =12*F35		
40	Annual variance		2.75%			7.75%	<-- =12*F36		
41	Annual stand. dev.		16.57%			27.83%	<-- =SQRT(F40)		

(Note that we have used **Varp( )** instead of **Var( )** and **Stdevp( )** instead of **Stdev( )**. For the difference between these functions, and the reasoning behind this choice, see Chapter 29.)

Next we want to calculate the *covariance* of the returns. The covariance (and the correlation coefficient, which is derived from it) measures the degree to which the returns on the two assets move together. The definition is

$$\text{Cov}(r_A, r_B) = \frac{1}{M} \sum_1 [r_{At} - E(r_A)] * [r_{Bt} - E(r_B)]$$

where M is the number of points in the distribution (in our case, $M = 12$). This equation is easily set up in Excel:

	A	B	C	D	E	F	G	H	I	J
44		COVARIANCE AND VARIANCE CALCULATION								
45		Stock A			Stock B	=D48-$F$35				
46	Return	Return-mean		Return	Return-mean		Product			
47										
48	-0.0358	-0.0682		-0.0033	-0.0380		0.00259	<-- =E48*B48		
49	-0.0316	-0.0640		0.0443	0.0096		-0.00061			
50	0.0574	0.0250		-0.0354	-0.0701		-0.00175			
51	0.0728	0.0404		0.1171	0.0824		0.00333			
52	-0.0045	-0.0369		0.0457	0.0110		-0.00041			
53	0.0551	0.0227		0.0000	-0.0347		-0.00079			
54	0.0309	-0.0015		0.1642	0.1295		-0.00019			
55	0.0297	-0.0027		0.0429	0.0082		-0.00002			
56	0.0533	0.0209		0.0207	-0.0140		-0.00029			
57	0.1443	0.1119		0.1603	0.1257		0.01406			
58	0.0240	-0.0084		-0.0064	-0.0411		0.00035			
59	-0.0068	-0.0392		-0.1338	-0.1685		0.00660			
60										
61					Covariance		0.00191	<-- =AVERAGE(G48:G59)		
62							0.00191	<-- =COVAR(A48:A59,D48:D59)		
63					Correlation		0.49589	<-- =G62/(F37*C37)		
64							0.49589	<-- =CORREL(A48:A59,D48:D59)		

The column **Product** contains the multiple of the deviation from the mean in each month, that is, the terms $[r_{At} - E(r_A)][r_{Bt} - E(r_B)]$, for $t = 1, ..., 12$. The covariance is **Average(Product)** = 0.00191. While it is worthwhile calculating the covariance this way at least once, there is a shorter way, which is also illustrated in the spreadsheets. Excel has an array function— **Covar(Array1,Array2)**—that calculates the covariance directly. To calculate the covariance using **Covar** there is no necessity to find the difference between the returns and the means. Simply use **Covar** directly on the columns, as illustrated in Cell G62 in the spreadsheet picture.

The covariance is a hard number to interpret, since its size depends on the units in which we measure the returns. (If we were to write the returns in percentages—i.e., 4 instead of 0.04—then the covariance would be 19.1, which is 10,000 times the number we just calculated.) We can also calculate the *correlation coefficient* ρ_{AB}, which is defined as

$$\rho_{AB} = \frac{\text{Cov}(r_A, r_B)}{\sigma_A \sigma_B}$$

The correlation coefficient is unit-free; calculating it for our example gives $\rho_{AB} = 0.4958$. As we have illustrated, the correlation coefficient can be calculated directly in Excel using the function **Correl(Array1, Array2)**, where the arrays are the same column vectors used to calculate the covariance using the function **Covar.**

The correlation coefficient measures the degree of linear relation between the returns of Stock A and Stock B. The following facts can be proven about the correlation coefficient:

- The correlation coefficient is always between $+1$ and -1: $-1 \leq \rho_{AB} \leq 1$.
- If the correlation coefficient is $+1$, then the returns on the two assets are linearly related with a positive slope; that is, if $\rho_{AB} = 1$, then

$r_{At} = c + dr_{Bt}$, where $d > 0$

- If the correlation coefficient is -1, then the returns on the two assets are linearly related with a negative slope; that is, if $\rho_{AB} = -1$, then

$r_{At} = c + dr_{Bt}$, where $d < 0$

- If the return distributions are independent, then the correlation coefficient will be zero. (The opposite is not true: If the correlation coefficient is zero, this fact does not necessarily mean that the returns are independent. See the exercises for an example.)

7.2.1   A Different View of the Correlation Coefficient

Another way to took at the correlation coefficient is to graph Stock A and B returns on the same axes and then use the Excel **Trendline** facility to regress the returns of Stock B on those of Stock A. (For a full discussion of **Trendline,** see chapter 29.) The correlation coefficient is the square root of the regression R^2:

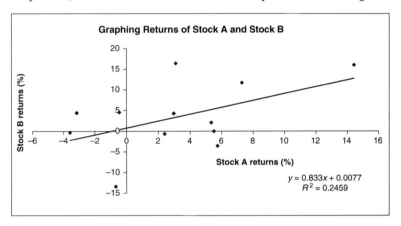

7.3   Calculating Portfolio Means and Variances

Now suppose we form a portfolio composed half of Stock A and half of Stock B. What will be the mean and the variance of this portfolio? It is worth doing the brute-force calculations at least once in Excel.

	A	B	C	D	E	F	G	H
1	CALCULATING THE MEAN AND SIGMA OF A PORTFOLIO							
2								
3	Proportion of A	0.5						
4								
5			Month	R$_{At}$	R$_{Bt}$	R$_{pt}$		
6			1	-3.58%	-0.33%	-1.96%	<-- =C6*$B$3+(1-$B$3)*D6	
7			2	-3.16%	4.43%	0.63%		
8			3	5.74%	-3.54%	1.10%		
9			4	7.28%	11.71%	9.50%		
10			5	-0.45%	4.57%	2.06%		
11			6	5.51%	0.00%	2.75%		
12			7	3.09%	16.42%	9.76%		
13			8	2.97%	4.29%	3.63%		
14			9	5.33%	2.07%	3.70%		
15			10	14.43%	16.03%	15.23%		
16			11	2.40%	-0.64%	0.88%		
17			12	-0.68%	-13.38%	-7.03%		
18					Mean	3.35%	<-- =AVERAGE(E6:E17)	
19					Variance	0.31%	<-- =VARP(E6:E17)	
20					St dev.	5.60%	<-- =STDEVP(E6:E17)	

It is easy to see that the mean portfolio return is exactly the average of the mean returns of the two assets:

Expected portfolio return $= E(r_p) = 0.5E(r_A) + 0.5E(r_B)$
$= 0.5 * 3.24\% + 0.5 * 3.47\% = 3.35\%$

In general the mean return of the portfolio is the *weighted average return* of the component stocks. If we denote by γ the proportion invested in Stock A, then

$$E(r_p) = \gamma E(r_A) + (1 - \gamma)E(r_B)$$

However, the portfolio's variance is *not* the average of the two variances of the stocks! The formula for the variance is

$$\text{Var}(r_p) = \gamma^2 \text{Var}(r_A) + (1 - \gamma)^2 \text{Var}(r_B) + 2\gamma(1 - \gamma)\text{Cov}(r_A, r_B)$$

Another way of writing this relation is

$$\sigma_P^2 = \gamma^2 \sigma_A^2 + (1 - \gamma)^2 \sigma_B^2 + 2\gamma(1 - \gamma)\rho_{AB}\sigma_A\sigma_B$$

A frequently performed exercise is to plot the means and standard deviations for various portfolio proportions γ. To do this we build a table using Excel's **Data|Table** command (see Chapter 26):

	A	B	C	D	E	F
23	**Proportion**	**Sigma**	**Mean**			
24		5.60%	3.35%	Table header: <-- =E18		
25	0	8.03%	3.47%			
26	0.075	7.62%	3.45%			
27	0.15	7.21%	3.43%			
28	0.225	6.82%	3.42%			
29	0.3	6.46%	3.40%			
30	0.375	6.11%	3.38%			
31	0.45	5.80%	3.37%			
32	0.525	5.51%	3.35%			
33	0.6	5.26%	3.33%			
34	0.675	5.06%	3.31%			
35	0.75	4.90%	3.30%			
36	0.825	4.80%	3.28%			
37	0.9	4.75%	3.26%			
38	0.975	4.77%	3.25%			
39	1.05	4.84%	3.23%			
40	1.125	4.96%	3.21%			
41	1.2	5.14%	3.19%			
42	1.275	5.36%	3.18%			
43	1.35	5.62%	3.16%			
44	1.425	5.92%	3.14%			
45	1.5	6.25%	3.13%			
46	1.575	6.60%	3.11%			

The graph of the means and standard deviations looks like the following figure. To make the figure come out in this way, you have to use the **Graph Type XY** option.

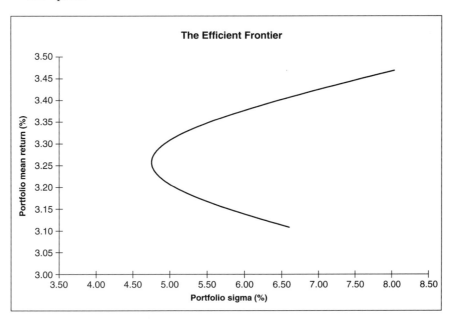

7.4   Portfolio Mean and Variance—The General Case

Matrix notation greatly simplifies the writing of the portfolio problem.[1] In the general case of N assets, suppose that the proportion of asset i in the portfolio is denoted by γ_i. It is often convenient to write the portfolio proportions as a column vector Γ:

$$\Gamma = \begin{bmatrix} \gamma_1 \\ \gamma_2 \\ \gamma_3 \\ \vdots \\ \gamma_N \end{bmatrix}$$

---

1. Chapter 27 gives an introduction to matrices sufficient to deal with all the problems encountered in this book. Since Excel has excellent matrix-handling capabilities, it is recommended that you study Chapter 27 before going on with the current chapter. The Excel matrix functions **MMult( )** and **MInverse( )** used in portfolio problems are discussed in Chapter 27.

We may then write Γ^T as the transpose of Γ:

$$\Gamma^T = [\gamma_1, \gamma_2, \gamma_3, ..., \gamma_N]$$

The expected return of the portfolio whose proportions are given by Γ is the weighted average of the expected returns of the individual assets:

$$E(r_p) = \sum_{i=1}^{N} \gamma_i E(r_i)$$

Now write $E(r)$ as the column vector of asset returns, and $E(r)^T$ as the row vector of the asset returns:

$$E(r) = \begin{bmatrix} E(r_1) \\ E(r)_2 \\ E(r_3) \\ \vdots \\ E(R_N) \end{bmatrix}$$

$$E(r)^T = [E(r_1), E(r_2), E(r_3), ..., E(r_N)]$$

Then we may write the expected portfolio return in matrix notation as

$$E(r_p) = \sum_{i=1}^{N} \lambda_i E(r_i) = \Gamma^T E(r) = E(r)^T \Gamma$$

The portfolio's variance is given by

$$\text{Var}(r_p) = \sum_{i=1}^{N} (\gamma_i)^2 \text{Var}(r_i) + 2 \sum_{i=1}^{N} \sum_{j=i+1}^{N} \gamma_i \gamma_j \text{Cov}(r_i, r_j)$$

This looks bad, but it is really a straightforward extension of the expression for the variance of a portfolio of two assets that we had before: Each asset's variance appears once, multiplied by the square of the asset's proportion in the portfolio; the covariance of each pair of assets appears once, multiplied by twice the product of the individual assets' proportions. Another way of writing the variance is to use the notation

$$\text{Var}(r_i) = \sigma_{ii}, \qquad \text{Cov}(r_i, r_j) = \sigma_{ij}$$

We may then write

$$\mathrm{Var}(r_p) = \sum_i \sum_j \gamma_i \gamma_j \sigma_{ij}$$

The most economical representation of the portfolio variance uses matrix notation. It is also the easiest representation to implement for large portfolios in Excel. In this representation we call the matrix that has σ_{ij} in the ith row and the jth column the *variance-covariance matrix:*

$$S = \begin{bmatrix} \sigma_{11} & \sigma_{12} & \sigma_{13} & \cdots & \sigma_{1N} \\ \sigma_{21} & \sigma_{22} & \sigma_{23} & \cdots & \sigma_{2N} \\ \sigma_{31} & \sigma_{32} & \sigma_{33} & \cdots & \sigma_{3N} \\ \vdots & & & & \\ \sigma_{N1} & \sigma_{N2} & \sigma_{N3} & \cdots & \sigma_{NN} \end{bmatrix}$$

Then the portfolio variance is given by $\mathrm{Var}(r_p) = \Gamma^T S \Gamma$.

Finally, if we denote by $\Gamma_1 = [\gamma_1, \gamma_2, \gamma_3, \ldots, \gamma_N]$ the proportions of Portfolio 1 and by $\Gamma_2 = [\delta_1, \delta_2, \delta_3, \ldots, \delta_N]$ the proportions of Portfolio 2, we can show that the covariance of the two portfolios is given by $\mathrm{Cov}(1, 2) = \Gamma_1 S \Gamma_2^T$.

We now give an example: Suppose that there are four risky assets that have the following expected returns and variance-covariance matrix:

	B	C	D	E	F	G	H
1	\multicolumn{7}{c}{**A FOUR-ASSET PORTFOLIO PROBLEM**}						
2							
3	Variance-covariance					Mean returns	
4	0.10	0.01	0.03	0.05		6%	
5	0.01	0.30	0.06	-0.04		8%	
6	0.03	0.06	0.40	0.02		10%	
7	0.05	-0.04	0.02	0.50		15%	

We wish to consider two portfolios of risky assets:

	B	C	D	E	F
9	Portfolio 1	0.2	0.3	0.4	0.1
10	Portfolio 2	0.2	0.1	0.1	0.6

For clarity of exposition, we first allocate space on the spreadsheet for the transposes of the two portfolios. We use the *array function* (see Chapter 29) **Transpose** to insert these cells.

	B	C	D
19	**Transposes**		
20	Portfolio 1		Portfolio 2
21	0.2		0.2
22	0.3		0.1
23	0.4		0.1
24	0.1		0.6

We next calculate the means, variances, and covariance of the two portfolios. We use the Excel function **Mmult** for all the calculations:

	B	C	D	E	F	G	H	I	J	K
12	**Portfolio 1**			**Portfolio 2**						
13	Mean	9.10%		Mean	12.00%	<-- =MMULT(C10:F10,$G$4:$G$7)				
14	Variance	12.16%		Variance	20.34%	<-- =MMULT(C10:F10,MMULT(B4:E7,D21:D24))				
15										
16	Covariance	0.0714	<-- =MMULT(C9:F9,MMULT(B4:E7,D21:D24))							
17	Correlation	0.4540	<-- =C16/SQRT(C14*F14)							

We can now calculate the standard deviation and return of combinations of portfolios 1 and 2. Note that once we have calculated the means, variances, and the covariance of the returns of the two portfolios, the calculation of the mean and the variance of any portfolio is the same as for the two-asset case.

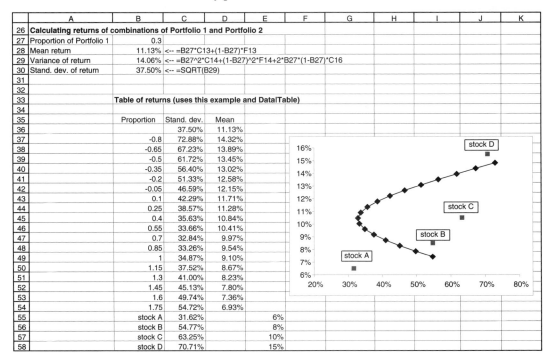

	A	B	C	D	E	F	G	H	I	J	K
26	**Calculating returns of combinations of Portfolio 1 and Portfolio 2**										
27	Proportion of Portfolio 1	0.3									
28	Mean return	11.13%	<-- =B27*C13+(1-B27)*F13								
29	Variance of return	14.06%	<-- =B27^2*C14+(1-B27)^2*F14+2*B27*(1-B27)*C16								
30	Stand. dev. of return	37.50%	<-- =SQRT(B29)								
31											
32											
33			**Table of returns (uses this example and DataTable)**								
34											
35			Proportion	Stand. dev.	Mean						
36				37.50%	11.13%						
37			-0.8	72.88%	14.32%						
38			-0.65	67.23%	13.89%						
39			-0.5	61.72%	13.45%						
40			-0.35	56.40%	13.02%						
41			-0.2	51.33%	12.58%						
42			-0.05	46.59%	12.15%						
43			0.1	42.29%	11.71%						
44			0.25	38.57%	11.28%						
45			0.4	35.63%	10.84%						
46			0.55	33.66%	10.41%						
47			0.7	32.84%	9.97%						
48			0.85	33.26%	9.54%						
49			1	34.87%	9.10%						
50			1.15	37.52%	8.67%						
51			1.3	41.00%	8.23%						
52			1.45	45.13%	7.80%						
53			1.6	49.74%	7.36%						
54			1.75	54.72%	6.93%						
55			stock A	31.62%		6%					
56			stock B	54.77%		8%					
57			stock C	63.25%		10%					
58			stock D	70.71%		15%					

7.5   Efficient Portfolios

An *efficient portfolio* is the portfolio of risky assets that gives the lowest variance of return of all portfolios having the same expected return. Alternatively, we may say that an efficient portfolio has the highest expected return of all portfolios having the same variance. Mathematically, we may define an efficient portfolio as follows: For a given return *m*, an efficient portfolio *p* is one that solves

$$\min \sum_i \sum_j x_i x_j \sigma_{ij} = \text{Var}(r_p)$$

subject to

$$\sum_i x_i r_i = \mu = E(r_p)$$

$$\sum_i x_i = 1$$

The *efficient frontier* is the set of all efficient portfolios. As shown by Black (1972), the efficient frontier is the locus of all convex combinations of any two efficient portfolios. Therefore, if $x = \{x_1, \ldots, x_N\}$ and $y = \{y_1, \ldots, y_N\}$, are efficient portfolios and if *a* is a constant, then the portfolio *z* defined by

$$z = ax + (1-a)y = \begin{bmatrix} ax_1 + (1-a)y_1 \\ ax_2 + (1-a)y_2 \\ \vdots \\ ax_N + (1-a)y_N \end{bmatrix}$$

is also efficient. Thus we can find the whole efficient frontier if we can find any two efficient portfolios.

By this theorem, once we have found two efficient portfolios *x* and *y*, we know that any other efficient portfolio is a convex combination of *x* and *y*. If we denote the mean and variance of *x* and *y* by $\{E(r_x), \sigma_x^2\}$ and $\{E(r_y), \sigma_y^2\}$, and if $z = ax + (1-a)y$, then

$$E(r_z) = aE(r_x) + (1-a)E(r_y)$$

$$\sigma_z^2 = a^2\sigma_x^2 + (1-a)^2\sigma_y^2 + 2a(1-a)\text{Cov}(x, y)$$

$$= a^2\sigma_x^2 + (1-a)^2\sigma_y^2 + 2a(1-a)x^T S y$$

Further details of the calculation of efficient portfolios are discussed in Chapter 9.

7.5.1   Return to the General Case (Section 7.4)

To show that efficiency is a nontrivial concept, we show that the two portfolios whose combinations are graphed in section 7.4 are *not efficient*. This point is easy to see if we extend the data table to include numbers for the individual stocks:

	A	B	C	D	E	F	G	H	I	J	K
26	**Calculating returns of combinations of Portfolio 1 and Portfolio 2**										
27	Proportion of Portfolio 1	0.3									
28	Mean return	11.13%	<-- =B27*C13+(1-B27)*F13								
29	Variance of return	14.06%	<-- =B27^2*C14+(1-B27)^2*F14+2*B27*(1-B27)*C16								
30	Stand. dev. of return	37.50%	<-- =SQRT(B29)								
31											
32											
33			**Table of returns (uses this example and DataTable)**								
34											
35			Proportion	Stand. dev.	Mean						
36				37.50%	11.13%						
37			-0.8	72.88%	14.32%						
38			-0.65	67.23%	13.89%						
39			-0.5	61.72%	13.45%						
40			-0.35	56.40%	13.02%						
41			-0.2	51.33%	12.58%						
42			-0.05	46.59%	12.15%						
43			0.1	42.29%	11.71%						
44			0.25	38.57%	11.28%						
45			0.4	35.63%	10.84%						
46			0.55	33.66%	10.41%						
47			0.7	32.84%	9.97%						
48			0.85	33.26%	9.54%						
49			1	34.87%	9.10%						
50			1.15	37.52%	8.67%						
51			1.3	41.00%	8.23%						
52			1.45	45.13%	7.80%						
53			1.6	49.74%	7.36%						
54			1.75	54.72%	6.93%						
55			stock A	31.62%		6%					
56			stock B	54.77%		8%					
57			stock C	63.25%		10%					
58			stock D	70.71%		15%					

Were the two portfolios efficient, then all of the individual stocks would fall on or inside the graph of the combinations. In Chapter 9 you will learn to compute efficient portfolios, but as you will see there, this requires considerably more computation.

7.6   Conclusion

In this chapter we have reviewed the basic concepts and mathematics of portfolios. In succeeding chapters we shall describe how to compute the variance-covariance matrix from asset returns and show how to calculate efficient portfolios.

Exercises

1. The spreadsheet **Problems 07.xls** includes price data for the Dow-Jones 30 Industrials from December 1993 through April 1999. Isolating the data for American Airlines (AA) and Sears-Roebuck (S), confirm the following statistics about the returns of these two stocks:

	A	B	C	D	E	F	G	H	I
1	AMERICAN AIRLINES (AA) and SEARS (S), RETURN DATA for Dec. 93 - April 99								
2									
3	Monthly statistics		AA			S			
4	Average		0.0257			0.0146			
5	Sigma		0.0955			0.0851			
6	Covariance		0.0020						
7									
8	Correlation		0.2401	<-- Uses the **Correl** function					
9			0.2401	<-- =C5/(C4*F4)					

2. Using the data from exercise 1, suppose you bought and held a portfolio composed of 50% American Airlines (AA) and 50% Sears (S) stock and held it throughout this period. Compute the following statistics for this portfolio:

   a. Average monthly return

   b. Standard deviation(σ) of monthly return

3. Following are annual return statistics for two mutual funds from the Vanguard family:

	A	B	C	D	E	F	G
1	**Vanguard's Windsor Fund and Index 500 Fund Returns**						
2	Source: http://www.vanguard.com						
3	The Index 500 fund mimics the SP500 index; the Windsor Fund is an "aggressive" growth fund						
4							
5	**Year Ended**	**SP 500**	**Windsor**				
6	**31 December**	**Index**	**Fund**				
7	1997	33.40%	22.00%				
8	1996	23.00%	26.40%				
9	1995	37.60%	30.10%				
10	1994	1.30%	-0.10%				
11	1993	10.10%	19.40%				
12	1992	7.60%	16.50%				
13	1991	30.50%	28.60%				
14	1990	-3.10%	-15.50%				
15	1989	31.70%	15.00%				
16	1988	16.60%	28.70%				
17	1987	5.30%	1.20%				
18	1986	18.70%	20.30%				
19	1985	31.80%	28.00%				
20	1984	6.30%	19.50%				
21							
22	Average	17.91%	17.15%				
23	Standard deviation	13.03%	12.82%				
24	Covariance of returns	0.0126					
25							
26	**Portfolio returns**						
27	Percentage of SP500	25%					
28	Percentage of Windsor	75%					
29							
30	Expected portfolio return	17.34%					
31	Variance of portfolio return	1.50%					
32	Standard dev. of port. return	12.26%					

Use Excel to graph the combinations of standard deviation of return (*x*-axis) and expected return (*y*-axis) by varying the percentage of SP 500 in the portfolio from 0% to 100%.

4.   Using the data base of the DJ Industrials—For American Airlines (AA), Procter & Gamble (PG), and General Electric (GE)—compute:

a. The average monthly returns

b. The covariances of the monthly returns:

- $\sigma_{AA,AA} = \text{Covariance}(R_{AA}, R_{AA})$, $\sigma_{PG,PG} = \text{Covariance}(R_{PG}, R_{PG})$, $\sigma_{GE,GE} = \text{Covariance}(R_{GE}, R_{GE})$—these are equal to the variance of AA, PG, and GE respectively.

- $\sigma_{AA,GE}$ = Covariance (R_{AA}, R_{GE}), $\sigma_{AA,PG}$ = Covariance (R_{AA}, R_{PG}), $\sigma_{PG,GE}$ = Covariance(R_{PG}, R_{GE}).

   c. What are the monthly expected return and monthly standard deviation of a portfolio which is equally invested in the three stocks?

5.   Suppose that X and Y are two random variables and that $Y = X^2$. Let X have values -5, -4, -2, 2, 4, 5 with equal probabilities. Show that the correlation coefficient between X and Y is zero. Does this mean that X and Y are independent random variables?

6.   Pfizer and Merck are two American pharmaceutical firms. The following table gives the end-of-year stock prices for each of the firms for the years 1981–92 as well as the dividends paid in the years 1982–92.

   a. For the decade 1982–92 calculate the following:

- Annual returns from each of the shares. (Don't forget the dividends!)
- The mean, variance, and standard deviation of each stock's return.
- The covariance and the correlation coefficient of the returns.

   b. Graph the mean portfolio return (y-axis) against the standard deviation of the portfolio return (x-axis) for portfolios of the two shares in which the weight of Pfizer goes from 0 to 1.4.

	A	B	C	D	E	F
1		**PFIZER AND MERCK**				
2						
3			**Pfizer**			**Merck**	
4			Stock price	Dividend		Stock price	Dividend
5	1981	11.85			4.95	
6	1982	16.35	0.46		4.25	0.16
7	1983	19.60	0.58		5.15	0.16
8	1984	17.95	0.66		4.85	0.17
9	1985	23.45	0.74		6.35	0.18
10	1986	29.75	0.82		10.95	0.21
11	1987	29.25	0.90		19.20	0.27
12	1988	26.90	1.00		17.95	0.43
13	1989	32.45	1.10		22.85	0.55
14	1990	34.10	1.20		26.35	0.64
15	1991	61.45	1.32		41.50	0.77
16	1992	76.05	1.48		51.15	0.90

7.   Consider two assets, A and B, which have the following means and variances:

$E(r_A) = 0.03$, $E(r_B) = 0.05$

$\mathrm{Var}(r_A) = 0.0025$, $\mathrm{Var}(r_B) = 0.0045$

Now consider three cases:

$\rho_{AB} = +1$, $\rho_{AB} = -1$, $\rho_{AB} = 0$

Graph the combinations of portfolio means and variances for each case. (Graphs like these appear in virtually all elementary finance books. The standard deviation usually appears on the *x*-axis and the portfolio mean return on the *y*-axis. In this case, if you want to put all three graphs on the same set of axes, you will have to reverse this arrangement or use a trick.)

8.   Consider a three-asset world with the following parameters:

$$\text{Means returns} = \begin{pmatrix} 10\% \\ 12\% \\ 14\% \end{pmatrix}, \text{Variance-covariance matrix} = \begin{pmatrix} 0.3 & 0.02 & -0.05 \\ 0.02 & 0.4 & 0.06 \\ -0.05 & 0.06 & 0.6 \end{pmatrix}$$

Suppose you have two portfolios with the following portfolio weights:

Portfolio 1 = (0.3   0.2   0.5)

Portfolio 2 = (0.5   0.4   0.1)

a. Calculate the following:

• The mean and variance of each portfolio's returns

• The covariance and correlation coefficient of the portfolios' returns

b. Create a graph of the means and variance of convex combinations of the portfolios.

Appendix 1: Adjusting for Dividends

In this appendix we discuss two ways of adjusting returns for dividends, which are ignored in the examples in the chapter. The first, and simplest, method of adjusting for dividends is to add them to the annual change in price. In the following example, if you purchased GM stock at the 1986 year-end price of $33 per share and held it for one year, you would, at the end of the year, have made 0.57 percent.

$$\text{Discretely compounded return, 1987} = \frac{30.69 + 2.50}{33.00} - 1 = 0.568 \text{ percent}$$

The continuously compounded return is calculated by

$$\text{Continuously compounded return, 1987} = \ln\left[\frac{30.69 + 2.50}{33.00}\right] = 0.567 \text{ percent}$$

(The choice between discrete and continuous compounding is discussed in Appendix 2.)

	B	C	D	E	F	G	H	I
6	**General Motors (GM)**							
7		**Year-end**	**Dividend**	**Discretely**	**Continuously**			
8		**stock**	**per**	**compounded**	**compounded**			
9	**Year**	**price**	**share**	**return**	**return**			
10	1986	33.00						
11	1987	30.69	2.50	0.568%	0.567%			
12	1988	41.75	2.50	44.196%	36.600%			
13	1989	42.25	3.00	8.383%	8.050%			
14	1990	34.38	3.00	-11.538%	-12.260%			
15	1991	28.88	1.60	-11.345%	-12.042%			
16	1992	32.25	1.40	16.537%	15.304%			
17	1993	54.88	0.80	72.636%	54.601%			
18	1994	42.13	0.80	-21.777%	-24.560%			
19	1995	52.88	1.10	28.131%	24.788%			
20	1996	55.75	1.60	8.463%	8.124%			
21							=LN((D20+C20)/C19)	
22	Arithmetic annual return			13.425%	9.92%			
23	Standard deviation of returns			27.148%	22.838%			
24								
25			=(C20+D20)/C19-1					
26								

Dividend Reinvestment

Another way of calculating returns is to assume that the dividends are reinvested in the stock:

	J	K	L	M	N	O	P	Q	R	S
3	**REINVESTED DIVIDENDS**									
4		**Effective**	**Share**	**Dividend**	**Total**	**Number**	**Value of**			
5		**shares**	**price**	**per share**	**dividends**	**of shares**	**shares**			
6		**held at**	**at end**		**received**	**at end of**	**end of**			
7	**Year**	**beg. year**	**year**			**year**	**year**			
8	1986		33.00				33.000	=K10+N10/L10		
9	1987	1.00	30.69	2.500	2.500	1.081	33.188			
10	1988	1.08	41.75	2.500	2.704	1.146	47.855	=O10*L10		
11	1989	1.15	42.25	3.000	3.439	1.228	51.867			
12	1990	1.23	34.38	3.000	3.683	1.335	45.882			
13	1991	1.33	28.88	1.600	2.136	1.409	40.677			
14	1992	1.41	32.25	1.400	1.972	1.470	47.403			
15	1993	1.47	54.88	0.800	1.176	1.491	81.835			
16	1994	1.49	42.13	0.800	1.193	1.520	64.014			
17	1995	1.52	52.88	1.100	1.672	1.551	82.021			
18	1996	1.55	55.75	1.600	2.482	1.596	88.963			
19										
20		Annualized continuous return					9.92%	<-- =LN(P18/P8)/10		
21		Compound geometric return					10.43%	<-- =(P18/P8)^(1/10)-1		
22				=K10*M10						
23										

Consider first 1987: Since we purchased the share at the end of 1986, we own one share at the end of 1987. If the 1987 dividend is turned into shares at the end-1987 price, we can use it to buy 0.081 additional shares:

$$\text{New shares purchased at end of 1987} = \frac{2.50}{30.69} = 0.081$$

Thus we start 1988 with 1.081 shares. Since the 1988 dividend per share is $2.50, the total dividend received on the shares is $1.081 * \$2.50 = \$2.704$. Reinvesting these dividends in shares gives

$$\text{New shares purchased at end of 1988} = \frac{2.704}{41.75} = 0.065$$

Thus, at the end of 1988, the holder of GM shares will have accumulated $1 + 0.081 + 0.065 = 1.146$ shares.

As the spreadsheet fragment shows, this reinvestment of dividends will produce a holding of 1.596 shares at the end of 1996, worth $88.963.

We can calculate the return on this investment in one of two ways:

$$\text{Continuously compounded return} = \ln\left[\frac{\text{End 1996 value}}{\text{Beginning investment}}\right] \Big/ 10$$

$$= \ln\left[\frac{88.963}{33.00}\right] \Big/ 10 = 9.92 \text{ percent}$$

Note that this continuously compounded return is the same as that calculated in the first spreadsheet fragment from the annual returns (cell F22).

An alternative is to calculate the geometric return:

$$\text{Compound geometric return} =$$

$$\left[\frac{\text{End 1996 value}}{\text{Initial investment}}\right]^{1/10} - 1 = \left[\frac{88.963}{33.00}\right]^{1/10} - 1 = 10.43 \text{ percent}$$

Appendix 2: Continuously Compounded versus Geometric Returns

Using the continuously compounded return assumes that $P_t = P_{t-1}e^{r_t}$, where r_t is the rate of return during the period $(t - 1, t)$. Suppose that $r_1, r_2, \ldots, r_{12}$ are the returns for 12 periods (a period could be a month or it could be a year), then the price of the stock at the end of the 12 periods will be

$$P_{12} = P_0 e^{r_1 + r_2 + \ldots + r_{12}}$$

This representation of prices and returns allows us to assume that the *average periodic return* is $r = (r_1 + r_2 + \dots + r_{12})/12$. Since we wish to assume that the return data for the 12 periods represent the distribution of the returns for the coming period, it follows that the continuously compounded return is the appropriate return measure, and not the discretely compounded return $r_t = (P_{At} - P_{A,t-1})/P_{A,t-1}$

How Different Are Continuously Compounded and Discretely Compounded Returns?

The continuously compounded return will always be smaller than the discretely compounded return, but the difference is usually not large. The following table shows the differences for the example in section 7.2:

	A	B	C	D	E	F	G	H	I	J
1				COMPARING DISCRETE TO CONTINUOUS RETURNS						
2										
3			Stock A				Stock B			
4			Continuous	Discrete			Continuous	Discrete		
5	Month	Price	return	return		Price	return	return		
6	0	25.00				45.00				
7	1	24.12	-3.58%	-3.52%		44.85	-0.33%	-0.33%		
8	2	23.37	-3.16%	-3.11%		46.88	4.43%	4.53%		
9	3	24.75	5.74%	5.91%		45.25	-3.54%	-3.48%		
10	4	26.62	7.28%	7.56%		50.87	11.71%	12.42%		
11	5	26.50	-0.45%	-0.45%		53.25	4.57%	4.68%		
12	6	28.00	5.51%	5.66%		53.25	0.00%	0.00%		
13	7	28.88	3.09%	3.14%		62.75	16.42%	17.84%		
14	8	29.75	2.97%	3.01%		65.50	4.29%	4.38%		
15	9	31.38	5.33%	5.48%		66.87	2.07%	2.09%		
16	10	36.25	14.43%	15.52%		78.50	16.03%	17.39%		
17	11	37.13	2.40%	2.43%		78.00	-0.64%	-0.64%		
18	12	36.88	-0.68%	-0.67%		68.23	-13.38%	-12.53%		
19										
20		Mean	3.24%	3.41%			3.47%	3.86%	<-- =AVERAGE(H7:H18)	
21		Sigma	4.78%	5.02%			8.03%	8.32%	<-- =STDEVP(H7:H18)	

Calculating Annual Returns and Variances from Periodic Returns

Suppose we calculate a series of continuously compounded *monthly* rates of return $r_1, r_2, \dots, r_n$ and we wish to then calculate the mean and the variance of the *annual* rate of return. Clearly the mean annual return is given by

$$\text{Mean annual return} = 12 \left[\frac{1}{n} \sum_{t=1}^{n} r_t \right]$$

To calculate the variance of the annual rate of return, we assume that the monthly rates of return are independent identically distributed random variables. It then follows that $\mathrm{Var}(r) = 12\left[\dfrac{1}{n}\sum_{t=1}^{n}\mathrm{Var}(r_t)\right] = 12\sigma^2_{\mathrm{Monthly}}$, and that the standard deviation of the annual rate of return is given by $\sigma = \sqrt{12}\sigma_{\mathrm{Monthly}}$.

To return to our example: Given our monthly return data, here are the annual rates of return, their variance, and their standard deviation:

	A	B	C	D	E	F	G	H
1			**MONTHLY AND ANNUAL MEANS AND VARIANCES**					
2								
3			**Stock A**			**Stock B**		
4			Continuous			Continuous		
5	**Month**	**Price**	**return**		**Price**	**return**		
6	0	25.00			45.00			
7	1	24.12	-3.58%		44.85	-0.33%		
8	2	23.37	-3.16%		46.88	4.43%		
9	3	24.75	5.74%		45.25	-3.54%		
10	4	26.62	7.28%		50.87	11.71%		
11	5	26.50	-0.45%		53.25	4.57%		
12	6	28.00	5.51%		53.25	0.00%		
13	7	28.88	3.09%		62.75	16.42%		
14	8	29.75	2.97%		65.50	4.29%		
15	9	31.38	5.33%		66.87	2.07%		
16	10	36.25	14.43%		78.50	16.03%		
17	11	37.13	2.40%		78.00	-0.64%		
18	12	36.88	-0.68%		68.23	-13.38%		
19								
20	**Monthly mean**		3.24%			3.47%	<-- =AVERAGE(F7:F18)	
21	**Monthly variance**		0.23%			0.65%	<-- =VARP(F7:F18)	
22	**Monthly stand. dev.**		4.78%			8.03%	<-- =STDEVP(F7:F18)	
23								
24	**Annual mean**		38.88%			41.62%	<-- =12*F20	
25	**Annual variance**		2.75%			7.75%	<-- =12*F21	
26	**Annual stand. dev.**		16.57%			27.83%	<-- =SQRT(12)*F22	

8 Calculating the Variance-Covariance Matrix

8.1 Overview

In order to calculate efficient portfolios, we must be able to calculate the variance-covariance matrix from return data for stocks. In this chapter we discuss this problem, showing how to do the calculations in Excel. We illustrate several methods for calculating the variance-covariance matrix, including a direct calculation in the spreadsheet using the excess return matrix, an implementation of this method with Visual Basic for Applications (VBA), and the single-index model.

Before starting this chapter, you may want to peruse the parts of Chapter 29 that discuss *array functions*. These are Excel functions whose arguments are vectors and matrices; their implementation is slightly different from standard Excel functions. This chapter makes heavy use of the array functions **Transpose( )** and **MMult( )**.

Throughout the chapter we shall use data for six stocks to illustrate our calculations.

	A	B	C	D	E	F	G	H
1	**RETURN DATA FOR VARIANCE-COVARIANCE CALCULATIONS**							
2								
3		**AMR**	**BS**	**GE**	**HR**	**MO**	**UK**	**SP500**
4	**1974**	-0.3505	-0.1154	-0.4246	-0.2107	-0.0758	0.2331	-0.2647
5	**1975**	0.7083	0.2472	0.3719	0.2227	0.0213	0.3569	0.3720
6	**1976**	0.7329	0.3665	0.2550	0.5815	0.1276	0.0781	0.2384
7	**1977**	-0.2034	-0.4271	-0.0490	-0.0938	0.0712	-0.2721	-0.0718
8	**1978**	0.1663	-0.0452	-0.0573	0.2751	0.1372	-0.1346	0.0656
9	**1979**	-0.2659	0.0158	0.0898	0.0793	0.0215	0.2254	0.1844
10	**1980**	0.0124	0.4751	0.3350	-0.1894	0.2002	0.3657	0.3242
11	**1981**	-0.0264	-0.2042	-0.0275	-0.7427	0.0913	0.0479	-0.0491
12	**1982**	1.0642	-0.1493	0.6968	-0.2615	0.2243	0.0456	0.2141
13	**1983**	0.1942	0.3680	0.3110	1.8682	0.2066	0.2640	0.2251
14								
15			AMR	American Airlines				
16			BS	Bethlehem Steel				
17			GE	General Electric				
18			HR	International Harvester				
19			MO	Philip Morris				
20			UK	Union Carbide				

This particular data set is calculated from annual price data for these six stocks. Thus, for example, AMR's return of -35.05 percent for 1974 is calculated as

$$r_{AMR, 1974} = \frac{Price_{AMR, Dec. 31, 1974} - Price_{AMR, Dec. 31, 1973}}{Price_{AMR, Dec. 31, 1973}}$$

As noted in Chapter 7, these return data are sometimes calculated using *total returns,* which include the dividend over the period. Were this the case for our data, we would have

$$r_{AMR, 1974} =$$

$$\frac{Price_{AMR, Dec. 31, 1974} - Price_{AMR, Dec. 31, 1973} + Dividend_{AMR, 1973}}{Price_{AMR, Dec. 31, 1973}}$$

Suppose we have return data for N assets over M periods. We can write the return of asset i in period t as r_{it}. Write the *mean return* of asset i as

$$\bar{r}_i = \frac{1}{N} \sum_{t=1}^{N} r_{it}, \, i = 1, \ldots$$

Then the covariance of the return of asset i and asset j is calculated as

$$\sigma_{ij} = \text{Cov}(i, j) = \frac{1}{M} \sum_{t=1}^{M} (r_{it} - \bar{r}_i * (r_{jt} - \bar{r}_j), \, i, j = 1, \ldots$$

Our problem is to calculate these covariances efficiently.

8.2   Using the Excess-Return Matrix in the Spreadsheet

By far the clearest method for calculating the variance-covariance matrix is an on-screen method involving the excess return matrix. Suppose that we have N risky assets and that for each asset we have return data for M periods. Then the excess return matrix will look like this:

$$A = \text{Matrix of excess returns} = \begin{bmatrix} r_{11} - \bar{r}_1 & \cdots & r_{N1} - \bar{r}_N \\ r_{12} - \bar{r}_1 & \cdots & r_{N2} - \bar{r}_N \\ \vdots & & \vdots \\ r_{1M} - \bar{r}_1 & \cdots & r_{NM} - \bar{r}_N \end{bmatrix}$$

The transpose of this matrix is

$$A^T = \begin{bmatrix} r_{11} - \bar{r}_1 & r_{12} - \bar{r}_1 & \cdots & \cdots & r_{1M} - \bar{r}_1 \\ r_{N1} - \bar{r}_N & r_{N2} - \bar{r}_N & \cdots & \cdots & r_{NM} - \bar{r}_N \end{bmatrix}$$

Multiplying A^T times A and dividing through by the number of periods M gives the variance-covariance matrix:

$$S = [\sigma_{ij}] = \frac{A^T \cdot A}{M}$$

8.3   Illustration

We illustrate this method with our numerical example. We first calculate the mean return for each asset (the last line of the following spreadsheet picture):

	A	B	C	D	E	F	G	H	I	J
1	CALCULATING THE VARIANCE-COVARIANCE MATRIX FROM EXCESS RETURNS									
2										
3		AMR	BS	GE	HR	MO	UK			
4	1974	-0.3505	-0.1154	-0.4246	-0.2107	-0.0758	0.2331			
5	1975	0.7083	0.2472	0.3719	0.2227	0.0213	0.3569			
6	1976	0.7329	0.3665	0.2550	0.5815	0.1276	0.0781			
7	1977	-0.2034	-0.4271	-0.0490	-0.0938	0.0712	-0.2721			
8	1978	0.1663	-0.0452	-0.0573	0.2751	0.1372	-0.1346			
9	1979	-0.2659	0.0158	0.0898	0.0793	0.0215	0.2254			
10	1980	0.0124	0.4751	0.3350	-0.1894	0.2002	0.3657			
11	1981	-0.0264	-0.2042	-0.0275	-0.7427	0.0913	0.0479			
12	1982	1.0642	-0.1493	0.6968	-0.2615	0.2243	0.0456			
13	1983	0.1942	0.3680	0.3110	1.8682	0.2066	0.2640			
14	Mean	0.2032	0.0531	0.1501	0.1529	0.1025	0.1210	<-- =AVERAGE(G4:G13)		

The means were calculated by using the Excel function **Average( )** on each column of data.

Next, we calculate the excess return matrix by subtracting each asset's mean return from each of the periodic returns:

	A	B	C	D	E	F	G	H	I
16		Excess return matrix							
17		AMR	BS	GE	HR	MO	UK		
18	1974	-0.5537	-0.1686	-0.5747	-0.3635	-0.1784	0.1121		
19	1975	0.5051	0.1940	0.2218	0.0698	-0.0812	0.2359		
20	1976	0.5297	0.3134	0.1049	0.4286	0.0250	-0.0429		
21	1977	-0.4066	-0.4802	-0.1991	-0.2466	-0.0313	-0.3931		
22	1978	-0.0369	-0.0984	-0.2074	0.1222	0.0347	-0.2555		
23	1979	-0.4691	-0.0374	-0.0603	-0.0736	-0.0810	0.1044		
24	1980	-0.1908	0.4220	0.1849	-0.3423	0.0977	0.2447		
25	1981	-0.2296	-0.2574	-0.1777	-0.8956	-0.0112	-0.0731		
26	1982	0.8610	-0.2024	0.5467	-0.4144	0.1217	-0.0754	<-- =G12-$G$14	
27	1983	-0.0090	0.3149	0.1609	1.7154	0.1041	0.1430	<-- =G13-$G$14	

The transpose of this matrix can be calculated by using the array function **Transpose( )**:

	A	B	C	D	E	F	G	H	I	J	K
29		Transpose of excess return matr									
30		1974	1975	1976	1977	1978	1979	1980	1981	1982	1983
31	AMR	-0.5537	0.5051	0.5297	-0.4066	-0.0369	-0.4691	-0.1908	-0.2296	0.8610	-0.0090
32	BS	-0.1686	0.1940	0.3134	-0.4802	-0.0984	-0.0374	0.4220	-0.2574	-0.2024	0.3149
33	GE	-0.5747	0.2218	0.1049	-0.1991	-0.2074	-0.0603	0.1849	-0.1777	0.5467	0.1609
34	HR	-0.3635	0.0698	0.4286	-0.2466	0.1222	-0.0736	-0.3423	-0.8956	-0.4144	1.7154
35	MO	-0.1784	-0.0812	0.0250	-0.0313	0.0347	-0.0810	0.0977	-0.0112	0.1217	0.1041
36	UK	0.1121	0.2359	-0.0429	-0.3931	-0.2555	0.1044	0.2447	-0.0731	-0.0754	0.1430
37		Cells B31:K36 contain the array formula =TRANSPOSE(B18:G27). To									
38		enter this formula:									
39		1. Mark the area B31:K36									
40		2. Type =TRANSPOSE(B18:G27)									
41		3. Instead of [Enter], finish with [Ctrl]-[Shift]-[Enter]									
42		The formula will appear as {=TRANSPOSE(B18:G27)}									
43											

We can now calculate our variance-covariance matrix by multiplying A^T times A. Again we use the array function **MMult(A_Transpose, A)/N**:

	A	B	C	D	E	F	G	H
45		Product of transpose[excess return] times [excess return] / 10						
46		AMR	BS	GE	HR	MO	UK	
47	AMR	0.2060	0.0375	0.1077	0.0493	0.0208	0.0059	
48	BS	0.0375	0.0790	0.0355	0.1028	0.0089	0.0406	
49	GE	0.1077	0.0355	0.0867	0.0443	0.0194	0.0148	
50	HR	0.0493	0.1028	0.0443	0.4435	0.0193	0.0274	
51	MO	0.0208	0.0089	0.0194	0.0193	0.0083	-0.0015	
52	UK	0.0059	0.0406	0.0148	0.0274	-0.0015	0.0392	
53		Cells B47:G52 contain the array formula =MMULT(B31:K36,B18:G27)/10 . To						
54		enter this formula:						
55		1. Mark the whole area						
56		2. Type =MMULT(B31:K36,B18:G27)/10						
57		3. Instead of [Enter], finish with [Ctrl]-[Shift]-[Enter]						
58		The formula will appear as {=MMULT(B31:K36,B18:G27)/10}						
59								

8.4   Other Ways of Calculating the Variance-Covariance Matrix

In this section we present two alternatives to calculating the variance-covariance matrix.[1] The first alternative uses a VBA function.[2]

---

1. This section, which can be skipped on first reading, requires some knowledge of Excel's programming language Visual Basic for Applications (VBA), which is discussed in Chapters 31 and 32.

2. I thank Amir Kirsh of Tel-Aviv University for showing me this function.

```
Function VarCovar(rng As Range) As Variant
    Dim i As Integer
    Dim j As Integer
    Dim numCols As Integer
    numCols = rng.Columns.Count
    Dim matrix( ) As Double
    ReDim matrix(numCols - 1, numCols - 1)

    For i = 1 To numCols
        For j = 1 To numCols
            matrix(i - 1, j - 1) = _
        Application.WorksheetFunction.
            Covar(rng.Columns(i), rng.Columns(j))
        Next j
    Next i

    VarCovar = matrix
End Function
```

This function is an *array function* (meaning that it has to be applied using [Ctrl]-[Shift]-[Enter]). Here's an example:

	A	B	C	D	E	F	G	H
1	A VBA FUNCTION FOR THE VARIANCE-COVARIANCE MATRIX							
2								
3	Return data for four stocks (in columns)							
4								
5	22.9%	3.6%	4.1%	9.5%				
6	37.4%	18.2%	8.6%	19.2%				
7	1.2%	-2.7%	0.1%	-1.7%				
8	9.9%	9.7%	6.3%	18.2%				
9	7.4%	7.1%	6.4%	14.2%				
10	30.2%	15.2%	9.5%	29.0%				
11	-3.3%	8.6%	7.0%	-5.8%				
12	31.4%	13.6%	8.1%	1.9%				
13	16.2%	7.4%	6.4%	13.6%				
14								
15	The variance-covariance matrix				These cells contain the formula			
16	0.0182	0.0057	0.0021	0.0080	=varcovar(A5:D13). To enter this			
17	0.0057	0.0035	0.0015	0.0034	formula:			
18	0.0021	0.0015	0.0007	0.0015	* Block off the area B16:E19			
19	0.0080	0.0034	0.0015	0.0110	* Enter the formula			
20					* Press [Ctrl]-[Shif]t-[Enter]			
21								

8.4.1   The Variance-Covariance Matrix Using Excel's Offset Function

Another way to calculate the variance-covariance function uses Excel's **Offset** function.[3] **Offset** takes a bit of getting used to: This function allows you to define a block of cells *relative* to some initial cell. Thus, for example, **Offset(initial cells, rows, columns)** refers to a block of cells of the same size as the initial cells, but **rows** and **columns** over from the initial cells. The technique is illustrated in the following spreadsheet. Note that the borders 0, 1, 2, 3 have been added to the variance-covariance matrix:

	A	B	C	D	E	F	G	H	I	J	K	L	M
1	USING THE OFFSET FUNCTION TO COMPUTE THE VAR-COV MATRIX												
2													
3		Return data for four stocks (in columns)											
4		22.9%	3.6%	4.1%	9.5%								
5		37.4%	18.2%	8.6%	19.2%								
6		1.2%	-2.7%	0.1%	-1.7%								
7		9.9%	9.7%	6.3%	18.2%								
8		7.4%	7.1%	6.4%	14.2%								
9		30.2%	15.2%	9.5%	29.0%								
10		-3.3%	8.6%	7.0%	-5.8%								
11		31.4%	13.6%	8.1%	1.9%								
12		16.2%	7.4%	6.4%	13.6%								
13													
14		The variance-covariance matrix											
15		0	1	2	3								
16	0	0.0182	0.0057	0.0021	0.0080		Cell B16 contains the formula						
17	1	0.0057	0.0035	0.0015	0.0034		=COVAR(OFFSET($B$4:$B$12,0,E$15),OFFSET($B$4:$B$12,0,$A16)).						
18	2	0.0021	0.0015	0.0007	0.0015		This can then be copied to all the other cells.						
19	3	0.0080	0.0034	0.0015	0.0110								

8.5   The Single-Index Model

The single-index model (SIM) is an attempt to simplify some of the computational complexities of calculating the variance-covariance matrix. The model's basic assumption is that the returns of each asset can be linearly regressed on some market index:

$$\tilde{R}_i = \alpha_i + \beta_i \tilde{R}_x + \tilde{\varepsilon}_i$$

---

3. Shay Zafrir, an M.B.A. student at Tel-Aviv University, suggested using this function to define the var-cov matrix.

Given this assumption, it is easy to establish the following two facts:

- $E(\tilde{R}_i) = \alpha_i + \beta_i E(\tilde{R}_x)$. This fact is trivial.
- $\sigma_{ij} = \beta_i \beta_j \sigma_x^2$. This fact requires a little more work. Writing the definition of σ_{ij} and expanding gives

$$\sigma_{ij} = E\{[\tilde{R}_i - E(\tilde{R}_i)][\tilde{R}_j - E(\tilde{R}_j)]\}$$
$$= E\{[\alpha_i + \beta_i \tilde{R}_x - [\alpha_i + \beta_i E(\tilde{R}_x)]\}\{\alpha_j + \beta_j \tilde{x} - [\alpha_j + \beta_j E(\tilde{R}_x)]\}$$
$$= E\{\beta_i[\tilde{x} - E(\tilde{R}_x)]\beta_j[\tilde{x} - E(\tilde{R}_x)]\}\beta_i \beta_j E\{[\tilde{x} - E(\tilde{R}_x)][\tilde{x} - E(\tilde{R}_x)]\}$$
$$= \beta_i \beta_j \sigma_x^2$$

The SIM can lead to great simplifications in the calculation of the variance-covariance matrix. We illustrate with our six-portfolio example, adding a seventh column for the returns on the S&P 500. Regressing the returns of each asset on the Standard & Poor's 500 portfolio, we get the following table of βs:

	A	B	C	D	E	F	G	H
1				SINGLE-INDEX MODEL				
2								
3		AMR	BS	GE	HR	MO	UK	SP500
4	1974	-0.3505	-0.1154	-0.4246	-0.2107	-0.0758	0.2331	-0.2647
5	1975	0.7083	0.2472	0.3719	0.2227	0.0213	0.3569	0.3720
6	1976	0.7329	0.3665	0.2550	0.5815	0.1276	0.0781	0.2384
7	1977	-0.2034	-0.4271	-0.0490	-0.0938	0.0712	-0.2721	-0.0718
8	1978	0.1663	-0.0452	-0.0573	0.2751	0.1372	-0.1346	0.0656
9	1979	-0.2659	0.0158	0.0898	0.0793	0.0215	0.2254	0.1844
10	1980	0.0124	0.4751	0.3350	-0.1894	0.2002	0.3657	0.3242
11	1981	-0.0264	-0.2042	-0.0275	-0.7427	0.0913	0.0479	-0.0491
12	1982	1.0642	-0.1493	0.6968	-0.2615	0.2243	0.0456	0.2141
13	1983	0.1942	0.3680	0.3110	1.8682	0.2066	0.2640	0.2251
14								
15	Beta	1.4820	1.0840	1.3107	1.2991	0.2622	0.4939	
16								
17		=SLOPE(B4:B13,$H$4:$H$13)						
18		=COVAR(B4:B13,$H$4:$H$13)/VARP($H$4:$H$13)						
19								

The circled formulas show two ways of calculating the betas of the shares (this topic will be discussed further in the next chapter).

To calculate the variance-covariance matrix, we have to calculate a matrix with entries $\beta_i \beta_j \sigma^2_{SP}$. This calculation is easily accomplished by putting the βs of the six assets on the borders of our variance-covariance matrix:

	B	C	D	E	F	G	H	I	J
11	Var(SP500)		0.0359						
12									
13			**AMR**	**BS**	**GE**	**HR**	**MO**	**UK**	
14			**1.482**	**1.084**	**1.311**	**1.299**	**0.262**	**0.494**	
15	**AMR**	**1.482**	0.0790	0.0578	0.0698	0.0692	0.0140	0.0263	
16	**BS**	**1.084**	0.0578	0.0422	0.0511	0.0506	0.0102	0.0192	
17	**GE**	**1.311**	0.0698	0.0511	0.0618	0.0612	0.0124	0.0233	
18	**HR**	**1.299**	0.0692	0.0506	0.0612	0.0607	0.0122	0.0231	
19	**MO**	**0.262**	0.0140	0.0102	0.0124	0.0122	0.0025	0.0047	
20	**UK**	**0.494**	0.0263	0.0192	0.0233	0.0231	0.0047	0.0088	
21									
22					=D$14*$C15*$D$11				

To create the entries of the matrix, we use the **mixed cell-reference** feature of the spreadsheet. Thus, for example, the upper right-hand cell of the variance-covariance matrix (which contains AMR's SIM variance of 0.0790) has the formula = D$14 * $C15 * $D$11. The cell D11 contains the index variance (in this case $\sigma^2_{SP} = 0.0359$) and D$14 and $C15 refer to the borders of the matrix, which contain the βs of the assets.[4] When this formula is copied to the whole matrix, we create the variance-covariance matrix according to the single-index model.

It is clear that the variance-covariance matrix as estimated by the SIM differs from the exact variance-covariance matrix computed from the returns (sections 8.2 and 8.3). In particular, as long as βs are positive (nearly always the case), the SIM's variance-covariance matrix will have no negative entries; it cannot thus accommodate the negative covariance between two assets. In our example, the *difference* between the two matrices is significant.

---

4. Note that the variance of the S&P 500 is equivalent to a standard deviation of about 19 percent. Over the period 1926–91 the standard deviation of S&P 500 annual returns was 20.22 percent. Over the period 1981–91, the standard deviation was somewhat less, 16.31 percent. (See Ibbotson Associates, *Stocks, Bonds, Bills, and Inflation—1992 Yearbook.* Chicago: Ibbotson Associates, 1992.

	B	C	D	E	F	G	H	I
13			AMR	BS	GE	HR	MO	UK
14			1.482	1.084	1.311	1.299	0.262	0.494
15	AMR	1.482	0.0790	0.0578	0.0698	0.0692	0.0140	0.0263
16	BS	1.084	0.0578	0.0422	0.0511	0.0506	0.0102	0.0192
17	GE	1.311	0.0698	0.0511	0.0618	0.0612	0.0124	0.0233
18	HR	1.299	0.0692	0.0506	0.0612	0.0607	0.0122	0.0231
19	MO	0.262	0.0140	0.0102	0.0124	0.0122	0.0025	0.0047
20	UK	0.494	0.0263	0.0192	0.0233	0.0231	0.0047	0.0088
21								
22					=D$14*$C15*$D$11			
23								
24	Variance-covariance matrix based on return data							
25		AMR	BS	GE	HR	MO	UK	
26	AMR	0.2060	0.0375	0.1077	0.0493	0.0208	0.0059	
27	BS	0.0375	0.0790	0.0355	0.1028	0.0089	0.0406	
28	GE	0.1077	0.0355	0.0867	0.0443	0.0194	0.0148	
29	HR	0.0493	0.1028	0.0443	0.4435	0.0193	0.0274	
30	MO	0.0208	0.0089	0.0194	0.0193	0.0083	-0.0015	
31	UK	0.0059	0.0406	0.0148	0.0274	-0.0015	0.0392	
32								
33	Difference between two var-cov matrices:							
34		AMR	BS	GE	HR	MO	UK	
35	AMR	0.1270	-0.0202	0.0379	-0.0200	0.0069	-0.0205	
36	BS	-0.0202	0.0368	-0.0156	0.0522	-0.0013	0.0213	
37	GE	0.0379	-0.0156	0.0250	-0.0169	0.0071	-0.0084	
38	HR	-0.0200	0.0522	-0.0169	0.3829	0.0070	0.0043	
39	MO	0.0069	-0.0013	0.0071	0.0070	0.0058	-0.0061	
40	UK	-0.0205	0.0213	-0.0084	0.0043	-0.0061	0.0304	

Exercises

1. In the following table you will find annual return data for six furniture companies between the years 1982 and 1992. Use these data to calculate the variance-covariance matrix of the returns.

	A	B	C	D	E	F	G
1		**DATA FOR SIX FURNITURE COMPANIES**					
2							
3					**Leggett**	**Herman**	**Shaw**
4		**La-Z-Boy**	**Kimball**	**Flexsteel**	**& Platt**	**Miller**	**Industries**
5	**1982**	36.67%	0.20%	41.54%	21.92%	26.13%	22.50%
6	**1983**	122.82%	61.43%	195.09%	62.27%	73.38%	117.89%
7	**1984**	14.44%	63.51%	-38.38%	-1.27%	45.15%	7.80%
8	**1985**	21.39%	28.42%	1.30%	81.17%	24.27%	38.14%
9	**1986**	45.36%	-7.44%	21.89%	19.83%	10.73%	54.48%
10	**1987**	20.19%	48.27%	9.11%	-10.21%	-11.92%	26.82%
11	**1988**	-8.94%	-11.28%	12.65%	13.77%	7.06%	-6.24%
12	**1989**	27.02%	12.85%	12.08%	32.55%	-7.55%	123.03%
13	**1990**	-11.64%	2.42%	-17.13%	-6.48%	1.31%	15.48%
14	**1991**	20.29%	6.90%	3.62%	50.12%	-5.54%	19.92%
15	**1992**	34.08%	22.21%	33.46%	84.40%	5.71%	62.76%
16							
17	**Beta**	0.80	0.95	0.65	0.85	0.85	1.40

2.   For the firms from exercise 1: Suppose that the standard deviation of the market index is 18 percent. Calculate the variance-covariance matrix using the single-index model.

3.   In the spreadsheet "DJ 30, raw data" which is part of Problems 08.xls on the disk accompanying this book, you will find end-of-month price data for the 30 stocks in the Dow-Jones Index of 30 Industrials. Use the data to calculate the variance-covariance matrix of the Index (in the next chapter you will use this matrix to calculate the efficient frontier for the index).

9   Calculating Efficient Portfolios When There Are No Short-Sale Restrictions

9.1   Overview

This chapter covers all the calculations necessary for both versions of the classical capital asset pricing model (CAPM)–both that which is based on a risk-free asset and Black's (1972) zero-beta CAPM (which does not require the assumption of a risk-free asset). You will find that using a spreadsheet enables you to do the necessary calculations easily.

The structure of the chapter is as follows: We begin with some preliminary definitions and notation. We then state the major results (proofs are given in the appendix to the chapter). In succeeding sections we implement these results, showing you

- How to calculate efficient portfolios.
- How to calculate the efficient frontier.

This chapter includes more theoretical material than most chapters in this book: Section 9.3 contains the propositions on portfolios that underlie the calculations of both efficient portfolios and the security market line (SML) in Chapter 10. If you find the theoretical material in section 9.3 difficult, skip it at first and try to follow the illustrative calculations in section 9.4.

9.2   Some Preliminary Definitions and Notation

Throughout this chapter we use the following notation: There are N risky assets, each of which has expected return $E(r_i)$. The variable R is the column vector of expected returns of these assets:

$$R = \begin{bmatrix} E(r_1) = \bar{r}_1 \\ E(r_2) = \bar{r}_2 \\ \vdots \\ E(r_N) = \bar{r}_N \end{bmatrix}$$

and S is the $N \times N$ variance-covariance matrix:

$$S = \begin{bmatrix} \sigma_{11} & \sigma_{21} & \cdots & \sigma_{N1} \\ \sigma_{12} & \sigma_{22} & \cdots & \sigma_{n2} \\ \vdots & & & \\ \sigma_{1N} & \sigma_{2N} & \cdots & \sigma_{NN} \end{bmatrix}$$

A *portfolio of risky assets* (when our intention is clear, we shall just use the word *portfolio*) is a column vector x whose coordinates sum to 1:

$$x = \begin{bmatrix} x_1 \\ x_2 \\ \vdots \\ x_N \end{bmatrix}, \quad \sum_{i=1}^{N} x_i = 1$$

Each coordinate x_i represents the proportion of the portfolio invested in risky asset i.

The *expected portfolio return* $E(r_x)$ of a portfolio x is given by the product of x and R :

$$E(r_x) = x^T * R \equiv \sum_{i=1}^{N} x_i E(r_i)$$

The *variance of portfolio x's return,* $\sigma_x^2 \equiv \sigma_{xx}$ is given by the product $x^T S x = \sum_{i=1}^{N} \sum_{j=1}^{N} x_i x_j \sigma_{ij}$.

The *covariance between the return of two portfolios x and y,* $\text{Cov}(r_x, r_y)$, is defined by the product $\sigma_{xy} = x^T S y = \sum_{i=1}^{N} \sum_{j=1}^{N} x_i y_j \sigma_{ij}$. Note that $\sigma_{xy} = \sigma_{yx}$.

The following graph illustrates four concepts. A *feasible* portfolio is any portfolio whose proportions sum to one. The *feasible set* is the set of portfolio means and standard deviations generated by the feasible portfolios; this feasible set is the area inside and to the right of the curved line. A feasible portfolio is on the *envelope* of the feasible set if for a given mean return it has minimum variance. Finally, a portfolio x is *an efficient portfolio* if it maximizes the return given the portfolio variance (or standard deviation). That is, x is efficient if there is no other portfolio y such that $E(R_y) > E(R_x)$ and $\sigma_y \leq \sigma_x$. The set of all efficient portfolios is called the *efficient frontier;* this frontier is the heavier line in the graph.

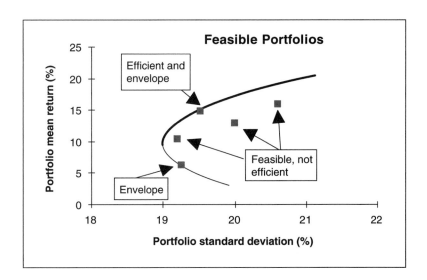

9.3   Some Theorems on Efficient Portfolios and the CAPM

In the appendix to this chapter we prove the following results, which are basic to the calculations of the CAPM. All of these propositions are used in deriving the efficient frontier and the security market line; numerical illustrations are given in the next section and in Chapter 10.

PROPOSITION 1   Let c be a constant. We use the notation $R - c$ to denote the following column vector:

$$R - c = \begin{bmatrix} E(r_1) - c \\ E(r_2) - c \\ E(r_N) - c \end{bmatrix}$$

Let the vector z solve the system of simultaneous linear equations $R - c = Sz$. Then this solution produces a portfolio x on the envelope of the feasible set in the following manner:

$$z = S^{-1}\{R - c\}$$
$$x = \{x_1, \ldots, x_N\}$$

where

$$x_i = \frac{z_i}{\displaystyle\sum_{j=1}^{N} z_j}$$

Furthermore, all envelope portfolios are of this form.

Intuition   A formal proof of the proposition is given in the appendix to this chapter, but the intuition is simple and geometric. Suppose we pick a constant c and we try to find an efficient portfolio x for which there is a tangency between c and the feasible set:

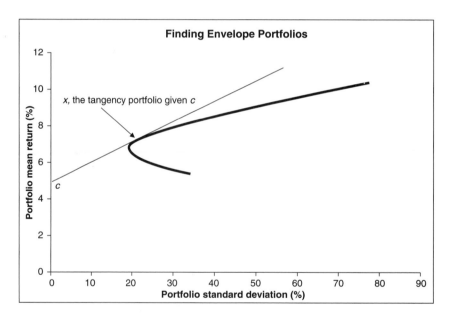

Then Proposition 1 gives a procedure for finding x; furthermore, the proposition states that all envelope portfolios (in particular: all efficient portfolios) are the result of the procedure outlined in the proposition. That is, if x is any envelope portfolio, then there exists a constant c and a vector z such that $Sz = R - c$ and $x = z \big/ \sum_i z_i$.

PROPOSITION 2   By a theorem first proved by Black (1972), any two envelope portfolios are enough to establish the whole envelope. Given any two envelope portfolios $x = \{x_1, \ldots, x_N\}$ and $y = \{y_1, \ldots, y_N\}$, all envelope portfolios are convex combinations of x and y. This means that given any constant a, the portfolio

$$ax + (1 - a)y = \begin{bmatrix} ax_1 + (1 - a)y_1 \\ ax_2 + (1 - a)y_2 \\ \vdots \\ ax_N + (1 - a)y_N \end{bmatrix}$$

is on the envelope of the efficient frontier.

PROPOSITION 3   If y is any envelope portfolio, then for any other portfolio (envelope or not) x, we have the relationship

$$E(r_x) = c + \beta_x [E(r_y) - c]$$

where

$$\beta_x = \frac{\text{Cov}(x, y)}{\sigma_y^2}$$

Furthermore, c is the expected return of a portfolio z whose covariance with y is zero:

$$c = E(r_z)$$

where

$$\text{Cov}(y, z) = 0$$

Notes   If y is on the envelope, the regression of any and all portfolios x on y gives a linear relationship. In this version of the CAPM (usually known as Black's zero-beta CAPM, in honor of Fisher Black, whose 1972 paper proved this result) the Sharpe-Lintner-Mossin security market line is replaced with an SML in which the role of the risk-free asset is played by a portfolio with a zero beta with respect to the particular envelope portfolio y. Note that this result is true for any envelope portfolio y.

If the market portfolio M is efficient (this is a big "if" as we shall see later on), Black's result is also true for the market portfolio. That is, the SML holds with $E(r_z)$ substituted for c:

$$E(r_x) = E(r_z) + \beta_x [E(r_M) - E(r_z)]$$

where

$$\beta_x = \frac{\mathrm{Cov}(x, M)}{\sigma_M^2}$$

$\mathrm{Cov}(z, M) = 0$

This version of the SML has received the most empirical attention of all the CAPM results. In Chapter 10 we show how to calculate β and how to calculate the SML; we go on to examine Roll's criticism of these empirical tests. From the following graph, it is easy to see how to locate a zero-beta portfolio on the envelope of the feasible set:

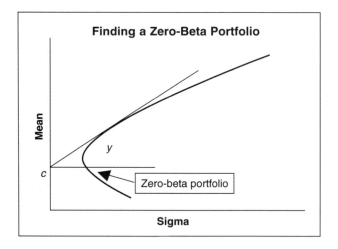

Finding a Zero-Beta Portfolio

When there is a risk-free asset, Proposition 3 specializes to the security market line of the classic capital asset pricing model.

PROPOSITION 4   If there exists a risk-free asset with return r_f, then there exists an envelope portfolio M such that

$$E(r_x) = r_f + \beta_x[E(r_M) - r_f]$$

where

$$\beta_x = \frac{\mathrm{Cov}(x, M)}{\sigma_M^2}$$

Note   If all investors choose their portfolios only on the basis of portfolio mean and standard deviation, then M is a portfolio composed of *all the risky assets in the economy,* with each asset taken in proportion to its value. To make this statement more specific: Suppose that there are N risky assets and that the market value of asset i is V_i. Then the market portfolio has the following weights:

$$\text{Proportion of asset } i \text{ in } M = \frac{V_i}{\displaystyle\sum_{h=1}^{N} V_h}$$

This result was first proved by Sharpe (1964), Lintner (1965), and Mossin (1966).

PROPOSITION 5   The converse of Proposition 3 is also true. Suppose that there exists a portfolio y such that for any portfolio x the following relation holds:

$$E(r_x) = c + \beta_x[E(r_y) - c]$$

where

$$\beta_x = \frac{\text{Cov}(x, y)}{\sigma_y^2}$$

Then the portfolio y is an envelope portfolio.

Two particular propositions to note are Propositions 3 and 5: These propositions show that *an SML relation holds if and only if we regress all portfolios on an envelope portfolio.* As Roll (1977, 1978) has forcefully pointed out, these propositions show that it is not enough to run a test of the CAPM by showing that the SML holds.[1] The only real test of the CAPM is *whether the true market portfolio is mean-variance efficient.* We shall return to this topic in Chapter 10.

In the remainder of this chapter, we explore the meaning of these propositions using numerical examples worked out on Excel.

---

1. Roll's 1977 paper is more frequently cited and more comprehensive, but his 1978 paper is much easier to read and more intuitive. If you're interested in this literature, start there.

9.4   Calculating the Efficient Frontier: An Example

In this section we calculate the efficient frontier using Excel. We consider a world with four risky assets having the following expected returns and variance-covariance matrix:

	A	B	C	D	E	F
4						Mean
5		Variance-covariance matrix				returns
6	0.400	0.030	0.020	0.000		0.06
7	0.030	0.200	0.001	-0.060		0.05
8	0.020	0.001	0.300	0.030		0.07
9	0.000	-0.060	0.030	0.100		0.08

We separate our calculations into two parts: First we calculate two portfolios on the envelope of the feasible set (section 9.4.1). In section 9.4.2 we calculate the efficient frontier.

9.4.1   Calculating Two Envelope Portfolios

By Proposition 2, we have to find two efficient portfolios in order to identify the whole efficient frontier. By Proposition 1, we must solve the system $R - c = Sz$ for z, where we use two different values for c. For each value of c, we solve for z and then set $x_i = z_i / \sum_h z_h$ to find an efficient portfolio.

The c's we solve for are somewhat arbitrary, but to make life easy, we first solve this system for $c = 0$. This procedure gives the following results:

	B	C
12	z	x
13	0.1019	0.0540
14	0.5657	0.2998
15	0.1141	0.0605
16	1.1052	0.5857

The formulas in the cells are as follows:

• For z: **=MMult(MInverse(A6:D9), F6:F9).** The range A6:D9 contains the variance-covariance matrix, and the cells F6:F9 contain the mean returns of the assets.

• For x: Each cell contains the associated value of z divided by the sum of all the z's. Thus, for example, cell C13 contains the formula **=B13/SUM(B$13:B$16).**

We now solve this system for some other constant c. This solution involves a few extra definitions, as the following picture from the spreadsheet shows:

	A	B	C	D	E	F	G
3							Mean
4						Mean	minus
5	Variance-covariance matrix					returns	constant
6	0.4	0.03	0.02	0		0.06	-0.005
7	0.03	0.2	0.001	-0.06		0.05	-0.015
8	0.02	0.001	0.3	0.03		0.07	0.005
9	0	-0.06	0.03	0.1		0.08	0.015
10							
11				Constant	0.065		
12		z	x		z	y	
13		0.1019	0.0540		-0.0101	-0.1163	
14		0.5657	0.2998		-0.0353	-0.4067	
15		0.1141	0.0605		0.0047	0.0544	
16		1.1052	0.5857		0.1274	1.4687	

Each cell of the column vector labeled **Mean minus constant** contains the mean return of the given asset minus the value of the constant c (in this case $c = 0.065$). The second set of z's and its associated envelope portfolio y is given by

	E	F
12	z	y
13	-0.0101	-0.1163
14	-0.0353	-0.4067
15	0.0047	0.0544
16	0.1274	1.4687

This vector *z* is calculated in a manner similar to that of the first vector, except that the array function in the cells is **MMult(MInverse(A6:D9), G6:G9).**

To complete the basic calculations, we compute the means, standard deviations, and covariance of returns for the portfolios *x* and *y*.

	B	C	D	E	F
19	Transpose x				
20	0.053986	0.299808	0.06049	0.585716	
21					
22	Transpose y				
23	-0.1163	-0.40674	0.054355	1.468681	
24					
25	Mean(x)	0.0693		Mean(y)	0.0940
26	Var(x)	0.0367		Var(y)	0.3341
27	Sigma(x)	0.1917		Sigma(y)	0.5780
28					
29	Cov(x,y)	0.0498			
30	Corr(x,y)	0.4496			

The transpose vectors of *x* and of *y* are inserted using the array function **Transpose** (see Chapter 29 for a discussion of array functions). Now we calculate the mean, variance, and covariance as follows:

Mean(x) uses the formula **MMult(transpose_x, means).**

Var(x) uses the formula **MMult(MMult(transpose_x, var_cov), x).**

Sigma(x) uses the formula **Sqrt(var_x).**

Cov(x, y) uses the formula **MMult(MMult(transpose_x, var_cov), y).**

Corr(x, y) uses the formula **cov(x, y)/(sigma_x ∗ sigma_y).**

The following spreadsheet illustrates everything that has been done in this subsection.

	A	B	C	D	E	F	G
3							Mean
4						Mean	minus
5		Variance-covariance matrix				returns	constant
6	0.4	0.03	0.02	0		0.06	-0.005
7	0.03	0.2	0.001	-0.06		0.05	-0.015
8	0.02	0.001	0.3	0.03		0.07	0.005
9	0	-0.06	0.03	0.1		0.08	0.015
10							
11				Constant	0.065		
12		z	x		z	y	
13		0.1019	0.0540		-0.0101	-0.1163	
14		0.5657	0.2998		-0.0353	-0.4067	
15		0.1141	0.0605		0.0047	0.0544	
16		1.1052	0.5857		0.1274	1.4687	
17							
18							
19		Transpose x					
20		0.053986	0.299808	0.06049	0.585716		
21							
22		Transpose y					
23		-0.1163	-0.40674	0.054355	1.468681		
24							
25		Mean (x)	0.0693		Mean (y)	0.0940	
26		Var(x)	0.0367		Var(y)	0.3341	
27		Sigma(x)	0.1917		Sigma(y)	0.5780	
28							
29		Cov(x,y)	0.0498				
30		Corr(x,y)	0.4496				

9.4.2   Calculating the Efficient Frontier

By Proposition 2 of section 9.3, convex combinations of the two portfolios calculated in section 9.4.1 allow us to calculate the whole envelope of the feasible set (which, of course, includes the efficient frontier). Suppose we let p be a portfolio that has proportion a invested in portfolio x and proportion $(1 - a)$ invested in y. Then—as discussed in Chapter 7—the mean and standard deviation of p's return are

$$E(R_p) = aE(R_x) + (1 - a)E(R_x)$$

$$\sigma_p = \sqrt{a^2\sigma_x^2 + (1 - a)^2\sigma_y^2 + 2a(1 - a)\text{Cov}(x, y)}$$

Here's a sample calculation for our two portfolios:

	A	B	C
34	**A single portfolio calculation**		
35	Proportion of x	0.3	
36	p's mean return	8.66%	
37	p's sigma	43.35%	

We can turn this calculation into a data table (see Chapter 26) to get the following table:

	D	E	F	G	H
33		**DATA TABLE**			
34	**FOR EFFICIENT FRONTIER**				
35		**GRAPH**			
36		**Sigma**	**Return**		
37		0.4335	0.0866	<-- Data table header	
38	-0.4	0.7778	0.1038		
39	-0.3	0.7274	0.1014	0.1014	Port. w
40	-0.2	0.6772	0.0989		
41	-0.1	0.6274	0.0965		
42	0	0.5780	0.0940	0.0940	Port. y
43	0.1	0.5291	0.0915		
44	0.2	0.4809	0.0891	0.0891	Port. z
45	0.3	0.4335	0.0866		
46	0.4	0.3874	0.0841		
47	0.5	0.3429	0.0817		
48	0.6	0.3010	0.0792		
49	0.7	0.2627	0.0767		
50	0.8	0.2298	0.0743		
51	0.9	0.2051	0.0718		
52	1	0.1917	0.0693	0.0693	Port. x
53	1.1	0.1919	0.0669		
54	1.2	0.2058	0.0644		
55	1.3	0.2309	0.0619		
56	1.4	0.2640	0.0595		
57	1.5	0.3024	0.0570		
58	1.6	0.3445	0.0545	0.0545	Port. q

The data table itself has been outlined in black. The five data points in the fourth column give the expected return of the portfolio in the cell to the left; these data points are graphed as a separate data series in the following figure.

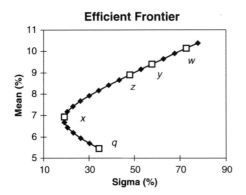

Note that the convex combinations all lie on the envelope, but may not necessarily be efficient. For example, z is an efficient portfolio that is a convex combination of the two efficient portfolios x and y; in this particular case the proportion of x is 20 percent and that of y is 80 percent. The portfolio w is also a convex combination of x and y (in this case with a positive weight on y and a negative weight on x); q is not efficient, but it is on the envelope of the set of feasible portfolios. Thus, while every efficient portfolio is a convex combination of any two efficient portfolios, it is *not true* that every convex combination of any two efficient portfolios is efficient.

9.4.3   Finding Efficient Portfolios in One Step

The examples in this section find efficient portfolios by writing out most of the components of the portfolio separately on the spreadsheet. However, for some uses we will want to calculate the efficient portfolio in one step. This approach requires a number of Excel tricks, most of which relate to the correct use of array functions.

1. Writing **=F6:F9-E11** as an array function (i.e., inserting it with [Ctrl]+[Shift]+[Enter]) gives the value of each coordinate in the vector **F6:F9** minus **E11**:

	A	B	C	D	E	F	G	H	I
3							Mean		
4						Mean	minus		
5		Variance-covariance matrix				returns	constant		
6	0.40	0.03	0.02	0.00		0.06	0.05		
7	0.03	0.20	0.00	-0.06		0.05	0.04		
8	0.02	0.00	0.30	0.03		0.07	0.06	<-- {=F6:F9-E11}	
9	0.00	-0.06	0.03	0.10		0.08	0.07		
10									
11				Constant	0.01				

This same trick can be used in the calculation of efficient portfolios:

	A	B	C	D	E	F	G	H	I	J	K	L
13		z	x						z	y			
14		0.10187	0.05399						0.08464	0.05257			
15		0.56570	0.29981						0.47324	0.29395			
16		0.11414	0.06049	<-- {=B14:B17/SUM($B$14:$B$17)}					0.09730	0.06044	<-- {=H14:H17/SUM(H14:H17)}		
17		1.10518	0.58572						0.95475	0.59304			
18													
19	{=MMULT(MINVERSE(A6:D9),F6:F9)}					{=MMULT(MINVERSE(A6:D9),G6:G9)}						
20													
21													

2. The Excel function **Transpose** can be used in a cell, but only as an array function. Consequently, any time we use **Transpose,** we have to enter the cell contents with [Ctrl]-[Shift]-[Enter] instead of simply [Enter]. Thus, for example:

	B	C	D	E	F	G	H	I
23	Mean x	0.0693	<-- {=MMULT(TRANSPOSE(C14:C17),F6:F9)}					
24	Var. x	0.0367	<-- {=MMULT(MMULT(TRANSPOSE(C14:C17),A6:D9),C14:C17)}					
25	St. dev. x	0.1917	<-- =SQRT(C24)					

Note the braces ({ }), indicating array functions (see Chapter 29). You do not type these braces—Excel inserts them when you hit [Ctrl]+[Shift]+[Enter].

With a little patience, you can now set up a spreadsheet in which the efficient portfolio mean and σ are each calculated in a single cell. The following example shows the calculation of the mean and standard deviation of the return of portfolio y for the constant $c = 0.01$:

	A	B	C	D	E	F	G	H	I
27				{=MMULT(TRANSPOSE(MMULT(MINVERSE(A6:D9),F6:F9-					
28	**One-step efficient portfolio**			E11)/SUM(MMULT(MINVERSE(A6:D9),F6:F9-E11))),F6:F9)}					
29	Portfolio mean	6.95% ◄							
30	Portfolio sigma	19.23% ◄							
31									
32				{=SQRT(MMULT(TRANSPOSE(MMULT(MINVERSE(A6:D9),F6:F9-					
33				E11)/SUM(MMULT(MINVERSE(A6:D9),F6:F9-					
34				E11))),MMULT(A6:D9,MMULT(MINVERSE(A6:D9),F6:F9-					
35				E11)/SUM(MMULT(MINVERSE(A6:D9),F6:F9-E11)))))}					
36									

This procedure is ugly, rather unintuitive, and hard to follow, but it can be handy. It also makes it easy to graph the efficient frontier as a function of the constant:

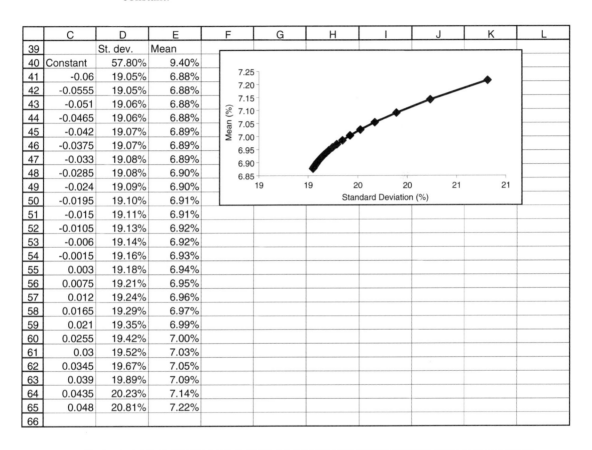

	C	D	E	F	G	H	I	J	K	L
39		St. dev.	Mean							
40	Constant	57.80%	9.40%							
41	-0.06	19.05%	6.88%							
42	-0.0555	19.05%	6.88%							
43	-0.051	19.06%	6.88%							
44	-0.0465	19.06%	6.88%							
45	-0.042	19.07%	6.89%							
46	-0.0375	19.07%	6.89%							
47	-0.033	19.08%	6.89%							
48	-0.0285	19.08%	6.90%							
49	-0.024	19.09%	6.90%							
50	-0.0195	19.10%	6.91%							
51	-0.015	19.11%	6.91%							
52	-0.0105	19.13%	6.92%							
53	-0.006	19.14%	6.92%							
54	-0.0015	19.16%	6.93%							
55	0.003	19.18%	6.94%							
56	0.0075	19.21%	6.95%							
57	0.012	19.24%	6.96%							
58	0.0165	19.29%	6.97%							
59	0.021	19.35%	6.99%							
60	0.0255	19.42%	7.00%							
61	0.03	19.52%	7.03%							
62	0.0345	19.67%	7.05%							
63	0.039	19.89%	7.09%							
64	0.0435	20.23%	7.14%							
65	0.048	20.81%	7.22%							
66										

9.5   Finding the Market Portfolio: The Capital Market Line (CML)

Suppose a risk-free asset exists, and suppose that this asset has expected return r_f. Let M be the efficient portfolio that is the solution to the following system of equations:

$$R - r_f = Sz$$

$$M_i = \frac{z_i}{\sum_{i=1}^{N} z_i}$$

Now consider a convex combination of the portfolio M and the risk-free asset rf; for example, and suppose that the weight of the risk-free asset in such a portfolio is a. It follows from the standard equations for portfolio return and σ that

$$E(r_p) = ar_f + (1 - a)E(r_M)$$

$$\sigma_p = \sqrt{a^2\sigma_{rf}^2 + (1 - a)^2\sigma_M^2 + 2a(1 - a)\text{Cov}(r_f, y)} = (1 - a)\sigma_M$$

The locus of all such combinations for $a \geq 0$ is known as the *capital market line*. It is graphed along with the efficient frontier as follows:

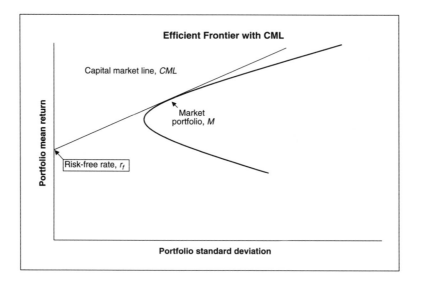

The portfolio M is called the *market portfolio* for several reasons:

• Suppose investors agree about the statistical portfolio information (i.e., the vector of expected returns R and the variance-covariance matrix S). Suppose furthermore that investors are interested only in maximizing expected portfolio return given portfolio standard deviation σ. Then it follows that *all optimal portfolios will lie on the CML.*

• In the case above, it further follows that *the portfolio M is the only portfolio of risky assets included in any optimal portfolio.* It must therefore include *all the risky assets, with each asset weighted in proportion to its market value. That is,*

$$\text{Weight of risky asset } i \text{ in portfolio } M = \frac{V_i}{\sum\limits_{i=1}^{N} V_i}$$

where V_i is the market value of asset i.

It is not difficult to find M when we know r_f: We merely have to solve for the efficient portfolio given that the constant $c = r_f$. When r_f changes, we get a different "market" portfolio—this is just the efficient portfolio given a constant of r_f. For example, in our numerical example, suppose that the risk-free rate is $r_f = 5$ percent. Then solving the system $R - r_f = Sz$ gives

	D	E	F	G	H	I	J
11	Constant	0.05					
12		z	M				
13		0.0157	0.0314		**Note:** the market portfolio		
14		0.1034	0.2059		**M** is the tangency portfolio		
15		0.0300	0.0597		for the constant.		
16		0.3531	0.7031				
17		**Mean(M)**	0.0726				
18		**Sigma(M)**	0.2121				

9.6   The SML When There Is a Risk-Free Asset

Proposition 4 guarantees that when there is a risk-free asset, the following linear relationship (known as the SML–the **security market line**) holds:

$$E(r_x) = r_f + \beta_x [E(r_m) - r_f]$$

where

$$\beta_x = \frac{\text{Cov}(x, M)}{\sigma_M^2}$$

In the next chapter we explore some statistical techniques for finding the SML that parallel those used by finance researchers.

Exercises

1. In Chapter 8 you were asked to calculate the variance-covariance matrix of returns for six furniture companies. The calculated variance-covariance matrix and mean returns for these firms are as follows:

	A	B	C	D	E	F	G	H	I
3	Variance-covariance matrix								
4		La-Z-Boy	Kimball	Flexsteel	Leggett	Miller	Shaw		Means
5	La-Z-Boy	0.1152	0.0398	0.1792	0.0492	0.0568	0.0989		29.24%
6	Kimball	0.0398	0.0649	0.0447	0.0062	0.0349	0.0269		20.68%
7	Flexsteel	0.1792	0.0447	0.3334	0.0775	0.0886	0.1487		25.02%
8	Leggett	0.0492	0.0062	0.0775	0.1033	0.0191	0.0597		31.64%
9	Miller	0.0568	0.0349	0.0886	0.0191	0.0594	0.0243		15.34%
10	Shaw	0.0989	0.0269	0.1487	0.0597	0.0243	0.1653		43.87%

a. Given this matrix, and assuming that the risk-free rate is 0 percent, calculate the efficient portfolio of these six firms.

b. Repeat, assuming that the risk-free rate is 10 percent.

c. Use these two portfolios to generate an efficient frontier for the six furniture companies. Plot this frontier.

d. Is there an efficient portfolio with only positive proportions of all the assets?[2]

2. A sufficient condition to produce positively weighted efficient portfolios is that the variance-covariance matrix be diagonal, that is, that $\sigma_{ij} = 0$, for $i \neq j$. By continuity, positively weighted portfolios will result if the off-diagonal elements of the variance-covariance matrix are sufficiently small compared to the diagonal. Consider a transformation of this matrix in which

$$\sigma_{ij} = \begin{cases} \varepsilon \sigma_{ij}^{\text{Original}} & \text{if } i \neq j \\ \sigma_{ii}^{\text{Original}} & \end{cases}$$

When $\varepsilon = 1$, this transformation will give the original variance-covariance matrix, and when $\varepsilon = 0$, the transformation will give a fully diagonal matrix.

For $r = 10$ percent find the maximum ε for which all portfolio weights are positive.

3. Consider the example given in section 9.4 Use Excel to find an envelope portfolio whose β with respect to the efficient portfolio y is zero. *Hint:* Notice that because the covariance is linear, so is β: Suppose that $z = \lambda x + (1 - \lambda)y$ is a convex combination of x and y, and that we are trying to find the β_z. Then

$$\beta_z = \frac{\text{Cov}(z, y)}{\sigma_y^2} = \frac{\text{Cov}[\lambda x + (1 - \lambda)y, y]}{\sigma_y^2}$$

$$= \frac{\lambda \text{Cov}(x, y)}{\sigma_y^2} + \frac{(1 - \lambda)\text{Cov}(y, y)}{\sigma_y^2} = \lambda \beta_x + (1 - \lambda)$$

---

2. The problem of when a portfolio contains only positive weights is nontrivial. See Green (1986) and Nielsen (1987).

4.   This problem returns to the four-asset problem considered in section 7.5:

	A	B	C	D	E	F	G
1	**A FOUR-ASSET PORTFOLIO PROBLEM**						
2							
3							
4	Variance-covariance					Mean returns	St. dev.
5	0.10	0.01	0.03	0.05		6%	31.62%
6	0.01	0.30	0.06	-0.04		8%	54.77%
7	0.03	0.06	0.40	0.02		10%	63.25%
8	0.05	-0.04	0.02	0.50		15%	70.71%

Calculate the envelope set for these four assets and show that the individual assets all lie within this envelope set. You should get a graph that looks something like the following:

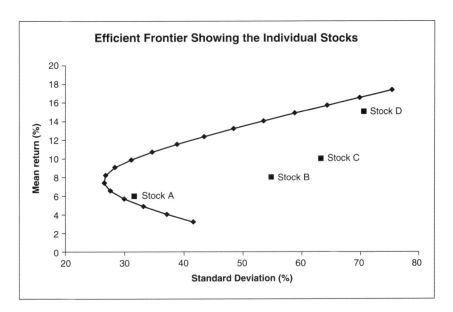

Appendix

In this appendix we collect the various proofs of statements made in the chapter. As in the chapter, we assume that we are examining data for N risky assets. It is important to note that all the definitions of "feasibility" and "optimality" are made relative to this set. Thus the word "efficient" really means "efficient relative to the set of the N assets being examined."

PROPOSITION 0   The set of all feasible portfolios of risky assets is convex.

Proof   A portfolio x is feasible if and only if the proportions of the portfolio add up to 1; that is, $\sum_{i=1}^{N} x_i = 1$, where N is the number of risky assets. Suppose that x and y are feasible portfolios and suppose that λ is some number between 0 and 1. Then it is clear that $z = \lambda x + (1 - \lambda)y$ is also feasible.

PROPOSITION 1   Let c be a constant, and denote by R the vector of mean returns. A portfolio x is on the envelope relative to the sample set of N assets if and only if it is the normalized solution of the system

$$R - c = Sz$$

$$x_i = \frac{z_i}{\sum_h z_h}$$

Proof   A portfolio x is on the envelope of the feasible set of portfolios if and only if it lies on the tangency of a line connecting some point c on the y-axis to the feasible set. Such a portfolio must either maximize or minimize the ratio $\frac{x(R - c)}{\sigma^2(x)}$, where $x(R - c)$ is the vector product that gives the portfolio's expected excess return over c, and $\sigma^2(x)$ is the portfolio's variance. Let this ratio's value, when maximized (or minimized), be λ. Then our portfolio must satisfy

$$\frac{x(R - c)}{\sigma^2(x)} = \lambda$$

$$\Rightarrow x(R - c) = \sigma^2(x)\lambda = xSx^T\lambda$$

Let h be a particular asset, and differentiate this last expression with respect to x_h. This step gives $\overline{R}_h - c = Sx^T\lambda$. Writing $z_h = \lambda x_h$, we see that a portfolio is efficient if and only if it solves the system $R - c = Sz$. Normalizing z so that its coordinates add to 1 gives the desired result.

PROPOSITION 2   The convex combination of any two envelope portfolios is on the envelope of the feasible set.

Proof   Let x and y be portfolios on the envelope. By Proposition 1, it follows that there exist two vectors z_x and z_y and two constants c_x and c_y such that

- x is the normalized-to-unity vector of z_x, that is, $x_i = \dfrac{z_{xi}}{\sum_h z_{xh}}$ and y is the normalized-to-unity vector of z_y.

- $R - c_x = Sz_x$ and $R - c_y = Sz_y$.

Furthermore, since z maximizes the ratio $\dfrac{z(R-c)}{\sigma^2(z)}$, it follows that any normalization of z also maximizes this ratio. With no loss in generality, therefore, we can assume that z sums to 1.

It follows that for any real number a the portfolio $az_x + (1-a)z_y$ solves the system $R - [ac_x + (1-a)c_y] = Sz$. This result proves our claim.

PROPOSITION 3   Let y be any envelope portfolio of the set of N assets. Then for any other portfolio x (including, possibly, a portfolio composed of a single asset) there exists a constant c such that the following relation holds between the expected return on x and the expected return on portfolio y:

$$E(r_x) = c + \beta_x[E(r_y) - c]$$

where

$$\beta_x = \frac{\text{Cov}(x, y)}{\sigma_y^2}$$

Furthermore, $c = E(r_z)$, where z is any portfolio for which $\text{Cov}(z, y) = 0$.

Proof   Let y be a particular envelope portfolio, and let x be any other portfolio. We assume that both portfolios x and y are column vectors. Note that

$$\beta_x \equiv \frac{\text{Cov}(x, y)}{\sigma_y^2} = \frac{x^T S y}{y^T S y}$$

Now since y is on the envelope, we know that there exist a vector w and a constant c that solve the system $Sw = R - c$ and that $y = w/\sum_i w_i = w/a$. Substituting this equation in the expression for β_x, we get

$$\beta_x = \frac{\text{Cov}(x, y)}{\sigma_y^2} = \frac{x^T S y}{y^T S y} = \frac{x^T(R-c)/a}{y^T(R-c)/a} = \frac{x^T(R-c)}{y^T(R-c)}$$

Next note that since $\sum_i x_i = 1$, it follows that $x^T I(R-c) = E(r_x) - c$ and that $y^T I(R-c) = E(r_y) - c$. This relation shows that

$$\beta_x = \frac{E(r_x) - c}{E(r_y) - c}$$

which can be rewritten as

$$E(r_x) = c + \beta_x[E(r_y) - c]$$

To finish the proof, let z be a portfolio that has zero covariance with y. Then the preceding logic shows that $c = E(r_z)$. This result proves the claim.

PROPOSITION 4   If in addition to the N risky assets, there exists a risk-free asset with return r_f, then the standard *security market line* holds:

$$E(r_x) = r_f + \beta_x[E(r_M) - r_f]$$

where

$$\beta_x = \frac{\text{Cov}(x, M)}{\sigma_M^2}$$

Proof   If there exists a risk-free security, then the tangent line from this security to the efficient frontier dominates all other feasible portfolios. Call the point of tangency on the efficient frontier M; then the result follows.

Note   It is important to repeat that the terminology "market portfolio" refers in this case to the "market portfolio relative to the sample set of N assets."

PROPOSITION 5   Suppose that there exists a portfolio y such that for any portfolio x the following relation holds:

$$E(r_x) = c + \beta_x[E(r_y) - c]$$

where

$$\beta_x = \frac{\text{Cov}(x, y)}{\sigma_y^2}$$

Then the portfolio y is on the envelope.

Proof   Substituting in for the definition of β_x it follows that for any portfolio x the following relation holds:

$$\frac{x^T S y}{\sigma_y^2} = \frac{x^T R - c}{y^T R - c}$$

Let x be the vector composed solely of the first risky asset: $x = \{1, 0, ..., 0\}$. Then the preceding equation becomes

$$S_1 y \frac{y^T R - c}{\sigma_y^2} = E(r_1) - c$$

which we write

$$S_1 ay = E(r_1) - c$$

where S_1 is the first row of the variance-covariance matrix S. Note that $a = \dfrac{y^T R - c}{\sigma_Y^2}$ is a constant whose value is independent of the vector x. If we let x be a vector composed solely of the ith risky asset, we get

$$S_i ay = E(r_i) - c$$

This result proves that the vector $z = ay$ solves the system $Sz = R - c$; by Proposition 1, therefore, the normalization of z is on the envelope. But this normalization is simply the vector y.

10 Estimating Betas and the Security Market Line

10.1 Overview

In this chapter we look at some typical capital-market data and replicate a simple test of the CAPM. We have to calculate the betas for a set of assets, and we then have to determine the equation of the security market line (SML). The test in this chapter is the simplest possible test of the CAPM. There is an enormous literature in which the possible statistical and methodological pitfalls of CAPM tests are discussed. Good places to begin are textbooks by Elton and Gruber (1995) and Haugen (1997).

10.2 Testing the CAPM

We illustrate the tests of the CAPM with a simple numerical example that uses the same data used in Chapter 8. This example starts with rates of return on six securities and the S&P 500 portfolio. As a first step in analyzing these data and testing the CAPM, we calculate the *mean return* and the *beta* of each security's return, where we use the following formulas:

Mean return for security i = **Average** (Security i's returns, 1972–1981)

$$\beta_i = \frac{\textbf{Covar} \text{ (Security } i\text{'s return, S\&P 500 returns)}}{\textbf{Varp} \text{ S\&P 500 returns)}}$$

Here **Average, Covar,** and **Varp** are Excel functions on the column vectors of returns.[1] Calculating these statistics gives the results in the following spreadsheet. Note that the $\beta_{SP500} = 1$, which is the way it should be if the S&P 500 is the market portfolio. Also note that instead of calculating the β using the **Covar( )** and **Varp( )** functions, we can also use Excel's **Slope( )** function.

---

1. As discussed in Chapters 7 and 9, Excel has two functions that give the variance: **Var**(array) gives the sample variance and **Varp**(array) gives the population variance. For reasons discussed in Chapter 7, we use the latter function here.

	A	B	C	D	E	F	G	H
3		AMR	BS	GE	HR	MO	UK	SP500
4	1974	-0.3505	-0.1154	-0.4246	-0.2107	-0.0758	0.2331	-0.2647
5	1975	0.7083	0.2472	0.3719	0.2227	0.0213	0.3569	0.3720
6	1976	0.7329	0.3665	0.2550	0.5815	0.1276	0.0781	0.2384
7	1977	-0.2034	-0.4271	-0.0490	-0.0938	0.0712	-0.2721	-0.0718
8	1978	0.1663	-0.0452	-0.0573	0.2751	0.1372	-0.1346	0.0656
9	1979	-0.2659	0.0158	0.0898	0.0793	0.0215	0.2254	0.1844
10	1980	0.0124	0.4751	0.3350	-0.1894	0.2002	0.3657	0.3242
11	1981	-0.0264	-0.2042	-0.0275	-0.7427	0.0913	0.0479	-0.0491
12	1982	1.0642	-0.1493	0.6968	-0.2615	0.2243	0.0456	0.2141
13	1983	0.1942	0.3680	0.3110	1.8682	0.2066	0.2640	0.2251
14								
15	Mean	0.2032	0.0531	0.1501	0.1529	0.1025	0.1210	0.1238
16	Beta	1.4820	1.0840	1.3107	1.2991	0.2622	0.4939	1.0000
17								
18		=SLOPE(B4:B13,$H$4:$H$13)						
19		=COVAR(B4:B13,$H$4:$H$13)/VARP($H$4:$H$13)						
20								
21								

The CAPM's security market line postulates that the mean return of each security should be linearly related to its beta. Assuming that the historic data provide an accurate description of the distribution of future returns, we postulate that $E(R_i) = \alpha + \beta_i \Pi + \varepsilon_i$. In the second step of our test of the CAPM, we examine this hypothesis by regressing the mean returns on the βs.

Excel offers us several ways of producing regression output. A simple way is to use the functions **Intercept( ), Slope( ),** and **Rsqr( )** to produce the basic ordinary least-squares results:

	A	B	C	D	E	F
23	**Regressing the means on the betas:**					
24	Intercept		0.0766	<-- =INTERCEPT(B15:G15,B16:G16)		
25	Slope		0.0545	<-- =SLOPE(B15:G15,B16:G16)		
26	R-squared		0.2793	<-- =RSQ(B15:G15,B16:G16)		

These results suggest that the SML is given by $E(R_i) = \alpha + \beta_i \Pi$, where $\alpha = 0.0766$ and $\Pi = 0.0545$. The R^2 of the regression (the percentage of the variability in the means explained by the betas) is 28 percent.

We can also use **Tools|Data Analysis|Regression** to produce a new worksheet that has much more output. However, this tool will only work if the data are in columns, so we first rewrite the data as

	C	D
29	**Mean**	**Beta**
30	0.2032	1.4820
31	0.0531	1.0840
32	0.1501	1.3107
33	0.1529	1.2991
34	0.1025	0.2622
35	0.1210	0.4939

Here is some sample output:

SUMMARY OUTPUT

Regression Statistics	
Multiple R	0.5285
R Square	0.2793
Adjusted R Square	0.0991
Standard Error	0.0485
Observations	6

ANOVA

	df	SS	MS	F	Significance F
Regression	1	0.0036	0.0036	1.5503	0.2811
Residual	4	0.0094	0.0023		
Total	5	0.0130			

	Coefficients	Standard Error	t Stat	P-value	Lower 95%	Upper 95%	Lower 95.0%	Upper 95.0%
Intercept	0.0766	0.0476	1.6094	0.1828	-0.0555	0.2087	-0.0555	0.2087
X Variable 1	0.0545	0.0438	1.2451	0.2811	-0.0670	0.1761	-0.0670	0.1761

Both the standard error figures and the *t*-statistics show that neither α nor Π is significantly different from zero.

The command that produced this output looks like this:

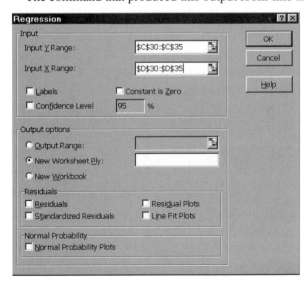

10.3   Testing the CAPM: General Rules

The previous section showed a specific numerical example in which we used some data to test the CAPM. In this section we summarize what we did in section 10.2.

Tests of the CAPM start with return data on a set of assets. The steps in the test are as follows:

• Determine a candidate for the market portfolio M. In the preceding example, we used the Standard & Poor's 500 Index (SP500) as a candidate for M. This is a critical step: In principle, the "true" market portfolio should—as pointed out in Chapter 9—contain all the market's risky assets in proportion to their value. It is clearly impossible to calculate this theoretical market portfolio, and we must therefore make do with a surrogate. As you will see in the next two sections, the propositions of Chapter 9 can shed much light on how the choice of the market surrogate affects the R-squared of our regression test of the CAPM.

• For each of the assets in question, determine the asset beta (β).

• Regress the mean returns of the assets on their respective betas; this step should give the security market line (SML).

Our "test" yielded the following SML:

$$E(r_i) = 7.66\% + 5.45\%\beta_i, \ R^2 = 27.93\%$$

If the intercept is the risk-free rate (or the return on the zero-beta portfolio), then the expected return on the market is $E(r_m) = 7.66\% + 5.45\% = 13.11\%$.

10.4   Why Are the Results So Bad? Is the "Market" Portfolio Efficient?

The experiment we did in section 10.3—checking the CAPM by plotting the security market line—does not appear to have worked out very well. There does not appear to be much evidence in favor of the SML: neither the R^2 of the regression nor the t-statistics give much evidence that there is a relation between expected return and portfolio β.

There are a number of reasons why these disappointing results may hold:

1. One reason is that perhaps the CAPM itself does not hold. This could be true for a variety of reasons.

a. Perhaps in the market short sales of assets are restricted. Our derivation of the CAPM (see Chapter 9 on efficient portfolios) assumes that there are no short-sale restrictions. Clearly this assumption is unrealistic. The computation of efficient portfolios when short sales are restricted is considered in Chapter 11. In this case, however, there are no simple relations (such as those proven in Chapter 9) between the returns of assets and their betas. In particular, if short sales are restricted, there is no reason to expect the SML to hold.

b. Perhaps individuals do not have homogeneous probability assessments, or perhaps they do not have the same expectations of asset returns, variances, and covariances.

2. Perhaps the CAPM holds only for portfolios and not for single assets.

3. Perhaps our set of assets isn't large enough: After all, the CAPM talks about *all risky assets,* whereas we have chosen—for illustrative purposes—to do our test on a very small subset of these assets. The literature on CAPM testing records tests in which the set of risky assets has been expanded to include bonds, real estate, and even nondiversifiable assets such as human capital.

4. Perhaps the "market portfolio" isn't efficient. This possibility is suggested by the mathematics of Chapter 9 on efficient portfolios, and it is this suggestion that we will explore in the next section.

10.5   The Nonefficiency of the "Market Portfolio"

When we calculated the SML in sections 10.2 and 10.3, we regressed the mean return of each asset on the returns of the market portfolio. The propositions of Chapter 9 on efficient portfolios suggest that our failure to find adequate results may stem from the fact that the S&P 500 portfolio is not efficient relative to the set of the six assets that we have chosen. Proposition 3 of Chapter 9 states that if we had chosen to regress our asset returns on a portfolio that is efficient with respect to the asset set itself, we would get an R-squared of 100 percent. Proposition 5 of Chapter 9 shows that—if we get an R-squared of 100 percent—then the portfolio on which we regress the asset returns is necessarily efficient with respect to the set of assets. In this section we give a numerical illustration of these propositions.

10.5.1   Is the S&P 500 Not Efficient?

We start by asking if the S&P 500 is indeed efficient with respect to the six assets we have chosen. In Chapter 8 we calculated the variance-covariance matrix for this data set. Now following the procedures outlined in Chapter 9, we can create the following spreadsheet to find two efficient portfolios:

	A	B	C	D	E	F	G	H	I	J	K	L
3		Variance-covariance matrix									Means	
4											Minus	
5			AMR	BS	GE	HR	MO	UK		Means	Constant	
6		AMR	0.2060	0.0375	0.1077	0.0493	0.0208	0.0059		0.2032	0.1032	
7		BS	0.0375	0.0790	0.0355	0.1028	0.0089	0.0406		0.0531	-0.0469	
8		GE	0.1077	0.0355	0.0867	0.0443	0.0194	0.0148		0.1501	0.0501	
9		HR	0.0493	0.1028	0.0443	0.4435	0.0193	0.0274		0.1529	0.0529	
10		MO	0.0208	0.0089	0.0194	0.0193	0.0083	-0.0015		0.1025	0.0025	
11		UK	0.0059	0.0406	0.0148	0.0274	-0.0015	0.0392		0.1210	0.0210	
12												
13												
14			Calculating two efficient portfolios									
15									Constant	10%		
16			z	x						z	y	
17	=MMULT(MINVERSE		5.9969	0.1065						1.5261	0.2036	
18	(C6:H11),J6:J11)		-15.4455	-0.2743						-5.2570	-0.7014	
19			-16.7869	-0.2982	<-- =C19/SUM($C$17:$C$22)					-2.0059	-0.2677	
20			0.9185	0.0163						0.7113	0.0949	
21			55.6285	0.9881						6.2721	0.8369	
22			25.9885	0.4616						6.2480	0.8337	
23												
24			Mean	0.1220	<-- =MMULT(TRANSPOSE(E17:E22),J6:J11)						0.1651	Mean
25			Variance	0.0022	<-- =MMULT(MMULT(TRANSPOSE(E17:E22),C6:H11),E17:E22)						0.0087	Variance
26			Sigma	0.0465	<-- =SQRT(E25)						0.0932	Sigma
27			Covariance	0.0029	<-- =MMULT(MMULT(TRANSPOSE(E17:E22),C6:H11),K17:K22)							

In this spreadsheet x and y are two efficient portfolios; by Proposition 2 of Chapter 9, convex combinations of these portfolios will produce the whole efficient frontier.

We intend to create a **Data|Table** with which to calculate the efficient frontier; however, before doing so we calculate the mean and standard deviation of the S&P 500 portfolio:

	O	P	Q	R	S
2	Data for SP500				
3		returns			
4	1974	-0.2647			
5	1975	0.3720			
6	1976	0.2384			
7	1977	-0.0718			
8	1978	0.0656			
9	1979	0.1844			
10	1980	0.3242			
11	1981	-0.0491			
12	1982	0.2141			
13	1983	0.2251			
14					
15	Mean	0.1238	<-- =AVERAGE(P4:P13)		
16	Sigma	0.1896	<-- =STDEVP(P4:P13)		

The data table that we create (inside the dark lines) shows a calculation for a single portfolio as well as the data for the S&P 500:

	C	D	E	F	G	H	I	J	K
29	**Calculations for a single portfolio**								
30	Prop. x	0.2500							
31	Prop. y	0.7500							
32									
33	Mean	0.1543							
34	Variance	0.0061							
35	Sigma	0.0783		**Data table**					
36									
37				**Portfolio**			**SP 500**		
38				**prop.**	**Sigma**	**Mean**	**mean**		
39	Step	0.2737			0.0783	0.1543		<-- Data table header	
40				-2.0000	0.2273	0.2514			
41	Cell D39 is the change			-1.7263	0.2084	0.2396			
42	in the portfolio proportion			-1.4526	0.1896	0.2278	0.1238		
43	in the data table to the			-1.1789	0.1709	0.2160			
44	right.			-0.9052	0.1523	0.2042			
45				-0.6315	0.1340	0.1924			
46				-0.3579	0.1160	0.1806			
47				-0.0842	0.0985	0.1688			
48				0.1895	0.0818	0.1570			
49				0.4632	0.0665	0.1451			
50				0.7369	0.0540	0.1333			
51				1.0106	0.0464	0.1215			
52				1.2843	0.0462	0.1097			
53				1.5580	0.0535	0.0979			
54				1.8317	0.0659	0.0861			
55				2.1054	0.0811	0.0743			
56				2.3790	0.0977	0.0625			
57				2.6527	0.1152	0.0507			
58				2.9264	0.1332	0.0389			
59				3.2001	0.1515	0.0270			

The cell marked **Step** is the difference between the various portfolio proportions; that is, if the initial portfolio proportion of x is -2, then the next portfolio proportion is $-2.000 + $ **Step** $ = -1.726$. We have used the Excel **GoalSeek** to manipulate **Step** so that one of the portfolio sigmas is equal to the standard deviation of the S&P 500:

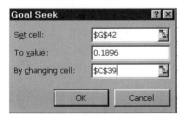

We have then added the S&P 500 mean return of 0.1238 in a separate column. All this work goes to produce a graph of the efficient frontier and the S&P 500:

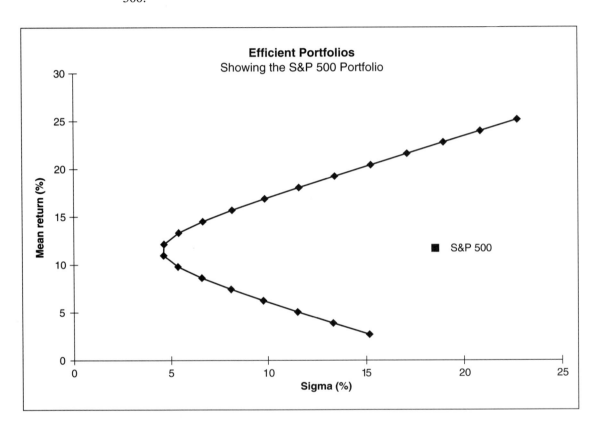

10.5.2   Redoing the SML with an Efficient Portfolio

The preceding graph shows the efficient set of portfolios created by the six assets, and it shows the S&P 500, which is clearly *inefficient* relative to this set of assets. The propositions of Chapter 9 suggest that as a consequence of this inefficiency, *it necessarily follows* that the SML will not have an R^2 of 100 percent. Proposition 3 of Chapter 9 also suggests that if we do the regression on an efficient portfolio, we will find an $R^2 = 100$ percent. In this subsection we show numerically that this conclusion is true.

We start by finding an efficient portfolio having the same standard deviation as the S&P 500. This portfolio can be read from the preceding data table: It has a proportion of -1.426 invested in x and a corresponding proportion of 2.4526 invested in y. For clarity, we repeat its statistics here:

	C	D
30	Prop. x	-1.4526
31	Prop. y	2.4526
32		
33	Mean	0.2278
34	Variance	0.0360
35	Sigma	0.1896

This portfolio is circled on the following graph:

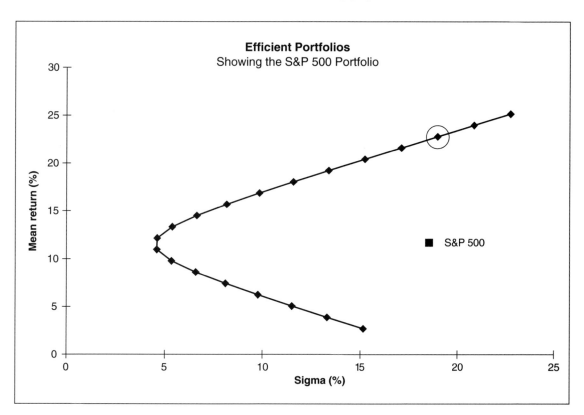

10.5.3   Rederiving the SML

We now perform the following experiment: We rederive the SML using as the "market portfolio" the efficient portfolio defined in section 10.5.2. In order to simplify the discussion, we shall call this portfolio the "market" portfolio, always using care to write this term within quotation marks.[2] The "market" portfolio is composed of -1.4526 of portfolio x and 2.4526 of portfolio y. Since we have already derived the portfolio proportions of x and y, it is easy to derive the composition of the "market" portfolio:

	C	D	E	F	G	H	I	J
30	Prop. x	-1.4526						
31	Prop. y	2.4526						
32								
33	Mean	0.2278						
34	Variance	0.0360						
35	Sigma	0.1896						
36								
37			Portfolio	Portfolio	"Market"			
38			x	y	portfolio			
39		AMR	0.1065	0.2036	0.3447	<-- =$D$30*E39+$D$31*F39		
40		BS	-0.2743	-0.7014	-1.3219			
41		GE	-0.2982	-0.2677	-0.2233			
42		HR	0.0163	0.0949	0.2091			
43		MO	0.9881	0.8369	0.6173			
44		UK	0.4616	0.8337	1.3741			

Furthermore, since we know the returns of each of the six assets in the years 1972–1981, we can derive the returns of the "market" portfolio in each of these years, by multiplying the return on each asset by the proportions in the "market" portfolio:

Simulated "market" portfolio return in year $t =$
$0.3447 * AMR - 1.3219 * BS - 0.2233 * GE + 0.2091 * HR + 0.6173 *MO + 1.3741 * UK$

In the next spreadsheet we calculate these returns and then regress each asset's mean return on its β with respect to the "market" portfolio.

---

2.   We of course don't know that the S&P 500 is the actual market portfolio either.

	D	E	F	G	H	I	J	K	L	M	N	O
47		ANNUAL RETURNS ON SIX ASSETS AND "MARKET" PORTFOLIO										
48									"Market"			
49		AMR	BS	GE	HR	MO	UK		portfolio			
50	1974	-0.3505	-0.1154	-0.4246	-0.2107	-0.0758	0.2331		0.3560			
51	1975	0.7083	0.2472	0.3719	0.2227	0.0213	0.3569		0.3845			
52	1976	0.7329	0.3665	0.2550	0.5815	0.1276	0.0781		0.0189			
53	1977	-0.2034	-0.4271	-0.0490	-0.0938	0.0712	-0.2721		0.1558			
54	1978	0.1663	-0.0452	-0.0573	0.2751	0.1372	-0.1346		0.0872		{==MMULT(E51:J51,	
55	1979	-0.2659	0.0158	0.0898	0.0793	0.0215	0.2254		0.2070		$G$39:$G$44)}	
56	1980	0.0124	0.4751	0.3350	-0.1894	0.2002	0.3657		-0.1121			
57	1981	-0.0264	-0.2042	-0.0275	-0.7427	0.0913	0.0479		0.2340			
58	1982	1.0642	-0.1493	0.6968	-0.2615	0.2243	0.0456		0.5550			
59	1983	0.1942	0.3680	0.3110	1.8682	0.2066	0.2640		0.3918			
60												
61	Mean	0.2032	0.0531	0.1501	0.1529	0.1025	0.1210		0.2278			
62	Beta with respect to "market"											
63		0.7938	-0.4647	0.3484	0.3716	-0.0504	0.1043		1.0000			
64												
65				=SLOPE(E50:E59,$L$50:$L$59)								
66												
67	Regressing the means on the betas											
68	Intercept	0.1086	<-- =INTERCEPT(E61:J61,E63:J63)									
69	Slope	0.1193	<-- =SLOPE(E61:J61,E63:J63)									
70	R-squared	1.0000	<-- =RSQ(E61:J61,E63:J63)									

As you can see, the results are perfect! As stated in Proposition 3 of Chapter 9, *when portfolio returns are regressed on their βs with respect to an efficient portfolio, an exact linear relationship holds*!

10.6   So What's the Real Market Portfolio? How Can We Test the CAPM?

A little reflection will reveal that although the "market" portfolio of the previous section may be efficient with respect to our six securities, it could not be the *true market portfolio,* even if the six stocks represented the whole universe of risky securities, because Bethleham Steel and General Electric appear in the "market" portfolio with a negative proportion. Surely a minimal characteristic of the market portfolio must be that all shares appear in it with *positive proportions.*

Roll (1977, 1978) suggests that the only test of the CAPM is to answer the question, *Is the true market portfolio mean-variance efficient?* If the answer to this question is yes, then it follows from Proposition 3 of Chapter 7 that a linear relation holds between the mean of each portfolio and its β. In our little example, we can shed some light on this question by building a table of the asset proportions of portfolios on the efficient frontier. Since we know that each efficient portfolio is composed of combinations of *x* and *y* (this is Proposition 2 in Chapter 9), the following table gives a good idea of the asset proportions in the efficient portfolios:

	B	C	D	E	F	G	H
3	**The Two Efficient Portfolios**						
4		**x**	**y**				
5	**AMR**	0.1065	0.2036				
6	**BS**	-0.2743	-0.7014				
7	**GE**	-0.2982	-0.2677				
8	**HR**	0.0163	0.0949				
9	**MO**	0.9881	0.8369				
10	**UK**	0.4616	0.8337				
11							
12	**Proportion**		**Individual Asset Proportions**				
13	**of x**	**AMR**	**BS**	**GE**	**HR**	**MO**	**UK**
14	-10	1.1747	(4.9725)	0.0375	0.8809	(0.6749)	4.5543
15	-9.5	1.1262	(4.7589)	0.0222	0.8416	(0.5993)	4.3682
16	-9	1.0776	(4.5454)	0.0070	0.8023	(0.5237)	4.1822
17	-8.5	1.0290	(4.3318)	(0.0083)	0.7630	(0.4481)	3.9962
18	-8	0.9805	(4.1183)	(0.0235)	0.7237	(0.3725)	3.8102
19	0	0.2036	(0.7014)	(0.2677)	0.0949	0.8369	0.8337
20	0.5	0.1551	(0.4879)	(0.2829)	0.0556	0.9125	0.6476
21	1	0.1065	(0.2743)	(0.2982)	0.0163	0.9881	0.4616
22	1.5	0.0580	(0.0608)	(0.3134)	(0.0230)	1.0637	0.2756
23	2	0.0094	0.1528	(0.3287)	(0.0623)	1.1392	0.0895
24	2.5	(0.0391)	0.3663	(0.3439)	(0.1016)	1.2148	(0.0965)
25	3	(0.0877)	0.5799	(0.3592)	(0.1409)	1.2904	(0.2825)
26	3.5	(0.1363)	0.7934	(0.3745)	(0.1802)	1.3660	(0.4685)
27	4	(0.1848)	1.0070	(0.3897)	(0.2195)	1.4416	(0.6546)
28	4.5	(0.2334)	1.2205	(0.4050)	(0.2588)	1.5172	(0.8406)
29	5	(0.2819)	1.4341	(0.4202)	(0.2981)	1.5928	(1.0266)
30	5.5	(0.3305)	1.6476	(0.4355)	(0.3374)	1.6684	(1.2127)
31	6	(0.3790)	1.8612	(0.4507)	(0.3767)	1.7440	(1.3987)
32	6.5	(0.4276)	2.0747	(0.4660)	(0.4160)	1.8195	(1.5847)
33	7	(0.4761)	2.2883	(0.4813)	(0.4553)	1.8951	(1.7708)
34	7.5	(0.5247)	2.5018	(0.4965)	(0.4946)	1.9707	(1.9568)
35	8	(0.5732)	2.7154	(0.5118)	(0.5338)	2.0463	(2.1428)
36	8.5	(0.6218)	2.9289	(0.5270)	(0.5731)	2.1219	(2.3289)
37	9	(0.6704)	3.1425	(0.5423)	(0.6124)	2.1975	(2.5149)
38	9.5	(0.7189)	3.3560	(0.5575)	(0.6517)	2.2731	(2.7009)
39	10	(0.7675)	3.5696	(0.5728)	(0.6910)	2.3487	(2.8869)
40	10.5	(0.8160)	3.7831	(0.5881)	(0.7303)	2.4243	(3.0730)

We have put negative proportions in parentheses to make it easy to identify portfolios with only positive proportions of all assets. Looking closely at this table, you can see that every potential "market" portfolio has at least one negative proportion of some stock! If the six stocks represent our universe, then we can reject the CAPM.

10.7   Does the CAPM Have Any Uses?

Is the game lost? Do we have to give up on the CAPM? Not totally.

• First of all, it could be that the mean returns are approximately described by their regression on a "market" portfolio. In this alternative description of the CAPM, we claim (with some justification, see footnote) that the β of an asset (which measures the dependence of the asset's returns on the market returns) is an important measure of the asset's risk.[3]

• Second, the CAPM might be a good normative description of how to choose portfolios. As we showed in the appendix of Chapter 2, larger diversified portfolios are quite well described by their betas, so that the average beta of a well-diversified portfolio may be a reasonable description of the portfolio's risk.

Exercise

In a well-known paper, Roll (1978), discusses tests of the SML in a four-asset context:

Variance-covariance matrix					Returns
0.10	0.02	0.04	0.05		0.06
0.02	0.20	0.04	0.01		0.07
0.04	0.04	0.40	0.10		0.08
0.05	0.01	0.10	0.60		0.09

a. Derive two efficient portfolios in this four-asset model.

---

3. The R^2 of 28 percent that we got for our regression of the basic SML is actually a respectable number in finance. Students—influenced by overenthusiastic statistics instructors and an overly linear view of the world—often feel that the R^2 of any convincing regression should be at least 90 percent. Finance does not appear to be a highly linear profession. A good rule of thumb is that any financial regression that gives an R^2 greater than 80 percent is misspecified and misleading.

b. Suppose that the market portfolio is composed of equal proportions of each asset (i.e., the market portfolio has proportions 0.25,0.25,0.25,0.25). Calculate the resulting SML. Is this portfolio efficient?

c. Roll claims that the following four portfolios are efficient:

Security 1	0.59600	0.40700	-0.04400	-0.49600
Security 2	0.27621	0.31909	0.42140	0.52395
Security 3	0.07695	0.13992	0.29017	0.44076
Security 4	0.05083	0.13399	0.33242	0.53129

Confirm this claim.

11.1 Introduction

In Chapter 9 we discussed the problem of finding an efficient portfolio. As shown there, this problem can be written as finding a tangent portfolio on the envelope of the feasible set of portfolios:

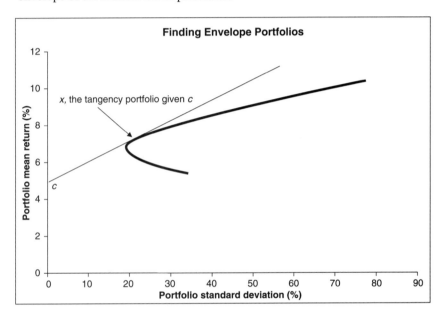

Our conditions for solving for such an efficient portfolio involved finding the solution to the following problem:

$$\max \Theta = \frac{E(r_x) - c}{\sigma_p}$$

such that

$$\sum_{i=1}^{N} x_i = 1$$

where

$$E(r_x) = x^T * R = \sum_{i=1}^{N} x_i E(r_i)$$

$$\sigma_p = \sqrt{x^T S x} = \sqrt{\sum_{i=1}^{N} \sum_{j=1}^{N} x_i x_j \sigma_{ij}}$$

Proposition 1 of Chapter 9 gives a methodology for solving this problem. So-lutions to the maximization problem allow *negative* portfolio proportions; when $x_i < 0$, this is equivalent to the following assumptions:

- The *i*th security is sold short by the investor.
- The proceeds from this short sale become immediately available to the investor.

Reality is, of course, considerably more complicated than this academic model of short sales. In particular, it is rare for all of the short-sale proceeds to become available to the investor at the time of investment, since brokerage houses typically escrow some or even all of the proceeds. It may also be that the investor is completely prohibited from making any short sales (indeed, most small investors seem to proceed on the assumption that short sales are impossible).

In this chapter we investigate these problems. We show how to use Excel's Solver to find efficient portfolios of assets when we restrict short sales.[1] Although the solutions are not perfect (in particular, they take too much time), they are instructive and easy to follow.

We start with the problem of finding an optimal portfolio when there are no short sales allowed. The problem we solve is similar to the maximization problem stated previously, with the addition of the short sales constraint:

$$\max\Theta = \frac{E(r_x) - c}{\sigma_p}$$

such that

$$\sum_{i=1}^{N} x_i = 1$$

$$x_i \geq 0, \, i = 1, \ldots, N$$

where

$$E(r_x) = x^T * R = \sum_{i=1}^{N} x_i E(r_i)$$

$$\sigma_p = \sqrt{x^T S x} = \sqrt{\sum_{i=1}^{N} \sum_{j=1}^{N} x_i x_j \sigma_{ij}}$$

---

1.   We do not go into the efficient set mathematics when short sales of assets are restricted. This involves the Kuhn-Tucker conditions, a discussion of which can be found in Elton and Gruber (1995).

11.2   A Numerical Example

Our problem can be solved in Excel using **Tools|Solver**.[2] We illustrate with the following numerical example, in which there are only four risky assets:

	B	C	D	E	F	G
3	Variance-covariance matrix					Means
4	0.1	0.03	-0.08	0.05		8%
5	0.03	0.2	0.02	0.03		9%
6	-0.08	0.02	0.3	0.2		10%
7	0.05	0.03	0.2	0.9		11%

In order to solve the portfolio problem with no short sales, we set up the following spreadsheet (which also illustrates a solution to the problem for the $c = 9$ percent):

	A	B	C	D	E	F	G	H	I
1			**NO SHORT SALES**						
2									
3			Variance-covariance matrix				Means		
4			0.1	0.03	-0.08	0.05	8%		
5			0.03	0.2	0.02	0.03	9%		
6			-0.08	0.02	0.3	0.2	10%		
7			0.05	0.03	0.2	0.9	11%		
8									
9			c		9.0%	<-- This is the constant			
10									
11			Optimal portfolio proportions						
12			x_1	0.0000					
13			x_2	0.0000					
14			x_3	0.5556					
15			x_4	0.4444					
16			Total	1	<-- =SUM(C12:C15)				
17									
18		Portfolio mean	10.44%	<-- {=MMULT(TRANSPOSE(C12:C15),G4:G7)}					
19		Portfolio sigma	60.76%	<-- {=SQRT(MMULT(TRANSPOSE(C12:C15),MMULT(B4:E7,C12:C15)))}					
20		Theta	2.38%	<-- =(B18-C9)/B19					
21									
22		**Note:** Because the formulas in cells B18 and B19 use the TRANSPOSE function,							
23		they must be entered as arrays, with Ctrl-Shift-Enter. The braces are entered							
24		automatically by Excel. See section 9.4 for more details.							

---

2.   If **Tools|Solver** doesn't work, you may not have loaded the Solver add-in. To do so, go to **Tools|Add-ins** and click next to the **Solver Add-in**.

The solution was achieved by use the **Tools|Solver** feature of Excel. The first time we bring up the Solver, we create the following dialogue box:

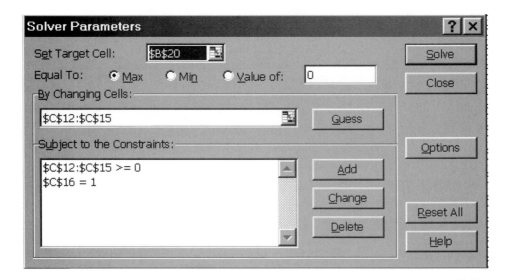

The nonnegativity constraints can be added by clicking on the **Add** button in the preceding dialogue box to bring up the following window (shown here filled in):

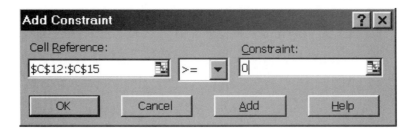

The second constraint (which constrains the portfolio proportions to sum to 1) is added in a similar fashion.

By changing the value of c in the spreadsheet, we can compute other portfolios; in the following example, we have set the constant c equal to 8.50 percent.

	A	B	C	D	E	F	G	H	I
1			**NO SHORT SALES**						
2									
3		**Variance-covariance matrix**					**Means**		
4		0.1	0.03	-0.08	0.05		8%		
5		0.03	0.2	0.02	0.03		9%		
6		-0.08	0.02	0.3	0.2		10%		
7		0.05	0.03	0.2	0.9		11%		
8									
9		c		8.5%	<-- This is the constant				
10									
11		Optimal portfolio proportions							
12		x_1	0.0000						
13		x_2	0.2514						
14		x_3	0.4885						
15		x_4	0.2601						
16		Total	1	<-- =SUM(C12:C15)					
17									
18	Portfolio mean	10.01%	<-- {=MMULT(TRANSPOSE(C12:C15),G4:G7)}						
19	Portfolio sigma	45.25%	<-- {=SQRT(MMULT(TRANSPOSE(C12:C15),MMULT(B4:E7,C12:C15)))}						
20	Theta	3.33%	<-- =(B18-C9)/B19						

In both examples, the short-sale restriction is effective: In the first example both x_1 and x_2 are equal to zero, whereas in the second example x_1 equals zero. However, not all values of c give portfolios in which the short-sale constraint is effective. For example, if the constant is 8 percent, we get

	A	B	C	D	E	F	G	H	I
1			**NO SHORT SALES**						
2									
3		**Variance-covariance matrix**					**Means**		
4		0.1	0.03	-0.08	0.05		8%		
5		0.03	0.2	0.02	0.03		9%		
6		-0.08	0.02	0.3	0.2		10%		
7		0.05	0.03	0.2	0.9		11%		
8									
9		c		8.0%	<-- This is the constant				
10									
11		Optimal portfolio proportions							
12		x_1	0.2004						
13		x_2	0.2587						
14		x_3	0.4219						
15		x_4	0.1190						
16		Total	1	<-- =SUM(C12:C15)					
17									
18	Portfolio mean	9.46%	<-- {=MMULT(TRANSPOSE(C12:C15),G4:G7)}						
19	Portfolio sigma	31.91%	<-- {=SQRT(MMULT(TRANSPOSE(C12:C15),MMULT(B4:E7,C12:C15)))}						
20	Theta	4.57%	<-- =(B18-C9)/B19						

As c gets lower, the short-sale constraint begins to be effective with respect to asset 4. For example, when $c = 3$ percent,

	A	B	C	D	E	F	G	H	I
9		c	3.0%	<-- This is the constant					
10									
11		Optimal portfolio proportions							
12		x_1	0.5856						
13		x_2	0.0965						
14		x_3	0.3179						
15		x_4	0.0000						
16		Total	1	<-- =SUM(C12:C15)					
17									
18	Portfolio mean		8.73%	<-- {=MMULT(TRANSPOSE(C12:C15),G4:G7)}					
19	Portfolio sigma		20.32%	<-- {=SQRT(MMULT(TRANSPOSE(C12:C15),MMULT(B4:E7,C12:C15)))}					
20	Theta		28.21%	<-- =(B18-C9)/B19					

For very high cs (the next case illustrates $c = 11$ percent) only asset 4 is included in the maximizing portfolio:

	A	B	C	D	E	F	G	H	I
9		c	11.0%	<-- This is the constant					
10									
11		Optimal portfolio proportions							
12		x_1	0.0000						
13		x_2	0.0000						
14		x_3	0.0000						
15		x_4	1.0000						
16		Total	1	<-- =SUM(C12:C15)					
17									
18	Portfolio mean		11.00%	<-- {=MMULT(TRANSPOSE(C12:C15),G4:G7)}					
19	Portfolio sigma		94.87%	<-- {=SQRT(MMULT(TRANSPOSE(C12:C15),MMULT(B4:E7,C12:C15)))}					
20	Theta		0.00%	<-- =(B18-C9)/B19					

11.3   The Efficient Frontier with Short-Sale Restrictions

We want to graph the efficient frontier with short-sale restrictions. Recall that in the case of no short-sale restrictions discussed in Chapter 9, it was enough to find two efficient portfolios in order to determine the whole efficient frontier. When we impose short-sale restrictions, this statement is no longer true. In this case the determination of the efficient frontier requires the plotting of a large number of points. The only efficient (pardon the pun!) way of doing so is with a VBA program that repeatedly applies the **Solver** and puts the solutions in a table.

In this section we describe such a program. One aim of the program is to create a graph of the efficient frontier without short sales.

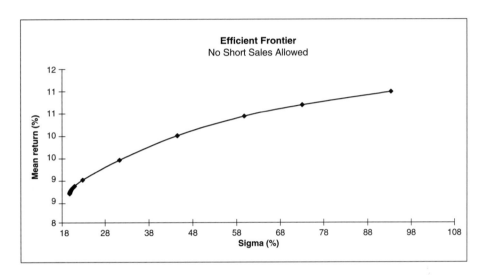

Once we have the program and the graph of the efficient frontier without short sales, we will also compare this efficient frontier to the efficient frontier *with* short sales allowed.

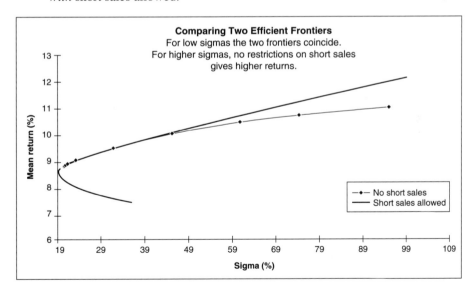

The relation between these two graphs is not all that surprising:

• In general, the efficient frontier with short sales dominates the efficient frontier without short sales. This statement must clearly be so, since the short-sales restriction imposes an extra constraint on the maximization problem.

- For some cases (for example, $c = 8$ percent, illustrated previously), the two efficient frontiers coincide.

Putting these two graphs on one set of axes shows that the effect of the short-sale restrictions is mainly for portfolios with higher returns and sigmas.

11.4   The VBA Program

The output for the restricted short-sale case shown in section 11.3 was produced with the following VBA program:

```
Sub Solve()
        SolverOk SetCell:="$B$20", MaxMinVal:=1,
          ValueOf:="0", ByChange:="$C$12:$C$15"
        SolverSolve UserFinish:=True
End Sub

Sub Doit()
    Range("Results").ClearContents
    For counter = 1 To 40
        Range("constant") = -0.04 + counter * 0.005
        Solve
        Application.SendKeys ("{Enter}")
        Range("Results").Cells(counter, 1) =
          ActiveSheet.Range("constant")
        Range("Results").Cells(counter, 2) =
          ActiveSheet.Range("portfolio_sigma")
        Range("Results").Cells(counter, 3) =
          ActiveSheet.Range("portfolio_mean")
        Range("Results").Cells(counter, 4) =
          ActiveSheet.Range("x_1")
        Range("Results").Cells(counter, 5) =
          ActiveSheet.Range("x_2")
        Range("Results").Cells(counter, 6) =
          ActiveSheet.Range("x_3")
        Range("Results").Cells(counter, 7) =
          ActiveSheet.Range("x_4")
    Next counter
End Sub                 ActiveSheet.Range("x_3")
        Range("Results").Cells(counter, 7) =
          ActiveSheet.Range("x_4")
    Next counter
End Sub
```

The program includes two subroutines: `Solve` calls the Excel Solver; and the subroutine `Doit` repeatedly calls the solver for different values of the range named `Constant` (this is cell C9 in the spreadsheet), putting the output in a range called Results.

The final output looks like this:

	M	N	O	P	Q	R	S
	c	Sigma	Mean	x_1	x_2	x_3	x_4
3							
4	-0.035	20.24%	8.70%	0.605	0.089	0.307	0.000
5	-0.03	20.25%	8.70%	0.604	0.089	0.307	0.000
6	-0.025	20.25%	8.70%	0.603	0.089	0.307	0.000
7	-0.02	20.25%	8.71%	0.603	0.089	0.308	0.000
8	-0.015	20.25%	8.71%	0.602	0.090	0.309	0.000
9	-0.01	20.26%	8.71%	0.601	0.090	0.309	0.000
10	-0.005	20.26%	8.71%	0.599	0.091	0.310	0.000
11	0	20.27%	8.71%	0.598	0.091	0.311	0.000
12	0.005	20.27%	8.71%	0.597	0.092	0.311	0.000
13	0.01	20.28%	8.72%	0.595	0.093	0.312	0.000
14	0.015	20.29%	8.72%	0.593	0.093	0.313	0.000
15	0.02	20.30%	8.72%	0.591	0.094	0.315	0.000
16	0.025	20.31%	8.73%	0.589	0.095	0.316	0.000
17	0.03	20.32%	8.73%	0.586	0.097	0.318	0.000
18	0.035	20.34%	8.74%	0.582	0.098	0.320	0.000
19	0.04	20.37%	8.74%	0.578	0.100	0.322	0.000
20	0.045	20.41%	8.75%	0.573	0.102	0.325	0.000
21	0.05	20.46%	8.76%	0.566	0.105	0.329	0.000
22	0.055	20.54%	8.78%	0.557	0.108	0.334	0.000
23	0.06	20.67%	8.80%	0.545	0.113	0.342	0.000
24	0.065	20.90%	8.82%	0.528	0.120	0.352	0.000
25	0.07	21.36%	8.87%	0.499	0.132	0.368	0.000
26	0.075	23.27%	9.01%	0.427	0.163	0.386	0.025
27	0.08	31.91%	9.46%	0.200	0.259	0.422	0.119
28	0.085	45.25%	10.01%	0.000	0.251	0.488	0.260
29	0.09	60.76%	10.44%	0.000	0.000	0.556	0.444
30	0.095	74.30%	10.70%	0.000	0.000	0.300	0.700
31	0.1	94.87%	11.00%	0.000	0.000	0.000	1.000
32	0.105	94.87%	11.00%	0.000	0.000	0.000	1.000
33	0.11	94.87%	11.00%	0.000	0.000	0.000	1.000
34	0.115	94.87%	11.00%	0.000	0.000	0.000	1.000
35	0.12	94.87%	11.00%	0.000	0.000	0.000	1.000
36	0.125	94.87%	11.00%	0.000	0.000	0.000	1.000
37	0.13	94.87%	11.00%	0.000	0.000	0.000	1.000
38	0.135	94.87%	11.00%	0.000	0.000	0.000	1.000
39	0.14	94.87%	11.00%	0.000	0.000	0.000	1.000
40	0.145	94.87%	11.00%	0.000	0.000	0.000	1.000
41	0.15	94.87%	11.00%	0.000	0.000	0.000	1.000
42	0.155	94.87%	11.00%	0.000	0.000	0.000	1.000
43	0.16	94.87%	11.00%	0.000	0.000	0.000	1.000

11.5   Conclusion

No one would claim that Excel offers a quick way to solve for portfolio maxi-mization, with or without short-sale constraints. However, it can be used to il-lustrate the principles involved, and the Excel Solver provides an easy-to-use and intuitive interface for setting up these problems.

Exercises

Both exercises relate to the data set given to you in Chapter 8 (this same data set was used in the first exercise to Chapter 9). In Chapter 8 you were asked to calculate the variance-covariance ma-trix of returns for six furniture companies. The calculated variance-covariance matrix and the mean returns for these firms are as follows:

Variance-covariance matrix								Means	
	La-Z-Boy	Kimball	Flexsteel	Leggett	Miller	Shaw		Means	
La-Z-Boy	0.1267	0.0438	0.1971	0.0541	0.0625	0.1088		La-Z-Boy	29.24%
Kimball	0.0438	0.0713	0.0492	0.0068	0.0384	0.0296		Kimball	20.68%
Flexsteel	0.1971	0.0492	0.3667	0.0853	0.0975	0.1636		Flexsteel	25.02%
Leggett	0.0541	0.0068	0.0853	0.1136	0.0210	0.0657		& Platt	31.64%
Miller	0.0625	0.0384	0.0975	0.0210	0.0654	0.0267		Miller	15.34%
Shaw	0.1088	0.0296	0.1636	0.0657	0.0267	0.1819		Shaw	43.87%

1.   Given these data, calculate the efficient frontier assuming no short sales are allowed.

2.   On the same set of axes, graph the efficient frontier for these six stocks with and without short sales.

12 Value at Risk (VaR)[1]

12.1 Overview

Value-at-Risk (VaR) measures the worst expected loss under normal market conditions over a specific time interval at a given confidence level. VaR answers the question: How much can I lose with x percent probability over a preset horizon? Another way of expressing this idea is that VaR is the lowest quantile of the potential losses that can occur within a given portfolio during a specified time period. The basic time period T and the confidence level (the quantile) q are the two major parameters that should be chosen in a way appropriate to the overall goal of risk measurement. The time horizon can differ from a few hours for an active trading desk to a year for a pension fund. When the primary goal is to satisfy external regulatory requirements, such as bank capital requirements, the quantile is typically very small (for example, 1 percent of worst outcomes). However, for an internal risk management model used by a company to control the risk exposure, the typical number is around 5 percent (visit the Internet sites in the references for more details). A general introduction to VaR can be found in Linsmeier and Pearson (1996) and Jorion (1997).

In the jargon of VaR, suppose that a portfolio manager has a daily VaR equal to $1 million at 1 percent. This statement means that there is only one chance in 100 that a daily loss bigger than $1 million occurs under normal market conditions.

12.2 A Very Simple Example

Suppose a manager has a portfolio that consists of a single asset. The return of the asset is normally distributed with mean return 20 percent and standard deviation 30 percent. The value of the portfolio today is $100 million. We want to answer various simple questions about the end-of-year distribution of portfolio value:

1. What is the distribution of the end-of-year portfolio value?

2. What is the probability of a loss of more than $20 million dollars by year-end (i.e., what is the probability that the end-of-year value is less than $80 million)?

3. With 1 percent probability what is the maximum loss at the end of the year? This is the VaR at 1 percent.

---

1. This chapter is based on an article written by Zvi Wiener of Hebrew University, Jerusalem, which first appeared in *Mathematica in Education and Research,* Vol. 7, 1998, pp. 39–45.

The probability that the end-of-year portfolio value is less than $80 million is about 9 percent. ("Million" is omitted in the example.)

	A	B	C	D	E	F	G
3	Mean	20%					
4	Sigma	30%					
5	Initial investment	100					
6	Cutoff	80					
7		9.12%	<-- =NORMDIST(B6,(1+B3)*B5,B5*B4,TRUE)				

Here's the way the screen looks when we apply the **NormDist** function:

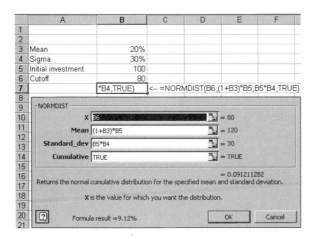

This picture shows that the Excel function **Normdist** can give both the cumulative normal distribution and the probability mass function. Using the latter option and a data table gives the standard bell-shaped graph:

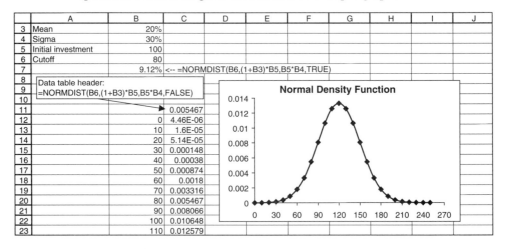

	A	B	C	D	E	F	G	H	I	J
3	Mean	20%								
4	Sigma	30%								
5	Initial investment	100								
6	Cutoff	80								
7		9.12%	<-- =NORMDIST(B6,(1+B3)*B5,B5*B4,TRUE)							
8	Data table header:									
9	=NORMDIST(B6,(1+B3)*B5,B5*B4,FALSE)									
10										
11			0.005467							
12		0	4.46E-06							
13		10	1.6E-05							
14		20	5.14E-05							
15		30	0.000148							
16		40	0.00038							
17		50	0.000874							
18		60	0.0018							
19		70	0.003316							
20		80	0.005467							
21		90	0.008066							
22		100	0.010648							
23		110	0.012579							

12.3   Defining Quantiles in Excel

With a probability of 1 percent the end-of-year portfolio value will be less than 50.20865; thus the VaR of the distribution is $100 - 50.20865 = 49.79135$.

	A	B	C	D	E	F	G
1	**CALCULATING THE QUANTILES**						
2							
3	Mean	20%					
4	Sigma	30%					
5	Initial investment	100					
6	Cutoff	50.20974	<-- =NORMINV(0.01,(1+B3)*B5,B5*B4)				
7		1.00%	<-- =NORMDIST(B6,(1+B3)*B5,B5*B4,TRUE)				
8							
9	VaR at 1.00% level	49.79026	<-- =B5-B6				
10							
11			Contains string formula which changes				
12			with contents of cell B6:				
13			="VaR at "&TEXT(B7,"0.00%")&" level"				
14							

The cutoff is known as the quantile of the distribution. We found this solution by using Excel's Solver:

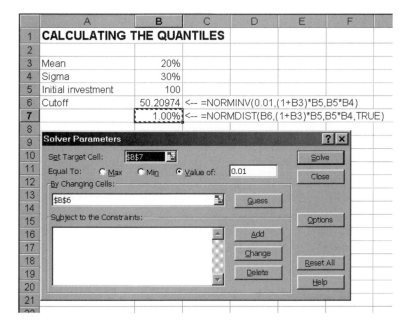

12.3.1   Finding Quantiles

We can use Solver to find the quantiles for any distribution. For two distributions we use—the normal and the lognormal distribution—Excel has built in functions that find the quantile. These functions—**Norminv, Normsinv,** and **Loginv**—find the inverse for the normal, standard normal, and lognormal distributions.

Here's an example for the numbers that we've been using; this time we have written the function **Norminv(0.01,(1 + B3)*B5,B4)** in cell B6. This function finds the cutoff point for which the normal distribution with a mean of 120 and a standard deviation of 30 has probability of 1 percent. You can see this point on the following graph, which shows part of the cumulative distribution:

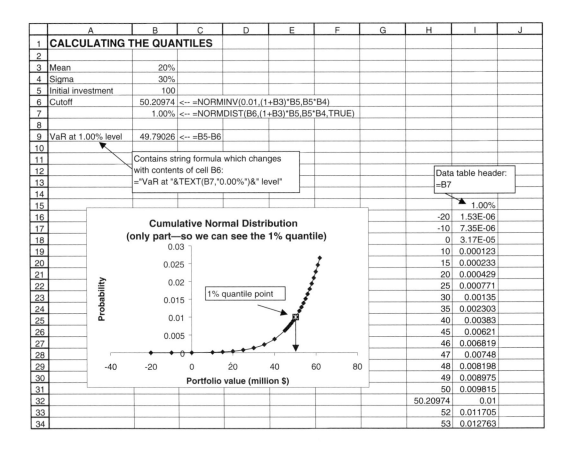

	A	B	C	D	E	F	G	H	I	J
1	**CALCULATING THE QUANTILES**									
2										
3	Mean	20%								
4	Sigma	30%								
5	Initial investment	100								
6	Cutoff	50.20974	<-- =NORMINV(0.01,(1+B3)*B5,B5*B4)							
7		1.00%	<-- =NORMDIST(B6,(1+B3)*B5,B5*B4,TRUE)							
8										
9	VaR at 1.00% level	49.79026	<-- =B5-B6							
10										
11			Contains string formula which changes							
12			with contents of cell B6:					Data table header:		
13			="VaR at "&TEXT(B7,"0.00%")&" level"					=B7		
14										
15									1.00%	
16								-20	1.53E-06	
17								-10	7.35E-06	
18								0	3.17E-05	
19								10	0.000123	
20								15	0.000233	
21								20	0.000429	
22								25	0.000771	
23								30	0.00135	
24								35	0.002303	
25								40	0.00383	
26								45	0.00621	
27								46	0.006819	
28								47	0.00748	
29								48	0.008198	
30								49	0.008975	
31								50	0.009815	
32								50.20974	0.01	
33								52	0.011705	
34								53	0.012763	

Cumulative Normal Distribution (only part—so we can see the 1% quantile)

1% quantile point

Probability

Portfolio value (million $)

12.3.2 The Lognormal Distribution

The lognormal distribution is a more reasonable distribution for many asset prices (which cannot become negative) than the normal distribution. Suppose that the return on the portfolio is normally distributed with annual mean μ and annual standard deviation σ. Furthermore, suppose that the current value of the portfolio is given by V_0. Then it follows (see Hull, 1997, Chapter 11) that the logarithm of the portfolio value at time T, V_T, is normally distributed:

$$\ln V_T \sim \text{Normal}\left[\ln(V_0) + \left(\mu - \frac{\sigma^2}{2}\right)T, \sigma\sqrt{T}\right]$$

Suppose, for example, that $V_0 = 100$, $\mu = 10$ percent, and $\sigma = 30$ percent. Thus the end-of-year log of the portfolio value is distributed normally:

$$\ln(V_1) \sim \text{Normal}\left[\ln(100) + \left(0.10 - \frac{0.3^2}{2}\right), 0.3\right] = \text{Normal}[4.666017, 0.3]$$

Thus a portfolio whose initial value is \$100 million and whose annual returns are lognormally distributed with parameters $\mu = 10$ percent and $\sigma = 30$ percent, has an annual VaR equal to \$47.42 million at 1 percent:

	A	B	C	D	E
3	Initial value, V_0	100			
4	Mean, μ	10%			
5	Sigma, σ	30%			
6	Time period, T	1	<-- in years		
7					
8	Parameters of normal distribution of $\ln(V_T)$				
9	Mean	4.6602	<-- =LN(B3)+(B4-B5^2/2)*B6		
10	Sigma	0.3000	<-- =B5*B6		
11					
12	Cutoff	52.57641	<-- =LOGINV(0.01,B9,B10)		
13	VaR at 1% level	47.42359	<-- =B3-B12		

Most VaR calculations are not concerned with annual value at risk. The main regulatory and management concern is with loss of portfolio value over a much shorter time period (typically several days or perhaps weeks). It is clear that the distribution formula

$$\ln(V_T) \sim \text{Normal}\left[\ln(V_0) + \left(\mu - \frac{\sigma^2}{2}\right)T, \sigma\sqrt{T}\right]$$

can be used to calculate the VaR over any horizon. Recall that T is measured in annual terms; if there are 250 business days in a year, then the daily VaR corresponds to $T = 1/250$ (for many fixed-income instruments one should use $1/360$, $1/365$, or $1/365.25$ depending on the market convention).

12.4 A Three-Asset Problem: The Importance of the Variance-Covariance Matrix

As can be seen from the preceding examples, VaR is not—in principle, at least—a very complicated concept. In the implementation of VaR, however, there are two big practical problems:

1. The first problem is the estimation of the parameters of asset return distributions. In "real-world" applications of VaR, it is necessary to estimate means, variances, and correlations of returns. This is a not-inconsiderable problem! In this section we illustrate the importance of the correlations between asset returns. In the following section we give a highly simplified example of the estimation of return distributions from market data. For example, you can imagine that a long position in euros and a short position in U.S. dollars is less risky than a position in only one of the currencies, because of a high probability that profits of one position will be mainly offset by losses of another.

2. The second problem is the actual calculation of position sizes. A large financial institution may have thousands of loans outstanding. The database of these loans may not classify them by their riskiness, nor even by their term to maturity. Or—to give a second example—a bank may have offsetting positions in foreign currencies at different branches in different locations. A long position in deutschemarks in New York may be offset by a short position in deutschemarks in Geneva; the bank's risk—which we intend to measure by VaR—is based on the net position.

We start with the problem of correlations between asset returns. We continue the previous example, but assume that there are three risky assets. As before, the parameters of the distributions of the asset returns are known: all the means, μ_1, μ_2, μ_3, as well as the variance-covariance matrix of the returns:

$$S = \begin{pmatrix} \sigma_{11} & \sigma_{12} & \sigma_{13} \\ \sigma_{21} & \sigma_{22} & \sigma_{23} \\ \sigma_{31} & \sigma_{32} & \sigma_{33} \end{pmatrix}$$

The matrix S is of course symmetric; σ_{ii} is the variance of the ith asset's return and σ_{ij} the covariance of the returns of assets i and j (if $i = j$, σ_{ij} is the variance of asset i's return).

Suppose that the total portfolio value today is \$100 million, with \$30 million invested in asset 1, \$25 million in asset 2, and \$45 million in asset 3. Then the return distribution of the portfolio is given by

$$\text{Mean return} = \{x_1, x_2, x_3\}\begin{pmatrix} \mu_1 \\ \mu_2 \\ \mu_3 \end{pmatrix} = x_1\mu_1 + x_2\mu_2 + x_3\mu_3$$

$$\text{Variance of return} = \{x_1, x_2, x_3\}S\{x_1, x_2, x_3\}^T$$

where $x = \{x_1, x_2, x_3\} = \{0.3, 0.25, 0.45\}$ is the vector of proportions invested in each of the three assets. Assuming that the returns are normally distributed (meaning that prices are lognormally distributed), we may calculate the VaR as in the following spreadsheet fragment:

	A	B	C	D	E	F	G	H	I
1			VaR FOR THREE-ASSET PROBLEM						
2									
3		**Mean**		**Variance-covariance**				**Portfolio**	
4		**returns**		**matrix**				**proportions**	
5	Asset 1	10%		0.1	0.04	0.03		0.30	
6	Asset 2	12%		0.04	0.2	-0.04		0.25	
7	Asset 3	13%		0.03	-0.04	0.6		0.45	
8									
9	Initial investment	100							
10	Mean return	0.1185	<-- {=MMULT(TRANSPOSE(B5:B7),H5:H7)}						
11	Portfolio sigma	0.3848	<-- {=SQRT(MMULT(MMULT(TRANSPOSE(H5:H7),D5:F7),H5:H7))}						
12									
13	Mean investment value	111.8500							
14	Sigma of investment value	38.4838							
15									
16	Cutoff	22.32361	<-- =NORMINV(0.01,(1+B10)*B9,B11*B9)						
17	Cumulative PDF	0.01	<-- =NORMDIST(B16,B13,B14,TRUE)						
18	VaR at 1.00% level	77.67639	<-- =B9-B16						
19									
20			Note that the functions in cells B10 and B11 are *array*						
21			*functions:* You must press Ctrl + Shift + Enter when						
22			after you write the function in the cell. The braces {}						
23			are not written—they appear automatically.						
24									

12.5 Simulating Data—Bootstrapping

Sometimes it helps to simulate data. In this section we give an example. Suppose that the current date is February 10, 1997, and consider a firm that has an investment in two assets:

• It is long two units of an index fund. The fund's current market price is 293, so that the investment in the index fund is worth $2 * 293 = 586$.

• It is short a foreign bond denominated in rubles. The bond is a zero-coupon bond (i.e., pays no interest), has face value of 100 rubles and maturity of May 8, 2000. If the current ruble interest rate is 5.30 percent, then the February 10, 1997, ruble value of the bond is

$$-100 * \exp\left[-5.30 \text{ percent} * (\text{May 8, 2000} - \text{Feb. 10, 1997})/365\right] = -84.2166$$

In dollars, the value of the bond is $-84.2166 * 3.40 = -286.3365$, so that the net portfolio value is $586 - 286.3365 = 299.66$.

This example is illustrated in the following display:

	A	B	C	D	E	F	G	H	I	J	K
3	Units of Index held	2									
4	Bond maturity	May 8, 2000									
5											
6				Ruble	Ruble		Total	Ruble	Dollar	Portfolio	
7			Index	interest	exchange		index	bond	bond	value	
8		Date	Value	rate	rate		value	value	value		
9		2/10/97	293	5.30%	3.40		586.00	-84.2166	-286.3365	299.66	
10											
11							=B3*C9			=G9+I9	
12								=H9*E9			
13											
14							=-100*EXP(-(B4-B9)/365*D9)				
15											

Now suppose we have exchange-rate and index data. We illustrate data for 40 days (the middle of the data has been hidden, but you will see that the rows go from 8 to 47):

	A	B	C	D	E	F
6			Foreign	Exchange		Portfolio
7	Day	Index	interest rate	rate		value
8	1/2/97	462.71	5.28%	3.50		632.13
9	1/3/97	514.71	5.26%	3.47		738.41
10	1/4/97	456.5	5.23%	3.46		622.49
11	1/5/97	487.39	5.24%	3.45		685.17
12	1/6/97	470.42	5.25%	3.45		651.28
45	2/8/97	467.14	5.31%	3.44		644.75
46	2/9/97	562.06	5.32%	3.41		837.17
47	2/10/97	481.61	5.30%	3.40		676.88

We want to use these data as a basis for generating "random" return data. We illustrate one technique for doing so, called *bootstrapping*. This term refers to random reshufflings of the data. For each iteration, we reorder the series of index prices, interest rates, and exchange rates and calculate the return on the portfolio.[2]

	A	B	C	D	E	F	G	H
1	**BOOTSTRAPPING RETURN DISTRIBUTIONS**							
2								
3	Units of Index held	2			Interations	5000	Start time	14:11:54
4	Bond maturity	May 8, 2000			Return	-0.36	Elapsed	0:14:42
5	Number of data points	40						
6								
7				Foreign		Exchange		Portfolio
8	Day	Index	Index rand	interest rate	Interest rand	rate	Exchange rand	value
9	1/2/97	670.63	0.0648	5.25%	0.0249	3.46	0.0585	1,051.03
10	1/3/97	669.12	0.0681	5.30%	0.0379	3.41	0.0967	1,052.64
11	1/4/97	467.14	0.1164	5.35%	0.0631	3.44	0.1051	646.61
12	1/5/97	757.02	0.1695	5.27%	0.0836	3.48	0.1206	1,222.20
13	1/6/97	740.74	0.1741	5.23%	0.1550	3.49	0.1244	1,188.37
14	1/7/97	645.5	0.1787	5.28%	0.1671	3.45	0.1598	1,001.69
15	1/8/97	462.71	0.1837	5.24%	0.1829	3.42	0.1926	638.20
16	1/9/97	562.06	0.2534	5.24%	0.2021	3.41	0.2183	837.70
17	1/10/97	445.77	0.2838	5.34%	0.2080	3.42	0.2280	605.19
18	1/11/97	605.37	0.3022	5.28%	0.2345	3.41	0.2457	924.62
19	1/12/97	654.17	0.3220	5.36%	0.2744	3.42	0.2761	1,022.10
20	1/13/97	639.95	0.3623	5.26%	0.2977	3.42	0.2932	992.67
21	1/14/97	790.82	0.3687	5.24%	0.3031	3.52	0.2961	1,285.77
22	1/15/97	458.26	0.4159	5.30%	0.3857	3.47	0.3607	625.39
23	1/16/97	640.43	0.4195	5.32%	0.3995	3.39	0.3847	996.59
24	1/17/97	500.71	0.4202	5.25%	0.4040	3.41	0.3990	714.77
25	1/18/97	705.27	0.4260	5.32%	0.4451	3.40	0.5175	1,125.35
26	1/19/97	786.16	0.4280	5.26%	0.4712	3.44	0.5292	1,283.16
27	1/20/97	487.39	0.4677	5.25%	0.4724	3.44	0.5313	685.23
28	1/21/97	459.27	0.5063	5.29%	0.4959	3.43	0.5544	630.42
29	1/22/97	514.71	0.5323	5.26%	0.5094	3.42	0.5711	741.81
30	1/23/97	475.49	0.5393	5.31%	0.5213	3.37	0.5882	668.00
31	1/24/97	533.4	0.6087	5.35%	0.5249	3.68	0.6141	758.15
32	1/25/97	450.91	0.6202	5.28%	0.5389	3.40	0.6309	615.96
33	1/26/97	687.33	0.6426	5.31%	0.5569	3.46	0.6673	1,084.00
34	1/27/97	456.5	0.7015	5.27%	0.6120	3.50	0.6924	618.55
35	1/28/97	636.02	0.7612	5.28%	0.6486	3.42	0.6948	984.37
36	1/29/97	561.88	0.7653	5.28%	0.6562	3.47	0.7066	831.85
37	1/30/97	461.79	0.7888	5.27%	0.6779	3.45	0.7210	633.21
38	1/31/97	615.93	0.8018	5.25%	0.6832	3.48	0.7210	938.73
39	2/1/97	466.45	0.8060	5.28%	0.7246	3.44	0.7336	643.38
40	2/2/97	470.42	0.8196	5.27%	0.7411	3.42	0.7406	652.87
41	2/3/97	584.41	0.8458	5.23%	0.8106	3.46	0.7516	877.06
42	2/4/97	581.5	0.8728	5.32%	0.8528	3.41	0.7919	876.26
43	2/5/97	444.27	0.8939	5.34%	0.8786	3.46	0.8126	597.74
44	2/6/97	472.35	0.9205	5.26%	0.8964	3.42	0.8215	656.47
45	2/7/97	544.75	0.9494	5.28%	0.9147	3.49	0.8253	795.52
46	2/8/97	453.69	0.9896	5.31%	0.9241	3.41	0.8449	620.38
47	2/9/97	651.99	0.9956	5.29%	0.9955	3.43	0.9186	1,015.07
48	2/10/97	481.61	0.8740	5.24%	0.4419	3.45	0.5562	672.11

---

2. The bootstrapping technique is illustrated in the appendix to this chapter.

The bootstrapped return data look like this:

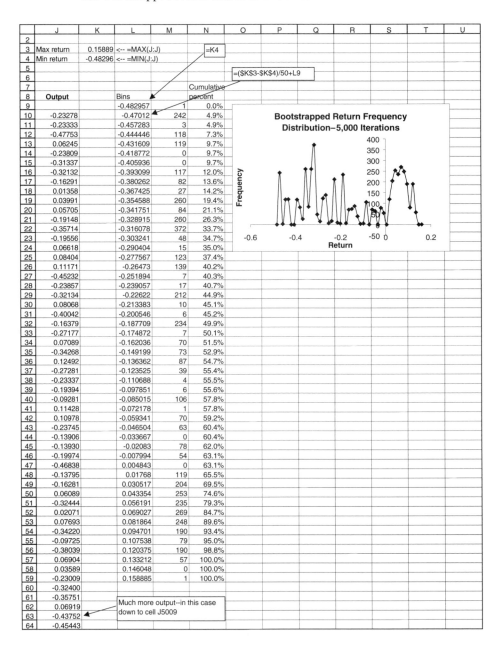

	J	K	L	M	N
3	Max return	0.15889	<-- =MAX(J:J)		=K4
4	Min return	-0.48296	<-- =MIN(J:J)		
5					=($K$3-$K$4)/50+L9
7					Cumulative
8	**Output**		**Bins**		percent
9			-0.482957	1	0.0%
10	-0.23278		-0.47012	242	4.9%
11	-0.23333		-0.457283	3	4.9%
12	-0.47753		-0.444446	118	7.3%
13	0.06245		-0.431609	119	9.7%
14	-0.23809		-0.418772	0	9.7%
15	-0.31337		-0.405936	0	9.7%
16	-0.32132		-0.393099	117	12.0%
17	-0.16291		-0.380262	82	13.6%
18	0.01358		-0.367425	27	14.2%
19	0.03991		-0.354588	260	19.4%
20	0.05705		-0.341751	84	21.1%
21	-0.19148		-0.328915	260	26.3%
22	-0.35714		-0.316078	372	33.7%
23	-0.19556		-0.303241	48	34.7%
24	0.06618		-0.290404	15	35.0%
25	0.08404		-0.277567	123	37.4%
26	0.11171		-0.26473	139	40.2%
27	-0.45232		-0.251894	7	40.3%
28	-0.23857		-0.239057	17	40.7%
29	-0.32134		-0.22622	212	44.9%
30	0.08068		-0.213383	10	45.1%
31	-0.40042		-0.200546	6	45.2%
32	-0.16379		-0.187709	234	49.9%
33	-0.27177		-0.174872	7	50.1%
34	0.07089		-0.162036	70	51.5%
35	-0.34268		-0.149199	73	52.9%
36	0.12492		-0.136362	87	54.7%
37	-0.27281		-0.123525	39	55.4%
38	-0.23337		-0.110688	4	55.5%
39	-0.19394		-0.097851	6	55.6%
40	-0.09281		-0.085015	106	57.8%
41	0.11428		-0.072178	1	57.8%
42	0.10978		-0.059341	70	59.2%
43	-0.23745		-0.046504	63	60.4%
44	-0.13906		-0.033667	0	60.4%
45	-0.13930		-0.02083	78	62.0%
46	-0.19974		-0.007994	54	63.1%
47	-0.46838		0.004843	0	63.1%
48	-0.13795		0.01768	119	65.5%
49	-0.16281		0.030517	204	69.5%
50	0.06089		0.043354	253	74.6%
51	-0.32444		0.056191	235	79.3%
52	0.02071		0.069027	269	84.7%
53	0.07693		0.081864	248	89.6%
54	-0.34220		0.094701	190	93.4%
55	-0.09725		0.107538	79	95.0%
56	-0.38039		0.120375	190	98.8%
57	0.06904		0.133212	57	100.0%
58	0.03589		0.146048	0	100.0%
59	-0.23009		0.158885	1	100.0%
60	-0.32400				
61	-0.35751				
62	0.06919				
63	-0.43752		Much more output--in this case		
64	-0.45443		down to cell J5009		

Chart: **Bootstrapped Return Frequency Distribution–5,000 Iterations** (Frequency vs. Return)

The graph on the right indicates the return distribution, which is far from normal. From columns L, M, and N, you can tell that the 5 percent VaR is about -47 percent, meaning that with a probability of 5 percent, the firm could lose 47 percent of its investment.

Appendix: How to Bootstrap: Making a Bingo Card in Excel

Bootstrapping refers to a technique of random shuffling of data to create more "data." This appendix gives a simple illustration of bootstrapping. It is based on the "Birthday Bingo" game created for Helena Benninga-Frank's 85th birthday. The game goes like this:

• Everyone gets a "Helen Bingo Card," which has five columns of five numbers each. The first column has five numbers from 1 to 17, the second column has five numbers between 18 and 34, and so on. A typical card looks like this:

Helen's
85th Birthday
bingo game

H	E	L	E	N
3	23	51	52	75
15	26	40	57	70
9	21	50	68	82
7	22	49	56	71
8	20	45	55	69

• We made up 85 question with answers from 1 to 85. When a card with a question was drawn, someone had to give the correct answer, and then everyone who had the number on his or her card could cross it out. For example, if we asked, "How many grandchildren does Helen have?" and someone answered "Thirteen," then everyone with a 13 in the first column could cross it out.

• The first person with five numbers in a line (a column, a row, or a diagonal) won the prize. (Note that it didn't take any talent to win—all you had to do was hear the right answers.)

We wanted to use Excel to create the cards, but it wasn't initially clear how to go about this task. Finally, the requisite trick, which is that we want to model the selection of balls from an urn without replacement, was discovered. (We will discuss this topic in greater detail later).

The Trick

The trick is very simple. As an illustration, suppose we want to make a random draw of five numbers between 1 and 17. (These will be the five numbers that will appear in the first column of a particular Helen Bingo card.) Here's how we go about it:

• First create a list of numbers from 1 to 17 and an adjoining column of random numbers. This step will give something that looks like the following:

	A	B	C
1	**EXPLAINING THE TRICK**		
2			
3		1	0.653152
4		2	0.425876
5		3	0.743173
6		4	0.911709
7		5	0.104356
8		6	0.09228
9		7	0.49608
10		8	0.210725
11		9	0.740506
12		10	0.724376
13		11	0.310175
14		12	0.437225
15		13	0.197224
16		14	0.145462
17		15	0.797405
18		16	0.52166
19		17	0.438188

The list of numbers was itself created in two stages: In the first stage =**Rand( )** was entered into each of the cells C3:C19. In the second stage C3:C19 were copied and were then pasted special back into their locations using **Edit|Paste Special|Values.** This procedure gets rid of the formulas behind the numbers (else **Rand( )** will change its values every time we hit Enter).

• Next, sort both columns using the second column as a sorting key. First mark off the relevant data, and then use the Excel command **Data|Sort.** This will bring up the following screen, in which I've chosen to sort the data by column C.

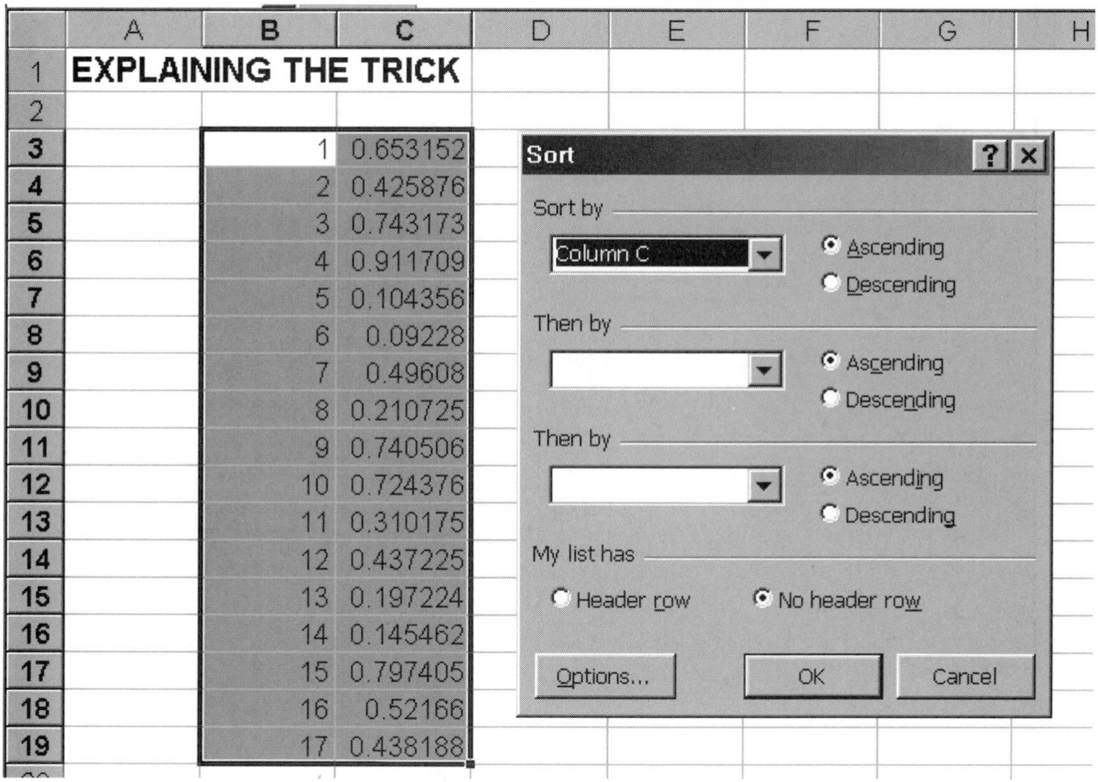

• In this case the sort command will give

	A	B	C
1	**EXPLAINING THE TRICK**		
2			
3		6	0.09228
4		5	0.104356
5		14	0.145462
6		13	0.197224
7		8	0.210725
8		11	0.310175
9		2	0.425876
10		12	0.437225
11		17	0.438188
12		7	0.49608
13		16	0.52166
14		1	0.653152
15		10	0.724376
16		9	0.740506
17		3	0.743173
18		15	0.797405
19		4	0.911709

- Finally, pick the first five numbers from the first column (in this example: 6, 5, 14, 13, 8). You could, of course, equally well pick the last five, the middle five, or any other five numbers from the column.

The Probabilistic Model

What we're doing here is just like picking random numbers out of an urn *without replacement*. This model, standard in all introductory probability books, imagines an urn filled with balls. Each ball has a different number—in our case, there are 17 balls with numbers between 1 and 17. The urn is shaken to mix up the balls, and then five balls are drawn out. Each ball, once drawn, is not placed back in the urn.

This model is somewhat different from the standard random-number generators, which pick random numbers with replacement (i.e., once the ball's number is recorded, it is placed back in the urn, so that it could possibly be drawn again).[3]

---

3. Excel has a function **Randbetween(low,high)** that lets you create random integers between **low** and **high**. Thus, to create five numbers between 1 and 17, you just copy **=Randbetween(1.17)** into five adjacent cells. However, this is like drawing numbers from the urn without replacement, and hence can give you multiple draws of the same number—a bingo no-no!

Writing a VBA Program

The next obvious step was to write a program in VBA to automate the procedure. Here is the spreadsheet:

Helen's
85th Birthday
bingo game

H	E	L	E	N
6	19	38	66	73
4	30	48	64	81
16	25	50	61	80
7	28	47	67	82
13	23	36	53	79

Note: Ctrl + A works macro.

Output1 number	Random	Output2 number	Random	Output3 number	Random	Output4 number	Random	Output5 number	Random
10	0.00250566	19	0.077980578	38	0.074950337	66	0.099409938	73	0.004019678
8	0.178693533	30	0.114332795	48	0.078708887	64	0.152676821	81	0.010293424
6	0.259060979	25	0.151756227	50	0.11143291	61	0.195534885	80	0.108785868
7	0.259541333	28	0.24314785	47	0.209698975	67	0.20504719	82	0.151656985
13	0.278589427	23	0.312288105	36	0.245173931	53	0.231596649	79	0.176886857
4	0.330300808	21	0.339375198	41	0.245678842	62	0.326157212	70	0.183076024
9	0.346957147	20	0.410631657	45	0.270359218	60	0.382569313	84	0.188131809
15	0.404864609	18	0.437663913	42	0.3786062	63	0.413233101	75	0.28871733
3	0.517192423	26	0.592991233	43	0.397243559	56	0.44121623	83	0.37740761
1	0.585937917	33	0.59885639	39	0.438826382	57	0.492006242	74	0.425849319
14	0.702970147	32	0.632975817	44	0.526573181	65	0.619831502	72	0.471391439
17	0.741780698	22	0.710554242	35	0.574864924	68	0.692517757	69	0.504459083
11	0.742342055	24	0.798773527	46	0.5811764	58	0.769506812	76	0.752542496
16	0.81157136	34	0.902569652	51	0.652376711	59	0.834893286	78	0.821931481
12	0.84088707	29	0.939971149	40	0.75997901	55	0.846187413	77	0.891279399
5	0.868453681	27	0.956236899	37	0.860162437	52	0.900333881	85	0.97953099
2	0.931559443	31	0.984253228	49	0.895446241	54	0.949905515	71	0.991402447

The VBA program repeats five bits of code (with some small and obvious changes); here's what a typical piece of code looks like.

```
For Row = 1 To 17
    Range ("output1").Cells(Row, 1) = Row
    Range ("output1").Cells(Row, 2) = Rnd
    Next Row
    Range ("output1").Select
    Selection.Sort   Key1:=Range("random1"),
        Order1:=xlAscending,
        Header:=xlGuess, _
        OrderCustom:=1, MatchCase:=False,
        Orientation:=xlTopToBottom
For Row = 1 To 5
    Range("card").Cells(Row, 1) =
        Range("Output1").Cells(Row, 1)
Next Row
```

The range **Output1** is a two-column-wide, 17-row range; the second column of this range is called **Random1.**

	B	C
13	Output1	
14	number	Random
15	10	0.00250566
16	8	0.178693533
17	6	0.259060979
18	7	0.259541333
19	13	0.278589427
20	4	0.330300808
21	9	0.346957147
22	15	0.404864609
23	3	0.517192423
24	1	0.585937917
25	14	0.702970147
26	17	0.741780698
27	11	0.742342055
28	16	0.81157136
29	12	0.84088707
30	5	0.868453681
31	2	0.931559443

If we want to print the card, we can name the print area something (here: **printarea**). We can then write out a macro for printing. We can even create a macro for creating multiple cards and printing each one out:

```
Sub cardprint()
 Range ("printarea").Select
    Selection.PrintOut Copies:=1, Collate:=True
End Sub

Sub multprint()
    For counter = 1 To 10
    doit
    Application.ScreenUpdating = True
    cardprint
    Next counter
End Sub
```

The main module **doit( )** (which is given in full at the end of this article) includes the line `Application.ScreenUpdating = False`. This command prevents the screen from updating until the end of the main module is reached; it both saves time and avoids a lot of needless screen garbage. However, when we run the module `multprint()` we want to undo this command at the end of every iteration in order to see the results; hence the line `Application.ScreenUpdating = True` which appears in `multprint()`.

Some Final Notes

- Obviously, the numbers on the card have been formatted using the appropriate Excel commands.

- The syntax for the `Selection.Sort` command was derived from a recorded macro, to which we made the appropriate changes.

The Whole Program

```
Sub doit()
    Application.ScreenUpdating = False

    For Row = 1 To 17
    Range("output1").Cells(Row, 1) = Row
    Range("output1").Cells(Row, 2) = Rnd
    Next Row
    Range("output1").Select
    Selection.Sort Key1:=Range("random1"),
      Order1:=xlAscending, Header:=xlGuess,
      OrderCustom:=1, MatchCase:=False,
      Orientation:=xlTopToBottom
    For Row = 1 To 5
    Range("card").Cells(Row, 1) =
      Range("output1").Cells(Row, 1)
    Next Row

    For Row = 1 To 17
    Range("output2").Cells(Row, 1) = Row + 17
    Range("output2").Cells(Row, 2) = Rnd
    Next Row
    Range("output2").Select
    Selection.Sort Key1:=Range("random2"),
      Order1:=xlAscending, Header:=xlGuess,
      OrderCustom:=1, MatchCase:Case:=False,
      Orientation:=xlTopToBottom
    For Row = 1 To 5
    Range("card").Cells(Row, 2) =
      Range("output2").Cells(Row, 1)
    Next Row

    For Row = 1 To 17
    Range("output3").Cells(Row, 1) = Row + 34
    Range("output3").Cells(Row, 2) = Rnd
    Next Row
    Range("output3").Select
```

```
      Selection.Sort Key1:=Range("random3"),
        Order1:=xlAscending, Header:=xlGuess,
        OrderCustom:=1, MātchCase:=False,
        Orientation:=xlTopToBottom
      For Row = 1 To 5
      Range("card").Cells(Row, 3) =
        Range("output3").Cells(Row, 1)
      Next Row

      For Row = 1 To 17
      Range("output4").Cells(Row, 1) = Row + 51
      Range("output4").Cells(Row, 2) = Rnd
      Next Row
      Range("output4").Select
      Selection.Sort Key1:=Range("random4"),
        Order1:=xlAscending, Header:=xlGuess,
        OrderCustom:=1, MātchCase:=False,
        Orientation:=xlTopToBottom
      For Row = 1 To 5
      Range("card").Cells(Row, 4) =
        Range("output1").Cells(Row, 1)
      Next Row

      For Row = 1 To 17
      Range("output5").Cells(Row, 1) = Row + 68
      Range("output5").Cells(Row, 2) = Rnd
      Next Row
      Range("output5").Select
      Selection.Sort Key1:=Range("random5"),
        Order1:=xlAscending, Header:=xlGuess,
        OrderCustom:=1, MātchCase:=False,
        Orientation:=xlTopToBottom
      For Row = 1 To 5
      Range("card").Cells(Row, 5) =
        Range("output5").Cells(Row, 1)
      Next Row
  End Sub
```

III   Option-Pricing Models

Chapters 13–19 deal with option pricing and applications. Chapter 13 is an introduction to options. After defining the option terminology, this chapter discusses option payoffs and basic option-pricing propositions. In Chapter 14 we discuss the binomial option-pricing model and its implementation in Excel. After showing how these binomial models work, we use Visual Basic for Applications (VBA; see Chapters 31–35) to build binomial option-pricing functions for both European and American options.

Chapter 15 discusses the lognormality of stock prices. The assumption of lognormality underlies the Black-Scholes pricing formulas. In Chapter 15 we use Excel to simulate lognormal price processes.

Chapter 16 discusses the Black-Scholes pricing formulas for European calls and puts. These formulas can be implemented either by direct calculation in the spreadsheet or by using VBA to build new spreadsheet functions. Both methods are illustrated in the chapter. In Chapter 17 we discuss an application of the Black-Scholes model—portfolio insurance. We use Excel to simulate the performance of portfolio insurance strategies; these simulations use the lognormal simulations developed in Chapter 15.

Real options are illustrated in Chapter 18. Real options are an application of optionlike concepts to the capital budgeting and valuation problems discussed in Chapters 1–4. Finally, Chapter 19 discusses early-exercise boundaries for puts and calls.

13 An Introduction to Options

13.1 Basic Option Definitions and Terminology

In this chapter we give a brief introduction to options. The chapter can, at best, serve as an introduction to the already informed. If you know nothing whatsoever about options, read an introduction to the topic in a basic finance text.[1] We start with the basic definitions and options terminology, go on to discuss graphs of option payoffs and "profit diagrams," and finally discuss some of the more important option arbitrage propositions (sometimes referred to as linear pricing restrictions). In subsequent chapters we discuss two methods of pricing options: the binomial option-pricing model (Chapter 14) and the Black-Scholes option-pricing model (Chapter 16).

An *option on a stock* is a security that gives the holder the right to buy or to sell one share of the stock on or before a particular date for a predetermined price. Here is a brief glossary of terms and notation used in the field of options:

- *Call, C:* An option that gives the holder the right to buy a share of stock on or before a given date at a predetermined price.

- *Put, P:* An option that gives the holder the right to sell a share of stock on or before a given date at a predetermined price.

- *Exercise price, X:* The price at which the holder can buy or sell the underlying stock; sometimes also referred to as the *strike price* .

- *Expiration date, T:* The date on or before which the holder can buy or sell the underlying stock.

- *Stock price, S_t:* The price at which the underlying stock is selling at date t. The current stock price is denoted S_0.

- *Option price:* The price at which the option is sold or bought.

American versus European Options   In the jargon of options markets, an American option is an option that can be exercised on or before the expiration

---

1. Good chapters can be found in the following books: John Hull (2000, Chapters 6–8); Bodie, Kane, and Marcus (1996, Chapters 19–20).

date $T,$ whereas a European option is one that can be exercised only on the expiration date $T.$ This terminology is confusing for two reasons:

1. The options sold on both European and American options exchanges are almost invariably American options.

2. The simplest option-pricing formulas (these include the famous Black-Scholes option pricing formula discussed in Chapter 16) are for *European options.* As we will show in section 13.5, in many cases we can price American options as if they were European options.

We shall use C_t to denote the price of a European call on date $t,$ and P_t to denote the European put price. If it is clear that the option price refers to today's price, we often drop the subscript, writing C or P instead of C_0 or $P_0.$ When we need fuller notation, we shall write $C_t(S_t, X, T)$ for the price of a call on date t when the price of the underlying stock is $S_t,$ the exercise price is $X,$ and the expiration date is $T.$ If we wish to specify that our option-pricing formula relates to an American option, we use the superscript A: $C_t^A,$ $C_t^A(S_t, X, T),$ or $P_t^A(S_t, X, T).$ When written without superscripts, the symbols refer to European options.

13.1.1   Writing Options versus Purchasing Options: Cash Flows

The purchaser of a call option acquires the right to buy a share of stock for a given price on or before date T and pays for this right at the time of purchase. The *writer* or seller of this call option is the seller of this right: The writer collects the option price today in return for obligating herself to deliver one share of stock in the future for the exercise price, if the purchaser of the call demands. In terms of cash flows, the purchaser of an option always has an initial negative cash flow (the price of the option) and a future cash flow that is at worst zero (if it is not worthwhile exercising the option) and otherwise positive (if the option is exercised). The cash-flow position of the writer of the option is reversed: An initial positive cash flow is followed by a terminal cash flow that is at best zero.

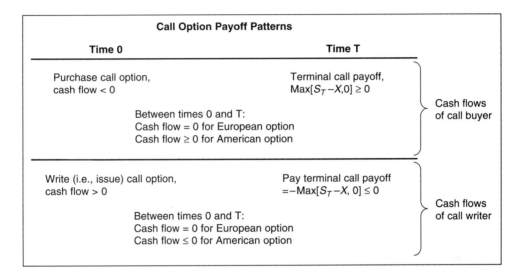

The same holds for the cash flows of the purchaser and writer of a put option on a stock:

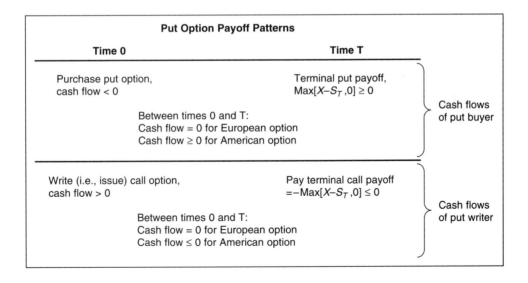

13.2 Some Examples

On pages 235 and 236 we have reprinted two excerpts from the options page of the *Wall Street Journal.*[2] A close-up of the options quotes for American Express (AmExpr; one of the most actively traded contracts of the same day, as you can see from the first excerpt) follows:

			-Call-		-Put-	
Option	Strike	Exp.	Vol.	Last	Vol.	Last
AmExpr	35	Feb	1000	8 5/8	...	...
43 1/8	35	Apr	602	9 7/8	18	5/16
43 1/8	37 1/2	Feb	650	6 3/8	722	1/8
43 1/8	37 1/2	Apr	10	6	405	11/16
43 1/8	40	Feb	2140	4 3/8	170	1/2
43 1/8	40	Jul	589	6 1/2	155	1 3/8
43 1/8	42 1/2	Feb	1831	2 1/16	815	1
43 1/8	42 1/2	Apr	250	3 5/8	16	2 3/16
43 1/8	42 1/2	Jul	85	4 7/8	1030	2 1/2
43 1/8	45	Feb	4830	1 3/8	218	2 3/4
43 1/8	45	Mar	836	1 15/16	223	3
43 1/8	45	Apr	1157	2 3/8	103	3 1/4
43 1/8	45	Jul	231	3 7/8	35	4 1/8
43 1/8	47 1/2	Jul	410	2 5/8	...	...
43 1/8	50	Apr	1977	1 1/16	2	6 3/8

Traded options on AmExpr have strike prices of 35, 37 1/2, 40, 42 1/2, 45, 47 1/2, and 50. Expiration dates for the options are February, April, and July of 1996. Not all months have options at all exercise prices: For example, there is no April option with an exercise price of 40. Not all options are traded (e.g., the July 47 1/2 put or the Feb 35 put).

The most actively traded AmExpr option on January 26, 1996, was the Feb 45 call option. We will examine this option in more detail. This option, which expires on Friday, February 17 (all options expire on the third Friday of their expiration month) gives its owner the right to purchase 100 shares of American Express stock for $45. On January 26, 4,830 such options were traded (i.e., the rights to purchase 483,000 shares); the price (per underlying share of stock) of each option was 1 3/8.[3] You pay this price for the privilege of being able,

2. The scans are from the international edition of the *Wall Street Journal* for Monday, January 29, 1996. Reprinted by permission of the *Wall Street Journal,* © Dow Jones & Company, Inc. All rights reserved worldwide.

3. In the rest of the discussion in this and the following chapters, we ignore the fact that each option relates to the purchase or sale of 100 shares. Thus if a listed AmExpr Feb 45 option is priced at 1 3/8, we examine the option as if the purchaser has bought (for $1.375) the right to purchase *one* share of AmExpr for $45 (whereas in actual fact the purchaser has spent $137.50 to buy the right to purchase 100 shares for $4,500).

U.S. LISTED OPTIONS QUOTATIONS

Friday, January 26, 1996

Volume and close for actively traded equity options with results for corresponding put or call contract as of 3 p.m. Volume figures are unofficial. Open interest is total outstanding for all exchanges and reflects previous trading day. Close when possible is shown for the underlying stock on primary market. CB-Chicago Board Options Exchange. AM-American Stock Exchange. PB-Philadelphia Stock Exchange. PC-Pacific Stock Exchange. NY-New York Stock Exchange. XC-Composite. c-Call. p-Put.

MOST ACTIVE CONTRACTS

Option	Strike	Vol.	Exch.	Last	Net Chg	Last Close	Open Int.
Compaq	Feb 50	11,851	PC	3/4 −	1/16	46 3/4	18,512
MicrTc	Feb 35	p10,505	XC	2 11/16 +	3/4	34 5/8	11,185
MicrTc	Feb 35	6,162	XC	2 1/8 −	7/8	34 5/8	13,642
MicrTc	Feb 30	p 5,339	XC	1 +	7/16	34 5/8	15,136
Loral	Apr 45	5,288	CB	1 7/8 +	5/8	45 1/2	10,128
AmExpr	Feb 45	4,830	XC	1 3/8 +	1 1/4	43 1/8	404
MicrTc	Feb 32 1/2	p 4,347	XC	1 5/8 +	1/2	34 5/8	1,702
BankAm	Jan 98 60	4,150	CB	11 1/4 +	3/4	63 5/8	564
AppleC	Feb 35	3,822	AM	5/8 +	1/16	30 5/8	12,396
Loral	Feb 45	3,712	CB	1 1/8 +	3/4	45 1/2	9,083
MicrTc	Feb 40	3,331	XC	11/16 −	7/16	34 5/8	18,476
Hasbro	Jul 45	3,301	PC	4 1/8	...	42 7/8	323
I B M	Feb105	3,280	CB	2 7/8 +	1/16	104 7/8	9,453
EMC	Feb 20	3,184	CB	3/4 −	11/16	19 3/4	8,257
Hasbro	Mar 45	2,982	PC	2	...	42 7/8	202
Hasbro	Feb 40	2,962	PC	4 3/8	...	42 7/8	1,901
I B M	Feb110	2,860	CB	15/16 −	3/16	104 7/8	7,117
GTelev	Feb 27 1/2	2,688	XC	1 11/16 +	13/16	28	6,292
I B M	Feb100	p 2,571	CB	1 3/16 −	5/16	104 7/8	11,050
Intel	Feb 55	2,544	AM	1 15/16 +	3/16	55	17,785
NwmtMn	Jun 50	p 2,500	PB	1 3/4	...	56 3/8	80
I B M	Feb 95	p 2,335	CB	1/2 −	3/16	104 7/8	8,494
Compaq	Feb 50	p 2,268	PC	3 3/4 +	5/8	46 3/4	7,293
MicrTc	Apr 35	2,222	XC	4 1/2 −	1/2	34 5/8	4,236
AmExpr	Feb 40	2,140	XC	4 3/8 +	2 1/2	43 1/8	1,394
BankAm	Mar 60	p 2,130	CB	1 −	7/8	63 5/8	408
Intel	Feb 55	p 2,129	AM	1 7/8 −	1/4	55	7,250
MicrTc	Feb 45	2,107	XC	1/4 −	1/8	34 5/8	11,414
Motrla	Feb 50	p 2,076	AM	9/16 −	3/16	53 1/4	11,407
Compaq	Feb 45	p 2,065	PC	1 +	1/4	46 3/4	5,533
AplMat	Feb 35	p 2,063	PC	1 5/8 +	1/4	36 7/8	1,402
Compaq	Feb 45	2,036	PC	3 1/8 −	1/4	46 3/4	4,037
GTriba	Feb 10	2,034	XC	1/2 −	1/16	9 5/8	13,869
BkBost	Jan 97 40	p 2,000	PB	2 3/4 +	3/8	43 1/2	244
SFeGld	Feb 12 1/2	2,000	XC	3 1/4 −	1/4	15 3/8	135
MicrTc	Mar 40	1,998	XC	1 11/16 −	7/16	34 5/8	2,800
Iomega	Feb 55	1,979	XC	1 3/16 −	1 1/8	48 1/2	4,518
AmExpr	Apr 50	1,977	XC	1 1/16 +	15/16	43 1/8	529
I B M	Feb105	p 1,968	CB	3 −	1/2	104 7/8	5,085
Hasbro	Feb 45	1,897	PC	1 5/16	...	42 7/8	2,307

Option	Strike	Exp.	-Call- Vol.	-Call- Last	-Put- Vol.	-Put- Last
ADT	12 1/2	Mar	...	...	625	3/16
A S A	45	Feb	234	1 3/4	53	7/8
46	47 1/2	Mar	345	1 1/4	...	...
AT&T	65	Mar	1021	1 3/4	...	...
64 3/4	70	Feb	531	1/8	50	6 1/8
Abbt L	40	Feb	546	1 1/8	45	1 1/16
A M D	20	Feb	302	1	510	3/4
AlaskA	20	Feb	1395	11/16	24	1 9/16
19 1/8	20	Apr	405	1 1/4	...	...
Altera	60	Feb	213	5 1/4	62	3
Alza	22 1/2	Jul	...	...	520	7/8
26 7/8	27 1/2	Apr	355	1 7/16	...	...
AmerOn	35	Feb	311	7 7/8	76	3/4
42	40	Feb	771	3 7/8	720	2
42	40	Apr	732	6 1/2	122	4 1/2
42	42 1/2	Apr	1070	5	20	6
42	45	Feb	1102	1 7/8	17	5 1/8
42	45	Apr	280	4 1/4	...	...
42	50	Feb	218	11/16	...	...
42	50	Apr	387	2 3/4	...	...
AmExpr	35	Feb	1000	8 5/8	...	...
43 1/8	35	Apr	602	9 7/8	18	5/16
43 1/8	37 1/2	Feb	650	6 3/8	722	1/8
43 1/8	37 1/2	Apr	10	6	405	11/16
43 1/8	40	Feb	2140	4 3/8	170	1/2
43 1/8	40	Jul	589	6 1/2	155	1 3/8
43 1/8	42 1/2	Feb	1831	2 1/16	815	1
43 1/8	42 1/2	Apr	250	3 5/8	16	2 3/16
43 1/8	42 1/2	Jul	85	4 7/8	1030	2 1/2
43 1/8	45	Feb	4830	1 3/8	218	2 3/4
43 1/8	45	Mar	836	1 15/16	223	3
43 1/8	45	Apr	1157	2 3/8	103	3 1/4
43 1/8	45	Jul	231	3 7/8	35	4 1/8
43 1/8	47 1/2	Jul	410	2 5/8	...	...
43 1/8	50	Apr	1977	1 1/16	2	6 3/8
Amgen	55	Feb	233	5	139	7/8
59 1/2	60	Feb	258	1 7/8	513	2 3/8
AnnTay	10	Feb	51	1	334	15/16
Epitpe	15	Apr	100	3 1/8	220	1 1/4
Exide	30	Feb	49	4 1/8	318	7/8
33 3/8	35	Feb	763	1 1/4	79	3
33 3/8	50	May	...	...	242	16
F N M	27 1/2	Feb	350	4 3/8	55	1/16
32	30	Feb	183	2 1/16	680	3/8
32	30	Mar	26	2 3/8	684	5/8
Ford	30	Feb	364	3/8	23	1 1/16
29 1/4	30	Jun	227	1 1/2	22	2 1/8
FounHl	40	Feb	370	2 5/8	380	1
FrMcRP	20	Jun	260	13/16	...	...
Gandlf	15	Feb	250	1 3/16	150	1 7/16
Gtwy2000	20	Feb	409	5 7/8	124	3/16
25 3/4	22 1/2	Feb	767	3 7/8	104	1/2
25 3/4	25	Feb	1253	2	44	1 1/8
25 3/4	25	Mar	436	3 1/8	270	2 1/4
25 3/4	30	Mar	380	1 1/16	...	...
25 3/4	30	Jun	255	2 3/4	...	...
GaylCn	10	Feb	266	5/16	130	1 1/2
9	10	Mar	273	3/4	5	1 3/4
G M	50	Feb	1729	2 1/16	351	7/8
51 1/8	50	Mar	460	2 3/4	94	1 1/4
51 1/8	50	Jun	227	4 1/8	38	2 1/4
51 1/8	55	Feb	363	3/8	42	3 3/4
51 1/8	55	Mar	1546	3/4	5	4 1/8
Genzym	75	Feb	260	1 1/2	...	...
GlenFd	15	Jul	...	...	210	7/8
Grace	60	Feb	320	2 1/8	3	2 1/16
GrdCasn	30	Feb	331	1 5/16	10	1 11/16
GTelev	25	Feb	400	3 1/4	250	1/2
28	27 1/2	Feb	2688	1 11/16	5	1 1/4
28	30	Feb	218	11/16	...	...
28	30	Mar	1856	1 7/16	...	...
GTriba	7 1/2	Feb	212	2 1/4	...	...
9 5/8	10	Feb	2034	1/2	250	7/8
9 5/8	10	Mar	778	13/16	44	1 5/16
9 5/8	10	Apr	599	1 1/8	...	...
Harley	30	Feb	228	4 1/2	27	1/4
53 1/4	50	Feb	171	4 1/8	2076	9/16
53 1/4	50	Mar	60	4 7/8	245	1 1/4
53 1/4	50	Jul	1	6 3/4	329	3
53 1/4	55	Feb	340	15/16	63	2 3/4
53 1/4	55	Apr	277	3	3	4 1/4
53 1/4	60	Apr	220	1 3/16	186	7 1/2
53 1/4	65	Jul	230	1 1/4	...	...
NewbNk	50	Feb	371	2	47	2 1/8
49 1/2	50	Mar	514	3 3/8	16	3 1/2
49 1/2	55	Mar	368	1 1/2	...	...
NwmtMn	50	Jun	1	8 5/8	2500	1 3/4
Nokia	35	Feb	230	3 3/8	...	...
NoramE	10	May	261	9/16	...	...
NthfldLb	20	Feb	357	2 11/16	100	2 3/4
20 3/8	20	May	1030	4	...	...
20 3/8	22 1/2	Feb	327	1 3/4	...	...
20 3/8	22 1/2	Aug	210	4 1/4	...	...
Novell	10	Aug	449	3 3/4	43	7/8
12 3/8	12 1/2	Feb	907	11/16	165	3/4
12 3/8	12 1/2	Mar	300	1 1/16	155	1 1/8
12 3/8	15	Feb	342	1/4	7	3
12 3/8	15	Mar	400	7/16	2	2 15/16
12 3/8	15	May	370	7/8	110	3 1/4
12 3/8	20	Feb	242	1/16	...	...
12 3/8	20	May	301	3/8	...	...
OakTch	60	Feb	471	1 9/16	...	...
52 1/2	60	Mar	209	3 3/4	...	...
OfceDp	15	Apr	...	...	1000	5/16
Oracle	50	Feb	447	3/4	108	3 3/8
47 3/8	50	Mar	473	1 7/8	26	3 7/8
OrbScl	17 1/2	Feb	225	1/2	...	...
Organo	17 1/2	Feb	629	13/16	15	1 3/4
ParmTc	50	Feb	...	...	1300	3/8
PepBys	30	Feb	539	1 9/16	17	2 3/4
Pepsi	55	Feb	615	5	...	...
59 1/8	60	Feb	812	1	...	...
Pfizer	60	Feb	310	5 7/8	30	3/8
65 7/8	65	Feb	1133	1 7/8	104	1 3/8

INDEX OPTIONS TRADING

Friday, January 26, 1996

Volume, close, net change and open interest for all contracts. Volume figures are unofficial. Open interest reflects previous trading day. p-Put. c-Call. The totals for call and put volume and open interest are closing figures.

RANGES FOR UNDERLYING INDEXES

	High	Low	Close	Net Chg.	From Dec. 31	% Chg.
S&P 100(OEX)	596.11	588.86	595.60	+ 5.09	+ 9.68	+ 1.7
S&P 500 -A.M.(SPX)	621.70	615.26	621.62	+ 4.59	+ 5.69	+ 0.9
S&P Banks(BIX)	329.97	327.93	329.41	+ 0.33	− 1.09	− 0.3
CB-Tech(TXX)	156.59	153.89	155.94	+ 0.55	− 0.59	− 0.4
CB-Mexico(MEX)	86.72	84.67	86.66	+ 1.07	+ 14.92	+ 20.8
CB-Lps Mex(VEX)	8.67	8.47	8.67	+ 0.11	+ 1.50	+ 20.9
Nasdaq 100(NDX)	577.05	568.33	577.05	+ 4.79	+ 0.82	+ 0.1
Russell 2000(RUT)	311.22	309.83	311.22	+ 0.66	− 4.75	− 1.5
Lps S&P 100(OEX)	59.61	58.89	59.56	+ 0.51	+ 0.97	+ 1.7
Lps S&P 500(SPX)	62.17	61.53	62.16	+ 0.46	+ 0.57	+ 0.9
S&P Midcap(MID)	216.57	214.98	216.57	+ 0.90	− 1.27	− 0.6
Major Mkt(XMI)	556.67	548.38	555.95	+ 6.65	+ 20.35	+ 3.8
Leaps MMkt(XLT)	55.67	54.84	55.60	+ 0.67	+ 2.04	+ 3.8
Hong Kong(HKO)			224.56	+ 0.27	+ 21.65	+ 10.7
Leaps HK(HKL)			22.46	+ 0.03	+ 2.17	+ 10.7
AM-Mexico(MXY)	103.67	101.41	103.67	+ 1.27	+ 20.05	+ 24.0
Institut'l -A.M.(XII)	644.51	636.06	644.14	+ 6.21	+ 7.42	+ 1.2
Japan(JPN)			209.78	+ 2.42	+ 7.94	+ 3.9
MS Cyclical(CYC)	342.02	339.14	341.84	+ 1.83	+ 1.62	+ 0.5
MS Consumr(CMR)	290.65	286.91	290.54	+ 2.90	+ 5.79	+ 2.0
MS Hi Tech(MSH)	315.56	310.57	314.41	+ 1.62	− 1.36	− 0.4
Pharma(DRG)	300.35	294.09	300.26	+ 4.68	+ 4.31	+ 1.5
Biotech(BTK)	138.43	135.00	137.78	+ 2.53	+ 4.01	+ 3.0
Comp Tech(XCI)	233.24	229.57	232.57	+ 1.49	+ 3.95	+ 1.7
NYSE(NYA)	332.89	329.72	332.84	+ 2.29	+ 3.33	+ 1.0
Gold/Silver(XAU)	140.34	138.57	139.83	+ 0.41	+ 19.41	+ 16.1
OTC(XOC)	424.49	418.49	424.45	+ 3.09	− 0.25	− 0.1
Utility(UTY)	282.27	280.80	282.21	+ 0.24	+ 4.61	+ 1.7
Value Line(VLE)	568.70	565.68	568.68	+ 1.95	− 1.22	− 0.2
Bank(BKX)	391.67	389.48	390.95	+ 0.30	− 2.90	− 0.7
Semicond(SOX)	188.69	183.85	187.89	+ 0.24	− 12.77	− 6.4
Top 100(TPX)	559.61	552.28	559.37	+ 5.38	+ 6.35	+ 1.2

CHICAGO

CB MEXICO INDEX(MEX)

CB TECHNOLOGY(TXX)

NASDAQ-100(NDX)

RUSSELL 2000(RUT)

S&P 100 INDEX(OEX)

AMERICAN

AM MEXICO INDEX(MXY)

BIOTECH(BTK)

COMP TECH(XCI)

S&P BANKS(BIX)

S&P MIDCAP(MID)

PHILADELPHIA

GOLD/SILVER(XAU)

OTC INDEX(XOC)

between now and February 17, to purchase one share of American Express stock for $45, irrespective of its market price at the time you exercise the option.[4]

An AmExpr 45 put option is the right to *sell* one share of American Express stock on or before February 17 for $45. Paying $2 3/4 for this put option today gives you the right to sell a share of AmExpr stock for $45 between now and February, irrespective of the market price of the stock. Of course, you will exercise this option only if the market price at the time of exercise is less than $45.[5]

13.3   Option Payoff and Profit Patterns

One of the attractions of options is that they allow their owners to change the payoff patterns of the underlying assets. In this section we consider

- The basic payoff and profit patterns of a call and a put option and a share.

- The payoff patterns of various combinations of options and shares.

13.3.1   Stock Profit Patterns

13.3.1.1   Payoff Pattern from a Purchased Stock

Suppose you buy a share of General Pills stock in July at its then-current market price of $40. If in September the price of the stock is $70, you will have made a $30 profit; if its price is $30, you will have a loss (or a negative profit) of $10.[6] Generalize this pattern by writing the price of the stock in September as S_T and its price in July by S_0. Then we write the profit function from the stock as

Profit from stock $= S_T - S_0$

---

4. As we show in section 13.5, it is usually not optimal to exercise a call before its expiration date. One of the remarkable theorems in option-pricing theory states that early exercise may be optimal only if the underlying stock pays dividends before the expiration date. The upshot of this theorem is that in many cases an American call option can be analyzed as if it were a European option.

5. As opposed to a call option, early exercise of an American put may be optimal even in the absence of dividend payments. See Chapter 16.

6. Our use of the word *profit* in this section constitutes a slight abuse of the English language and the standard finance concept of the word, since we are ignoring the interest costs associated with buying the asset. In the case at hand, this abuse of language is both traditional and harmless.

13.3.1.2   Payoff from the Short Sale of a Stock

Suppose we had sold one share of GP stock short in July, when its market price was $40. If in September the market price of GP was $70, and if at that point we undid the short sale (i.e., we purchase a share at the market price in order to return the share to the lender of the original short), then our profit would be $-\$30$:

$$\text{Profit from short sale of stock} = S_0 - S_T$$
$$= -(\text{Profit from purchase of stock})$$

Notice that the profit from the short sale is the *negative* of the profit from the purchase; this is always the case (also for options, considered in section 13.3.2).

13.3.1.3   Graphing Stock Profit Patterns

The following Excel graph shows the profit patterns from both a purchase and a short sale of the GP stock.

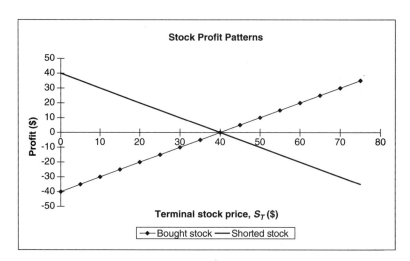

13.3.2   Call Option Profit Patterns

13.3.2.1   Payoff Pattern from a Purchased Call

Returning to the General Pills (GP) options of the previous section, suppose that in July you bought one GP September 40 call for $4.[7] In September you

---

7. Because the exercise price of this call is equal to the current market price of the stock, it is called an *at-the-money* call. When the exercise price of the call is higher than the current market price, it is called an *out-of-the-money* call, and when the exercise price is lower than the current market price, the call is an *in-the-money* call.

will exercise the call only if the market price of GP is higher than $40. If we write the initial (July) call price as C_0, we can write the profit function from the call in September as follows:

$$\text{Call profit in September} = \max(0, S_T - X) - C_0$$
$$= \max(0, S_T - 40) - 4$$
$$= \begin{cases} -4 & \text{if } S_T \leq 40 \\ S_T - 44 & \text{if } S_T > 40 \end{cases}$$

13.3.2.2   Payoff Pattern from a Written Call

In options markets the purchaser of a call buys the call from a counterparty who issues the call. In the jargon of options, the issuer of the call is called the *call writer.* It is worthwhile to spend a few minutes considering the difference between the securities bought by the call purchaser and the call writer:

• The call purchaser buys a security that *gives the right to buy a share of stock on or before date T for price X.* The cost of this privilege is the *call price C,* which is paid at the time of the call purchase. Thus the call purchaser has an initial negative cash flow (the purchase price C); however, his cash flow at date T is always nonnegative: $\max(S_T - X, 0)$.

• The call writer gets C at the date of the call purchase. In return for this price, the writer of the call *agrees to sell a share of the stock for price X on or before date T.* Notice that whereas the call purchaser has an option, the call writer has undertaken an obligation. Furthermore, note that the cash flow pattern of the call writer is opposite to that of the call purchaser: The writer's initial cash flow is positive $(+C)$, and her cash flow at date T is always nonpositive: $-\max(S_T - X, 0)$.

The profit of a call writer is the opposite of that of the call purchaser. For the case of the GP options:

$$\text{Call writer's profit in September} = C_0 - \max(0, S_T - X)$$
$$= 4 - \max(0, S_T - 40)$$
$$= \begin{cases} +4 & \text{if } S_T \leq 40 \\ 44 - S_T & \text{if } S_T > 40 \end{cases}$$

Graphing the profit patterns of the bought call and the written call gives the following:

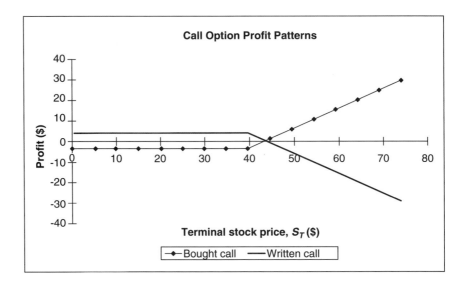

13.3.3   Put Option Profit Patterns

13.3.3.1   Payoff Pattern from a Purchased Put

If in July you bought one GP September 40 put for $2, then in September you will exercise the put only if the market price of GP is lower than $40. If we write the initial (July) put price as P_0, we can write the profit function from the put in September as follows:

$$\text{Put profit in September} = \max(0, X - S_T) - P_0$$
$$= \max(0, 40 - S_T) - 2$$
$$= \begin{cases} 38 - S_T & \text{if } S_T \leq 40 \\ -2 & \text{if } S_T > 40 \end{cases}$$

13.3.3.2   Payoff Pattern from a Written Put

The *put writer* obligates herself to purchase one share of GP stock on or before date T for the put exercise price of X. For putting herself in this invidious position, the writer of the put receives, at the time the put is written, the put price P_0. The payoff pattern from writing the GP September 40 put is therefore

Put writer's profit in September $= P_0 - \max(0, X - S_T)$

$$= 2 - \max(0, 40 - S_T)$$

$$= \begin{cases} -38 + S_T & \text{if } S_T \leq 40 \\ 2 & \text{if } S_T > 40 \end{cases}$$

Graphing the profit patterns of the bought and the written put gives the following:

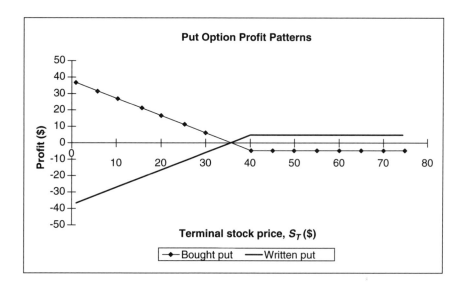

13.4   Option Strategies: Payoffs from Portfolios of Options and Stocks

There is some interest in graphing the combined profit pattern from a portfolio of options and stocks. These patterns give an indication of how options can be used to *change the payoff patterns* of "standard" securities such as stocks and bonds. Here are a few examples.

13.4.1   The Protective Put

Consider the following combination:

- One share of stock, purchased for S_0.

- One put, purchased for P with exercise price X.

This option strategy is often called a "protective put" strategy or "portfolio insurance"; in Chapter 17 we return to this topic, exploring it in further detail. The payoff pattern of the protective put is given by

$$\text{Stock profit} + \text{Put profit} = S_T - S_0 + \max(X - S_T, 0) - P$$

$$= \begin{cases} S_T - S_0 + X - S_T - P & \text{if } S_T \leq X \\ S_T - S_0 - P & \text{if } S_T \geq X \end{cases}$$

$$= \begin{cases} X - S_0 - P & \text{if } S_T \leq X \\ S_T - S_0 - P & \text{if } S_T \geq X \end{cases}$$

When applied to the GP example (i.e., buying a share at \$40 and a put with $X = \$40$ for \$2) this formula gives the following graph:

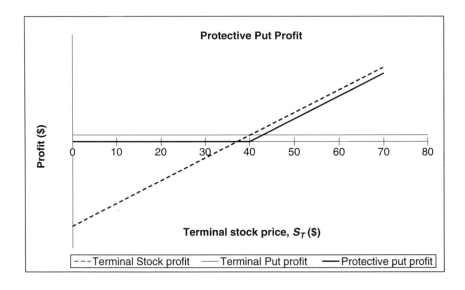

Protective Put Profit

Profit (\$)

Terminal stock price, S_T (\$)

---Terminal Stock profit   ——Terminal Put profit   ——Protective put profit

This pattern looks very much like the payoff pattern from a call.[8]

13.4.2   Spreads

Another combination involves buying and writing calls with different exercise prices. When the bought call has a low exercise price and the written call has a

---

8.   In section 13.5 we prove and illustrate the *put-call parity theorem*. It follows from this theorem that a call must be priced at a price C such that $C = P + S_0 - Xe^{-rT}$. Thus, when calls are correctly priced according to this theorem, the payoff from a put + stock combination is the same as that from a call + bond combination.

higher exercise price, the combination is called a *bull spread.* As an example, suppose you bought a call (for $4) with an exercise price of $40 and wrote a call (for $2) with an exercise price of $50. This bull spread gives a profit of

$$\max (S_T - 40, 0) - 4 - [\max (S_T - 50, 0) - 2] =$$

$$\begin{cases} -4 + 2 & \text{if } S_T \leq 40 \\ S_T - 40 - 4 + 2 = S_T - 42 & \text{if } 40 \leq S_T \leq 50 \\ S_T - 40 - 4 - (S_T - 50 - 2) = 8 & \text{if } S_T \geq 50 \end{cases}$$

The following Excel graph shows each of the two calls and the resulting spread profit:

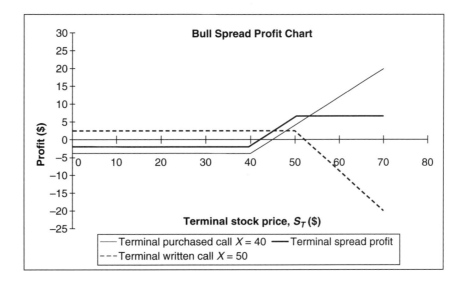

13.5   Option Arbitrage Propositions

In succeeding chapters we price options given specific assumptions about the probability distribution of the underlying asset (usually the stock) on which the option is written. However, there is much that can be learned about the pricing of options without making these specific probability assumptions. In this section we consider a number of these *arbitrage restrictions* on option pricing. Our list is by no means exhaustive, and we have concentrated on those propositions which provide insight into the pricing of options or which will be used in later sections.

Throughout we assume that there is a single risk-free interest rate that prices bonds; we also assume that this risk-free rate is continuously compounded, so that the present value of a riskless security that pays off X at time T is given by $e^{-rT}X$.

PROPOSITION 1   Consider a call option written on a stock that pays no dividends before the option's expiration date T. Then the lower bound on a call option price is given by

$$C \geq \max (S_0 - Xe^{-rT}, 0)$$

Comment   Before proving this proposition, it will be helpful to consider its meaning: Suppose that the riskless interest rate is 10 percent, and suppose we have a American call option with maturity $T = 1/2$ (i.e., the expiration date of the option is one-half year from today) with $X = 80$ written on a stock whose current stock price $S_0 = 83$. A naive approach to determining a lower bound on this option's price would be to state that it is worth at least $3, since it could be exercised immediately with a profit of $3. Proposition 1 shows that the option's value is *at least* $83 - e^{-0.10*0.5}80 = 6.90$. Furthermore, a careful examination of the following proof will show that this fact *does not* depend on the option's being an American option—it is also true for a European option.

	A	B	C	D	E
1	**Proposition 1–Higher Lower Bounds for Call Prices**				
2					
3	Current stock price, S_0	83			
4	Option time to maturity, T	0.5			
5	Option exercise price, X	80			
6	Interest rate, r	10%			
7					
8	Naive minimum option price, Max(S_0-X,0)		3	<-- =MAX(B3-B5,0)	
9	Proposition 1 lower bound on option price, Max(S_0 - Exp(-rT)X,0)		6.902	<-- =MAX(B3-EXP(-B6*B4)*B5,0)	

Proof   Standard arbitrage proofs are built on the consideration of the cash flows from a particular strategy. In this case the strategy is the following:

At Time 0 (Today)

- Buy one share of the stock.
- Borrow the present value (PV) of the option exercise price X.
- Write a call on the option.

At Time T

- Exercise the option if it is profitable to do so.
- Repay the borrowed funds.

This strategy produces the following cash-flow table:

Today		At Time T	
Action	Cash Flow	$S_T < X$	$S_T \geq X$
Buy stock	$-S_0$	$+S_T$	$+S_T$
Borrow PV of X	$+Xe^{-rT}$	$-X$	$-X$
Write call	$+C$	0	$-(S_T - X)$
Total	$-S_0 + Xe^{-rT} + C$	$S_T - X \leq 0$	0

Note that at time T the cash flow resulting from this option is either negative (if the call is not exercised) or zero (when $S_T \geq X$). Now a financial asset (in this case, the combination of purchasing a stock, borrowing X, and writing a call) that has only nonpositive payoffs in the future must have a positive initial cash flow; therefore,

$$C - S_0 + Xe^{-rT} > 0 \qquad \text{or} \qquad C > S_0 - Xe^{-rT}$$

To finish the proof, we note that in no case can the value of a call be less than zero. Thus we have $C \geq \max(S_0 - Xe^{-rT}, 0)$, which proves the proposition.

Proposition 1 has an immediate and very interesting consequence: In many cases the early-exercise feature of an American call option is worthless; therefore, an American call option can be valued as if it were a European call. The precise conditions are the following:

PROPOSITION 2   Consider an American call option written on a stock that will not pay any dividends before the option's expiration date T. Then it is never optimal to exercise the option before its maturity.

Proof   Suppose the holder of the option is considering exercising it early, at some date $t < T$. The only reason to consider such early exercise is that $S_t - X > 0$, where S_t is the price of the underlying stock at time t. However, by Proposition 1 the market value of the option at time t is at least $S_t - Xe^{-r(T-t)}$, where r is the risk-free rate of interest. Since $S_t - Xe^{-r(T-t)} > S_t - X$, it follows that the option's holder is better off selling the option in the market than exercising it.

Proposition 2 means that many American call options can be priced as if they were European calls. Note that this statement is not true for American puts, even if the underlying stock pays no dividends (we give an example in Chapter 16).

PROPOSITION 3 (PUT BOUNDS)   The lower bound on the value of a put option is

$$P \geq \max (0, Xe^{-rT} - S_0)$$

Proof The proof of this proposition has the same form as the proof of the previous theorem. We set up a table of strategies:

Today		At Time T	
Action	Cash Flow	$S_T < X$	$S_T \geq X$
Short stock	$+S_0$	$-S_T$	$-S_T$
Lend PV of X	$+Xe^{-rT}$	$+X$	$+X$
Write put	$+P$	$-(X - S_T)$	0
Total	$P + S_0 - Xe^{rT}$	0	$X - S_T \leq 0$

Since the strategy has only negative or zero payoffs in the future, it must have a positive cash flow today, so that we can conclude that

$$P - Xe^{-rT} + S_0 \geq 0$$

Combined with the fact that in no case can a put value be negative, this proves the proposition.

PROPOSITION 4 (PUT-CALL PARITY)   Let C be the price of a European call with exercise price X written on a stock whose current price is S_0. Let P be the price of a European put on the same stock with the same exercise price X. Suppose both put and call have exercise date T, and suppose that the continuously compounded interest rate is r. Then,

$$C + Xe^{-rT} = P + S_0$$

Proof The proof is similar in style to that of the two previous propositions. We consider a combination of the four assets (the put, the call, the stock, and a bond), and show that the pricing relation must hold.

Today		At Time T	
Action	Cash Flow	$S_T < X$	$S_T \geq X$
Buy a call	$-C$	0	$+S_T - X$
Buy a bond with payoff X at time T	$-Xe^{-rT}$	X	X
Write a put	$+P$	$-(X - S_T)$	0
Short one share of the stock	$+S_0$	$-S_T$	$-S_T$
Total	$C - Xe^{-rT} + P + S_0$	0	0

Since the strategy has future payoffs that are zero no matter what happens to the price of the stock, it follows that the initial cash flow of the strategy must also be zero.[9] Therefore,

$$C + Xe^{-rT} - P - S_0 = 0$$

which proves the proposition.

Put-call parity states that the stock price S_0, the price of a call C with exercise price X and the price of a put P with exercise price X, are simultaneously determined with the interest rate r. Following is an illustration that uses the call price C, the option exercise price X, the current stock price S_0, and the interest rate r to compute the price of a put with exercise price X and time to maturity T:

	A	B	C	D	E
1	**Put-Call Parity**				
2					
3	Current stock price, S_0	55			
4	Option time to maturity, T	0.5			
5	Option exercise price, X	60			
6	Interest rate, r	10%			
7	Call price, C	3			
8	Put price	5.0738	<-- =B7+B5*EXP(-B6*B4)-B3		
9					
10	This spreadsheet uses put-call parity to derive the put price				
11	from the call price C, the interest rate r, the time to maturity				
12	T, and the exercise price X.				

---

9. This is a very fundamental fact of finance: If a financial strategy has future payoffs that are identically zero, then its current cost must also be zero. Likewise, if a financial strategy has future payoffs that are nonnegative, then its time-zero payoff must be negative (that is, it must cost something).

PROPOSITION 5 (CALL OPTION PRICE CONVEXITY)   Consider three European calls, all written on the same non-dividend-paying stock and with the same expiration date T. We suppose that the exercise prices on the calls are X_1, X_2, and X_3, and denote the associated call prices by C_1, C_2, and C_3. We further assume that $X_2 = (X_1 + X_3)/2$. Then

$$C_2 < \frac{C_1 + C_3}{2}$$

It follows that the call option price is a convex function of the exercise price.

Proof   To prove the proposition, we consider the following strategy:

At Time 0		At Time T			
Action	Cash Flow	$S_T < X_1$	$X_1 \leq S_T < X_2$	$X_2 \leq S_T < X_3$	$X_3 \leq S_T$
Buy call with exercise price X_1	$-C_1$	0	$S_T - X_1$	$S_T - X_1$	$S_T - X_1$
Buy call with exercise price X_3	$-C_3$	0	0	0	$S_T - X_3$
Write two calls with exercise price X_2	$+2C_2$	0	0	$-2(S_T - X_2)$	$-2(S_T - X_2)$
Total	$2C_2 - C_1 - C_3$	0	$S_T - X_1 \geq 0$	$2X_2 - X_1 - S_T$ $= X_3 - S_T > 0$	0

Since the payoffs in the future are all nonnegative (with a positive probability of being positive), it follows that the initial cash flow from the position must be negative:

$$2C_2 - C_1 - C_3 < 0 \Rightarrow C_2 < \frac{C_1 + C_3}{2}$$

This proves the proposition. [Note that the assumption that $X_2 = (X_1 + X_3)/2$ is made for convenience and does not affect the generality of the argument.]

Without proof we state a similar proposition for puts:

PROPOSITION 6 (PUT PRICE CONVEXITY)   Consider three European puts, all written on the same non-dividend-paying stock and with the same expiration date

T. We suppose that the exercise prices on the calls are X_1, X_2, and X_3, and denote the associated call prices by P_1, P_2, and P_3. We further assume that $X_2 = (X_1 + X_3)/2$. Then the put price is a convex function of the exercise price:

$$P_2 < \frac{P_1 + P_3}{2}$$

Finally, we state the following proposition:

PROPOSITION 7 (CALL OPTION BOUNDS WITH A KNOWN FUTURE DIVIDEND)   Consider a call with exercise price X and maturity date T. Suppose that at some time $t < T$, the stock will, with certainty, pay a dividend D. Then the lower bound on the call option price is given by

$$C \geq \max (S_0 - De^{-rt} - Xe^{-rT}, 0)$$

Proof   The proof involves only a minor modification of the proof of Proposition 1.

Today		Time T	At Time T	
Action	Cash Flow		$S_T < X$	$S_T \geq X$
Buy stock	$-S_0$	$+D$	$+S_T$	$+S_T$
Borrow the PV of dividend D	$+De^{-rT}$	$-D$		
Borrow PV of X	$+Xe^{-rT}$		$-X$	$-X$
Write call	$+C$		0	$-(S_T - X)$
Total	$-S_0 + De^{-rT}$ $+ Xe^{-rT} + C$	0	$S_T - X \leq 0$	0

This proves the proposition.

In Chapter 16, exercise 7, we apply Proposition 7 to the pricing of index options.

Exercises

1. Look at the prices of the American Express options in the chapter. The February call option with $X = 37.5$ is priced at 6 3/8, whereas the April option with the same exercise price is priced at 6. Can you devise an arbitrage out of these prices? Do you have an explanation for the newspaper quotes?

2. An American call option is written on a stock whose price today is $S = 50$. The exercise price of the call is $X = 45$. If the call price is 2, explain how you would use arbitrage to make an immediate profit.

   If the option is exercisable at time $T = 1$ year and if the interest rate is 10 percent, what is the minimum price of the option? Use Proposition 1.

3. A European call option is written on a stock whose current price $S = 80$. The exercise price is $X = 80$, the interest rate is $r = 8$ percent, and the time to option exercise is $T = 1$. The stock is assumed to pay a dividend of 3 at time $t = 1/2$. Use Proposition 7 to determine the minimum price of the call option.

4. A put with an exercise price of 50 has a price of 6, and a call on the same stock with an exercise price of 60 has a price of 10. Both put and call have the same expiration date. On the same set of axes, draw the "profit" diagram for

   a. One put bought and one call bought.

   b. Two puts bought and one call bought.

   c. Three puts bought and one call bought.

   d. All three lines cross each other for the same value of S_T. Derive this value.

5. Consider the following two calls:

   Both calls are written on shares of ABC Corporation, whose current share price is $100. ABC does not pay any dividends.

   Both calls have one year to maturity.

   One call has $X_1 = 90$ and has price of 30; the second call has $X_2 = 100$ and has price of 20.

   The riskless, continuously compounded interest rate is 10 percent.

   By designing a spread position (i.e., buying one call and writing another), show that the difference between the two call prices is *too large* and that a riskless arbitrage exists.

6. A share of ABC Corporation sells for $95. A call on the share with exercise price $90 sells for $8.

   a. Graph the profit pattern from buying one share and one call on the share.

   b. Graph the profit pattern from buying one share and two calls.

   c. Consider the profit pattern from buying one share and N calls. At which share price do all of the profit lines cross?

7. A European call with a maturity of six months and exercise price $X = 80$ written on a stock with a current price of 85 is selling for $12.00; a European put written on the same stock with the same maturity and with the same exercise price is selling for $5.00. If the annual interest rate (continuously compounded) is 10 percent, construct an arbitrage from this situation.

8.   Prove Proposition 6. Then solve the following problem:

Three puts on shares of XYZ with the same expiration date are selling at the following prices:

Exercise price 40: 6
Exercise price 50: 4
Exercise price 60: 1

Show an arbitrage strategy that allows you to profit from these prices and prove that it works.

9.   The current stock price of ABC Corporation is 50. Prices for six-month calls on ABC are given in the following table:

Call	Price
40	16.5
50	9.5
60	4.5
70	2

Draw a profit diagram of the following strategy: Buy one 40 call, write two 50 calls, buy one 60 call, and write two 70 calls.

10.   Consider the following option strategy, which consists only of calls:

Exercise price	Bought/Written? Number?	Price per call option
20	1 written	45
30	2 bought	33
40	1 written	22
50	1 bought	18
60	2 written	17
70	1 bought	16

a. Draw the profit diagram for this strategy.

b. The prices given include one violation of an arbitrage condition. Identify this violation and explain.

14 The Binomial Option-Pricing Model

14.1 Two-Date Binomial Pricing

Next to the Black-Scholes model (discussed in Chapter 16), the binomial option-pricing model is probably the most widely used option-pricing model. It has many advantages: It is a simple model that is easily programmed and adapted to numerous, and often quite complicated, option-pricing problems. In addition, it gives many insights into option pricing. When extended to many periods, the binomial model becomes one of the most powerful ways of valuing securities like options whose payoffs are contingent on the market prices of other assets.

To illustrate the use of the binomial model, we start with the following very simple example:

- There are two dates: date 0 represents today, and date 1 is one year from now.

- There are two "fundamental" assets: a stock and a bond. There is also a call option written on the stock.

- The stock price today is $50. At date 1 it will either go up by 10 percent or go down by 3 percent.

- The one-period interest rate is 6 percent.

- The call option matures at date 1 and has exercise price $X = \$50$.

Here is a picture from a spreadsheet that embodies this model:

	A	B	C	D	E	F	G	H	I	J	K
1					**TWO-DATE BINOMIAL OPTION PRICING**						
2											
3	Up	10%									
4	Down	-3%									
5											
6	Initial stock price	50									
7	Interest rate	6%									
8	Exercise price	50									
9											
10		**Stock price**					**Bond price**				
11				55	<-- =$B$12*(1+B3)				1.06	<-- =$G$12*(1+$B$7)	
12		50					1				
13				48.5	<-- =$B$12*(1+B4)				1.06	<-- =$G$12*(1+$B$7)	
14											
15		**Call option**									
16				5	<-- =MAX(D11-$B$8,0)						
17		???									
18				0	<-- =MAX(D13-$B$8,0)						

We wish to price the call option. We do so by showing that there is a *combination of the bonds and stocks that exactly replicates the call option's payoffs.* To show this fact, we use some basic linear algebra; suppose we find *A* shares of the stock and *B* bonds such that

$$55A + 1.06B = 5$$
$$48.5A + 1.06B = 0$$

This system of equations solves to give $A = 0.769231$, $B = -35.1959$. Thus purchasing 0.77 of a share of the stock and borrowing \$35.20 at 6 percent for one period will give payoffs of \$5 if the stock price goes up and \$0 if the stock price goes down—the payoffs of the call option. It follows that the price of the option must be equal to the cost of replicating its payoffs; that is,

Call option price $= 0.7692 * \$50 - \$35.1959 = \$3.2656$

This logic is called *pricing by arbitrage:* If two assets or sets of assets (in our case—the call option and the portfolio of 0.77 of the stock and $-\$35.20$ of the bonds) have the same payoffs, they must have the same market price.

	A	B	C	D	E	F	G	H
21		A	0.7692	<-- =(D16-D18)/(B12*(B3-B4))				
22								
23		B	-35.1959	<-- =((1+B3)*D18-(1+B4)*D16)/((1+B7)*(B3-B4))				
24								
25	Call price		3.2656	<-- =C21*B6+C23				

In succeeding sections we show that this simple arbitrage argument can be extended to multiple periods. But in the meantime we confine ourselves in the next section to generalizing the logic.

14.2   State Prices

There is actually a simpler (and more general) way to solve this problem: Viewed from today, there are only two possibilities for tomorrow: Either the stock price goes up, or it goes down. Think about the market determining a price q_u for \$1 in the "up" state of the world and a price q_d for \$1 in the "down" state of the world. Then both the bond and the stock have to be priced using these *state prices:*

$$q_u * S * (1 + u) + q_d * S * (1 + d) = S \Rightarrow q_u(1 + u) + q_d(1 + d) = 1$$
$$q_u * (1 + i) + q_d * (1 + i) = 1$$

These solve to give

$$q_u = \frac{i - d}{(1 + i)(u - d)}$$

$$q_d = \frac{u - i}{(1 + i)(u - d)}$$

We can now use these state prices to price the call option:

$$C = q_u \max [S(1 + u) - X, 0] + q_d \max [S(1 + d) - X, 0]$$

If the stock price can move up in one period by a factor u and down by a factor d, and if the one-period interest rate is i, then any other asset will be priced by discounting its payoff in the "up" state by q_u and by discounting its payoff in the "down" state by q_d.

In our case these state prices are given by

	A	B	C	D	E	F	G	H	I
27						Check: confirm that state prices			
28	**State prices**					actually price the stock and the bond			
29	q$_u$	0.6531	<-- =(B7-B4)/((1+B7)*(B3-B4))			1.06	<-- =1/(B29+B30)		
30	q$_d$	0.2903	<-- =(B3-B7)/((1+B7)*(B3-B4))			50	<-- =B29*D11+B30*D13		

Note that in cells F29 and F30 we check that the state prices indeed give back the interest rate and the stock price. Using these state prices to price the call of the previous section (with $S = 50, X = 50, u = 0.10, d = -0.03, i = 0.06$) gives

$$C = q_u \max [S(1 + u) - X, 0] + q_d \max [S(1 + d) - X, 0]$$
$$= 0.6531 * 5 + 0.2903 * 0 = 3.27$$

which is, of course, the result we got previously. Note that we can also use the state prices to price a put option; given the same parameters, we get

$$P = q_u \max [X - S(1 + u), 0] + q_d \max [X - S(1 + d), 0]$$
$$= 0.6531 * \max (50 - 55, 0) + 0.2903 * \max (50 - 48.5, 0) = 0.4354$$

We also note that—as expected—the put-call parity theorem holds for this particular put and call:

$$P + S = 0.4354 + 50 = C + \frac{X}{1+i} = 3.27 + \frac{50}{1.06}$$

Putting this all together gives:

	A	B	C	D	E	F	G	H	I	J
1	**TWO-DATE BINOMIAL OPTION PRICING WITH STATE PRICES**									
2										
3	Up	10%		**State prices**						
4	Down	-3%		q_u	0.6531	<-- =(B7-B4)/((1+B7)*(B3-B4))				
5				q_d	0.2903	<-- =(B3-B7)/((1+B7)*(B3-B4))				
6	Initial stock price	50								
7	Interest rate	6%								
8	Exercise price	50								
9										
10	**Call payoff**									
11	In up state	5	<-- =MAX($B$6*(1+B3)-$B$8,0)							
12	In down state	0	<-- =MAX($B$6*(1+B4)-$B$8,0)							
13	Call price	3.2656	<-- =$E$4*B11+$E$5*B12							
14										
15	**Put payoff**									
16	In up state	0	<-- =MAX($B$8-(1+B3)*$B$6,0)							
17	In down state	1.5	<-- =MAX($B$8-(1+B4)*$B$6,0)							
18	Put price	0.4354	<-- =$E$4*B16+$E$5*B17							
19										
20	**Put-call parity**						**Note about PV(X) in put-call parity:**			
21	Stock + put	50.4354	<-- =B6+B18				In the continuous-time framework (the standard			
22	Call + PV(X)	50.4354	<-- =B13+B8/(1+B7)				Black-Scholes framework), PV(X) = X*Exp(-i*T).			
23							Because the framework here is discrete time,			
24							PV(X) also has to be discrete-time: PV(X) =			
25							X/(1+i) .			
26										

14.3   Multiperiod Binomial Model

The binomial model can easily be extended to more than two periods. Consider, for example, a three-period binomial model that has the following characteristics:

• In each period the stock price goes up by 10 percent or down by 3 percent from what it was in the previous period.

• In each period the interest rate is 6 percent.

Recall that these movements of the stock price and this interest rate give state prices

$$q_u = \frac{i - d}{(1 + i)(u - d)} = 0.6531$$

$$q_d = \frac{u - i}{(1 + i)(u - d)} = 0.2903$$

We can now use these state prices to price a call option written on the stock after two periods. As before, we assume that the stock price is $50 initially and that the call exercise price X is 50 after two periods. These assumptions give the following picture:

Stock price

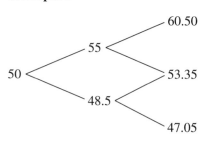

Bond price

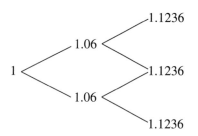

Call option

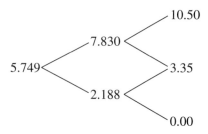

How was the call option price of 5.749 determined? To make this determination, we go backward, starting at period 2:

At date 2: At the end of two periods the stock price is either $60.50 (corresponding to two "up" movements in the price), $53.35 (one "up" and one "down" movement), or $47.05 (two "down" movements in the price). Given the exercise price of $X = 50$, therefore, the terminal option payoff in period 2 is either $10.50, $3.35, or $0.

At date 1: At date 1, there are two possibilities: The first is that we have reached an "up" state, in which case the current stock price is $55 and the option will pay off $10.50 or $3.35 in the next period:

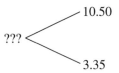

We use the state prices of $q_u = 0.6531$, $q_d = 0.2903$ to price the option at this state:

Option price at "up" state period 1 = $0.6531 * 10.50 + 0.2903 * 3.35 = 7.830$

The second possibility is that we are in the "down" state of period 1:

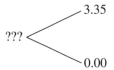

Using the same state prices (which, after all, depend only on the "up" and "down" movements of the stock price and the interest rate), we get

Option price at "down" state period 1 = $0.6531 * 3.35 + 0.2903 * 0 = 2.188$

At date 0: Going backwards in this way, we've now filled in the following picture:

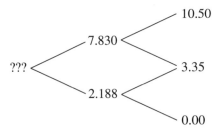

Thus at period 0 the buyer of an option owns a security that will be worth $7.83 if the underlying stock has an "up" movement in its return and that will be worth $2.19 if the stock has a "down" movement in its return. We can again use the state prices to value this option:

Option price at period 0 = $0.6531 * 7.830 + 0.2903 * 2.188 = 5.749$

	A	B	C	D	E	F	G	H	I	J	K
1		THREE DATE BINOMIAL OPTION PRICING									
2											
3	Up	10%									
4	Down	-3%		state prices							
5				q_u	0.6531						
6	Initial stock price	50		q_d	0.2903						
7	Interest rate	6%									
8	Exercise price	50									
9											
10											
11	Stock price						Bond price				
12					60.50						1.1236
13			55						1.06		
14		50			53.35		1				1.1236
15			48.5						1.06		
16					47.05						1.1236
17											
18											
19	Call option price										
20			=q_u*E21+q_d*E23								
21					10.50						
22			7.830								
23		5.749			3.35						
24			2.188								
25					0.00						
26	=q_u*C22+q_d*C24		=q_u*E23+q_d*E25								
27											
28											

14.3.1   Extending the Binomial Pricing Model to Many Periods

It is clear that the logic of the example can be extended to many periods. Here's another graphic showing a five-date model using the same "up" and "down" parameters as before:

Stock price

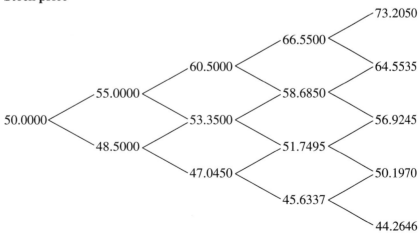

Bond price

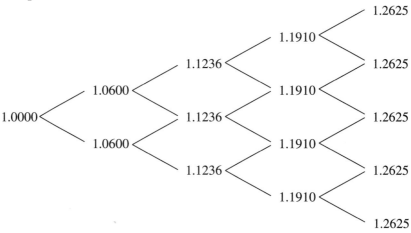

Call price

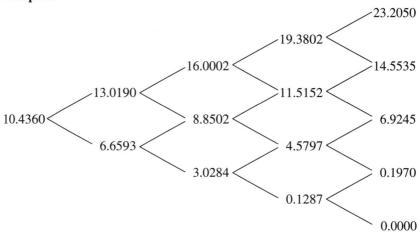

14.3.2 Do You Really Have to Price Everything Backward?

The answer is no. There's no necessity to price the call-price payoffs "back-ward" at each node back from the terminal date, *as long as the call is European.* It is enough to price each of the terminal payoffs by the state prices, providing you count properly the number of paths to each terminal node. Here's an illustration, using the same example.

	B	C	D	E	F	G	H	I	J
43				q_u^(# up steps)*q_d^(# down steps)					
44									
45	Terminal						Value =		
46	stock	Terminal	Number	Number			payoff *		
47	price	payoff	of "up"	of "down"	State	Number	price *		
48			steps	steps	price	of paths	# paths		
49	73.2050	23.2050	4	0	0.1820	1	4.2224	<-- =G49*F49*I34	
50									
51	64.5535	14.5535	3	1	0.0809	4	4.7078	<-- =G51*F51*I36	
52									
53	56.9245	6.9245	2	2	0.0359	6	1.4933	<-- =G53*F53*I38	
54									
55	50.1970	0.1970	1	3	0.0160	4	0.0126	<-- =G55*F55*I40	
56									
57	44.2646	0.0000	0	4	0.0071	1	0.0000	<-- =G57*F57*I42	
58									
59					Option value		10.4360	<-- =SUM(H49:H57)	

An explanation for the preceding spreadsheet follows. For each terminal option payoff, we consider these questions:

How was this terminal payoff reached? How many "up" steps did the stock make, and how many "down" steps did it make?		Example: The terminal payoff of 14.5535 arises when the stock price is 64.5535. This result occurs when the stock price goes up three times and down once.
What is the price per dollar of the payoff in the particular state?	State price = $q_u^{\text{# up steps}} q_d^{\text{# down steps}}$	Example: The value at time 0 of the terminal payoff considered above is $0.6531^4 * 0.2903^1 = 0.0809$
How many paths are there with the same terminal payoff?	The answer is given by the binomial coefficient $\binom{\text{Number of periods}}{\text{Number of "up" steps}}$	Example: There are $\binom{4}{3} = 4$ paths that give the terminal stock price of 64.5535. The Excel function **Combin(4,3)** gives this binomial coefficient.
What is the value at time 0 of a particular terminal payoff?	The answer is the product of the payoff times the price times the number of paths.	Example: $14.5535 * 0.0809 * 4 = 4.7078$
What is the value at time 0 of the option?	The sum of the values of each payoff.	Total value: 10.4360. This is the multiperiod call option value in the five-date (four-period) binomial model.

It follows that the price of a European call option in a binomial model with n periods is given by

$$\text{Call price} = \sum_{i=0}^{n} \binom{n}{i} q_u^i q_d^{n-i} \max\left[S_0(1+u)^i(1+d)^{n-i} - X, 0\right]$$

$$\text{Put price} = \sum_{i=0}^{n} \binom{n}{i} q_u^i q_d^{n-i} \max\left[X - S_0(1+u)^i(1+d)^{n-1}, 0\right]$$

The following section applies this method to the valuation of American options. In section 14.5 we implement these formulas in VBA.

14.4   Pricing American Options Using the Binomial Pricing Model

We can use the binomial pricing model to calculate the prices of American options as well as European options.[1] We reconsider the same basic model, in which "up" is 10 percent, "down" is 3 percent, $S = 50$, $X = 50$, and $i = 6$ percent. We examine the three-date version of the model. The payoff patterns for the stock and the bond have been given, and it remains only to consider the payoff patterns for a put option with $X = 50$. We reference the states of the world by using the following labels:

State labels

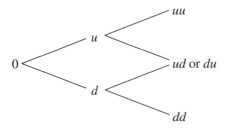

Here are the values of the stock and the date-3 put payoffs:

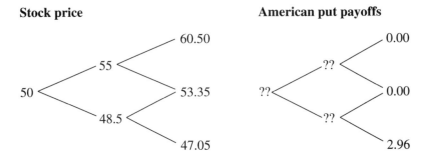

---

1.   Recall from Chapter 13 that an American call option on a non-dividend-paying stock has the same value as a European call option. In this section we consider *put* options, leaving the (less interesting!) call options as an exercise. In Chapter 19 we consider the valuation of American options in more detail.

At date 2, the holder of an American put can choose whether to hold the put or to exercise it. We now have the following value function:

$$
\begin{aligned}
\text{Put value} \\
\text{at date} & = \max \left\{ \begin{array}{l} \text{Value of put if exercised,} \\ q_u * \text{Put payoff in state } uu + q_d * \text{Put payoff in state } ud \end{array} \right\} \\
\text{2, state } u &
\end{aligned}
$$

$$
= \max \left\{ \begin{array}{l} \max (X - S_u), \\ q_u * \text{Put payoff in state } uu + q_d * \text{Put payoff in state } ud \end{array} \right\}
$$

A similar function holds for the put value in state d at date 2. The resulting tree now looks like this:

American put payoffs

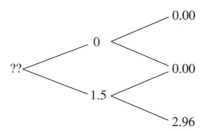

Here's the explanation: In state u, when the stock price is $55, it is not worth-while to exercise the put; since the future put payoffs from state u are zero, the put is worthless. In state d, on the other hand, the holder of the put gets max $(50 - 48.5, 0) = 1.5$ if he exercises the put; however, if he holds the put without exercise, its market value is the state-dependent value of the future payoffs:

$$
q_u * 0 + q_d * 2.96 = 0.6531 * 0 + 0.2903 * 2.96 = 0.8578
$$

It is clearly preferable to exercise the put in this state rather than hold onto it.
At date 0, a similar value function recurs:

$$
\begin{aligned}
\text{Put value} \\
\text{at date 0} & = \max \left\{ \begin{array}{l} \text{Value of put if exercised,} \\ q_u * \text{Put payoff in state } u + q_d * \text{Put payoff in state } d \end{array} \right\}
\end{aligned}
$$

$$
= \max \left\{ \begin{array}{l} \max (X - S), \\ q_u * \text{Put payoff in state } u + q_d * \text{Put payoff in state } d \end{array} \right\}
$$

The value tree for the American put is as follows:

American put option

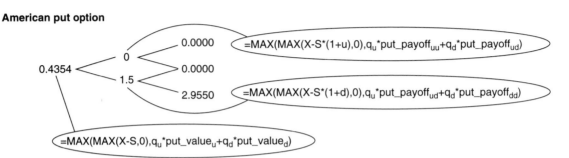

This should be compared to the value for a European put option:

European put option

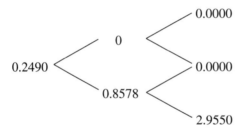

Thus we have used the binomial pricing model to value both an American and a European put option. In the process, we have shown that the American put may be worth more than a European put.

14.5   Programming the Binomial Option-Pricing Model in VBA

The pricing procedure used in the preceding examples is a bit cumbersome, but it can easily be programmed using Excel's Visual Basic for Applications programming language. In the binomial model the price can move *up* or *down* in any time period. If q_u is the state price associated with an up move and if q_d is the state price associated with a down move, then the binomial call option price is

$$\text{Call price} = \sum_{i=0}^{n} \binom{n}{i} q_u^i \, q_d^{n-i} \max [S_0(1 + u)^i(1 + d)^{n-i} - X, 0]$$

where u is an up move in the stock price, d is a down move, and $\binom{n}{i}$ is the binomial coefficient (the number of up moves in n total moves):

$$\binom{n}{i} = \frac{n!}{i!\,(n-i)!}$$

We use Excel's **Combin(n, i)** to give values for the binomial coefficients.

Whenever we consider a finite approximation to the option-pricing formulas, we have to use an approximation to the up and the down movements. We translate the interest rate and the stock's volatility σ binomial coefficients in the following manner:

$$\Delta t = 1/n \qquad R = e^{r\Delta t}$$

$$1 + \text{Up} = e^{\sigma \Delta t} \qquad q_u = \frac{R - \text{Down}}{R * (\text{Up} - \text{Down})}$$

$$1 + \text{Down} = e^{-\sigma \Delta t} \qquad q_d = \frac{1}{R} - q_u$$

This approximation guarantees that as $\Delta t \rightarrow 0$ (i.e., as $n \rightarrow \infty$), the resulting distribution of the stock returns approaches the lognormal distribution.[2]

Given this approximation, we are ready to define the VBA functions for the European binomial option-pricing formulas. We use this function in defining the VBA functions for the binomial call-pricing and put-pricing formulas:

```
Function EurCall(S, X, T, rf, sigma, n)
'VBA is not case sensitive, so we use "rf" instead of
'"r" and below we use "r" instead of "R"
'Note that we use "up" and "down" instead of "1 + up"
'and "1 + down"
    delta_t = T / n
    up = Exp(sigma * Sqr(delta_t))
    down = Exp(-sigma * Sqr(delta_t))
    r = Exp(rf * delta_t)
    q_up = (r - down) / (r * (up - down))
    q_down = 1 / r - q_up
    EurCall = 0
```

---

2. This is not the only approximation that converges to a lognormal price process: see Omberg (1987); Hull (2000); and Benninga, Steinmetz, and Stroughair (1993).

```
    For Index = 0 To n
        EurCall = EurCall + Application.Combin(n, Index) *_
            q_up ^ Index * q_down ^ (n - Index) * _
            Application.Max(S * up ^ Index * down ^ _
            (n - Index) - X, 0)
    Next Index
End Function

Function (EurPut(S, X, T, rf, Sigma, n)
    delta_t = T / n
    up = Exp(sigma * Sqr(delta_t))
    r = Exp(rf * delta_t)
    q_up = (r - down) / (r * (up - down))
    q_down = 1 / r - q_up
    EurPut = 0
    For Index = 0 To n
        EurPut = EurPut + Application.Combin(n, Index) *_
            q_up ^ Index * q_down ^ (n - Index) *_
            Application.Max(X - up ^ Index * down ^_
            (n - Index) * S, 0)
    Next Index
End Function
```

Note that while we defined the European binomial put formula directly, we could have used the put-call parity theorem.

14.6 American Put Pricing

As discussed in Chapter 13, a well-known theorem states that the price of an American call on a non-dividend-paying stock is the same as that of a European option. The pricing of American put, however, can be different. The following VBA function uses a binomial option-pricing model like the one from section 14.4 to price American puts.

```
Function AmericanPut(S, X, T, rf, sigma, n)
'VBA is not case sensitive, so we use "rf" instead of
'"r" and below we use "r" instead of "R"
'Note that we use "up" and "down" instead of "1 + up"
'and "1 + down"
    delta_t = T / n
    up = Exp(sigma * Sqr(delta_t))
    down = Exp(-sigma * Sqr(delta_t))
    r = Exp(rf * delta_t)
    q_up = (r - down) / (r * (up - down))
    q_down = 1 / r - q_up
    DimOptionReturnEnd() As Double
    DimOptionReturnMiddle() As Double
    ReDim OptionReturnEnd(n + 1)

    For State = 0 to n
        OptionReturnEnd(State) = Application.Max(X - _
            S * up ^ State * down ^ (n - State), 0)

    Next State

    For Index = n - 1 To 0 Step -1
        ReDim OptionReturnMiddle(Index)
        For State = 0 To Index
            OptionReturnMiddle(State) = _
                Application.Max(X - S * up ^ State *_
                down ^ (Index - State), q_down *_
                OptionReturnEnd(State) + q_up *_
                OptionReturnEnd(State + 1))
        Next State
        ReDim OptionReturnEnd(Index)
        For State = 0 To Index
            OptionReturnEnd(State) = _
                OptionReturnMiddle(State)
        Next State
    Next Index
    AmericanPut = OptionReturnMiddle(0)
End Function
```

In this function we use two arrays, called **OptionReturnEnd** and **Option-ReturnMiddle,** to store the values, at each date *t* of the option values at *t* + 1 and *t,* respectively. Note also that since VBA does not have a function that calculates the maximum, we use **Application.Max** to invoke Excel's **Max** function.

We can also define a similar function for American calls, although this will only confirm what we already knew—that the values of an American and a European call on a non-dividend-paying stock are the same:

```
Function AmericanCall(S, X, T, rf, sigma, n)
'VBA is not case sensitive, so we use "rf" instead of
'"r" and below we use "r" instead of "R"
'Note that we use "up" and "down" instead of "1 + up"
'and "1 + down"
    delta_t = T / n
    up = Exp(sigma * Sqr(delta t))
    down = Exp(-sigma * Sqr(delta_t))
    r = Exp(rf * delta_t)
    q_up = (r - down) / (r * (up - down))
    q_down = 1 / r - q_up
    DimOptionReturnEnd() As Double
    DimOptionReturnMiddle() As Double
    ReDim OptionReturnEnd(n + 1)

    For State = 0 to n
        OptionReturnEnd(State) = Application.Max(S * _
            up ^ State * down ^ (n - State) - X, 0)

    Next State

    For Index = n - 1 To 0 Step -1
        ReDim OptionReturnMiddle(Index)
        For State = 0 To Index
            OptionReturnMiddle(State) = _
                Application.Max(S * up ^ State * down ^_
                (Index - State) - X, q_down *_
                OptionReturnEnd(State) + q_up *_
                OptionReturnEnd(State + 1))
        Next State
        ReDim OptionReturnEnd(Index)
        For State = 0 To Index
            OptionReturnEnd(State) = _
                OptionReturnMiddle(State)
        Next State
    Next Index
    AmericanCall = OptionReturnMiddle(0)
End Function
```

Here's the way this program looks when implemented in a spreadsheet. Note that the spreadsheet also shows that put-call parity does not hold for American calls.

	A	B	C	D	E	F
1	**AMERICAN BINOMIAL OPTION PRICING IN EXCEL**					
2						
3	S	60	Current stock price			
4	X	60	Option exercise price			
5	T	0.5000	Time to option exercise (in years)			
6	r	8%	Annual interest rate			
7	Sigma	30%	Riskiness of stock			
8	n	20	Number of subdivisions of T			
9						
10	American put price	4.0905	<-- =AmericanPut(S,X,T,interest,sigma,n)			
11	American call price	6.1701	<-- =AmericanCall(S,X,T,interest,sigma,n)			
12						
13	European put price	3.8175	<-- =EurPut(S, X,T,interest,sigma,n)			
14	European call price	6.1701	<-- =EurCall(S, X,T,interest,sigma,n)			
15						
16	**Put-call parity?**					
17	Delta t, Δt	0.0250	<-- =B5/B8			
18	$R = e^{r\Delta t}$	1.0020	<-- =EXP(B6*B17)			
19						
20	American put + Stock	64.0905	<-- =B10+B3			
21	American call + Bond	63.8175	<-- American call price+X/R^n			
22						
23	European put + Stock	63.8175	<-- =B13+B3			
24	European call + Bond	63.8175	<-- European call price+X/R^n			

The spreadsheet illustrates a number of things:

• The European put price is *lower* (in general) than the corresponding American put price. This difference exists because, for a put, the possibility of early exercise is valuable.

• Because an American call written on a non-dividend-paying stock will never be exercised early, the European and American call prices are the same.

• Put-call parity does not hold for American options, whereas it holds (of course) for European options.[3]

---

3. For bounds on the difference between American puts and calls see Jarrow and Rudd (1983).

14.7 The Convergence of the Binomial Option-Pricing Model to the Black-Scholes Price[4]

In section 14.5 we defined the function **EurCall(S, X, T, r, σ, n),** which uses a binomial model to value a call option; in this function n is the number of subdivisions of the time period T. In Chapter 16 we describe the Black-Scholes option-pricing model, which is the most widely used model for option pricing. At this juncture, we note that the binomial model converges to the Black-Scholes pricing formula for large n.

To demonstrate this point, we define the following spreadsheet:

	A	B	C	D	E	F	G	H	I	J
1	**CONVERGENCE OF BINOMIAL TO BLACK-SCHOLES**									
2										
3	S	60	Current stock price							
4	X	50	Option exercise price							
5	T	0.5000	Time to option exercise (in years)							
6	r	8%	Annual interest rate							
7	Sigma	30%	Riskiness of stock							
8	n	20	Number of subdivisions of T							
9										
10	European binomial call price	12.8055	<-- =EurCall(S, X,interest,sigma,T,n)							
11	European binomial put price	0.8450	<-- =EurCall(S, X,interest,sigma,T,n)							
12										
13	Black-Scholes call price	12.8226	<-- =BSCall(S, X,interest,sigma,T)							
14	Black-Scholes put price	0.8621	<-- =BSPut(S, X,interest,sigma,T)							
15										
16			Data table: As n gets large,							
17			binomial price -> Black-Scholes							
18										
19				Binomial call	Black-Scholes					
20						<-- The data table header in cell C20 is hidden				
21			10	12.8593	12.8226					
22			50	12.8108	12.8226					
23			75	12.8238	12.8226					
24			100	12.8255	12.8226					
25			125	12.8251	12.8226					
26			150	12.8240	12.8226					
27			175	12.8226	12.8226					
28			200	12.8205	12.8226					
29			225	12.8204	12.8226					
30		n -->	250	12.8230	12.8226					
31			275	12.8243	12.8226					
32			300	12.8243	12.8226					
33			325	12.8232	12.8226					
34			350	12.8210	12.8226					
35			375	12.8226	12.8226					
36			400	12.8238	12.8226					
37			425	12.8236	12.8226					
38			450	12.8221	12.8226					
39			475	12.8223	12.8226					
40			500	12.8236	12.8226					

---

4. We're getting a bit ahead of ourselves here; since the Black-Scholes option pricing formula is discussed in Chapter 16 you may want to skip this section and come back to it later.

The function **BSCall(S, X, interest, sigma, T)** is a VBA function that gives the Black-Scholes call price. This function is further described in Chapter 16.

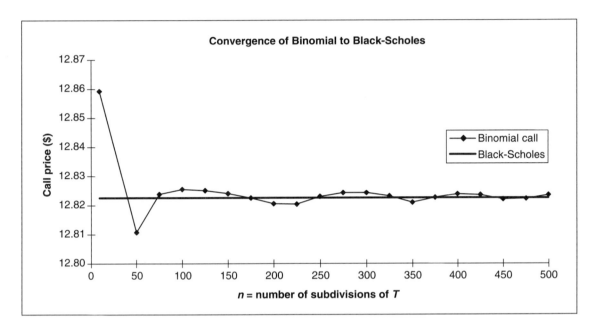

In the exercises for this chapter you are asked to show that the binomial put-pricing formula also converges to the Black-Scholes formula for a put.

14.8   Using the Binomial Model to Price Nonstandard Options: An Example

The binomial model can also be used to price nonstandard options. Consider the following example: You hold an option to buy a share of a company. The option allows for early exercise, but the exercise price varies with the time at which you choose to exercise. For the case we consider, the option has the following conditions:

• There are n possible exercise dates *only* (that is, the option is exercisable only on these dates).

• Exercise at date t precludes exercise at all dates $s > t$. However, if you don't exercise at date s, you may still exercise at date $t > s$.

- The exercise price at date t is X_t. In other words, the exercise price can vary with time.

We want to value this option using a binomial framework. To do so, we recognize that basically this is just an American option with three separate exercise prices. Here's how we set this problem up in a spreadsheet, using the logic of the early-exercise problem described in section 14.4:

	A	B	C	D	E	F	G	H	I	J	K	L
1		TIME-DEPENDENT EXERCISE PRICES										
2												
3	Initial stock price	100		Exercise prices								
4	Up	10%		Date 1	100							
5	Down	-5%		Date 2	105							
6	Interest rate	6%		Date 3	112							
7												
8	State prices											
9	q_u	0.6918	<-- =(B6-B5)/((1+B6)*(B4-B5))									
10	q_d	0.2516	<-- =(B4-B6)/((1+B6)*(B4-B5))									
11												
12	Check											
13	$1/(q_u+q_d)$	1.06	<-- =1/(B9+B10)									
14	$q_u*(1+up)+q_d*(1+down)$	1	<-- =B9*(1+B4)+B10*(1+B5)									
15												
16			Stock price					133.100				
17						121.000						
18					110.000			114.950				
19			100.000			104.500						
20					95.000			99.275				
21						90.250						
22								85.738				
23									=MAX(q_u*H26+q_d*H28,MAX(F17-E5,0))			
24			Date 0		Date 1		Date 2		Date 3			
25												
26			Value at each node					21.100	<-- =MAX(H16-E6,0)			
27						16.000						
28					11.583			2.950	<-- =MAX(H18-E6,0)			
29			8.368			2.041						
30					1.412			0.000				
31						0.000						
32								0.000				
33												
34			Early exercise?									
35							yes					
36					no				=IF(q_u*H26+q_d*H28>=			
37						no			MAX(F17-E5,0),"no","yes")			
38					no							
39						no						
40												

Most of this spreadsheet follows section 14.4. Cells B16:H22 describe the stock price over time, which follows a binomial process with the "up" = 10 percent and "down" = −5 percent (cells B4 and B5). Where things get interesting is in the valuation:

	A	B	C	D	E	F	G	H	I	J	K	L
23									=MAX(q$_u$*H26+q$_d$*H28,MAX(F17-E5,0))			
24		Date 0		Date 1		Date 2		Date 3				
25												
26		Value at each node						21.100	<-- =MAX(H16-E6,0)			
27						16.000						
28				11.583				2.950	<-- =MAX(H18-E6,0)			
29		8.368				2.041						
30				1.412				0.000				
31						0.000						
32	=MAX(q$_u$*F29+q$_d$*F31,MAX(D20-E4,0))							0.000				
33												

As is usual for an American option, at each node of the tree we consider whether the option is worth more whether exercised or whether held. But note that in the preceding picture, the exercise price varies with the date, so that the exercise price at date 3 is E6, that of date 2 is E5, and that of date 1 is E4.

As you can see in cell B29, the value of the American call option is 8.368.

Exercises

1. A stock selling for $25 today will, in one year, be worth either $35 or $20. If the interest rate is 8 percent, what is the value today of a one-year call option on the stock with exercise price $30? Use the simultaneous-equation approach of section 14.1 to price the option.

2. In exercise 1, compute the state prices q_u and q_d, and use these prices to calculate the value today of a one-year put option on the stock with exercise price $30. Show that put-call parity holds: That is, using your answer from this problem and the previous problem, show that

$$\text{Call price} + \frac{X}{1+r} = \text{Stock price today} + \text{Put price}$$

3. In a binomial model a call option and a put option are both written on the same stock. The exercise price of the call option is 30, and the exercise price of the put option is 40. The call option's payoffs are 0 and 5 and the put option's payoffs are 20 and 5. The price of the call is 2.25 and the price of the put is 12.25.

   a. What is the riskless interest rate? Assume that the basic period is one year.

   b. What is the price of the stock today?

4. All reliable analysts agree that a share of ABC Corporation, selling today for $50, will be priced at either $65 or $45 one year from today. They further agree that the probabilities of these events are 0.6 and 0.4, respectively. The market risk-free rate is 6 percent. What is the value of a call option on ABC whose exercise price is $50 and which matures in one year?

5. A stock is currently selling for 60. The price of the stock at the end of the year is expected either to increase by 25 percent or to decrease by 20 percent. The riskless interest rate is 5 percent. Calculate the price of a European put on the stock with exercise price 55. Use the binomial option-pricing model.

6.   Fill in all the cells labeled ??? in the following spreadsheet:

THREE-DATE BINOMIAL OPTION PRICING										
Up	35%									
Down	-5%	State prices								
		q_u	???							
Initial stock price	40	q_d	???							
Interest rate	25%									
Exercise price	40									
Stock price					**Bond price**					
				???						???
		???						???		
40				???	1					???
		???						???		
				???						???
Call option price					**European put option price**					
				???						???
		???						???		
???				???	???					???
		???						???		
				???						???
American put option										
				???						
		???								
???				???						
		???								
				???						

7.   Consider the following 3-date binomial model, in which the annual interest rate is 9 percent and in which the stock price goes up by 15 percent or down by 10 percent per period:

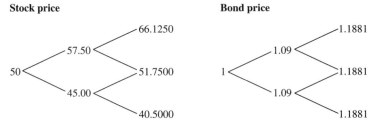

Stock price   **Bond price**

a. Price a European call on the stock with exercise price 60.

b. Price a European put on the stock with exercise price 60.

c. Price an American call on the stock with exercise price 60.

d. Price an American put on the stock with exercise price 60.

8.   Consider the following three-date binomial model, in which the stock price either goes up by 30 percent or decreases by 10 percent in each period, and in which the one-period interest rate is 25 percent:

Stock price   **Bond price**

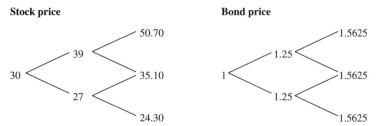

a. Consider a European call with $X = 30$ and $T = 2$. Fill in the blanks in the tree:

Call option price

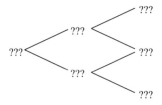

b. Price a European put with $X = 30$ and $T = 2$.

c. Now consider an American put with $X = 30$ and $T = 2$. Fill in the blanks in the tree:

American put option price

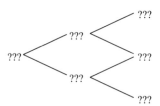

9.   A prominent securities firm recently introduced a new financial product. This product, called the Best of Both Worlds (BOBOW for short), costs $10. It matures in five years, at which point it repays the investor the $10 cost *plus* 120 percent of any positive return in the S&P 500 index. There are no payments before maturity.

For example, if the S&P 500 is currently at 1500, and if it is at 1800 in five years, a BOBOW owner will receive back $12.40 = $10 * [1 + 1.2 * (1800/1500 − 1)]. If the S&P is at or below 1500 in 5 years, the BOBOW owner will receive back $10.

Suppose that the annual interest rate on a five-year, continuously compounded, pure-discount bond is 6 percent. Suppose further that the S&P 500 is currently at 1500 and that you believe that in five years it will be at either 2500 or 1200. Use the binomial option-pricing model to show that BOBOWs are underpriced.

10. This problem is a continuation of the discussion of section 14.6. Show that as $n \to \infty$, the binomial European put price converges to the Black-Scholes put price. (Note that, as part of the spreadsheet **Chapter14.xls,** we have included a function called **BSPut** that computes the Black-Scholes put price.)

11. Here's an advanced version of exercise 10. Consider an alternative parameterization of the binomial:

$$\Delta t = 1/n \qquad\qquad R = e^{r\Delta t}$$

$$1 + \text{Up} = e^{(r - \sigma^2/2)\Delta t + \sigma\sqrt{\Delta t}} \qquad q_u = \frac{R - \text{Down}}{R * (\text{Up} - \text{Down})}$$

$$1 + \text{Down} = e^{(r - \sigma^2/2)\Delta t - \sigma\sqrt{\Delta t}} \qquad q_d = \frac{1}{R} - q_u$$

Construct binomial European call and put option-pricing functions in VBA for this parameterization and show that they also converge to the Black-Scholes formula. (The message here is that the parameterization of the binomial σ is not unique.)

12. A call option is written on a stock whose current price is $50. The option has maturity of three years, and during this time the annual stock price is expected to increase by 25 percent or to decrease by 10 percent. The annual interest rate is constant at 6 percent. The option is exercisable at date 1 at a price of $55, at date 2 for a price of $60, and at date 3 for a price of $65. What is its value today? Will you ever exercise the option early?

13. Reconsider exercise 12. Show that if the date-1 exercise price is X, the date-2 exercise price is $X * (1 + r)$, and the date-3 exercise price is $X * (1 + r)^2$, you will not exercise the option early.[5]

---

5. It can also be shown that this property holds if the exercise prices grow more slowly than the interest rate. Thus for the problem considered in section 14.7, there will be early exercise of the American call only when the exercise prices grow at a rate faster than the interest rate.

15 The Lognormal Distribution

15.1 Introduction

In the previous chapter we discussed the pricing of options using the binomial option-pricing model. The binomial model—besides being an attractive and intuitive way to price options and other derivative securities—also has a deeper message for derivative asset pricing: It shows us that, given some assumptions about the uncertainty governing the stock price and given a risk-free interest rate, we can price options and other assets whose prices are dependent on the price of an underlying stock.

A problem with the binomial option-pricing approach is that we were not able to give simple formulas for the pricing of options. The pricing approach developed in the previous chapter is computational, not analytic. In order to develop a *formula* for the pricing of options (such as the Black-Scholes formula, which will be discussed in Chapter 16), we need to make some assumptions about the statistical properties of the underlying stock price.

A central assumption of the Black-Scholes (BS) pricing model is that prices are distributed lognormally. In this chapter we attempt to give this assumption enough content so that you will be happy using it. Our method is as follows: We shall not, in this book, prove the Black-Scholes option-pricing formula. Instead, we shall try to convince you in this chapter that the basic assumption made by the BS model with regard to stock prices—the lognormality of stock prices—is reasonable. If we can convince you that it is, then we will leave the technical details of the BS proof to other, more advanced, texts.

The structure of this chapter is as follows:

• We start with a discussion of what constitute "reasonable" assumptions about stock prices.

• We then discuss why the lognormal distribution is a reasonable distribution for stock prices.

• Finally, we show how to simulate lognormal price paths.

15.2   What Do Stock Prices Look Like?

What are reasonable assumptions about the way stock prices behave over time? Clearly the price of a stock (or any other risky financial asset) is uncertain. What is its distribution? This is a perplexing question. One way to answer it is to ask what the reasonable statistical properties of a stock price are. Here are five reasonable properties:

1. The stock price is uncertain. Given the price today, we do not know the price tomorrow.

2. Changes in the stock's price are continuous. Over short periods of time, changes in a stock's price are very small, and the change goes to zero as the time span goes to zero.[1]

3. The stock price is never zero. This property means that we exclude the stocks of "dead" companies.

4. The average return from holding a stock tends to increase over time. Notice the word "tends": We do not *know* that holding a stock for a longer time will lead to higher return; however, we *expect* that holding a risky asset over a longer term will lead to a higher *average* return.

5. The *uncertainty* associated with the return from holding a stock also tends to increase the longer the stock is held. Thus, given the stock's price today, the variance of the stock price tomorrow is small; however, the price variance in one month is larger, and the variance in one year is larger still.

15.2.1   Reasonable Stock Properties and Stock Price Paths

One way of viewing these five "reasonable properties" of stock prices is to think about *price paths*. A stock price path is a graph of a stock price over a period of time. Following, for example, is the price of path of several actual stocks.

---

1. If you have watched stock prices, you know that continuity is usually not a bad assumption. Sometimes, however, it can be disastrous (look at the way stock market prices behaved in October 1987 for a dramatic example of price *discontinuities*). It is possible to build a stock-price model that assumes that prices are usually continuous but have occasional (and random) jumps. See Cox and Ross (1976), Merton (1976), and Jarrow and Rudd (1983).

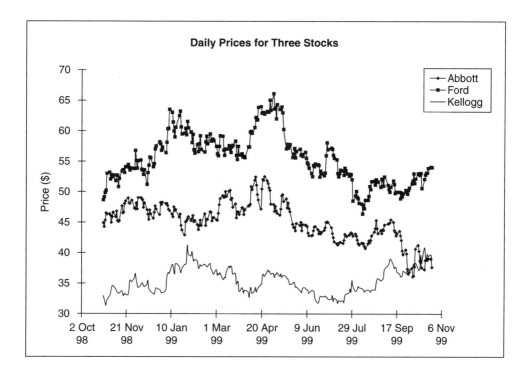

If we simulated stock price paths (something we shall do using the lognormal model later on in this chapter), how would we expect them to look? Our five properties imply that we would expect

1. Wiggly lines.

2. Lines that are continuous (solid), with no jumps.

3. Lines that are always positive and never cross zero, no matter how low they get.

4. That at a given point in time, the average over all plausible lines is greater than the initial price of the stock. The farther out we go, the higher this average becomes.

5. That the standard deviation over all plausible lines is greater the farther out we go.

Here's another way of thinking about stock prices. Suppose we take the daily returns on the Standard & Poor's 500 index.[2]

	A	B	C	D	E	F
1	**SOME DAILY RETURN DATA FOR S&P 500**					
2						
3		**SP 500**				
4	**Date**	**Price**	**Return**			
5	26-Oct-98	1072.32				
6	27-Oct-98	1065.34	-0.0065	<-- =LN(B6/B5)		
7	28-Oct-98	1068.09	0.0026	<-- =LN(B7/B6)		
8	29-Oct-98	1085.93	0.0166			
9	30-Oct-98	1098.67	0.0117			
10	2-Nov-98	1111.60	0.0117			
11	3-Nov-98	1110.84	-0.0007			
12	4-Nov-98	1118.67	0.0070			
13	5-Nov-98	1133.85	0.0135			
14	6-Nov-98	1141.01	0.0063			
15	9-Nov-98	1130.20	-0.0095			

If we graph these returns over a year, it is difficult to interpret them:

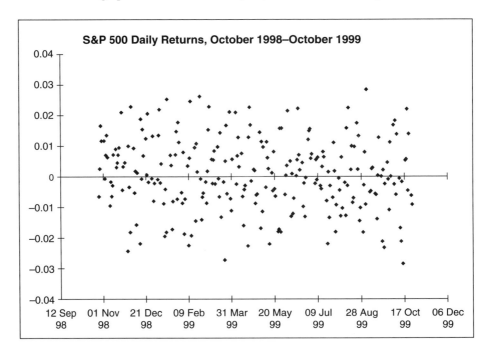

---

2. By taking the natural logarithm of the price relatives, we implicitly assume that the return-generating process is continuous. For example, if the stock price is 30 on day 1 and 31 on day 2, the continuously compounded return on the stock over the day is $\ln(31/30) = 3.279$ percent.

However, if we use the Excel function **Frequency** (see Chapter 29) to do a frequency distribution of these returns, we see that they are approximately normally distributed:

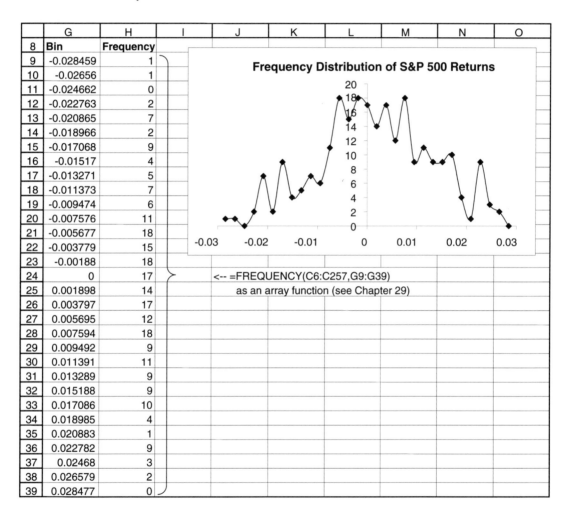

	G	H	I	J	K	L	M	N	O
8	Bin	Frequency							
9	-0.028459	1							
10	-0.02656	1							
11	-0.024662	0							
12	-0.022763	2							
13	-0.020865	7							
14	-0.018966	2							
15	-0.017068	9							
16	-0.01517	4							
17	-0.013271	5							
18	-0.011373	7							
19	-0.009474	6							
20	-0.007576	11							
21	-0.005677	18							
22	-0.003779	15							
23	-0.00188	18							
24	0	17		<-- =FREQUENCY(C6:C257,G9:G39)					
25	0.001898	14		as an array function (see Chapter 29)					
26	0.003797	17							
27	0.005695	12							
28	0.007594	18							
29	0.009492	9							
30	0.011391	11							
31	0.013289	9							
32	0.015188	9							
33	0.017086	10							
34	0.018985	4							
35	0.020883	1							
36	0.022782	9							
37	0.02468	3							
38	0.026579	2							
39	0.028477	0							

As we shall see in the next section, the assumption that stock returns are normally distributed underlies the lognormal distribution.

15.3   Lognormal Price Distributions and Geometric Diffusions

In this section we get a bit more formal and describe what we mean by a lognormal price distribution. We then relate the lognormal price process to a geometric diffusion.

Suppose we denote by S_t the price at time t of a share of stock. The lognormal distribution assumes that *the natural logarithm of one-plus-the-return from holding a share of stock between time t and time $t + \Delta t$ is normally distributed with mean μ and standard deviation σ*. Denote the (uncertain) rate of return over an interval Δt by $\tilde{r}_{\Delta t}$. Then we can write $S_{t+\Delta t} = S_t \exp[\tilde{r}_{\Delta t} \Delta t]$. In the lognormal distribution, we assume that the rate of return $\tilde{r}_{\Delta t}$ over a short period Δt is normally distributed with mean $\mu \Delta t$ and variance $\sigma^2 \Delta t$.

Another way of writing this relation is to write the stock price $S_{t+\Delta t}$ at time $t + \Delta t$ in the following way:

$$\frac{S_{t+\Delta t}}{S_t} = \exp\left[\mu \Delta t + \sigma Z \sqrt{\Delta t}\right]$$

where Z is a standard normal variable (mean $= 0$, standard deviation $= 1$).[3]

To see what this assumption means, suppose first that $\sigma = 0$. In this case we have

$$S_{t+\Delta t} = S_t \exp[\mu \Delta t]$$

which simply says that the stock price grows at an exponential rate with certainty. In this case the stock is like a riskless bond that bears interest rate μ, continuously compounded.

Now suppose that $\sigma > 0$. In this case, the lognormal assumption says that, although the tendency is for the stock price to increase, there is an uncertain element (normally distributed) that must be taken into account. The best way to think about this process is in terms of a simulation. Suppose, for example, that we're trying to simulate a lognormal price process in which $\mu = 15$ percent, $\sigma = 30$ percent, and $\Delta t = 0.004$. Suppose the price at time 0 is $S_0 = 35$. To simulate the possible stock prices at time Δt we first have to pick (at random) a

---

3. If you know about diffusion processes, then the lognormal price process is a *geometric diffusion:* $\frac{dS}{S} = \mu\, dt + \sigma\, dB$, where dB is a Wiener process ("white noise"): $dB = Z\sqrt{dt}$, where Z is a standard random variable.

number Z from a standard normal distribution.[4] Suppose that this number is 0.1165. Then the stock price $S\Delta t$ at time Δt will be

$$S_{\Delta t} = S_0 * \exp\left[\mu\Delta t + \sigma Z\sqrt{\Delta t}\right]$$

$$= 35 * \exp\left[0.15 * 0.004 + 0.3 * 0.1165 * \sqrt{0.004}\right] = 35.0985$$

Of course we could have drawn a different random number. If, for example, our random number Z had been 0.9102, then we would have

$$S_{\Delta t} = S_0 * \exp\left[\mu\Delta t + \sigma Z\sqrt{\Delta t}\right]$$

$$= 35 * \exp\left[0.15 * 0.004 + 0.3 * 0.9102 * \sqrt{0.004}\right] = 34.421$$

This process is illustrated in the next spreadsheet picture, where we generated a list of 250 numbers picked from a standard-normal distribution (the technical nomenclature is "standard normal deviates").[5] Each is an equally likely potential candidate to be Z. Having picked Z for a particular time interval Δt, the price $S_{t+\Delta t}$ follows.

	A	B	C	D	E	F	G	H	I	J
1	**Conceptualizing the Lognormal Distribution**									
2			A Simple Example							
3										
4			Time	Normal	Stock					
5				deviates	price					
6	Mean	15%	0		35.0000	<-- B9				
7	Sigma	30%	1	-0.876878	34.4432	<-- =E6*EXP($B$6*$B$8+$B$7*D7*SQRT($B$8))				
8	Δt	0.004	2	1.387725	35.3833	<-- =E7*EXP($B$6*$B$8+$B$7*D8*SQRT($B$8))				
9	Initial stock price	35	3	1.234612	36.2437					
10			4	0.683103	36.7386					
11			5	0.715531	37.2631					
12			6	-0.652362	36.8268					
13			7	-1.910576	35.5370					
14			8	-0.030415	35.5378					
15			9	0.159681	35.6671					
16			10	0.511053	36.0362					
17			11	-0.929388	35.4276					
18			12	-1.36386	34.5433					
19			13	0.929804	35.1792					
20			14	-0.272737	35.0186					
21			15	-0.742007	34.5498					
22			16	0.331329	34.7885					

Simulated Stock Price Path

---

4. See Chapter 25 for some techniques (using both Excel and VBA) for generating random numbers.

5. The number of business days in a year is approximately 250. Thus when we define $\Delta t = 1/250 = 0.004$, we are simulating the stock price on a daily basis over the course of a year.

The spreadsheet uses **Tools|Data Analysis|Random Number Generation** to generate a list of 250 standard-normal deviates. The command looks like this:

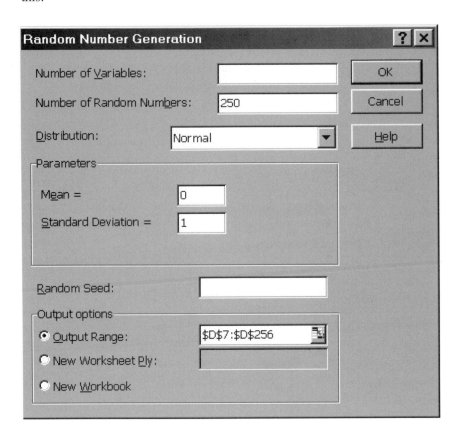

To summarize: In order to simulate *the growth of the stock price,* when the price follows a lognormal price distribution,

• Multiply Δt (the elapsed time interval) by μ (the average rate of growth). This step gives the certain portion of the return.

• Take a draw from a random variable that is standard normal, multiply this draw by $\sigma\sqrt{\Delta t}$. This step gives the uncertain portion of the return. (The square root implies that the variance of the stock's return is linear in time. See the next section.)

• Add the two results and exponentiate.

15.4   What Does the Lognormal Distribution Look Like?

We know that the normal distribution produces a bell curve. What about the lognormal distribution? In the following experiment we simulate 1,000 random end-of-year stock prices. The experiment is a continuation of the experiment performed in the previous section; since we are simulating end-of-year prices, we set $\Delta t = 1$. To perform this experiment:

- We produce a list of 1,000 normal deviates.

- We use each normal deviate to produce an end-of-period stock price

$$S_1 = S_0 * \exp\left[\mu\Delta t + \sigma Z\sqrt{\Delta t}\right] = S_0 * \exp[\mu + \sigma Z], \; since \; \Delta t = 1$$

- We put the stock prices into bins and produce a histogram.

Here's what the spreadsheet for this experiment looks like:

	A	B	C	D	E	F	G	H	I	J
1	**The Lognormal Histogram**									
2										
3										
4				List of 1000 normally	Lognormal					
5				distributed numbers	exp(μΔt + σ Z √Δt)					
6	Mean	15%		0.726111011	1.4446	<-- =EXP($B$6*$B$8+$B$7*D6*SQRT($B$8))				
7	Sigma	30%		-0.75691446	0.9258					
8	Δt	1		0.054451448	1.1810					
9				1.616244845	1.8868					
10				-0.009147243	1.1587					
11	We used Tools|Data			1.130981673	1.6312					
12	Analysis|RandomNumber			2.550623321	2.4972					
13	Generation to produce the list of			-0.230678552	1.0842					
14	1,000 normally distributed random			1.092166713	1.6123					
15	numbers(with mean = 0 and			-2.794113243	0.5025					
16	standard deviation = 1) onthe			0.724598976	1.4439					
17	right.			0.433137757	1.3231					
18				-1.047612841	0.8485					
19				1.33371941	1.7335					

Having produced 1,000 lognormal price relatives, $\exp\left[\mu\Delta t + \sigma Z\sqrt{\Delta t}\right]$, we can use the array function **Frequency( )** (this function is discussed in Chapter 29) to put them into bins.

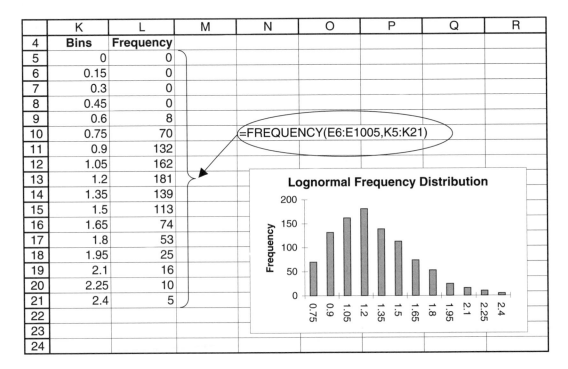

	K	L	M	N	O	P	Q	R
4	**Bins**	**Frequency**						
5	0	0						
6	0.15	0						
7	0.3	0						
8	0.45	0						
9	0.6	8						
10	0.75	70		=FREQUENCY(E6:E1005,K5:K21)				
11	0.9	132						
12	1.05	162						
13	1.2	181						
14	1.35	139						
15	1.5	113						
16	1.65	74						
17	1.8	53						
18	1.95	25						
19	2.1	16						
20	2.25	10						
21	2.4	5						
22								
23								
24								

When we do this simulation for a large number of points, the resulting density curve becomes smooth. Here, for example, is the frequency distribution of 100,000 trials with $\mu = 10$ percent, $\sigma = 20$ percent, and $\Delta t = 1$ (this sample was done with VBA on a 166-mHz Pentium in 7 seconds):

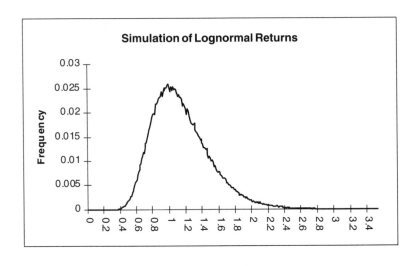

The VBA program that produced this output follows:

```
'Simulating the lognormal distribution
'Note that I take delta = 1!
Sub RandomNumberSimulation()
Application.ScreenUpdating = False
Range("starttime") = Time
N = Range("runs").Value
mean = Range("mean")
sigma = Range("sigma")
ReDim Frequency(0 To 1000) As Integer

For Index = 1 to N
start:
    Static rand1, rand2, S1, S2, X1, X2
    rand1 = 2 * Rnd - 1
    rand2 = 2 * Rnd - 1
    S1 = rand1 ^ 2 + rand2 ^ 2
    If S1 > 1 Then GoTo start
    S2 = Sqr(-2 * Log(S1) / S1)
    X1 = rand1 * S2
    X2 = rand2 * S2

    Return1 = Exp(mean + sigma * X1)
    Return1 = Exp(mean + sigma * X2)

    Frequency(Int(Return1 / 0.01)) = _
        Frequency(Int(Return1 / 0.01)) + 1
    Frequency(Int(Return2 / 0.01)) = _
        Frequency(Int(Return2 / 0.01)) + 1
Next Index

For Index = 0 To 400
    Range("output").Cells(Index + 1, 1) = _
        Frequency(Index) / N
Next Index

Range("stoptime" = Time
Range("elapsed") = Range("stoptime") - Range("starttime")
Range("elapsed").NumberFormat = "hh:mm:ss"

End Sub
```

The routine that produces randomly distributed standard normal deviates is contained in the eight lines following the word `start`; this routine is further explained in Chapter 25.

15.5   Simulating Lognormal Price Paths

We now return to the problem of simulating lognormal price paths that we started to discuss in section 15.3. We shall try to understand, through a simulation written in VBA, the meaning of the following sentences: "The price of a stock today is $25. The price of the stock is distributed lognormally, with an annual log mean return of 10 percent and an annual log standard deviation of 20 percent." We want to know how the price of the stock might behave on a daily basis throughout the next year. There are an infinite number of price paths for the stock. What we will do is simulate (randomly) one of these paths. If we want another price path, we can merely rerun the simulation.

There are about 250 business days in a year. Therefore, the daily price movement of the stock between day t and day $t + 1$ can be simulated by setting $\Delta t = 1/250 = 0.004$, $\mu = 10$ percent, and $\sigma > 20$ percent. If the initial price of the stock $S_0 = \$25$, then the price after one day will be

$$S_{\Delta t} = S_0 * \exp\left[\mu \Delta t + \sigma Z \sqrt{\Delta t}\right]$$
$$= 25 * \exp\left[0.15 * 0.004 + 0.20 * Z\sqrt{0.004}\right]$$

and the price after two days will be

$$S_{0.008} = S_{0.004} * \exp\left[0.15 * 0.004 + 0.20 * Z\sqrt{0.004}\right]$$

and so on. At each step the random normal deviate Z is the uncertain factor in the price return. Because of this uncertainty, all paths produced will be different.

Here is a VBA program `PricePathSimulation` that reproduces a typical price path.

```
Sub PricePathSimulation()
Range("starttime") = Time

Application.ScreenUpdating = False

N = Range("runs").Value
mean = Range("mean")
sigma = Range("sigma")
delta_t = 1 / (2 * N)

ReDim price(0 To 2 * N) As Double

price(0) = Range("initial_price")

For Index = 1 to N
start:
    Static rand1, rand2, S1, S2, X1, X2
    rand1 = 2 * Rnd - 1
    rand2 = 2 * Rnd - 1
    S1 = rand1 ^ 2 + rand2 ^ 2
    If S1 > 1 Then GoTo start
    S2 = Sqr(-2 * Log(S1) / S1)
    X1 = rand1 * S2
    X2 = rand2 * S2

    price(2 * Index - 1) = price(2 * Index - 2) * _
        Exp(mean * delta_t + sigma * Sqr(delta_t) * X1)
    price(2 * Index) = price(2 * Index - 1) * _
        Exp(mean * delta_t + sigma * Sqr(delta_t) * X2)
Next Index

For Index = 0 To 2 * N
    Range("output").Cells(Index + 1, 1) = Index
    Range("output").Cells(Index + 1, 2) = price(Index)
Next Index

Range("stoptime" = Time
Range("elapsed") = Range("stoptime") - Range("starttime")
Range("elapsed").NumberFormat = "hh:mm:ss"

End Sub
```

The output from this program looks like this on the spreadsheet:

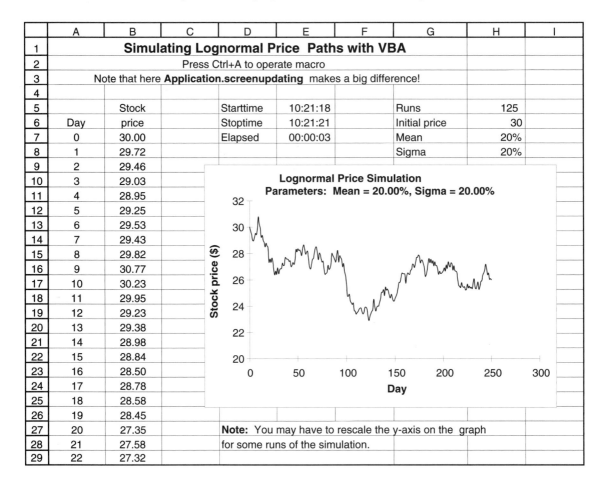

	A	B	C	D	E	F	G	H	I
1				**Simulating Lognormal Price Paths with VBA**					
2				Press Ctrl+A to operate macro					
3			Note that here **Application.screenupdating** makes a big difference!						
4									
5		Stock		Starttime	10:21:18		Runs	125	
6	Day	price		Stoptime	10:21:21		Initial price	30	
7	0	30.00		Elapsed	00:00:03		Mean	20%	
8	1	29.72					Sigma	20%	
9	2	29.46							
10	3	29.03							
11	4	28.95							
12	5	29.25							
13	6	29.53							
14	7	29.43							
15	8	29.82							
16	9	30.77							
17	10	30.23							
18	11	29.95							
19	12	29.23							
20	13	29.38							
21	14	28.98							
22	15	28.84							
23	16	28.50							
24	17	28.78							
25	18	28.58							
26	19	28.45							
27	20	27.35		**Note:** You may have to rescale the y-axis on the graph					
28	21	27.58		for some runs of the simulation.					
29	22	27.32							

As you can see from the VBA program, we prevent the screen from updating using the command `Application.screenupdating = false`. This speeds up the simulation greatly. (Try turning this command off, and see the difference.)

We can modify the program slightly to produce many lognormal price paths (see exercise 1). The output from this program is shown in the following graph.

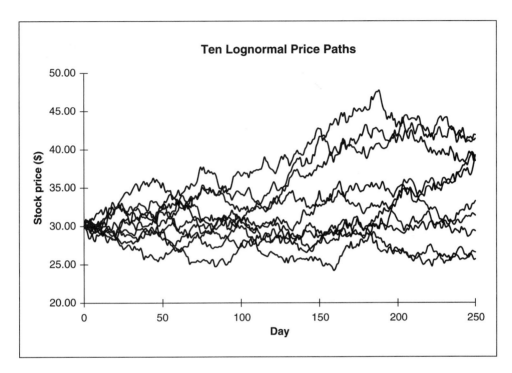

As you can see, on average the price of the asset increases over time, as does the variance of the returns. These results accord with properties 4 and 5 of stock prices in section 15.2—we expect both the return on an asset and the uncertainty associated with this return to increase over time.

15.6   Technical Analysis

Security analysis are divided into "fundamentalists" and "technicians." This division has nothing to do with their outlook on the Creator of the Universe, but rather with the way they regard stock prices. Fundamentalists believe that the value of a stock is ultimately determined by underlying economic variables. Thus, when a fundamentalist analyzes a company, she will look at its earnings, its debt/equity ratio, its markets, and so forth.

Technicians, in contrast, think that stock prices are determined by patterns. They believe that, by examining the pattern of past prices of a stock, they can predict (or at least make sensible statements about) the stock's future prices. A technician may tell you that "we're currently in a head-and-shoulders pattern," by which he means that a graph of the stock price looks like the following figure:

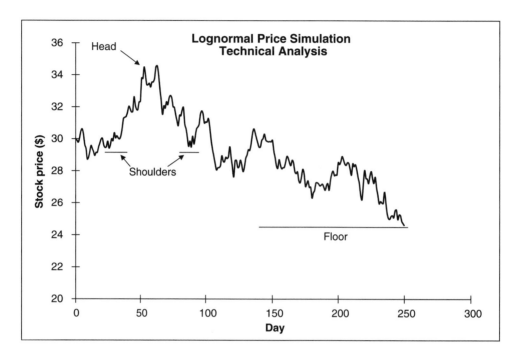

Other terms used by technicians include "floors" (there's one in the graph), "rebound levels," and "pennants."[6]

The orthodox (some would say ivory-tower) view of technical analysis is that it is worthless. A basic supposition of financial theory says that markets efficiently incorporate the information known about the securities traded on them. There are several versions of this theory; one of them, the *weak efficient-markets hypothesis,* says that at the very least all information about past prices is incorporated into the current price. The weak efficient-markets hypothesis means that technical analysis cannot make predictions about futures prices, since technical analysis is based solely on past price information.[7]

---

6. The Chicago Board of Trade has published an excellent introduction to technical analysis and nomenclature entitled "An Introduction to Speculating." It is available free from the Chicago Board of Trade, Publications Division, 141 W. Jackson, Chicago, IL 60604.

7. For a discussion of this point, see Chapter 13 of Brealey and Myers (1996); for a more advanced treatment, see Chapter 9 of Copeland and Weston (1983).

Nevertheless, a lot of people believe in technical analysis. (This belief in it-self may give technical analysis some validity.) The simulations we are running in this chapter allow us to generate a myriad of patterns which, when analyzed, will yield "good" predictions of future prices. For example, in the preceding figure it appears that $24 is a floor for the stock price, since it never goes any lower. A perspicacious analyst can detect a clear head-and-shoulders pattern between days 40 and 100. There appears to be a ceiling of $35. Thus a techni-cian might predict that the stock price will stay below $35 unless it rises above that level. (If you are going to be a technician, you have to learn to say these things with a straight face.)

15.7   Calculating the Parameters of the Lognormal Distribution from Stock Prices

The main purpose of this section is to show you how stock-price data can be used to compute the μ and σ needed in the lognormal simulations (and—in the next chapter—the σ needed as an input to the Black-Scholes formula). First, however, note that the mean and variance of the logarithm of the stock return over an interval Δt are

$$E\left[\ln\left(\frac{S_{t+\Delta t}}{S_t}\right)\right] = E\left(\mu\Delta t + \sigma Z\sqrt{\Delta t}\right) = \mu\Delta t$$

$$\text{Var}\left[\ln\left(\frac{S_{t+\Delta t}}{S_t}\right)\right] = \text{Var}\left(\mu\Delta t + \sigma Z\sqrt{\Delta t}\right) = \sigma^2\Delta t$$

These expressions indicate that both the expected log return and the variance of the log return are linear in time.

Now suppose we want to estimate the lognormal μ and σ from data on his-torical prices. It follows that

$$\mu = \frac{\text{Mean}[\ln{(S_{t+\Delta t}/S_t)}]}{\Delta t}, \quad \sigma^2 = \frac{\text{Var}[\ln{(S_{t+\Delta t}/S_t)}]}{\Delta t}.$$

To make things specific, the following spreadsheet gives monthly prices for a particular stock. From these prices we calculate the log returns and the *annual-ized* mean and standard deviation. Note that we have used the function **Stdevp** to calculate σ; it is assumed that the data represent the actual distribution.

	A	B	C	D	E	F	G
1	**Calculating Lognormal Mean and Sigma from Stock-Price Data**						
2							
3			Monthly				
4	**Month**	**Price**	**return**				
5	0	12.00					
6	1	12.90	7.23%	=LN(B6/B5)			
7	2	12.35	-4.36%	=LN(B7/B6)			
8	3	12.88	4.20%				
9	4	13.80	6.90%				
10	5	13.20	-4.45%				
11	6	13.55	2.62%				
12	7	12.65	-6.87%				
13	8	14.50	13.65%				
14	9	15.35	5.70%				
15	10	14.85	-3.31%				
16	11	15.25	2.66%				
17	12	15.50	1.63%				
18							
19	Monthly average		2.13%	<--=AVERAGE(C6:C17)			
20	Monthly standard deviation		5.74%	=STDEVP(C6:C17)			
21							
22	Annual average		25.59%	<--=C19*12			
23	Annual standard deviation		19.88%	<--=C20*SQRT(12)			

Note that the annual average log return is 12 times the monthly average log return, whereas the annual standard deviation is $\sqrt{12}$ the monthly standard deviation. In general if the return data are generated for n periods per year, then

$$\text{mean}_{\text{annual return}} = n * \text{mean}_{\text{periodic return}}, \ \sigma_{\text{annual return}} = \sqrt{n} \cdot \sigma_{\text{periodic return}}$$

Of course, this is not the only way to calculate the parameters of the lognormal distribution. We should mention at least two other methods:

• We can use some other procedure to extrapolate the mean and standard deviation of *future* returns from the past history of returns. One example would be to use a moving average.

• We can use the Black-Scholes formula to find the *implied volatility:* the σ of the stock's log returns that fits the price of an option on the stock. This method is illustrated in section 16.4.

Exercises

1. Write a VBA program that reproduces the lognormal frequency distribution for an arbitrary number of runs. That is, this program should

   a. Produce N normal random deviates.
   b. For each deviate produce a lognormal price relative $\exp\left[\mu\Delta t + \sigma Z\sqrt{\Delta t}\right]$.
   c. Classify each price relative into a set of bins running from 0, 0.1, …, 3.
   d. Put the frequencies on the spreadsheet and produce a frequency graph like the one in section 15.4.

2. Run a few of the lognormal price-path simulations. Examine the price pattern for trends. Find one or more of the following technical patterns:

   support area

   resistance area

   uptrend/downtrend

   head and shoulders

   inverted head and shoulders

   double top/bottom

   rounded top/bottom

   triangle (ascending, symmetrical, descending)

   flag

3. Write a VBA program that produces a set of 10 price paths and graph them on a spreadsheet (as in section 15.5).

4. The notebook **Problems 15.xls** contains daily price data for the S&P 500 index and for Abbott Laboratories from 26 October 1998 through 26 October 1999. Use this data to compute the annual average, variance, and standard deviation of the logarithmic returns for the S&P and for Abbott. What is the correlation between the returns of the S&P 500 and Abbott?

16 The Black-Scholes Model

16.1 Introduction

In a famous paper published in 1973, Fisher Black and Myron Scholes proved a formula for pricing European call and put options on non-dividend-paying stocks. Their model is probably the most famous model of modern finance. The Black-Scholes formula is relatively easy to use, and it is often an adequate approximation to the price of more complicated options.

In this chapter we make no pretense at a full-blown development of the model; this would require a knowledge of stochastic processes and a not-inconsiderable mathematical investment. Instead, we shall describe the mechanics of the model and show how to implement it in Excel.[1]

16.2 The Black-Scholes Model

Consider a stock whose price is lognormally distributed. The Black-Scholes model uses the following formula to price calls on the stock:

$$C = SN(d_1) - Xe^{-rT}N(d_2)$$

where

$$d_1 = \frac{\ln(S/X) + (r + \sigma^2/2)T}{\sigma\sqrt{T}}$$

$$d_2 = d_1 - \sigma\sqrt{T}$$

Here C denotes the price of a call, S is the price of the underlying stock, X is the exercise price of the call, T is the call's time to exercise, r is the interest rate, and σ is the standard deviation of the logarithm of the stock's return. $N(\ )$ denotes a value of the standard normal distribution. It is assumed that the stock will pay no dividends before date T.

By the put-call parity theorem (see Chapter 13), a put with the same exercise date T and exercise price X written on the same stock will have price $P = C - S + Xe^{-rT}$. Substituting for C in this equation and doing some algebra gives the Black-Scholes put-pricing formula:

$$P = Xe^{-rT}N(-d_2) - SN(-d_1)$$

---

1. In the exercises to Chapter 14 we hinted at one form of the proof of Black-Scholes formula. There it was noted that the Black-Scholes formula coincided with the binominal option-pricing model formula when (a) the length of a typical period $\rightarrow 0$; (b) the "up" and the "down" moves in the binominal model converge to a lognormal price process, and (c) the term structure of interest rates is flat.

16.2.1   Implementing the Black-Scholes Formulas in a Spreadsheet

The Black-Scholes formulas for call and put pricing are easily implemented in a spreadsheet. The following example shows how to calculate the price of a call option written on a stock whose current price $S = 25$, when the exercise price $X = 25$, the annualized interest rate $r = 6$ percent, and $\sigma = 30$ percent. The option has $T = 0.5$ years to exercise. Note that all three of the parameters T, r, and σ are assumed to be in annual terms.[2]

	A	B	C	D	E	F	G
1			**Black-Scholes Option-Pricing Formula**				
2							
3	S	25	Current stock price				
4	X	25	Exercise price				
5	r	6.00%	Risk-free rate of interest				
6	T	0.5	Time to maturity of option (in years)				
7	Sigma	30%	Stock volatility				
8							
9	d_1	0.2475	<-- (LN(S/X)+(r+0.5*sigma^2)*T)/(sigma*SQRT(T))				
10	d_2	0.0354	<-- d_1-sigma*SQRT(T)				
11							
12	$N(d_1)$	0.5977	<-- Uses formula NormSDist(d_1)				
13	$N(d_2)$	0.5141	<-- Uses formula NormSDist(d_2)				
14							
15	Call price	2.47	<-- S*N(d_1)-X*exp(-r*T)*N(d_2)				
16	Put price	1.73	<-- call price - S + X*Exp(-r*T): by Put-Call parity				
17		1.73	<-- X*exp(-r*T)*N(-d_2) - S*N(-d_1): direct formula				

Note that we have calculated the put price twice: Once by using put-call parity, the second time by the direct Black-Scholes formula.

We can use this spreadsheet to do the usual sensitivity analysis. For example, the following **Data|Table** (see Chapter 26) gives—as the stock price S varies—the Black-Scholes value of the call compared to its intrinsic value [i.e., max $(S - X, 0)$]. Note that we have not shown the header of the data table (Row 21).

---

2. The last section of Chapter 15 discusses how to calculate the annualized σ of the lognormal process given nonannual data.

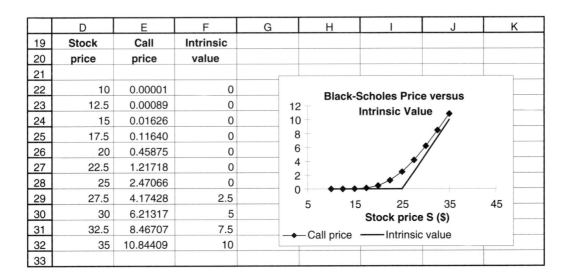

	D	E	F	G	H	I	J	K
19	**Stock**	**Call**	**Intrinsic**					
20	**price**	**price**	**value**					
21								
22	10	0.00001	0					
23	12.5	0.00089	0					
24	15	0.01626	0					
25	17.5	0.11640	0					
26	20	0.45875	0					
27	22.5	1.21718	0					
28	25	2.47066	0					
29	27.5	4.17428	2.5					
30	30	6.21317	5					
31	32.5	8.46707	7.5					
32	35	10.84409	10					
33								

16.3 Using VBA to Define a Black-Scholes Pricing Function

Although the spreadsheet implementation of the Black-Scholes formulas illustrated in the previous section is sufficient for some purposes, we are sometimes interested in having a closed-form function that we can use directly in Excel. We can do so with Visual Basic for Applications. Here is a VBA function that prices calls:

```
Function dOne (Stock, Exercise, Time, Interest, sigma)
    dOne = (Log(Stock / Exercise) + Interest * Time) / _
        (sigma * Sqr(Time)) + 0.5 * sigma * Sqr(Time)
End Function

Function CallOption (Stock, Exercise, Time, Interest, sigma)
    CallOption = Stock * Application.NormSDist(dOne(Stock,_
        Exercise, Time, Interest, sigma)) - Exercise * _
        Exp(-Time * Interest) *_
        Application.NormSDist(dOne(Stock, Exercise,_
        Time, Interest, sigma) - sigma * Sqr(Time))
End Function
```

The first function defines d_1, and the second function (**CallOption**) defines the Black-Scholes call price. Note the use of the Excel fuction **NormSDist,** which gives the standard normal distribution; in order to use this function in VBA, we must write **Application.NormSDist.**

16.3.1 Pricing Puts

By the put-call parity theorem we know that a put is priced by the formula $P = C - S + Xe^{-rT}$. We can implement this in another VBA function:

```
Function PutOption (Stock, Exercise, Time, Interest, sigma)
    PutOption = CallOption(Stock, Exercise, Time,_
        Interest, sigma) + Exercise * Exp(-Interest * _
        Time) - Stock
End Function
```

16.3.2 Using These Functions in an Excel Spreadsheet

Here's an example of these functions used in Excel. The graph was created by a data table. (In presentations, we usually hide the first row of such a table; here we have shown it.)

	A	B	C	D	E	F	G	H	I	J	K	L	M
1			BLACK-SCHOLES MODEL IN VBA										
2										=B10			
3	S	100					=B9						
4	X	100						Call	Put				
5	T	1.00						20.3185	10.8022	<--This is the header of the Data Table			
6	Interest	10.00%					40	0.1802	50.6639				
7	Sigma	40.00%					45	0.4104	45.8941				
8							50	0.8081	41.2918				
9	Call price	20.3185	<-- =CallOption(B3,B4,B5,B6,B7)				55	1.4241	36.9079				
10	Put price	10.8022	<-- =PutOption(B3,B4,B5,B6,B7)				60	2.3019	32.7857				
11							65	3.4739	28.9576				
12							70	4.9600	25.4437				
13	To the right is a data						75	6.7683	22.2520				
14	table that gives the						80	8.8965	19.3803				
15	call and put values for						85	11.3341	16.8179				
16	various exercise						90	14.0645	14.5482				
17	prices.						95	17.0669	12.5506				
18							100	20.3185	10.8022				
19							105	23.7954	9.2791				
20							110	27.4740	7.9578				

16.4 Calculating the Implied Volatility

A common problem in option pricing is the following: Given a price C for a call option, and given the current stock price S, interest rate r, time to maturity of the option T, and option exercise price X, find the volatility σ at which the option is priced. Consider the following call option for example.

Call price $C = 4$

Current stock price $S = 45$

Option exercise price $X = 50$

Interest rate $r = 8$ percent

Time to maturity $T = 1$

We want to know the *implied volatility* σ, that is, the standard deviation for which the Black-Scholes call-pricing formula gives the price of 4, given the other parameters. This problem is easily solved by trial and error by noting that the option price is monotonically increasing in σ. Here's a data table from the previous spreadsheet:

	A	B	C	D	E	F	G	H
1		**Black-Scholes Option-Pricing Formula**						
2								
3	S	45	Current stock price					
4	X	50	Exercise price					
5	r	8.00%	Risk-free rate of interest					
6	T	1	Time to maturity of option (in years)					
7	Sigma	10.00%	Stock volatility					
8								
9	d_1	-0.2036	<--(LN(S/X)+(r+0.5*sigma^2)*T)/(sigma*SQRT(T))					
10	d_2	-0.3036	<--d_1-sigma*SQRT(T)					
11								
12	$N(d_1)$	0.4193	<---Uses formula NormSDist(d_1)					
13	$N(d_2)$	0.3807	<---Uses formula NormSDist(d_2)					
14								
15	Call price	1.2977	<--S*N(d_1)-X*exp(-r*T)*N(d_2)					
16								
17		DATA TABLE						
18			1.2977	<-- =B15, Table header				
19		15%	2.18575					
20		16%	2.36461					
21		17%	2.54368					
22		18%	2.72290					
23		19%	2.90225					
24		20%	3.08168					
25		21%	3.26116					
26		22%	3.44067					
27		23%	3.62020					
28		24%	3.79971					
29		25%	3.97921					
30		26%	4.15866					
31		27%	4.33806					

Call Price and Sigma

It is clear from the data table that the option price of 4 implies that the σ must be slightly above 25 percent. Some trial and error leads us to $\sigma = 25.116$ percent:

	A	B	C	D	E	F	G
1	**Black-Scholes Option-Pricing Formula**						
2							
3	S	45	Current stock price				
4	X	50	Exercise price				
5	r	8.00%	Risk-free rate of interest				
6	T	1	Time to maturity of option (in years)				
7	Sigma	25.116%	Stock volatility				
8							
9	d_1	0.0246	<--(LN(S/X)+(r+0.5*sigma^2)*T)/(sigma*SQRT(T))				
10	d_2	-0.2266	<--d_1-sigma*SQRT(T)				
11							
12	$N(d_1)$	0.5098	<---Uses formula NormSDist(d_1)				
13	$N(d_2)$	0.4104	<---Uses formula NormSDist(d_2)				
14							
15	Call price	4.0000	<--S*N(d_1)-X*exp(-r*T)*N(d_2)				

16.5   A VBA Function to Find the Implied Variance

We can use Visual Basic for Applications to define a function **CallVolatility** that finds the σ for a call option. The function is defined as **CallVolatility(Stock, Exercise, Time, Interest, Target),** where the definitions are as follows:

Stock $\rightarrow$ is the stock price S.

Exercise $\rightarrow$ is the option's exercise price X.

Time $\rightarrow$ is the time to the option's maturity T.

Interest $\rightarrow$ is the interest rate r.

Target $\rightarrow$ is the call price C.

The function finds σ for which the Black-Scholes formula $= C$.

```
Function CallVolatility(Stock, Exercise, Time, _
    Interest, Target)
    High = 1
    Low = 0
    Do While (High - Low) > 0.0001
    If CallOption(Stock, Exercise, Time, Interest, _
        (High + Low) / 2) > Target
Then
            High = (High + Low) / 2
            Else Low = (High + Low) / 2
    End If
    Loop
    CallVolatility = (High + Low) / 2
End Function
```

The technique used by the function is very similar to the technique used in trial and error: We start with two estimates for the possible σ. A **High** estimate of 100 percent and a **Low** estimate of 0 percent. We now do the following:

• Plug the average of the **High** and the **Low** into the Black-Scholes formula. This gives us **CallOption(Stock, Exercise, Time, Interest, (High + Low) / 2).** (Note that the function **CallVolatility** assumes that the function **CallOption** is available to the spreadsheet.)

• If **CallOption(Stock, Exercise, Time, Interest, (High + Low) / 2) > Target,** then the current σ estimate of **(High + Low) / 2** is too high and we replace **High** by **(High + Low) / 2**.

• If **CallOption(Stock, Exercise, Time, Interest, (High + Low) / 2) < Target,** then the current σ estimate of **(High + Low) / 2** is too low and we replace **Low** by **(High + Low) / 2**.

We repeat this procedure until the difference **High-Low** is less than 0.0001 (or some other arbitrary constant).[3]

---

3. This stopping rule always works (meaning that the procedure eventually grinds to a halt) for bisection applied to a monotonic function. We could have replaced this criterion with the following stopping rule: **|CallOption(Stock,Exercise,Time,Interest,(High+Low)/2)-Target|** < 0.0001. For the case of finding the implied volatility, this will work equally well; however, for other cases a rule of this type may not always work.

Here's an example of this function, including a data table and a graph that shows the implied volatility as a function of the call price:

	A	B	F	G	H	I	J	K
1	**BLACK-SCHOLES IMPLIED VOLATILITY**							
2								
3	The VBA module attached to this spreadsheet defines a function called							
4	CallVolatility(S,X,T,interest,target_call_price).To use this function fill in the relevant rows							
5	(in boldface). The cell labeled "Implied call volatility"contains the function.							
6								
7	**S**	**51.00**						
8	**X**	**50.00**						
9	**T**	**1**						
10	**Interest**	**8.00%**						
11	**Target call price**	**6.00**						
12								
13	Implied call volatility	15.35%	<-- =CallVolatility(B7,B8,B9,B10,B11)					
14								
15								
16	**Data Table**							
17		15.35%						
18	5.00	7.51%						
19	5.50	11.96%						
20	6.00	15.35%						
21	6.50	18.45%						
22	7.00	21.39%						
23	7.50	24.25%						
24	8.00	27.07%						
25	8.50	29.84%						
26	9.00	32.59%						
27	9.50	35.33%						
28	10.00	38.05%						
29	10.50	40.77%						
30								

Implied Call Volatility — plot of Implied volatility vs. Target call price ($)

16.6   Bang for the Buck with Options

This section presents a simple application of the Black-Scholes formula. Suppose that you are convinced that a given stock will go up in a very short period of time. You want to buy calls on the stock that have a maximum "bang for the buck"—that is, you want the percentage profit on your option investment to be maximal. Using the Black-Scholes formula, it is easy to show that you should

- Buy calls with the shortest possible maturity.
- Buy calls that are most highly out of the money (i.e., with the highest exercise price possible).

Here's a spreadsheet illustration:

	A	B	C	D	E	F	G
1			"Bang for the Buck" with Options				
2							
3	S		25	Current stock price			
4	X		25	Exercise price			
5	r		6.00%	Risk-free rate of interest			
6	T		0.5	Time to maturity of option (in years)			
7	Sigma		30%	Stock volatility			
8							
9	d_1		0.2475	<-- (LN(S/X)+(r+0.5*sigma^2)*T)/(sigma*SQRT(T))			
10	d_2		0.0354	<-- d_1 - sigma*SQRT(T)			
11							
12	$N(d_1)$		0.5977	<--- Uses formula NormSDist(d_1)			
13	$N(d_2)$		0.5141	<--- Uses formula NormSDist(d_2)			
14							
15	Call price		2.47	<-- S*N(d_1)-X*exp(-r*T)*N(d_2)			
16	Put price		1.73	<-- call price - S + X*Exp(-r*T): by put-call parity			
17							
18	Call bang	6.048317	<-- =B12*B3/B15				
19	Put bang	5.807036	<-- =NORMSDIST(-B9)*B3/B16				

The "call bang" defined in cell B18 is simply the percentage change in the call price divided by the percentage change in the stock price (in economics this is known as the *price elasticity*):

$$\text{Call bang} = \frac{\partial C/C}{\partial S/S} = \frac{\partial C}{\partial S}\frac{S}{C} = N(d_1)\frac{S}{C}$$

Similarly, for a put, the "bang for the buck" is defined by the following formula (of course, the story behind the put "bang for the buck" is that you are convinced that the stock price will go down):

$$\text{Put bang} = \frac{\partial P/P}{\partial S/S} = \frac{\partial P}{\partial S}\frac{S}{P} = -N(-d_1)\frac{S}{P}$$

This is defined in cell B19. To make the numbers easier to understand, we have dropped the initial minus sign, making the "put bang" $= N(-d_1)\dfrac{S}{P}$.

The following graph shows the "bang for the buck" for both calls and puts:

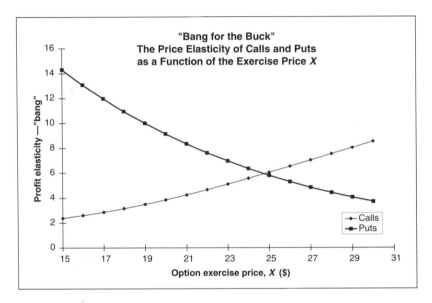

If you play with the spreadsheet, you will see that the longer the time to maturity, the less the bang for the buck. (Another way of saying all this is that the most risky options are the most out-of-the-money and the shortest-term options.)

	F	G	H	I	J	K	L	M
24				Data table: Effect of S and T on "call bang"				
25								
26		Data table header:			T--option time to exercise			
27		=B19		6.0483	0.25	0.5	0.75	1
28				15	25.8856	14.1771	10.1696	8.1112
29		S, stock price -->		16	23.3305	12.9884	9.4123	7.5625
30				17	20.9954	11.9033	8.7218	7.0623
31				18	18.8590	10.9121	8.0914	6.6057
32				19	16.9052	10.0067	7.5154	6.1882
33				20	15.1222	9.1805	6.9891	5.8062
34				21	13.5007	8.4274	6.5082	5.4565
35				22	12.0334	7.7424	6.0691	5.1362
36				23	10.7137	7.1205	5.6682	4.8426
37				24	9.5347	6.5572	5.3025	4.5737
38				25	8.4893	6.0483	4.9691	4.3272
39				26	7.5694	5.5896	4.6655	4.1012
40				27	6.7664	5.1773	4.3892	3.8941
41				28	6.0706	4.8074	4.1379	3.7043
42				29	5.4720	4.4764	3.9094	3.5303
43				30	4.9598	4.1807	3.7019	3.3708

Exercises

1. Use the Black-Scholes model to price the following:

    a. A call option on a stock whose current price is 50, with exercise price $X = 50$, $T = 0.5$, $r = 10$ percent, $\sigma = 25$ percent.

    b. A put option with the same parameters.

2. Use the data from exercise 1 and **Data|Table** to produce graphs that show

    a. The sensitivity of the Black-Scholes call price to changes in the initial stock price S.

    b. The sensitivity of the Black-Scholes put price to changes in σ.

    c. The sensitivity of the Black-Scholes call price to changes in the time to maturity T.

    d. The sensitivity of the Black-Scholes call price to changes in the interest rate r.

    e. The sensitivity of the put price to changes in the exercise price X.

3. Produce a graph comparing a call's *intrinsic value* [defined as $\max(S - X, 0)$] and its Black-Scholes price. From this graph you should be able to deduce that it is never optimal to exercise early a call priced by the Black-Scholes formula.

4. Produce a graph comparing a put's intrinsic value [$\max(X - S, 0)$] and its Black-Scholes price. From this graph you should be able to deduce that it may be optimal to exercise early a put priced by the Black-Scholes formula.

5. Refer back to the American Express options in Chapter 13. Assume that the current date is Friday, January 26, 1996, and that the expiration dates of the options are as follows:

    "Feb" = February 16, 1996
    "Mar" = March 15, 1996
    "Apr" = April 19, 1996
    "Jul" = July 19, 1996

    Generate two tables:

    a. One table showing the prices (using the Black-Scholes model) of all of the American Express call options. Assume that the interest rate is $r = 6$ percent, and that the relevant volatility is $\sigma = 30$ percent.

    b. A second table for the American Express put options.

6. Use the Excel **Solver** to find the stock price for which there is the maximum difference between the Black-Scholes call option price and the option's intrinsic value. Use the following values: $S = 45$, $X = 45$, $T = 1$, $\sigma = 40$ percent, $r = 8$ percent.

7. As shown in proposition 7, Chapter 13, a European option on a stock should be priced by netting out from the underlying asset price all the dividends to be paid before the option matures. Merton (1973) shows that for the case of an asset with price S paying a continuously compounded dividend yield k, this approach leads to the following call-option-pricing formula:

    $$C = Se^{-kT}N(d_1) - Xe^{-rT}N(d_2)$$

where

$$d_1 = \frac{\ln(S/X) + (r - k + \sigma^2/2)T}{\sigma\sqrt{T}}$$
$$d_2 = d_1 - \sigma\sqrt{T}$$

This formula is often applied to the pricing of options on indexes, where the aggregation of many stock dividends makes the continuous-dividend assumption an appropriate approximation. Use this formula to price a call option on an index whose current price is $S = 500$ when the option's maturity $T = 1$, the dividend yield is $k = 2.2$ percent, its standard deviation $\sigma = 20$ percent, and the interest rate $r = 7$ percent.

8. The Merton model in exercise 7 can also be used to price options on currencies. Suppose, for example, we are pricing a call option to buy € 10,000 for a rate of $1.10 per € in 3 months. Suppose that the U.S. interest rate is 5.5 percent and that the Euro interest rate is 3.8 percent. The following spreadsheet illustrates how to use the Merton model to price this option (note the low volatility—typical of currencies).

Use this model to perform a sensitivity analysis that shows the effects of the current exchange rate on the option price.

	A	B	C	D	E	F	G	H
1			**Pricing Currency Options**					
2								
3	S	1.04	Current exchange rate: U.S. dollar price of one Euro					
4	X	1.10	Exercise price					
5	r_{US}	5.50%	U.S. interest rate					
6	$r_€$	3.80%	Euro interest rate					
7	T	0.25	Time to maturity of option (in years)					
8	Sigma	6.00%	Stock volatility					
9	d_1	-1.7130	<--(LN(S/X)+(r_{US}-$r_€$ +0.5*sigma^2)*T)/(sigma*SQRT(T))					
10	d_2	-1.7430	<-- d_1 - sigma*SQRT(T)					
11								
12	Number of Euros per call contract	10,000						
13								
14	N(d_1)	0.0434	<--- Uses formula NormSDist(d_1)					
15	N(d_2)	0.0407	<--- Uses formula NormSDist(d_2)					
16								
17	Call price	5.42	<-- S*Exp(-$r_€$*T)*N(d_1)-X*exp(-r_{US}*T)*N(d_2)					
18	Put price	553.53	<-- X*exp(-r_{US}*T)*N(-d_2)-S*Exp(-$r_€$*T)*N(d_1): direct formula					

9. Note that you can use the Black-Scholes formula to calculate the call option premium as a percentage of the exercise price in terms of S/X:

$$C = SN(d_1) - Xe^{-rT}N(d_2) \Rightarrow \frac{C}{X} = \frac{S}{X}N(d_1) - e^{-rT}N(d_2)$$

where

$$d_1 = \frac{\ln(S/X) + (r + \sigma^2/2)T}{\sigma\sqrt{T}}$$

$$d_2 = d_1 - \sigma\sqrt{T}$$

Implement this in a spreadsheet.

10. Note that you can also calculate the Black-Scholes put option premium as a percentage of the exercise price in terms of S/X:

$$P = -SN(-d_1) + Xe^{-rT}N(-d_2) \Rightarrow \frac{P}{X} = e^{-rT}N(-d_2) - \frac{S}{X}N(-d_1)$$

where

$$d_1 = \frac{\ln(S/X) + (r + \sigma^2)T}{\sigma\sqrt{T}}$$

$$d_2 = d_1 - \sigma\sqrt{T}$$

Implement this in a spreadsheet. Find the ratio of S/X for which C/X and P/X cross when $T = 0.5$, $\sigma = 25\%$, $r = 10\%$. (You can use a graph or you can use Excel's Solver.) Note that this crossing point is affected by the interest rate and the option maturity, but not by σ.

17 Portfolio Insurance

17.1 Introduction: Insuring Stock Returns

Options can be used to guarantee minimum returns from stock investments. As we showed in our discussion of option strategies in Chapter 13, when you purchase a stock (or a portfolio of stocks) and simultaneously purchase a put on the stock (or the portfolio), you are assured that the dollar return from the purchase will never be lower than the exercise price on the put. However, it is not always possible to find marketed puts on all portfolios; in this case the Black-Scholes option-pricing formula can show us how to *replicate* a put by a dynamic strategy in which the investment in a risky asset (be it a single stock or a portfolio) and the investment in riskless bonds changes over time to mimic the returns of a put option. Such *replication strategies* are at the heart of the portfolio insurance strategies discussed here.

We start by considering the following simple example: You decide to invest in one share of General Pills stock, which currently costs $56. The stock pays no dividends. You hope for a large capital gain at the end of the year, but you worry that the stock's price may decline. To guard against a decline in the stock's price, you decide to purchase a European put on the stock. The put you purchase allows you to sell the stock at the end of one year for $50. The cost of the put, $2.38, is derived from the Black-Scholes model (see Chapter 16) using the following data: $S_0 = \$56$, $X = \$50$, $\sigma = 30$ percent, and $r = 8$ percent:

	A	B	C	D	E	F	G
1			**Black-Scholes Option-Pricing Formula**				
2			**Applied to General Pills Put**				
3							
4	S	56	Stock price				
5	X	50	Exercise price				
6	T	1	Time remaining				
7	r	8.00%	Risk-free rate of interest				
8	Sigma	30%	Stock volatility				
9							
10	d_1	0.7944	<-- (LN(S/X)+(r+0.5*sigma^2)*T)/(sigma*SQRT(T))				
11	d_2	0.4944	<-- d_1-Sigma*SQRT(T)				
12							
13	$N(d_1)$	0.7865	<-- Uses formula NormSDist(d_1)				
14	$N(d_2)$	0.6895	<-- Uses formula NormSDist(d_2)				
15							
16	Call price	12.22	<-- S*N(d_1)-X*exp(-r*T)*N(d_2)				
17	Put price	2.38	<-- call price - S + X*Exp(-r*T): by Put-Call parity				

This *protective put* or *portfolio insurance* strategy guarantees that you will lose no more than $6 on your share of General Pills stock. If the stock's price at the end of the year is more than $50, you will simply let the put expire without exercising it. However, if the stock's price at the end of the year is less than $50, you will exercise the put and collect $50. It is as if you had purchased an insurance policy on the stock with a $6 deductible.

Of course, this protection doesn't come for free: Instead of investing $56 in your single share of stock, you have invested $58.38. You could have deposited the additional $2.38 in the bank and earned interest of 8 percent $*$ $2.38 = \$0.19$ in the course of the year; alternatively, you could have used the $2.38 to buy more shares.

17.2   Portfolio Insurance on More Complicated Assets

In the example, we have implemented a portfolio insurance strategy by purchasing a put whose underlying asset exactly corresponds to our share portfolio. But this technique may not always be possible:

• It could be that there is no traded put option on the shares we wish to insure.

• It could also happen that we want to purchase portfolio insurance on a more complicated basket of assets, such as a portfolio of shares. Puts on some portfolios do exist (for example, puts on the S&P 100 and S&P 500 portfolios are traded) but clearly there are no traded puts on most portfolios.

It is here that the Black-Scholes option-pricing model comes to our aid. From this formula it follows that a put option on a stock (from here on, "stock" will be used to refer to a portfolio of stocks as well as a single stock) is simply a portfolio consisting of a short position in the stock and a long position in the risk-free asset, with both positions being adjusted continuously. For example, consider the Black-Scholes formula for a put with expiration date $T = 1$ and exercise price X. At time t, $0 \leq t < 1$, the put has value

$$P_t = -S_t N(-d_1) + X e^{-r(1-t)} N(-d_2)$$

where

$$d_1 = \frac{\ln\left(S_t/X\right) + \left(r + \sigma^2/2\right)(1 - t)}{\sigma\sqrt{1 - t}}$$

$$d_2 = d_1 - \sigma\sqrt{1 - t}$$

where $1 - t$ is the time remaining to maturity and S_t is the price of the stock at time t.

Thus, buying a put is equivalent to investing $Xe^{-r(1-t)}N(-d_2)$ in a risk-free bond that matures at time 1 and investing $-S_t N(-d_1)$ in the stock. Since the investment in the stock is negative, a put is equivalent to a short position in the stock and a long position in the risk-free asset.

The total investment required to buy one share of the stock plus a put on the stock is $S_t + P_t$. Writing this out and substituting in the Black-Scholes put formula gives

$$\text{Total investment, protective put} = S_t + P_t$$

$$= S_t - S_t N(-d_1) + Xe^{-r(1-t)}N(-d_2)$$

$$= S_t[1 - N(-d_1)] + Xe^{-r(1-t)}N(-d_2)$$

$$= S_t N(d_1) + Xe^{-r(1-t)}N(-d_2)$$

where the last equality uses the fact that for the standard normal distribution $N(x) + N(-x) = 1$. An even more useful way of looking at this problem is to regard the total investment $S_t + P_t$ at time t as a portfolio of a stock and a bond; we can then ask what is the proportion ω_t of this portfolio invested in the stock at time t. Rewriting the preceding formula in terms of portfolio proportions gives

$$\text{Proportion invested in stock} = \omega_t$$

$$= \frac{S_t N(d_1)}{S_t N(d_1) + Xe^{-r(1-t)}N(-d_2)}$$

$$\text{Proportion invested in risk-free asset} = 1 - \omega_t$$

$$= \frac{Xe^{-r(1-t)}N(-d_2)}{S_t N(d_1) + Xe^{-r(1-t)}N(-d_2)}$$

In summary, if you want to buy a specific portfolio of assets *and* an insurance policy guaranteeing that at $t = 1$ your total investment will not be worth less than *X,* then at each point in time, *t,* you should invest a proportion ω_t of your wealth in the specific portfolio you have chosen, and a proportion $1 - \omega_t$ in riskless, pure-discount bonds that mature at $t = 1$. The Black-Scholes put-pricing formula can be used to determine these proportions.

17.3 An Example

Suppose you decide to invest $1,000 in General Pills stock (currently selling at $56) and in protective puts on the shares with an exercise price of $50 and an expiration date one year from now. This method insures that your dollar value per share at the end of one year will be no less than $50. Suppose that there is no traded put on General Pills, so that you will have to create your own put by investing in the share and in riskless discount bonds. The riskless rate of interest is 8 percent, and the standard deviation of General Pills' log return is 30 percent.

   We will construct a series of portfolios that implements this strategy on a week-by-week basis.[1]

17.3.1 Week 0

At the beginning of week 0, the initial investment in shares of General Pills should be

$$\omega_0 = \frac{S_0 N(d_1)}{S_0 + P_0} = \frac{56 * 0.7865}{56 + 2.38} = 75.45 \text{ percent}$$

with the remaining proportion, $1 - \omega_0 = 24.55$ percent, invested in riskless discount bonds maturing in one year. If traded European puts on GP existed and if these puts had an exercise price of 50 with an exercise date one year from now, these would be trading at $2.38. Your strategy would consist of buying 17.13 shares of GP (cost = $959.23) and 17.13 puts (cost = $40.77). Buying $754.40 of shares and $245.60 of bonds exactly duplicates the initial investment in 17.13 shares and 17.13 puts. This equivalence is guaranteed by Black and Scholes. The calculations of the option price and the appropriate portfolio proportions are shown in the following spreadsheet picture.

---

1. There's an implicit contradiction here between the finite updating strategy and the continuous rebalancing that underlies the Black-Scholes model. This is discussed at the end of this section.

	A	B	C	D	E	F	G
1		**Black-Scholes Option-Pricing Formula**					
2		**Applied to General Pills Put**					
3							
4	S	56	Stock price				
5	X	50	Exercise price				
6	T	1	Time remaining				
7	r	8.00%	Risk-free rate of interest				
8	Sigma	30%	Stock volatility				
9							
10	d_1	0.7944	<-- (LN(S/X)+(r+0.5*sigma^2)*T)/(sigma*SQRT(T))				
11	d_2	0.4944	<-- d_1-Sigma*SQRT(T)				
12							
13	$N(d_1)$	0.7865	<-- Uses formula NormSDist(d_1)				
14	$N(d_2)$	0.6895	<-- Uses formula NormSDist(d_2)				
15							
16	Call price	12.22	<-- S*N(d_1)-X*exp(-r*T)*N(d_2)				
17	Put price	2.38	<-- call price - S + X*Exp(-r*T): by Put-Call parity				
18							
19	**Calculating the portfolio insurance proportions**						
20	Omega	75.45%	<-- =B4*B13/(B4+B17): proportion in shares				
21	1-omega	24.55%	<-- =1-B20: proportion in bonds				

We now turn to the end of week 1. You started at $t = 0$ with an initial investment of $1,000; now suppose that by the end of the first week the price of GP shares had increased to $60. Then your portfolio value at the beginning and end of the first week would look like this.

Week	Stock price at begin. of week	Stock price at end of week	d_1 at begin. of week	Omega, begin. of week	Portfolio value, beginning of week			Portfolio value, end of week		
					Stocks	Bonds	Portfolio value	Stocks	Bonds	Portfolio value
0	56.00	60.00	0.7944	0.7545	754.50	245.50	1000.00	808.39	245.88	1054.27

Note that the value of your bonds at the end of the week is known in advance; this value grows by a factor of $1.00154 = e^{(1/52)0.08}$ per week.[2] The value of your shares, however, depends on the rate of growth in the price of General Pills stock. During week 0, this rate of growth was $60/56 = 1.0714$.

---

2. Throughout we assume that the interest rate does not change. As an approximation to reality, this assumption is acceptable in this situation (meaning that the effect of interest-rate changes is much smaller than the effect of changes in the stock price). If we wished to account for interest-rate changes, then this factor would add another source of uncertainty to the model.

17.3.2   Week 1

At the beginning of week 1 you rebalance your portfolio, increasing the proportion of equity and decreasing the amount invested in the bonds. The new portfolio proportions reflect the time to maturity (time after one week is $t = 1/52 = 0.0192$), the stock price at the beginning of the week ($60), and the total portfolio value at the beginning of the week ($1,054.27). As the next spreadsheet picture shows, you should now *rebalance* your portfolio, investing

$$\omega_{0.0192} = \frac{SN(d_1)}{S + P} = \frac{60 * 0.8476}{60 + 1.63} = 82.53 \text{ percent}$$

in shares of General Pills and the remainder, 17.47 percent, in bonds. Here $1.63 is the Black-Scholes cost of a European put, calculated with the correct parameters:

	A	B	C	D	E	F	G
1	\multicolumn{7}{c}{**Black-Scholes Option-Pricing Formula**}						
2	\multicolumn{7}{c}{**Applied to General Pills Put**}						
3							
4	S	60	Stock price				
5	X	50	Exercise price				
6	T	0.980769	Time remaining = 51/52				
7	r	8.00%	Risk-free rate of interest				
8	Sigma	30%	Stock volatility				
9							
10	d_1	1.0263	<-- (LN(S/X)+(r+0.5*sigma^2)*T)/(sigma*SQRT(T))				
11	d_2	0.7292	<-- d_1-Sigma*SQRT(T)				
12							
13	$N(d_1)$	0.8476	<-- Uses formula NormSDist(d_1)				
14	$N(d_2)$	0.7671	<-- Uses formula NormSDist(d_2)				
15							
16	Call price	15.40	<-- S*N(d_1)-X*exp(-r*T)*N(d_2)				
17	Put price	1.63	<-- call price - S + X*Exp(-r*T): by Put-Call parity				
18							
19	\multicolumn{7}{l}{**Calculating the portfolio insurance proportions**}						
20	Omega	82.53%	<-- =B4*B13/(B4+B17): proportion in shares				
21	1-omega	17.47%	<-- =1-B20: proportion in bonds				

Suppose that at the end of week 1, the price of a share of General Pills tumbled to 52. Your position now looks like this:

	Stock price at begin. of week	Stock price at end of week	d_1 at begin. of week	Omega, begin. of week	Portfolio value, beginning of week			Portfolio value, end of week		
Week					Stocks	Bonds	Portfolio value	Stocks	Bonds	Portfolio value
0	56.00	60.00	0.7944	0.7545	754.50	245.50	1000.00	808.39	245.88	1054.27
1	60.00	52.00	1.0263	0.8253	870.06	184.21	1054.27	754.05	184.50	938.55

17.3.3   Week 2

Since another week has passed, the proportion of your investment in General Pills should now be

$$\omega_{0.0385} = \frac{S * N(d_1)}{S + P} = \frac{52 * 0.7061}{52 + 3.33} = 66.35 \text{ percent}$$

This gives

	Stock price at begin. of week	Stock price at end of week	d_1 at begin. of week	Omega, begin. of week	Portfolio value, beginning of week			Portfolio value, end of week		
Week					Stocks	Bonds	Portfolio value	Stocks	Bonds	Portfolio value
0	56.00	60.00	0.7944	0.7545	754.50	245.50	1000.00	808.39	245.88	1054.27
1	60.00	52.00	1.0263	0.8253	870.06	184.21	1054.27	754.05	184.50	938.55
2	52.00	???	0.5419	0.6635	622.73	315.82	938.55	???	316.30	???

The uncertainty will be resolved only when we know the value of the shares at the end of the week.

Of course this example is somewhat misleading because the Black-Scholes model assumes that portfolio proportions are continuously adjusted, whereas we have waited a whole week to readjust our proportions. In the background lurks a pious hope that finite (but short) adjustment intervals will approximate the Black-Scholes continuous-readjustment scheme. (Since we are only human, we can't in fact make continuous adjustments to our portfolio. Moreover, since readjustment of the portfolio involves transaction costs to the investor, only finite adjustment is possible.)

17.4   Some Properties of Portfolio Insurance

The preceding example illustrates some of the typical properties of portfolio insurance. Three important properties are the following:

PROPERTY 1   When the stock price is above the exercise price X, then the proportion ω invested in the risky asset is greater than 50 percent.

Proof   The proof of this property requires a little manipulation of our formula for ω. Rewrite ω as

$$\omega = \frac{SN(d_1)}{SN(d_1) + Xe^{-r(1-t)}N(-d_2)} = \frac{1}{1 + \dfrac{Xe^{-r(1-t)}N(-d_2)}{SN(d_1)}}$$

We will show that when $S \geq X$, the denominator of ω is < 2, which will prove the proposition: First note that when $S \geq X$, $X/S \leq 1$. Next note that $e^{-r(1-t)} < 1$ for all $0 \leq t \leq 1$. Finally, examine the expression

$$\frac{N(-d_2)}{N(d_1)} = \frac{N(\sigma\sqrt{1-t} - d_1)}{N(d_1)}$$

$$= \frac{N\{0.5\sigma\sqrt{1-t} - [\ln(S/X) + r(1-t)]/(1-t)\}}{N\{0.5\sigma\sqrt{1-t} + [\ln(S/X) + r(1-t)]/(1-t)\}} < 1$$

This proves the property.

PROPERTY 2   When the stock's price increases, the proportion ω invested in the stock increases and vice versa.

Proof   To see this property, it is enough to see that when S increases, the value of the put decreases and $N(-d_1)$ decreases. Rewrite the original definition of ω as

$$\omega = \frac{S[1 - N(-d_1)]}{S + P} = \frac{[1 - N(-d_1)]}{1 + P/S}$$

Thus, when S increases, the denominator of ω decreases and the numerator increases, which proves Property 2.

PROPERTY 3   As $t \to 1$, one of two things happens: If $S_t > X$, then $\omega_t \to 1$. If $S_t < X$, then $\omega_t \to 0$.

Proof   To see this property, note that when $S_t > X$ and $t \to 1$, $N(d_1) \to 1$ and $N(-d_1) \to 0$; thus for this case $\omega_t \to 1$. Conversely, when $S_t < X$ and $t \to 1$, $N(d_1) \to 0$ and $N(-d_1) \to 1$ and thus $\omega_t \to 0$. (Strictly speaking these statements are only true as "probability limits"—see Billingsley, 1968. What about the case when, as $t \to 1$, $S_t/X \to 1$? In this case $\omega_t \to 1/2$. However, the probability of this occuring is zero.)

17.5   What Do Portfolio Insurance Strategies Look Like? A Simulation

What do portfolio insurance strategies look like? In this section we consider this question by simulating such a strategy. Throughout we assume that the interest rate is constant and that the stock price is lognormally distributed. Here is a sample from the output of a simulation:

Week	Stock price at begin. of week	Stock price at end of week	d_1 at begin. of week	Omega, begin. of week	Portfolio value, beginning of week			Portfolio value, end of week			Standard Normal Deviates
					Stocks	Bonds	Portfolio value	Stocks	Bonds	Portfolio value	
0	56.00	56.87	0.7944	0.7545	754.50	245.50	1000.00	766.21	245.88	1012.09	0.300952
1	56.87	54.19	0.8459	0.7717	781.06	231.04	1012.09	744.32	231.39	975.71	-1.22724
2	54.19	52.27	0.6824	0.7163	698.89	276.83	975.71	674.09	277.25	951.35	-0.93746
3	52.27	52.82	0.5571	0.6699	637.27	314.08	951.35	643.95	314.56	958.51	0.181024
4	52.82	52.87	0.5907	0.6832	654.82	303.68	958.51	655.46	304.15	959.61	-0.04603
5	52.87	52.01	0.5919	0.6841	656.46	303.15	959.61	645.76	303.62	949.38	-0.46433
6	52.01	56.28	0.5315	0.6614	627.90	321.47	949.38	679.42	321.97	1001.39	1.826256
7	56.28	56.02	0.8114	0.7625	763.61	237.78	1001.39	760.13	238.15	998.28	-0.17924
8	56.02	57.31	0.7953	0.7576	756.30	241.97	998.28	773.72	242.35	1016.07	0.478002
9	57.31	62.79	0.8791	0.7848	797.38	218.69	1016.07	873.60	219.03	1092.63	2.125198
10	62.79	62.39	1.2192	0.8743	955.28	137.35	1092.63	949.21	137.56	1086.78	-0.2224
11	62.39	59.12	1.2011	0.8705	946.06	140.72	1086.78	896.49	140.93	1037.42	-1.36308
12	59.12	61.93	1.0023	0.8216	852.33	185.09	1037.42	892.77	185.38	1078.15	1.044987
13	61.93	63.29	1.1842	0.8672	934.95	143.20	1078.15	955.48	143.42	1098.90	0.452768
14	63.29	66.81	1.2750	0.8867	974.34	124.56	1098.90	1028.64	124.75	1153.39	1.234253
15	66.81	67.42	1.4970	0.9251	1067.05	86.34	1153.39	1076.78	86.47	1163.26	0.148917
16	67.42	73.92	1.5444	0.9319	1084.09	79.17	1163.26	1188.61	79.29	1267.90	2.143097
17	73.92	76.54	1.9305	0.9706	1230.57	37.32	1267.90	1274.18	37.38	1311.56	0.767639
18	76.54	77.82	2.0923	0.9801	1285.44	26.12	1311.56	1306.87	26.16	1333.03	0.32804
19	77.82	78.48	2.1829	0.9842	1311.92	21.10	1333.03	1323.15	21.13	1344.28	0.135394
20	78.48	77.20	2.2427	0.9865	1326.07	18.21	1344.28	1304.44	18.23	1322.68	-0.46467
21	77.20	84.76	2.1972	0.9848	1302.55	20.13	1322.68	1430.10	20.16	1450.26	2.176184
22	84.76	88.17	2.6329	0.9954	1443.65	6.60	1450.26	1501.62	6.61	1508.24	0.876967
23	88.17	85.89	2.8429	0.9976	1504.63	3.61	1508.24	1465.75	3.61	1469.36	-0.69867
24	85.89	87.58	2.7634	0.9969	1464.86	4.50	1469.36	1493.64	4.50	1498.15	0.398409
25	87.58	87.82	2.8930	0.9980	1495.10	3.05	1498.15	1499.24	3.05	1502.29	-0.00287
26	87.82	88.87	2.9498	0.9983	1499.75	2.54	1502.29	1517.67	2.55	1520.22	0.216135
27	88.87	88.01	3.0538	0.9988	1518.39	1.82	1520.22	1503.66	1.83	1505.48	-0.30376
28	88.01	89.15	3.0571	0.9988	1503.70	1.78	1505.48	1523.20	1.79	1524.99	0.240398
29	89.15	88.06	3.1754	0.9992	1523.78	1.21	1524.99	1505.17	1.21	1506.38	-0.36476
30	88.06	90.69	3.1715	0.9992	1505.17	1.21	1506.38	1550.23	1.21	1551.44	0.63972
31	90.69	90.28	3.3882	0.9996	1550.87	0.57	1551.44	1543.84	0.57	1544.41	-0.17854
32	90.28	94.25	3.4346	0.9997	1543.93	0.48	1544.41	1611.84	0.48	1612.32	0.965367
33	94.25	97.47	3.7479	0.9999	1612.17	0.15	1612.32	1667.23	0.15	1667.38	0.737782
34	97.47	95.65	4.0272	1.0000	1667.33	0.05	1667.38	1636.07	0.05	1636.12	-0.52423
35	95.65	99.84	4.0196	1.0000	1636.07	0.05	1636.12	1707.79	0.05	1707.84	0.961959
36	99.84	106.44	4.3867	1.0000	1707.83	0.01	1707.84	1820.70	0.01	1820.71	1.468939
37	106.44	111.94	4.9129	1.0000	1820.71	0.00	1820.71	1914.88	0.00	1914.88	1.142803
38	111.94	118.18	5.3938	1.0000	1914.88	0.00	1914.88	2021.57	0.00	2021.57	1.233925
39	118.18	112.63	5.9428	1.0000	2021.57	0.00	2021.57	1926.62	0.00	1926.62	-1.22561
40	112.63	114.89	5.8350	1.0000	1926.62	0.00	1926.62	1965.39	0.00	1965.39	0.409448
41	114.89	119.86	6.2214	1.0000	1965.39	0.00	1965.39	2050.33	0.00	2050.33	0.947721
42	119.86	113.38	6.8285	1.0000	2050.33	0.00	2050.33	1939.43	0.00	1939.43	-1.40597
43	113.38	120.76	6.7330	1.0000	1939.43	0.00	1939.43	2065.68	0.00	2065.68	1.446579
44	120.76	120.41	7.6570	1.0000	2065.68	0.00	2065.68	2059.67	0.00	2059.67	-0.13941
45	120.41	122.59	8.1373	1.0000	2059.67	0.00	2059.67	2096.99	0.00	2096.99	0.362387
46	122.59	123.23	8.9420	1.0000	2096.99	0.00	2096.99	2108.03	0.00	2108.03	0.056831
47	123.23	127.51	9.8260	1.0000	2108.03	0.00	2108.03	2181.17	0.00	2181.17	0.750497
48	127.51	135.13	11.3669	1.0000	2181.17	0.00	2181.17	2311.45	0.00	2311.45	1.325138
49	135.13	137.50	13.8971	1.0000	2311.45	0.00	2311.45	2352.13	0.00	2352.13	0.350079
50	137.50	132.82	17.2761	1.0000	2352.13	0.00	2352.13	2272.03	0.00	2272.03	-0.90219
51	132.82	132.56	23.5414	1.0000	2272.03	0.00	2272.03	2267.53	0.00	2267.53	-0.11704
52	132.56						2267.53				0.350079

All of the columns of the simulation have already been explained, except the last column: This column contains a series of random numbers drawn from a standard normal distribution. The price of the stock at the end of each week is determined by these random numbers. In this example, the stock price of 56.87 at the end of week 0 is—as explained in Chapter 15—determined by the lognormal assumption $S_t = S_{t-1} * e^{\mu\Delta t + \sigma Z\sqrt{\Delta t}}$, which for this particular case becomes $56.87 = 50 * e^{0.15*1/52 + 0.30*0.300952\sqrt{1/52}}$. As explained in Chapter 15, these standard normal deviates were created with the Excel command **Tools|Data Analysis|Random Number Generation.**

When graphed, the results look like this:

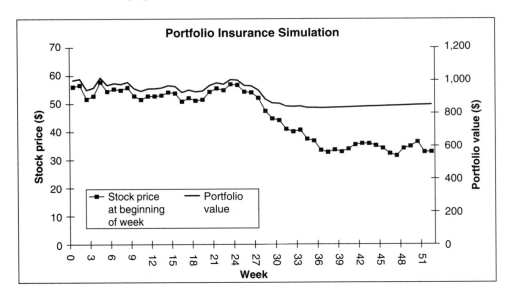

In this particular graph the stock price (graphed on the left axis) declined over the year, so that the portfolio insurance strategy (the heavy line) pays off more than a straight stock strategy would have. In effect, we have used the puts that are implicit in this strategy.

In this example, the stock price declines below \$50 per share. As we pointed out in section 17.3, at date 0 the portfolio insurance strategy involved the equivalent of purchasing 17.13 shares of the stock and a put on each of these shares. In this particular simulation, the portfolio value never dips below \$856.50 ($= 17.13 * \$50$), even though the stock price at $t = 1$ is just above \$40. As suggested by Proposition 3 of section 17.4, by the end of the year, the portfolio insurance strategy is wholly invested in bonds. By week 47 there is no investment in stocks whatsoever.

We can rerun the simulation and graph the output, tracking both the stock price and the total portfolio value over the course of the year.

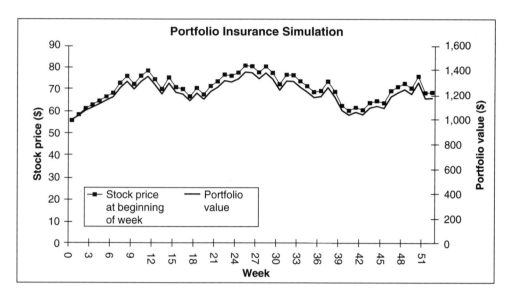

In this example, by year-end the portfolio insurance strategy will be wholly invested in stocks (again this result follows from Proposition 3 of section 17.4). In this example the portfolio insurance proves more expensive than an uninsured investment (i.e., ex post, we would have been better off not following an insurance policy.

We can use the **Tools|Record Macro** feature of Excel to produce a macro that automates the simulation procedure.

```
Sub Simulation()
'Simulation Macro
'Macro recorded 10/28/1999 by Simon Benninga
'
    Application.SendKeys ("{Enter}")
    Application.Run "ATPVBAEN.XLA!Random", _
    ActiveSheet.Range("$O$11:$O$62"),, _
        , 2, , 0, 1
End Sub
```

The first line of the macro `Application.SendKeys ("{Enter}")` was added because each run of the random-number generator brings up the following dialogue box.

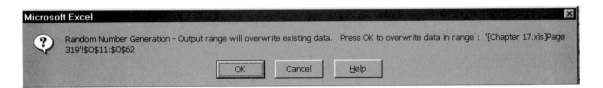

The first line of the macro sends an Enter to answer this dialogue box, so that the macro automatically enters the data into the range.

17.6   Insuring Total Portfolio Returns

So far we have considered only the problem of constructing artificial puts, one per share. A slightly different version of this problem involves constructing a portfolio of puts and shares that guarantees the *total* dollar returns on the *total* initial investment. A typical story goes like this:

You have $1,000 to invest, and you want to guarantee that a year from now you will have at least $1,000z. Here z is some number, generally between 0 and 1; for example, a z equal to 0.93 would mean that you want your final wealth to be at least $930.[3] You want to invest in a stock whose current price is S_0 and in a put on the stock with an exercise price X. You want the number of puts to be equal to the number of shares. Given X and S_0, the put price is $P(S_0, X)$. To implement the strategy, you must therefore buy α shares, where

$$\alpha = \frac{1,000}{S_0 + P(S_0, X)}$$

Since you have bought α shares and α puts with an exercise price of X, the minimum dollar return from your portfolio is αX. You want this to be equal to $1,000\ z$, and therefore you solve to get $\alpha = 1,000z/X$. Thus you can guarantee your minimum return if

$$S_0 + P(S_0, X) = X/z$$

Substituting in the Black-Scholes put-option-pricing formula with $T = 1$ gives

$$\frac{X}{z} = S_0 + P(S_0, X) = S_0 - S_0 N(-d_1) + Xe^{-r}N(-d_2)$$
$$= S_0[1 - N(-d_1)] + Xe^{-r}N(-d_2) = S_0 N(d_1) + Xe^{-r}N(-d_2)$$
$$= S_0 N(d_1) + Xe^{-r}N(\sigma - d_1)$$

---

3.   As we will show, it is possible to insure (up to a point) even with $z > 1$.

where

$$d_1 = \frac{\ln(S_0/X) + (r + \sigma^2/2)}{\sigma}, \quad d_2 = d_1 - \sigma$$

In order to solve this equation for X, we must thus solve

$$\frac{X}{z} = S_0 N(d_1) + Xe^{-r}N(\sigma - d_1)$$

Divide through by X and bring all the terms to one side to get

$$\frac{1}{z} - \frac{S_0}{X}N(d_1) - e^{-r}N(\sigma - d_1) = 0$$

A spreadsheet implementation of this equation follows. The data table shows the graph of the left-hand side of the equation; where this graph crosses the x-axis is the solution for the synthetic put exercise price X when $S_0 = 56$, $\sigma = 30$ percent, $r = 8$ percent, $T = 1$, and $z = 93$ percent.

	A	B	C	D	E	F	G	H	I	J
1		CHOOSING A SYNTHETIC PUT EXERCISE PRICE								
2										
3	z		0.9300	Insurance level						
4										
5	S		56	Current stock price						
6	X		57	Exercise price						
7	T		1	Time to maturity of option (in years)						
8	r		8.00%	Risk-free rate of interest						
9	Sigma		30%	Stock volatility						
10	d_1		0.3577	<-- (LN(S/X)+(r+0.5*sigma^2)*T)/(sigma*SQRT(T))						
11	d_2		0.0577	<-- d_1 - sigma*SQRT(T)						
12										
13	N(d_1)		0.6397	<-- Uses formula NormSDist(d_1)						
14	N(d_2)		0.5230	<-- Uses formula NormSDist(d_2)						
15										
16	Equation		0.0065	<-- 1/z - S_0/X*N(d_1)-exp(-r*T)*(1-N(d_2))						
17										
18			Data Table							
19			data table header -->		0.0065					
20				40	-0.3375					
21			Synthetic	45	-0.1960					
22			put	50	-0.0923					
23			exercise	55	-0.0172					
24			price	60	0.0363					
25				65	0.0738					
26				70	0.0996					
27				75	0.1172					
28				80	0.1291					
29				85	0.1370					
30										

At Which X to Create a Synthetic Put?

As you can see, the left-hand side of this equation is always an increasing function of *X*. In this case we can use **Tools|Solver** to find that *X* = 56.4261 is the exact solution:

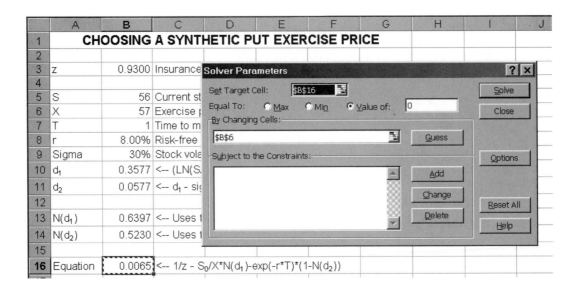

	A	B	C	D	E	F	G
1	**CHOOSING A SYNTHETIC PUT EXERCISE PRICE**						
2							
3	z	0.9300	Insurance level				
4							
5	S	56	Current stock price				
6	X	56.42616	Exercise price				
7	T	1	Time to maturity of option (in years)				
8	r	8.00%	Risk-free rate of interest				
9	Sigma	30%	Stock volatility				
10	d_1	0.3914	<-- (LN(S/X)+(r+0.5*sigma^2)*T)/(sigma*SQRT(T))				
11	d_2	0.0914	<-- d_1 - sigma*SQRT(T)				
12							
13	$N(d_1)$	0.6522	<-- Uses formula NormSDist(d_1)				
14	$N(d_2)$	0.5364	<-- Uses formula NormSDist(d_2)				
15							
16	Equation	0.0000	<-- 1/z - S_0/X*N(d_1)-exp(-r*T)*(1-N(d_2))				

17.6.1 What Is the Effect of Raising the Insurance Level?
Can You Insure for More Than Your Initial Investment?

When we raise the insurance level, the implied exercise price of the put must go up. Therefore, as we buy more insurance, we spend relatively more of our $1,000 on puts (insurance) and relatively less on the stocks (which have the upside potential).

Can we insure for more than our current level of investment? To put it another way, can we set $z > 1$? We would be picking an insurance level that would guarantee that we will end up with *more* than our initial investment. A little thought and some calculations reveal that we can indeed choose $z > 1$ as long as $z \leq 1 + r$. That is, we cannot guarantee ourselves a return greater than the riskless interest rate!

The following graph illustrates the answers to both our questions:

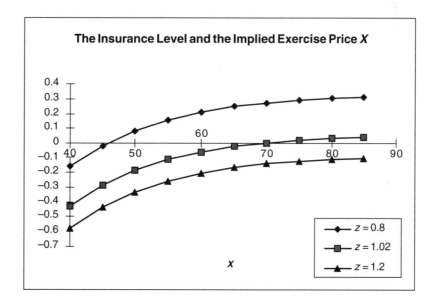

As the graph shows, you can insure for $z = 1.02$; that is, you can guarantee yourself at least $1,020 from your initial investment of $1,000. However, since there is no intersection point between the $x =$ axis and the curve for this value of z, you cannot insure for $z = 1.2$.

17.7   Implicit Puts and Asset Values

Up to this point, we have been discussing the construction of puts in order to construct portfolio insurance. We will now reverse the logic and consider situations in which we are offered a package that includes an implicit put. The problem is how to deduce the true value of the underlying asset that is part of the package.

Many commonly encountered situations include implicit puts. Consider the situation in which you are offered an asset plus an option to have the seller repurchase the asset. Some examples that come to mind are irrevocable tender offers, "satisfaction guaranteed or your money back" offers, and computer sales where you get to return the item but have to pay a 15 percent "restocking charge." (See Bhagat, Brickley, and Loewenstein, 1987, for an application of these ideas to cash tender offers.)

Were you in possession of the asset's variance, you could deduce from the offer the true value of the asset. Without this information, you can deduce the locus of the asset's standard deviation and its true value. To do so, let V_a denote the true value of the asset stripped of any puts or repurchase offers. Let V_p denote the value of the put. Let Y denote the purchase price (which, of course, includes the put), and let X denote the price at which you can get your money back. Then it follows that

$$Y = V_a + V_p$$

If we assume that the put option can be priced by the Black-Scholes formula, we will have

$$V_p = -V_a N(-d_1) + Xe^{-rT} N(\sigma\sqrt{T} - d_1)$$

where

$$d_1 = \frac{\ln(V_a/X) + \left(rT + \frac{\sigma}{2}\sqrt{T}\right)}{\sigma\sqrt{T}}$$

Thus, to solve this problem, we must find a σ and V_a that simultaneously solve

$$Y = V_a N(d_1) + Xe^{-rT} N(\sigma\sqrt{T} - d_1)$$

The right-hand side of this equation is increasing in σ and in V_a.

Here is an example: You are offered a risky asset for $100. If not satisfied with the asset, you may return it within one year and get back $85 (the remaining $15 is a "restocking charge"). How much is the asset worth? If you think that the asset's σ is 30 percent, then we have to solve:

$$Y = V_a N(d_1) + Xe^{-rT}N(\sigma\sqrt{T} - d_1)$$

where $Y = 100$, $\sigma = 30$ percent, $T = 1$, $r = 10$ percent, and $X = 85$. The answer, calculated in the following spreadsheet using **Tools|Solver,** is that the underlying asset value $V_a = \$96.71$:

	A	B	C	D	E	F	G
1		**IMPLICIT PUTS AND ASSET VALUES**					
2							
3	V_a	96.70586	Actual asset value				
4	X	85	Money-back guarantee				
5	r	10.00%	Risk-free rate of interest				
6	T	1	Time to maturity of option (in years)				
7	sigma	30%	Stock volatility				
8	d_1	0.9134	<-- (LN(S/X)+(r+0.5*sigma^2)*T)/(sigma*SQRT(T))				
9	d_2	0.6134	<-- d_1 - sigma*SQRT(T)				
10							
11	$N(d_1)$	0.8195	<-- Uses formula NormSDist(d_1)				
12	$N(d_2)$	0.7302	<-- Uses formula NormSDist(d_2)				
13							
14	Put price	3.29	<-- =-B3*(1-B11)+B4*EXP(-B5*B6)*(1-B12)				
15	Put + asset value	100.00	<-- =B3+B14				

Exercises

1. You are a portfolio manager, and you want to invest in an asset having $\sigma = 40$ percent. You want to create a put on the investment so that at the end of the year you have losses no greater than 5 percent. Since there is no put on this specific asset, you plan to create a synthetic put by engaging in a dynamic investment strategy—purchasing a portfolio composed of dynamically changing proportions of the risky asset and riskless bonds. If the interest rate is 6 percent, how much should your initial investment be in the portfolio and in the riskless bond?

2. Simulate the strategy of exercise 1, assuming weekly rebalancing of the portfolio.

3. Go back to the numerical example of section 17.6. Write a VBA function that solves for the implied asset value V_a. (Hint: Use the bisection method.) Then use this function to create a graph showing the trade-off between the implied asset value and the asset volatility.

4. You have been offered the chance to purchase stock in a firm. The seller wants $55 per share, but offers to repurchase the stock at the end of one-half year for $50 per share. If the σ of the share's log returns is 80 percent, determine the true value per share. Assume that the interest rate is 10 percent.

18 Real Options

18.1 Introduction

The standard net present values (NPV) analysis of capital budgeting values a project by discounting its expected cash flows at a risk-adjusted cost of capital. This technique is by far the most widely used technique for evaluating capital projects, be they acquisitions of companies or purchases of machines. However, standard NPV analysis does not take account of the *flexibility* inherent in the capital budgeting process. Part of the complexity of the capital budgeting process is that we can change our decision dynamically, depending on the circumstances.

Here are two examples:

1. A firm is considering replacing some of its machines with a new type of machine. Instead of replacing all the machines together, it can first replace one machine. Based on the performance of the first machine replaced, the firm can then decide whether to replace the rest of the machines. This *option to wait* (or perhaps "option to expand") is not valued in the standard NPV process. It is essentially a call option.

2. A firm is considering investing in a project that will produce (uncertain) cash flows over time. One option—not valued in the standard NPV framework—is to *abandon* the project if its performance is not satisfactory. The *abandonment option,* as we will see, is a put option that is implicit in many projects. It is also sometimes called the *option to contract scale.*

There are many other real options. In the leading book on the valuation of real options, Trigeorgis (1996) lists the following common ones:

• The option to defer or to wait when developing a natural resource or building a plant.

• The time-to-build option (staged investment): At each stage the investment can be re-evaluated and (possibly) abandoned or expanded.

• The option to alter operating scale (expand, contract, shut down, or restart).

• The option to abandon.

• The option to switch inputs or outputs.

• The growth option—an early investment in a project constitutes an option to "get into the market" at a later date.

The recognition of real options is an important extension of the NPV techniques. However, one of the difficulties inherent in the real-option technique is the computational difficulty. Modeling and valuing real options is more difficult than modeling and valuing standard cash flows. Our examples in this chapter illustrate these difficulties. Often it is best to implement real options by *recognizing* that the NPV technique misjudges the value of a project because it ignores the project's real options. Our usual conclusion will be that real options *add* to the value of a project, and that the NPV thus *underestimates* the true value.

18.2   A Simple Example of the Option to Expand

In this section we give a simple example of the option to expand. Consider ABC Corporation, which has six widget machines. It is considering replacing each of the old machines with a new machine that costs $1,000. The new machines have a five-year life. The anticipated cash flows for the new machine are as follows:[1]

A	B	C	D	E	F	G
3 Year	0	1	2	3	4	5
4 CF of single machine	-1000	220	300	400	200	150

The financial analyst working on the replacement project has estimated a cost of capital for the project of 12 percent. Using these anticipated cash flows and the 12 percent cost of capital, the analyst has concluded that the replacement of a single old machine by a new machine is unprofitable, since the NPV is negative:

$$-1000 + \frac{220}{1.12} + \frac{300}{(1.12)^2} + \frac{400}{(1.12)^3} + \frac{200}{(1.12)^4} + \frac{150}{(1.12)^5} = -67.48$$

Now comes the (real options) twist. The line manager in charge of the widget line says, "I want to try one of the new machines for a year. At the end of the year, if the experiment is successful, I want to replace five other similar machines on the line with the new machines."

---

1. These cash flows are the incremental cash flow of replacing a single old machine by a new machine. The computations include taxes, incremental depreciation, and the sale of the old machine.

Does this plan change our previously negative conclusion about replacing a single machine? The answer is yes. To see this point, we now realize that what we have is a package:

- Replacing a single machine today. This move has an NPV of -67.48.

- The *option* of replacing five more machines in one year. Suppose that the risk-free rate is 6 percent. Then we view each such option as a call option on an asset that has the following current value:

$$S = \frac{220}{1.12} + \frac{300}{(1.12)^2} + \frac{400}{(1.12)^3} + \frac{200}{(1.12)^4} + \frac{150}{(1.12)^5} = 932.52$$

and which has exercise price $X = 1,000$. Of course these call options can be exercised only if we purchase the first machine now.[2]

Suppose we assume that the Black-Scholes option-pricing model can price this option. In this case we have the following:

	A	B	C	D	E	F	G
1	THE OPTION TO EXPAND						
2							
3	Year	0	1	2	3	4	5
4	CF of single machine	-1000	220	300	400	200	150
5							
6	Discount rate for machine cash flows	12%					
7	Riskless discount rate	6%					
8	NPV of single machine	-67.48					
9							
10	Number of machines bought next year	5					
11	Option value of single machine purchased in one more year	143.98	<-- =B24				
12	NPV of total project	652.39	<-- =B8+B10*B11				
13							
14	**Black-Scholes Option Pricing Formula**						
15	S	932.52	PV of machine CFs				
16	X	1000.00	Exercise price = Machine cost				
17	r	6.00%	Risk-free rate of interest				
18	T	1	Time to maturity of option (in years)				
19	Sigma	40%	<-- Volatility				
20	d_1	0.1753	<-- (LN(S/X)+(r+0.5*sigma^2)*T)/(sigma*SQRT(T))				
21	d_2	-0.2247	<-- d_1 - sigma*SQRT(T)				
22	$N(d_1)$	0.5696	<--- Uses formula NormSDist(d_1)				
23	$N(d_2)$	0.4111	<--- Uses formula NormSDist(d_2)				
24	Option value = BS call price	143.98	<-- S*N(d_1)-X*exp(-r*T)*N(d_2)				

---

2. What we're really doing is pricing the cost of learning!

As cell B12 shows, the value of the whole project is $652.39.

Our conclusion: Buying one machine today, and knowing that we have the option to purchase five more machines in one year is a worthwhile project. One critical element here is the volatility. The lower the volatility (i.e., the lower the uncertainty), the less worthwhile this project is:

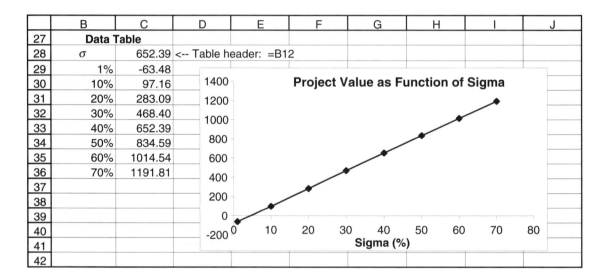

	B	C	D	E	F	G	H	I	J
27	**Data Table**								
28	σ	652.39	<-- Table header: =B12						
29	1%	-63.48							
30	10%	97.16							
31	20%	283.09							
32	30%	468.40							
33	40%	652.39							
34	50%	834.59							
35	60%	1014.54							
36	70%	1191.81							
37									
38									
39									
40									
41									
42									

This outcome is not very surprising: The value of the project as a whole comes from our uncertainty about the actual cash flows one year from now. The less is this uncertainty (measured by σ), the less valuable is the project.

18.2.1 Is Black-Scholes the Appropriate Valuation Tool for Real Options?

The answer is almost certainly no, Black-Scholes is not the appropriate tool. However—being realistic—the Black-Scholes model is by far the most numerically tractable (that is, the easiest) model we have for valuing options of any kind. In valuing real options we often use the Black-Scholes model, realizing that at best it can give an approximation to the actual option value. Such is life.

You should realize that the assumptions of the Black-Scholes option-valuation model—continuous trading, constant interest rate, no exercise before final option maturity—are not really appropriate to the real options considered in this chapter. In many cases real options involve what, in a securities-option context, would be considered dividend-paying securities and/or early exercise. Here are two examples:

• The staged-investment real option, when we have the opportunity to expand or contract the investment over time, is intrinsically an option with early exercise.

• When an option to abandon an investment exists, as long as the investment is still in place and not abandoned, it continues to pay "dividends," in the form of cash flows.

We can only hope that the Black-Scholes model gives an *approximation* to the option value intrinsic in the real options.

18.3   The Abandonment Option

Consider the following capital budgeting project:

	A	B	C	D	E
7	Project cash flows				
8					
9					150
10			100		
11					80
12	-50				
13					80
14			-50		
15					-60

As you can see, the initial cost of this project is $50. In one period the project will produce cash flows of either $100 or −$50; that is, under certain circumstances, it will lose money. Two periods hence the project again has chances of either losing money (in the worst case) or making money.

18.3.1   Valuing the Project

In order to value the project, we use the state prices from option pricing.[3] The state price q_u is the price today of $1 to be paid in the succeeding period in the "up" state; and the price q_d is the price today of $1 to be paid in the "down" state. The following spreadsheet fragment shows all the relevant details, leading to a project valuation of −$29.38 (implying rejection of the project).

---

3.   See section 18.3.4 on how to calculate these state prices.

	A	B	C	D	E	F	G	H	I	J	K	L
1					PRICING AN ABANDONMENT OPTION							
2												
3	**Market data**				**State prices**							
4	Expected market return	12%			q$_u$	0.3087	<-- =(1+B6-B10)/((1+B6)*(B9-B10))					
5	Sigma of market return	30%			q$_d$	0.6347	<-- =(B9-1-B6)/((1+B6)*(B9-B10))					
6	Risk-free rate	6%										
7												
8	**One-period "up" and "down" of market**											
9	up	1.521962	<-- =EXP(B4+B5), note that a valid alternative is "up" = EXP(B5)									
10	down	0.83527	<-- =EXP(B4-B5), note that a valid alternative is "down" = EXP(-B5)									
11												
12												
13	**Project cash flows**						**State-dependent present value factors**					
14												
15					150						0.0953	<-- =E4^2
16			100						0.3087			
17					80						0.1959	<-- =E4*E5
18		-50						1				
19					80						0.1959	<-- =E4*E5
20			-50						0.6347			
21					-60						0.4028	<-- =E5^2
22			=C16*I16									
23	**State-by-state present value**											
24					14.2981	<-- =E15*K15						
25			30.8740									
26					15.6755	<-- =E17*K17						
27		-50										
28					15.6755	<-- =E19*K19						
29			-31.7328									
30					-24.1673	<-- =E21*K21						
31												
32	**Net present value**				-29.38	<-- =SUM(A24:E30)						

The methodology is to calculate state-dependent present value factors (discussed later) and to multiply these factors times the individual state-dependent cash flows. Each node of the tree is discounted by the relevant state price for the node; for example, the cash flow of 80 that occurs at date 2 is discounted by $q_u q_d$. The NPV of the project is the sum of all the discounted cash flows plus the initial cost (cell C32).

18.3.2   The Abandonment Option Can Enhance Value

Now suppose that we can abandon the project at date 1 if its cash flow "threatens" to be −$50; suppose, furthermore, that this abandonment means that all subsequent cash flows will also be zero. As the following picture shows, this *option to abandon the project* enhances its value:

	A	B	C	D	E	F	G	H	I	J	K
35	**Cash flows with abandonment**						**Present value with abandonment**				
36											
37					150						14.29808
38			100						30.87402		
39					80						15.67551
40		-50						-50			
41					0						0
42			0						0		
43					0						0
44											
45											
46							**Present value with abandonment**				10.85

Thinking about this topic further, it is clear that it might even be worthwhile to *pay to abandon the project.* Here's what the project looks like when we pay $10 to abandon it in the troublesome state (this payment can be thought of as representing the cost of closing down a facility, for example):

	A	B	C	D	E	F	G	H	I	J	K
35	Cash flows with abandonment						Present value with abandonment				
36											
37					150						14.29808
38			100						30.87402		
39					80						15.67551
40	-50						-50				
41					0						0
42			-10						-6.34656		
43					0						0
44											
45											
46							Present value with abandonment				4.50

18.3.3   Abandonment When We Sell the Equipment

Another possibility is, of course, that "abandonment" means selling the equipment. In this case there might even be a positive cash flow from abandonment. As an example, suppose that we can sell the asset for $15:

	A	B	C	D	E	F	G	H	I	J	K
35	Cash flows with abandonment						Present value with abandonment				
36											
37					150						14.29808
38			100						30.87402		
39					80						15.67551
40	-50						-50				
41					0						0
42			15						9.51984		
43					0						0
44				Sale of asset for $15							
45											
46							Present value with abandonment				20.37

18.3.4   Determining the State Prices

The method we have used to determine the state prices was explained in greater detail in Chapter 14. We assume that in each period the market portfolio (by which we mean some large, diversified stock-market portfolio such as the S&P 500) moves either "up" or "down"; the size of these moves is determined by the mean return μ of the market portfolio and by the standard deviation σ of the market portfolio's returns. Assuming that the returns on the market portfolio have mean $\mu = 12$ percent and standard deviation of returns $\sigma = 30$ percent, we have—in the preceding examples—calculated

$$\text{Up} = \exp(\mu + \sigma) = 1.53, \text{ Down} = \exp(\mu - \sigma) = 0.8$$

Denote by q_u the price today for one dollar in the "up" state in one period, and denote by q_d the price today for one dollar in the "down" state in one period. Then, as explained in Chapter 14, the state prices are calculated by solving the following system of linear equations:

$$1 = q_u * \text{Up} + q_d * \text{Down}$$

$$\frac{1}{1+r} = q_u + q_d$$

The solution to this system of equations is

$$q_u = \frac{1 + r - \text{Down}}{(1 + r) * (\text{Up} - \text{Down})}, \, q_u = \frac{\text{Up} - 1 - r}{(1 + r) * (\text{Up} - \text{Down})}$$

18.3.5   Alternative State Price Determinations

An alternative method of calculating the state prices is to try to match them to the project's cost of capital. Reconsider the project discussed before, and suppose that the actual probability of each state's occurrence is $1/2$. Furthermore suppose that the risk-free rate is 6 percent. Finally, assume that the project's discount rate—if it has no options whatsoever—is 22 percent. Then we can calculate the project's NPV without real options as $12.48:

	A	B	C	D	E	F	G	H
28	**Method 2**: Matching state prices to the cost of capital							
29								
30	Project cost of capital	22%	<-- This is the discount rate for the project if it has **no options**					
31	Risk-free rate	6%						
32								
33	**Project cash flows**							
34					150			
35			100					
36					80			
37	-50							
38					80			
39			-50					
40					-60			
41								
42						=AVERAGE(C35:C39)		
43	**Project expected cash flows**: Assumes equal state probabilities							
44	Year	0	1	2				
45	Expected CF	-50	25	62.5	=AVERAGE(E34:E40)			
46	Project NPV	12.48	<-- =NPV(B30,C45:D45)+A37					
47								

We now look for state prices q_u and q_d, which have two properties:

1. They are consistent with the risk-free interest rate; therefore,

$$q_u + q_d = \frac{1}{1+r} = \frac{1}{1.06}$$

2. The state prices give the same NPV for the project as that calculated by the cost of capital.

The second requirement means that we have to use the Excel Solver to determine the state prices. Here's what the solution looks like (the discussion of how Solver was used follows this spreadsheet picture):

	A	B	C	D	E	F	G	H
28	**Method 2**: Matching state prices to the cost of capital							
29								
30	Project cost of capital	22%	<-- This is the discount rate for the project if it has **no options**					
31	Risk-free rate	6%						
32								
33	**Project cash flows**							
34					150			
35			100					
36					80			
37		-50						
38					80			
39			-50					
40					-60			
41								
42					=AVERAGE(C35:C39)			
43	**Project expected cash flows**: Assumes equal state probabilities							
44	Year	0	1	2				
45	Expected CF	-50	25	62.5	=AVERAGE(E34:E40)			
46	Project NPV	12.48	<-- =NPV(B30,C45:D45)+A37					
47								
48								
49	**State prices**							
50	q_u	0.4241	<-- =1/(1+B31)-B51					
51	q_d	0.5193	<-- Determined by Solver					
52								
53					=C35*B50			
54	**Project state-by-state discounting**							
55					26.9797	<-- =E34*B50^2		
56			42.4105					
57					17.6187	<-- =E36*B50*B51		
58		-50						
59					17.6187	<-- =E38*B50*B51		
60			-25.9646					
61					-16.1798	<-- =E40*B51^2		
62								
63			=C39*B51					
64								
65								
66	State-by-state NPV	12.48	<-- =SUM(D54:H60)					
67								
68	Target cell	(0.00)	<-- =B66-B46					

To determine the state prices, we use the Solver (**Tools|Solver**):

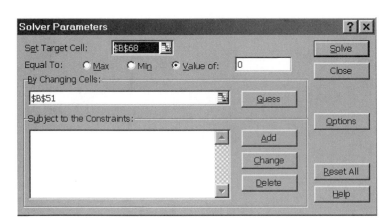

You can also use Goal Seek (**Tools|Goal Seek**) to get the same result. However, Excel's Goal Seek does not remember its previous settings; as a result, each time you repeat this calculation you will have to reset the cell references. Here's what the Goal Seek dialogue box looks like:

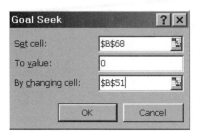

18.4   Valuing the Abandonment Option as a Series of Puts

The preceding example shows how and why the abandonment option can have value. It also illustrates another, more troublesome, feature of the abandonment option, namely, that it may be very difficult to value. While it is difficult enough to project expected cash flows, it is even more difficult to project state-by-state cash flows and state prices for a complex project.

A possible compromise in the valuation of an abandonment option is to value a project as a series of cash flows *plus* a series of Black-Scholes put options. Consider the following example: You are valuing a four-year project with the expected cash flows given in the following spreadsheet and with a risk-adjusted discount rate of 12 percent. As you can see, the project has a negative NPV.

	A	B	C	D	E	F
3	**Project cash flows**					
4	Year	0	1	2	3	4
5	Cash flow	-750	100	200	300	400
6						
7	Risk-adjusted discount rate	12%	The project's cost of capital			
8						
9	NPV without options	-33.53	<-- =NPV(B7,C5:F5)+B5			

Suppose that we can abandon the project at the end of any of the next four years, selling the equipment for $300. Although this abandonment option is an American option and not a Black-Scholes option, we value it as a series of Black-Scholes put options. In each case we suppose that we first get the year-end cash flow; we then value the abandonment option on the remaining project value.

- *End of year 1:* The asset's expected value at the end of year 1 will be the discounted value of its future expected cash flows: $702.44 = \dfrac{200}{1.12} + \dfrac{300}{(1.12)^2} + \dfrac{400}{(1.12)^3}$. The abandonment option means that we can get $300 for the asset during the next three years. If the value has a volatility of 50 percent, then valuing this option as a Black-Scholes put with one year to maturity gives its value as $19.53. The following spreadsheet uses the VBA function **Putoption** defined in Chapter 16:

	A	B	C	D	E	F
1	**ABANDONMENT VALUE--DETAILS OF YEAR 1 CALCULATION**					
2						
3	**Project cash flows**					
4	Year	0	1	2	3	4
5	Cash flow	-750	100	200	300	400
6						
7	Risk-adjusted discount rate	12%	The project's cost of capital			
8						
9	**Valuing the year-1 abandonment put**					
10	Value of project, end year 1	702.44	Like asset value in put formula			
11	Abandonment value	300	Like strike price in put formula			
12	Time to option maturity (years)	3				
13	Risk-free rate	6%				
14	Sigma	50%				
15						
16	Put value	19.53	<-- =putoption(B10,B11,B12,B13,B14)			

- *End of year 2:* We have a put option with exercise price $300 on an asset worth $586.73 = \dfrac{300}{1.12} + \dfrac{400}{(1.12)^2}$. Valuing the abandonment option as a Black-Scholes put with two years to exercise gives its value (when $\sigma = 50$ percent) as $17.74.

- *End of year 3:* We have a put option with exercise price \$300 on an asset worth $357.14 = \dfrac{400}{1.12}$. The option has one more year remaining and is worth \$32.47.

- *End of year 4:* The asset is worthless in terms of future anticipated cash flows, but it can be abandoned for \$300 (its scrap or salvage value). The abandonment option is worth \$300.

In the next spreadsheet the asset has been valued as the sum of

- The present value of the future expected cash flows. As we showed, this is −\$33.53.

- The present value (at the risk-free rate) of a series of Black-Scholes puts. This value is \$299.10.

The total value of the project is −\$33.53 + \$299.10 = \$265.57.

	A	B	C	D	E	F	G	H
1	**PRICING AN ABANDONMENT OPTION AS A SERIES OF PUTS**							
2								
3	**Project cash flows**							
4	Year		0	1	2	3	4	
5	Cash flow		-750	100	200	300	400	
6								
7	Risk-adjusted discount rate		12%	The project's cost of capital				
8								
9	NPV without options		-33.53	<-- =NPV(B7,C5:F5)+B5				
10								
11	Sigma		50%					
12	Risk-free rate		6%					
13	Abandonment value		300	Project can be abandoned at end of any year for this amount				
14								
15	NPV of cash flows at RADR		-33.53	<-- =B9				
16	Value of abandonment option		299.10	<-- =NPV(B16,C13:F13)				
17	Adjusted present value		265.57			=NPV($B$7,E5:$F$5)		
18								
19	End-year value of remaining cash flows			702.44	586.73	357.14	0.00	
20	Put option value			19.53	17.74	32.47	300.00	
21								
22								
23								
24				=putoption(D19,$B$13,$F$4-D4+1,$B$12,$B$11)				
25				the parameters are:				
26				Asset value -> D19				
27				Exercise price -> B13				
28				Time to exercise -> $F$4-D4				
29				Risk-free rate -> B12				
30				Volatility (sigma) -> B11				
31								

18.5   Conclusion

Recognizing that capital budgeting should include option aspects of projects is clear and obvious. Valuing these options is often difficult. In this chapter we have tried to emphasize the intuitions and—insofar as is possible—to give some implementation of the valuation.

Exercises

1. Your company is considering purchasing 10 machines, each of which has the following expected cash flows (the entry −$550 is the cost of the machine):

Year	Cash Flow of Single Machine
0	−550
1	100
2	200
3	300
4	400

You estimate the appropriate discount rate for the machines as 25 percent.

a. Would you recommend buying just one machine, if there are no options effects?

b. Your purchase manager recommends buying one machine today and then—after seeing how the machine operates—reconsidering the purchase of the other nine machines in six months. Assuming that the cash flows from the machines have a standard deviation of 30 percent and that the risk-free rate is 10 percent, value this strategy.

2. Your company is considering the purchase of a new piece of equipment. The equipment costs $50,000, and your analysis indicates that the PV of the future cash flows from the equipment is $45,000. Thus the NPV of the equipment is −$5,000. This estimated NPV is based on some initial numbers provided by the manufacturer plus some creative thinking on the part of your financial analyst.

The seller of the new piece of equipment is offering a course on how it works. The course costs $1,500. You estimate that the σ of the equipment's cash flows is 30 percent, the risk-free rate is 6 percent, and you will have another half-year after the course to purchase the equipment at the price of $50,000. Is it worth taking the course?

3. Consider a project whose cash flows are as follows:

Project cash flows

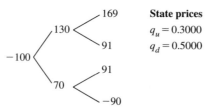

a. Using the state prices, value the project.

b. Suppose that at date 2 the project can be abandoned at no cost. What does this fact do to its value?

c. Suppose that at any time the project can be sold for $100. Show the tree of cash flows and value the project.

4.   Suppose that the market portfolio has mean $\mu = 15$ percent and standard deviation $\sigma = 20$ percent.

a. If the risk-free rate of interest is 8 percent, calculate the one-period state prices for an "up" and a "down" state.

b. Show the effect (in a data table) of the risk-free rate on the state prices.

c. Show the effect of the σ on the state prices.

5.   Consider the following cash flows:

Project cash flows

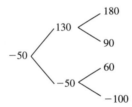

a. If the cost of capital is 30 percent and the risk-free rate is 5 percent, find the state prices that match the project's NPV.

b. If there exists an abandonment option so that we can change all negative cash flows to zero, value the project.

19 Early Exercise Boundaries[1]

19.1 Introduction

In Chapter 14 we showed that it may be optimal to exercise a put option before maturity, so that an American put may be valued at more than an otherwise-equivalent European put. We start this chapter by considering this problem in greater depth; we ask how to determine the early exercise boundary for a put—defined as the *highest stock price* at time t for which the put might be exercised early. We show how to compute this boundary.

We then go on to consider a similar problem for calls. We know from Chapter 13 that an American call on a stock that does not pay dividends will never be exercised early. Thus the only case in which early exercise of calls is possible is if the stock underlying the call pays dividends. We consider this problem in some detail and derive the early exercise boundary for a call—the *lowest stock price* at time t for which the call might be exercised early.

19.2 Why Would You Want to Exercise a Put Early?

The first spreadsheet of this chapter calculates the Black-Scholes price for a put with one year to maturity. Recall that the Black-Scholes price is always for European options. In this spreadsheet the initial option price calculation—in rows 2 through 15—calculates the put price when $S = X = 50$ (i.e., for an at-the-money put).

The data table that starts in row 21 calculates the value of the put for various values of the stock price S. These values are graphed against the option's intrinsic value [i.e., max $(X - S, 0)$, where $X = 50$). What we see in the graph is that for low stock prices the Black-Scholes put value is below the option's intrinsic value. For these low stock prices the holder of a European put would pay to be able to exercise it early. Hence—for these low stock prices—the value of an American put is higher than the value of a European put.

---

1. This chapter deals with a somewhat advanced topic. You may want to skip it on first reading.

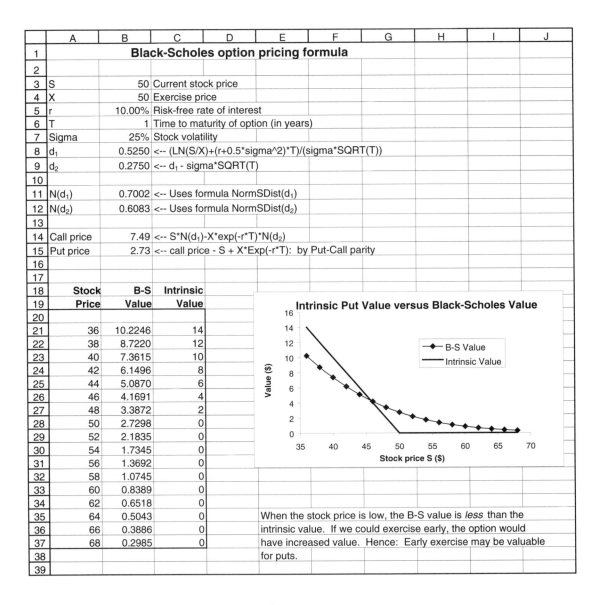

	A	B	C	D	E	F	G	H	I	J
1		**Black-Scholes option pricing formula**								
2										
3	S	50	Current stock price							
4	X	50	Exercise price							
5	r	10.00%	Risk-free rate of interest							
6	T	1	Time to maturity of option (in years)							
7	Sigma	25%	Stock volatility							
8	d_1	0.5250	<-- (LN(S/X)+(r+0.5*sigma^2)*T)/(sigma*SQRT(T))							
9	d_2	0.2750	<-- d_1 - sigma*SQRT(T)							
10										
11	$N(d_1)$	0.7002	<-- Uses formula NormSDist(d_1)							
12	$N(d_2)$	0.6083	<-- Uses formula NormSDist(d_2)							
13										
14	Call price	7.49	<-- S*N(d_1)-X*exp(-r*T)*N(d_2)							
15	Put price	2.73	<-- call price - S + X*Exp(-r*T): by Put-Call parity							
16										
17										
18		**Stock**	**B-S**	**Intrinsic**						
19		**Price**	**Value**	**Value**						
20										
21		36	10.2246	14						
22		38	8.7220	12						
23		40	7.3615	10						
24		42	6.1496	8						
25		44	5.0870	6						
26		46	4.1691	4						
27		48	3.3872	2						
28		50	2.7298	0						
29		52	2.1835	0						
30		54	1.7345	0						
31		56	1.3692	0						
32		58	1.0745	0						
33		60	0.8389	0						
34		62	0.6518	0						
35		64	0.5043	0	When the stock price is low, the B-S value is *less* than the					
36		66	0.3886	0	intrinsic value. If we could exercise early, the option would					
37		68	0.2985	0	have increased value. Hence: Early exercise may be valuable					
38					for puts.					
39										

19.2.1   No Early Exercise for American Calls

It is worthwhile noting that comparing the Black-Scholes value for a European call with its intrinsic value shows a different pattern. (As in the case of all Black-Scholes valuations, the call is written on a stock with no dividends before option maturity.)

	A	B	C	D	E	F	G	H	I	J
42	**Stock**	**B-S call**	**Intrinsic**							
43	**price**	**value**	**value**							
44										
45	20	0.001083	0							
46	23	0.008322	0							
47	26	0.039814	0							
48	29	0.13549	0							
49	32	0.358386	0							
50	35	0.783616	0							
51	38	1.480176	0							
52	41	2.494929	0							
53	44	3.845132	0							
54	47	5.519967	0							
55	50	7.487899	0							
56	53	9.705828	3							
57	56	12.12728	6							
58	59	14.70815	9							
59	62	17.40995	12							
60	65	20.20104	15							
61	68	23.05661	18							
62										

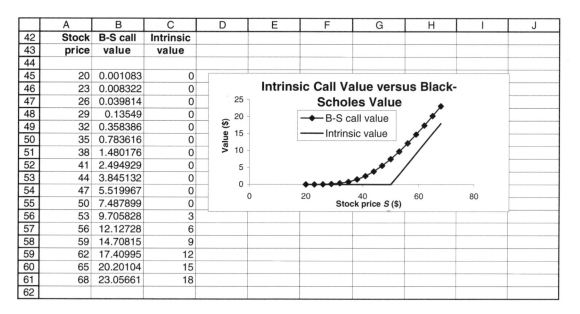

Since the Black-Scholes price of the call is always above the intrinsic option value, there is no reason to want to exercise the call early. When we return to this case later, in section 19.5, we introduce dividends to induce the call option holder to desire early exercise.

19.3   The Early Exercise Boundary for Puts

For an American put, the early exercise boundary refers to the *highest stock price at time t* for which it is worthwhile to exercise the put early. Consider the following example, which follows the procedure outlined in Chapter 14 for calculating the value of an American put.

	A	B	C	D	E	F	G	H	I
1			FIVE DATE AMERICAN BINOMIAL PUT OPTION PRICING						
2									
3	Up	0.2214		**State prices**					
4	Down	-0.1813		q_u	0.4904	<-- =(B8-B4-1)/(B8*(B3-B4))			
5				q_d	0.4898	<-- =1/B8-E4			
6	Initial stock price	50							
7	Exercise price	55		Sigma	40%				
8	1+r(Δt)	1.020201		r	8%				
9				T	1				
10									
11						**Note: The period T = 1 is divided into four**			
12						subperiods. "Up" for each period is defined			
13						as exp[σ*Δt] and "down" is exp[-σ*Δt],			
14						where σ = 40%. The annual interest rate of			
15						8% is discretized as exp[8%/4] -1 for each			
16						subperiod.			
17									
18			**Stock price**: Circled cells indicate put exercise.						
19									111.2770
20							91.1059		
21					74.5912				74.5912
22			61.0701				61.0701		
23	50.0000				50.0000				50.0000
24			40.9365				40.9365		
25					33.5160				33.5160
26							27.4406		
27									22.4664
28									
29		t=0		t=0.25		t=0.5		t=0.75		t=1
30									
31									0.0000
32			**American put price**				0.0000		
33					1.1994				0.0000
34			4.5499				2.4489		
35	9.3278				8.0889				5.0000
36			14.4893				14.0635		
37					21.4840				21.4840
38							27.5594		
39									32.5336
40									

The calculations proceed from the end of the tree to the beginning. As in Chapter 14, the put price at each node was calculated as follows.

$$\max \left\{ \begin{array}{l} \text{Immediate exercise at the node,} \\ q_u * (\text{Put value at following ``up'' node}) \\ \quad + q_d * (\text{Put value at following ``down'' node}) \end{array} \right\}$$

In the preceding figure, the nodes at which the put was exercised have been put in ovals. The *early exercise boundary* for the put is defined as the highest price at each time t for which the put is exercised:

American Put Early Exercise Boundary

t	Early Exercise Boundary
0	0
0.25	0
0.5	33.5160
0.75	40.9365
1	50

We note two things before going on:

• The nomenclature "early exercise boundary" takes a slight liberty with language by including terminal points at which the put is exercised.

• A second, more important note is this: If a put is exercised early at a price S that occurs at time t, then the put will be exercised early at all prices *below* S that occur at the same time. This fact is proved in the appendix to this chapter.

19.4   A VBA Program to Find the Put Early Exercise Boundary

In this section we construct a VBA program to find the early exercise boundary. The VBA program takes its parameters from the Excel spreadsheet to which it is attached, and the output from the program is entered into this same spreadsheet. The spreadsheet (the front end of the program) is as follows (with the output entered into the columns **Time** and **Early exercise boundary**).

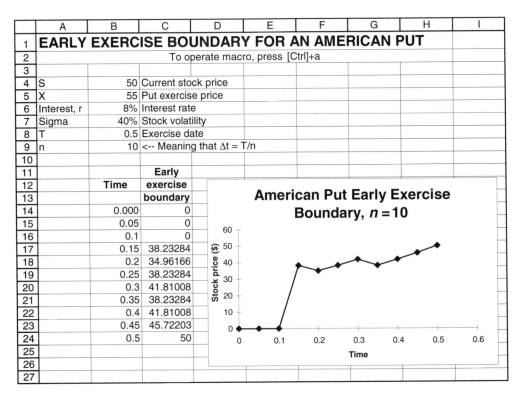

	A	B	C	D	E	F	G	H	I
1	**EARLY EXERCISE BOUNDARY FOR AN AMERICAN PUT**								
2			To operate macro, press [Ctrl]+a						
3									
4	S		50	Current stock price					
5	X		55	Put exercise price					
6	Interest, r		8%	Interest rate					
7	Sigma		40%	Stock volatility					
8	T		0.5	Exercise date					
9	n		10	<-- Meaning that Δt = T/n					
10									
11			**Early**						
12		**Time**	**exercise**						
13			**boundary**						
14		0.000	0						
15		0.05	0						
16		0.1	0						
17		0.15	38.23284						
18		0.2	34.96166						
19		0.25	38.23284						
20		0.3	41.81008						
21		0.35	38.23284						
22		0.4	41.81008						
23		0.45	45.72203						
24		0.5	50						
25									
26									
27									

What the graph shows is that when the put option still has a lot of time until maturity, it is not optimal to exercise early (in the graph, the early exercise boundary for $t \leq 0.1$ is 0). When the time gets closer to the option's maturity, the early exercise boundary increases, meaning that the holder of the option gets increasingly impatient about holding on to the put. For example, in this case, at time $t = 0.4$ (when the option is one-tenth of a year from exercise), the put holder will find it optimal to exercise the option if the stock price is more than 41.81.[2]

The VBA program to find the early exercise boundary is a modification of the program given in Chapter 14 for calculating the value of an American put. We have used named ranges (see Chapter 30) to make it easier to identify the specific cells.

---

2. We would expect that early exercise boundary to be smooth and increasing in time, and this expectation will indeed be fulfilled for the continuous-time case. The "wiggly" nature of the boundary calculated here is typical of what happens when we use a finite approximation to the boundary. This same "wiggle" also occurred in the Chapter 14's discussion of the convergence of the binomial model to the Black-Scholes option price.

```
Sub PutBoundary()
   Application.ScreenUpdating = False
   n = Worksheets("Early exercise").Range("n")
   S = Worksheets("Early exercise").Range("S")
   X = Worksheets("Early exercise").Range("X")
   delta_t = Worksheets("Early exercise").Range("T") /_
      Worksheets("Early exercise").Range("n")
   up = Exp(Worksheets("Early exercise").Range("sigma")_
      * Sqr(delta_t))
   down = Exp(-Worksheets("Early exercise").Range("sigma")_
      * Sqr(delta_t))
   R = Exp(Worksheets("Early exercise").Range("interest")_
      * delta_t)
   qup = (R - down) / (R * (up - down))
   qdown = 1 / R - qup

   Dim OptionReturnEnd() As Double
   Dim OptionReturnMiddle() As Double
   Dim boundary() As Double
   ReDim OptionReturnEnd(n + 1)
   ReDim boundary(n + 1, n + 1)

   Worksheets("Early exercise").Range("output").Clear

   For Index = 0 To n
      boundary(Index, 1) = Index
      boundary(Index, 2) = 0
   Next Index

   For state = 0 To n + 1
      OptionReturnEnd(state) = 0
   Next state

   For Index = n To 0 Step -1
      ReDim OptionReturnMiddle(Index + 1)
      For state = 0 To Index
         OptionReturnMiddle(state) = Application.Max(X - _
            S * up ^ state * down ^ (Index - state), _
            qdown * OptionReturnEnd(state) + _
            qup * OptionReturnEnd(state + 1))
         If X - S * up ^ state * down ^ (Index - state) > _
            qdown * OptionReturnEnd(state) + qup *_
            OptionReturnEnd(state + 1) Then boundary(Index, _
            2) = S * up ^ state * down ^(Index - state)
         End If
```

```
      Next state
      ReDim OptionReturnEnd(Index)
      For state = 0 To Index
            OptionReturnEnd(state) = _
               OptionReturnMiddle(state)
      Next state
   Next Index

   For Index = 0 To n
      Worksheets("Early exercise").Range("output"). _
         Cells(Index, 1)= boundary(Index, 1) * delta_t
      Worksheets("Early exercise").Range("output"). _
         Cells(Index, 2) = boundary(Index, 2)
   Next Index
End Sub
```

When the program is run for a larger number of iterations, the boundary gets finer:

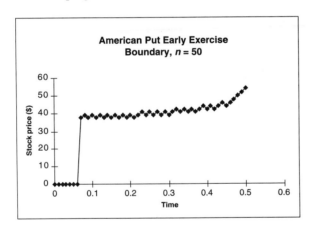

19.5   A Note on Dividend-Equivalent Price Processes

In the next section we consider early exercise bounds on American calls on dividend-paying stocks. But first we need to discuss dividend processes and their effects on the state prices.

We start by considering what we mean by two price processes that are "dividend equivalent." In the first price process we have no dividends. The stock price today S rises tomorrow to either Su or Sd. In the second price process, the stock price today is $\hat{S}$ and rises tomorrow to either $\hat{S}\hat{u}$ or $\hat{S}\hat{d}$; but in this second price process there are dividends paid at each node: D_0 at time 0, and D_u or D_d depending on the up or down node at time 1.[3]

We call these two price processes *equivalent* if $S = \hat{S} + D_0$, $Su = \hat{S}\hat{u} + D_u$, and $Sd = \hat{S}\hat{d} + D_d$. Note that these equivalent price processes do not have the same state prices. To see this fact, consider first the state prices for the process without dividends:

$$q_u Su + q_d Sd = S$$

$$q_u + q_d = \frac{1}{1+r} \equiv \frac{1}{R}$$

$$\Rightarrow q_d = \frac{u-R}{R(u-d)}, q_u = \frac{R-d}{R(u-d)}$$

Now consider the process with dividends. We have to look at *when the dividends are received*. We model the stock prices as if the dividends are received *at the beginning of the period, before the share is sold.* Another way of saying this is that we are modeling share prices that are ex-dividend when the share is sold. This said, what we get is

$$q_u(\hat{S}\hat{u} + D_u) + q_d(\hat{S}\hat{d} + D_d) = \hat{S} \Rightarrow q_u Su + q_d Sd = \hat{S}$$

$$q_u + q_d = \frac{1}{1+r} \equiv \frac{1}{R}$$

$$\Rightarrow q_d = \frac{Su - \hat{S}R}{RS(u-d)}, q_u = \frac{\hat{S}R - Sd}{RS(u-d)}$$

If we assume that $\hat{S} = S*(1-\delta)$, where δ is the rate of dividend payment, then we have

$$q_d = \frac{Su - \hat{S}R}{RS(u-d)} = \frac{Su - S(1-\delta)R}{RS(u-d)} = \frac{u - (1-\delta)R}{R(u-d)}, q_u = \frac{(1-\delta)R - d}{R(u-d)}$$

Thus equivalent dividend processes have different state prices.

---

3. Note that here u and d denote the returns including "1." This usage is slightly different from that in Chapter 14, where u and d denoted the returns without "1." For example, whereas u might be equal to 20 percent in Chapter 14, here the equivalent would be $u = 1.2$.

19.6   Early Exercise of American Calls: A Numerical Example

We start with an example of an American call on a stock that pays dividends. The following picture explains most of the concepts. The total payoff (dividend plus stock price) in each period either goes up by 41.91 percent or goes down by 22.22 percent. The top tree in the picture gives the total payoff tree.

In each period, two percent of the total payoff is paid out as dividend, with the remaining payout being the ex-dividend stock price shown in the middle tree. The bottom of the three trees is the dividend payout.

	A	B	C	D	E	F	G	H	I	J	K	L
1			FIVE-DATE AMERICAN BINOMIAL CALL OPTION PRICING									
2												
3	Up-down–including dividends			State prices					Note: The period T = 1 is divided into four			
4	Up	1.4191		q_u	0.3374	<-- =((1-E14)*B9-B5)/(B4-B5)			subperiods. "Up" for each period is defined			
5	Down	0.7788		q_d	0.6626	<-- =(B4-(1-E14)*B9)/(B4-B5)			as exp[mean*Δt+sigma*sqrt(Δt)] and "down"			
6									is exp[mean*Δt-sigma*sqrt(Δt)] , where			
7	Initial stock price	50		Mean	20%				mean = 20% and sigma = 60%. The annual			
8	Exercise price	30		Sigma	60%				interest rate of 6% is discretized as			
9	1+r(Δt)	1.0151		r	6%				exp[6%/4] -1 for each subperiod.			
10				T	1							
11									The dividend rate of 8% is paid out			
12				Dividend rate					quarterly.			
13				Annual	8%							
14				in Δt	2.00%	<-- =E13/4						
15												
16			Stock price including dividends (same as if div. yld. = 0%)									
17									202.7600			
18							142.8826					
19					100.6876				111.2770			
20			70.9534				78.4156					
21	50.0000				55.2585				61.0701			
22			38.9400				43.0354					
23					30.3265				33.5160			
24							23.6183					
25									18.3940			
26												
27			Stock price after dividend payout									
28									198.7048			
29							140.0249					
30					98.6739				109.0515			
31			69.5343				76.8473					
32	49.0000				54.1534				59.8487			
33			38.1612				42.1747					
34					29.7200				32.8457			
35							23.1460					
36									18.0261			
37												
38	t=0		t=0.25		t=0.5		t=0.75		t=1			
39												
40			Dividends: Difference between two preceding trees									
41									4.0552			
42							2.8577					
43					2.0138				2.2255			
44			1.4191				1.5683					
45	1.0000				1.1052				1.2214			
46			0.7788				0.8607					
47					0.6065				0.6703			
48							0.4724					
49									0.3679			

We consider the early exercise problem in the following illustration:

	A	B	C	D	E	F	G	H	I
50									
51					=MAX(G29-X,q_u*I53+q_d*I55)				
52					G29 is stock price *after* dividend payout				
53									168.7048
54		**American call price**					110.0249		
55					68.6739				79.0515
56			39.5343				46.8473		
57	20.8202				24.1534				29.8487
58			11.2920				12.1747		
59					4.7436				2.8457
60							0.9601		
61									0.0000
62							=q_u*I64+q_d*I66		
63									
64		**European call price on after-dividend stock**							168.7048
65							109.2983		
66					67.6525				79.0515
67			38.4574				46.4485		
68	20.2992				23.5928				29.8487
69			11.0539				11.9558		
70					4.6698				2.8457
71							0.9601		
72									0.0000
73					=IF(G29-X > q_u*I53+q_d*I55,"early","no")				
74									
75									
76		**Early exercise points**					Early		
77					Early				
78			Early				Early		
79		No			Early				
80			No				Early		
81					No				
82							No		
83									

In order to price the American call, at every node we compare the following:

- The price of the call—defined as the state-dependent present value of its next period value (for example, q_u I53 + q_d I55 in one of the preceding cells.
- The value of the call as immediately exercised (in the examples, G29 − X).

If the latter is larger, we exercise the call early.

19.7   A VBA Program for the Call Early Exercise Boundary with Dividends

Writing a program to compute the early exercise boundary of the call, defined as the *lowest stock price* at time t for which it is worthwhile to exercise the call, produces the following output:

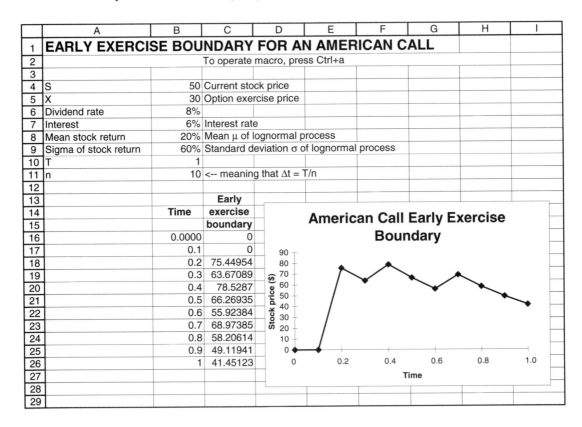

	A	B	C	D	E	F	G	H	I
1	**EARLY EXERCISE BOUNDARY FOR AN AMERICAN CALL**								
2			To operate macro, press Ctrl+a						
3									
4	S		50	Current stock price					
5	X		30	Option exercise price					
6	Dividend rate	8%							
7	Interest	6%	Interest rate						
8	Mean stock return	20%	Mean μ of lognormal process						
9	Sigma of stock return	60%	Standard deviation σ of lognormal process						
10	T	1							
11	n	10	<-- meaning that Δt = T/n						
12									
13			**Early**						
14		**Time**	**exercise**						
15			**boundary**						
16		0.0000	0						
17		0.1	0						
18		0.2	75.44954						
19		0.3	63.67089						
20		0.4	78.5287						
21		0.5	66.26935						
22		0.6	55.92384						
23		0.7	68.97385						
24		0.8	58.20614						
25		0.9	49.11941						
26		1	41.45123						
27									
28									
29									

Take note of the following general observations:

- When current time is far away from the option exercise date T, it is not optimal to exercise the option early.

- Once early exercise becomes potentially optimal, the early exercise boundary declines as time approaches the option exercise date T.[4] The explanation is

---

4.   As noted for the case of put early exercise boundaries, the "wiggliness" of the call early exercise boundary has to do with the binomial approximation to the price process.

that early exercise of the call catches the trade-off between dividend capture (achieved by early exercise of the option) and the value of waiting for the stock price to rise.

When we substitute in the case of no dividends, the spreadsheet gives us the standard result that it is never optimal to exercise the call early:

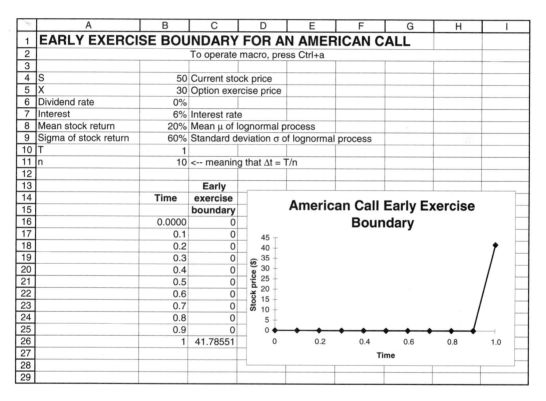

	A	B	C	D	E	F	G	H	I
1	**EARLY EXERCISE BOUNDARY FOR AN AMERICAN CALL**								
2			To operate macro, press Ctrl+a						
3									
4	S	50	Current stock price						
5	X	30	Option exercise price						
6	Dividend rate	0%							
7	Interest	6%	Interest rate						
8	Mean stock return	20%	Mean μ of lognormal process						
9	Sigma of stock return	60%	Standard deviation σ of lognormal process						
10	T	1							
11	n	10	<-- meaning that $\Delta t = T/n$						
12									
13			Early						
14		Time	exercise						
15			boundary						
16		0.0000	0						
17		0.1	0						
18		0.2	0						
19		0.3	0						
20		0.4	0						
21		0.5	0						
22		0.6	0						
23		0.7	0						
24		0.8	0						
25		0.9	0						
26		1	41.78551						
27									
28									
29									

The VBA program is as follows.

```
Sub CallBoundary()
    Application.ScreenUpdating = False
    n = Worksheets("Early exercise").Range("n")
        'divisions of year
    S = Worksheets("Early exercise").Range("S")
        'initial stock price
    X = Worksheets("Early exercise").Range("X")
        'call exercise price
    divYld = Worksheets("Early exercise").Range("divrate") _
        / n 'periodic div. yield
    delta_t = Worksheets("Early exercise").Range("T") / n
    up = Exp(Worksheets("Early exercise").Range("mean") / _
        n + Worksheets("Early exercise").Range("sigma") _
        * Sqr(delta_t))
    down = Exp(Worksheets("Early exercise").Range("mean") _
        / n - Worksheets("Early exercise").Range("sigma") _
        * Sqr(delta_t))
    R = Exp(Worksheets("Early exercise").Range("interest") _
        * delta_t)
    qup = (R * (1 - divYld) - down) / (R * (up - down))
    qdown = 1 / R - qup

    Dim OptionReturnEnd() As Double
    Dim OptionReturnMiddle() As Double
    Dim boundary() As Double
    ReDim OptionReturnEnd(n + 1)
    ReDim boundary(n + 1, 2)

    Worksheets("Early exercise").Range("output").Clear

    For Index = 0 To n
        boundary(Index, 1) = Index
        boundary(Index, 2) = 0
    Next Index
```

```
    For state = 0 To n + 1
            OptionReturnEnd(state) = 0
    Next state

    For Index = n To 0 Step -1
        ReDim OptionReturnMiddle(Index + 1)
        For state = Index To 0 Step -1

        stock = S * up ^ state * down ^ (Index - state) _
            * (1 - divYld)
        optionalive = qdown * OptionReturnEnd(state) + _
            qup * OptionReturnEnd(state + 1)
        If stock - X > optionalive Then
                boundary(Index, 2) = stock:
                OptionReturnMiddle(state) = stock - X:
            Else: OptionReturnMiddle(state) = qdown * _
                OptionReturnEnd(state) _
                + qup * OptionReturnEnd(state + 1)
            End If
        Next state
        ReDim OptionReturnEnd(Index)
        For state = 0 To Index
            OptionReturnEnd(state) = _
                OptionReturnMiddle(state)
        Next state
    Next Index

    For Index = 0 To n
        Worksheets("Early exercise").Range("output"). _
            Cells(Index, 1) = boundary(Index, 1) * delta_t
        Worksheets("Early exercise").Range("output"). _
            Cells(Index, 2) = boundary(Index, 2)
    Next Index
End Sub
```

Exercises

1.   Consider an at-the-money American put on a stock whose current price is $S = 50$. Find the early exercise boundary point for $t = 0.5$ for a series of these puts, when $T = 1, 2, 3, 4, \ldots, 10$. Assume that the risk-free interest rate is 8 percent and that $\sigma = 30$ percent. Can you draw any conclusions from this exercise?

2.   Consider a series of American puts on a stock whose current price is $S = 100$. Suppose that all the puts have exercise price $X = 120$ and maturity $T = 1$. Divide this interval into sub-intervals of length $\Delta t = 0.1$ (i.e., let $n = 10$ in the spreadsheet). Compare the early exercise boundary for $\sigma = 20$ percent and $\sigma = 40$ percent. (Make a graph!) Can you give an intuitive explanation of your results?

Appendix: Proof

We want to prove the following about early exercise: If at time t the put option is exercised at stock price S, then it will be exercised for all stock prices at time t that are lower than S.

We start by considering one time period before the end. Suppose early exercise is optimal at a higher node, where the preceding stock price is S:

$$X - Su > q_u * \max(X - Su^2, 0) + q_d * \max(X - Sud, 0)$$

Now in order to decide on early exercise at Sd we have to show that

$$X - Sd > q_u * \max(X - Sud, 0) + q_d * \max(X - Sd^2, 0)$$

First note that since $X - Su > 0$, it follows that

$$\max(X - Sud, 0) = X - Sud \quad \text{and that} \quad \max(X - Sd^2, 0) = X - Sd^2$$

so that we can write the question as

$$X - Sd > q_u * (X - Sud) + q_d * (X - Sd^2)$$

Taking the right-hand side gives

$$q_u * (X - Sud) + q_d * (X - Sd^2) = \frac{X}{1 + r} - Sd$$

(this follows, since $q_u + q_d = \dfrac{1}{1 + r}$ and $q_u * Su + q_d * Sd = S$). Thus we want to know whether

$$X - Sd > \frac{X}{1 + r} - Sd \Rightarrow X > \frac{X}{1 + r}$$

which is clearly true, provided that the interest rate $r > 0$. Note that this proof will also work for nonconstant state prices (i.e., not a Black-Scholes world).

Two Periods before the End: The General Case

Now consider two periods (or more) before the end. At Su we assume there is early exercise, that is,

$$X - Su > q_u * C_{uu} + q_d * C_{ud}$$

Stock price

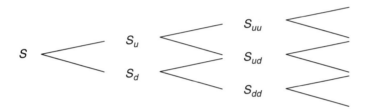

American put

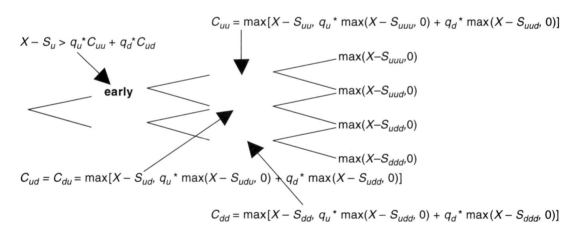

We want to prove that there will be early exercise also at Sd: $X - Sd > q_u * C_{du} + q_d * C_{dd}$. We know the following rules: $C > C_{ud} > C_{udd} \dots$. Similarly $C < C_d < C_{dd} < \dots$. Thus we know that since $X - Su > q_u * C_{uu} + q_d * C_{ud}$, it follows that

$$X - Su > q_u * C_{uu} + q_d * C_{ud} > q_u * C_{uud} + q_d * C_{udd}$$

Furthermore, $X - Sud > X - Su$. It therefore follows that we have early exercise at *ud,* and from the first part of this proof, it follows that we have early exercise at *dd.* Thus we can establish the following.

American put

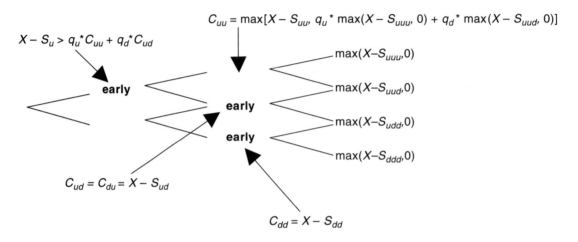

Now it remains to establish whether $X - Sd > q_u * C_{du} + q_d * C_{dd}$. However, by doing a little work, we can now show that this is true if the interest rate is $r > 0$:

$$X - Sd > q_u * C_{du} + q_d * C_{dd}$$
$$= q_u * (X - Sud) + q_d * (X - Sdd)$$
$$= \frac{X}{1+r} - q_u Sud - q_d Sdd = \frac{X}{1+r} - Sd$$

The rest of the proof follows the same kind of induction.

IV Bonds and Duration

Chapters 20–24 cover topics related to bonds and term structure. Chapters 20 and 21 concentrate on the classic duration and immunization formulations. In Chapter 20 we develop the basic Macauley duration concept. Excel's **Duration( )** formula is somewhat cumbersome to use; we use VBA to build a new, easier-to-use formula. Chapter 21 discusses the use of duration to immunize bond portfolios. Chapter 22 shows how to model the term structure using a polynomial approximation. These approximations are in wide use and appear to work well for certain purposes. Chapter 23 uses a Markov process and much information about default probabilities and bond recovery ratios to model the expected rate of return on a risky corporate bond. Finally, Chapter 24 (written jointly with Zvi Wiener) discusses the relation between duration and the cheapest-to-deliver bond on the Treasury bond futures contract.

20 Duration

20.1 Introduction

Duration is a measure of the sensitivity of the price of a bond to changes in the interest rate at which the bond is discounted. It is widely used as a risk measure for bonds (i.e., the higher a bond's duration, the more risky it is). In this chapter we consider a basic duration measure—Macauley duration—which is defined for the case when the term structure is flat. In Chapter 21 we examine the uses of duration in immunization strategies.

Consider a bond with payments C_t, where $t = 1, \ldots, N$. Ordinarily, the first $N - 1$ payments will be interest payments, and C_N will be the sum of the repayment of principal and the last interest payment. If the term structure is flat and the discount rate for all of the payments is r, then the bond's market price today will be

$$P = \sum_{t=1}^{N} \frac{C_t}{(1 + r)^t}$$

The Macauley duration measure (throughout this chapter and the next, when we use the word "duration" we shall always refer to this measure) is defined as

$$D = \frac{1}{P} \sum_{t=1}^{N} \frac{t C_t}{(1 + r)^t}$$

In section 20.3 we will consider the meaning of this formula. Before doing so, however, we show how to calculate the duration in Excel.

20.2 Two Examples

Consider two bonds. Bond A has just been issued. Its face value is $1,000, it bears the current market interest rate of 7 percent, and it will mature in 10 years. Bond B was issued five years ago, when interest rates were higher. This bond has $1,000 face value and bears a 13 percent coupon rate. When issued, this bond had a 15-year maturity, so its remaining maturity is 10 years. Since the current market rate of interest is 7 percent, bond B's market price is given by

$$\$1,421.41 = \sum_{t=1}^{10} \frac{\$130}{(1.07)^t} + \frac{\$1,000}{(1.07)^{10}}$$

It is worthwhile calculating the duration of each of the two bonds (just once!) the long way. We set up a table in Excel:

	A	B	C	D	E	F	G	H
1			BASIC DURATION CALCULATION					
2								
3	YTM	7%						
4								
5	Year	$C_{t,A}$	$t{*}C_{t,A}/P_A{*}(1{+}YTM)^t$		$C_{t,B}$	$t{*}C_{t,B}/P_B{*}(1{+}YTM)^t$		
6	1	70	0.0654		130	0.0855		
7	2	70	0.1223		130	0.1598		
8	3	70	0.1714		130	0.2240		
9	4	70	0.2136		130	0.2791		
10	5	70	0.2495		130	0.3260		
11	6	70	0.2799		130	0.3657		
12	7	70	0.3051		130	0.3987		
13	8	70	0.3259		130	0.4258		
14	9	70	0.3427		130	0.4477		
15	10	1070	5.4393		1130	4.0413		
16		Bond price	Duration		Bond price	Duration		
17		$ 1,000	7.5152		$ 1,421	6.7535		
18								
19		=NPV(B3,B6:B15)				=SUM(F6:F15)		
20								
21	Excel formula		7.5152		<-- =DURATION(DATE(1996,12,3),DATE(2006,12,3),7%,B3,1)			
22								

As might be expected, the duration of bond A is longer than that of bond B, since the average payoff of bond A takes longer than that of bond B. To look at this relationship another way, the net present value of bond A's first-year payoff ($70) represents 6.54 percent of the bond's price, whereas the net present value of bond B's first-year payoff ($130) is 8.55 percent of its price. The figures for the second-year payoffs are 6.11 percent and 7.99 percent, respectively. (For the second-year figures, you have to divide the appropriate line of the preceding table by 2, since in the duration formula each payoff is weighted by the period in which it is received.)

20.2.1   Using an Excel Formula

Excel has two duration formulas, **Duration( )** and **MDuration( )**. **MDuration**—somewhat inaccurately termed Macauley duration by Excel—is defined as

$$\text{MDuration} = \cfrac{\text{Duration}}{\left(1 + \cfrac{\text{Yield to maturity}}{\text{Number of coupon payments per year}}\right)}$$

Both formulas have the same syntax; for example, for **Duration( )** the syntax is as follows:

Duration(settlement, maturity, coupon, yield, frequency, basis)

where

settlement is the settlement date (i.e., the purchase date) of the bond.

maturity is the bond's maturity date.

coupon is the bond's coupon.

yield is the bond's yield to maturity.

frequency is the number of coupon payments per year.

basis is the "day count basis" (i.e., the number of days in a year). This is a code between 0 and 4:

0 or omitted	US (NASD) 30/360
1	Actual/actual
2	Actual/360
3	Actual/365
4	European 30/360

The **Duration** formula gives the standard Macauley duration. The **MDuration** formula can be used in calculating the price volatility of the bond (see section 20.3).

Both duration formulas may require a bit of trickery to implement because they demand a date serial number for both the settlement and the maturity. In the preceding spreadsheet picture, the Excel formula is implemented in cell C21 by assuming that bond A's settlement date (for our purposes: the current date) is December 3, 1996, and that the bond's maturity date is December 3, 2006. The choice of dates is arbitrary. The last parameter of the Excel duration formula, which gives the basis, is optional and could be omitted.[1]

---

1. The insertion of serial date formats in the Excel duration formula is often unhandy. Later in the chapter we use VBA to define a simpler duration formula that overcomes this problem; we postpone this topic until we discuss the calculation of bond duration when the payments are unevenly spaced (section 20.5).

20.3   What Does Duration Mean?

In this section we present three different meanings of duration. Each is interesting and important in its own right.

20.3.1   Duration as the Weighted Average of the Bond's Payments

As originally defined by Macauley (1938), duration is a weighted average of the bond's payments. Rewrite the duration formula as follows:

$$D = \frac{1}{P} \sum_{t=1}^{N} \frac{tC_t}{(1+r)^t} = \sum_{t=1}^{N} \left[\frac{C_t/P}{(1+r)^t} \right] * t$$

Note that the bracketed terms $\left[\dfrac{C_t/P}{(1+r)^t} \right]$ sum to 1. This fact follows from the definition of the bond price; each of these terms is the proportion of the bond's price represented by the payment at time t. In the duration formula, each of the terms $\left[\dfrac{C_t/P}{(1+r)^t} \right]$ is multiplied by its time of occurrence: Thus *the duration is the time-weighted average of the bond's discounted payments as a proportion of the bond's price.*

20.3.2   Duration as the Bond's Price Elasticity with Respect to Its Discount Rate

Viewing duration another way—as the bond's price elasticity with respect to its discount rate—explains why the duration measure can be used to measure the bond's price volatility; it also shows why duration is often used as a risk measure for bonds. To derive this interpretation, we take the derivative of the bond's price with respect to the current interest rate:

$$\frac{dP}{dr} = \sum_{t=1}^{N} \frac{-tC_t}{(1+r)^{t+1}}$$

A little algebra shows that

$$\frac{dP}{dr} = \sum_{t=1}^{N} \frac{-tC_t}{(1+r)^{t+1}} = -\frac{DP}{1+r}$$

This formula transforms into two useful interpretations of duration.

- First, duration can be regarded as the *discount-factor elasticity of the bond price,* where by "discount factor" we mean $1 + r$:

$$\frac{dP/P}{dr/(1+r)} = \frac{\text{Percent change in bond price}}{\text{Percent change in discount factor}} = -D$$

- Second, we can use duration to measure the *price volatility* of a bond by rewriting the previous equation as

$$\frac{dP}{P} = -D\frac{dr}{1+r}$$

Let's go back to the examples of the previous section. Suppose that the market interest rate rises by 10 percent, from 7 percent to 7.7 percent. What will happen to the bond prices? The price of bond A will be

$$952.39 = \sum_{t=1}^{10} \frac{\$70}{(1.077)^t} + \frac{\$1.070}{(1.077)^{10}}$$

A similar calculation shows the price of bond B to be

$$1,360.50 = \sum_{t=1}^{10} \frac{\$130}{(1.077)^t} + \frac{\$1,000}{(1.077)^{10}}$$

As predicted by the price-volatility formula, the changes in the bond prices are approximated by $\Delta P \cong -DP\Delta r/(1+r)$. To see this relationship, work out the numbers for each bond:

	A	B	C	D	E	F	G	H	I
24			**Approximating Price Changes Using Duration**						
25									
26		**Actual**							
27	**Bond**	**ΔP**	**D**	**P**	**Δr**	**-DPΔr/(1+r)**			
28	A	-47.61	7.5152	$ 1,000	0.007	-49.17	<-- =-C28*D28*E28/(1.07)		
29	B	-60.92	6.7535	$ 1,421	0.007	-62.80			
30									
31			=-(-PV(7%,10,70)+1000/(1.07)^10-(-PV(7.7%,10,70)+1000/(1.077)^10))						
32									

Note that instead of using the Excel **Duration** function and multiplying by $\Delta r/(1+r)$, we could have used the **MDuration** function and multiplied by Δr.

	A	B	C	D	E	F	G	H
34	**Using Excel's MDuration formula:**							
35	MDuration of bond A		7.0236	<-- =MDURATION(DATE(1996,12,3),DATE(2006,12,3),7%,7%,1)				
36	Δr		0.007					
37	Bond price		1000					
38	-DPΔr/(1+r)		49.17	Product of 3 terms above = -DPΔr/(1+r)				
39								
40	MDuration of bond B		6.3117	<-- =MDURATION(DATE(1999,10,31),DATE(2009,10,31),13%,7%,1)				
41	Δr		0.007					
42	Bond price		1,421					
43	-DPΔr/(1+r)		62.80	<-- =C42*C41*C40				
44								
45	**Note** that the formulas in cells C35 and C40 use different dates! This doesn't matter in the							
46	Excel functions **Duration** and **MDuration**, as long as the time between the dates is correct							
47	(in this case--10 years).							

20.3.3 Babcock's Formula: Duration as the Convex Combination of Bond Yields

A third interpretation of duration is Babcock's (1985) formula, which shows that duration is a weighted average of two factors:

$$D = N\left(1 - \frac{y}{r}\right) + \frac{y}{r}PVIF(r, N) * (1 + r)$$

where the "current yield" of the bond is

$$y = \frac{\text{Bond coupon}}{\text{Bond price}}$$

and the present value of an N = period annuity is

$$PVIF(r, N) = \sum_{i=1}^{N} \frac{1}{(1 + r)^i}$$

This formula gives two useful insights into the duration measure:

• Duration is a weighted average of the maturity of the bond and of $(1 + r)$ times the PVIF associated with the bond. (Note that the PVIF is given by the Excel formula **PV(r, N, –1).**)

• In many cases the current yield of the bond, y, is not greatly different from its yield to maturity r. In these cases, duration is not very different from $(1 + r)PVIF$.

Unlike the two previous interpretations, Babcock's formula holds only for the case of a bond with constant coupon payments and single repayment of principal at time N; that is, the formula does not extend to the case where the payments C_t differ over time.

Here's an implementation of Babcock's formula for bond B:

	A	B	C	D	E	F
49	**Babcock's Formula**					
50	N	10	Bond maturity			
51	r	7%	Current market interest rate			
52	C	13%	Bond coupon			
53	Price	1,421.41	<-- =PV(B51,B50,-B52*1000)+1000/(1+B51)^B50			
54	y	9.15%	Current yield			
55	PVIF(r,N)	7.02	<-- =PV(B51,B50,-1)			
56	D	6.7535	<-- =B50*(1-B54/B51)+B54/B51*B55*(1+B51)			

20.4   Duration Patterns

Intuitively we would expect that duration is an increasing function of a bond's maturity and a decreasing function of a bond's coupon. However, as the following examples show, this expectation is not always fulfilled:

	A	B	C	D	E	F	G	H
1	**EFFECTS OF COUPON AND MATURITY ON DURATION**							
2								
3	Current date	05/21/1996	<-- =DATE(1996,5,21)					
4	Maturity, in years	21						
5	Maturity date	05/21/2017	<-- =DATE(1996+B4,5,21)					
6	YTM	15%	Yield to maturity (i.e., discount rate)					
7	Coupon	4%						
8	Face value	1,000						
9								
10	Duration	9.0110	<-- =DURATION(B3,B5,B7,B6,1)					
11								
12	**Data table: Effect of maturity on duration**							
13			9.0110	<-- =B10 -- Table header				
14		5	4.5163					
15		10	7.4827					
16		15	8.8148					
17		20	9.0398					
18		25	8.7881					
19		30	8.4461					
20		35	8.1633					
21		40	7.9669					
22		45	7.8421					
23		50	7.7668					
24		55	7.7228					
25		60	7.6977					
26		65	7.6837					
27		70	7.6759					

Effect of Maturity on Duration
Coupon rate = 4.00%, YTM = 15.00%

As the coupon increases, the bond's duration unequivocally decreases. The following data table and graph (based on the previous example) show this effect:

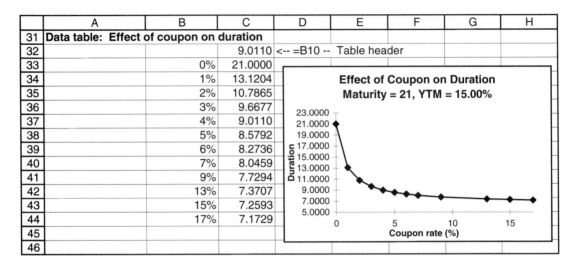

	A	B	C	D	E	F	G	H
31	Data table: Effect of coupon on duration							
32			9.0110	<-- =B10 --	Table header			
33		0%	21.0000					
34		1%	13.1204					
35		2%	10.7865					
36		3%	9.6677					
37		4%	9.0110					
38		5%	8.5792					
39		6%	8.2736					
40		7%	8.0459					
41		9%	7.7294					
42		13%	7.3707					
43		15%	7.2593					
44		17%	7.1729					
45								
46								

Effect of Coupon on Duration
Maturity = 21, YTM = 15.00%

Duration (y-axis): 5.0000 to 23.0000
Coupon rate (%) (x-axis): 0 to 15

20.5 The Duration of a Bond with Uneven Payments

The duration formulas that we have discussed assume that bond payments are evenly spaced. This is almost invariably the case for bonds, *except for the first payment.* For example, consider a bond that pays interest on May 1 of each of the years 1997, 1998, ..., 2010, with repayment of its face value on the last date. All the payments are spaced one year apart; however, if this bond is purchased on September 1, 1996, then the time to the first payment is eight months, not one year. We shall refer to such a bond as a *bond with uneven payments.* In this section we discuss two aspects of this (extremely common) problem:

1. The calculation of the duration of such a bond, when the YTM is known. We show that the duration has a very simple formula, related to the duration of a bond with even payments (i.e., the standard duration formula). In the process of the discussion we develop a simpler duration formula in Excel.

2. The calculation of the YTM of a bond with uneven payments. This requires a bit of trickery, and ultimately leads us to another VBA function.

20.5.1   Duration of a Bond with Uneven Payments

Consider a bond with N payments, the first of which occurs at time $\alpha < 1$, and the rest of which are evenly spaced. In the derivation that follows, we show that the duration of such a bond is given by the sum of two terms:

• The duration of a bond with N payments spaced at even intervals (i.e., the standard duration discussed earlier).

• $\alpha - 1$

The derivation is relatively simple. Denote the payments on the bond by $C_\alpha, C_{\alpha+1}, C_{\alpha+2}, \ldots, C_{\alpha+N-1}$, where $0 < \alpha < 1$. The price of the bond is given by

$$P = \sum_{t=1}^{N} \frac{C_{\alpha+t-1}}{(1+r)^{\alpha+t-1}} = (1+r)^{1-\alpha} \sum_{t=1}^{N} \frac{C_{\alpha+t-1}}{(1+r)^t}$$

The duration of this bond is given by

$$D = \frac{1}{P} \sum_{t=1}^{N} \frac{(\alpha + t - 1)C_{\alpha+t-1}}{(1+r)^{\alpha+t-1}}$$

Rewrite this last expression as follows:

$$D = \frac{1}{P}(1+r)^{1-\alpha} \left[\sum_{t=1}^{N} \frac{t C_{t+\alpha}}{(1+r)^t} + \sum_{t=1}^{N} \frac{(\alpha-1)C_{t+\alpha}}{(1+r)^t} \right]$$

$$= \frac{1}{(1+r)^{1-\alpha} \sum_{t=1}^{N} \dfrac{C_{t+\alpha}}{(1+r)^t}} (1+r)^{1-\alpha} \left[\sum_{t=1}^{N} \frac{t C_{t+\alpha}}{(1+r)^t} + (\alpha-1) \sum_{t=1}^{N} \frac{C_{t+\alpha}}{(1+r)^t} \right]$$

$$= \frac{1}{\sum_{t+1}^{N} \dfrac{C_{t+\alpha}}{(1+r)^t}} \left[\sum_{t=1}^{N} \frac{t C_{t+\alpha}}{(1+r)^t} \right] + \alpha - 1$$

Here is an example of the calculation of the duration of a bond with uneven periods. Recall that when there is α until the first payment, the duration formula is given by

$$D = \sum_{t=1}^{N} \frac{1}{P} \frac{(\alpha + t - 1)C_{\alpha+t}}{(1+r)^{\alpha+t-1}}$$

Each of the cells D11:D15 calculates the value of a term of this formula:

	A	B	C	D	E	F	G	H
1	DURATION OF BOND WITH UNEVEN PERIODS--Brute Force Calculation							
2								
3	Alpha	0.3	Time until first coupon payment (in years)					
4	N	5	Number of payments					
5	YTM	6%						
6	Coupon	100						
7	Face	1,000						
8	Bond price	1,217	<-- =NPV(B5,C11:C15)*(1+B5)^(1-B3)					
9								
10		Period	Payment					
11		0.3	100	0.0242	<-- =(C11*B11)/(1+$B$5)^B11/$B$8			
12		1.3	100	0.0990				
13		2.3	100	0.1653				
14		3.3	100	0.2237				
15		4.3	1,100	3.0249				
16		Duration		3.5371	<-- =SUM(D11:D15)			
17								
18		Newly defined VBA formula			3.5371	<-- =dduration(B4,B6/B7,B5,B3)		

As noted in section 20.2, the Excel formula **Duration( )** is somewhat difficult to use because of the insertion of the dates. We therefore write a simpler duration formula using VBA; the syntax of this formula is **DDuration(numberPayments, couponRate, YTM, timeToFirstPayment):**

```
Function dduration(numberPayments, couponRate, YTM,
        timeToFirstPayment)
    price = 1 / (1 + YTM) ^ numberPayments
    dduration = numberPayments / (1 + YTM) ^ numberPayments

    For Index = 1 To numberPayments
        price = couponRate / (1 + YTM) ^ Index + price
    Next Index

    For Index = 1 To numberPayments
        dduration = couponRate * Index / (1 + YTM) ^ _
            Index + dduration
    Next Index

    dduration = dduration / price + timeToFirstPayment - 1
End Function
```

Our homemade formula **DDuration** requires only the number of payments on the bond, the coupon rate, and the time to the first payment α. The use of the formula is illustrated in the previous spreadsheet picture, in cell E18.

20.5.2   Calculating the YTM for Uneven Periods

As the preceding discussion shows, the calculation of duration requires us to know the bond's yield to maturity (YTM); this YTM is just the internal rate of return of the bond's payments and its initial price. Often the YTM is given, but when it is not, we can run into a problem that requires us to make an adjustment to the Excel **IRR** function. The problem has to do with unevenly spaced bond payments. This section gives a simple example of this problem and shows how a small trick can solve it.

Consider a bond that currently costs $1,123 and that pays a coupon of $89 on January 1 of each year. On January 1, 2001, the bond will pay $1,089, the sum of its annual coupon and its face value. The current date is October 3, 1996. The problem in finding the YTM of this bond is that while most of the bond payments are spaced one year apart, there is only 0.2466 of a year until the first coupon payment: $0.2466 = [\text{Date}(1997, 1, 1) - \text{Date}(1996, 10, 3)]/365$. Thus we wish to use Excel to solve the following equation:

$$-1{,}123 + \sum_{t=0}^{3} \frac{89}{(1 + YTM)^{t+0.2466}} + \frac{1{,}089}{(1 + YTM)^{4.2466}} = 0$$

To solve this problem, we can use the Excel function **XIRR:**

	A	B	C	D	E	F
1	**Using XIRR to Calculate The IRR with Uneven Payments**					
2						
3	Current date	03-Oct-96				
4	Annual coupon	89	Paid January 1 for each of next five years			
5	Maturity date	01-Jan-01				
6	Face value	1,000				
7	Price of bond	1,123				
8						
9	Time to first payment	0.246575				
10						
11		**Date**	**Payment**			
12		03-Oct-96	-1123			
13		01-Jan-97	89			
14		01-Jan-98	89			
15		01-Jan-99	89			
16		01-Jan-00	89			
17		01-Jan-01	1089			
18						
19		YTM	7.300%	<-- =XIRR(C12:C17,B12:B17)		

To use the **XIRR** function, you first have to make sure that the Analysis ToolPak is loaded into Excel. Go to **Tools|Add-Ins.** This brings up the following menu, in which you have to make sure that **Analysis ToolPak** is checked:

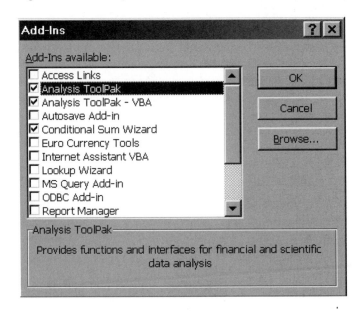

You can now use **XIRR,** which returns the internal rate of return for a schedule of cash flows that is not necessarily periodic. To use this function you have to specify the list of cash flows and the list of dates. As in the case of the Excel function **IRR,** you can also provide a guess for the IRR, although this may be left out.[2]

20.5.3   Calculating the YTM for Uneven Payments Using a VBA Program

If you do not know the payment dates, you can use VBA to calculate the YTM for a series of uneven payments. The following program is composed of two functions. The first function, **annuityvalue,** calculates the value $\sum_{t+1}^{n} \frac{1}{(1 + r)^t}$. The second function, **unevenYTM,** uses the simple bisection technique to calculate the YTM of a series of uneven payments, leaving you to choose the accuracy **epsilon** of the desired result.

---

2.   There is also a function **XNPV** for finding the present value of a series of payments paid out at uneven dates.

```
Function annuityvalue(interest, numberPeriods)
    annuityvalue = 0

    For Index = 1 To numberPeriods
        annuityvalue = annuityvalue + 1 / (1 + interest) _
            ^ Index
    Next Index
End Function

Function unevenYTM(couponRate, faceValue, bondPrice, _
        numberPayments, timeToFirstPayment, epsilon)
    Dim YTM As Double
    high = 1
    low = 0

    While Abs(annuityvalue(YTM, numberPayments) * _
            couponRate * faceValue + faceValue / (1 + _
            YTM) ^ numberPayments - bondPrice / (1 + _
            YTM) ^ (1 - timeToFirstPayment)) >= epsilon

        YTM = (high + low) / 2

        If annuityvalue(YTM, numberPayments) * _
            couponRate * faceValue + faceValue / (1 + _
            YTM) ^ numberPayments - bondPrice / (1 + _
            YTM) ^ (1 - timeToFirstPayment) > 0 Then
                low = YTM
        Else
                high = YTM
        End If

        Wend

    unevenYTM = (high + low) / 2

End Function
```

Here's an illustration of the use of this function:

	A	B	C	D	E	F
1	**ILLUSTRATION OF CALCULATION OF YTM OF UNEVEN PERIODS**					
2	This spreadsheet illustrates the **unevenYTM** VBA function:					
3	The syntax of this function:					
4	**unevenYTM(couponRate,faceValue,bondPrice,#payments,timeToFirstPayment,epsilon)**					
5						
6	Coupon rate	7.90%				
7	Face value	1,000.00				
8	Bond price	1,123.00				
9	Number of payments	5				
10	Time to first payments	0.25				
11	Epsilon	0.00001				
12						
13	YTM	6.138%	<-- =unevenYTM(B6,B7,B8,B9,B10,B11)			

20.6   Nonflat Term Structures and Duration

In a general model of the term structure, payments at time t are discounted by rate r_t, so that the value of a bond is given by

$$P = \sum_{t=1}^{N} \frac{C_t}{(1 + r_t)^t}$$

The duration measure discussed in this chapter assumes either a flat term structure (i.e., $r_t = r$ for all t) or a term structure that shifts in a parallel fashion. When the term structure exhibits parallel shifts, we can write the bond price as

$$P = \sum_{t=1}^{N} \frac{C_t}{(1 + r_t + \Delta t)^t}$$

and then derive a measure of duration by taking the derivative with respect to Δt.

A general model of the term structure should explain how the discount rate r_t for time-t payments comes about, and how the rates at time t change. This is a difficult problem, one aspect of which we discuss in Chapter 22.[3]

Does the difficulty of the problem mean that the simple duration measure we present in this chapter is useless? Not necessarily. It may be that the Macauley

---

3.   In Chapter 22 we discuss polynomial approximations to the term structure. For a further reference on general term structure models, see Hull (2000, Chapters 21–22).

duration measure gives a good approximation for changes in bond value as a result of changes in the term structure, even for the case when the term structure itself is relatively complex and not flat.[4] In this section, we explore this possibility, using data from a file **TermStruc.XLS,** which is on the CD that accompanies this book.[5] The file contains monthly information on the term structure of interest rates in the United States for the period 12.1949–2.87 (i.e., December, 1949–February, 1987). A typical row of this file looks like this:

	0mo	1mo	2mo	3mo	4mo	5mo	6mo
12.1946	0.18	0.32	0.42	0.48	0.52	0.55	0.58

9mo	1yr	2 yr	3yr	4yr	5yr	10yr	15yr	20yr
0.65	0.72	0.95	1.15	1.3	1.41	1.82	2.16	2.32

This particular row gives the term structure of interest rates in December 1946. Interest rates are given in *annual percentage terms;* that is, 0.32 means 0.32 percent per year. The next two graphs present some pictures of term structures, taken from the file.[6] Each line in the graphs represents the term structure in a particular month. In 1948 the term structures were very closely correlated, and all were upward sloping:

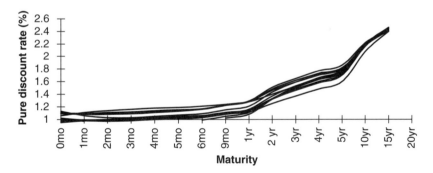

Term Structures, 1947

---

4. A paper by Gultekin and Rogalski (1984) seems to confirm that it is.

5. The data are from McCullogh (1990).

6. The interest rates are pure discount rates, calculated so that the value of a bond with price P and with N payments, $C_1, C_2, ..., C_N$ is $P = \sum_{t=1}^{N} C_t / (1 + r_t)^t$. The column market "0mo" gives the *instantaneous interest rate*—the shortest-term interest rate in the market. You can think of this as the rate paid by a money-market fund on a one-day deposit.

Contrast this graph with the term structures in 1981, when there were upward- and downward-sloping term structures, as well as term structures with "humps":

Term Structures, 1981

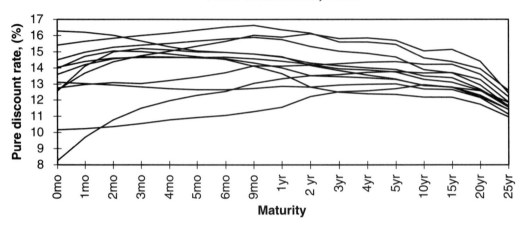

Despite this great variety of term structure shapes, you will see in exercise 7 that the Macauley duration can give an adequate approximation to the change in bond value over short periods.

Exercises

1. What is the effect of *raising* the coupon payment on the duration of a bond? Assume that the bond's yield to maturity does not change. Use a numerical example and plot the answer.

2. What is the effect on a bond's duration of increasing the bond's maturity? As in exercise 1, use a numerical example and plot the answer. Note that as $N \to \infty$. the bond becomes a consol (a bond that has no repayment of principal but an infinite stream of coupon payments). The duration of a consol is given by $(1 + YTM)/YTM$. Show that your numerical answers converge to this formula.

3. "Duration can be viewed as a proxy for the riskiness of a bond. All other things being equal, the riskier of two bonds should have lower duration." Check this claim with an example. What is its economic logic?

4. A pure discount bond with maturity N is a bond with *no payments* at times $t = 1, ..., N - 1$; at time $t = N$, a pure discount bond has a single terminal payment of both principal and interest. What is the duration of such a bond?

5. Replicate the two graphs in section 20.4.

6.   On January 23, 1987, the market price of a West Jefferson Development bond was $1,122.32. The bond pays $59 in interest on March 1 and September 1 of each of the years 1987–93. On September 1, 1993, the bond is redeemed at its face value of $1,000. Calculate the yield to maturity of the bond, and then calculate its duration.

7.   This exercise relates to the file **TermStruc.XLS.** You are asked to do the following:

   a. Produce at least three graphs of six term structures each for 10 typical subperiods. For example, the term structures from January to June 1953, July to December 1980, and so on.

   b. For January 1980, what would have been the coupon rate on a five-year bond with annual coupons? A 10-year bond? To answer this question you have to solve the following equation:

$$1,000 = \sum_{t=1}^{5} \frac{c*1,000}{(1+r_t)^t} + \frac{1,000}{(1+r_5)^5}$$

   where c is the coupon rate on the bond and r_t is the pure discount rate for period t. Note that for a 10-year bond you will have to *interpolate* the data.

   c. Calculate the coupon rate on five-year bonds *for all the data*. Graph the results.

   d. Now for duration: Return to exercise 7b. Suppose that you have calculated $c_{Jan.80}$, and that immediately following this calculation, the term structure changes to that of February 1980. What will be the effect on the price of the bond? How well is this change approximated by the Macauley duration measure (assuming that the change in the interest rate Δr is the change in the short-term rate)?

   e. Repeat the calculation of exercise 7c for at least 10 periods. Report on the results in an attractive and understandable way.

8.   Rewrite the formula **DDuration** in section 20.5.1, so that if the **timeToFirstPayment** α is not inserted, then α automatically defaults to 1.

21 Immunization Strategies

21.1 Introduction

A bond portfolio's value in the future depends on the interest-rate structure prevailing up to and including the date at which the portfolio is liquidated. If a portfolio has the same payoff at some specific future date, no matter what interest-rate structure prevails, then it is said to be *immunized*. This chapter discusses immunization strategies, which are closely related to the concept of duration discussed in Chapter 20. Immunization strategies have been discussed for many concepts of duration, but this chapter is restricted to the simplest duration concept, that of Macauley.

21.2 A Basic Simple Model of Immunization

Consider the following situation: A firm has a known future obligation, Q. (A good example would be an insurance firm, which knows that it has to make a payment in the future.) The discounted value of this obligation is

$$V_0 = \frac{Q}{(1 + r)^N}$$

where r is the appropriate discount rate.

Suppose that this future obligation is currently hedged by a bond held by the firm. That is, the firm currently holds a bond whose value V_B is equal to the discounted value of the future obligation V_0. If $P_1, P_2, \ldots, P_M$ is the stream of anticipated payments made by the bond, then the bond's present value is given by

$$V_B = \sum_{t=1}^{M} \frac{P_t}{(1 + r)^t}$$

Now suppose that the underlying interest rate, r, changes to $r + \Delta r$. Using a first-order linear approximation, we find that the new value of the future obligation is given by

$$V_0 + \Delta V_0 \approx V_0 + \frac{dV_0}{dr} \Delta r = V_0 + \Delta r \left[\frac{-NQ}{(1 + r)^{N+1}} \right]$$

However, the new value of the bond is given by

$$V_B + \Delta V_B \approx V_B + \frac{dV_B}{dr} \Delta r = V_B + \Delta r \sum_{t=1}^{N} \frac{-tP_t}{(1+r)^{t+1}}$$

If these two expressions are equal, a change in r will not affect the hedging properties of the company's portfolio. Setting the expressions equal gives us the condition

$$V_B + \Delta r \sum_{t=1}^{N} \frac{-tP_t}{(1+r)^{t+1}} = V_0 + \Delta r \left[\frac{-NQ}{(1+r)^{N+1}} \right]$$

Recalling that

$$V_B = V_0 = \frac{Q}{(1+r)^N}$$

we can simplify this expression to get

$$\frac{1}{V_B} \sum_{t=1}^{M} \frac{tP_t}{(1+r)^t} = N$$

This statement is worth restating as a formal proposition:

Suppose that the term structure of interest rates is always flat (that is, the discount rate for cash flows occurring at all future times is the same) or that the term structure moves up or down in parallel movements. Then a necessary and sufficient condition that the market value of an asset be equal under all changes of the discount rate r to the market value of a future obligation Q is that the duration of the asset equal the duration of the obligation. Here we understand the word "equal" to mean equal in the sense of a first-order approximation.

An obligation against which an asset of this type is held is said to be *immunized*.
   The preceding statement has two critical limitations:

• The immunization discussed applies only to first-order approximations. When we get to a numerical example in the succeeding sections, we shall see that there is a big difference between first-order equality and "true" equality. In *Animal Farm,* George Orwell made the same observation about the barnyard: "All animals are equal, but some animals are more equal than others."

• We have assumed either that the term structure is flat or that the term structure moves up or down in parallel movements. At best, this assumption might be considered to be a poor approximation to reality (recall the term structure graphs in section 20.6). Alternative theories of the term structure lead to alternative definitions of duration and immunization (for alternatives, see Bierwag et al., 1981, 1983a, 1983b; Cox, Ingersoll, and Ross, 1985; Vasicek, 1977). In an empirical investigation of these alternatives, Gultekin and Rogalski (1984) found that the simple Macauley duration we use in this chapter works at least as well as any of the alternatives.

21.3   A Numerical Example

In this section we consider a basic numerical immunization example. Suppose you are trying to immunize a year-10 obligation whose present value is $1,000. (For example, at a current interest rate of 6 percent, its future value would be $1,000 * 1.06^{10} = $1,790.85.) You intend to immunize the obligation by purchasing $1,000 worth of a bond or a combination of bonds.

You consider three bonds:

1. Bond 1 has 10 years remaining until maturity, a coupon rate of 6.7 percent, and a face value of $1,000.

2. Bond 2 has 15 years until maturity, a coupon rate of 6.988 percent, and a face value of $1,000.

3. Bond 3 has 30 years until maturity, a coupon rate of 5.9 percent, and a face value of $1,000.

At the existing yield to maturity of 6 percent, the prices of the bonds differ. Bond 1, for example is worth $1,051.52 = $\sum_{t}^{10} \dfrac{67}{(1.06)^t} + \dfrac{1,000}{(1.06)^{10}}$; thus, in order to purchase $1,000 worth of this bond, you have to purchase $951 = $1,000/$1,051.52 of *face value* of the bond.

However, Bond 3 is currently worth $986.24, so that in order to buy $1,000 of market value of this bond, you will have to buy $1,013.96 of face value. If you intend to use this bond to finance a $1,790.85 obligation 10 years from now, following is a schematic of the problem you face.

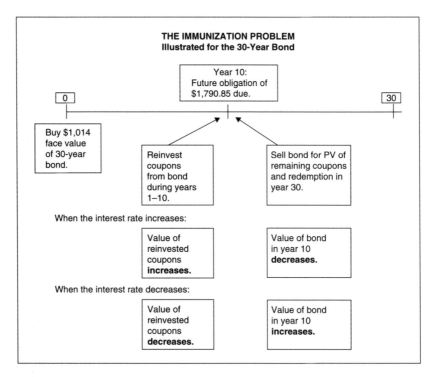

As we will see, the 30-year bond will exactly finance the future obligation of $1,790.85 only for the case in which the current market interest rate of 6 percent remains unchanged.

Here is a summary of price and duration information for the three bonds:

	A	B	C	D
1	**BASIC IMMUNIZATION EXAMPLE WITH THREE BONDS**			
2				
3	Yield to maturity	6%		
4				
5		**Bond 1**	**Bond 2**	**Bond 3**
6	Coupon rate	6.70%	6.988%	5.90%
7	Maturity	10	15	30
8	Face value	1,000	1,000	1,000
9				
10	Bond price	$1,051.52	$1,095.96	$986.24
11	Face value equal to $1,000 of market value	$ 951.00	$ 912.44	$ 1,013.96
12				
13	Duration	7.6655	10.0000	14.6361
14				
15		<-- =dduration(B7,B6,$B$3,1)		
16				

Note that to calculate the duration, we have used the "homemade" **DDuration** function defined in Chapter 20.

If the yield to maturity does not change, then you will be able to reinvest each coupon at 6 percent. Thus, bond 2, for example, will give a terminal wealth at the end of 10 years of

$$\sum_{t=0}^{9} 69.88 * (1.06)^t + \left[\sum_{t=1}^{5} \frac{69.88}{(1.06)^t} + \frac{1,000}{(1.06)^5} \right] = 921.07 + 1,041.62$$

$$= 1,962.69$$

The first term in this expression, $\sum_{t=0}^{9} 69.88 * (1.06)^t$, is the sum of the reinvested coupons. The second and third terms, $\sum_{t=1}^{5} \frac{69.88}{(1.06)^t} + \frac{1,000}{(1.06)^5}$, represent the market value of the bond in year 10, when the bond has five more years until maturity. Since we will be buying only $912.44 of face value of this bond, we have, at the end of 10 years, $0.91244 * \$1,962.69 = \$1,790.85$. This is exactly the amount we wanted to have at this date. The results of this calculation for all three bonds, provided there is no change in the yield to maturity, are given in the following table:

	A	B	C	D	E	F	G	H	I
19	New yield to maturity	6%							
20									
21		Bond 1	Bond 2	Bond 3					
22	Bond price	$1,000.00	$1,041.62	$988.53	<-- =PV($B$19,D7-10, D6*D8)+D8/(1+$B$19)^(D7-10)				
23	Reinvested coupons	$883.11	$921.07	$777.67	<-- =FV($B$19,10, D6*D8)				
24	Total	$1,883.11	$1,962.69	$1,766.20					
25									
26	Multiply by percent of face value bought	95.10%	91.24%	101.40%					
27	Product	$ 1,790.85	$ 1,790.85	$ 1,790.85					

The upshot of this table is that purchasing $1,000 of any of the three bonds will provide—10 years from now—funding for your future obligation of $1,790.85, *provided the market interest rate of 6 percent doesn't change.*

Now suppose that, immediately after you purchase the bonds, the yield to maturity changes to some new value and stays there. This change will obviously affect the calculation we already did. For example, if the yield falls to 5 percent, the table will now look as follows.

	A	B	C	D
19	New yield to maturity	5%		
20				
21		**Bond 1**	**Bond 2**	**Bond 3**
22	Bond price	$1,000.00	$1,086.07	$1,112.16
23	Reinvested coupons	$842.72	$878.94	$742.10
24	**Total**	$1,842.72	$1,965.01	$1,854.26
25				
26	Multiply by percent of face value bought	95.10%	91.24%	101.40%
27	**Product**	$ 1,752.43	$ 1,792.97	$ 1,880.14

Thus, if the yield falls, bond 1 will no longer fund our obligation, whereas bond 3 will overfund it. Bond 2's ability to fund the obligation—not surprisingly, in view of the fact that its duration is exactly 10 years—hardly changes. We can repeat this calculation for any new yield to maturity. The results are shown in the following figure:

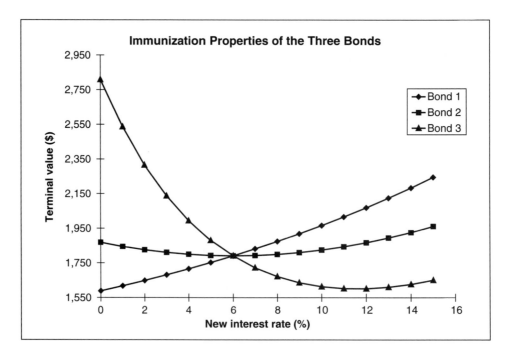

Clearly, if you want an immunized strategy, you should buy bond 2!

21.4   Convexity: A Continuation of Our Immunization Experiment

The duration of a portfolio is the weighted average duration of the assets in the portfolio. As a result, there is another way to get a bond investment with a duration of 10: If we invest \$665.09 in bond 1 and \$344.91 in bond 3, the resulting portfolio also has a duration of 10. These weights are calculated as follows:

$$\lambda * D_{\text{bond1}} + (1 - \lambda) * D_{\text{bond2}} = 7.665\lambda + 14.636(1 - \lambda)$$

$$= 10 \Rightarrow \lambda = 0.66509$$

Suppose we repeat our experiment with this portfolio of bonds. Starting in row 16 of the next spreadsheet, we repeat the experiment of the previous section (varying the YTM), but add in the portfolio of bond 1 and bond 3. The results show that the future value in row 24 does not vary for the portfolio.

	A	B	C	D	E	F	G	H	I
1	**EXPERIMENTING WITH BOND PORTFOLIOS AND CONVEXITY**								
2									
3	Yield to maturity (YTM)	6%							
4									
5		**bond 1**	**bond 2**	**bond 3**					
6	Coupon rate	6.70%	6.988%	5.90%					
7	Maturity	10	15	30					
8	Face value	1,000	1,000	1,000					
9									
10	Bond price	$1,051.52	$1,095.96	$986.24					
11	Face value equal to $1,000 of market value	$ 951.00	$ 912.44	$ 1,013.96					
12									
13	Duration	7.6655	10.0000	14.6361					
14									
15									
16	New YTM	7%							
17						**bond 1 & 3**			
18		**Bond 1**	**Bond 2**	**Bond 3**		**portfolio**			
19	Bond price	$1,000.00	$999.51	$883.47					
20	Reinvested coupons	$925.70	$965.49	$815.17					
21	**Total**	$1,925.70	$1,965.00	$1,698.64					
22									
23	Multiply by percent of face value bought	95.10%	91.24%	101.40%					
24	**Product**	$ 1,831.35	$ 1,792.95	$ 1,722.34		$ 1,794.84	<-- =B27*B24+(1-B27)*D24		
25									
26	Portfolio of bonds 1 and 3								
27	Proportion of bond 1	0.6651	<-- =(10-D13)/(B13-D13)						
28	Proportion of bond 3	0.3349	<-- =1-B27						

Building a data table based on this experiment and graphing the results shows that the portfolio's performance is better than that of bond 2 by itself.

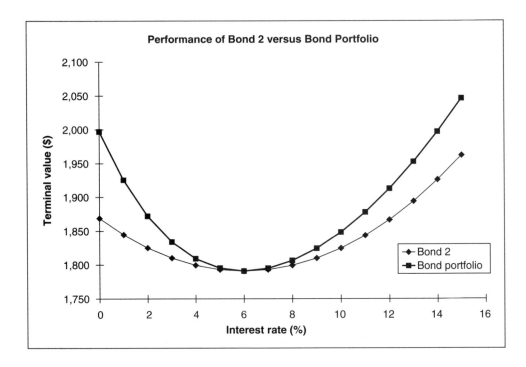

Look again at the graph: Notice that, while the terminal value is somewhat convex in the yield to maturity for both bond 2 and the bond portfolio, the terminal value of the portfolio is *more convex* than that of the single bond. Redington (1952), one of the influential propagators of the concept of duration and immunization, thought this convexity very desirable, and we can see why: No matter what the change in the yield to maturity, the portfolio of bonds provides *more overfunding* of the future obligation than the single bond. This is obviously a desirable property for an immunized portfolio, and it leads us to formulate the following rule:

In a comparison between two immunized portfolios, both of which are to fund a known future obligation, the portfolio whose terminal value is more convex with respect to changes in the yield to maturity is preferable.[1]

---

1.   There is another interpretation of the convexity shown in this example: It shows the impossibility of parallel change in the term structure! If such changes describe the uncertainty relating to the term structure, a bond position can be chosen that always benefits from changes in the term structure. This is an arbitrage, and therefore impossible. I thank Zvi Wiener for pointing this fact out to me.

21.5   Building a Better Mousetrap

Despite what was said in the preceding section, there is some interest in deriving the characteristics of a bond portfolio whose terminal value is as insensitive to changes in the yield as possible. One way of improving the performance (when so defined) of the bond portfolio is not only to match the first derivatives of the change in value (which, as we saw in section 21.2, leads to the duration concept), but also to match the second derivatives.

A direct extension of the analysis of section 21.2 leads us to the conclusion that matching the second derivatives requires:

$$N(N+1) = \sum_{t=1}^{M} \frac{t(t+1)P_t}{(1+r)^t}$$

The following example illustrates the kind of improvement that can be made in a portfolio where the second derivatives are also matched. Consider four bonds, one of which, bond 2, is our old friend from the previous example, whose duration is exactly 10. The bonds are described in the following table:

	A	B	C	D	E	F	G	H	I	J
1		BOND CONVEXITY								
2										
3	Yield to maturity	6%								
4										
5		Bond 1	Bond 2	Bond 3	Bond 4					
6	Coupon rate	4.50%	6.988%	3.50%	11.00%					
7	Maturity	20	15	14	10					
8	Face value	1,000	1,000	1,000	1,000					
9										
10	Bond price	$827.95	$1,095.96	$767.63	$1,368.00					
11	Face value equal to $1,000 of market value	$ 1,207.80	$ 912.44	$ 1,302.72	$ 730.99					
12										
13	Duration	12.8964	10.0000	10.8484	7.0539					
14	Second derivative of duration	229.0873	136.4996	148.7023	67.5980	<-- =secondDur(E7,E6,$B$3)/bondprice(E7,E6,$B$3)				

Here secondDur(numberPayments, couponRate, YTM) is a VBA function we have defined to calculate the second derivative of the duration:

```
Function secondDur(numberPayments, couponRate, YTM)

    For Index = 1 To numberPayments
        If Index < numberPayments Then
            secondDur = couponRate * Index * (Index + 1) _
                / (1 + YTM) ^ Index + secondDur
```

```
        Else
                secondDur = (couponRate + 1) * Index * _
                    (Index + 1) / (1 + YTM) ^ Index secondDur
        End If

        secondDur = secondDur
    Next Index

End Function
```

We need three bonds in order to calculate a portfolio of bonds whose duration and whose second duration derivative are exactly equal to those of the liability. The proportions of a portfolio that sets both the duration and its second derivative equal to those of the liability are bond 1 = −0.56185, bond 2 = 1.641528, and bond3 = −0.07967. (The negative proportions of bonds 1 and 3 mean that we are short-selling these bonds.) As the following figure shows, this portfolio provides an even better hedge against the terminal value than bond 2:

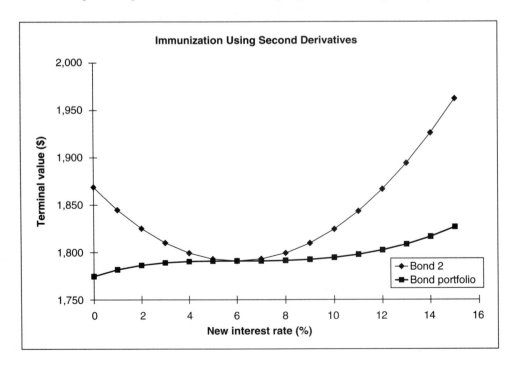

Exercises

1. Prove that the duration of a portfolio is the weighted average duration of the portfolio assets.

2. Set up a spreadsheet that enables you to duplicate the calculations of section 21.5.

3. a. Using the example of section 21.3, find a combination of bonds 1 and 3 with a duration of 8.

   b. Find a combination of bonds 1 and 2 with a duration of 8.

4. In exercise 3, which portfolio (a or b) would you prefer to immunize an obligation with a duration of 8?

5. In exercise 3, recalculate the portfolio proportions assuming that you need a target duration of 12. Which portfolio would you prefer now?

22 Modeling the Term Structure

22.1 Introduction

In this chapter we model the term structure using polynomial and other regression models.

22.2 Polynomial Regressions

We illustrate some of the term-structure modeling concepts by using the same set of U.S. Treasury interest rate data mentioned in Chapter 20 (McCullogh, 1990). We use a subset of the data, from 1980 to 1987. Here's what part of the data set looks like:

McCULLOGH'S TERM-STRUCTURE DATA SET							
	1	2	3	4	5	6	7
Date	0mo	1mo	2mo	3mo	4mo	5mo	6mo
1.1980	11.03	11.87	12.28	12.36	12.39	12.43	12.43
2.1980	13.29	13.92	14.26	14.32	14.37	14.54	14.73
3.1980	13.89	15.07	15.44	15.24	15.19	15.53	15.92
4.1980	10.28	10.39	10.52	10.68	10.82	10.95	11.04
5.1980	8.22	7.85	7.76	7.91	8.1	8.25	8.36
6.1980	4.09	6.66	7.94	8.16	8.11	8.13	8.2
7.1980	6.47	7.84	8.57	8.8	8.87	8.9	8.93
8.1980	8.27	9.2	9.86	10.26	10.5	10.64	10.71
9.1980	10.98	11.2	11.42	11.63	11.79	11.89	11.95
10.1980	10.23	11.66	12.58	12.99	13.14	13.21	13.27

The data on interest rates go out to 20 or 25 years, but because of space considerations we cannot show the length of the rows. Recall that the percentage interest rates are in whole numbers; for example, the three-month interest rate in January 1980 was 12.36 percent.

We first normalize the data by considering the excess of each rate over the short-term rate. We subtract out the 0-month rate (which should be conceived of as the rate on a very short-term, say one-day, money market fund) from the rest of its row, as follows.

	A	B	C	D	E	F	G	H
4		1	2	3	4	5	6	7
5	Date	0mo	1mo	2mo	3mo	4mo	5mo	6mo
6	**Time**	**0.000**	**0.083**	**0.167**	**0.250**	**0.333**	**0.417**	**0.500**
7	1.1980	0	0.84	1.25	1.33	1.36	1.4	1.4
8	2.1980	0	0.63	0.97	1.03	1.08	1.25	1.44
9	3.1980	0	1.18	1.55	1.35	1.3	1.64	2.03
10	4.1980	0	0.11	0.24	0.4	0.54	0.67	0.76
11	5.1980	0	-0.37	-0.46	-0.31	-0.12	0.03	0.14
12	6.1980	0	2.57	3.85	4.07	4.02	4.04	4.11
13	7.1980	0	1.37	2.1	2.33	2.4	2.43	2.46
14	8.1980	0	0.93	1.59	1.99	2.23	2.37	2.44
15	9.1980	0	0.22	0.44	0.65	0.81	0.91	0.97
16	10.1980	0	1.43	2.35	2.76	2.91	2.98	3.04

Note that we have also added a row to the spreadsheet. In row 6 the maturity dates are annualized.

There appears to be considerable evidence that polynomial regressions work well in modeling the term structure.[1] Consider, as an example, the term structure in January 1980:

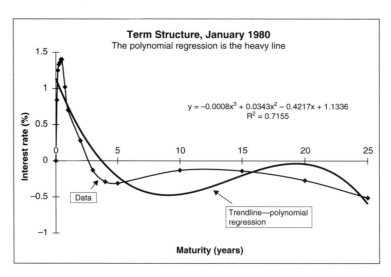

Term Structure, January 1980
The polynomial regression is the heavy line

$y = -0.0008x^3 + 0.0343x^2 - 0.4217x + 1.1336$
$R^2 = 0.7155$

Data

Trendline—polynomial regression

Interest rate (%)

Maturity (years)

The regression was performed with Excel's **Trendline** facility. First the data were graphed using an XY graph. We then marked the data on the graph and clicked the right mouse button, choosing **Add Trendline.** This brings up the following menu (note that we have already chosen to do a polynomial regression of order 3).

---

1. See, for example, papers by Litterman and Scheinkman (1991), Mann and Ramanlal (1997).

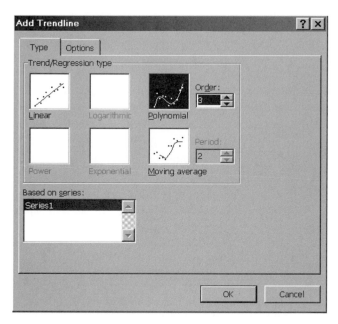

Before clicking OK on the dialogue box, we go to the **Options** tab, so that Excel will present the data on the graph in the form desired:

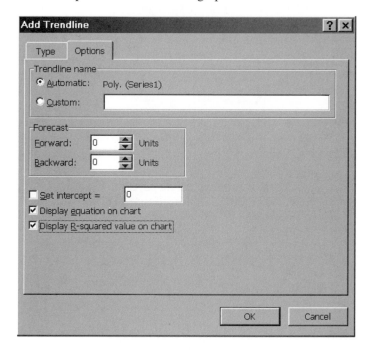

The regression line is

$$y = -0.0008x^3 + 0.0343x^2 - 0.4217x + 1.1336, R^2 = 0.7155$$

Thus 70 percent of the variability in this particular term structure is explained by the time (x), the square of the time (x^2), and the cube of the time (x^3). Litterman and Scheinkman (1991) call the coefficient of x the *level* factor affecting interest rates. When this factor increases, there is a parallel shift in the term structure. They call the coefficient of x^2 the *steepness* factor and the coefficient of x^3 the *curvature factor* of the term structure.

We can also use Excel's **Linest** function to do this regression. To use this function to do a 3rd-degree polynomial regression, we add the square of the time and the cube of the time to our data set (as before, we show only part of the row):

	A	B	C	D	E	F	G	H	I
1	**USING EXCEL'S LINEST FUNCTION**								
2	All data are presented as excess over short-term rate								
3									
4		1	2	3	4	5	6	7	8
5	Date	0mo	1mo	2mo	3mo	4mo	5mo	6mo	9mo
6	Time	0.000	0.083	0.167	0.250	0.333	0.417	0.500	0.750
7	Time^2	0	0.0069	0.0278	0.0625	0.1111	0.1736	0.2500	0.5625
8	Time^3	0	0.0006	0.0046	0.0156	0.0370	0.0723	0.1250	0.4219
9	1.1980	0	0.84	1.25	1.33	1.36	1.4	1.4	1.02
10	2.1980	0	0.63	0.97	1.03	1.08	1.25	1.44	1.63

We now block off a 5×4 range and enter the **Linest** function as an array (for a fuller description, see Chapter 29):

	T	U	V	W	X	Y
7			**LINEST output**			
8		t^3	t^2	t	Intercept	
9	Coefficients	-0.000807202	0.034285199	-0.421704381	1.133605149	
10	Standard errors	0.000337542	0.012168429	0.110592888	0.161789951	
11	R^2 and S.E.(y)	0.715538244	0.428807141	#N/A	#N/A	
12	F, d	10.90011454	13	#N/A	#N/A	
13	SS$_{req}$, SS$_{resid}$	6.012794135	2.390382336	#N/A	#N/A	
14	T-statistics	-2.391410786	2.817553427	-3.813123867	7.006647481	<-- =X9/X10
15						
16	Formula in U9:X13 (this is an array function):					
17		=LINEST(B9:R9,B6:R8,,TRUE)				

From the T-statistic line, we see that all three of the coefficients are significant.

22.3   What Happens to the Coefficients over Time?

We can repeat this experiment on the McCullogh term structures, creating a spreadsheet in which the coefficients vary over time. Following are some lines from this spreadsheet.

	A	B	C	D	E	F	G	H	I	J	K
1	USING EXCEL'S LINEST FUNCTION										
2	We use Linest to show the variation in time of the coefficients										
3											
4											
5											
6											
7											
8	Date	t^3	t^2	t	Intercept	R²					
9	1.1980	-0.0008	0.0343	-0.4217	1.1336	71.55%	Note: Cells B9:E9 contain {=LINEST(L9:AB9,$M$5:$AC$7)}				
10	2.1980	-0.0001	0.0086	-0.2762	1.1587	86.54%	The cells M5:AC5 contain the time, time², time³.				
11	3.1980	-0.0014	0.0593	-0.8209	1.6074	88.38%	This formula has then been copied.				
12	4.1980	-0.0003	0.0113	-0.0916	0.4556	17.78%	Cell F9 contains the formula				
13	5.1980	0.0005	-0.0268	0.4586	-0.1996	96.93%	=INDEX(LINEST(L9:AB9,$M$5:$AC$7,,TRUE),3,1)				
14	6.1980	0.0010	-0.0505	0.7208	3.1846	60.88%					
15	7.1980	0.0007	-0.0363	0.5698	1.8186	77.91%					
16	8.1980	0.0010	-0.0441	0.5313	1.6942	51.13%					
17	9.1980	-0.0001	0.0009	0.0152	0.6400	31.47%					
18	10.1980	0.0001	-0.0063	0.0315	2.3198	20.02%					
19	11.1980	-0.0010	0.0423	-0.5951	1.1428	91.68%					
20	12.1980	-0.0009	0.0376	-0.4909	2.9244	51.87%					
21	1.1981	-0.0015	0.0638	-0.7865	0.7615	91.32%					
22	2.1981	-0.0006	0.0250	-0.3482	0.8460	90.08%					
23	3.1981	-0.0002	0.0009	0.0072	-0.2530	91.69%					
24	4.1981	-0.0003	0.0088	-0.1584	2.0541	64.87%					
25	5.1981	-0.0014	0.0585	-0.7609	-0.5463	94.97%					
26	6.1981	-0.0004	0.0152	-0.2326	0.5594	96.10%					

Notice that over this 16-month period, the biggest changes were in the intercepts—the base case, date-0 interest rates. The next biggest changes were in the coefficient of t, which measures the change in the term structure as a function of time. Changes in the t^2 and t^3 coefficients were much smaller, indicating that these coefficients are important mostly for the long end of the term structure. Graphing the intercepts and coefficients for the regression $r_{jt} = \beta_0 + \beta_1 t + \beta_2 t^2 + \beta_3 t^3$ for the whole period through 1987 emphasizes this fact:

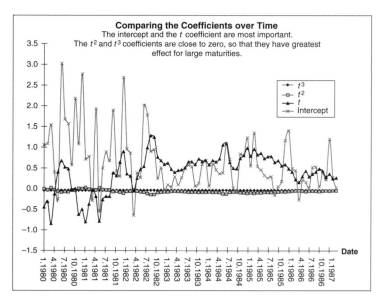

We can also graph the *R*-squared coefficients to get a rough idea of the fit. Throughout much of the 1980s, the regression gave an excellent fit to the data, though the fit is much poorer for the highly volatile term structures of the beginning of the decade:

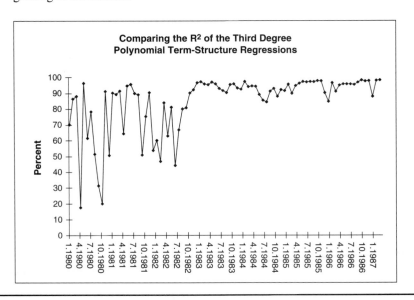

22.4   Academic Term-Structure Models

The term-structure model that we have used—a 3rd-degree polynomial approximation to the term structure—is very useful. However, the academic literature contains a much richer variety of term-structure models. In this section we briefly discuss one of these models, that of Vasicek (1977). The Vasicek term-structure model makes two basis assumptions about interest rates: (1) The whole term structure depends on the interest rate for the very shortest term to maturity. This interest rate, termed the *spot interest rate,* is denoted by *r*. (2) The spot rate *r* is mean-reverting. Changes in *r* can be written as

$$\Delta r = \alpha(\gamma - r)\Delta t + \rho Z\sqrt{\Delta t}$$

where γ is the long-term mean spot interest rate, α is the "push" toward the long-run mean spot rate, and ρ is the instantaneous standard deviation.

Vasicek shows that the present value factor $v(t, s, r)$ at time t for time $s > t$ is given by

$$v[t, s, r, R(\infty)] = \exp\left\{\frac{1}{\alpha}(1 - e^{-\alpha(s-t)})[R(\infty) - r]\right.$$

$$\left. - (s - t)R(\infty) - \frac{\rho^2}{4\alpha^3}(1 - e^{-\alpha(s-t)})^2\right\}, t \leq s$$

where $R(\infty)$ is the long-run interest rate. If we were to price a bond using the Vasicek model, we might specify α, γ, ρ, and $R(\infty)$. We could then write the price of the bond as a function of the current spot rate r:

$$P = \sum_{s=1}^{N} v[0, s, r, R(\infty)]C_t$$

The Vasicek model is easily programmable in Excel, but a full discussion of the model and its properties is beyond the purview of this book.

23 Calculating Default-Adjusted Expected Bond Returns

23.1 Introduction

In this chapter we discuss the effects of default risk on the returns from holding bonds to maturity. The *expected return* on a bond that may possibly default is different from the bond's *promised return*. The latter is defined as the bond's *yield to maturity,* the internal rate of return calculated from the bond's current market price and its *promised* coupon payments and *promised eventual return* of principal in the future. The bond's expected return is less easily calculated: We need to take into account both the bond's probability of future default and the percentage of its principal that holders can expect to recover in the case of default. To complicate matters still further, default can happen in stages, through the gradual degradation of the issuing company's creditworthiness.[1]

In this chapter we use a Markov model to solve for the expected return on a risky bond. Our adjustment procedure takes into account all three of the factors mentioned: the probability of default, the transition of the issuer from one state of creditworthiness to another, and the percentage recovery of face value when the bond defaults. After illustrating the problem and using Excel to solve a small-scale problem, we use some publicly available statistics to program a fuller spreadsheet model. Finally, we show that this model can be used to derive bond betas, the CAPM's risk measure for securities (discussed previously in Chapters 7–12).

23.1.1 Some Preliminaries

Before proceeding, we define a number of terms:

• A bond is issued with a given amount of *principal* or *face value.* When the bond matures, the bondholder is promised the return of this principal. If the bond is issued *at par,* then it is sold for the principal amount.

• A bond bears an interest rate called the *coupon rate.* The periodic payment promised to the bondholders is the product of the coupon rate times the bond's face value.

---

1. Besides default risk, bonds are also subject to term-structure risk: The prices of bonds may show significant variations over time as a result of changing term structure. This statement will be especially true for long-term bonds. In this chapter we abstract from term-structure risk, confining ourselves only to a discussion of the effects of default risk on bond expected returns.

- At any given moment, a bond will be sold in the market for a *market price*. This price may differ from the bond's coupon rate.[2]
- The bond's *yield to maturity* (YTM) is the internal rate of return of the bond, assuming that it is held to maturity and that it does not default.

American corporate bonds are rated by various agencies on the basis of the bond issuer's ability to make repayment on the bonds. The classification scheme for two of the major rating agencies, Standard & Poor's (S&P) and Moody's, is given in the following table:

Long-Term Senior Debt Ratings

Investment-Grade Ratings			Speculative-Grade Ratings		
S&P	Moody's	Interpretation	S&P	Moody's	Interpretation
AAA	Aaa	Highest quality	BB+	Ba1	Likely to fulfill obligations; ongoing uncertainty
			BB	Ba2	
			BB−	Ba3	
AA+	Aa1	High quality	B+	B1	High-risk obligations
AA	Aa2		B	B2	
AA−	AA3		B−	B3	
A+	A1	Strong payment capacity	CCC+	Caa	Current vulnerability to default
AA	A2		CCC		
AA−	A3		CCC−		
BBB+	Baa1	Adequate payment capacity	C	Ca	In bankruptcy or default, or other marked shortcomings
BBB	Baa2		D	D	
BBB−	Baa3				

When a bond defaults, its holders will typically receive some payoff, though less than the promised bond coupon rate and return of principal. We refer to the percent of face value paid off in default as the *recovery percentage*.

---

2. Just to complicate matters, in the United States the convention is to add to a bond's listed price the *prorated coupon* between the time of the last coupon payment and the purchase date. The sum of these two is termed the *invoice price* of the bond; the invoice price is the actual cost at any moment to a purchaser of buying the bond. In our discussion in this chapter we use the term *market price* to denote the invoice price.

23.2   Calculating the Expected Return in a One-Period Framework

The bond's yield to maturity is *not* its expected return: It is clear that both a bond's rating and the anticipated payoff to bondholders in the case of bond default should affect its expected return. All other things being equal, we would expect that if two newly issued bonds have the same term to maturity, then the lower-rated bond (having the higher default probability) should have a higher coupon rate. Similarly, we would expect that an issued and traded bond whose rating has been lowered would experience a decrease in price. We might also expect that the lower is the anticipated payoff in the case of default, the lower will be the bond's expected return.

As a simple illustration, we calculate the expected return of a one-year bond that can default at maturity. We use the following symbols:

F = face value of the bond

P = price of bond

Q = annual coupon rate of the bond

π = probability that the bond will *not* default at end of year

λ = fraction of bond's value that bondholders collect upon default

The bond's expected end-of-year cash flow is $\pi * (1 + Q) * F + (1 - \pi) * \lambda * F$, and its *expected return* is given by

$$\text{Expected return} = \frac{\text{Expected year-end cash flow}}{P} - 1$$

$$= \frac{\pi * (1 + Q) * F + (1 - \pi) * \lambda * F}{P} - 1$$

This calculation is illustrated in the following spreadsheet:

	A	B	C	D	E	F	G
1	**EXPECTED RETURN ON A ONE-YEAR BOND**						
2	**WITH AN ADJUSTMENT FOR DEFAULT PROBABILITY**						
3							
4	Face value, F	100					
5	Price, P	98					
6	Annual coupon rate, Q	16%					
7	Nondefault probability, π	90%					
8	Recovery percentage, λ	80%					
9							
10	Expected cash flow	112.4	<-- =B7*(1+B6)*B4+(1-B7)*B8*B4				
11	Expected return	14.69%	<-- =B10/B5-1				

23.3   A Multiperiod, Multistate Markov Chain Problem

We now introduce multiple periods into the problem. In this section we define a basic model using a very simple set of ratings, much simpler than the complex rating system illustrated in section 23.1. Section 23.5 will use more realistic data.

We suppose that at any date there are four possible bond "ratings":

A   The highest rating.

B   The next highest rating.

D   The bond is in default for the first time (and hence pays off λ of the face value).

E   The bond was in default in the previous period; it therefore pays off 0 in the current period and in any future periods.

The *transition probability* matrix Π is given by

$$\Pi = \begin{bmatrix} \pi_{AA} & \pi_{AB} & \pi_{AD} & 0 \\ \pi_{BA} & \pi_{BB} & \pi_{BD} & 0 \\ 0 & 0 & 0 & 1 \\ 0 & 0 & 0 & 1 \end{bmatrix}$$

The probabilities π_{ij} indicate the probability that in *one period* the bond will go from a rating of i to a rating of j. In the numerical example in section 23.4, we will use the following Π:

$$\Pi = \begin{bmatrix} 0.99 & 0.01 & 0 & 0 \\ 0.03 & 0.96 & 0.01 & 0 \\ 0 & 0 & 0 & 1 \\ 0 & 0 & 0 & 1 \end{bmatrix}$$

What does this matrix Π mean?

• If a bond is rated A in the current period, there is a probability of 0.99 that it will still be rated A in the next period. There is a probability 0.01 that it will be rated B in the next period, but it is *impossible* for the bond to be rated A today and D or E in the subsequent period. While it is possible to go from ratings A and B to any of ratings A, B, and D, it is *not* possible to go from A or B to E. This statement is true because E denotes that default took place in the *previous period*.

• In the example of Π, a bond that starts off with a rating of B can—in a subsequent period—be rated A (with a probability of 0.03); be rated B (with a probability of 0.96); or rated D (and hence in default) with a probability of 0.01.

• A bond that is currently in state D (i.e., first-time default), will necessarily be in E in the next period. Thus the third row of our matrix Π will always be [0 0 0 1].

• Once the rating is in E, it remains there permanently. Therefore, the fourth row of the matrix Π also will always be [0 0 0 1].

23.3.1   The Multiperiod Transition Matrix

The matrix Π defines the transition probabilities over one period. The two-period transition probabilities are given by the matrix product $\Pi * \Pi$ (see discussion of matrix products and array functions in Chapter 27):

Two-period transition probability

$$
= \Pi * \Pi = \begin{bmatrix} 0.99 & 0.01 & 0 & 0 \\ 0.03 & 0.96 & 0.01 & 0 \\ 0 & 0 & 0 & 1 \\ 0 & 0 & 0 & 1 \end{bmatrix} * \begin{bmatrix} 0.99 & 0.01 & 0 & 0 \\ 0.03 & 0.96 & 0.01 & 0 \\ 0 & 0 & 0 & 1 \\ 0 & 0 & 0 & 1 \end{bmatrix}
$$

$$
= \begin{bmatrix} 0.9804 & 0.0195 & 0.0001 & 0 \\ 0.0585 & 0.9219 & 0.0096 & 0.0100 \\ 0 & 0 & 0 & 1 \\ 0 & 0 & 0 & 1 \end{bmatrix}
$$

Thus if a bond is rated B today, there is a probability of 5.85 percent that in two periods it will be rated A, a probability of 92.19 percent that in two periods it will be rated B, a probability of 0.96 percent that in two periods it will default (and hence be rated D), and a probability of 1 percent that in two periods it will be rated E. The last rating means, of course, that the bond went into default in the first period.

We can use the array function **MMult** function of Excel (see Chapter 27) to calculate multiyear transition probability matrices:

	A	B	C	D
3	**One-period transition matrix**			
4	0.9900	0.0100	0.0000	0.0000
5	0.0300	0.9600	0.0100	0.0000
6	0.0000	0.0000	0.0000	1.0000
7	0.0000	0.0000	0.0000	1.0000
8				
9				
10	**Two-period transition matrix**			
11	0.9804	0.0195	0.0001	0.0000
12	0.0585	0.9219	0.0096	0.0100
13	0.0000	0.0000	0.0000	1.0000
14	0.0000	0.0000	0.0000	1.0000
15	Cells A11:D14 contain array formula {=MMULT(A4:D7,A4:D7)}			
16				
17				
18				
19	**Three-period transition matrix**			
20	0.9712	0.0285	0.0002	0.0001
21	0.0856	0.8856	0.0092	0.0196
22	0.0000	0.0000	0.0000	1.0000
23	0.0000	0.0000	0.0000	1.0000
24	Cells A20:D23 contain array formula {=MMULT(A4:D7,A11:D14)}			
25				
26				
27				

In general, the year-t transition matrix is given by the matrix power Π^t. Calculating these matrix powers by the procedure that we have illustrated is cumbersome, so we first define a VBA function that can compute powers of matrices:

```
Function matrixpower(matrix, n)
    If n = 1 Then
        matrixpower = matrix
        Else: matrixpower =
            Application.MMult(matrixpower(matrix,
            n - 1), matrix)
    End If
End Function
```

The use of this function is illustrated in the following spreadsheet. The function **Matrixpower** allows a one-step computation of the power of any transition matrix:

	A	B	C	D
1	USING THE FUNCTION MATRIXPOWER			
2				
3	One-period transition matrix			
4	0.9900	0.0100	0.0000	0.0000
5	0.0300	0.9600	0.0100	0.0000
6	0.0000	0.0000	0.0000	1.0000
7	0.0000	0.0000	0.0000	1.0000
8				
9	t		10	
10				
11	t-period transition matrix			
12	0.9159	0.0802	0.0007	0.0032
13	0.2405	0.6754	0.0070	0.0771
14	0.0000	0.0000	0.0000	1.0000
15	0.0000	0.0000	0.0000	1.0000
16				
17				
18		Cells A12:D15 contain array formula		
19		{=MATRIXPOWER(A4:D7,B9)}		
20				

From this example it follows that if a bond started out with an A rating, there is a probability of 0.3 percent that the bond will be in default at the end of ten periods, and there is a probability of 0.07 percent that it will default before the tenth period.

23.3.2 Bond Payoff Vector

Recall that Q denotes the bond's coupon rate and λ denotes the percentage payoff of face value if the bond defaults. The payoff vector of the bond depends on whether the bond is currently in its last period N or whether $t < N$:

$$
\text{Payoff}(t) = \begin{cases} \begin{bmatrix} Q \\ Q \\ \lambda \\ 0 \end{bmatrix} & \text{if } t < N \\[1em] \begin{bmatrix} 1+Q \\ 1+Q \\ \lambda \\ 0 \end{bmatrix} & \text{if } t = N \end{cases}
$$

The first two elements of each vector denote the payoff in nondefaulted states, the third element λ is the payoff if the rating is D, and the fourth element 0 is the payoff if the bond rating is E. The distinction between the two vectors depends, of course, on the repayment of principal in the terminal period.

Before we can define the expected payoffs, we need to define one further vector, which will denote the *initial state of the bond*. This current-state vector is a vector with a 1 for the current rating of the bond and zeros elsewhere. For example, if the bond has rating A at date 0, then Initial = [1 0 0 0]; if it has date-0 rating of B, then Initial = [0 1 0 0].

We can now define the expected bond payoff in period t:

$$E[\text{Payoff}(t)] = \text{Initial} * \Pi^t * \text{Payoff}(t)$$

23.4   A Numerical Example

We continue using the numerical Π from the previous section, and we further suppose that $\lambda = 0.8$, meaning that a defaulted bond will pay off 80 percent of face value in the first period of default. We consider a bond having the following characteristics:

- The bond is currently rated B.
- Its coupon rate $Q = 8$ percent.
- The bond has five more years to maturity.
- The bond's current market price is 98 percent of its face value.

The following spreadsheet shows the facts in the preceding list as well as the payoff vectors of the bond at dates before maturity (in cells F4:F7) and on the maturity date (cells I4:I7). The transition matrix is given in cells C10:F13, and the initial vector is given in B15:E15.[3]

The expected bond payoffs are given in cells B19:G19. Before we explain how they were calculated, we note the important economic fact that—if the expected payoffs are as given—then the *bond's expected return* is calcu-

---

3.   Note the use of the **IF** statement in translating the bond's initial rating (cell B7) to the initial vector given in B15:E15. To avoid confusion, we might improve this statement by writing it as **IF(Upper(B7)="A", 1, 0)**, etc. This method guarantees that even if the bond's rating is entered as a lower case letter, the initial vector will come out correctly.

lated by **IRR(B19:G19, 0).** As cell B20 shows, this expected return is 7.2447 percent.[4]

	A	B	C	D	E	F	G	H	I	J
1		CALCULATING THE EXPECTED BOND RETURN								
2										
3	Bond price	98.00%				Payoff(t<N)			Payoff(N)	
4	Coupon rate, Q	7%			Cells F4:F7	7%		Cells I4:I7	107%	
5	Recovery rate, λ	80%			are called	7%		are called	107%	
6	Bond term, N	5			"payoff1"	80%		"payoff2"	80%	
7	Initial rating	B			in row 19	0		in row 19	0	
8										
9			A	B	D	E				
10	Transition matrix	A	0.9990	0.0010	0.0000	0.0000				
11		B	0.0300	0.9600	0.0100	0.0000				
12		D	0.0000	0.0000	0.0000	1.0000				
13		E	0.0000	0.0000	0.0000	1.0000				
14										
15	Initial vector	0	1	0	0					
16	=IF(B7="A",1,0)			=IF(B7="B",1,0)						
17	="A",1,0)			="A",1,0)						
18	Year	0	1	2	3	4	5	6	7	8
19	Expected payoffs	-0.9800	0.0773	0.0763	0.0754	0.0744	1.0274	0.0000	0.0000	0.0000
20	Expected yield	7.2447%								
21										
22										
23	=IRR(B19:AN19,0)			=IF(C18>bondterm,0,						
24				IF(C18=bondterm,MMULT(initial,MMULT(matrixpower(transition,C18),payoff2)),							
25				MMULT(initial,MMULT(matrixpower(transition,C18),payoff1))))							
26										

23.4.1   How to Calculate the Expected Bond Payoffs

As indicated in the previous section, the period-t expected bond payoff is given by the following formula $E[\text{Payoff}(t)] = \text{Initial} * \Pi^t * \text{Payoff}(t)$. The formula in row 19 uses two **IF** statements to implement this formula:

=IF(C18>bondterm, 0,

**IF(C18=bondterm, MMULT(initial, MMULT
(matrixpower(transition, C18), payoff2)),**

MMULT(initial, MMULT(matrixpower(transition, C18), payoff1))))

---

4.   The actual formula in Cell B20 is **IRR(B19:AN19)**. This allows the calculation of the IRR of bonds of maturing up to 40 years.

Here's what these statements mean:

- First **IF:** If the current year is greater than the bond term N (in our example $N = 5$), then the payoff on the bond is 0.

- Second **IF:** If the current year is equal to the bond term N, then the expected payoff on the bond is **MMULT(initial, MMULT(matrixpower(transition, C18), payoff2)).** Here **transition** is the name for the transition matrix in cells C10:F13 and **payoff2** is the name for the cells I4:I7.

- If the current year n is less than the bond term, then the expected payoff on the bond is **MMULT(initial, MMULT(matrixpower(transition, C18), payoff1),** where **payoff1** is the name for the cells F4:F7.

Copying this formula gives the whole vector of expected bond payoffs.

23.5   Transition Matrices and Recovery Percentages: What Do We Know?

From an extensive survey of bond defaults conducted by Standard & Poor's, it is possible to calculate average rating-transition probabilities:

Initial Rating	Rating at End of Year							
	AAA	AA	A	BBB	BB	B	CCC	D
AAA	0.9050	0.0859	0.0074	0.0006	0.0011	0.0000	0.0000	0.0000
AA	0.0076	0.9074	0.0762	0.0064	0.0007	0.0014	0.0002	0.0000
A	0.0009	0.0262	0.9069	0.0547	0.0078	0.0028	0.0001	0.0006
BBB	0.0003	0.0027	0.0615	0.8653	0.0536	0.0131	0.0014	0.0020
BB	0.0003	0.0016	0.0070	0.0738	0.8040	0.0924	0.0096	0.0113
B	0.0000	0.0008	0.0034	0.0053	0.0658	0.8384	0.0370	0.0494
CCC	0.0015	0.0000	0.0046	0.0109	0.0163	0.1148	0.6730	0.1790
D	0.0000	0.0000	0.0000	0.0000	0.0000	0.0000	0.0000	0.0000
E	0.0000	0.0000	0.0000	0.0000	0.0000	0.0000	0.0000	0.0000

There is also a considerable amount of data on the recovery rates from bankruptcy in various industries. A table from an article by Edward Altman and Velore M. Kishore follows; from this table we can see that the average recovery rate from a variety of industries was 41 percent.

Recovery Rates by Industry: Defaulted Bonds by Three-Digit SIC Code, 1971–95

Industry	SIC Code	Number of Observations	Recovery Rate			
			Average	Weighted Observation	Median Average	Standard Deviation Weighted
Public utilities	490	56	70.47	65.48	79.07	19.46
Chemicals, petroleum, rubber and plastic products	280, 290, 300	35	62.73	80.39	71.88	27.10
Machinery, instruments, and related products	350, 360, 380	36	48.74	44.75	47.50	20.13
Services—business and personal	470, 632, 720, 730	14	46.23	50.01	41.50	25.03
Food and kindred products	200	18	45.28	37.40	41.50	21.67
Wholesale and retail trade	500, 510, 520	12	44.00	48.90	37.32	22.14
Diversified manufacturing	390, 998	20	42.29	29.49	33.88	24.98
Casino, hotel, and recreation	770, 790	21	40.15	39.74	28.00	25.66
Building materials, metals, and fabricated products	320, 330, 340	68	38.76	29.64	37.75	22.86
Transportation and transportation equipment	370, 410, 420, 450	52	38.42	41.12	37.13	27.98
Communication, broadcasting, movies, printing, publishing	270, 480, 780	65	37.08	39.34	34.50	20.79
Financial institutions	600, 610, 620, 630, 670	66	35.69	35.44	32.15	25.72
Construction and real estate	150, 650	35	35.27	28.58	24.00	28.69
General merchandise stores	530, 540, 560, 570, 580, 000	89	33.16	29.35	30.00	20.47
Mining and petroleum drilling	100, 103	45	33.02	31.83	32.00	18.01
Textile and apparel products	220, 230	31	31.66	33.72	31.13	15.24
Wood, paper, and leather products	240, 250, 260, 310	11	29.77	24.30	18.25	24.38
Lodging, hospitals, and nursing facilities	700 through 890	22	26.49	19.61	16.00	22.65
Total		**696**	**41.00**	**39.11**	**36.25**	**25.56**

Source: E. Altman and V. M. Kishore, "Almost Everything You Wanted to Know about Recoveries on Defaulted Bonds," Table 3, *Financial Analysts Journal,* November/December 1996, pp. 57–64.

Using the Altman-Kishore and Standard & Poor's data, we can calculate the following spreadsheet:

	A	B	C	D	E	F	G	H	I	J
1	**CALCULATING EXPECTED RETURNS USING HISTORIC TRANSITION MATRIX**									
2										
3						Payoff(t<N)		Payoff(N)		
4	Bond price	99.00%			AAA	11%		AAA	111%	
5	Coupon rate, C	11.00%			AA	11%		AA	111%	
6	Recovery rate, λ	41%			A	11%		A	111%	
7	Bond term, N	5			BBB	11%		BBB	111%	
8	Initial rating	B			BB	11%		BB	111%	
9					B	11%		B	111%	
10					CCC	11%		CCC	111%	
11					D	41%		D	41%	
12					E	0		E	0%	
13										
14	Transition matrix									
15						Rating at end of year				
16	**Initial Rating**	AAA	AA	A	BBB	BB	B	CCC	D	E
17	AAA	0.9050	0.0859	0.0074	0.0006	0.0011	0.0000	0.0000	0.0000	0.0000
18	AA	0.0076	0.9074	0.0762	0.0064	0.0007	0.0014	0.0002	0.0000	0.0000
19	A	0.0009	0.0262	0.9069	0.0547	0.0078	0.0028	0.0001	0.0006	0.0000
20	BBB	0.0003	0.0027	0.0615	0.8653	0.0536	0.0131	0.0014	0.0020	0.0000
21	BB	0.0003	0.0016	0.0070	0.0738	0.8040	0.0924	0.0096	0.0113	0.0000
22	B	0.0000	0.0008	0.0034	0.0053	0.0658	0.8384	0.0370	0.0494	0.0000
23	CCC	0.0015	0.0000	0.0046	0.0109	0.0163	0.1148	0.6730	0.1790	0.0000
24	D	0.0000	0.0000	0.0000	0.0000	0.0000	0.0000	0.0000	0.0000	1.0000
25	E	0.0000	0.0000	0.0000	0.0000	0.0000	0.0000	0.0000	0.0000	1.0000
26										
27										
28		AAA	AA	A	BBB	BB	B	CCC	D	E
29	Initial vector	0	0	0	0	0	1	0	0	0
30										
31					=IF(UPPER($B$8)=D28,1,0)					
32										
33	Year	0	1	2	3	4	5	6	7	8
34	Expected payoff	-99.00%	0.12483	0.119207	0.113183	0.1071731	0.872328	0	0	0
35	Expected bond return	7.726%								
36		=IF(E33>$B$7,0,								
37	=IRR(B34:L34,0)	IF(E33=$B$7,MMULT($B$29:$J$29,MMULT(matrixpower($B$17:$J$25,E33)),$I$4:$I$12)),								
38		MMULT($B$29:$J$29,MMULT(matrixpower($B$17:$J$25,E33)),$F$4:$F$12))))								
39										

The specific example calculates the expected return on a bond with five more years until maturity, currently rated B, with a coupon rate of 11 percent and a current price of 99 percent of par. The assumption is that the bond's payoff in default will match the Altman-Kishore 41 percent average.[5]

---

5. The transition matrix given here represents some reworking of publicly available data from Standard & Poor's. S&P data do not give information on transitions beyond CCC.; for purposes of this example, we assume that any transition below CCC is into default D. The reworking of the data was done by the author and not by S&P, and the reworking is for illustrative purposes only.

23.6   Adjusting the Expected Return for Uneven Periods

The spreadsheet of the previous section will calculate the expected bond returns adjusted for default probability and recovery percentage, but it still has one major problem: It assumes that all payments on the bond are evenly spaced; that is, it assumes that there is a full period from the current date to the next coupon payment, two periods to the following coupon, etc. In many cases, of course, the time to the first coupon payment is less than a full period. As discussed in Chapter 20, there is a simple solution to this problem. We illustrate this solution in the spreadsheet below, which is a simple modification of the previous spreadsheet:

	A	B	C	D	E	F	G	H	I	J
1	**CALCULATING EXPECTED RETURNS USING HISTORIC TRANSITION MATRIX**									
2					**Adjusted for uneven periods**					
3						Payoff(t<N)		Payoff(N)		
4	Bond price	102.00%			AAA	12%		AAA	112%	
5	Coupon rate, C	12%			AA	12%		AA	112%	
6	Recovery rate, λ	55%			A	12%		A	112%	
7	Bond term, N	7			BBB	12%		BBB	112%	
8	Initial rating	B			BB	12%		BB	112%	
9	Time until first payment	0.8			B	12%		B	112%	
10					CCC	12%		CCC	112%	
11					D	55%		D	55%	
12					E	0		E	0%	
13										
14	Transition matrix									
15						Rating at end of year				
16	**Initial Rating**	AAA	AA	A	BBB	BB	B	CCC	D	E
17	AAA	0.9050	0.0859	0.0074	0.0006	0.0011	0.0000	0.0000	0.0000	0.0000
18	AA	0.0076	0.9074	0.0762	0.0064	0.0007	0.0014	0.0002	0.0000	0.0000
19	A	0.0009	0.0262	0.9069	0.0547	0.0078	0.0028	0.0001	0.0006	0.0000
20	BBB	0.0003	0.0027	0.0615	0.8653	0.0536	0.0131	0.0014	0.0020	0.0000
21	BB	0.0003	0.0016	0.0070	0.0738	0.8040	0.0924	0.0096	0.0113	0.0000
22	B	0.0000	0.0008	0.0034	0.0053	0.0658	0.8384	0.0370	0.0494	0.0000
23	CCC	0.0015	0.0000	0.0046	0.0109	0.0163	0.1148	0.6730	0.1790	0.0000
24	D	0.0000	0.0000	0.0000	0.0000	0.0000	0.0000	0.0000	0.0000	1.0000
25	E	0.0000	0.0000	0.0000	0.0000	0.0000	0.0000	0.0000	0.0000	1.0000
26										
27										
28		AAA	AA	A	BBB	BB	B	CCC	D	E
29	Initial	0	0	0	0	0	1	0	0	0
30										
31	=-B4/(1+B35)^(1-B9)				=IF(UPPER($B$8)=D28,1,0)					
32										
33	Year	0	1	2	3	4	5	6	7	8
34	Expected payoff	-100.11%	0.141257	0.135058	0.128264	0.1214055	0.114779	0.108535	0.802214	0
35	Expected bond return	9.122%								
36				=IF(E33>$B$7,0,						
37		=IRR(B34:L34,0)		IF(E33=$B$7,MMULT($B$29:$J$29,MMULT(matrixpower($B$17:$J$25,E33),$I$4:$I$12)),						
38				MMULT($B$29:$J$29,MMULT(matrixpower($B$17:$J$25,E33),$F$4:$F$12))))						
39										

The spreadsheet calculates the expected return of a bond rated B, with coupon rate 12 percent, a market price of 102 percent of par, and a recovery percentage of 55 percent. The bond has seven more payments, the last being the payment of interest plus principal (the principal here is assumed to be 1).[6] The bond has only 0.8 year until the first payment.

23.7   Computing Bond Betas

A vexatious problem in corporate finance is the computation of bond betas. The model presented in this chapter can be easily used to compute the beta of a bond. Recall that the capital asset pricing model's *security market line* (SML) is given by

$$E(r_d) = r_f + \beta_d[E(r_m) - r_f]$$

where $E(r_d)$ is expected return on debt, r_f is return on riskless debt, and $E(r_m)$ is return on equity market portfolio.

If we know expected return on debt, we can calculate the debt β. provided we know the risk-free rate r_f and the expected rate of return on the market $E(r_m)$. Suppose, for example, that the market risk premium $E(r_m) - r_f = 8.4$ percent, and that $r_f = 7$ percent. Then a bond having an expected return of 8 percent will have a β of 0.119:

	A	B	C	D
1	**CALCULATING A BOND'S BETA**			
2				
3	Market risk premium, E(r$_m$) - r$_f$	8.40%		
4	r$_f$	7%		
5	Expected bond return	8.00%		
6	Implied bond beta	0.119	<-- =(B5-B4)/B3	

If we use the Benninga-Sarig tax adjustment to the SML (see section 2.7), then the bond SML becomes r_d = cost of debt = $r_f + \beta_{\text{Debt}}[E(r_m) - r_f(1 - T_c)]$. This gives the bond beta as:

---

6. Note that in all the examples of this chapter, the payments on bonds are assumed to be annual. In point of fact, the payments on many corporate bonds are semiannual, or even quarterly. The adjustment to the spreadsheet is easily made. A bond with a coupon of 11 percent and with semiannual payments will pay 5.5 percent of the face value each half year. Thus all the calculations should be made with 5.5 percent, and a "period" will represent one-half year.

	A	B	C	D	E
8	**Benninga-Sarig tax-adjusted SML (see section 2.7)**				
9	Market risk premium, $E(r_m) - r_f$	8.40%			
10	r_f	7%			
11	Corporate tax rate, T_C	40%			
12	Expected bond return	8.00%			
13	Implied bond beta	0.089	<-- =(B12-B10)/(B9+B10*B11)		

Exercises

1. A newly issued bond with one year to maturity has a price of 100, which equals its face value. The coupon rate on the bond is 15 percent; the probability of default in one year is 35 percent; and the bond's payoff in default will be 65 percent of its face value. Calculate the bond's expected return.

2. Consider the case of five possible rating states, A, B, C, D, and E. The states A, B, and C are initial bond ratings; D symbolizes first-time default; and E indicates default in the previous period. Assume that the transition matrix Π is given by:

$$\Pi = \begin{bmatrix} 1 & 0 & 0 & 0 & 0 \\ 0.06 & 0.90 & 0.03 & 0.01 & 0 \\ 0.02 & 0.05 & 0.88 & 0.05 & 0 \\ 0 & 0 & 0 & 0 & 1 \\ 0 & 0 & 0 & 0 & 1 \end{bmatrix}$$

   A 10-year bond issued today at par with an A rating is assumed to bear a coupon rate of 7 percent.

   a. If a bond is issued today at par with a B rating and with a recovery percentage of 50 percent, what should be its coupon rate so that its expected return will also be 7 percent?

   b. If a bond is issued today at par with a C rating and with a recovery percentage of 50 percent, what should be its coupon rate so that its expected return will be 7 percent?

3. A bond of XYZ Corporation has the following characteristics:

   Market price: 108.32 percent of par

   Coupon rate: 15 percent

   Number of annual payments (including return of principal) left on bond: 15

   Time to first payment: 8 months

   XYZ Corporation's debt is currently rated CCC. Use the model of section 23.5 to calculate the bond's expected return. Assume a recovery percentage $\lambda = 78$ percent.

4. An underwriter issues a new seven-year B bond with a coupon rate of 9 percent. If the expected rate of return on the bond is 8 percent, what is the bond's implied recovery percentage λ? Assume the transition matrix given in section 23.5.

5. An underwriter issues a new seven-year CCC bond. The anticipated recovery rate in default of the bond is expected to be 55 percent. What should be the coupon rate on the bond so that its expected return is 9 percent? Assume the transition matrix given in section 23.5.

24 Duration and the Cheapest-to-Deliver Problem for Treasury Bond Futures Contracts

24.1   Introduction

In this chapter we consider the problem of the cheapest to deliver (CTD) on a Treasury bond futures contract.[1] This problem has received a great deal of attention in the finance literature; interest in it derives from the fact that the Treasury bond futures contract—one of the most widely traded of all financial futures contracts—allows for the delivery of a wide range of Treasury bonds and the fact that the procedure for adjusting the delivery price of these bonds rarely conforms to the differences in market prices.

An extensive literature dealing with the CTD when the term structure is flat has somehow become mired in the misconception that the CTD is characterizable in terms of the duration. We use Excel to show that this assumption is not always true and that the exceptions to the duration rule contain a large number of economically relevant scenarios.[2]

24.2   A General Model of the CTD

In this section we set out a general model of the CTD for any term-structure model. For convenience, we shall use notation that assumes a one-factor term-structure model, but extensions to more factors are trivial.

• The discount factor at time t for a one-dollar payment at time $\tau \geq t$ when the time-t spot rate is r is denoted by $v(t, \tau, r)$.

• The set of all deliverable T-bonds is assumed to be convex; bonds are assumed to pay continuous coupons. By writing $\{c, M\}$ we denote a T-bond paying a continuous coupon c and having maturity M.

• The notation $g(t, T, c, M, r)$ denotes *a bond-specific* forward contract at time t; the contract calls for delivery of a T-bond $\{c, M\}$ at time T.

---

1.   This chapter was written jointly with Zvi Wiener of the Hebrew University of Jerusalem, Israel.

2.   We have not succeeded in tracking down the source of this misconception. Jones (1985)—basing his analysis on papers by Kilcollin (1982) and Kane and Marcus (1984)—seems to have been the first to have stated that duration is the determining factor in choosing the CTD. We have found similar statements in textbooks (e.g., Edwards and Ma, 1992) and in the internal manuals of a number of investment banks.

- We ignore the effects of marking to market on the price of the futures contract. This presupposition enables us to examine only a forward contract.[3]
- The *price* today of a Treasury bond with coupon c and maturity M is given by

$$Price(c, M) = \int_t^M c * v(t, \tau, r)d\tau + v(t, M, r)$$

- The value $CF(c, M, T)$—the conversion factor for a T-bond with maturity M and coupon c delivered at time T against the forward contract—is calculated using a continuous version of the Chicago Board of Trade (CBOT) formula:

$$CF(c, M, T) = \int_0^{M-T} c * e^{-0.08\tau}d\tau + e^{-0.08(M-T)}$$

$$= \frac{ce^{-0.08\tau}}{-0.08} \bigg|_0^{M-T} + e^{-0.08(M-T)}$$

$$= \frac{c(1 - e^{-0.08(M-T)})}{0.08} + e^{-0.08(M-T)}$$

24.2.1 Nonoption Forward Contracts

Suppose that we are offered a nonoption forward contract on a specific bond $\{c, M\}$ at time t, and suppose that the forward price of this contract is $g(t, T, c, M, r)$.[4] Denote by $f(t, T, c, M, r)$ the profit from buying the specific bond $\{c, M\}$ today and holding it for delivery on the forward contract. It is clear that the forward contract will be priced so that the profit to its participants will be zero:

$$f(t, T, c, M, r) = v(t, T, r)g(t, T, c, M, r)CF(c, M, T)$$

$$- \left[\int_T^M c * v(t, \tau, r)d\tau + v(t, M, r) \right]$$

$$= 0 \Rightarrow g(t, T, c, M, r)$$

$$= \frac{\int_t^M c * v(t, \tau, r)d\tau + v(t, M, r)}{v(t, T, r)CF(c, M, T)}$$

---

3. Although in principle marking to market is a factor in futures versus forward pricing (see, for example, Cox, Ingersoll, and Ross, 1981; Jarrow and Oldfield, 1981; Richard and Sundaresan, 1981), there seems to be a general agreement that marking to market is not an important pricing consideration for financial future contracts. See Sundaresan (1991), Benninga and Protopapadakis (1994), and Hanweck (1995).

4. The contract $g(t, T, c, M)$ is a version of a standard bond repo contract.

For the moment we assume that the set of deliverable bonds is convex and compact; convexity implies that if $\{c_1, M_1\}$ is the coupon and maturity on a particular deliverable bond, and $\{c_2, M_2\}$ is a combination of coupon and maturity on a second bond, then $\{\lambda c_1 + (1 - \lambda)c_2, \lambda M_1 + (1 - \lambda)M_2\}$ is also the specification of a deliverable bond.[5]

In the Treasury bond futures contract, the short chooses the delivery instrument. This means that the forward price $g(t, T, c, M, r)$ that minimizes the preceding function for all deliverable $\{c, M\}$ will be the market forward price.

The next two sections discuss the optimal delivery bond given this forward price.

24.3 The Extremal Coupon as a General Solution for the CTD

Denote by $g^*(t, T)$ the minimum of the $g(t, T, c, M, r)$ for all $\{c, M\}$. Suppose this minimum is achieved for $c^*(t, T, r)$, $M^*(t, T, r)$; when no confusion is caused, we will write $\{c^*, M^*\}$. Proposition 1 shows that $\{c^*, M^*\}$ is always achieved for either the highest or lowest coupon bond, independent of any assumptions on the term structure.[6]

PROPOSITION 1   Given maturity M, $g^*(t, T, r) = \min\limits_{\{c,M\}} g(t, T, c, M, r)$ is achieved for extremal c.

According to Proposition 1, the cheapest-to-deliver bond will *always*—irrespective of the term structure—be a bond with either the lowest or the highest coupon of all the deliverable bonds.

24.4 Choosing the Optimal Maturity for CTD: The Case of Flat Term Structure

In section 24.3 we showed that—independent of the term-structure model—the optimal CTD will have either the highest or lowest coupon c. In this section we

---

5. The assumptions on convexity and compactness of the set of deliverable bonds are standard in the CTD literature, although they are not always made explicitly. Compactness is a fairly harmless assumption, but the assumption of convexity is not entirely trivial. For example, consider the convex combination of two bonds: if the bonds have the same maturity but different coupons, this convex combination will give a bond with an intermediate coupon; however, the convex combination of two bonds having the same coupon but different maturities is not a bond with an intermediate maturity.

6. The proofs of the propositions can be found in Benninga & Wiener (1999).

consider the optimal maturity of the CTD for the case of a flat term structure. It can be shown that all economically reasonable term structures are approximately flat for large maturities. Since the T-bond futures contract is written on long-maturity bonds, we shall claim that the assumption of flat term structure is a good approximation of the results for actual term structures.

In order to set the stage, we first prove the following proposition, which extends the results of the Proposition 1 for the case of a flat (or approximately flat) term structure.

PROPOSITION 2   Suppose that the long-run term structure is approximately flat and let r_L be the long-run interest rate. Then when $r_L > 8$ percent, we will choose the *lowest* coupon, and when $r_L < 8$ percent, we will choose the *highest* coupon c for delivery.

Proposition 2 shows that when the term structure is flat, if interest rates are above 8 percent it will be optimal to deliver the smallest coupon, and vice versa. In Proposition 3, we show the taxonomy given in Table 24.1 for the optimal choice of $\{c, M\}$ for the case of a flat term structure:

Table 24.1
Characterization of Optimal CTD

Case	Characterization	Optimal Coupon	Optimal M
Case 1	$8\% > r > \max c$	Largest c	Smallest M (there could be another local minimum, but this possibility is unrealistic since the value of M is usually larger than 50 years)
Case 2	$8\% > r$	Largest c	Smallest M
Case 3	$r > 8\%$ $\min c > 8\%$	Smallest c	Largest M
Case 4	$r > 8\% > \min c$	Smallest c	$\max M \geq M^* \geq \min M$, with possibility of an interior optimum

PROPOSITION 3   If the term structure is flat, then $g^*(t, T, r) = \min_{\{c,M\}} g(t, T, c, M, r)$ is determined by Table 24.1.

To sum up the results of this and the previous section: Independent of the term-structure model, the delivery specifications on the Treasury-bond futures contract lead to a CTD with either the lowest or highest coupon. When the term structure is flat, we can completely characterize the optimal maturity of the CTD; we have shown that this will fall in one of four cases. The following section compares our characterization to the commonly cited duration rules in the literature.

24.5   Using Excel to Plot the CTD and Duration

A number of authors (e.g., Jones, 1985; Kane and Marcus, 1984, p. 236; and Edwards and Ma, 1992, p. 333) state that the solution to the CTD-bond problem when the term structure is flat is the deliverable bond with

- Highest duration if the market interest rate is greater than 8 percent.
- Lowest duration if the market interest rate is less than 8 percent.

In this section we discuss this duration-based rule and compare it to our characterization of the optimal delivery problem proved in Propositions 1–3. We show that the duration-based rule is *not true* in three out of four of the cases of Table 24.1. For convenience of exposition, we set out, in Table 24.2, our characterization of the CTD and a comparison to the duration rule.

Table 24.2
Comparing Optimal CTD to Duration-Based Rules

	Interest Rates	Optimal Coupon	Optimal M	Duration Rule	Agreement?
Case 1	$8\% > r > \max c$	Largest c	In general, smallest M	Shortest duration	For most economically relevant cases
Case 2	$8\% > r$ $\max c > r$	Largest c	Smallest M	Shortest duration	Always
Case 3	$r > 8\%$ $\min c > 8\%$	Smallest c	Largest M	Longest duration	Not always
Case 4	$r > 8\% > \min c$	Smallest c	$\max M \geq M^* \geq \min M$, with possibility of an interior optimum	Longest duration	Not always

24.5.1 The Excel Spreadsheet

We use Excel to do simulations with which we illustrate the results claimed in Table 24.2. The spreadsheet showing the simulations is on page 423. Some features of this spreadsheet are:

• To simplify the reading of the formulas, we have used the **Name** feature of Excel. Thus references to cell B2 are named **T_** (the underscore is used to avoid confusion with the column by the same name), references to cell B3 are named **c_**, etc.

There are several ways to name cells in Excel: you can use **Insert|Name|Define,** or (after first blocking the range B2:C5) you can use **Insert|Name|Create.** You can also put the cursor on B2, go to the **name box** at the end of the formula bar. Click on this box and put in the name you want.

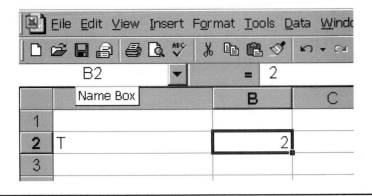

• Cell B14 is used to generate a correct title for the graph automatically. This cell uses a concatenation of text and cell contents (note the use of the ampersand [&] to connect the elements of the cell).

• The graph is generated by a Data Table whose headers (cells D21 and E21) have been hidden.

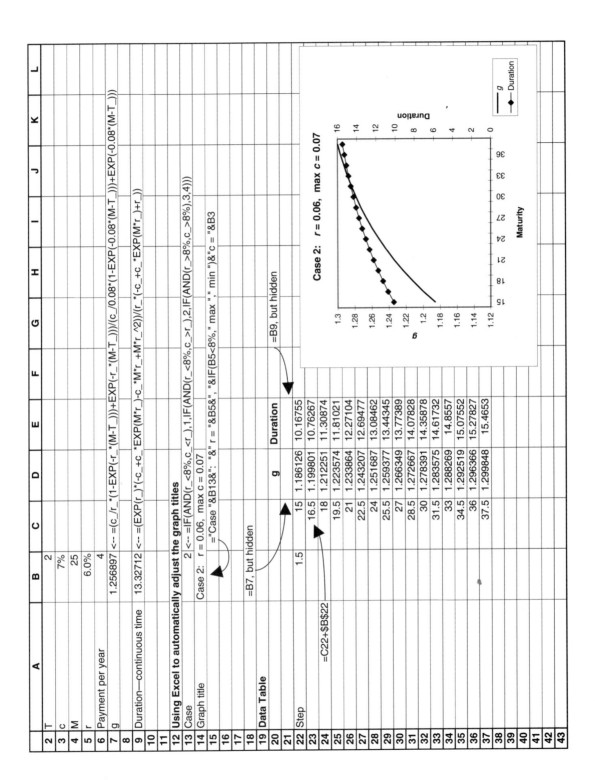

	A	B	C	D	E
2	T	2			
3	c	7%			
4	M	25			
5	r	6.0%			
6	Payment per year	4			
7	g	1.256897	<-- =(c_/r_*(1-EXP(-r_*(M-T_)))+EXP(-r_*(M-T_)))/(c_/0.08*(1-EXP(-0.08*(M-T_)))+EXP(-0.08*(M-T_)))		
8					
9	Duration—continuous time	13.32712	<-- =(EXP(r_)*(-c_+c_*EXP(M*r_)-c_*M*r_+M*r_^2))/(r_*(-c_+c_*EXP(M*r_)+r_))		
10					
11					
12	**Using Excel to automatically adjust the graph titles**				
13	Case	2	<-- =IF(AND(r_<8%,c_<r_),1,IF(AND(r_<8%,c_>r_),2,IF(AND(r_>8%,c_>8%),3,4)))		
14	Graph title	Case 2: r = 0.06, max c = 0.07			
15			="Case "&B13&": "&" r = "&B5&", "&IF(B5<8%," max "," min ")&"c = "&B3		
16					
17					
18		=B7, but hidden			
19	Data Table				
20				g	Duration
21					=B9, but hidden
22	Step		1.5		
23			15	1.186126	10.16755
24	=C22+$B$22		16.5	1.199801	10.76267
25			18	1.212251	11.30874
26			19.5	1.223574	11.81021
27			21	1.233864	12.27104
28			22.5	1.243207	12.69477
29			24	1.251687	13.08462
30			25.5	1.259377	13.44345
31			27	1.266349	13.77389
32			28.5	1.272667	14.07828
33			30	1.278391	14.35878
34			31.5	1.283575	14.61732
35			33	1.288269	14.8557
36			34.5	1.292519	15.07552
37			36	1.296366	15.27827
38			37.5	1.299848	15.4653
39					
40					
41					
42					
43					

Case 2: r = 0.06, max c = 0.07

24.5.2   The Numerical Simulation Results

We now proceed to demonstrate our results.

CASE 1   8 percent $> r >$ max c. When 8 percent $> r$, it is optimal to choose the largest available coupon for the delivery bond. If this coupon is less than 8 percent (which is not a very reasonable case, since it is unlikely that there are no deliverable bonds with coupons less than 8 percent), then we show it is optimal to choose the smallest available M. The duration rule for this case is to choose the smallest duration bond in the deliverable set; for most cases of this type, the duration rule works. The following graph shows the case where $r = 6$ percent and max $c = c^* = 5$ percent:

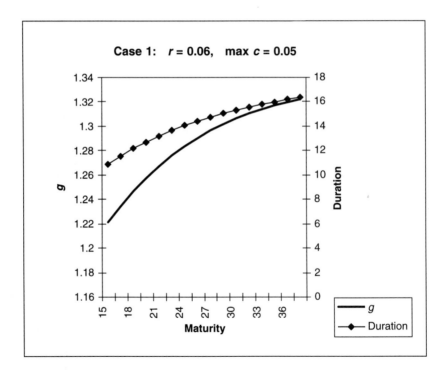

We stress that in this case the duration rule does not always work. It is easy to construct an example where 8 percent $> r >$ max c for which the duration has an internal maximum, and hence two local minima. Benninga and Wiener (1999) show that in order for this internal maximum to be at bond maturities less than 30 years, r must be greater than 8 percent. Thus the intuitive rule is correct for this case, provided there are no deliverable T-bonds with maturities longer than 30 years. If very long-term deliverable bonds exist, it is possible that the smallest g and the lowest duration no longer coincide.

CASE 2   8 percent $> r$, max $c > r$. When 8 percent $> r$, it is optimal to choose the largest available coupon for the delivery bond. If this coupon is greater than 8 percent, then we show that it is optimal to choose the smallest available M. For this case duration increases with increasing bond maturity (see, for example, Bierwag, Kaufman, and Toevs, 1983). It is therefore optimal to choose the bond with the lowest duration. The following graph shows the case where $r = 6$ percent and max $c = c^* = 11$ percent:

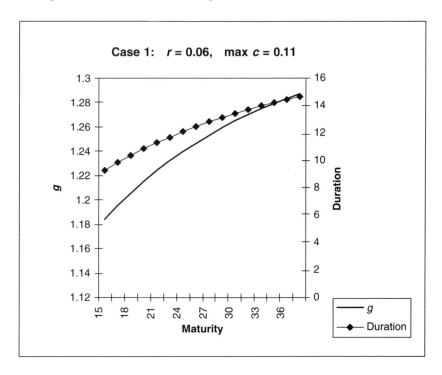

CASE 3 $r > 8$ percent, min $c > 8$ percent. When $r > 8$ percent, it is optimal to choose the smallest available coupon for the delivery bond. The standard claim in the literature is that it is—in this case—also optimal to choose the highest duration bond. The following example (in which $r = 18$ percent and min $c = c^* = 10$ percent) shows a counterexample for which this claim does not hold.

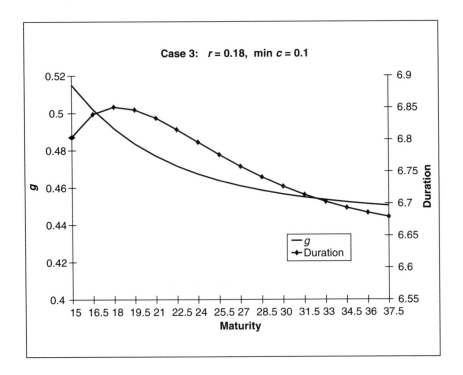

The intuition behind this result is that although a discount bond's duration ultimately declines, it can initially rise with increasing maturity. Thus the duration can have an internal maximum, whereas for this case—as proven in Proposition 3—the function g has a minimum for the largest deliverable maturity.

CASE 4 $r > 8$ percent $>$ min c. When $r > 8$ percent, it is optimal to choose the smallest available coupon for the delivery bond. If this coupon is smaller than *8 percent,* then it is not *optimal* to choose the highest duration. As we will show, it is easy to construct examples in which the value of M for which the duration is at a maximum is different from the value of M for which g has a minimum (it is this latter value which determines the optimal deliverable bond). In our example, $r = 14$ percent and min $c = c^* = 7$ percent.[7]

---

7. For graphical clarity, we have chosen quite a large r, but other examples with smaller values of r can also be constructed.

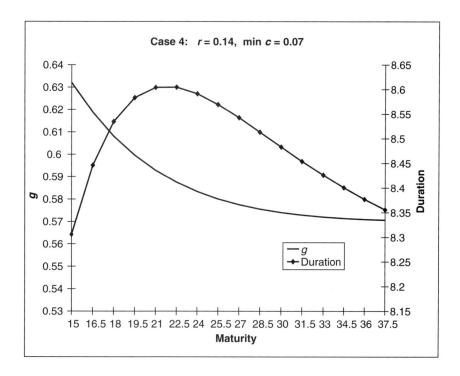

In summary, for the flat-term-structure case, whenever $r > 8$ percent, the duration rule (which, for this case, would have us choose as CTD a bond with maximal duration) is not true. The duration rule does not necessarily hold for the case where $r < 8$ percent and the optimal deliverable coupon $c^* < r$.

24.6   Conclusion

In this chapter we have used Excel to examine the problem of the optimal delivery instrument on the Treasury bond futures contract. Our conclusions may be summarized as follows:

1. The cheapest-to-deliver bond always has either the highest (if the market interest rate is less than 8 percent) or lowest coupon of all deliverable bonds. This result assumes that the set of deliverable bonds is convex, but it is independent of the term structure.

2. The maturity of the cheapest to deliver is the shortest maturity of all deliverable bonds if the market interest rate is less than 8 percent. If the market interest rate is greater than 8 percent, the maturity of the CTD is the largest deliverable maturity if the optimal coupon is greater than 8 percent; if the optimal coupon is less than 8 percent, then there is the possibility of an optimal deliverable maturity which is neither the largest nor the smallest deliverable maturity (an interior optimum).

3. In contradistinction to the prevailing (and published) belief, the CTD is—in many cases— *not* a bond with extremal duration.

V Technical Considerations

Chapters 25–30 cover a variety of technical subjects that are used in the book. Chapter 25 discusses the generation of random numbers. The book uses random-number generation extensively in Chapter 15 (simulating lognormal prices) and Chapter 17 (simulating portfolio insurance). Chapter 26 considers data tables. This is a basic Excel tool that allows us to build sophisticated sensitivity tables. It is used throughout *Financial Modeling*. Chapter 27 deals with matrices, used in the book to do portfolio optimization (Chapters 7–12). Chapter 28 discusses the Gauss-Seidel iterative method for solving simultaneous equations. This method, though never explicitly used in *Financial Modeling,* underlies the pro forma models of Chapters 3 and 4. Chapter 29 is a compendium of Excel functions used in the book. A special feature of this chapter is its discussion of array functions (section 29.3). Chapter 30 discusses a grab bag of Excel tricks that are used in various places in this book: fast copying; graph titles that update automatically; creating multiline cells; putting Greek symbols, subscripts, and superscripts into Excel text; naming cells; and hiding cells.

25 Random Numbers

25.1 Introduction

A random-number generator on a computer is a function that produces a seemingly unrelated set of numbers. The question of *what is* a random number is a philosophical one.[1] In this chapter we will ignore philosophy and concentrate on some simple random-number generators—primarily the Excel random-number generator **Rand( )** and the VBA random-number generator **Rnd.**

To imagine a set of uniformly distributed random numbers think of an urn filled with 1,000 little balls, numbered 000, 001, 002, ..., 999. Suppose we perform the following experiment: Having shaken the urn to mix up the balls, we draw one ball out of the urn and record the ball's number. Next we put the ball back into the urn, shake the urn thoroughly so that the balls are mixed up again, and then draw out a new ball. The series of numbers produced by repeating this procedure many times should be *uniformly distributed* between 000 and 999.

A random-number generator on a computer is a function that imitates this procedure. The random-number generators considered in this chapter are sometimes termed *pseudo-random-number generators,* since they are actually deterministic functions whose values are indistinguishable from random numbers. All pseudo-random-number generators have cycles (that is, they eventually start to repeat themselves). The trick is to find a random-number generator with a long cycle. The Excel **Rand( )** function has a very long cycle and is a respectable random-number generator.

In the option chapters of this book (Chapters 13–19), we use random-number generators to simulate stock prices. If you've never used a random-number generator, open an Excel spreadsheet and type **=Rand( )** in any cell. You will see a 15 digit number between 0.000000000000000 and 0.999999999999999. Every time you recalculate the spreadsheet (for example, by hitting the **F9** button), the number changes. The series of numbers thus produced should be (to use Lehmer's terminology from footnote 1) "unpredictable to the uninitiated."

In this chapter we shall deal with two kinds of random-number generators: We first examine the uniform random-number generators that come with Excel and VBA. Subsequently we generate normally distributed random numbers.[2]

---

1. Knuth (1981, p. 142) gives the following quote: "A random sequence is a vague notion embodying the idea of a sequence in which each term is unpredictable to the uninitiated and whose digits pass a certain number of tests, traditional with statisticians and depending somewhat on the uses to which the sequence is to be put" (from D. H. Lehmer, 1951).

2. A common nomenclature speaks of "random deviates." Only in this field can one find "normal deviates"!

25.2   Testing the Excel Random-Number Generator

Suppose you simply wanted to generate a list of random numbers. One way to do so would be to copy the Excel function **Rand( )** to a range of cells.

	A	B	C	D	E	F
1						
2	0.0476	0.0307	0.0566	0.2900	<-- Rand()	
3	0.3308	0.6487	0.9282	0.2670		
4	0.9501	0.5388	0.4760	0.3977		
5	0.3315	0.4088	0.7248	0.5463		
6	0.4508	0.4252	0.0297	0.2548		
7	0.2183	0.4249	0.6687	0.4921		
8	0.9956	0.7920	0.0623	0.2962		
9	0.2945	0.2327	0.3599	0.9290		
10	0.1301	0.7369	0.4279	0.3980		
11						
12	Each cell contains the function Rand().					
13	Each time you update the spreadsheet or					
14	press F9 the block of cells will produce a					
15	new set of random numbers.					

Another way is to use VBA's **Rnd** function, illustrated in the following program **randomlist:**

```
Sub randomlist() 'Produces a simple list of random numbers
    Range("output").Range(Cells(1, 1), _
        Cells(250, 1)).Clear
    N = Range("runs").Value
    .
    For Index = 1 To N
        Range("output").Cells(Index, 1) = Rnd
    Next Index

End Sub
```

The names "runs" and "output" refer to named ranges in the worksheet where the program is run. In the sample output that follows, for example, "runs" refers to cell B4 and "output" refers to cells B7:B16.[3] The second line of the program clears the results of previous runs (up to 250 results).

	A	B	C	D	E
1		**Most Elementary Random List**			
2		To run VBA "randomlist": press [Ctrl]+q			
3					
4	Runs	10			
5					
6		Output			
7		0.524868429	<-- This cell is named "output,"		
8		0.767111659	and this name is used in the		
9		0.053504527	VBA routine in clearing		
10		0.592458248	previous results.		
11		0.468700111			
12		0.298165441			
13		0.622696698			
14		0.647821188			
15		0.263792932			
16		0.279342055			

By itself, this result is interesting, though a bit uninformative. Is the list of numbers thus produced really uniformly distributed? A simple test is to generate each number and determine whether it falls into the interval [0, 0.1), [0.1, 0.2), ..., [0.9, 1). (The notation [a,b) denotes the *half-open* interval between a and b; a number x is in this interval if $a \leq x < b$. If the list of numbers is really uniformly distributed, we would expect roughly an even number of the "random" numbers to be in each of the ten intervals.

One way to test uniformity is to generate a list of random numbers on the spreadsheet by copying **Rand( )** to many cells and then using the Excel array function **Frequency(data_array, bins_array).**[4] This procedure is illustrated in the following spreadsheet picture.

---

3. The technique of naming cells is explained in Chapter 30.

4. Array functions are explained in Chapter 29.

	A	B	C	D	E	F	G	H
1	USING EXCEL'S FREQUENCY FUNCTION							
2								
3	Random							
4	numbers		Bin	Frequency				
5	0.2374		0.1	1				
6	0.2421		0.2	0				
7	0.3985		0.3	2				
8	0.5713		0.4	1				
9	0.0905		0.5	0	<-- =FREQUENCY(A5:A14,C5:C14)			
10	0.7608		0.6	2				
11	0.8230		0.7	1				
12	0.5389		0.8	1				
13	0.8883		0.9	2				
14	0.6689		1	0				
15								
16	Each cell in the range A5:A14 contains the formula							
17	Rand(). Pressing F9 will produce a new set							
18	of random numbers and frequencies.							

This method is obviously not efficient (or even feasible) when we want to test the random-number generator for large numbers of random draws. The following program use VBA to generate many random numbers and puts them into the same kind of *bins:*

```
Sub uniformRandom()
'Puts random numbers into bins
    Application.screenupdating = False

    Range("starttime") = Time
    N = Range("runs").Value 'the number of random draws

    Dim distribution(10) As Long 'bins

    For k = 1 To N
        draw = Rnd
        distribution(Int(draw * 10) + 1) = _
            distribution(Int(draw * 10) + 1) + 1
Next k

    For Index = 1 To 10
        Range("output").Cells(Index, 1) = distribution(Index)
    Next Index

    Range("stoptime") = Time

End Sub
```

The output from this program produces the following spreadsheet:

	A	B	C	D	E	F	G	H	I
1		**Uniformly Distributed Random Numbers**							
2				Using VBA's **Rnd** function					
3				To run VBA program "uniformrandom," use [Ctrl] +a .					
4									
5	Runs	100,000							
6				Starttime	18:18:28				
7	Bin	Output		Stoptime	18:18:29				
8	1	10,097		Elapsed	0:00:01				
9	2	9,911							
10	3	10,010							
11	4	9,966							
12	5	9,870							
13	6	9,946							
14	7	9,977							
15	8	10,273							
16	9	9,978							
17	10	9,972							
18									
19									
20									
21									
22									
23									
24									

Here are some things to note about **uniformrandom:**

• The program uses **Application.screenupdating = False** to stop Excel from updating the screen while the program runs (the screen is automatically updated after the program ends; if you want intermediate updating, you can use the command **Application.screenupdating = True**).

• The program has a "clock" to measure the amount of time it takes to run. At the start of the program, we use **Range("Starttime")=Time** to put the current time into the cell labeled **Starttime.** At the end of the program, **Range("Stoptime")=Time** puts in the ending time. The cell **Elapsed** contains the formula **=Stoptime-Starttime.** Note that in order for the cells to read correctly, you have to use the command **Format|Cells|Number|Time** on the relevant cells.

• The heart of the program uses the function Int (draw * 10) + 1. Multiplying the random draw by 10 produces a number whose first digit is 0, 1, ..., or 9. The VBA function **Int** gives this integer. **Distribution** is a VBA array numbered 1 to 10, with **Distribution(1)** being the number of random numbers in [0, 0.1), **Distribution(2)** the number of random numbers in [0.1, 0.2), and so on. Thus `Int(draw * 10) + 1` is the proper place in **Distribution** to which the current random draw belongs.

25.3   Generating Normally Distributed Random Numbers

In the preceding sections we have generated numbers that are uniformly distributed. We now want to generate normally distributed random numbers. One way to do so is to use the Excel command **Tools|Data Analysis|Random Number Generation.** Here's how we get Excel to produce 1,000 random numbers that are normally distributed (with $\mu = 0$ and $\sigma = 1$) in column G of the spreadsheet:

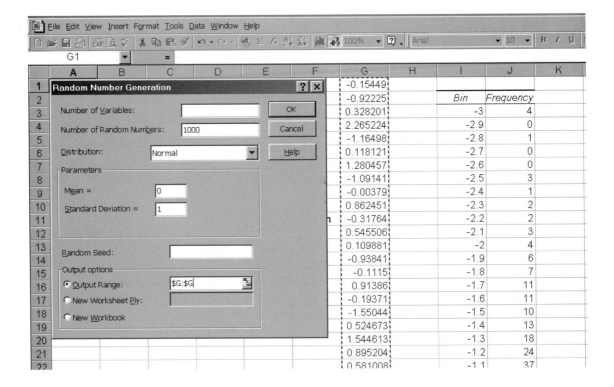

If we want to see whether the output is distributed normally we can have Excel do a frequency distribution (either by using the array function **Frequency** or by using **Tools|Data Analysis|Histogram**). Here's a graph produced from the output:

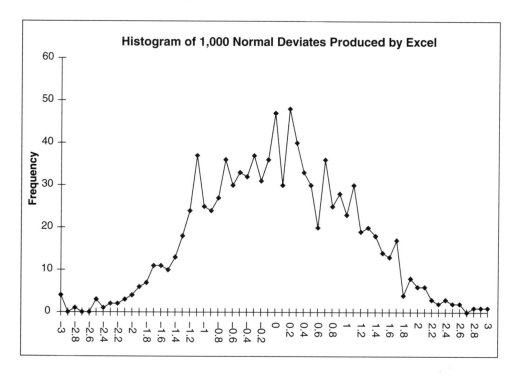

While this is an easy way to produce normally distributed random deviates, it is not efficient, especially if we have to produce many numbers. The solution is to use VBA to produce the random numbers. The VBA program **normalSimulation** uses the following algorithm to produce normal deviates:

• Produce two random numbers (in the program they are called **rand1** and **rand2**)

• Let $S1 = rand1^2 + rand2^2$

• If $S1 > 1$, produce two new random numbers. Otherwise proceed and let $S2 = [-2 * \text{Log}(S1)/S1]^{1/2}$. (Note that here *Log* refers to the natural logarithm; in Excel this is written with the function **Ln( )**, but in VBA it is written as **Log**.)

• The two random deviates are $X1 = rand1 * S2$ and $X2 = rand2 * S2$.

Here is the program:

```
Sub normalSimulation()
Range("starttime") = Time

Application.screenupdating = False

ReDim sample(2 * N) As Double
Dim distribution(-30 To 30) As Integer

N = Range("runs").Value

For Index = 1 To N
start:
   Static rand1, rand2, S1, S2, X1, X2
   rand1 = 2 * Rnd - 1
   rand2 = 2 * Rnd - 1
   S1 = rand1 ^ 2 + rand2 ^ 2
   If S1 > 1 Then GoTo start
   S2 = Sqr(-2 * Log(S1) / S1)
   X1 = rand1 * S2
   X2 = rand2 * S2

   If X1 < -3 Then
       distribution(-30) = distribution(-30) + 1
   ElseIf X1 > 3 Then
       distribution(30) = distribution(30) + 1
   Else distribution(Int(X1 / 0.1)) = _
       distribution(Int(X1 / 0.1)) + 1
   End If

   If X2 < -3 Then
       distribution(-30) = distribution(-30) + 1
   ElseIf X2 > 3 Then
       distribution(30) = distribution(30) + 1
   Else distribution(Int(X2 / 0.1)) = _
       distribution(Int(X2 / 0.1)) + 1
End If

Next Index

For Index = -30 To 30
   Range("output").Cells(Index + 31, 1) = _
       distribution(Index) / (2 * N)
Next Index

Range("stoptime") = Time

End Sub
```

There are a few things to note about this program:

• Note how we sent the normal deviate routine back to the beginning, in the case where $S1 > 1$. Here are the first few lines of the relevant part of **normalSimulation** :

```
For Index = 1 To N
start:
Static rand1, rand2, S1, S2, X1, X2
rand1 = 2 * Rnd - 1
rand2 = 2 * Rnd - 1
S1 = rand1 ^ 2 + rand2 ^ 2
If S1 > 1 Then GoTo start
.  .  .  .
```

By labeling the point start, we can refer to it in the line that tests $S1$.

• Most of the results of the normal distribution are between -3 and $+3$. When, in **normalSimulation,** we classify the output into bins, we want these bins to be $(-\infty, -2.9]$, $(-2.9, -2.8]$, ..., $(-2.9, \infty)$. To do so we first define an array `distribution(-30 To 30)`; this array has 61 indices. To classify a particular random number (say $X1$) into the bins of this array, we use the following function:

```
If X1 < -3 Then
    distribution(-30) = distribution(-30) + 1
  ElseIf X1 > 3 Then
    distribution(30) = distribution(30) + 1
  Else distribution(Int(X1 / 0.1)) =
    distribution(Int(X1 / 0.1)) + 1
```

• **NormalSimulation** produces not a histogram (which is a *count* of how many times a number falls into a particular bin), but a *frequency distribution.* We produce this by dividing by twice the number of runs (remember that each successful run produces two random numbers), *2N,* before we output the data to the spreadsheet:

```
For Index = -30 To 30
    Range("output").Cells(Index + 31, 1) = _
        distribution(Index) / (2 * N)
Next Index
```

• Finally, note that the command `Application.ScreenUpdating = False` makes a big difference! This command prevents the updating of the output both in the cells and in the Excel chart. Try running the program with and without this command to see the effect.

Here's what the output for this routine looks like:

	A	B	C	D	E	F	G	H	I
1		**Simulating the Normal Distribution Using VBA**							
2		Note that here **Application.screenupdating** makes a big difference!							
3		[Ctrl]+r runs the macro							
4									
5	Runs	200,000		Starttime	14:54:25				
6				Stoptime	14:54:29				
7	Bin	Output		Elapsed	0:00:04				
8	-3	0.0019							
9	-2.9	0.0007							
10	-2.8	0.0009							
11	-2.7	0.0012							
12	-2.6	0.0015							
13	-2.5	0.0020							
14	-2.4	0.0025							
15	-2.3	0.0031							
16	-2.2	0.0039							
17	-2.1	0.0050							
18	-2	0.0061							
19	-1.9	0.0070							
20	-1.8	0.0084							
21	-1.7	0.0104							
22	-1.6	0.0122							
23	-1.5	0.0139							
24	-1.4	0.0161							

Note that our graph has "fat tails." These occur because we have thrown all the output below -3 into the lowest bin and all the output above $+3$ into the highest bin.

Exercises

1. Use the program **randomlist** from section 25.2 to produce a list of 200 random numbers. Use the Excel function **frequency** to produce a histogram of the results.

2. Here is a random-number generator you can make yourself:

   a. Start with some number, *Seed.*

   b. Let $X_1 = Seed + \pi$. Let $X_2 = e^{5 + \ln(X_1)}$.

   c. The first random number is $Random = X_2 - Integer(X_2)$, where $Integer(X_2)$ is the integer part of X_2.

   d. Repeat the process, letting $Seed = Random.$

   Implement this random-number generator in a VBA program similar to **randomlist,** and produce a list of 50 random numbers.

3. Define *AmodB* as the *remainder* when *A* is divided by *B*. For example, $36 \bmod 25 = 11$. Excel has this function; it is written **Mod(A,B).** Now here is another random-number generator:

   a. Let $X_0 = 1$.

   b. Let $X_{n+1} = (7 * X_n) \bmod 10^8$.

   c. Let $U_{n+1} = X_{n+1}/10^8$.

   The list of numbers $U_1, U_2, \ldots$ contains the pseudo-random numbers generated by this random-number generator. (This is one of the many random-number generators given in Abramowitz and Stegun, 1972.) Use VBA to produce this random-number generator, and use it in a program similar to **uniformrandom.**

4. Many states have daily lotteries, which are played as follows: Sometime during the day, you buy a lottery ticket, on which the seller inscribes a number you choose, between 000 and 999. That night there is a drawing on television in which a three-digit number is drawn. If the number on your ticket matches the number drawn, you win and collect $500 (for a $1 wager). If you lose, you get nothing.

   a. Write an Excel function that produces a random number between 000 and 999. (Hint: Use **Rand()** and **Int()** .)

   b. Write a VBA program that reproduces 250 random draws of the daily lottery (about one year's worth, if there are no drawings on weekends). Assuming that each ticket costs $1, and assuming that you choose the same number each day, how much would you have won during the year?

5. Program **normalSimulation,** but put the output into more bins. (Can you make the number of bins and their size controllable from the spreadsheet?) Does this method get rid of the "fat tails" in the distribution graph?

6. It is well-known that if *Z* is a standard normal random variable (i.e., with mean $\mu = 0$ and standard deviation $\sigma = 1$) then $X = aZ + b$ is normally distributed with $\mu = b$ and $\sigma = a$. Modify **normalSimulation** to produce normal, nonstandard distributions, with the mean and the standard deviation being inputted from the spreadsheet.

26 Data Tables

26.1 Introduction

Data table commands are powerful commands that make it possible to do complex sensitivity analyses. Excel offers the opportunity to build a table in which only one variable is changed, or one in which two variables are changed. Excel data tables are array functions and thus change dynamically when related spreadsheet cells are changed.

In this chapter you will learn how to build both one-dimensional and two-dimensional Excel data tables.

26.2 An Example

Consider a project that has an initial cost of $1,150 and seven subsequent cash flows. The cash flows in year 1–7 grow at rate g, so that the cash flow in year t is $CF_t = CF_{t-1} * (1 + g)$. Given a discount rate r, the net present value (NPV) of the project is

$$NPV = -1,150 + \frac{CF_1}{(1+r)^1} + \frac{CF_1(1+g)}{(1+r)^2} + \frac{CF_1(1+g)^2}{(1+r)^3}$$
$$+ \dots + \frac{CF_1(1+g)^6}{(1+r)^7}$$

The internal rate of return (IRR), i, is the rate at which the NPV equals zero:

$$0 - 1,150 + \frac{CF_1}{(1+i)^1} + \frac{CF_1(1+g)}{(1+i)^2} + \frac{CF_1(1+g)^2}{(1+i)^3} + \dots + \frac{CF_1(1+g)^6}{(1+i)^7}$$

These calculations are easily done in Excel. In the following example the initial cash flow is 234, the growth rate $g = 10$ percent, and the discount rate $r = 15$ percent:

	A	B	C	D	E	F	G	H	I
1	CF$_1$	234							
2	Growth rate	10%							
3	Discount rate	15%							
4									
5	Year	0	1	2	3	4	5	6	7
6	Cash flow	-1150.00	234.00	257.40	283.14	311.45	342.60	376.86	414.55
7									
8	NPV		101.46	<-- =+B6+NPV(B3,C6:I6)					
9	IRR		17.60%	<-- =IRR(B6:I6,0)					

Note the cell addresses for the growth rate, the discount rate, the NPV, and the IRR. They will be needed in this chapter.

26.3   Setting Up a Data Table

Suppose we want to know how the NPV and IRR are affected by a change in the growth rate. The command **Data Table** allows us to find this information simply. The first step is to set up the table's structure. In the next example, we put the formulas for the NPV and IRR on the top row, and we put the variable we wish to vary (in this case the growth rate) in the first column. At this point the table looks like this:

	F	G	H	I	J
10					
11		=B8			=B9
12					
13			NPV	IRR	
14			101.46	17.6%	
15		0			
16	Growth	5%			
17	rate	10%			
18		15%			
19					

The actual table (as opposed to the labels for the columns and the rows) is outlined in the dark border. The numbers directly under the labels "NPV" and "IRR" refer to the corresponding formulas in the previous picture. Thus, if the cell B8 contains the calculation for the NPV, then the cell under the letters "NPV" contains the formula "=B8." Similarly, if the cell B9 contains the original calculation for the IRR, then the cell under "IRR" in the table contains the formula "=B9."

We like to think of a data table spreadsheet as having two parts:

1. A basic example.

2. A table that does a sensitivity analysis on the basic example. In our example, the first row of the table contains references to calculations done in our basic example. While there are other ways to do data tables, this structure is both typical and easy to understand.

Now do the following:

- Highlight the table area (outlined in the dark border).

- Activate the command **Data|Table.** You will get a dialogue box that asks you to indicate a **Row Input Cell** and/or a **Column Input Cell.**

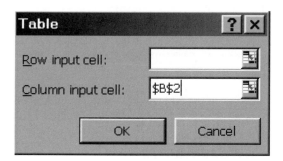

In this case, the variable we wish to change is in the left-hand column of our table, so we leave the Row Input Cell blank and indicate the cell B2 (which contains the growth rate in our basic example) in the Column Input Cell box. Here's the result:

	F	G	H	I	J
10					
11		=B8			=B9
12					
13			NPV	IRR	
14			101.46	17.60%	
15		0	-176.46	9.71%	
16	Growth	5%	-47.82	13.67%	
17	rate	10%	101.46	17.60%	
18		15%	274.35	21.50%	
19					

26.4   Building a Two-Dimensional Data Table

We can also use the **Data Table** command to vary *one* formula while changing *two* parameters. Suppose, for example, that we want to calculate the NPV of the cash flows for different growth rates and different discount rates. We create a new table that looks like this:

	E	F	G	H	I	J	K
19							
20	=B8						
21				Discount rate			
22			101.46	7%	10%	12%	
23		Growth	0				
24		rate	5%				
25			10%				
26			15%				
27							

The upper left-hand corner of the table contains the formula "=B8" as a reference to the basic example.

We now use the **Data Table** command again. This time we fill in both the **Row Input Cell** (indicating cell B3, the site of the discount rate in our basic example) and the **Column Input Cell** (indicating B2).

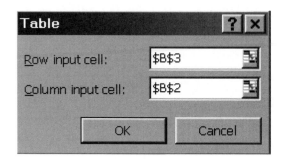

Here's the result:

	E	F	G	H	I	J	K
19							
20	=B8						
21				Discount rate			
22			101.46	7%	10%	12%	
23		Growth	0	111.09	-10.79	-82.08	
24		rate	5%	297.62	150.74	65.13	
25			10%	515.79	339.09	236.44	
26			15%	770.34	558.25	435.41	
27							

26.5   An Aesthetic Note: Hiding the Formula Cells

Data tables tend to look a bit strange because the formula being calculated shows up in the data table (in our examples: in the top row of the first data table, and in the left-hand top corner of the second data table). You can make your tables look nicer by *hiding* the formula cells. To do so, mark the offending cells and use the **Format Cells** command (or press the right mouse button and go to the **Number| Custom**). In the dialogue box go to the box marked **Type** and insert a semicolon into the box. Here's the way this screen looks for the previous example:

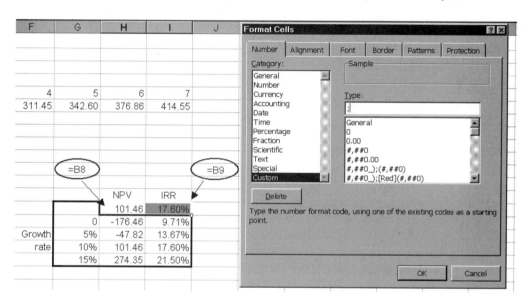

The cell contents will now be hidden. The result looks like this:

	F	G	H	I	J
10					
11		=B8			=B9
12					
13			NPV	IRR	
14					
15			0	-176.46	9.71%
16		Growth	5%	- 47.82	13.67%
17		rate	10%	101.46	17.60%
18			15%	274.35	21.50%
19					

26.6   Excel Data Tables Are Arrays

Excel data tables are dynamically linked to your initial example. When you change a parameter in the original example, the corresponding column or row of the data table changes. For example, if we change the initial cash flow from 234 to 300, here's what will happen in the preceding data table:

	A	B	C	D	E	F	G	H	I	J
1	CF$_1$	300								
2	Growth rate	10%								
3	Discount rate	15%								
4										
5	Year	0	1	2	3	4	5	6	7	
6	Cash flow	-1150.00	300.00	330.00	363.00	399.30	439.23	483.15	531.47	
7										
8	NPV	454.43	<-- =+B6+NPV(B3,C6:I6)							
9	IRR	26.01%	<-- =IRR(B6:I6,0)							
10										
11							=B8			=B9
12										
13								NPV	IRR	
14										
15							0	98.13	17.80%	
16						Growth	5%	263.06	21.92%	
17						rate	10%	454.43	26.01%	
18							15%	676.09	30.07%	

Exercises

1.   a. Use **Data Table** to graph the function $f(x) = 3x^2 - 2x - 15$.

b. Use **Solver** or **Goal|Seek** to find two values of x for which $f(x) = 0$.

2.   As explained in Chapter 29, the Excel function **PV(rate, number_periods, payment)** calculates the present value of a constant payment. For example, **PV(15%,15,–10) = 58.47**. (Note that we have put the payment as a negative number; otherwise, Excel returns a negative value! This little irritation is discussed in Chapters 1 and 29). Use **Data Table** to graph the present value as a function of the discount rate.

3.   Consider a project that costs $500 today and which has cash flows in years 1–5 of $100, $100 * (1 + g), $100 * (1 + g)^2, \ldots, (100 * (1 + g)^4$. Use **Data Table** to do a sensitivity analysis on the NPV of the project, varying the discount rates from 0 percent, 3 percent, 6 percent, . . . 21 percent and varying the growth rates from 0 percent, 3 percent, . . . , 12 percent.

4.   Using **Data Table**, graph the function $Sin(x * y)$ for $x = 0$, 0.2, 0.4, . . . 1.8, 2 and $y = 0$, 0.2, 0.4 . . . 1.8, 2. Use the "Surface" graph option to make a three-dimensional graph of the function.

27.1 Introduction

Chapter 9 makes extensive use of matrices to find efficient portfolios. This chapter contains enough information about matrices to make it possible for you to follow the discussion (and do the calculations!) required for portfolio mathematics.

A matrix is a rectangular array of numbers. All of the following are matrices:

	A	B	C	D	E	F	G	H	I	J
1					**MATRICES IN EXCEL**					
2										
3									Matrix C	
4									(a column	
5	Matrix A (a row vector)				Matrix B (a square 3 x 3 matrix)				vector)	
6	2	3	4		13	-8	-3		13	
7					-8	10	-1		-8	
8					-3	-1	11		-3	
9										
10	Matrix D (a 4 x 3 matrix)									
11	13	-8	-3							
12	-8	10	-1							
13	-3	-1	11							
14	0	13	3							

A matrix with only one row is also called a *row vector;* a matrix with only one column is also called a *column vector.* A matrix with an equal number of rows and columns is called a *square matrix* .

A single letter is often used to denote a matrix or a vector. In this case we often write, for example, $\mathbf{B} = [b_{ij}]$, where b_{ij} stands for the entry in row i and column j of the matrix. For a vector we might write $\mathbf{A} = [a_i]$ or $\mathbf{C} = [c_i]$. Thus, for the examples given,

$$a_3 = 4 \qquad b_{22} = 10 \qquad c_1 = 13 \qquad d_{41} = 0$$

The matrix $\mathbf{B}$ is *symmetric,* meaning that $b_{ij} = b_{ji}$.

27.2   Matrix Operations

27.2.1 Multiplication by a Scalar

Multiplying a matrix by a scalar multiplies every entry in the matrix by the scalar. For example:

	A	B	C	D	E	F
3	**Multiplication by a Scalar**					
4						
5	Scalar	6				
6						
7	Matrix B	13	-8	-3		
8		-8	10	-1		
9		-3	-1	11		
10						
11	Scalar*Matrix B					
12		78	-48	-18	<-- =D7*$B$5	
13		-48	60	-6		
14		-18	-6	66		

27.2.2 Addition

Matrices may be added together provided they have the same number of rows and columns. Adding two vectors or matrices is accomplished by adding their corresponding entries. Thus if $A = [a_{ij}]$ and, $B = [b_{ij}]$, $A + B = [a_{ij} + b_{ij}]$:

	A	B	C	D	E	F	G	H	I	J
17	**Addition of Matrices**									
18										
19	**Matrix A**			**Matrix B**			**Sum of A + B**			
20	1	3		0.1	0		1.1	3	<-- =B20+E20	
21	3	0		23	0		26	0		
22	6	-9		8	-33.4		14	-42.4		
23	5	11		-15	0		-10	11		
24	7	12		2.33	1.2		9.33	13.2		

27.2.3 Transposition

Transposition is an operation by which the rows of a matrix are turned into columns and vice versa. Thus for the matrix **E**:

	A	B	C	D	E	F	G	H	I	J	K	L
27	**Transposition of Matrix**											
28												
29	**Matrix E**					**Transpose of E = E^T**						
30	1	2	3	4		1	0	16	The framed area contains			
31	0	3	88	-9		2	3	7	the array function			
32	16	7	7	2		3	88	7	=Transpose(A30:D32) .			
33						4	-9	2	To use this function: Mark off			
34									the whole area; put in the formula,			
35									then finish by pressing			
36									[Ctrl]+[Shift]+[Enter].			

This illustration uses the array function **Transpose.** Each cell in the array giving the transpose contains the array formula {**=Transpose(A30:D32)**}, where **A30:D32** is the range that contains the matrix **E**. Note that to use this formula,

- You must first block off the whole area into which it will put its results (cells F30:G33 in the example).
- You then type in **=Transpose(A30:D32)** .
- When you have finished, you press [Ctrl] + [Shift] + [Enter]. Excel adds the braces, so that what you see in the cells is {**=Transpose(A30:D32)**} .

27.2.4 Multiplication of Matrices

Suppose that **X** is a row vector and that **Y** is a column vector, both with n coordinates:

$$\mathbf{X} = [x_1 \cdots x_n], \qquad \mathbf{Y} = \begin{bmatrix} y_1 \\ \vdots \\ y_n \end{bmatrix}$$

Then the *product of* **X** *and* **Y** is defined by

$$\mathbf{XY} = [x_1 \cdots x_n] \begin{bmatrix} y_1 \\ \vdots \\ y_n \end{bmatrix} = \sum_{i=1}^{n} x_i y_i$$

Now suppose that $\mathbf{A}$ and $\mathbf{B}$ are two matrices, and that $\mathbf{A}$ has n columns and p rows and $\mathbf{B}$ has n rows and m columns:

$$\mathbf{A} = \begin{bmatrix} a_{11} & a_{12} & \cdots & a_{1n} \\ \vdots & & & \\ a_{p1} & a_{p2} & \cdots & a_{pn} \end{bmatrix} \qquad \mathbf{B} = \begin{bmatrix} b_{11} & \cdots & b_{1m} \\ b_{21} & \cdots & b_{2m} \\ \vdots & & \\ b_{n1} & \cdots & b_{nm} \end{bmatrix}$$

Then the product of $\mathbf{A}$ and $\mathbf{B}$, written $\mathbf{AB}$, is defined by the matrix

$$\mathbf{AB} = \begin{bmatrix} \sum\limits_{h=1}^{n} a_{1h}b_{h1} & \sum\limits_{h=1}^{n} a_{1h}b_{h2} & \cdots & \sum\limits_{h=1}^{n} a_{1h}b_{hm} \\ \vdots & & & \\ \vdots & & & \\ \sum\limits_{h=1}^{n} a_{ph}b_{h1} & \cdots & & \sum\limits_{h=1}^{n} a_{ph}b_{hm} \end{bmatrix},$$

with ijth element $= \sum\limits_{h=1}^{n} a_{ih}b_{hj}$

Note that the ijth coordinate of $\mathbf{AB}$ is simply the product of the ith row of $\mathbf{A}$ times the jth column of $\mathbf{B}$. For example, if

$$\mathbf{A} = \begin{bmatrix} 2 & -6 \\ -9 & 3 \end{bmatrix}, \quad \mathbf{B} = \begin{bmatrix} 6 & 9 & -12 \\ -5 & 2 & 4 \end{bmatrix}$$

then

$$\mathbf{AB} = \begin{bmatrix} 42 & 6 & -48 \\ -69 & -75 & 120 \end{bmatrix}$$

The order of matrix multiplication is critical. Multiplication of matrices is not commutative; that is, $\mathbf{AB} \neq \mathbf{BA}$. As the example shows, the fact that it is possible to multiply $\mathbf{A}$ times $\mathbf{B}$ does not always imply that the multiplication $\mathbf{BA}$ is even defined.

In order to multiply matrices in Excel, we use the array function **MMult**.

	A	B	C	D	E	F
39	**Multiplication of matrices**					
40						
41	**Matrix A**					
42	2	-6		6	9	-12
43	-9	3		-5	2	4
44						
45						
46	**Product AB**					
47	42	6	-48	**<--Array contains formula**		
48	-69	-75	120	**=MMULT(A42:B43,D42:F43)**		

To multiply two matrices together, the number of columns in the first matrix must equal the number of rows in the second. Thus we can multiply **A** times **B,** but we cannot multiply **B** times **A.** If you try to do so in Excel, the function **MMult** will give you an error message:

	A	B	C	D
52	**Product BA -- this won't work**			
53	#VALUE!	**<-- =MMULT(D42:F43,A42:B43)**		

27.3   Matrix Inverses

A square matrix **I** is called the *identity matrix* if all its off-diagonal entries are 0 and all its diagonal entries are 1. Thus

$$
\mathbf{I} = \begin{bmatrix} 1 & 0 & \cdots & 0 & 0 \\ 0 & 1 & \cdots & 0 & 0 \\ \vdots & \vdots & & \vdots & \vdots \\ 0 & 0 & & 1 & 0 \\ 0 & 0 & \cdots & 0 & 1 \end{bmatrix}
$$

It is easy to confirm that multiplying any matrix **A** by the identity matrix of the proper dimension leaves that **A** unchanged. Thus, if $\mathbf{I}_n$ is an $n \times n$ identity matrix and **A** is an $n \times m$ matrix, $\mathbf{IA} = \mathbf{A}$. Similarly, if $\mathbf{I}_m$ is an $m \times m$ identity matrix, $\mathbf{AI} = \mathbf{A}$.

Now suppose we are given a *square* matrix **A** of dimension n. The $n \times n$ matrix $\mathbf{A}^{-1}$ is called the *inverse* of **A** if $\mathbf{A}^{-1}\mathbf{A} = \mathbf{A}\mathbf{A}^{-1} = \mathbf{I}$. The computation of an inverse matrix can be a lot of work; fortunately, however, Excel has the array function **MInverse** that does the calculations for us. Here's an example:

	A	B	C	D	E	F	G	H	I	J
1	MATRIX INVERSE									
2										
3	Matrix A					Inverse of A: Array function **Minverse(A4:D7)**				
4	1	-9	16	1		-0.0217	1.8913	0.5362	-1.1449	
5	3	3	2	3		0.0000	-1.0000	-0.1667	0.6667	
6	2	4	0	-2		0.0652	-0.6739	-0.1087	0.4348	
7	5	7	3	4		-0.0217	-0.1087	-0.2971	0.1884	
8										
9	Verifying the inverse									
10	We multiply A*Inverse A: cells contain array function **MMULT(A4:D7,F4:I7)**									
11	1	1.07E-15	-2.22045E-16	-9.4369E-16						
12	0	1	-1.11022E-16	2.22045E-16						
13	6.94E-18	8.33E-17	1	5.55112E-16						
14	1.39E-17	1.17E-15	-4.44089E-16	1						

As the spreadsheet shows, you can use **MMult** to verify that the product of the matrix and its inverse indeed give the identity matrix (expressions like 1.07E-15 mean $1.07 * 10^{-15}$, and are thus virtually zero).

A square matrix that has an inverse is called a *nonsingular matrix*. The conditions for a matrix to be nonsingular are the following: Consider a square matrix **A** of dimension n. It can be shown that $\mathbf{A} = [a_{ij}]$ is nonsingular if and only if the only solution to the n equations

$$\sum_i a_{ij} x_i = 0, \quad j = 1, \ldots, n$$

is $x_i = 0$, $i = 1, \ldots, n$. Matrix inversion is a tricky business. If there exists a vector **X** whose components are almost zero and which solves the system, then the matrix is *ill-conditioned,* and it may be very difficult to find an accurate inverse.

27.4   Solving Systems of Simultaneous Linear Equations

A system of n linear equations in m unknown is written as

$$a_{11}x_1 + a_{12}x_2 + \cdots + a_{1n}x_n = y_1$$
$$a_{21}x_1 + a_{22}x_1 + \cdots + a_{2n}x_1 = y_2$$
$$\vdots$$
$$a_{n1}x_1 + a_{n2}x_1 + \cdots + a_{nn}x_1 = y_n$$

Writing the matrix of coefficients as $\mathbf{A} = [a_{ij}]$, the column vector of unknowns as $\mathbf{X} = [x_j]$, and the column vector of constants as $\mathbf{Y} = [y_j]$, we may write this system in matrix notation as $\mathbf{AX} = \mathbf{Y}$.

Not every system of linear equations has a solution, and not every solution of such a system is unique. The system $\mathbf{AX} = \mathbf{Y}$ *always* has a unique solution, however, if the matrix $\mathbf{A}$ is square and nonsingular. In this case the solution is found by premultiplying both sides of the equation $\mathbf{AX} = \mathbf{Y}$ by the inverse of $\mathbf{A}$:

since $\mathbf{AX} = \mathbf{Y} \Rightarrow \mathbf{A}^{-1}\mathbf{AX} = \mathbf{A}^{-1}\mathbf{Y} \Rightarrow \mathbf{X} = \mathbf{A}^{-1}\mathbf{Y}$

Here is an example. Suppose we want to solve the following 3×3 system of equations:

$$3x_1 + 4x_2 + 66x_3 = 16$$
$$-33x_2 + x_3 = 77$$
$$42x_1 + 3x_2 + 2x_3 = 12$$

We set up this problem and solve it in Excel as follows:

	A	B	C	D	E	F	G
1	**SOLVING SIMULTANEOUS EQUATIONS**						
2							
3					**Column**		**Solution**
4	**Matrix A of coefficients**				**vector Y**		**A⁻¹ Y**
5	3	4	66		16		0.4343
6	0	-33	1		77		-2.3223
7	42	3	2		12		0.3634
8							
9							
10					=MMULT(MINVERSE(A5:C7),E5:E7)		
11							
12	**Checking that the solution works**						
13		16					
14		77		Contains the array function			
15		12		=MMULT(A5:C7,G5:G7)			
16							

In cells B13:B15 we check that the solution indeed solves the system by multiplying the matrix $\mathbf{A}$ times the column vector G5:G7.

Exercises

1. Use Excel to perform the following matrix operations:

    a. $\begin{bmatrix} 2 & 12 & 6 \\ 4 & 8 & 7 \\ 1 & 0 & -9 \end{bmatrix} + \begin{bmatrix} 1 & 1 & 2 \\ 8 & 0 & -23 \\ 1 & 7 & 3 \end{bmatrix}$

    b. $\begin{bmatrix} 2 & -9 \\ 5 & 0 \\ 6 & -6 \end{bmatrix} \begin{bmatrix} 3 & 1 & 1 \\ 2 & 3 & 2 \end{bmatrix}$

    c. $\begin{bmatrix} 2 & 0 & 6 \\ 4 & 8 & 7 \\ 1 & 0 & -9 \end{bmatrix} \begin{bmatrix} 1 & 1 & 2 \\ 8 & 0 & -2 \\ 1 & 7 & 3 \end{bmatrix}$

2. Find the inverses of the following matrices:

    a. $\begin{bmatrix} 1 & 2 & 8 & 9 \\ 2 & 5 & 3 & 0 \\ 4 & 4 & 2 & 7 \\ 5 & -2 & 1 & 6 \end{bmatrix}$

    b. $\begin{bmatrix} 3 & 2 & 1 \\ 6 & -1 & 3 \\ 7 & 4 & 3 \end{bmatrix}$

    c. $\begin{bmatrix} 20 & 2 & 3 & -3 \\ 2 & 10 & 2 & -2 \\ 3 & 2 & 40 & 9 \\ -3 & -2 & 9 & 33 \end{bmatrix}$

3. Solve the equations $\mathbf{AX} = \mathbf{Y}$, where

    $$\mathbf{A} = \begin{bmatrix} 13 & -8 & -3 \\ -8 & 10 & -1 \\ -3 & -1 & 11 \end{bmatrix}, \mathbf{Y} = \begin{bmatrix} 20 \\ -5 \\ 0 \end{bmatrix}, \mathbf{X} = \begin{bmatrix} x_1 \\ x_2 \\ x_3 \end{bmatrix}$$

4. An ill-conditioned matrix is a matrix that "almost doesn't have" an inverse. A set of examples of such matrices are Hilbert matrices. An n-dimensional Hilbert matrix looks like this:

    $$\mathbf{H}_n = \begin{bmatrix} 1 & 1/2 & \cdots & 1/n \\ 1/2 & 1/3 & \cdots & 1/(n+1) \\ \vdots & & & \\ 1/n & 1/(n+1) & & 1/(2n-1) \end{bmatrix}$$

    a. Calculate the inverses of $\mathbf{H}_2$, $\mathbf{H}_3$, and $\mathbf{H}_8$.

    b. Consider the following system of equations:

    $$\mathbf{H}_n \begin{bmatrix} x_1 \\ x_2 \\ \vdots \\ x_n \end{bmatrix} = \begin{bmatrix} 1 + 1/2 + \cdots + 1/n \\ 1/2 + 1/3 + \cdots + 1/(n+1) \\ \vdots \\ 1/n + 1/(n+1) + \cdots + 1/(2n-1) \end{bmatrix}$$

    Find the answers to these problems by inspection.

    c. Now solve $\mathbf{H}_n * \mathbf{X} = \mathbf{Y}$ for $n = 2, 8, 14$. How do you explain the differences?

28 The Gauss-Seidel Method

28.1 Overview

Many simultaneous equations can be solved by *recursive iteration*. In these methods we successively substitute a solution for one equation into another of the simultaneous equations until a solution is reached. These *Gauss-Seidel* methods are often efficient in solving complicated systems of equations. We use them in Chapter 3 to find the solutions of pro forma financial statements (though we let Excel do the work!).

28.2 A Simple Example

Suppose we are trying to solve the simultaneous linear equations

$$2x + 3y = 10$$
$$x - 4y = 2$$

The first equation solves to give $x = (10 - 3y)/2$, and from the second equation we obtain $y = (x - 2)/4$. To use the Gauss-Seidel method, we set some initial value for y; for example, we can let $y = 0$. If $y = 0$, then $x = (10 - 3*0)/2 = 5$. But if $x = 5$, then $y = (x - 2)/4 = (5 - 2)/4 = 0.75$. If we keep going, we will see that ultimately the values of x and y converge to a solution to the equations. Here is the problem, set up as a table in Excel:

	A	B	C	D	E	F	G	H	I
1	GAUSS-SEIDEL METHOD--SOLUTION BY ITERATIVE SUBSTITUTION								
2									
3				y	x				
4				0	5				
5		=(E4-2)/4		0.75	3.875		=(10-3*D5)/2		
6				0.46875	4.296875				
7				0.574219	4.138672				
8				0.534668	4.197998				
9				0.5495	4.175751				
10				0.543938	4.184093				
11				0.546023	4.180965				
12				0.545241	4.182138				
13				0.545535	4.181698				
14				0.545425	4.181863				
15				0.545466	4.181801				

As you can see, the values converge. It follows from the way we have constructed the values that the limits of the two sequences are the solutions to the equations.

28.3   A More Concise Solution

A neater way of solving the same problem is to set up the following spreadsheet:

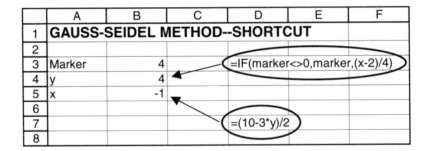

Marker refers to the cell B3, **x** refers to the cell B5, **y** refers to the cell B4. The formula for **y** says that if **marker** $\neq$ **0,** then $y = (x - 2)/4$. The formula for **x** is obvious.

How does this technique work? If you set **marker** equal to some nonzero value, then you see, as in the preceding spreadsheet picture, that $x = 4$ and $y = -1$. Once you let **marker** equal zero, then the iterative process starts, and if there is a solution, Excel will find it.[1] Here's the solution:

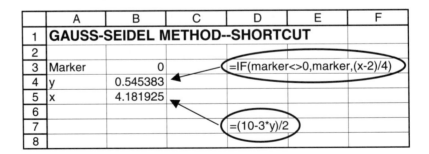

---

1.   To make sure your spreadsheet recalculates, you have to go to the **Tools|Options|Calculation** box and click *Iteration*. See box on this topic in section 3.2.

28.4   Conclusion

The Gauss-Seidel method is a somewhat untidy way of solving simultaneous equations. The solution may not always converge, and convergence may depend on whether x or y is solved for first. The advantage of the method is that it assures us that what we do in many financial models makes sense by allowing us to construct a model in which we set up the relations between the variables without asking how the equations are to be solved. If we observe convergence, then we have a solution. The models of Chapters 3 and 4 are examples of how powerful the Gauss-Seidel method can be.

Exercise

Solve the following system using the Gauss-Seidel method:

$13x - 8y - 3z = 20$
$-8x + 10y - z = -5$
$-3x - y + 11z = 0$

Note that in order to get a solution, you may have to hit the **F9** (recalculate spreadsheet) key a few times. You will have gotten a solution if the numbers on the screen stop changing.

29 Excel Functions

29.1 Introduction

Excel contains several hundred functions. Sections 29.2–29.6 survey the functions used in this book, and section 29.7 adds others you may find useful. The structure of the chapter is as follows:

- Section 29.2 discusses some of Excel's financial functions. Many of these functions are also discussed in Chapter 1.

- Section 29.3 discusses array functions. These functions are used especially in the chapters on portfolio modeling (Chapters 7–12)

- Section 29.4 looks at some statistical functions.

- Section 29.5 shows how to do regression with Excel. Regressions are used in Chapters 2, 10, and 22.

- Section 29.6 discusses three of Excel's conditional functions.

- Section 29.7 introduces ranking functions.

29.2 Financial Functions

29.2.1 NPV( )

The Excel definition of **NPV( )** differs somewhat from the standard finance definition. In the finance literature, the net present value of a sequence of cash flows C_0, C_1, C_2, ..., C_n at a discount rate r refers to the expression:

$$\sum_{t=0}^{n} \frac{C_t}{(1+r)^t} \quad \text{or} \quad C_0 + \sum_{t=0}^{n} \frac{C_t}{(1+r)^t}$$

In many cases C_0 represents the cost of the asset purchased and is therefore negative.

The Excel definition of **NPV( )** always assumes that the first cash flow occurs after one period. The user who wants the standard finance expression must therefore calculate $\text{NPV}(r, \{C_1, \ldots, C_n\}) + C_0$. Here is an example:

	A	B	C	D	E	F	G
1	EXCEL'S NPV FUNCTION						
2							
3	Discount rate	10%					
4	Year	0	1	2	3	4	5
5	Cash flow	-100	35	33	34	25	16
6							
7	NPV	$11.65	<-- =NPV(B3,C5:G5)+B5				

29.2.2   IRR( )

The internal rate of return (IRR) of a sequence of cash flows $C_0, C_1, C_2, ..., C_n$ is an interest rate r such that the net present value of the cash flows is zero:

$$\sum_{t=0}^{n} \frac{C_t}{(1+r)^t} = 0$$

The Excel syntax for the **IRR( )** function is **IRR(cash flows, guess)**. Here **cash flows** represents the whole sequence of cash flows, including the first cash flow C_0, and **guess** is a starting point for the algorithm that calculates the IRR.

First a simple example—consider the cash flows given previously:

Note that **guess** is not necessary when there is only one IRR (see cell B14).

	A	B	C	D	E	F	G
8							
9	**EXCEL'S IRR FUNCTION**						
10	Year	0	1	2	3	4	5
11	Cash flow	-100	35	33	34	25	16
12							
13	IRR	15.00%	<-- =IRR(B13:G13,0)				
14		15.00%	<-- =IRR(B13:G13)				

The choice of **guess** can make a difference when there is more than one IRR. Consider, for example, the following cash flows:

	A	B	C	D	E	F	G	H
1	**MULTIPLE IRRs**							
2								
3			Cash		NPV of Cash Flows			
4		Year	flow					
5		0	-11,000					
6		1	15,000					
7		2	15,000					
8		3	15,000					
9		4	15,000					
10		5	15,000					
11		6	15,000					
12		7	15,000					
13		8	15,000					
14		9	15,000					
15		10	-135,000					
16								
17		IRR	1.86%	<-- =IRR(C5:C15,0)				
18		IRR	135.99%	<-- =IRR(C5:C15,2)				

The graph (created from a **Data|Table** that is not shown) shows that there are two IRRs, since the NPV curve crosses the *x*-axis twice. To find both these IRRs, we have to change the **guess** (though the precise value of guess is still not critical). In the next example we have changed both guesses, but still get the same answer:

	B	C	D	E
17	IRR	1.86%	<-- =IRR(C5:C15,0.1)	
18	IRR	135.99%	<-- =IRR(C5:C15,0.8)	

Note A given set of cash flows typically has more than one IRR if there is more than one change of sign in the cash flows—in the preceding example, the initial cash flow is negative, and CF_1–CF_9 are positive, accounting for one change of sign; but then CF_{10} is negative, making a second change of sign. If you suspect that a set of cash flows has more than one IRR, the first thing to do is to use Excel to make a graph of the NPVs, as we did. The number of times that the NPV graph crosses the *x*-axis identifies the number of IRRs (and also their approximate values).

29.2.3   PV( )

The **PV( )** function calculates the present value of an annuity (a series of fixed periodic payments). For example:

	A	B	C	D
1	THE PV FUNCTION			
2				
3	Payments made at the end of the period			
4	Rate	10%		
5	Number of periods	10		
6	Payment	100		
7	Present value	(614.46)	<-- =PV(B4,B5,B6)	

Thus $\$614.46 = \sum_{t=1}^{10} \dfrac{100}{(1.10)^t}$. Here are two things to note about the **PV( )** function:

• Writing **PV(B4,B5,B6)** assumes that payments are made at dates 1, 2, …, 10. If the payments are made at dates 0, 1, 2, …, 9, you should write

	A	B	C	D	E
10	**Payments made at the beginning of the period**				
11	Rate	10%			
12	Number of periods	10			
13	Payment	100			
14	Present value	(675.90)	<-- =PV(B11,B12,B13,,1)		

- Irritatingly, the **PV( )** function [like the **PMT( )** function—see the next sub-section] produces a negative number. (There is a logic here, but it's not worth explaining.) The solution is obvious: Either write **-PV(B4,B5,B6)** or let the payment be negative by writing **PV(B4,B5,-B6).**

29.2.4   PMT( )

The **PMT( )** function calculates the payment necessary to pay off a loan with equal payments over a fixed number of periods. For example, the first calculation in the following spreadsheet shows that a loan of $1,000 to be paid off over 10 years at an interest rate of 8 percent will require equal annual payments of interest and principal of $149.03. The calculation performed is the solution of the following equation:

$$\sum_{t=1}^{n} \frac{X}{(1 + r)^t} = \text{Initial loan principal}$$

	A	B	C	D	E
1		**THE PMT FUNCTION**			
2					
3		**Payments made at the end of the period**			
4		Rate	8%		
5		Number of periods	10		
6		Principal	1000		
7		Payment	(149.03)	<-- =PMT(C4,C5,C6)	
8					
9					
10		**Payments made at the beginning of the period**			
11		Rate	8%		
12		Number of periods	10		
13		Principal	1000		
14		Payment	(137.99)	<-- =PMT(C11,C12,C13,,1)	

Loan tables can be calculated using the **PMT( )** function. These tables—explained in detail in Chapter 1—show the split between interest and principal of each payment. In each period, the payment on the loan [calculated with **PMT( )**] is split:

• We first calculate the interest owing for that period on the principal outstanding at the beginning of the period. In the following table, at the end of year 1, we owe $80 (8 percent of $1,000) of interest on the loan principal outstanding at the beginning of the year.

• The remainder of the payment (for year 1, $69.03) goes to reduce the principal outstanding.

	A	B	C	D	E
1		**Loan Table**			
2					
3	Interest	8%			
4	Number of periods	10			
5	Principal	1,000			
6	Annual payment	149.03	<-- =-PMT(B3,B4,B5)		
7					
8		**Principal at**		**Split of payment between**	
9		**beginning**			**Repayment**
10	**Year**	**of year**	**Payment**	**Interest**	**of principal**
11	1	1,000.00	149.03	80.00	69.03
12	2	930.97	149.03	74.48	74.55
13	3	856.42	149.03	68.51	80.52
14	4	775.90	149.03	62.07	86.96
15	5	688.95	149.03	55.12	93.91
16	6	595.03	149.03	47.60	101.43
17	7	493.60	149.03	39.49	109.54
18	8	384.06	149.03	30.73	118.30
19	9	265.76	149.03	21.26	127.77
20	10	137.99	149.03	11.04	137.99

Note that at the end of the 10 years the repayment of principal is exactly equal to the principal outstanding at the beginning of the year (i.e., the loan has been paid off).

29.3   Array Functions

Array functions are a special feature of Excel. These functions manipulate matrices and vectors (i.e., they manipulate rectangular ranges of contiguous cells).

The functions we discuss here are **Transpose( ), MMult( ), MInverse( ),** and **Frequency( ).**

Suppose we're trying to calculate the transpose of a 4×2 (4 rows, 2 columns) matrix that is in cells B4:C7 of the spreadsheet.

	A	B	C	D
1	**MATRIX ARRAY FUNCTIONS**			
2				
3		**Original matrix**		
4		3	2	
5		1	-9	
6		5	7	
7		2	19	

Excel has a function called **Transpose( ),** but, like all array functions, its use requires care.

• First, block off the cells E4:H5 into which you intend to put the transposed matrix. Of course, you can use the usual tricks to show Excel which cells by showing ranges (e.g., pointing or using named ranges).

• Now type "=Transpose(B4:C7)." This will appear in the top left-hand corner of the blocked-off cells. At this point your spreadsheet looks like this:

SUM	▼	✕	✓	=	=transpose(B4:C7)

	A	B	C	D	E	F	G	H
1	**MATRIX ARRAY FUNCTIONS**							
2								
3		**Original matrix**			**Transposed matrix**			
4		3	2		=transpose(B4:C7)			
5		1	-9					
6		5	7					
7		2	19					

• When you've finished typing the formula, *don't press Enter!* Instead use **[Ctrl]+[Shift]+[Enter].** This action will put the array function into all of the blocked-off cells. Here's what the final product will look like:

	A	B	C	D	E	F	G	H
1	**MATRIX ARRAY FUNCTIONS**							
2								
3		**Original matrix**			**Transposed matrix**			
4		3	2		3	1	5	2
5		1	-9		2	-9	7	19
6		5	7					
7		2	19					

In this book we have used—in addition to **Transpose**—the following matrix array functions:

• **MMult(range1,range2)** multiplies the matrix in **range1** times that in **range2.** Of course this function can be performed only if the number of columns in **range1** equals the number of rows in **range2.**

• **MInverse(range)** calculates the inverse of the matrix in **range.** Note that **range** must be rectangular.

For illustrations of these functions, you are referred to Chapter 27.

29.3.1   Frequency( )

The Excel array function **Frequency(data_array,bins_array)** allows us to calculate the frequency distribution of a data set. The following spreadsheet picture shows four years of monthly return data for a particular asset. In column D we have put the bins, taking care that the first bin will be *below* the minimum monthly return over the period and that the last bin will be *above* the maximum monthly return. The range E7:E25 contains the array function **Frequency(B4:B51,D7:D25).** From the output we can, for example, deduce that in the four-year period there were three monthly returns between -5.5 percent and -3 percent, and six monthly returns between 7 percent and 9.5 percent.

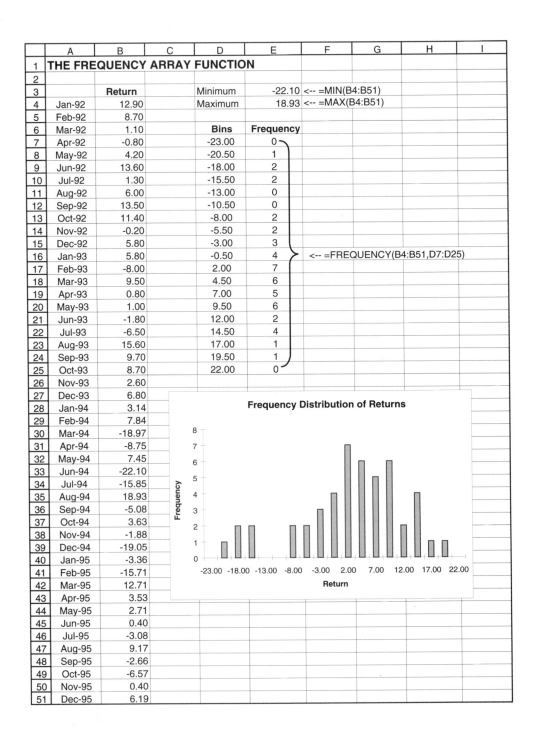

	A	B	C	D	E	F	G	H	I
1	**THE FREQUENCY ARRAY FUNCTION**								
2									
3		**Return**		Minimum	-22.10	<-- =MIN(B4:B51)			
4	Jan-92	12.90		Maximum	18.93	<-- =MAX(B4:B51)			
5	Feb-92	8.70							
6	Mar-92	1.10		**Bins**	**Frequency**				
7	Apr-92	-0.80		-23.00	0				
8	May-92	4.20		-20.50	1				
9	Jun-92	13.60		-18.00	2				
10	Jul-92	1.30		-15.50	2				
11	Aug-92	6.00		-13.00	0				
12	Sep-92	13.50		-10.50	0				
13	Oct-92	11.40		-8.00	2				
14	Nov-92	-0.20		-5.50	2				
15	Dec-92	5.80		-3.00	3				
16	Jan-93	5.80		-0.50	4	<-- =FREQUENCY(B4:B51,D7:D25)			
17	Feb-93	-8.00		2.00	7				
18	Mar-93	9.50		4.50	6				
19	Apr-93	0.80		7.00	5				
20	May-93	1.00		9.50	6				
21	Jun-93	-1.80		12.00	2				
22	Jul-93	-6.50		14.50	4				
23	Aug-93	15.60		17.00	1				
24	Sep-93	9.70		19.50	1				
25	Oct-93	8.70		22.00	0				
26	Nov-93	2.60							
27	Dec-93	6.80							
28	Jan-94	3.14							
29	Feb-94	7.84							
30	Mar-94	-18.97							
31	Apr-94	-8.75							
32	May-94	7.45							
33	Jun-94	-22.10							
34	Jul-94	-15.85							
35	Aug-94	18.93							
36	Sep-94	-5.08							
37	Oct-94	3.63							
38	Nov-94	-1.88							
39	Dec-94	-19.05							
40	Jan-95	-3.36							
41	Feb-95	-15.71							
42	Mar-95	12.71							
43	Apr-95	3.53							
44	May-95	2.71							
45	Jun-95	0.40							
46	Jul-95	-3.08							
47	Aug-95	9.17							
48	Sep-95	-2.66							
49	Oct-95	-6.57							
50	Nov-95	0.40							
51	Dec-95	6.19							

Frequency Distribution of Returns

29.3.2   Index( )

We sometimes want to pick an individual value out of an array. In the next example, the range of cells B3:D5 contains a mixture of numbers and names. To pick out an individual item from this range, we use **=Index(B3:D5, row, column),** where **row** and **column** are relative to the range itself. Thus "Howie" appears in row 2 and column 3 of the range B3:D5.

	A	B	C	D	E
1	**USING THE INDEX FUNCTION**				
2					
3		a	b	3	
4		Simon	6	Howie	
5		q	7	Jack	
6					
7		Howie	<-- =INDEX(B3:D5,2,3)		

In section 29.5.2 we use the **Index** function to pick out a single item in the **Linest** array. This use also occurred in section 22.3.

29.4   Statistical Functions

Excel contains a number of statistical functions. We illustrate these functions using the following data set:

	A	B	C	D	E	F	G
1	**BASIC STATISTICAL FUNCTIONS**						
2							
3		Observation	X	Y			
4		1	35.3	10.98			
5		2	29.7	11.13			
6		3	30.8	12.51			
7		4	58.8	8.4			
8		5	61.4	9.27			
9		6	71.3	8.73			
10		7	74.4	6.36			
11		8	76.7	8.5			
12		9	70.7	7.82			
13		10	57.5	9.14			
14							
15	Average		56.6600	9.2840	<-- =AVERAGE(D4:D13)		
16	Sample variance		334.1493	3.2342	<-- =VAR(D4:D13)		
17	Population variance		300.7344	2.9108	<-- =VARP(D4:D13)		
18	Sample standard deviation		18.2798	1.7984	<-- =STDEV(D4:D13)		
19	Population standard deviation		17.3417	1.7061	<-- =STDEVP(D4:D13)		
20							
21	Correlation			-0.9049	<-- =CORREL(D4:D13,C4:C13)		
22	Covariance			-26.7746	<-- =COVAR(D4:D13,C4:C13)		

The functions **Varp( )** and **Stdevp( )** calculate the population variance and standard deviation, whereas the functions **Var( )** and **Stdev( )** calculate the sample variance and standard deviation. The difference between these two functions is that **Varp** assumes that your data include the whole population and thus divides by the number of data points, whereas **Var** assumes that the data are a sample from the distribution:[1]

$$\mathrm{Varp}(x_1, \ldots, x_N) = \frac{1}{N} \sum_{i=1}^{N} [x_i - \mathrm{Average}(x_1, \ldots, x_N)]^2$$

$$\mathrm{Stdevp}(x_1, \ldots, x_N) = \sqrt{\mathrm{Varp}(x_1, \ldots, x_N)}$$

$$\mathrm{Var}(x_1, \ldots, x_N) = \frac{1}{N-1} \sum_{i=1}^{N} [x_i - \mathrm{Average}(x_1, \ldots, x_N)]^2$$

$$\mathrm{Stdev}(x_1, \ldots, x_N) = \sqrt{\mathrm{Var}(x_1, \ldots, x_N)}$$

Here's an example:

	A	B	C	D	E	F
1			**VAR VERSUS VARP**			
2						
3	**Observation**	**X**	**$(X_i$ - average$)^2$**			
4	1	35.3	456.2496	<-- =(B4-$B$15)^2		
5	2	29.7	726.8416			
6	3	30.8	668.7396			
7	4	58.8	4.5796			
8	5	61.4	22.4676			
9	6	71.3	214.3296			
10	7	74.4	314.7076			
11	8	76.7	401.6016			
12	9	70.7	197.1216			
13	10	57.5	0.7056			
14						
15	Average	56.66				
16	Var	334.1493	334.1493	<-- =SUM(C4:C13)/9		
17	Varp	300.7344	300.7344	<-- =SUM(C4:C13)/10		

---

1. We cannot resist a quote from *Numerical Recipes,* a wonderful book by W. H. Press, B. P. Flannery, S. P. Teukolsky, and W. T. Vetterling (Cambridge University Press, 1986): "There is a long story about why the denominator [of **Var**] is $N - 1$ instead of N. If you have never heard that story, you may consult any good statistics text. Here we will be content to note that the $N - 1$ *should* be changed to N if you are ever in the situation of measuring the variance of

29.5   Doing Regressions with Excel

There are several techniques to produce an ordinary least-squares regression with Excel. We illustrate two techniques using the data from the previous section.

The first technique involves the functions **Slope( )**, **Intercept( )**, and **Rsq( )**; these functions give the parameters for a simple regression of the data in column D on column C.

	A	B	C	D	E	F	G
1		**REGRESSIONS WITH EXCEL**					
2							
3		**Observation**	**X**	**Y**			
4		1	35.3	10.98			
5		2	29.7	11.13			
6		3	30.8	12.51			
7		4	58.8	8.4			
8		5	61.4	9.27			
9		6	71.3	8.73			
10		7	74.4	6.36			
11		8	76.7	8.5			
12		9	70.7	7.82			
13		10	57.5	9.14			
14							
15	Regression intercept		14.3285	<-- =INTERCEPT(D4:D13,C4:C13)			
16	Regression slope		-0.0890	<-- =SLOPE(D4:D13,C4:C13)			
17	Regression r-squared		0.8189	<-- =RSQ(D4:D13,C4:C13)			

Using these numbers, the best linear explanation of the relation between y and x is

$$y = 14.3285 - 0.089x$$

About 82 percent of the variation in the data is explained by this linear relation.

Another way that we can produce a simple regression is to graph the data and let Excel calculate the ordinarily least squares (OLS) regression coefficients. To do so:

• First plot the data.

• Double-click on the data and then go to **Insert|Trendline.** As the following picture shows, this function allows us to choose several types of regressions.

---

a distribution whose mean $\bar{x}$ is known *a priori* rather than being estimated from the data. (We might also comment that if the difference between N and $N - 1$ ever matters to you, then you are probably up to no good anyway—e.g., trying to substantiate a questionable hypothesis with marginal data.)"

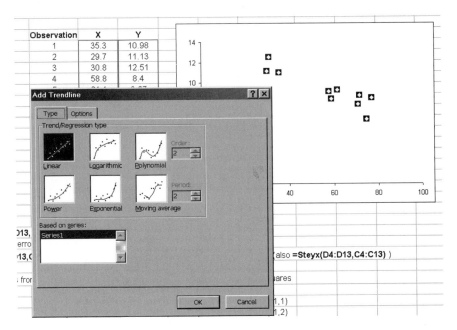

Choosing **Linear** produces the following plot (the equation and the R^2 are displayed by clicking the appropriate boxes on the **Options** tab of the dialog box):

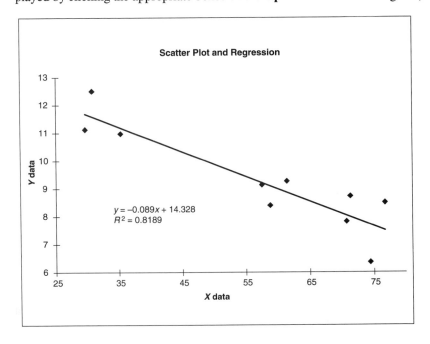

29.5.1   Using Linest( )

Excel has an array function **Linest( )** whose output consists of a number of regression statistics for an ordinary least-squares regression.[2] Here is a picture of the spreadsheet and the **Linest** dialogue box:

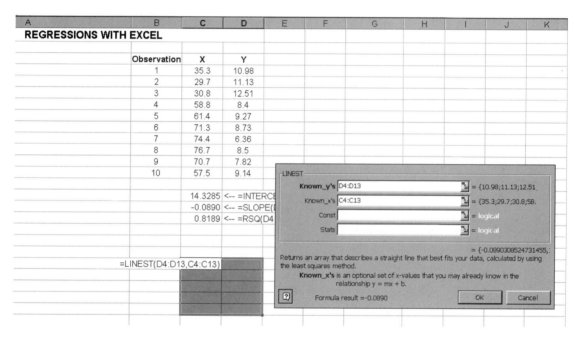

With the data from this example, we can use **Linest** to produce the following output:

	A	B	C	D	E	F	G	H	I	J
19			Linest output							
20			slope	intercept						
21	Slope (also =slope(D4:D13,C4:C13))-->		-0.0890	14.3285	<-- Intercept					
22	Standard error of slope -->		0.0148	0.8770	<-- Standard error of intercept					
23	R² (also =Rsq(D4:D13,C4:C13)) -->		0.8189	0.8117	<-- Standard error of y values (also =Steyx(D4:D13,C4:C13))					
24	F statistic -->		36.1825	8	<-- Degrees of freedom					
25	SSxy = Slope*(summed product of observations from means) -->		23.8377	5.2705	<-- SSE = Residual sum of squares					
26										
27		Slope	-0.0890	<-- =INDEX(LINEST(D4:D13,C4:C13,,1),1,1)						
28		Intercept	14.3285	<-- =INDEX(LINEST(D4:D13,C4:C13,,1),1,2)						
29		R²	0.8189	<-- =INDEX(LINEST(D4:D13,C4:C13,,1),3,1)						
30										
31		Slope	-0.0890	<-- =INDEX(LINEST(D4:D13,C4:C13,,TRUE),1,1)						
32		S.e. of slope	0.0148	<-- =INDEX(LINEST(D4:D13,C4:C13,,TRUE),2,1)						
33		t-statistic	-6.0152	<-- =C31/C32						

---

2.   There is also an Excel function **Logest( )**, whose syntax is exactly the same as that of **Linest( )**. **Logest( )** calculates the parameters to fit an exponential curve.

Linest produces a block of output without column headers or row labels to identify the output. Excel's Help provides a good explanation of the meaning of the output; in the preceding picture, we have added the explanations.

Note the syntax of this function: **Linest(y-range,x-range,constant,statistics).** The **y-range** is the range of dependent variables, and the **x-range** is the range of the independent variables. If **constant** is omitted (as in this case) or set to **True,** then the regression is calculated normally; if **constant** is set to **False,** then the intercept is forced to be zero. If **statistics** is set to **True** (as in this case), then the range of statistics is calculated; otherwise only the slope and intercept are calculated.

Recall from section 29.3 on array functions how to produce this output:

- First mark the whole area C20:D24 in which the output for **Linest** will be placed.

- Next write in the formula **=Linest(D4:D13,C4:C13,,TRUE).** As we have shown, you can use the function dialogue box to enter the cell references.

- Now press **[Ctrl]+[Shift]+[Enter]** simultaneously.

29.5.2   Using Index( ) to Pick Out Individual Entries of Linest( )

Individual items of this output can be accessed by using the function **Index( ).** Suppose, for example, that we want to do a simple t-test on the slope; we need to divide the slope value by its standard error. The following picture shows how to do this test using **Index** :

	A	B	C	D	E	F	G	H	I	J
19			Linest output							
20			slope	Intercept						
21	Slope (also **=slope(D4:D13,C4:C13)**)-->		-0.0890	14.3285	<-- Intercept					
22	Standard error of slope -->		0.0148	0.8770	<-- Standard error of intercept					
23	R² (also **=Rsq(D4:D13,C4:C13)**) -->		0.8189	0.8117	<-- Standard error of y values (also **=Steyx(D4:D13,C4:C13)**)					
24	F statistic -->		36.1825	8	<-- Degrees of freedom					
25	SS$_{xy}$ = Slope*(summed product of observations from means) -->		23.8377	5.2705	<-- SSE = Residual sum of squares					
26										
27		Slope	-0.0890	<-- =INDEX(LINEST(D4:D13,C4:C13,,1),1,1)						
28		Intercept	14.3285	<-- =INDEX(LINEST(D4:D13,C4:C13,,1),1,2)						
29		R²	0.8189	<-- =INDEX(LINEST(D4:D13,C4:C13,,1),3,1)						

29.5.3   Multiple Regressions

Linest( ) can also be used to do a multiple regression, as in the following illustration.

	A	B	C	D	E	F	G
1	**USING LINEST TO DO A MULTIPLE REGRESSION**						
2							
3		**Observation**	X_1	Z_2	**Y**		
4		1	35.3	81.2	10.98		
5		2	29.7	22.5	11.13		
6		3	30.8	77.3	12.51		
7		4	58.8	34.8	8.4		
8		5	61.4	55.1	9.27		
9		6	71.3	124.8	8.73		
10		7	74.4	18.5	6.36		
11		8	76.7	234.6	8.5		
12		9	70.7	22.5	7.82		
13		10	57.5	123.3	9.14		
14							
15			x_2 **coeff.**	x_1 **coeff.**	**intercept**		
16		Slope -->	0.0089	-0.0987	14.1705	<-- Intercept	
17		Standard error -->	0.0030	0.0110	0.6271		
18		R^2 -->	0.9196	0.5783	#N/A		
19		F statistic -->	40.0228	7.0000	#N/A		
20		SS_{xy} -->	26.7674	2.3408	#N/A		
21							
22							
23							
24			={LINEST(E4:E13,C4:D13,,TRUE)}				
25							
26							

29.6   Conditional Functions

If( ), **VLookup( )**, and **HLookup( )** are three functions that allow you to put in conditional statements.

The syntax of Excel's **If** statement is **If(condition,output if condition is true, output if condition is false).** In the following example, if the initial number in B3 is less than or equal to 3, then the desired output is 15. If B3 is greater than 3, then the output is 0:

	A	B	C	D
1	**THE IF FUNCTION**			
2				
3	Initial number	2		
4	If statement	15	<-- =IF(B3<=3,15,0)	

You can make **If** print text also, by enclosing the desired text in quotation marks:

	A	B	C	D	E	F	G
6	Initial number	2					
7	If statement	less than or equal to 3	<-- =IF(B6<=3,"Less than or equal to 3", "More than 3")				

Since **VLookup( )** and **HLookup( )** both have the same structure, we will concentrate on **VLookup( )** and leave you to figure out **HLookup( )** for yourself. **VLookup( )** is a way to introduce a table search in your spreadsheet. Here is an example: Suppose the marginal tax rates on income are given by the following table (i.e., for income less than $8,000, the marginal tax rate is 0 percent; for income above $8,000, the marginal tax rate is 15 percent, etc.). Cell B11 illustrates how the function **VLookup** is used to look up the marginal tax rate.

	A	B	C	D	E
1		VLOOKUP FUNCTION			
2					
3		Tax			
4	Income	rate			
5	0	0%			
6	8,000	15%			
7	14,000	25%			
8	25,000	38%			
9					
10	Income	15,000			
11	Tax rate	25%	<-- =VLOOKUP(B10,A5:B8,2)		

The syntax of this function is **VLookup(lookup_value,table,column).** The first column of the lookup table, A5:A8, must be arranged in ascending (increasing) order. The **lookup_value,** in this case the income of 15,000, is used to determine the applicable row of the **table.** The row is the first row whose value is less than or equal to the **lookup_value;** in this case, this is the row that starts with 14,000. The **column** entry determines from which column of the applicable row the answer is taken; in this case the marginal tax rates are in column 2.

29.7   Large( ) and Rank( ), Percentile( ), and Percentrank( )

We have not used these functions in this book, but they may be useful to a financial analyst. **Large(array, k)** returns the kth largest number of the **array,** and **Rank(number, array)** returns the rank in **array** of **number.**

Here is an example of each function:

	A	B	C	D	E	F
1	LARGE, RANK, PERCENTILE, PERCENTRANK					
2						
3	Data					
4	10.98					
5	11.13					
6	12.51					
7	8.4					
8	9.27					
9	8.73					
10	6.36					
11	8.5					
12	7.82					
13	9.14					
14						
15	Ranking, k	3				
16	K-th largest	10.98	<-- =LARGE(A4:A13,B15)			
17						
18	Specific number	9.27				
19	Rank from top	4	<-- =RANK(B18,A4:A13)			
20	Rank from bottom	7	<-- =RANK(B18,A4:A13,1)			
21						
22	Percentile rank	0.8				
23	Percentile	11.01	<-- =PERCENTILE(A4:A13,B22)			
24						
25	Specific number	9.27				
26	Percentile ranking	0.666	<-- =PERCENTRANK(A4:A13,B25)			

Thus the third-largest number in the range A4:A13 is 10.98, and the fourth-largest number in the range A4:A13 is 9.27. If, as in cell B20, you specify an additional parameter in the function **Rank,** you will see that 9.27 is the seventh-ranking number from the bottom of the range A4:A13.

As illustrated, Excel has similar functions for percentiles: **Percentile** and **PercentRank.**

30 Some Excel Hints

30.1 Introduction

This chapter covers a grab bag of Excel hints on dealing with problems and needs that we sometimes run into. The chapter makes no pretense at uniformity or extensiveness of coverage. Topics covered include

- Fast fills and copy
- Graph titles that change when data changes
- Creating multiline cells (useful for putting line breaks in cells and linked graph titles)
- Typing Greek symbols
- Typing sub- and superscripts (but not both)
- Naming cells
- Hiding cells

30.2 Fast Copy: Filling in Data Next to Filled-In Column

Usually, we copy cells by dragging on the fill handle of the cell with the formula. There is sometimes an easier method. Consider the following situation:

	A	B	C
1	**AUTO FILL/COPY**		
2			
3	1	2	
4	2	5	<-- B3+3
5	3		
6	4		
7	5		
8	6		
9	7		
10	8		

Now double-click on "fill handle" (shown in the following figure with the cross). After double-clicking, the range B5:B10 will automatically fill with the formula in B4.

	A	B	C	D
1	**AUTO FILL/COPY**			
2				
3	1	2		
4	2	5	<-- B3+3	
5	3			
6	4			
7	5			
8	6			
9	7			
10	8			
11				

Here's the result:

	A	B	C	D	E	F	G
1	**AUTO FILL/COPY**						
2							
3	1	2					
4	2	5	<-- B3+3				
5	3	8					
6	4	11					
7	5	14					
8	6	17					
9	7	20					
10	8	23					
11							
12	Double-clicking on the "fill handle" of a cell will fill in the rest of the column						
13	provided there's a filled cell next to it.						

30.3   Multiline Cells

It is sometimes useful to put a line break in a cell, thus creating a multiline cell. Do this with [Alt]+[Enter] where you want a line break.

	A	B
1	**PUTTING LINE BREAKS IN CELLS**	
2		
3	This is a multi-line cell. The break was entered by inserting Alt+Enter at the desired break points.	

30.4   Text Functions in Excel

Excel lets you change formulas to text. Here's an example:

	A	B	C	D	E
1	**TEXT FUNCTIONS**				
2					
3	Income	15,000			
4	Tax rate	35%			
5	Taxes owed	5,250	<-- =B4*B3		
6					
7					
8	Tax rate as text	35.00%	<-- =TEXT(B4,"0.00%")		
9		0.4	<-- =TEXT(B4,"0.0")		
10					
11	Income as date	Jan. 24, 1941	<-- =TEXT(B3,"mmm. dd, yyyy")		

Note that you can choose different ways of formatting the cell B4 in text form: In cell B8 we have formatted the tax rate as a percentage with two decimal points, whereas in cell B9 we have formatted the tax rate as one decimal, causing it to be rounded off.

Note also the somewhat stupid example in cell B11: Since dates in Excel are just numbers that express the number of days from January 1, 1900, we can express the income of $15,000 in cell B3 as a date.

30.5   Graph Titles That Update

You want to have the graph title change when a parameter on the spreadsheet changes. For example, in the next spreadsheet, you want the graph title to indicate the growth rate.

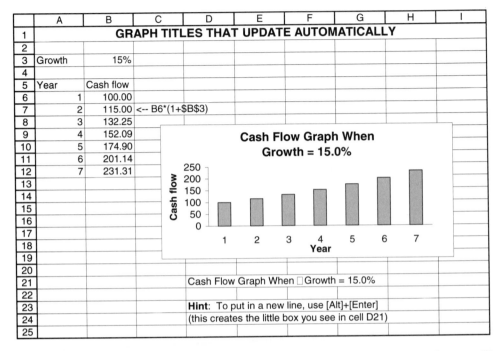

Once we have completed the necessary steps, changing the growth rate will change both the graph *and* its title, as follows:

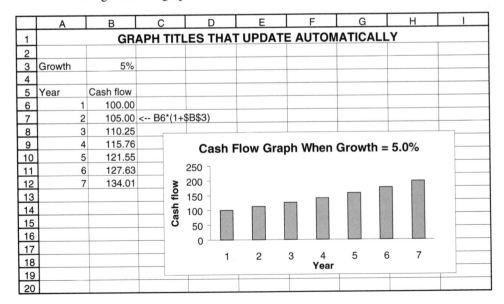

To make graph titles update automatically, carry out the following steps:

• Create the graph you want in the format you want it. Give the graph a "proxy title." (It makes no difference what; you're going to eliminate it soon.) At this stage your graph might look like this:

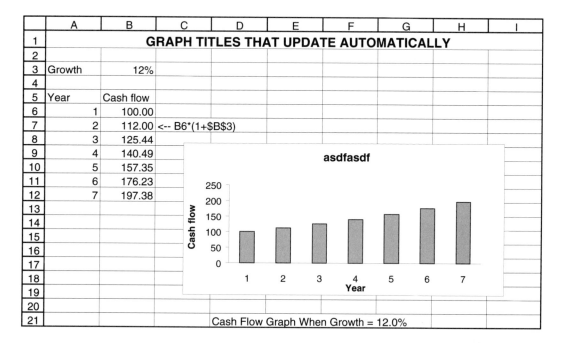

	A	B	C	D	E	F	G	H	I
1			**GRAPH TITLES THAT UPDATE AUTOMATICALLY**						
2									
3	Growth	12%							
4									
5	Year	Cash flow							
6	1	100.00							
7	2	112.00	<-- B6*(1+$B$3)						
8	3	125.44							
9	4	140.49							
10	5	157.35							
11	6	176.23							
12	7	197.38							
13									
14									
15									
16									
17									
18									
19									
20									
21			Cash Flow Graph When Growth = 12.0%						

• Create the title you want in a cell. In this example, cell D21 contains the formula:="Cash Flow Graph When Growth = "&TEXT(B3,"0.0%")

• Click on the graph title to mark it, and then go to the formula bar and insert an equal sign to indicate a formula. Then **point** at cell D21 with the formula and click [Enter]. In the next picture, you see the chart title highlighted and "='Section 30.5'!021" in the formula bar indicating the title of the graph.

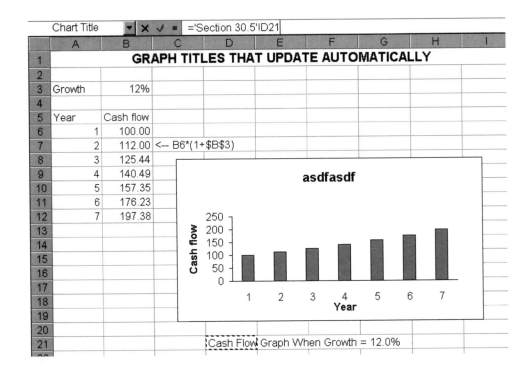

30.6   Putting Greek Symbols in Cells

How do we type Greek letters in a spreadsheet?

	A	B
3	Initial stock price	30
4	Mean, μ	15%
5	Standard deviation, σ	20%
6	Delta t, Δt	0.004

This task is fairly simple, if you know the Greek equivalents for the Greek letters. (For example, μ and σ are lowercase *m* and *s,* respectively, Σ and Δ are uppercase *S* and *D.*) Thus, we first typed "Delta t, Dt" into cell A6 and then marked the *D* in the formula bar.

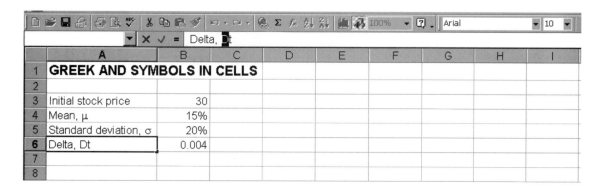

We then changed the font from "Arial" to "Symbol":

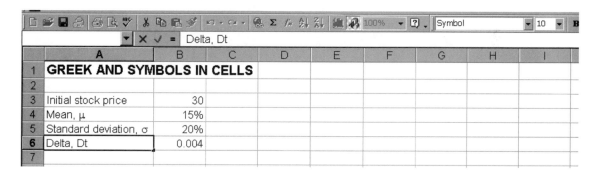

Pressing [**Enter**] produces the desired result.

30.7   Superscripts and Subscripts

Superscripts and subscripts are no problem to enter in Excel. Enter text in a cell, and then mark the letters you want to turn into a subscript or superscript:

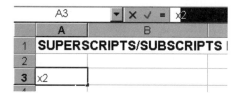

Now go to **Format|Cells** and mark the **Superscript** box.

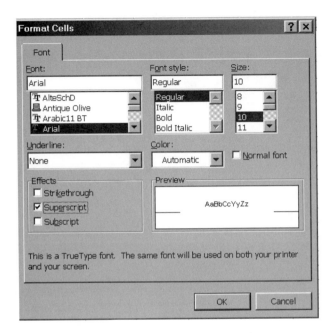

Here's the result:

	A	B	C	D
1	**SUPERSCRIPTS/SUBSCRIPTS IN CELLS**			
2				
3	x^2			

Note that you cannot put a subscript and a superscript on the same letter. That is, you cannot create x_i^2. The best you can do is

	A	B
5	x^2_i	Cannot put superscript and subscript in same column.

30.8   Named Cells

It is sometimes useful to give a name to a cell. Following is an example.

	A	B	C	D
1	**NAMED CELLS**			
2				
3	Income	15,000		
4	Tax rate	33%		
5	Tax paid	4,950	<-- =B4*B3	

We want to be able to refer to cell B4 by the name "tax." To do so, we mark the cell and then go to the name tab on the toolbar:

B4		▼	=	33%	
	A	B	C	D	
1	**NAMED CELLS**				
2					
3	Income	15,000			
4	Tax rate	33%			
5	Tax paid	4,950	<-- =tax*B3		
6					

Typing in the word "tax" in the highlighted B4 allows us to refer to B4 by this name anywhere in the Excel notebook:

	A	B	C	D
1	**NAMED CELLS**			
2				
3	Income	15,000		
4	Tax rate	33%		
5	Tax paid	4,950	<-- =tax*B3	

Sometimes Excel lets us use cell names without ever actually going through the procedure just described. In the next example, Excel lets us use the column headers as cell names:

	A	B	C	D	E
8	Sales	Margin	Profit		
9	1000	20%	200	<-- =Sales*Margin	
10	5000	30%	1500	<-- =Sales*Margin	

30.9   Hiding Cells

In this text we have often hidden the cell contents of data table headers. (This topic is discussed in detail in Chapter 26.) Here's a simple data table.

	A	B	C	D	E	F
1	**HIDING CELLS**					
2						
3	Payment	100				
4	Number of payments	15				
5	Discount rate	15%				
6	Present value	$584.74	<-- =PV(B5,B4,-B3)			
7						
8			**PV of payments**			
9	Data table		$584.74	<-- Data table header, =B6		
10		0%	$1,500.00			
11		3%	$1,193.79			
12		6%	$971.22			
13		9%	$806.07			
14		12%	$681.09			
15		15%	$584.74			
16		18%	$509.16			
17		21%	$448.90			

The data table header in cell C9 is necessary for the table to work, but it is ugly and may be confusing if the table is copied into other documents. To hide the contents of C9, mark the cell and go to the **Format|Cells** menu (or click on the right mouse button):

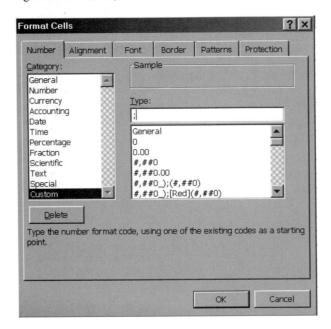

In the **Number|Custom|Type** box we have put in a semicolon. This preserves the cell contents but prevents them from being seen. Now when you copy the cells, they will appear as follows:

	PV of payments
0%	$1,500.00
3%	$1,193.79
6%	$971.22
9%	$806.07
12%	$681.09
15%	$584.74
18%	$509.16
21%	$448.90

Note   We advise you to always *annotate* your spreadsheet, so that when you come back to it after a few weeks or months, you will know that cell C9 really does have something in it.

VI Introduction to Visual Basic for Applications

Chapters 31–35 (written by Benjamin Czaczkes) cover the basic Visual Basic for Applications (VBA) techniques needed in this book. While they are far from being a complete VBA programming guide, these chapters should enable you to do a competent job of programming financial functions.

Chapter 31 introduces VBA and shows you how to write user-defined functions; we have used these functions in several places throughout this book, including Chapter 16 (to define the Black-Scholes option prices) and Chapters 20 and 21 (to define the duration). Chapter 32 discussed types and loops. An example of the use of a loop is the function that calculates an option's implied volatility in Chapter 16. Chapter 33 discusses macros and user intervention, allowing you to write routines that ask the user for input—typically through a message box to be filled in on the spreadsheet. Chapter 34 shows you how to use VBA arrays (used in the lognormal simulations of Chapter 15). Finally, Chapter 35 discusses the use of VBA objects.

31 User-Defined Functions with Visual Basic for Applications

31.1 Overview

The next few chapters discuss the uses of Excel's programming language, Visual Basic for Applications (VBA). VBA provides a complete programming language and environment fully integrated with Excel and all other Microsoft Office applications. In this chapter we introduce user-defined functions, which are used in various places in this book.

The examples and screen shots depict the Excel 2000 working environment but are fully compatible (unless otherwise noted) with all versions of Excel using Visual Basic for Applications (version 5 and above).

31.2 Using the VBA Editor to Build a User-Defined Function

A user function is a saved list of instructions for Excel that produces a value. Once defined, a user function can be used inside a worksheet like any other function.[1]

In this section we will write our first user-defined function. Before you can perform this task, you need to activate the VBA editor. You can do so either from the Excel menu (**Tools|Macro|Visual Basic Editor**) or by using the keyboard shortcut [Alt + F11]. The result in both cases is a new window looking something like the following screen shot.

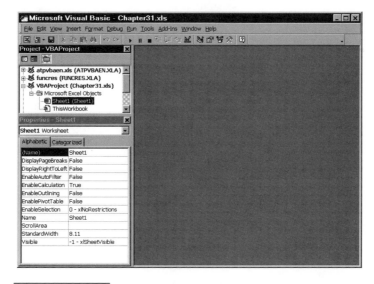

---

1. User-defined functions are usually attached to a specific workbook, and are only available if that workbook is currently open in Excel.

A user-defined function needs to be written in a module. To open a new module, select **Insert|Module** from the menu in the VBA editor environment. This step will open a new window, as follows:

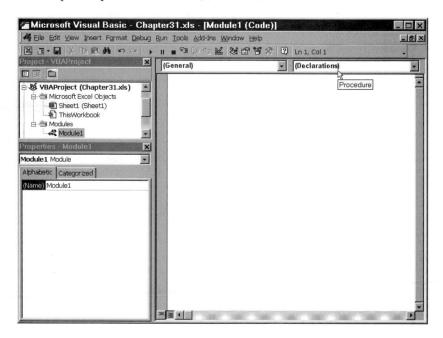

We are now ready to write our first function. A user-defined function in Excel has three obligatory elements:

1. A header line with the name of the function and a list of parameters.
2. A closing line (usually inserted by VBA).
3. Some program lines between the header and the closing line.

Start writing the first line of the function:

```
function Function1 (Parameter)
```

As soon as you end the line with a tap on the [Enter] key, VBA will do a cleanup job. The color of all the words that VBA recognizes as part of its programming language ("reserved words") will change. All reserved words will be capitalized. The closing line for the function will be inserted, and the cursor will be in position between the header and the closing line ready for you to go on typing.

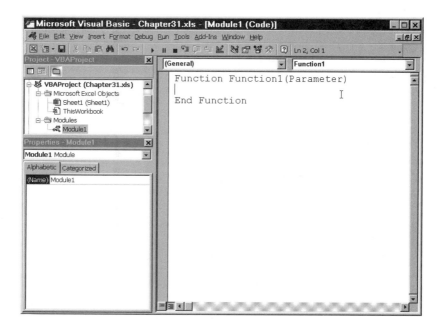

We are now ready to type our function line. This is the line that makes our function do something.[2] Our first function will take a variable, multiply it by 3 and add 1:

```
Function Function1(Parameter)
  Function1 = Parameter * 3 + 1
End Function
```

You can now use this function in your spreadsheet:

	A	B	C	D
1	**Functions in Action**			
2				
3	Parameter	1.25		
4	Function1	4.75	<-- =Function1(B3)	

You can also use the function in the Excel Function Wizard. Clicking on the *fx* icon on the toolbar and going to user-defined functions, you will find the function **Function1**.

---

2. The indentation of lines in VBA code is not required by VBA but makes reading the code much easier.

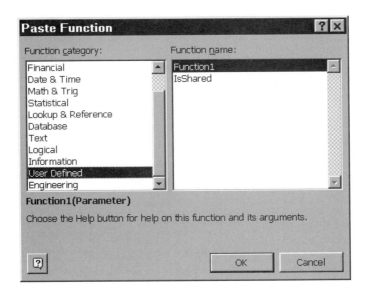

When you select **Function1,** and click OK, you will see that Excel treats this like any other function, bringing up a dialogue box that asks for the location or value of **Parameter**:

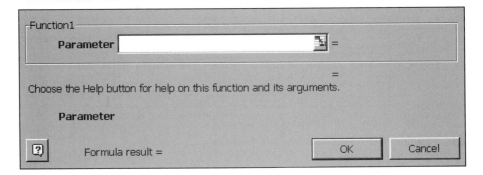

Notice that at this point there is no explanation or help for the function. The next section provides part of the remedy (the simple part).

31.3   Providing Help for User-Defined Functions in the Function Wizard

Excel's Function Wizard provides a short help line (an explanation of what the function does). Excel explains its own functions in the Function Wizard as follows.

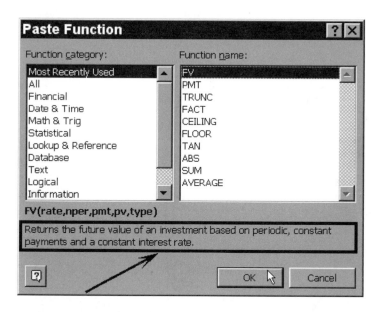

To attach a text description to **Function1,** activate the macro selection box. You can do so either from the Excel menu (**Tools|Macro|Macros**) or by using the keyboard shortcut [Alt + F8].

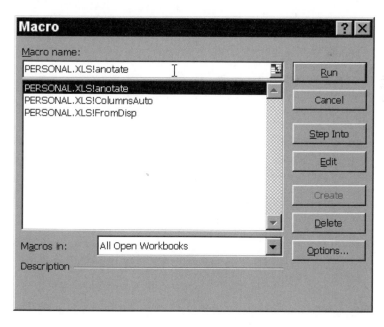

Click in the Macro name box, and replace its contents with the name of the function. (Notice that you don't see the function name in the macro dialogue box; you have to type it in.)

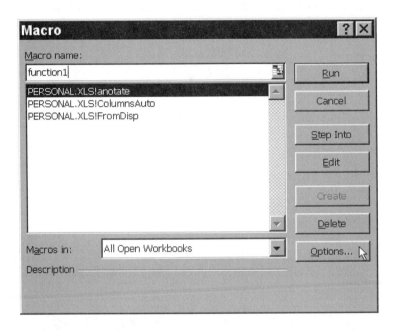

Click on the Options button

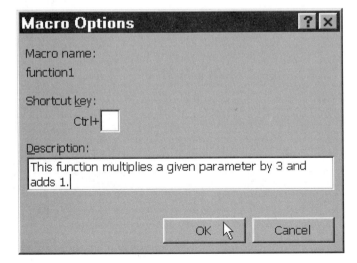

Type the description in the <u>D</u>escription box. Click OK, and close the macro selection box using either the cancel button or the corner X. **Function1** now has a help line.

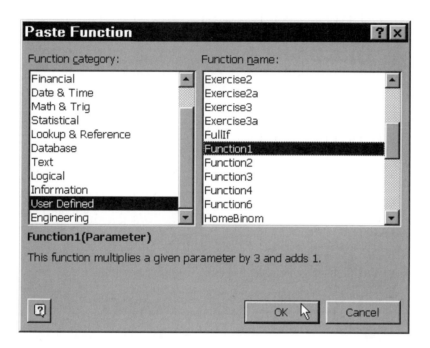

31.4   Fixing Mistakes in VBA

Once you start using VBA, you're sure to make mistakes. In this section we illustrate several typical mistakes and help you correct them. This list is not meant to be exhaustive—we have selected mistakes typically made by VBA beginners.

31.4.1   Mistake 1: Using the Wrong Syntax

Suppose that in writing **Function1** you forget the plus sign between **Parameter*3** and the **1** (recall that the function is supposed to return **Parameter*3+1**). Once you hit the Enter key, you get the following error message.

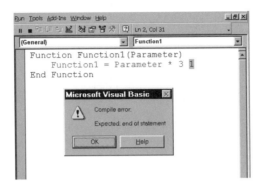

Clicking the OK button allows you to correct this problem.

31.4.2   Mistake 2: Right Syntax with a Typing Error

It's easy to make typing errors that will only be detected once you try to use the function. In this example we define two functions—**Function1** and **Function2.** Unfortunately, the program line for **Function2** mistakenly calls the function "Function1":

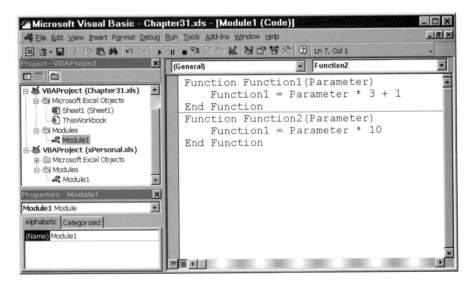

The VBA editor does not recognize this mistake.[3] Only when you try to use the function in a worksheet will Excel notify you that you've made a mistake. This mistake will take you to the VBA editor.

---

3.   Unless we use the Option Explicit statement, which is discussed in section 32.3.

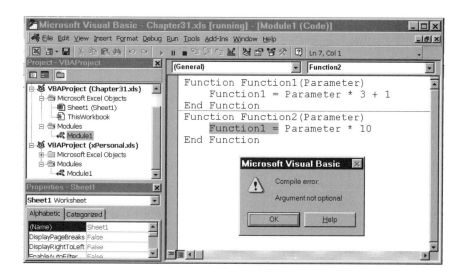

If you recognize your mistake, you can correct it. You can also try to go the VBA help by clicking **Help.** (In many cases this attempt will lead to an incomprehensibly complicated explanation.)

Suppose you recognize your mistake. You click OK, and get ready to correct the error by replacing the word "Function1" by "Function2." At this point your screen looks like this:

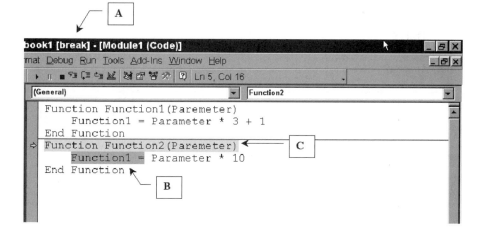

Notice the following.

A. The word "break" appears in the title bar.

B. The offending symbol is selected.

C. The function line is highlighted and pointed to by an arrow in the margin.

Because VBA found an error while trying to execute the function, it moved into a special execution mode called debug-break mode. For now all we need to do is get out of this special mode so we can get on with our work. We do so by clicking the appropriate icon on the VBA toolbar (a small dark square). Now you can fix the function and use it.

31.5   Conditional Execution: Using If Statements in VBA Functions

In this section we explore the **If** statements available to you in VBA. Not all things in life are linear, and sometimes decisions have to be made. **If** statements are one way of making decisions in VBA.

31.5.1   The One-Line If Statement

The one-line **If** statement is the simplest way to control the execution of a VBA function: One statement is executed if a condition is true, and another is executed if a condition is not true. The complete condition and its statement should be on one line. Here's an example:

```
Function SimpleIf(Parameter)
  If Parameter > 5 Then SimpleIf = 1 Else SimpleIf = 15
End Function
```

We can now use the function **SimpleIf** in Excel. When **Parameter** is > 5, **SimpleIf** returns 1:

	A	B	C	D
1	**If Statements**			
2				
3	Parameter	12		
4	SimpleIf	1	<-- =SimpleIf(B3)	

When **Parameter** is ≤5, **SimpleIf** returns 15:

	A	B	C	D
1	**If Statements**			
2				
3	Parameter	3		
4	SimpleIf	15	<-- =SimpleIf(B3)	

The one-line **If** statement doesn't even need the **Else** part. The following function, **SimpleIf2,** returns 0 if the condition "Parameter > 5" is not fulfilled:

```
Function SimpleIf2(Parameter)
    If Parameter > 5 Then SimpleIf2 = 1
End Function
```

31.5.2 Good Programming Practice: Assign a Value to Your Function *First*

In the preceding functions, it would be good programming practice to first assign a value to the function before introducing the **If** statement:

```
Function SimpleIf3(Parameter)
    SimpleIf3 = -16
    If Parameter > 5 Then SimpleIf3 = 1
End Function
```

This way we know that **SimpleIf3** defaults to −16 if the condition on **Parameter** is not fulfilled:

	A	B	C	D
1	**If Statements**			
2				
3	Parameter	-7		
4	SimpleIf	15	<-- =SimpleIf(B3)	
5	SimpleIf2	0	<-- =SimpleIf2(B3)	
6	SimpleIf3	-16	<-- =SimpleIf3(B3)	

31.5.3   If ... ElseIf Statements

If more then one statement is to be conditionally executed, the block **If ...**
ElseIf statement can be used. It uses the following syntax:

```
If Condition0 Then
    Statements
ElseIf Condition1 Then
    Statements
[... More ElseIfs ...]
Else
    Statements
End If
```

The Else and ElseIf clauses are both optional. You may have as many ElseIf
clauses as you want following an If, but none can appear after an Else clause.

If statements can be contained within one another. Here's an example:

```
Function BlockIf(Parameter)
    If Parameter < 0 Then
        BlockIf = -1
    ElseIf Parameter = 0 Then
        BlockIf = 0
    Else
        BlockIf = 1
    End If
End Function
```

Here's how this function works in Excel:

	A	B	C	D
9	Parameter	BlockIf		
10	-3	-1	<-- =BlockIf(A10)	
11	0	0	<-- =BlockIf(A11)	
12	13	1	<-- =BlockIf(A12)	

31.5.4 Nested If Structures

As stated in the previous subsection, If statements can be used as part of the statements used in another If statement. A program structure that has some If statements inside others is called a *nested If* structure. Each If statement in the structure must be a complete If statement. Either the one-line or the block version can be used.

The following function demonstrates the use of the nested If structure.

```
Function NestedIf(P1, P2)
    If P1 > 10 Then
        If P2 > 5 Then NestedIf = 1 Else _
            NestedIf = 2
    ElseIf P1 < -10 Then
        If P2 > 5 Then
            NestedIf = 3
        Else
            NestedIf = 4
        End If
    Else
        If P2 > 5 Then
            If P1 = P2 Then NestedIf = 5 Else _
                NestedIf = 6
        Else
            NestedIf = 7
        End If
    End If
End Function
```

This is how it looks in Excel:

	A	B	C	D
1	**Nested If Function**			
2				
3	P1	P2	NestedIf(P1, P2)	
4	11	6	1	<-- =NestedIf(A4,B4)
5	22	3	2	
6	-22	6	3	
7	-57.3	4	4	
8	6	6	5	
9	-5	7	6	
10	4	3	7	

Here is a flow chart diagramming program flow for the function:

31.6   The Select Case Statement

The **Select Case** statement is used to execute one of several groups of statements, depending on the value of an expression. The following function demonstrates its use in a very simple case. For more information see the VBA help file.

```
Function SimpleSelect(Parameter)
    Select Case Parameter
    Case 1
        SimpleSelect = 111
    Case 2
        SimpleSelect = 222
    Case 3, 5, 6
        SimpleSelect = 333
    Case 4, 2
        SimpleSelect = 444
    Case Else
        SimpleSelect = 555
    End Select
End Function
```

And this is how it looks in Excel:

	A	B	C
1	**SimpleSelect In Action**		
2			
3	**Parameter**	**SimpleSelect**	
4	0	555	<-- =simpleselect(A4)
5	1	111	
6	2	222	<-- Notice it's 222 and not 444
7	3	333	
8	3.5	555	
9	4	444	
10	5	333	
11	6	333	

Following is a flow chart of the function.

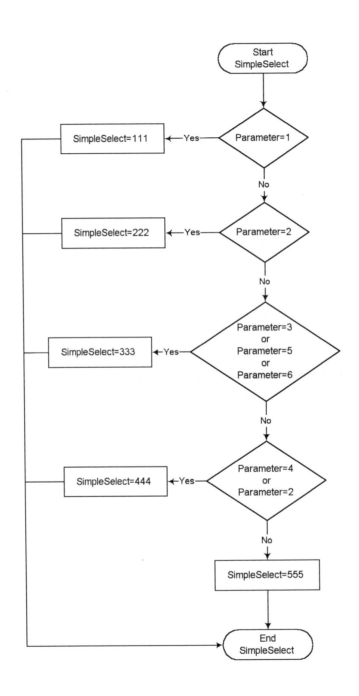

31.7   Using Excel Functions in VBA

VBA can make extensive use of Excel's worksheet functions. We illustrate by showing how to define the binomial distribution (even though this, itself, is an Excel function). The probability distribution of a binomial random variable is defined as

$$\text{binom } (p, n, x) = \binom{n}{x} p^x (1 - p)^{n-x}$$

where p is the probability of success; x is the number of successes, and n is the number of trials. The binomial coefficient is

$$\binom{n}{x} = \frac{n!}{(n - x)!x!}$$

which gives the number of ways of choosing x elements from among n elements. For example, suppose you want to form a two-person team from eight candidates and you want to know how many possible teams can be formed. The answer is given by

$$\binom{8}{2} = \frac{8!}{6!2!} = \frac{8 \cdot 7 \cdot 6 \cdot 5 \cdot 4 \cdot 3 \cdot 2 \cdot 1}{6 \cdot 5 \cdot 4 \cdot 3 \cdot 2 \cdot 1 * 2 \cdot 1} = 28$$

The Excel function **Combin** (8, 2) does this calculation.

We use this Excel function in the following VBA function:

```
Function Binomial(p, n, x)
    Binomial = Application.Combin(n, x) _
        * p ^ x * (1 - p) ^ (n - x)
End Function
```

As usual, this can be applied inside a spreadsheet:

	A	B	C	D	E
1	**Binomial function**				
2					
3	p	0.5			
4	n	10			
5	x	6			
6	Binomial	0.205078	<-- =Binomial(B3,B4,B5)		

Note that we used **Application.Combin(n, x)** to compute $\binom{n}{x}$ in our function. As you might guess from its name (**Application.Something**), this function is the Excel worksheet function **Combin( ).** Most Excel worksheet functions can be used in VBA in exactly the same way. Some examples will be given in subsequent parts of this section. For a complete list see the Help file.

> One more thing to notice is the underscore (_) preceded by a space at the end of line 2. If a line gets too long to handle, it can be continued on the next line using this contraption. (What's *too long*? This is a matter of programming taste, but for our purposes 70–80 characters is considered too long.) The second and third lines of **Binomial** are one line as far as VBA is concerned.

Suppose we try to use our **Binomial** function to calculate **Binomial(0.5, 10, 15).** This attempt won't work:

	A	B	C	D	E
1	**Binomial function**				
2					
3	p	0.5			
4	n	10			
5	x	15			
6	Binomial	#VALUE!	<-- =Binomial(B3,B4,B5)		

The reason for the problem is that in the computation $\binom{n}{x}$ used in **Binomial,** we have to have $x < n$. In this case, VBA causes Excel to return the error message **#Value!** The subject of Excel error values is somewhat obscure, and therefore we cover it in the chapter appendix.

31.8   Using User-Defined Functions in User-Defined Functions

User-defined functions can be used in other user-defined functions, just like Excel functions. The next function is a replacement for the COMBIN worksheet function. COMBIN is defined as

$$c(n, x) = \frac{n!}{(n - x)! x!}$$

where ! stands for the factorial function. [Recall that the factorial function $n!$ is defined for any $n \geq 0$: $0! = 1$, and for $n > 0$, $n! = n * (n - 1) * (n - 2) * \ldots * 1$.]

We will now write our VBA version of the two functions: the factorial function and the COMBIN function.

```
1    Function HomeFactorial(n)
2        If Int(n) <> n Then
3            HomeFactorial = CVErr (xlErrValue)
4        ElseIf n < 0 Then
5            HomeFactorial = CVErr (xlErrNum)
6        ElseIf n = 0 Then
7            HomeFactorial = 1
8        Else
9            HomeFactorial =
                 HomeFactorial(n - 1) * n
10       End If
11   End Function
```

Line 2 checks whether the input is an integer by comparing the integer part of "n" to "n." The function "Int" is a part of VBA. If we have erred, for example by asking for **HomeFactorial(3.3),** then line 3 of the program will cause Excel to return **#VALUE!** Similarly, lines 4 and 5 check if we have improperly asked for **HomeFactorial** of a negative number; if this is the case, then line 5 causes Excel to return **#NUM!** For a fuller explanation of the use of error values, see the appendix.

On line 9 something new happens: the function uses itself to calculate the value it should return. This new ability is called recursion. Here's an illustration of the function in action:

	A	B	C	D	E
1	**Recursion in Action**				
2					
3	N	Factorial		HomeFactorial(n)	
4	0	1	<-- 1	1	<-- =HomeFactorial(A4)
5	1	1	<-- =B4*A5	1	<-- =HomeFactorial(A5)
6	2	2	<-- =B5*A6	2	
7	3	6	<-- =B6*A7	6	
8	4	24	<-- =B7*A8	24	
9	5	120	<-- =B8*A9	120	

We can now use **HomeFactorial** to create our VBA version of **Combin** (which we will call **HomeCombin**).

```
Function HomeCombin(n, x)
    HomeCombin = HomeFactorial(n) / _
        (HomeFactorial(n - x) * _
            HomeFactorial(x))
End Function
```

Finally, we can use **HomeCombin** to create a VBA version of the binomial function:

```
Function HomeBinom(p, n, x)
    If n < 0 Then
        HomeBinom = CVErr (xlErrValue) 'Make the
            'function return #VALUE!
    ElseIf x > n Or x < 0 Then
        HomeBinom = CVErr (xlErrNum) 'Make the
            'function return #NUM!
    Else
        HomeBinom = HomeCombin(n, x) _
            * p ^ x * p ^ (n - x)
    End If
End Function
```

Putting comments in VBA code is illustrated in the preceding function. By using a single apostrophe, you can put comments in VBA code. VBA will ignore anything on a line that follows an apostrophe. (Note that each new line of comments has to begin with an apostrophe.)

Exercises

1.   Write a VBA function for $f(x) = x^2 - 3$.

	A	B	C
1	**Exercise 1**		
2			
3	X		
4	1		-2 <-- =Exercise1(A4)
5	2		1 <-- =Exercise1(A5)
6	3		6 <-- =Exercise1(A6)

2. Write a VBA function for $f(x) = \sqrt{2x^2} + 2x$. Note that there are two ways to carry out this assignment. The first is to use the VBA function **Sqr.** The second is to use the VBA operator ^. We suggest you try both.

	A	B	C
8	**Exercise 2**		
9			
10	X	Exercise2	
11	1	3.414213562	<-- =Exercise2(A10)
12	2	6.828427125	<-- =Exercise2(A10)
13	1	3.414213562	<-- =Exercise2a(A12)
14	2	6.828427125	<-- =Exercise2a(A13)

3. Suppose a share was priced at price P_0 at time 0, and suppose that at time 1 it will be priced P_1. Then the continuously compounded return is defined as $\ln\left(\dfrac{P_1}{P_0}\right)$. Implement this function in VBA. There are two ways to perform this calculation. You can use **Application.Ln** or the VBA function **Log.**

	A	B	C	D
18	**Exercise 3**			
19				
20	P0	P1		
21	100	110	0.09531018	<-- =Exercise3(A21,B21)
22	100	200	0.693147181	<-- =Exercise3(A22,B22)
23	100	110	0.09531018	<-- =Exercise3a(A23,B23)
24	100	200	0.693147181	<-- =Exercise3a(A24,B24)

4. A bank offers different yearly interest rates to its customers based on the size of the deposit in the following way:

For deposits up to $1,000 the interest rate is 5.5 percent.

For deposits from $1,000 up to $10,000 the interest rate is 6.3 percent.

For deposits from $10,000 up to $100,000 the interest rate is 7.3 percent.

For all other deposits the interest rate is 7.8 percent.

Implement the function **Interest(Deposit)** in VBA. Note that you can use the **Block If** structure or the **Select Case** structure

	A	B	C
31	**Exercise 4**		
32			
33	Deposit		
34	-1	#VALUE!	<-- =Interest(A34)
35	100	5.50%	<-- =Interest(A35)
36	1100	6.30%	
37	9999.99	6.30%	
38	10000	6.30%	
39	10000.001	7.30%	
40	100000.001	7.80%	
41	-1	#VALUE!	<-- =Interesta(A41)
42	100	5.50%	<-- =Interesta(A42)
43	1100	6.30%	
44	9999.99	6.30%	
45	10000	6.30%	
46	10000.001	7.30%	
47	100000.001	7.80%	

5. Using the function in exercise 4 implement a function **NewDFV(Deposit, Years).** The function will return the future value of a deposit with the bank assuming that the deposit and accrued interest are reinvested for a given number of years. Thus, for example **NewDFV(10000, 10)** will return $10000*(1.063)$ ^ 10.

	A	B	C	D
51	**Exercise 5**			
52				
53	Deposit	Years		
54	10000	10	18,421.8247	<-- =NewDFV(A54,B54)
55	10000.001	10	20,230.0643	<-- =NewDFV(A55,B55)

6. An investment company offers a bond linked to the FT100 index. On redemption the bond pays the face value plus the larger of (a) the face value times the change in the index or (b) 5 percent yearly interest compounded monthly. For example, 100 invested when the index was 110 and redeemed a year later when the index was 125 will pay (a) $100 + 100*(125 - 110)/110 = 113.636$ and not (b) $100*(1 + 0.05/12)\wedge 12 = 105.116$. Implement a VBA function **Bond(Deposit, Years, FT0, FT1)**

	A	B	C	D	E	F
64	**Exercise 6**					
65						
66	Deposit	Years	FT0	FT1		
67	100	1	110	125	113.636	<-- =Bond(A67,B67,C67,D67)
68	100	1	110	100	105.116	<-- =Bond(A68,B68,C68,D68)
69	100	12	110	125	1,261.394	<-- =Bond(A69,B69,C69,D69)
70	100	12	110	1387.53	1,261.394	<-- =Bond(A70,B70,C70,D70)
71	100	12	110	1387.535	1,261.395	<-- =Bond(A71,B71,C71,D71)

7. Implement a VBA function **ChooseBond(Deposit, Years, FT0, FT1).** The function will return the value 1 if the superior investment is the bank in exercise 5 or the value 2 if it is the company in exercise 6.

	A	B	C	D	E	F
76	**Exercise 7**					
77						
78	Deposit	Years	FT0	FT1		
79	100	1	110	125	2	<-- =ChooseBond(A79,B79,C79,D79)
80	100	1	110	110	1	
81	100	1	110	116.04	1	
82	100	1	110	116.05	2	
83	100000	1	110	125	2	<-- =ChooseBond(A83,B83,C83,D83)
84	100000	1	110	110	1	
85	100000	1	110	118.02	1	
86	100000	1	110	118.03	2	

8. A bank offers the following saving scheme: Invest a fixed amount on the first of each month for a set number of years. On the first of the month after your last installment get your money plus the accrued interest. The bank quotes a yearly interest rate, but interest is calculated and compounded on a monthly basis. Eight different interest rates are offered depending on the monthly deposit and the number of years the program is to run.

The following table lists the interest rates offered:

	For sums $\leq$ \$100 a Month	For sums $>$ \$100 a Month
For a period of two years	3.5%	3.9%
For a period of three years	3.7%	4.5%
For a period of four years	4.2%	5.1%
For a period of five years	4.6%	5.6%

Write a two-argument function **DFV(Deposit, Years),** returning the future value of such an investment.

	A	B	C	D
40	**Exercise 8**			
41				
42	Deposit	Years	DFV	
43	1	1	#NUM!	<-- =DFV(A43,B43)
44	14.79846406	5	1000	<-- =DFV(A44,B44)
45	19.10180565	4	1000	<-- =DFV(A45,B45)
46	99.999999	2	2489.488348	<-- =DFV(A46,B46)
47	100.000001	2	2499.973424	<-- =DFV(A47,B47)

9. Using the information provided in exercise 8, write a two-argument function **DEP(DFV, Years)** that will return the monthly contribution necessary to get a certain sum in the future (two, three, four, or five years). Note: This problem is more interesting; remember that the interest rate is dependent on the monthly contribution.

	A	B	C	D
50	**Exercise 9**			
51				
52	DFV	Years	DEP	
53	-1000	2	-40.16889619	<-- =DEP(A53,B53)
54	1000	5	14.79846406	<-- =DEP(A54,B54)
55	1000	4	19.10180565	<-- =DEP(A55,B55)
56	2489.488348	2	99.999999	<-- =DEP(A56,B56)
57	2499.973424	2	100.000001	<-- =DEP(A57,B57)

10. Fibonacci numbers (named after Leonardo Fibonacci, 1170–1230, an outstanding European mathematician of the medieval period) are defined as follows:

$F(0) = 0$

$F(1) = 1$

$F(2) = F(0) + F(1) = 1$

$F(3) = F(1) + F(2) = 2$

$F(4) = F(2) + F(3) = 3$

and so on

In general, $F(n) = F(n-2) + F(n-1)$.

Write a VBA function that computes the nth number in the series. Note: Recursion is necessary.

Appendix: Cell Errors in Excel and VBA

Excel uses a special kind of value to report errors. The **CVErr()** function is part of VBA. It converts a value supplied by you to the special kind of value used for errors in Excel. Excel has a number of error values that a function can return to signal that something went wrong. Here's an example: The function **NewMistake(x,y)** returns the result x/y. However, if $y = 0$, the function outputs the (cryptic) error message #DIV0!

```
Function NewMistake(x, y)
    If y <> 0 Then NewMistake = x / y Else _
        NewMistake = CVErr(xlErrDiv0)
End Function
```

> To avoid future confusion, all the VBA error values are written "xlErr . . . ."
> Because the typed alphabet letter *l* also looks like the number 1, it would
> have been easier had Microsoft used capital letters "XLErr . . . ." But . . .

This is **NewMistake** in Excel:

	A	B	C	D
1	**NewMistake in Action**			
2				
3	X	Y	NewMistake	
4	1	2	0.5	<-- =NewMistake(A4,B4)
5	2	1	2	<-- =NewMistake(A5,B5)
6	0	1	0	<-- =NewMistake(A6,B6)
7	1	0	#DIV/0!	<-- =NewMistake(A7,B7)

Error values and their explanations are listed in the following table. Each
error is explained by a short example following the table.

Error Value	VBA Name	Possible causes
#NULL!	XlErrNull	The #NULL! error value occurs when you specify an intersection of two areas that do not intersect.
#DIV/0!	XlErrDiv0	The #DIV/0! error value occurs when a formula divides by 0 (zero).
#VALUE!	XlErrValue	The #VALUE! Error value occurs when the wrong type of argument is used.
#REF!	XlErrRef	The #REF! error value occurs when a cell reference is not valid.
#NAME?	XlErrName	The #NAME? Error value occurs when Microsoft Excel doesn't recognize text in a formula.
#NUM!	XlErrNum	The #NUM! error value occurs when a problem occurs with a number in a formula or function.
#N/A	XlErrNA	The #N/A error value occurs when a value is not available to a function or formula.

The following worksheet demonstrates the most common causes for these
errors.

	A	B	C	D
9				
10	**NULL! in Action**			Notice comma omitted by mistake.
11				
12	1	4	#NULL!	<-- =SUM(A12:A14 B12:B14)
13	2	5	21	<-- =SUM(A12:A14,B12:B14)
14	3	6	21	<-- =SUM(A12:B14)

	A	B	C	D
17	**#VALUE! in Action**			
18				
19	Ben		#VALUE!	<-- =A19+A20+A21
20	3		5	<-- =SUM(A19:A21)
21	2			

	A	B	C
24	**#REF! in Action**		
25			
26		#REF!	<-- =Sheet1!B1
27			
28			
29		Sheet1 deleted	

	A	B	C
24	**#NAME! in Action**		
25			
26		#NAME?	<-- =Benny+3
27			
28			
29		They don't know me!	

	A	B	C
32	**#NUM! in Action**		
33			
34		#NUM!	<-- =IRR(A34:A36,0.1)
35			
36			

	A	B	C
37	**#N/A in Action**		
38			
39	3	#N/A	<-- =VLOOKUP(2,A39:A42,1)
40	4	2	<-- =VLOOKUP(2,A39:A42,1,FALSE)
41	1	#N/A	<-- =VLOOKUP(2,A39:A42,1,TRUE)
42	2		

32 Types and Loops

32.1 Introduction

In this chapter we introduce variable and function types. Using typed variables and functions can make your program more readable and allow it to run faster and use less computer memory. (The jargon "typed variable" or "typed function" means a variable or function that has a type, not something that is typed on a keyboard.) Section 32.5 introduces the looping structures. Looping structures are a way to make your program perform a task repeatedly.

32.2 Using Types

When a function is used in a spreadsheet, the end result is a value. You can use VBA to categorize this value, so that your user-defined function returns only values of a particular type. Values in VBA are categorized into types, either by default or explicitly. The default type associated with a value returned from a function is **Variant. Variant** is a category of values that includes all other categories. If we know that a function should return a specific type of value, it is good practice to explicitly declare the function as returning that type. This technique makes the function work faster and use less computer memory.

You can declare that a function must return a specific type of value by appending the reserved word **As,** followed by the type, to the function declaration line. We demonstrate by rewriting the Chapter 31 function **Function1** to return only an integer value. (This function from the previous chapter multiplies a variable by 3 and adds 1.) We start by writing the first line of the function:

```
function Function2(Parameter) as
```

As soon as you type the space after the word "as," VBA offers you a list of all the available types to choose from:

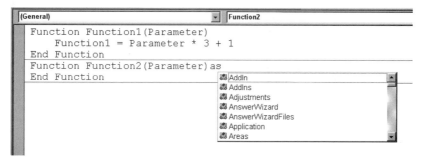

If you continue typing, the options will narrow automatically.

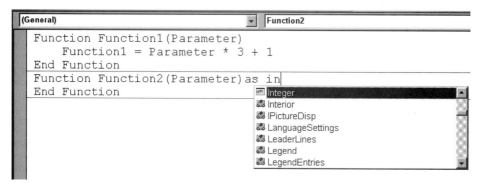

When the word you want is highlighted in the selection window, type the space to follow the word and the word will be inserted for you. Notice we didn't type the reserved words **Function** and **As** with capitals (these will be added by the VBA editor). Now hit [Enter] or the [down arrow] key. VBA will do the capitalization for you. Continue typing; the full function should look like this:

```
Function Function2(Parameter) As Integer
    Function2 = Parameter * 3 + 1
End Function
```

You can now use the new function in Excel. Comparing the results returned with those of **Function1,** you can see that **Function2** returns an integer value by rounding off the results:

	A	B	C
1	**Functions in Action**		
2			
3	Parameter	Function	
4	1.1667	4.5001	<-- =Function1(A4)
5	1.1667	5	<-- =Function2(A5)
6	1.16666	4.49998	<-- =Function1(A6)
7	1.1666	4	<-- =Function2(A7)

The list of Excel and VBA types is very extensive. Some of the more important types will be covered in the next section.

32.3   Variables and Variable Types

This section looks at two kinds of variables: variables internal to the function and parameter variables. Here's an example:

```
Function Function3(Parameter)
    Temp = Parameter * 3 + 1
    Function3 = Temp
End Function
```

In **Function3** the variable **Parameter** is a "parameter variable," which gets its value from the applications that activate the function (either Excel or another function). Parameter variables, like most other variables, are recognized only in the function in which they were created. In contrast, the variable **Temp** stores the value to be returned before actually assigning it to the function's name. **Temp** is *internal* to **Function3,** and is not recognized by Excel or by other VBA functions.

Whenever you assign a value to a name, VBA creates the corresponding variable. This is what happened in **Function3**—we simply typed `Temp = Parameter * 3 + 1`, and VBA created the variable **Temp.** However, letting VBA create variables for you is not always a good idea, since a small typing mistake can completely alter the results of a function (for an example, see **Function4E** later in this section). A much better way of using variables is to explicitly declare our intention before actually using the variable. Variables are declared using the **Dim** statement. The following function uses the **Dim** statement to declare "Temp" before its use.

```
Function Function4(Parameter)
    Dim Temp
    Temp = Parameter * 3 + 1
    Function4 = Temp
End Function
```

	A	B	C
10	**Functions in Action**		
11			
12	Parameter	Function	
13	1.1667	4.5001	<-- =Function3(A12)
14	1.1667	4.5001	<-- =Function4(A13)

We can make VBA alert us if we use an undeclared variable by inserting the **Option Explicit** statement as the first line in the module. With this statement any use of an undeclared variable will result in an error and not the creation of a new variable. The **Option Explicit** statement holds for all the routines in the module. Unfortunately there is no global **Option Explicit** statement. You can have VBA insert the **Option Explicit** statement in every new module. Select (**Tools|Options . . .**) from the VBA menu, tick the **Require Variable Declaration** line, and click the **OK** button

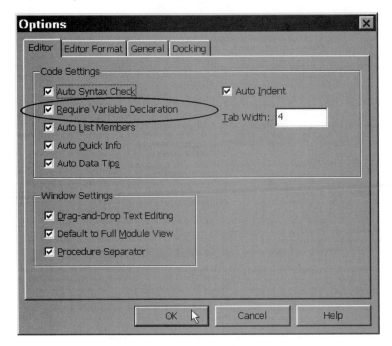

The following function contains a typing error.

```
Function Function4E(Parameter)
    Dim Temp
    remp = Parameter * 3 + 1
    Function4E = Temp
End Function
```

Without the **Option Explicit** statement, Excel merrily displays the following result.

	A	B	C
17	**Functions in Action**		
18			
19	Parameter	Function	
20	1.1667	4.5001	<-- =Function4(A20)
21	1.1667	0	<-- =Function4E(A21)

But, inserting the **Option Explicit** statement before the VBA code and re-calculating the worksheet results in the following "Run Time Error":

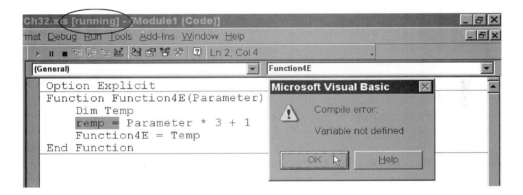

Once we are alerted to the problem, we can click the OK button, stop VBA from running, and fix the problem by replacing "remp" with "Temp." (Recall from Chapter 31 that after you fix the mistake in VBA, you have to press the button with a small square on the VBA editor toolbar.)

Like values, variables have types. Variables declared without a specific type (like Temp) are given the type **Variant.** Using variables and functions of the type **Variant** involves quite a lot of overhead. It is therefore recommended that functions and variables be given a specific type.[1]

You can declare a variable of a specific type by appending the reserved word **As** to the variable declaration. The following function is an integer version of **Function4.** We can now use this function in Excel and compare the results with **Function2** and **Function4.**

---

1. Attentive readers will notice that we violate this rule quite often in this book! Oh well . . .

```
Function Function5(Parameter As Integer)_
    As Integer
    Dim Temp As Integer
    Temp = Parameter * 3 + 1
    Function5 = Temp
End Function
```

	A	B	C
24	**Functions in Action**		
25			
26	Parameter	Function	
27	1.1667	5	<-- =Function2(A27)
28	1.1667	4.5001	<-- =Function4(A28)
29	1.1667	4	<-- =Function5(A29)
30	1.16666	4	<-- =Function2(A30)
31	1.16666	4.49998	<-- =Function4(A31)
32	1.16666	4	<-- =Function5(A32)

A Short List of VBA Types

Data Type	Range
Byte	0 to 255
Boolean	True or False
Integer	$-32,768$ to $32,767$
Long (integer)	$-2,147,483,648$ to $2,147,483,647$
Single (floating point)	$-3.403E38$ to $-1.401E-45$ for negative values;
	$1.401E-45$ to $3.403E38$ for positive values
Double (floating point)	$-1.798E308$ to $-4.941E-324$ for negative values;
	$4.941E-324$ to $1.798E308$ for positive values
Currency (scaled integer)	$-922,337,203,685,477.5808$ to $922,337,203,685,477.5807$
Decimal	$\pm79,228,162,514,264,337,593,543,950,335$ with no decimal point;
	$\pm7.9228162514264337593543950$ with 28 places to the right of the decimal
Date	January 1, 100 to December 31, 9999
String (variable length)	0 to approximately 2 billion
String (fixed length)	1 to approximately 65,400
Variant (with numbers)	Any numeric value up to the range of a Double
Variant (with characters)	Same range as for variable-length String

32.4   The Boolean and Comparison Operators

Usually the expressions used as conditions in an **If** statement are constructed using the Comparison and/or Boolean operators. The following is a list of the most common comparison operators:

Operator	Meaning
$<$	Less than
$<=$	Less than or equal to
$>$	Greater than
$>=$	Greater than or equal to
$=$	Equal to
$<>$	Not equal to

The next function uses a Boolean operator to check whether both **Parameter1 < 10** *and* whether **Parameter2 > 15**:

```
Function AndDemo(Parameter1, Parameter2)
    If (Parameter1 < 10) And (Parameter2 > 15) _
    Then
        AndDemo = 3
    Else
        AndDemo = 12
    End If
End Function
```

Here are two illustrations:

	A	B	C
1	**AndDemo in Action**		
2			
3	Parameter1	3	? < 10 ?
4	Parameter2	12	? > 15 ?
5	AndDemo	12	<-- =AndDemo(B3,B4)

	A	B	C
1	**AndDemo in Action**		
2			
3	Parameter1	3	? < 10 ?
4	Parameter2	33	? > 15 ?
5	AndDemo	3	<-- =AndDemo(B3,B4)

Notice what **AndDemo** does: It checks whether *both* Parameter1 < 10 *and* Parameter2 > 15. If both conditions hold, then the function returns a value of 3. Otherwise (that is, if either of the conditions is violated) it returns 12. (Note that both conditions are in parentheses.)

The following function and the activation screen shot demonstrate all four possible combinations of two conditions and the resulting combined condition:

```
Function AndDemoTable(Parameter1, Parameter2)
    AndDemoTable = Parameter1 And Parameter2
End Function
```

	A	B	C	D
1	**AndDemoTable in Action**			
2				
3	Parameter1	Parameter2		
4	TRUE	TRUE	TRUE	<-- =AndDemoTable(A4,B4)
5	TRUE	FALSE	FALSE	<-- =AndDemoTable(A5,B5)
6	FALSE	TRUE	FALSE	<-- =AndDemoTable(A6,B6)
7	FALSE	FALSE	FALSE	<-- =AndDemoTable(A7,B7)

The function **OrDemo,** as follows, checks whether at least one of the two conditions holds:

```
Function OrDemo(Parameter1, Parameter2)
    If (Parameter1 < 10) Or (Parameter2 > 15) _
    Then
        AndDemo = 3
    Else
        AndDemo = 12
    End If
End Function
```

	A	B	C	D
22	**OrDemo in Action**			
23				
24	Parameter1	Parameter2		
25	1	1	3	<-- =OrDemo(A25,B25)
26	1	30	3	<-- =OrDemo(A26,B26)
27	11	1	12	<-- =OrDemo(A27,B27)
28	11	30	3	<-- =OrDemo(A28,B28)

Notice what **OrDemo** does: It checks whether *either* Parameter1 < 10 *or* Parameter2 > 15 *or both* conditions hold. Only if both conditions are violated will the function return a value of 12. Otherwise (that is, if either or both of the conditions hold) it returns 3. (Note that both conditions are in parentheses.)

The following function and the activation screen shot demonstrate all four possible combinations of two conditions and the resulting combined condition:

```
Function OrDemoTable(Parameter1, Parameter2)
    OrDemoTable = Parameter1 Or Parameter2
End Function
```

	A	B	C	D
10	**OrDemoTable in Action**			
11				
12	Parameter1	Parameter2		
13	TRUE	TRUE	TRUE	<-- =OrDemoTable(A13,B13)
14	TRUE	FALSE	TRUE	<-- =OrDemoTable(A14,B14)
15	FALSE	TRUE	TRUE	<-- =OrDemoTable(A15,B15)
16	FALSE	FALSE	FALSE	<-- =OrDemoTable(A16,B16)

32.5 Loops

Looping structures are used when you need to do something repeatedly. As always, there is more than one way to achieve the desired effect. In general there are two major looping constructs:

• *A top-checking loop:* The loop condition is checked before anything else gets done. The something to be done can be left undone if the condition is not fulfilled on entry to the loop.

• *A bottom-checking loop:* The loop condition is checked after the something to be done is done. The something to be done will always be done at least once.

VBA has the two major looping structures covered from all possible angles by the **Do** statement and its variations. All the following subsections will use a version of the factorial function for demonstration purposes. The function used is defined as

$$f(0) = 1 \qquad f(1) = 1 \qquad f(2) = 2 * f(1) = 2 \quad \dots \quad f(n) = n * f(n-1)$$

32.5.1   The Do While Statement

The **Do While** statement is a member of the top-checking loop family. It makes VBA execute one or more statements zero or more times while a condition is true. The following function demonstrates this behavior:

```
Function DoWhileDemo(N As Integer) As Integer
    Dim i, j As Integer
    If N < 2 Then
        DoWhileDemo = 1
    Else
        i = 1
        j = 1
        Do While i <= N
            j = j * i
            i = i + 1
        Loop
        DoWhileDemo = j
    End If
End Function
```

	A	B	C
1	**DoWhileDemo in Action**		
2			
3	N		
4	1	1	<-- =DoWhileDemo(A4)
5	1.4	1	<-- =DoWhileDemo(A5)
6	2	2	<-- =DoWhileDemo(A6)
7	7	5040	<-- =DoWhileDemo(A7)
8	8	#VALUE!	<-- =DoWhileDemo(A8)

Notice that noninteger values get rounded to the nearest integer when transferred to an integer parameter in the function. Also notice that the function cannot handle values greater then 7, because—as explained in section 32.3—the type **Integer** is restricted to values between −32,678 and +32,767. The following function solves the problem by using the **Long** variable type, which allows larger integer values.

```
Function DoWhileDemo(N As Integer) As Long
    Dim i As Integer
    Dim j As Long
    If N < 2 Then
        DoWhileDemo = 1
    Else
        i = 1
        j = 1
        Do While i <= N
            j = j * i
            i = i + 1
        Loop
        DoWhileDemo = j
    End If
End Function
```

	A	B	C
1	**DoWhileDemo in Action**		
2			
3	N		
4	1	1	<-- =DoWhileDemo(A4)
5	1.4	1	<-- =DoWhileDemo(A5)
6	2	2	<-- =DoWhileDemo(A6)
7	7	5040	<-- =DoWhileDemo(A7)
8	8	40320	<-- =DoWhileDemo(A8)

32.5.2   The Do . . . Loop While Statement

The **Do . . . Loop While** statement is a member of the bottom-checking loop family. It makes VBA execute one or more statements one or more times while a condition is true. The following function demonstrates this behavior.

```
Function DoLoopWhileDemo(N As Integer) As Long
    Dim i As Integer
    Dim j As Long
    If N < 2 Then
        DoLoopWhileDemo = 1
    Else
        i = 1
        j = 1
        Do
            j = j * i
            i = i + 1
        Loop While i <= N
        DoLoopWhileDemo = j
    End If
End Function
```

	A	B	C
11	**DoLoopWhileDemo in Action**		
12			
13	N		
14	1	1	<-- =DoLoopWhileDemo(A14)
15	1.4	1	<-- =DoLoopWhileDemo(A15)
16	2	2	<-- =DoLoopWhileDemo(A16)
17	7	5040	<-- =DoLoopWhileDemo(A17)
18	8	40320	<-- =DoLoopWhileDemo(A18)

32.5.3   The Do Until Statement

The **Do Until** is a member of the top-checking loop family. It makes VBA execute one or more statements zero or more times until a condition is met. The following function demonstrates this behavior:

```
Function DoUntilDemo(N As Integer) As Long
    Dim i As Integer
    Dim j As Long
    If N < 2 Then
        DoUntilDemo = 1
    Else
        i = 1
        j = 1
```

```
            Do Until i > N
                j = j * i
                i = i + 1
            Loop
            DoUntilDemo = j
        End If
End Function
```

	A	B	C
21	**DoUntilDemo in Action**		
22			
23	N		
24	1	1	<-- =DoUntilDemo(A24)
25	1.4	1	<-- =DoUntilDemo(A25)
26	2	2	<-- =DoUntilDemo(A26)
27	7	5040	<-- =DoUntilDemo(A27)
28	8	40320	<-- =DoUntilDemo(A28)

32.5.4   The Do . . . Loop Until Statement

The **Do . . . Loop Until** statement is a member of the bottom-checking loop family. It makes VBA execute one or more statements one or more times until a condition becomes true. The following function demonstrates this behavior:

```
Function DoLoopUntilDemo(N As Integer) As Long
    Dim i As Integer
    Dim j As Long
    If N < 2 Then
        DoLoopUntilDemo = 1
    Else
        i = 1
        j = 1
        Do
            j = j * i
            i = i + 1
        Loop Until i > N
        DoLoopUntilDemo = j
    End If
End Function
```

	A	B	C
31	**DoLoopUntilDemo in Action**		
32			
33	N		
34	1	1	<-- =DoLoopUntilDemo(A34)
35	1.4	1	<-- =DoLoopUntilDemo(A35)
36	2	2	<-- =DoLoopUntilDemo(A36)
37	7	5040	<-- =DoLoopUntilDemo(A37)
38	8	40320	<-- =DoLoopUntilDemo(A38)

32.5.5   The While Statement

The **While** statement is a leftover from Quick Basic (a forerunner of VBA).[2] The **While** statement, a member of the top-checking loop family, executes a series of statements as long as a given condition is true. The following function demonstrates its workings.

```
Function WhileDemo(N As Integer) As Long
    Dim i As Integer
    Dim j As Long
    If N <= 1 Then
        WhileDemo = 1
    Else
        i = 1
        j = 1
        While i <= N
            j = j * i
            i = i + 1
        Wend
        WhileDemo = j
    End If
End Function
```

---

2. A quotation from the Microsoft VBA help file: "**Tip:** The **Do . . . Loop** statement provides a more structured and flexible way to perform looping."

	A	B	C
41	**WhileDemo in Action**		
42			
43	N		
44	1	1	<-- =WhileDemo(A44)
45	1.4	1	<-- =WhileDemo(A45)
46	2	2	<-- =WhileDemo(A46)
47	7	5040	<-- =WhileDemo(A47)
48	8	40320	<-- =WhileDemo(A48)

32.5.6   The For Loop

One last (for now) variation on the loopy theme, the **For** loop, is used mainly for loops where the number of times the action is repeated is known in advance. The following functions demonstrate its use and variations.

```
Function ForDemo1(N As Integer) As Long
    Dim i As Integer
    Dim j As Long
    If N <= 1 Then
        ForDemo1 = 1
    Else
        j = 1
        For i = 1 To N Step 1
            j = j * i
        Next i
        ForDemo1 = j
    End If
End Function
```

	A	B	C
51	**ForDemo1 in Action**		
52			
53	N		
54	1	1	<-- =ForDemo1(A54)
55	1.4	1	<-- =ForDemo1(A55)
56	2	2	<-- =ForDemo1(A56)
57	7	5040	<-- =ForDemo1(A57)
58	8	40320	<-- =ForDemo1(A58)

The **Step** part of the statement can be dropped if (as is in our case) the increment is 1. For example,

```
For i = 1 To N
    j = j * i
Next i
```

If you want the loop to count down, the **Step** argument can be negative, as demonstrated in the next function:

```
Function ForDemo2(N As Integer) As Long
    Dim i As Integer
    Dim j As Long
    If N <= 1 Then
        ForDemo2 = 1
    Else
      j = 1
        For i = N To 1 Step -1
            j = j * i
        Next i
        ForDemo2 = j
    End If
End Function
```

	A	B	C
61	**ForDemo2 in Action**		
62			
63	N		
64	1	1	<-- =ForDemo2(A64)
65	1.4	1	<-- =ForDemo2(A65)
66	2	2	<-- =ForDemo2(A66)
67	7	5040	<-- =ForDemo2(A67)
68	8	40320	<-- =ForDemo2(A68)

The **For** loop can be exited early by using the **Exit For** statement, as demonstrated in the next function:

```
Function ExitForDemo(Parameter1, Parameter2)
    Dim i As Integer
    Dim Sum As Long
    Sum = 0
    For i = 1 To Parameter1
        Sum = Sum + i
        If Sum > Parameter2 Then Exit For
    Next i
    ExitForDemo = Sum
End Function
```

	A	B	C	D
71	**ExitForDemo in Action**			
72				
73	Parameter1	Parameter2		
74	5	22	15	<-- =ExitForDemo(A74,B74)
75	6	22	21	<-- =ExitForDemo(A75,B75)
76	7	22	28	<-- =ExitForDemo(A76,B76)
77	8	22	28	<-- =ExitForDemo(A77,B77)

Exercises

1. Fibonacci numbers, introduced in exercise 10 of Chapter 31, are defined as follows:

    $F(0) = 0$
    $F(1) = 1$
    $F(2) = F(0) + F(1) = 1$
    $F(3) = F(1) + F(2) = 2$
    $F(4) = F(2) + F(3) = 3$
    and so on.

    In general, $F(n) = F(n-2) + F(n-1)$.

    Rewrite the function in exercise 10 of Chapter 31 without using recursion.

	A	B	C
1	**Fibonacci in Action**		
2			
3	n	Fibonacci	
4	1	1	<-- =Fibonacci(A4)
5	2	1	<-- =Fibonacci(A5)
6	3	2	<-- =Fibonacci(A6)
7	6	8	<-- =Fibonacci(A7)
8	12	144	<-- =Fibonacci(A8)
9	24	46368	<-- =Fibonacci(A9)

2.   Write a version of the function **HomeFactorial** (see section 31.8) that does not use recursion. Hint: We can describe the workings of the factorial function by saying, "To calculate 6! multiply the numbers from 1 to 6."

	A	B	C
12	**HomeFactorial in Action**		
13			
14	n	HomeFactorial	
15	-1	0	<-- =HomeFactorial(A15)
16	0	0	<-- =HomeFactorial(A16)
17	1	1	<-- =HomeFactorial(A17)
18	2	2	<-- =HomeFactorial(A18)
19	3	6	<-- =HomeFactorial(A19)
20	8	40320	<-- =HomeFactorial(A20)

3.   Write a function **NewPV(CF, r)** that calculates the present value of a given cash flow CF at interest rate r for five periods:

$$NewPV(CF, r) = \frac{CF}{(1+r)^1} + \frac{CF}{(1+r)^2} + \frac{CF}{(1+r)^3} + \frac{CF}{(1+r)^4} + \frac{CF}{(1+r)^5}$$

	A	B	C	D
23	**NewPV in Action**			
24				
25	CF	r	NewPV	
26	100.0000	10%	379.0787	<-- =NewPV(A26,B26)
27	50.0000	10%	189.5393	<-- =NewPV(A27,B27)
28	100.0000	1%	485.3431	<-- =NewPV(A28,B28)
29	50.0000	1%	242.6716	<-- =NewPV(A29,B29)

4.   Rewrite the function in exercise 3 as **BetterNewPV(CF, r, n),** so it can deal with *n* periods.

	A	B	C	D	E
32	**BetterNewPV in Action**				
33					
34	CF	r	n	BetterNewPV	
35	100.0000	10%	5	379.0787	<-- =BetterNewPV(A35,B35,C35)
36	50.0000	10%	5	189.5393	<-- =BetterNewPV(A36,B36,C36)
37	100.0000	1%	10	947.1305	<-- =BetterNewPV(A37,B37,C37)
38	50.0000	1%	10	473.5652	<-- =BetterNewPV(A38,B38,C38)

5.   A bank offers different interest rates on loans. The rate is based on the size of the periodical repayment (**CF**) and the following table. Rewrite the function in exercise 4 as **BankPV(CF, r, n)** so that it reflects the present value of a loan in the bank.

For Periodical Repayments <=	The Interest Rate Is
100.00	r
500.00	$r - 0.5\%$
1,000.00	$r - 1.1\%$
5,000.00	$r - 1.7\%$
1,000,000.00	$r - 2.1\%$

	A	B	C	D	E
41	**BankPV in Action**				
42					
43	CF	r	n	BankPV	
44	$100.00	5%	5	$432.95	<-- =BankPV(A44,B44,C44)
45	$100.01	5%	5	$439.04	<-- =BankPV(A45,B45,C45)
46	$1,000.00	5%	5	$4,464.36	<-- =BankPV(A46,B46,C46)
47	$1,000.01	5%	5	$4,540.79	<-- =BankPV(A47,B47,C47)
48	$5,000.00	5%	5	$22,703.71	<-- =BankPV(A48,B48,C48)
49	$5,000.01	5%	5	$22,964.11	<-- =BankPV(A49,B49,C49)

6.   A bank offers different interest rates on deposit accounts. The rate is based on the size of the periodical deposit (**CF**) and the following table. Write a future value function **BankFV(CF, r, n).**

For Periodical Deposits	The Interest Rate Is
$<=100.00$	r
$<=500.00$	$r + 0.5\%$
$<=1,000.00$	$r + 1.1\%$
$<=5,000.00$	$r + 1.7\%$
$>5,000.00$	$r + 2.1\%$

	A	B	C	D	E
52	**BankFV in Action**				
53					
54	CF	r	n	**BankFV**	
55	$100.00	5%	5	$580.19	<-- =BankFV(A55,B55,C55)
56	$100.01	5%	5	$588.86	<-- =BankFV(A56,B56,C56)
57	$1,000.00	5%	5	$5,992.91	<-- =BankFV(A57,B57,C57)
58	$1,000.01	5%	5	$6,099.47	<-- =BankFV(A58,B58,C58)
59	$5,000.00	5%	5	$30,497.07	<-- =BankFV(A59,B59,C59)
60	$5,000.01	5%	5	$30,856.78	<-- =BankFV(A60,B60,C60)

7.   Another bank offers a 1 percent increase in interest rate to savings accounts with a balance of more then $10,000.00. Write a future value function **Bank1FV(CF, r, n)** that reflects this policy.

	A	B	C	D	E
63	**Bank1FV in Action**				
64					
65	CF	r	n	**BankFV**	
66	$100.00	5%	5	$580.19	<-- =Bank1FV(A66,B66,C66)
67	$1,000.00	5%	5	$5,801.91	<-- =Bank1FV(A67,B67,C67)
68	$5,000.00	5%	5	$29,691.39	<-- =Bank1FV(A68,B68,C68)

8.   The bank in exercise 7 changed its bonus policy and now offers the interest rate increase based on the following table. Rewrite **Bank1FV(CF, r, n)** to reflect this change.

Balance	Interest Rate
$\leq 1{,}000.00$	$r + 0.2\%$
$\leq 5{,}000.00$	$r + 0.5\%$
$\leq 10{,}000.00$	$r + 1.0\%$
$> 10{,}000.00$	$r + 1.3\%$

	A	B	C	D	E
71	**Bank2FV in Action**				
72					
73	CF	r	n	**BankFV**	
74	$1,000.00	5%	5	$5,884.33	<-- =Bank2FV(A74,B74,C74)
75	$1,000.01	5%	5	$5,884.39	<-- =Bank2FV(A75,B75,C75)
76	$5,000.00	5%	5	$30,033.93	<-- =Bank2FV(A76,B76,C76)
77	$5,000.01	5%	5	$30,033.99	<-- =Bank2FV(A77,B77,C77)

33 Macros and User Interaction

33.1 Introduction

A macro is a VBA user routine used to automate routine or repetitive operations in Excel. Macros are also called subroutines; we use the names interchangeably. Some of the VBA user interaction routines are covered in sections 33.3 and 33.4. Modules (briefly mentioned in Chapter 31) are given fuller coverage as the last subject of the chapter.

33.2 Macro Subroutines

The first line of a macro subroutine gives the macro a name and lists the parameters if any. It is very similar to the first line of a function:

```
Sub MacroName()
```

The last line indicates the end of the macro and so looks (very appropriately) like this:

```
End Sub
```

Separating the first and last line are the statements that the macro executes. The following is a very simple macro that puts a message on the screen.

```
Sub SayHi()
    MsgBox "Hi", , "I say Hi"
End Sub
```

The macro introduces a built-in VBA macro called **MsgBox.** It also introduces the way a macro is activated (called) from a VBA routine. **MsgBox** is named as a command on a line followed by a list of arguments separated by commas. Notice the syntax:

```
MsgBox "Hi", , "I say Hi"
```

There are three arguments:

• "Hi" is the message that will be displayed.

• The second argument is empty: notice the space between the commas. This argument can be used to define buttons for the message box.

• The third argument is "I say Hi"—this is the message box title.

A macro can be activated (run) from Excel in various ways. The simplest way of running a macro is from the tools menu (**Tools|Macro|Macros . . .),** or by using the keyboard shortcut [Alt + F8]. Either way, the macro selection box appears. The box lists all available macros alphabetically. Find our macro, click on its name, and click the run button.

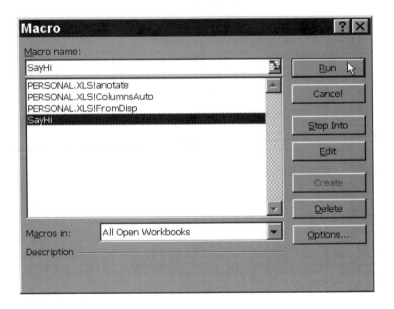

And this is what you will see:

At this point Excel is locked up. You have to click the **OK** button before you can proceed.

33.2.1   Keyboard Shortcut for Macros

Using a keyboard shortcut is a faster way to make a macro run. To attach a shortcut to our macro:

1. Select the **Options** button from the macro selection box.
2. Type a character in the provided space, and click **OK**.
3. Close the macro selection box using the corner **X**.

You can now activate the macro using the shortcut ([Ctrl + h] in our case).

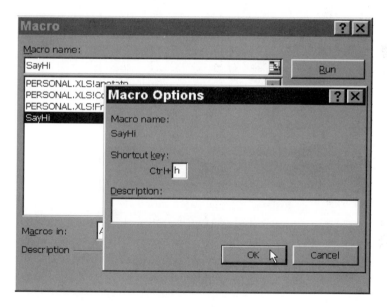

33.2.2   Attaching Macros to a Toolbar

You can attach macros to a button on a tool bar, and later activate the macro by clicking the button. To attach **SayHi** to a button, open the toolbars menu (**View|Toolbars|Customize . . .**) and select the **Commands** pane.

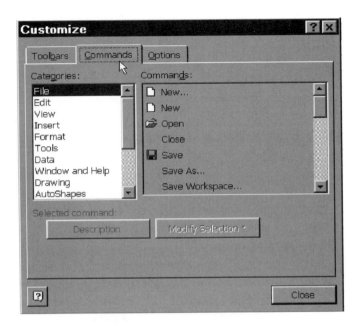

Scroll down the **Categories** subwindow to the Macros item.

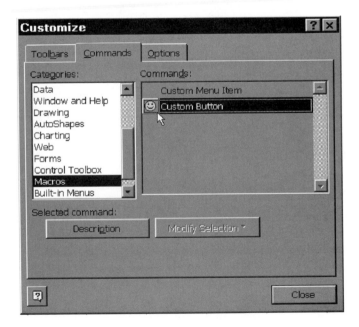

Select the Custom Button and drag it to a toolbar. (Keep the left mouse button pressed while moving the mouse.)

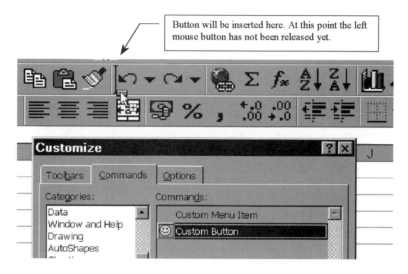

Right click on the newly inserted button, and select **AssignMacro** from the menu.

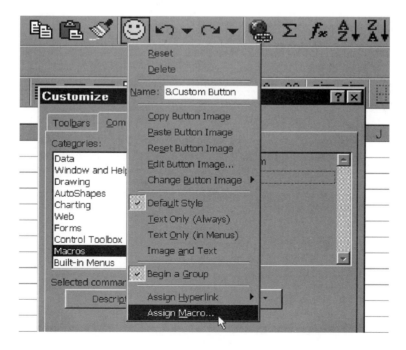

Select our macro from the list and click the **OK** button. Click the **Close** button. **SayHi** is now attached to the smiling button on the tool bar.

The image on the button and the tool tip attached to it can also be customized. For details refer to the Excel Help file.

33.3   User Output and the MsgBox Function

The **MsgBox** function displays a message on the screen and returns a value based on the button clicked. Some of the different options available with this function are demonstrated in the following macros:

```
Sub MsgBoxDefault()
    Dim Temp As Integer
    Temp = MsgBox("Default Message", , _
        "Default Title")
    MsgBox "The value returned by MsgBox is: _
        " & Temp
End Sub
```

Note: The default configuration of **MsgBox** produces one **OK** button. The Default title is "Microsoft Excel." Clicking the **OK** button makes **MsgBox** return the value 1.

```
Sub MsgBoxOKCancel()
    Dim Temp As Integer
    Temp = MsgBox("Default Message", vbOKCancel)
    MsgBox "The value returned by MsgBox is: _
        " & Temp
End Sub
```

As previously noted, the second argument to **MsgBox** determines which buttons are going to be displayed. This incarnation of the demo macro uses the constant **vbOKCancel** to produce the two buttons **OK** and **Cancel.** Note that if the **Cancel** button is clicked, **MsgBox** returns the value 2.

The following is a list of some of the constants that can be used as the second argument of **MsgBox,** together with the message box they produce:

VbOKOnly

VbOKCancel

VbAbortRetryIgnore

VbYesNoCancel

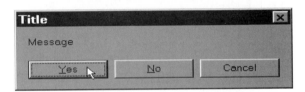

VbYesNo

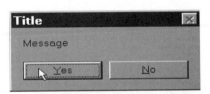

VbRetryCancel

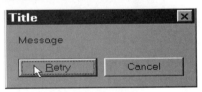

VbCritical

VbQuestion

VbExclamation

VbInformation

The values that can be returned by **MsgBox** are as follows:

Constant	Value	Description
vbOK	1	**OK** button clicked
vbCancel	2	**Cancel** button clicked
vbAbort	3	**Abort** button clicked
vbRetry	4	**Retry** button clicked
vbIgnore	5	**Ignore** button clicked
vbYes	6	**Yes** button clicked
vbNo	7	**No** button clicked

33.4   User Input and the InputBox Function

InputBox is an internal VBA function used to get textual information from the user into a variable in a subroutine (a macro by any other name . . .). The workings of the function are demonstrated in the following present-value calculator macro. The macro **PVCalculator** calculates $\sum\limits_{t=1}^{10} \dfrac{CF}{(1.05)^t}$, where CF is a number entered by the user:

```
Sub PVCalculator()
    Dim CF
    CF = InputBox("Enter the cash flow value _
        please", "PV calculator", "100")
    MsgBox "The present value of " & CF & _
        " At 5% for 10 periods is: " & _
        Round(Application.PV(0.05, 10, -CF), _
        2),vb Information, "PV calculator"
End Sub
```

Note the syntax:

```
CF = InputBox("Enter the cash flow value _
    please", "PV calculator", "100")
```

• "Enter ... please," the first argument to **InputBox,** is the message to display.

• "PV calculator," the second argument, is the title for the box.

• "100," the third argument, is the default string to place in the box.

• If you do not replace the default value by some other value, running the macro should result in the following:

At this point you can replace "100" with some other number. (In this example, we've chosen to leave it.) Clicking on the OK box produces the following box:

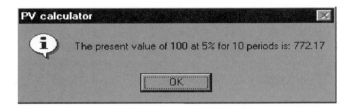

The macro also introduces a new VBA operator **&**. This operator is used to concatenate (combine) its two operands into one string of characters. It merits a small demo function on its own. Notice that nonstring operands are converted into strings.

```
Function ConcatDemo(Parameter1, Parameter2)
    ConcatDemo = Parameter1 & Parameter2
End Function
```

	A	B	C	D
1	**ConcatDemo in Action**			
2				
3	Parameter1	Parameter2		
4	1	2	12	<-- =ConcatDemo(A4,B4)
5	Ben	Jerry	BenJerry	<-- =ConcatDemo(A5,B5)
6	Ben	1	Ben1	<-- =ConcatDemo(A6,B6)
7	Jerry	2	Jerry2	<-- =ConcatDemo(A7,B7)

33.5   Modules

VBA organizes user-defined functions and subroutines in units called modules. We can (and sometimes should) have more then one module in a VBA project (that is, the part of the workbook that has our functions and subroutines). Modules have names: By default VBA uses the name "Module" followed by a number to indicate the module's name, but you might find it useful (as we have done on the workbook accompanying this book) to give them somewhat more descriptive names.

To rename a module (in the VBA editor), select the module on the project explorer pane.

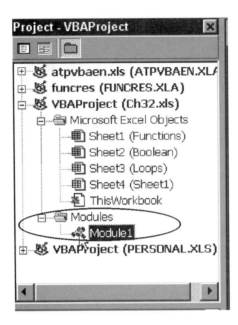

If the project explorer pane is not visible, select **Project Explorer** from the **View** menu.

Once a module is selected, the module's list of properties should appear in the properties pane. Click on the module's name (it should be the only property available) and change it (use one word only, and only digits and alphabetic characters).

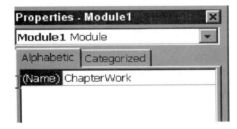

Once you tap the [Enter] key the name is changed. Notice the change in the project explorer.

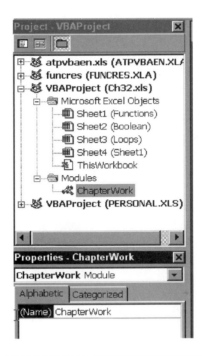

Exercises

1.   Write a macro that displays the following message box. The message box should be on top of all other windows, and it should prevent the user from doing anything in any application until one of the buttons is clicked.

Hint: You need to use some options of **MsgBox** that were not covered in the text; use the VBA Help system.

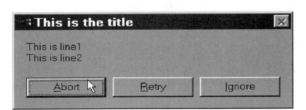

2.   Write a present-value calculator macro similar to the one that appears in section 33.4. However—as illustrated here—your macro should ask the user for the cash flow value, the interest rate, and the number of periods. It should then display the result in a message box. Sensible default values should be supplied for all arguments. Do not use the excel function **PV;** write your own present-value function and use it. A reminder:

$$PV(CF, r, n) = \sum_{i=1}^{n} \frac{CF}{(1+r)^i}$$

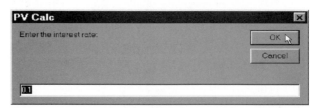

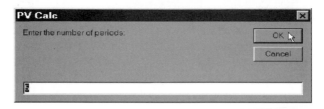

	A	B	C
1			
2			
3		100	
4		10%	
5		5	
6		379.0787	<-- =-PV(B4,B5,B3)
7			
8			
9			
10			
11			
12			

PV Calc

PV is:379.078676940845

OK

You can use the **PV** function provided by Excel, as we did, to verify the correctness of your macro.

3.   Rewrite the macro in the previous exercise so that the user interface is as demonstrated in the following screen shots. Some of the functions needed to write the macro were not covered in the text. We used the following functions:

- **Val**—A function used to convert a string of digits to a number.
- **Left**—A function used to return the left part of a string.
- **Right**—A function used to return the right part of a string.
- **FormatPercent**—A function used to format a number.
- **FormatCurrency**—A function used to format a number.

More information about these functions is available from the VBA Help file; we recommend you use it.

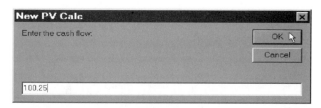

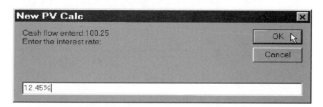

	A	B	C
1			
2			
3			
4		100.2500	
5		12.4500%	
6		13	
7		£630.0580	<-- =-PV(B4,B5,B3)

Note: Your computer might display a different currency symbol.

4. Rewrite the macro in the previous exercise so that it deals properly with the **Cancel** button.

    • A simple version of the new macro will abort the macro if **Cancel** is clicked in any stage.

    • A more sophisticated version of the new macro will allow the user to reenter the data from scratch.

    • The most sophisticated version of the new macro will allow reentering the data using the old data as a default.

Note: The last version is a slightly more complicated exercise using loops within loops.

5.   Write a payment-schedule calculator macro; the macro is to ask the user for the sum of the loan, the number of payments, and the interest rate. Assume payment at the end of the period. The output should look like the following example:

Hints:

- You may want to use the worksheet function **PMT** .
- The following macro and its output might be of interest.

```
Sub StringConcat()
    Dim S As String
    S = "Col1" & Chr(9) & "Col2" ' Chr(9) _
        is the Tab
    S = S & Chr(13) & "aaa" & Chr(9) & "bbb"
    MsgBox S
End Sub
```

Here is an example of the requested macro in action:

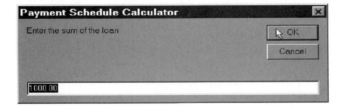

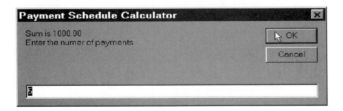

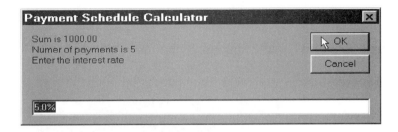

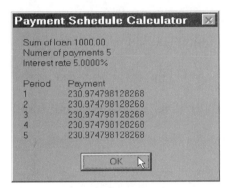

6. Rewrite the payment-schedule calculator macro so that it displays the payments broken down to interest and capital payments. The input boxes in the example were removed for compactness.

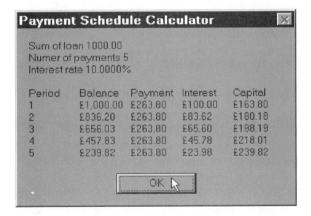

7. Write a payment-schedule calculator macro; the macro is to ask the user for the sum of the loan, the payment, and the interest rate. Assume payment at the end of the period. The macro should display the payments broken down to interest and capital payments. Obviously, the last payment can be smaller (but not larger) than the payment supplied by the user. The output should look like the following example (input boxes removed for compactness).

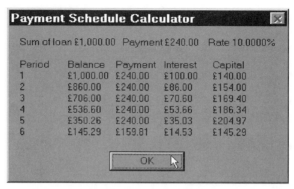

8.   A somewhat more complicated version of the macro in exercise 7 would produce the following better-looking results. Write this version of the macro. *Note:* A quick look at the Help file for the **Format** function might be advantageous at this point.

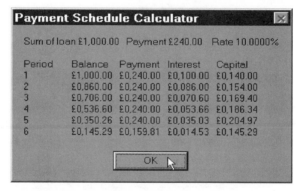

9.   A sliding payment schedule involves payment that changes by a fixed percent over the life of the loan. Write a sliding-payment version of the payment-schedule calculator in exercise 8. In addition to all the inputs described previously, the macro will get a payment rate of change (as percent) from the user. This is what it should look like in action.

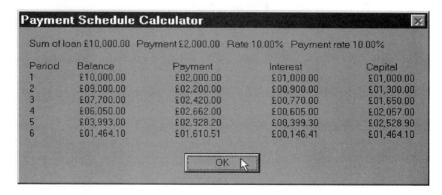

34 Arrays

34.1 Introduction

An array is a group of variables of the same type sharing the same name and referenced individually using an index. Vectors and matrices are good examples of one- and two-dimensional arrays. The first part of the chapter presents simple arrays. Dynamic arrays (whose size can be changed at run time) are discussed in sections 34.4 through 34.6. The chapter concludes with a section on the use of arrays as parameters and the relationship between arrays and worksheet ranges.

34.2 Simple Arrays

There are several ways to declare arrays, all using the **Dim** statement. The simplest way to declare an array is simply to tell VBA the largest value the array index can take. Unless you indicate otherwise, VBA arrays always start with index 0. In the following macro, **MyArray** has six elements numbered 0, 1, 2, …, 5.

```
Sub ArrayDemo1()
    Dim MyArray(5)
    Dim i As Integer
    Dim Temp As String
    For i = 0 To 5
        MyArray(i) = i * i
    Next i
    Temp = ""
    For i = 0 To 5
        Temp = Temp & " # " & MyArray(i)
    Next i
    MsgBox Temp
End Sub
```

If you use **ArrayDemo1** in a spreadsheet, here is the result.

Notice the following:

• **MyArray** has six elements (variables), the first being **MyArray(0)** and the last **MyArray(5).** All Excel arrays start from 0, unless you specify otherwise (see discussion of **Option Base** in section 34.2.3).

• An array element is treated just like a variable; that is, **MyArray(2)** is a variable, and so is **MyArray(i-3)** (assuming that i-3 has an integer value $>=0$ and $<=5$).

• The use of the concatenation operator **&**. This operator concatenates (combines) its two operands to create a string. If an operand to the concatenation operator is not a string, it is converted to a string, and then the concatenation takes place.

If you try to access an array element that is not part of the array, VBA will complain, as demonstrated by the following macro:

```
Sub ArrayDemo2()
    Dim MyArray(5)
    Dim i As Integer
    i = 6
    MsgBox MyArray(i)
End Sub
```

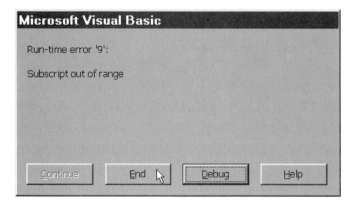

For now just click the **End** button and try to correct the problem. A full treatment of the debugger is beyond the scope of this book.

34.2.1   LBound and UBound

LBound and **UBound** are two internal VBA functions that are very useful when dealing with arrays. These functions return the minimum value (**LBound**), and maximum value (**UBound**) that an array index can have. The following macro demonstrates their use; the message box tells us that **MyArray** has lowest index 0 and highest index 5.

```
Sub ArrayDemo3()
    Dim MyArray(5)
    MsgBox "Minimum value for MyArray index _
        is: " & LBound (MyArray) & Chr(13) _
        & "Maximum value for MyArray index _
        is: " & UBound (MyArray), , _
            "Ubound and Lbound functions demo"
End Sub
```

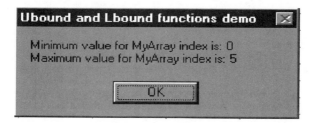

Note the use of **Chr(13)** to break the message line.

34.2.2   Explicitly Declared Index Boundaries

On occasion it is clearer to have an array with the index not starting at zero. You can create such an array by specifying a starting and ending value for the index. This approach is demonstrated in the following function.

```
Sub ArrayDemo4()
    Dim MyArray(6 To 10)
    Dim i As Integer
    MsgBox "Index of MyArray Starts at:" _
        & LBound (MyArray)
    MsgBox "Index of MyArray Stops at:" _
        & UBound (MyArray)
    For i = LBound (MyArray) To UBound (MyArray)
        MyArray(i) = i * i
    Next i
    MsgBox "The Value in MyArray(7) is: " &
MyArray(7)
End Sub
```

And here is the output in quick succession (click the **OK** button to close a message box and move to the next one):

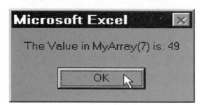

34.2.3   The Option Base Statement

Since most Excel (as opposed to VBA) array indices start at 1, we can use a module option to make all array indices that are not specifically declared start at 1. The following module demonstrates this procedure:

```
Option Explicit
Option Base 1
Sub ArrayDemoBase1()
    Dim MyArray(5)
    MsgBox "Minimum value for MyArray index _
        is: " & LBound (MyArray) & Chr(13) _
        & "Maximum value for MyArray index _
        is: " & UBound (MyArray), , "?bound _
        functions demo"
End Sub
```

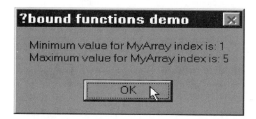

The **Option Base** 1 statement, like all option statements, should be inserted before all functions and subroutines in a module. Like all option statements, its effect is limited to all routines in the current module.

34.3   Multidimensional Arrays

Arrays can have more then one index. In a two-dimensional array the first index refers to the rows and the second to the columns. There is no formal limit to the number of indices you can declare an array with. The syntax for declaring a multidimensional array is demonstrated in the following macros; and so is the fact that array elements can (or indeed should) be typed.

```
Sub Matrix1()
    Dim MyMat(2, 2) As Integer
    Dim I, J As Integer
    Dim Temp As String
```

```
    For I = 0 To 2
        For J = 0 To 2
            MyMat(I, J) = I * J
        Next J
    Next I
    Temp = ""
    For I = 0 To 2
        For J = 0 To 2
            Temp = Temp & MyMat(I, J) & " # "
        Next J
        Temp = Temp & Chr(13)
    Next I
    MsgBox Temp
End Sub
```

Here's the output of this macro:

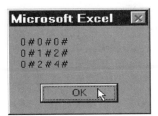

As the following macro demonstrates, we can use explicit index declaration for one or more of the dimensions in multidimensional arrays.

```
Sub Matrix2()
    Dim MyMat1(1 To 3, 1 To 2) As Integer
    Dim I, J As Integer
    Dim Temp As String
    For I = 1 To 3
        For J = 1 To 2
            MyMat1(I, J) = I * J
        Next J
    Next I
    Temp = ""
```

```
      For I = 1 To 3
          For J = LBound (MyMat1, 2) To UBound _
              (MyMat1, 2)
                  Temp = Temp & MyMat1(I, J) & " # "
          Next J
          Temp = Temp & Chr(13)
      Next I
      MsgBox Temp
  End Sub
```

Note the use of the second argument (optional and defaulting to one) to **LBound** and **UBound** (line 12 of the macro).

34.4   Dynamic Arrays and the ReDim Statement

Every so often it can be handy to have the size of an array set (and reset) when the program is running. Dynamic arrays are arrays that can have their size changed at run time. You declare dynamic arrays using the **Dim** statement but with nothing in the parentheses, as in

```
Dim SomeName() As SomeType
```

Before you can use the array you need to set its size using the **ReDim** Statement, as in

```
ReDim ArrayName(SomeIntegerExpression)
```

The **ReDim** Statement can also be used to change the size of a dynamic array (or indeed any array). If you change the size of an array, all the data in the array are lost. Use **ReDim Preserve** to keep the old data, as in

```
ReDim Preserve ArrayName(SomeIntegerExpression)
```

The following macro calculates the present value of a series of future cash flows. To simplify the macro, the interest rate is fixed at 5 percent per period.

```
Sub DynPV()
    Dim n As Integer ' Number of periods
    Dim CF() As Double ' Dynamic array for _
        cash flows
    Dim Temp As Double
    Dim i As Integer
    n = InputBox("Enter number of periods", _
        "Present value calculator", 3)
    ReDim CF(1 To n) ' redimension the array
        ' for demonstration purpose only
    MsgBox "Index starts at: " & LBound(CF) & _
        " and stops at: " & UBound(CF), _
        vbInformation, "Present value calculator"
    For i = 1 To n
        CF(i) = InputBox("Enter value for _
        period " & i, "Present value _
        calculator", 0)
    Next i
    Temp = 0
    For i = 1 To n
        Temp = Temp + CF(i) / 1.05 ^ i
    Next i
    MsgBox "Present value is: " & Temp, _
        vbInformation, "Present value calculator"
End Sub
```

Running the macro produces the following in quick succession.

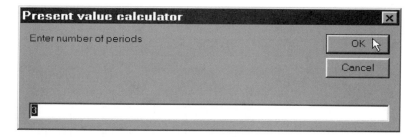

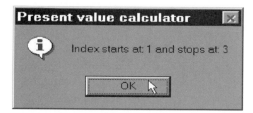

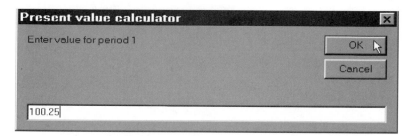

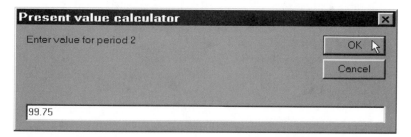

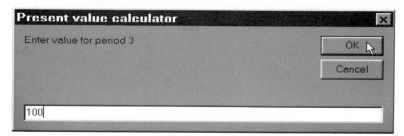

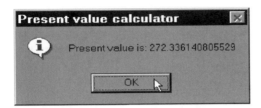

Trying to use a dynamic array that has not been initialized produces the following result:

```
Sub DynaArrayDemo1()
    Dim DynArray() As Integer
    MsgBox DynArray(0)
End Sub
```

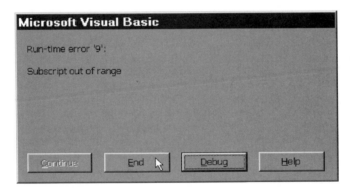

34.4.1   Using the ReDim Preserve Statement

As stated previously, the **Preserve** part of the **ReDim** statement prevents the loss of data from the redimensioned array. The use of **Preserve** imposes two major limitations on the use of **ReDim:**

- The inability to change the lower boundary of the index.
- The inability to change the number of dimensions.

The following macro is an interactive present-value calculator. It asks the user for the number of periods. Using the information supplied by the user, the macro redimensions an array to hold the cash flows for the periods. Once a present value has been calculated, the user is offered the choice of either stopping the macro or calculating the present value of another series of cash flows. As a by-product the macro demonstrates the use of **ReDim** and **Preserve**.

```vba
Sub MoreDynPV()
    Dim n, OldN As Integer ' Number of periods
    Dim CF() As Double ' Dynamic array for _
        cash flows
    Dim Temp As Double
    Dim i, Temp1 As Integer
    Do '******Begin main program loop
        OldN = n
        n = InputBox("Enter number of periods", _
            "Present value calculator", 3)
        Temp1 = MsgBox("Keep old Data?", _
            vbQuestion + vbYesNo, _
            "Present value calculator")
        If Temp1 = vbYes Then
            ReDim Preserve CF(1 To n) ' Redimension
            ' the array and keep the old data
        Else
            ReDim CF(1 To n)
                ' Redimension the array
                ' do not keep the old data
        End If
        For i = 1 To n
            CF(i) = InputBox("Enter value for _
                period" & i, "Present value _
                calculator", CF(i))
        Next i
        Temp = 0
        For i = 1 To n
            Temp = Temp + CF(i) / 1.05 ^ i
        Next i
        MsgBox "Present value is: " & Temp, _
            vbInformation, "Present value _
            calculator"
        Temp1 = MsgBox("Give it another go?", _
            vbQuestion + vbYesNo, _
            "Present value calculator")
    Loop While Temp1 = vbYes '*****End main _
        ' program loop
End Sub
```

One possible activation of the macro might look like the following screen shots, in which the button that has the arrow on it was clicked:

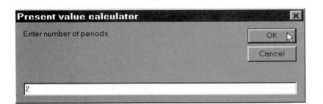

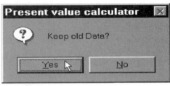

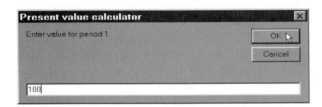

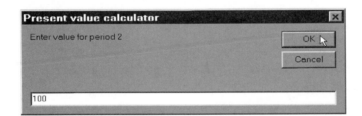

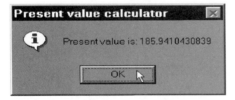

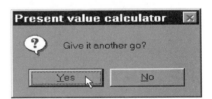

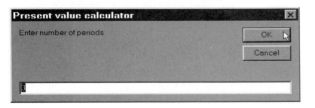

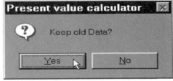

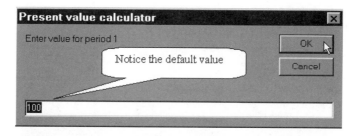

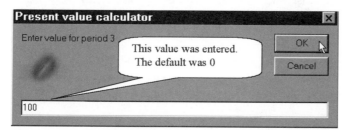

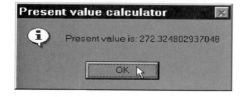

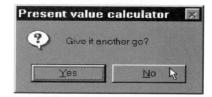

34.5 Array Assignment

Here's an error that's easy to make: In the following example we want to tell VBA that **Array2** is equal to **Array1.** VBA doesn't allow us to do so, as you can see.

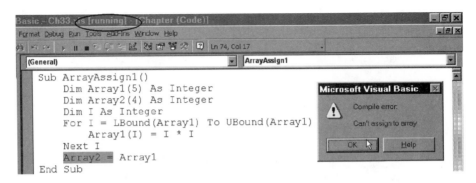

Obviously one way to assign arrays is to assign each element separately using a **For** loop.

```
Sub ArrayAssign()
    Dim Array1(5), Array2(4), I As Integer
    Dim Temp As String
    Temp = ""
    For I = 0 To 5: Array1(I) = I * I: Next I
    For I = 0 To 5
        Temp = Temp & Array1(I) & ":"
    Next I
    I = Len(Temp)
    Temp = Left(Temp, I - 1)
    MsgBox Temp, , "Array1"
    For I = 0 To 4: Array2(I) = Array1(I): Next I
    Temp = ""
    For I = 0 To 4
        Temp = Temp & Array2(I) & ":"
    Next I
    I = Len(Temp)
    Temp = Left(Temp, I - 1)
    MsgBox Temp, , "Array2"
End Sub
```

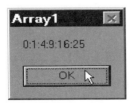
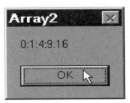

Note the following:

1. The use of the **:** operator to signal the end of a statement (line 5). This way we can put two or more short statements on the same line.

2. The use of the **Len** function to get the length of a string (line 9).

3. The use of the **Left** function to get the left part of a string (line 18). (Yes, a **Right** function is available.)

Another, much shorter, way of assigning arrays is discussed in the next section.

34.6   Variants Containing an Array

A **Variant** type variable can contain an array. The procedure is somewhat more complicated than the declaration of a normal array, but the reward in terms of assignment is sometimes worth the inconvenience (and the cost in program memory allocated to the array). The following macro demonstrates the use of a **Variant** containing an array:

```
Sub VarArrayAssign()
    Dim Array1 'This is a variant
    Dim I As Integer, Temp As String
    Array1 = Array()
    Temp = ""
    ReDim Array1(5) As Integer
    For I = LBound (Array1) To UBound (Array1)
        Array1(I) = I * I
    Next I
    For I = LBound (Array1) To UBound (Array1)
        Temp = Temp & Array1(I) & ":"
    Next I
    I = Len(Temp)
    Temp = Left(Temp, I - 1)
    MsgBox Temp, , "Array1"
End Sub
```

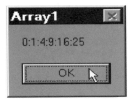

The **Array( )** function (line 4) returns an array. The assignment on the same line makes **Array1** into an array (not initialized at the moment). The **ReDim** statement two lines down makes **Array1** into a five-element **Integer** array.

And now for the reward, as demonstrated by the following macro (compare the macro with **ArrayAssign** in the preceding section):

```
Sub VarArrayAssign()
    Dim Array1 'This is a variant
    Dim Array2 'This is a variant
    Dim I As Integer
    Dim Temp As String
    Array1 = Array()
    Temp = ""
    ReDim Array1(5) As Integer
    For I = LBound (Array1) To UBound (Array1)
        Array1(I) = I * I
    Next I
    For I = LBound (Array1) To UBound (Array1)
        Temp = Temp & Array1(I) & ":"
    Next I
    I = Len(Temp)
    Temp = Left(Temp, I - 1)
    MsgBox Temp, , "VarArray1"
    Temp = ""
'********************Watch this spot
    Array2 = Array1 'Watch this spot
'********************Watch this spot
    For I = LBound (Array2) To UBound (Array2)
        Temp = Temp & Array2(I) & ":"
    Next I
    I = Len(Temp)
    Temp = Left(Temp, I - 1)
    MsgBox Temp, , "VarArray2"
End Sub
```

34.7 Arrays as Parameters to Functions

Arrays can be used as parameters to functions. The following set of functions and subroutines presents an improved version of **MoreDynPV.** Notice how much easier it is to read the main macro **NewDynPV** when all the auxiliary tasks are relegated to separate functions and subroutines.

A function **ComputePV(CF( ), n)** is used to compute the present value of a series of cash flows contained in an array of **Doubles.**

```
Function ComputePV(CF() As Double, n As _
        Integer) As Double
    Dim Temp As Double, i As Integer
    Temp = 0
    For i = 1 To n
        Temp = Temp + CF(i) / 1.05 ^ i
    Next i
    ComputePV = Temp
End Function
```

A subroutine **GetCF(CF( ), n)** is used to query the user for the cash flow values and store them in the **CF** array.

```
Sub GetCf(CF() As Double, n As Integer)
    Dim i As Integer
    For i = 1 To n
        CF(i) = InputBox("Enter value for _
            period " & i, "Present value _
            calculator", CF(i))
    Next i
End Sub
```

Note the fact that in both **ComputePV(CF( ), n)** and **GetCF(CF( ), n),** **CF( )** has to be declared without index information. Consequently, index information has to be transferred to the function. We could use **Lbound** and **Ubound** as an alternative to providing index information.

This is the main macro:

```
Sub NewDynPV()
    Dim n As Integer ' Number of periods
    Dim OldN As Integer ' Old number of periods
    Dim CF() As Double ' Dynamic array for cash flows
    Dim Temp As Double
    Dim i As Integer, Temp1 As Integer
    Dim FirstTime As Boolean
    FirstTime = True
    Do  '************************Begin main loop
        OldN = n
        n = GetN()
        If FirstTime Then
            ReDim CF(1 To n)  ' Redimension the
                              ' array
                              ' No old data to keep
            FirstTime = False ' not the first time
                              ' anymore
        Else
            If KeepOld() Then
                ReDim Preserve CF(1 To n)
                    ' Redimension the array
                    ' and keep the old data
            Else
                ReDim CF(1 To n) ' Redimension the
                                 ' array
                                 ' do not keep the
                                 ' old data
            End If
        End If
        GetCf CF(), n
        Temp = ComputePV(CF, n)
        DisplayPV (Temp)
    Loop While AnotherGo() '*********End main loop
End Sub
```

Here are the auxiliary functions and subroutines, dealing with all sorts of maintenance tasks:

```
Function GetN() As Integer
    GetN = InputBox("Enter number of periods", _
        "Present value calculator", 3)
End Function
Function AnotherGo() As Boolean
    Dim Temp As Integer
    Temp = MsgBox("Give it another go?", _
        vbQuestion + vbYesNo, "Present value _
        calculator")
    AnotherGo = (Temp = vbYes)
End Function
Function KeepOld() As Boolean
    Dim Temp As Integer
    Temp = MsgBox("Keep old Data?", vbQuestion _
        + vbYesNo, "Present value calculator")
    KeepOld = (Temp = vbYes)
End Function
Sub DisplayPV(PV As Double)
    MsgBox "Present value is: " & PV, _
        vbInformation, "Present value calculator"
End Sub
```

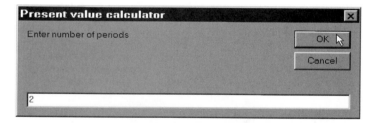

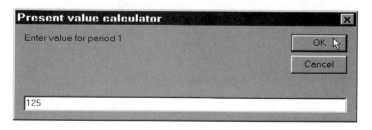

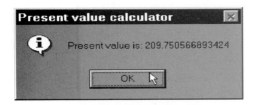

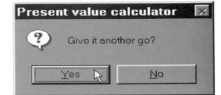

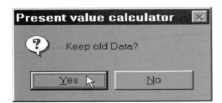

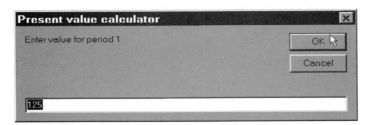

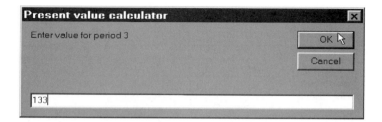

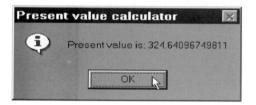
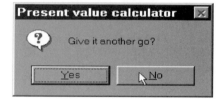

34.7.1 Arrays from a Worksheet

Arrays bear some resemblance to worksheet ranges. We might want to write a function that accepts a range as a parameter. Unfortunately the resemblance is only skin deep, and some manipulation is needed to achieve our goal. A full discussion of worksheet objects is beyond the scope of this book, though an introduction to the subject is provided in Chapter 35. The following function (based on **ComputePV** from the previous section), can actually accept a column range of cells as a parameter, because its parameter is defined as **Variant**.

```
Function VarPV(CF As Variant) As Double
    Dim X As Variant, Temp As Double, _
        i As Integer
    X = CF
    Temp = 0
    For i = LBound (X) To UBound (X)
        Temp = Temp + X(i, 1) / 1.05 ^ i
    Next i
    VarPV = Temp
End Function
```

The declaration of the internal variable "X as Variant" is necessary, and so is the assignment "X = CF" on the third line.

Here is how it looks in Excel:

	A	B	C	D	E
1	VarPV in Action				
2					
3	CF	VarPV		NPV	
4	100	432.9477	<-- =VarPV(A4:A$8)	432.9477	<-- =NPV(0.05,A4:A$8)
5	100	354.5951	<-- =VarPV(A5:A$8)	354.5951	<-- =NPV(0.05,A5:A$8)
6	100	272.3248	<-- =VarPV(A6:A$8)	272.3248	<-- =NPV(0.05,A6:A$8)
7	100	185.9410	<-- =VarPV(A7:A$8)	185.9410	<-- =NPV(0.05,A7:A$8)
8	100	#VALUE!	<-- =VarPV(A8:A$8)	95.2381	<-- =NPV(0.05,A8:A$8)

Notice that a single cell is not an array.

A range of cells is always a two-dimensional array (even if it is only a row or a column); the indices always run from one and not from zero.

If we want to emulate the way the worksheet function **NPV** works, then our function has to be modified.

```
Function VarPV(CF As Variant) As Double
    Dim X As Variant
    Dim Temp As Double
    Dim i As Integer
    X = CF
    Temp = 0
    If IsArray(X) Then
        For i = LBound(X) To UBound(X)
            Temp = Temp + X(i, 1) / 1.05 ^ i
        Next i
    Else
        Temp = X / 1.05
    End If
    VarPV = Temp
End Function
```

	A	B	C	D	E
1	VarPV in Action				
2					
3	CF	VarPV		NPV	
4	100	432.9477	<-- =VarPV(A4:A$8)	432.9477	<-- =NPV(0.05,A4:A$8)
5	100	354.5951	<-- =VarPV(A5:A$8)	354.5951	<-- =NPV(0.05,A5:A$8)
6	100	272.3248	<-- =VarPV(A6:A$8)	272.3248	<-- =NPV(0.05,A6:A$8)
7	100	185.9410	<-- =VarPV(A7:A$8)	185.9410	<-- =NPV(0.05,A7:A$8)
8	100	95.2381	<-- =VarPV(A8:A$8)	95.2381	<-- =NPV(0.05,A8:A$8)

Notice the use of the VBA function **IsArray** to determine whether a variable is an array.

___

Exercises

1.   Write a version of the present-value function **VarPV(CF( ))** that will work with column and row ranges. (Recall that the original version works only on column ranges.)

   Hint: Remember that

   - Ranges are always 2-dimentional arrays.
   - The lower bound for ranges is always 1.
   - The upper bound is the boundary that sets the size of the array.

	A	B	C	D	E
1	**RCMyPV in Action**				
2					
3	100	100	100	272.3248	<-- =RCMyPv(A3:C3)
4	100				
5	100				
6	272.3248	<-- =RCMyPv(A3:A5)			

2.   Write a version of the present-value function with two interest rates, one for positive cash flows and another for negative cash flows. The function should be written for use in a worksheet, and should accept both column and row ranges as parameters. The function declaration line should be

```
Function MyPV(CF As Variant, PositiveR _
      As Double, NegativeR As Double) _
      As Double
```

	A	B	C	D	E	F	G
10	**MyPV in Action**						
11							
12	PositiveR	5%	100	100	100	272.3248	<-- =MyPV(C12:E12,$B$12,$B$13)
13	NegativeR	10%	-100	-100	-100	-248.685	<-- =MyPV(C13:E13,$B$12,$B$13)
14			-100	100	100	86.17762	<-- =MyPV(C14:E14,$B$12,$B$13)
15			-63	<-- =MyPV(C12:C14,$B$12,$B$13)			

3.   Write a future-value version of the function in exercise 1.

4.   Write a future-value version of the function in exercise 2.

5.   A bank offers different interest rates on loans. The rate is based on the size of the periodical repayment (CF_i) and the following table. Write a present-value function **BankPV(CF, r)** so that it reflects the present value of a loan in the bank. The function should be usable as a worksheet function. **CF** could be either a row range or a column range.

For Periodical Repayments <=	The Interest Rate Is
100.00	r
500.00	$r - 0.5\%$
1,000.00	$r - 1.1\%$
5,000.00	$r - 1.7\%$
1,000,000.00	$r - 2.1\%$

6. A bank offers different interest rates on deposit accounts. The rate is based on the size of the periodical deposit (CF_i) and the following table. Write a future-value function **BankFV(CF, r)**. The function should be usable as a worksheet function. **CF** could be either a row range or a column range.

For Periodical Deposits	The Interest Rate Is
<=100.00	r
<=500.00	$r + 0.5\%$
<=1,000.00	$r + 1.1\%$
<=5,000.00	$r + 1.7\%$
>5,000.00	$r + 2.1\%$

7. Another bank offers a 1 percent increase in interest rate for savings accounts with a balance of more then 10,000.00. Write a future-value function **Bank1FV(CF, r)** that reflects this policy. The function should be usable as a worksheet function. **CF** could be either a row range or a column range.

8. The bank in exercise 7 changed its bonus policy and now offers the interest rate increase based on the following table. Rewrite **Bank1FV(CF, r, n)** to reflect this change.

Balance	Interest rate
<=1,000.00	$r + 0.2\%$
<=5,000.00	$r + 0.5\%$
<=10,000.00	$r + 1.0\%$
>10,000.00	$r + 1.3\%$

35 Objects

35.1 Introduction

This chapter deals with some of the more advanced subjects in VBA. The first part of the chapter introduces worksheet objects, **With** statements, collections, names, and the object browser are also discussed.

35.2 Worksheet Objects: An Introduction

Objects are the basic building blocks of VBA. Although you may not be aware that you are using objects, most things you do in VBA require the manipulation of objects. We can think of an object as a sort of a container with variables, functions, and subroutines inside. All of Excel's components (workbooks, worksheets, ranges, and so on) are represented by an object in the VBA object hierarchy (see appendix). The object's data are held in special variables called properties. You can access the properties using the Dot (.) operator. The following macro uses the VBA object variable **ActiveCell** and three of its properties: **Address, Formula,** and **Value:**

```
Sub ActivecellDemo()
    Dim Temp
    MsgBox "You are at: " & ActiveCell.Address _
        & Chr(13) & "The Formula in the cell _
        is: " & ActiveCell.Formula & _
        Chr(13) & "The value of the cell _
        is: " & ActiveCell.Value
    ActiveCell.Formula = ActiveCell.Formula _
        & "* 2"
End Sub
```

This macro uses the **ActiveCell** object to do two things:

1. It uses a message box to inform you of the contents of cell A2. This procedure uses a VBA Message Box and the properties **ActiveCell.Formula** and **ActiveCell.Value.**

2. It uses **ActiveCell.Formula** to change the formula in the cell. Note the way the formula is changed: The last element in the formula is multiplied by 2. Thus, if you have the formula 2 + A1 in cell A2, the new formula will be

2 + A1 ∗ 2. If you run the macro again on the same cell, the new formula will be 2 + A1 ∗ 2 ∗ 2.

The macro produces the following results:

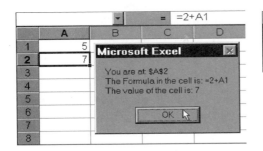

Methods are functions contained within an object. Methods are used to manipulate the object. Like properties, methods can be accessed using the Dot (**.**) operator. The line between methods and properties is sometimes very fuzzy. The following macro activates the **BorderAround** and **Cells** methods of **ActiveCell**:

```
Sub ActivecellDemo1()
    MsgBox "You are at: " & ActiveCell.Address
    ActiveCell.BorderAround xlDouble, xlThick, 3
    ActiveCell.Cells(2, 2).Select
End Sub
```

And it looks like this:

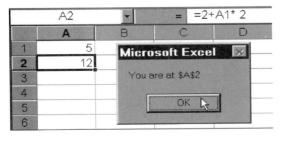

Notice that the active cell in the worksheet moved as a result of the last line in the macro.

35.3   The Range Object

Objects have types. One of the most important object types in VBA is the
Range. A worksheet cell and a range of cells are all objects of the type **Range.**
For example, the VBA object variable **ActiveCell** we encountered in the previous section is of the type **Range.** This section presents some of the properties
and methods of the **Range** object.

35.3.1   A Range as a Parameter to a Function

Suppose we define the return of an asset for period t as $r_t = \dfrac{\text{Price}_t - \text{Price}_{t-1}}{\text{Price}_{t-1}}$

and the mean return of an asset as $\bar{r} = \dfrac{1}{N} \sum_{t=1}^{N} r_t$. The function **MeanReturn**
accepts a column range of asset prices as a parameter and computes the mean
return of the asset. An auxiliary function **AssetReturn** is used to compute r_t.

```
Function AssetReturn(P0 As Variant, P1 As _
        Variant) As Double
    AssetReturn = (P1 - P0) / P0
End Function
```

```
Function MeanReturn(Rng As Range) As Double
    Dim NumRows As Integer
    Dim Prices As Variant
    Dim Temp As Double
    Dim i As Integer
    NumRows = Rng.Rows.Count
    Prices = Rng.Value
    Temp = 0
    For i = 2 To NumRows
        Temp = Temp + _
            AssetReturn(Prices(i - 1, 1), _
                Prices(i, 1))
    Next i
    MeanReturn = Temp / (NumRows - 1)
End Function
```

This is the function in action:

	A	B	C
5	**MeanReturn in Action**		
6			
7	100.000	0.160	<-- =meanreturn(A7:A12)
8	110.000	0.100	<-- =meanreturn(A7:A9)
9	121.000	0.200	<-- =meanreturn(A9:A12)
10	145.200		
11	174.240		
12	209.088		

Lines of note:

```
• NumRows = Rng.Rows.Count
```

The **Dot** operator is used twice. **Rng** is our **Range** object. **Rows** is property of the **Range** object, so **Rng.Rows** is an object of the **Collection** type that represents all the rows in our range. **Count** is a property of **Collection** type objects that stores the number of members in the collection, so **Rng.Rows.Count** is a variable that stores the number of rows in our range.

```
• Prices = Rng.Value
```

Value is a property of the **Range** object containing the values of all the cells in the range. **Value** is of the type **Variant.** If the range is more then one cell in size, **Value** is a two-dimensional array. The first index of **Value** is the row index starting from 1, and the second index is the column index starting from 1.

35.3.2   Type Considerations with Variants and Objects as Parameters

Sometimes **Variant** variables get typed too late for VBA to use the type information. The problem is illustrated by the **AssetReturn** function in the previous subsection. A better declaration for the **AssetReturn** function would have been

```
Function AssetReturn(P0 As Double, P1 As _
        Double) As Double
```

Unfortunately, when we try to use the function, VBA checks the correctness of our program. When the check is performed (just before the function is used), the **Prices** variables is not yet an array of doubles. As a consequence the following error is issued:

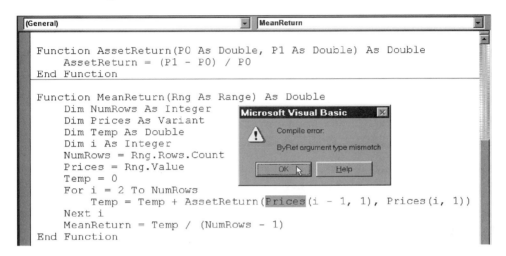

```
(General)                                    MeanReturn

Function AssetReturn(P0 As Double, P1 As Double) As Double
    AssetReturn = (P1 - P0) / P0
End Function

Function MeanReturn(Rng As Range) As Double
    Dim NumRows As Integer
    Dim Prices As Variant          Microsoft Visual Basic
    Dim Temp As Double                  Compile error:
    Dim i As Integer
    NumRows = Rng.Rows.Count            ByRef argument type mismatch
    Prices = Rng.Value
    Temp = 0                             OK          Help
    For i = 2 To NumRows
        Temp = Temp + AssetReturn(Prices(i - 1, 1), Prices(i, 1))
    Next i
    MeanReturn = Temp / (NumRows - 1)
End Function
```

35.3.3   The Item Property of the Range Object

The **Item** property of the **Range** object allows us to address a specific cell in the worksheet of which the range is part. Although **Item** is referred to as a property in the documentation, it actually behaves like a both a property and a method. The following function returns the formula in the cell three rows down and two columns to the left of its argument:

```
Function TwoLeftThreeDown(Rng As Range) As String
    TwoLeftThreeDown = Rng.Item(4, 3).Formula
End Function
```

	A	B	C	D
16	TwoLeftThreeDown in Action			
17				
18				
19			8	<-- =3+5
20			=3+5	<-- =TwoLeftThreeDown(A16)

Note **Rng.Item(1, 1)** is the cell in the top left-hand corner of **Rng.**

35.3.4   The Range Property

The **Range** property is one way to access a range on a worksheet. **Range** is a property of many Excel objects. When used on its own, as in the next macro, **Range** is a short way of writing **ActiveSheet.Range**.

```
Sub RangeDemo()
    Range("A1").Formula = 23
End Sub
```

As expected the macro will set the formula in cell "A1" of the active worksheet to 23. The next macro sets the formula of each cell in the range "A1:B2" of the active worksheet to 23.

```
Sub RangeDemo1()
    Range("A1:B2").Formula = 23
End Sub
```

The next macro sets the formula of each cell in the range "A1:B2" of the active worksheet to 23, using the alternative calling sequence of **Range.** The first argument is the cell in the top left corner of the range. The second is the cell in the bottom right corner of the range.

```
Sub RangeDemo2()
    Range("A1", "B2").Formula = 23
End Sub
```

Range is also a property of the **Range** object. The range returned by **Range** when used this way is relative to the **Range** object. The next macro sets the formula of the cell "C2" of the active worksheet to 23.

```
Sub RangeDemo3()
    Range("B1").Range("B2").Formula = 23
End Sub
```

Note: **Range("B1")** returns the range (or cell) "B1" of the active worksheet. **Range("B1").Range("B2")** returns the cell "B2" of the range that has "B1" as the top left corner. In worksheet terms, **Range("B1").Range("B2")** returns the cell "C2."

The next macro sets the formula of each cell in the range "C2:D3" of the active worksheet to 23. The macro uses the cell "C2" as a starting point, as well as the alternative calling sequence of **Range.**

```
Sub RangeDemo4()
    Range("C2").Range("A1", "B2").Formula = 23
End Sub
```

35.4   The With Statement

The **With** statement allows you to perform a series of statements on a specified object without restating the obvious (the object's name and its pedigree, which can be very long). If you have more then one property to change or more then one method to use for a single object, use the **With** statement. **With** statements make your procedures run faster and help you avoid repetitive typing. The following, somewhat contrived, macro sets some properties of the font of the cell in the top left-hand corner of the current region of the active cell. The font is set to be Arial, bold, red, and 15 points in size.

```
Sub WithoutDemo()
    ActiveCell.CurrentRegion.Range("A1").Font _
        .Bold = True
    ActiveCell.CurrentRegion.Range("A1").Font _
        .ColorIndex = 3
    ActiveCell.CurrentRegion.Range("A1").Font _
        .Name = "Arial"
    ActiveCell.CurrentRegion.Range("A1").Font _
        .Size = 15
End Sub
```

Following is the same macro using the **With** statement.

```
Sub WithDemo()
    With ActiveCell.CurrentRegion.Range("A1").Font
        .Bold = True
        .ColorIndex = 3
        .Name = "Arial"
        .Size = 15
    End With
End Sub
```

Notice the **Dot(.)** operator before the properties in the **With** statement.

35.5   Collections

A **Collection** is an ordered set of items that can be referred to as a unit. The **Collection** object provides a convenient way to refer to a related group of items as a single object. The items, or members, in a **Collection,** need only be related by the fact that they exist in the **Collection.** Members of a **Collection** don't have to share the same data type.

A **Collection** can be created the same way other objects are created. Members can be added using the **Add** method and removed using the **Remove** method. Specific members can be referred to using an integer index. The number of members currently in a **Collection** is available via the **Count** method. Our use of **Collections** will be restricted to using the (quite numerous) arsenal of **Collections** that are part of the Excel Object Model, like the **Rows Collection** mentioned in the previous section.

35.5.1   The For Each Statement in Use with Arrays and Collections

The **For Each** statement is a variation of the **For** loop unique to VBA. This statement comes in two distinct flavors. The first variation uses the statement to loop over an array as demonstrated in the following function:

```
Function ForEachSum(Rng As Range) As Double
    Dim Element As Variant
    Dim Sum As Double
    Sum = 0
    For Each Element In Rng.Value
        Sum = Sum + Element
```

```
        Next Element
        ForEachSum = Sum
    End Function
```

	A	B	C	D	E
23	**ForEachSum Demo**				
24					
25	1	4	7	6	<-- =ForEachSum(A25:A27)
26	2	5	8	12	<-- =ForEachSum(A25:C25)
27	3	6	9	45	<-- =ForEachSum(A25:C27)

Points to note:

• The current member of the array is available to the statements within the loop body through the loop variable (**Element** in the function).

• The loop variable has to be of the type **Variant** irrespective of array's type.

• Changes to **Element** will not be reflected in the actual array (a read-only situation).

• You don't need to know the number of dimensions or the range of indices to loop over the array. The preceding function works on column ranges (as in cell E25), row ranges (as in cell E26), and rectangular ranges (as in cell E27) in the same fashion

35.5.2   The For Each statement in Use with Collections

The second version of the **For Each** statement loops over **Collections:**

```
Sub ZeroRange()
    Dim Rng As Range
    Dim Cell As Variant
    Set Rng = ActiveCell.CurrentRegion
    MsgBox "The current region is: " & Rng.Address
    For Each Cell In Rng
        Cell.Formula = 0
    Next Cell
End Sub
```

Points to note:

• **Element** is a variable used to iterate over *all* the members of the collection.

• **Element** has to be one of the following types: **Variant,** Generic Object, or the specific type of element the **Collection** is made of.

• **Element** refers to the actual member of the **Collection,** and changes to **Element** will be reflected in the **Collection**.

• The use of the **CurrentRegion** property of the **Range** object. **CurrentRegion** is a **Range** object that represents the current region. The current region is a range bounded by any combination of blank rows and blank columns.

• The use of the **Set** statement. A complete explanation is beyond the scope of this book. For our purposes just prefix the reserved word **Set** to all object assignments. If you don't, the following might ensue:

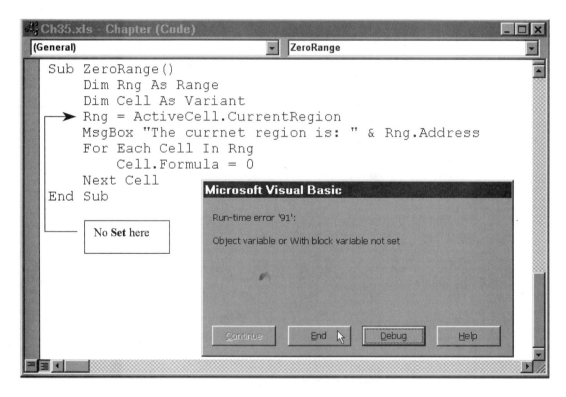

35.5.3   The Workbooks Collection and the Workbook Object

All the currently open workbooks are represented by a **Workbook** object in the **Workbooks Collection.** The following macro lists all open workbooks in a column of cells starting from the active cell:

```
Sub ListOpenWorkbooks()
    Dim i As Integer
    Dim Element As Workbook
    ActiveCell.Item(2, 1).Formula = _
        "List of open Workbooks"
    ActiveCell.Item(4, 1).Formula = _
        "Created on:" & FormatDateTime(Date, _
        & vbLongDate) " At: " _
        & FormatDateTime(Time, vbLongTime)
    With ActiveCell.Item(2, 1).Font
        .Bold = True
        .Name = "Arial"
        .Size = 12
    End With
    i = 5
    For Each Element In Workbooks
        ActiveCell.Item(i, 1).Formula = _
            Element.FullName
        i = i + 1
    Next Element
End Sub
```

This is the worksheet after the macro was run:

	A
59	**List of open Workbooks**
60	
61	Created on:17 January 2000 At: 17:43:42
62	C:\WINDOWS\Application Data\Microsoft\Excel\XLSTART\PERSONAL.XLS
63	C:\My Documents\book\Ch35\Ch35.xls
64	C:\My Documents\book\Ch34\Ch34.xls

Lines of note:

```
ActiveCell.Item(4, 1).Formula = _
    "Created on:" & FormatDateTime(Date, _
    vbLongDate) & " At: " & _
    FormatDateTime(Time, vbLongTime)
```

• The **Date** function returns the current system date.

- The **Time** function returns the current system time.
- The **FormatDateTime** function formats **Date** and **Time** variables for display.

```
For Each Element In Workbooks
    ActiveCell.Item(i, 1).Formula = _
        Element.FullName
    i = i + 1
Next Element
```

The **For** statement loops over the entire **Workbooks Collection.** On each iteration **Element** is one of the **Workbook** objects in the **Collection. FullName** is a property of the **Workbook** object containing the full path name of the workbook.

The next macro adds a workbook to the **Workbooks Collection:**

```
Sub AddWorkbook()
    Dim Wkbk As Workbook
    Dim OldWkbk As Workbook
    Set OldWkbk = ActiveWorkbook
    Set Wkbk = Workbooks.Add
    OldWkbk.Activate
    MsgBox Wkbk.FullName & " Added"
End Sub
```

Adding a workbook to the **Workbooks Collection** makes the newly added workbook the active workbook. If we want to stay where we are, we need to re-activate the old workbook.

35.5.4   The Worksheets Collection and the Worksheet Object

All the worksheets in a workbook are **Worksheet** objects in the **Worksheets Collection** that is a property of the **Workbook** object. We can use the **Worksheets Collection** without an object as a short form for **ActiveWorkbook.Worksheets**.

35.6   Names

35.6.1   Naming a Range Using a Macro

The following macro names the current region:

```
Sub NameCurrentRegion()
    Dim Rng As Range
    Dim MyName As String
    Set Rng = ActiveCell.CurrentRegion
    MyName = InputBox("The current region _
        is: " & Rng.Address & Chr(13) & "Enter _
            Name please: ", "Namer", "MyName")
    Names.Add Name:=MyName, RefersTo:="=" _
        & Rng.Address
End Sub
```

The interesting line in the macro is

```
Names.Add Name :=MyName, RefersTo:="=" & _
        Rng.Address
```

Names is a **Collection** of all the names in the active workbook. **Add** is a method of the **Names Collection** used to add members to the collection. We use only the first two parameters of the method. The first parameter **MyName** is the name to add to the **Names Collection.** The second parameter is a string containing the address that the added name is to refer to, preceded by "=".

35.6.2   Looking for Defined Names

The following function looks for a defined name in the current workbook. The function returns the **Boolean** value "True" if the name is defined, and "False" if it is not part of the **Names Collection.**

```
Function IsName(Name As String) As Boolean
    Dim Element As Variant
    Dim Flag As Boolean
    Flag = False
    For Each Element In Names
        If Name = Element.Name Then
            Flag = True
            Exit For
        End If
    Next Element
    IsName = Flag
End Function
```

	B	C	D
37	**IsName in Action**		
38			
39	**Name**	**IsName**	
40	Benny	FALSE	<-- =IsName(B40)
41	MyName	TRUE	<-- =IsName(B41)
42	myname	FALSE	<-- =IsName(B42)
43	MYNAME	FALSE	<-- =IsName(B43)

Note that

- Names are case sensitive.

- The **Exit For** statement can be used with **For Each** .

35.6.3   Referring to a Named Range

The following function computes the *Mean Return* on a named range of asset prices.

```
Function NamedMeanReturn(RangeName As String) _
        As Double
    Dim Rng As Range
    Dim Prices As Variant
    Dim Temp As Double
    Dim i As Integer
    Set Rng = Range(RangeName)
    Prices = Rng.Value
    Temp = 0
    For i = 2 To UBound (Prices, 1)
        Temp = Temp + _
        (Prices(i, 1) - Prices(i - 1, 1)) / _
            Prices(i - 1, 1)
    Next i
    NamedMeanReturn = Temp / (UBound _
        (Prices, 1) - 1)
End Function
```

	A	B	C	D
47	**NamedMeanReturn in Action**			
48				
49	**Asset1**	**Asset2**		
50	100.000	100.000	0.1000	<-- =meanreturn($A$50:$A$54)
51	110.000	120.000	0.2000	<-- =meanreturn($B$50:$B$54)
52	121.000	144.000	0.1000	<-- =NamedMeanReturn("Asset1")
53	133.100	172.800	0.2000	<-- =NamedMeanReturn("Asset2")
54	146.410	207.360	0.2000	<-- =NamedMeanReturn("aSsEt2")

Note the new way to use the **Range** property introduced in the macro:

```
Set Rng = Range(RangeName)
```

35.7   Using the Object Browser

The **Object Browser** is a convenient way to learn about the different objects that are available for use in VBA. The object browser can be activated by pressing its button on the VBA tool bar

or from the menu (**View|Object Browser**).

The object browser window is made of two panes, a selection box, and a few buttons. From the selection box you can choose a master set of objects to look at (two master sets, VBA and Excel, are always available). Select the VBA master set to look at objects that are internal to the working of VBA. The Excel master set deals with objects that are specific to Excel. (It's all part of a Microsoft master plan, no pun intended, where VBA is a center of many applications, not just Excel.)

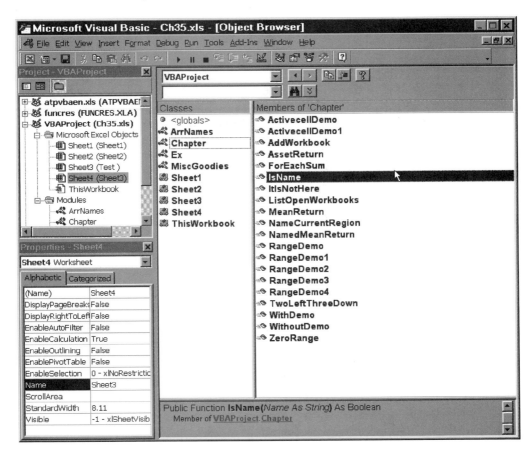

Once a master set of objects is selected, the two other panes change their contents to reflect the master set selected. The left pane is a list of categories (sorted in ascending alphabetical order). The right pane is a list of **Properties** or **Methods** attributable to the selected object in the left pane. Clicking the question-mark button causes the appropriate help screen to be displayed. Clicking a name in the right pane (**IsName** in the screen shot) displays information about it on the bottom of the screen.

Exercises

1. Suppose you have a spreadsheet with a series of numbers and formulas:

	A	B	C
1	Price	Return	
2	1,000.00		
3	1,019.66	0.019656	<-- =A3/A2-1
4	1,020.79	0.001116	<-- =A4/A3-1
5	1,025.36	0.00447	<-- =A5/A4-1
6	1,045.42	0.019564	<-- =A6/A5-1
7	1,065.90	0.019595	<-- =A7/A6-1
8	1,076.74	0.010165	<-- =A8/A7-1
9	1,091.68	0.013883	<-- =A9/A8-1
10	1,101.61	0.009094	<-- =A10/A9-1

Suppose you want to turn this into the following:

	A	B	C
1	Price	Return	
2	1,000.00		
3	1,019.66	1.965552	<-- =(A3/A2-1)*100
4	1,020.79	0.1116	<-- =(A4/A3-1)*100
5	1,025.36	0.446954	<-- =(A5/A4-1)*100
6	1,045.42	1.956373	<-- =(A6/A5-1)*100
7	1,065.90	1.959535	<-- =(A7/A6-1)*100
8	1,076.74	1.016492	<-- =(A8/A7-1)*100
9	1,091.68	1.388299	<-- =(A9/A8-1)*100
10	1,101.61	0.909361	<-- =(A10/A9-1)*100

Write a macro that accomplishes this purpose. Your macro (roughly based on the macro **ActiveCellDemo** of section 35.2) should

- Put in a set of parentheses and multiply the cell contents by 100.
- Move down one cell (see **ActiveCellDemo1,** section 35.2).
- Ask if you want to repeat the process. (If "yes," it should do it; if "no," the macro should exit).

Note: The parentheses have to come after the "=." The **Right** function might be used for this operation.

You may want to refer to section 33.3 for more information on the **MsgBox** function and the values it returns.

2. Rewrite the macro in exercise 1 so that it deals correctly with the end of the series. One possible treatment is not to ask to repeat the process when the last cell in the series is dealt with.

    Hint: For this macro it might be useful to think of the last cell in the series as the cell that fulfills the criterion **Cell.Item(2,1).Formula="\"** (see section 35.3).

3. Write a macro that multiplies all cells in the current region by 2.

4. Rewrite the macro in exercise 3 so that its action is dependent on the cell's contents

    - If the cell contents is a formula it will be replaced by the same formula multiplied by 2.
    - If the cell contents is a number it will be replaced by a number equal to the old number multiplied by 2.
    - On all other cells in the current region nothing will be done.

    Note: For the purposes of this exercise a formula is anything beginning with "=," and a number is anything beginning with the characters "0" to "9."

5. Rewrite the macro in exercise 4 so that it uses another method (the correct one) to detect the existence of a formula in a cell. Look at the different properties of the **Range** object in the help file.

6. The annotations for worksheet formulas in this book were done with a macro. For example running the macro on this worksheet, "B16" being the active cell:

	B	C	D
15	1		
16	1		
17	2		
18	4		
19	8		

Produces the following worksheet:

	B	C	D
15	1		
16	1	<-- =SUM($B$15:$B15)	
17	2		
18	4		
19	8		

Notice the changed column width. Write a macro to perform the annotation. If the cell immediately to the right of the active cell is not empty, the macro should overwrite it only after receiving confirmation from the user.

7. The **Selection** object represents the current selection in the worksheet. **Selection** is usually, and for our purposes always, a **Range** object. Rewrite the macro in exercise 6 so that it works on a selected range.

Note the following:

*   If the selected range is a single cell activatate the macro in exercise 6.

*   If the selected range is a row range the annotations should go below the selected range.

*   If the selected range is more than one column or one row, the macro should abort with an appropriate message.

8. Array functions are functions that return more than one value. For example, the TRANSPOSE worksheet function returns its argument turned by 90 degrees, as the following worksheet demonstrates:

	A	B	C	D	E	F
1	TRANSPOSE in Action					
2						
3	1	2	3	4	1	<--{=TRANSPOSE(A3:D3)}
4					2	<--{=TRANSPOSE(A3:D3)}
5					3	<--{=TRANSPOSE(A3:D3)}
6					4	<--{=TRANSPOSE(A3:D3)}

The curly brackets were not typed in but were added by Excel to indicate an array formula. The following macro created the preceding worksheet.

```
Sub TransposeMe()
    Range("E3:E6").FormulaArray = _
        "=Transpose(A3:D3)"
End Sub
```

The next macro is a more complicated version that could deal with any size or place in the row range.

```
Sub TransposeMeToo()
    Dim R As Integer, C As Integer
    C = Selection.Columns.Count
    R = Selection.Rows.Count
    If C = 1 Then                       'Its a Column
        MsgBox "I don't do Columns"
    ElseIf R = 1 Then                       'Its a Row
        Selection.Cells(1, C + 1).Range("A1:A" _
        & C). FormulaArray = "=Transpose(" & _
            Selection.Address(False, False) & ")"
    Else                                'What is it?
        MsgBox "What is it?"
    End If
End Sub
```

Rewrite **TransposeMeToo** so it could deal with column ranges as well as row ranges.

9.   Rewrite **TransposeMeToo** of exercise 8 so it could deal with all ranges. Note: it is not as easy as it looks at first sight.

Appendix: Excel Object Hierarchy

Microsoft Excel Objects

```
Application
    ├─ Workbooks (Workbook)
    │      ├─ Worksheets (Worksheet)
    │      ├─ Charts (Chart)
    │      ├─ DocumentProperties (DocumentProperty)
    │      ├─ VBProject
    │      ├─ CustomViews (CustomView)
    │      ├─ CommandBars (CommandBar)
    │      ├─ HTMLProject
    │      ├─ PivotCaches (PivotCache)
    │      ├─ Styles (Style)
    │      │      ├─ Borders (Border)
    │      │      ├─ Font
    │      │      └─ Interior
    │      ├─ Windows (Window)
    │      │      └─ Panes (Pane)
    │      ├─ Names (Name)
    │      ├─ RoutingSlip
    │      ├─ PublishObjects (PublishObject)
    │      └─ WebOptions
    │
    ├─ AddIns (AddIn)
    ├─ AnswerWizard
    ├─ AutoCorrect
    ├─ Assistant
    ├─ COMAddIns (COMAddIn)
    ├─ Debug
    ├─ Dialogs (Dialog)
    ├─ CommandBars (CommandBar)
    ├─ LanguageSettings
    ├─ Names (Name)
    ├─ Windows (Window)
    │      └─ Panes (Pane)
    ├─ WorksheetFunction
    ├─ RecentFiles (RecentFile)
    ├─ FileSearch
    ├─ VBE
    ├─ ODBCErrors (ODBCError)
    ├─ OLEDBErrors (OLEDBError)
    └─ DefaultWebOptions
```

Microsoft Excel Objects (Worksheet)

Worksheets (Worksheet)

- Names (Name)
- Range
  - Areas
  - Borders (Border)
  - Font
  - Interior
  - Characters
    - Font
  - Name
  - Style
    - Borders (Border)
    - Font
    - Interior
  - FormatConditions (FormatCondition)
  - Hyperlinks (Hyperlink)
  - Validation
  - Comment
  - Phonetics (Phonetic)
  - Shapes (Shape)

- Comments (Comment)
- HPageBreaks (HPageBreak)
- VPageBreaks (VPageBreak)
- Hyperlinks (Hyperlink)
- Scenarios (Scenario)
- OLEObjects (OLEObject)
- Outline
- PageSetup
- QueryTables (QueryTable)
  - Parameters (Parameter)
- PivotTables (PivotTable)
  - PivotCache
  - PivotFormulas (PivotFormula)
  - PivotFields (PivotField)
    - PivotItems (PivotItem)
  - CubeFields (CubeField)
- OLEObjects (OLEObject)
- ChartObjects (ChartObject)
  - Chart
  - PivotLayout
- AutoFilter
  - Filters (Filter)

References

Chapters 1–4: Corporate Finance and Valuation

Benninga, S. Z., and O. H. Sarig. 1997. *Corporate Finance: A Valuation Approach.* New York: McGraw-Hill.

Brealey, R. A., and S. C. Myers. 1996. *Principles of Corporate Finance,* 5th ed. New York: McGraw-Hill.

Gordon, M. J. 1959. "Dividends, Earnings, and Stock Prices." *Review of Economics and Statistics* 41 (May): 99–105.

Chapters 5–6: Leasing

Abdel-Khalik, R. 1981. *Economic Effects on Lessees of FASB Statement No. 13, Accounting for Leases.* Stamford, CT: Financial Accounting Standards Board.

Brealey, R. A., and S. C. Myers. 1996. *Principles of Corporate Finance,* 5th ed. New York: McGraw-Hill.

Copeland, T. E., and J. F. Weston. 1982. "A Note on the Evaluation of Cancelable Operating Leases." *Financial Management* (Summer): 68–72.

El-Gazzar, S., S. Lilien, and V. Pastena. 1986. "Accounting for Leases by Lessees." *Journal of Accounting and Economics* 8:217–237.

Financial Accounting Standards Board. 1976. Statement No. 13: Accounting for Leases. Stamford, CT.

Franks, J. R., and S. D. Hodges. 1978. "Valuation of Financial Lease Contracts: A Note." *Journal of Finance* 33 (May): 647–669.

Levy, H., and M. Sarnat. 1979. "On Leasing, Borrowing and Financial Risk." *Financial Management* 8 (Winter): 47–54.

Lewellen, W. G., M. S. Long, and J. J. McConnell. 1979. "Asset Leasing in Competitive Capital Markets." *Journal of Finance* 31 (June): 787–798.

McConnell, J. J., and J, S. Schallheim. 1983. "Valuation of Asset Leasing Contracts." *Journal of Financial Economics* 12 (August): 237–261.

Miller, M. H., and C. W. Upton. 1976. "Leasing, Buying, and the Cost of Capital Services." *Journal of Finance* 31 (June): 761–786.

Myers, S. C., D. A. Dill, and A. J. Bautista. 1976. "Valuation of Financial Lease Contracts." *Journal of Finance* 31 (June): 799–819.

Nakayama, M., S. Lilien, and M. Benis. 1981. "Due Process and FASB No. 13." *Management Accounting* 52:49–53.

Ofer, A. R. 1976. "The Evaluation of the Lease versus Purchase Alternative." *Financial Management* (Summer): 67–74.

Ross, S. A., R. W. Westerfield, and J. Jaffe. 1996. *Corporate Finance,* 4th edition, Burr Ridge, IL: Irwin.

Chapters 7–11: Portfolio

Black, F. 1972. "Capital Market Equilibrium with Restricted Borrowing." *Journal of Business* 45 (July): 444–455.

Bodie, Z., A. Kane, and A. J. Marcus. 1996. *Investments,* 3rd ed. Burr Ridge, IL: Irwin.

Elton, E. J., and M. J. Gruber. 1995. *Modern Portfolio Theory and Investment Analysis,* fifth ed. New York: Wiley.

Green, R. C. 1986. "Positively Weighted Portfolios on the Minimum-Variance Frontier." *Journal of Finance* 41 (December): 1051–1068.

Haugen, R. A. 1977. *Modern Investment Theory.* Englewood Cliffs, NJ: Prentice Hall.

Jensen, M. C., ed. 1972. *Studies in the Theory of Capital Markets.* New York: Praeger.

Lintner, J. 1965. "The Valuation of Risky Assets and the Selection of Risky Investments in Stock Portfolios and Capital Budgets." *Review of Economics and Statistics* 47 (February): 13–37.

Markowitz, H. M. 1952. "Portfolio Selection." *Journal of Finance* 7 (March): 77–91.

Merton, R. C. 1973. "An Analytic Derivation of the Efficient Portfolio Frontier." *Journal of Financial and Quantitative Analysis* 7 (September): 1851–1872.

Modigliani, F., and G. A. Pogue. 1974. "An Introduction to Risk and Return." *Financial Analysts Journal* 30 (March-April): 68–80; (May-June): 69–88.

Mossin, J. 1966. "Equilibrium in a Capital Market." *Econometrica,* October.

Nielsen, L. T. 1987. "Positively Weighted Frontier Portfolios: A Note." *Journal of Finance* 42 (June): 471.

Roll, R. 1977. "A Critique of the Asset Pricing Theory's Tests, Part I: On Past and Potential Testability of the Theory." *Journal of Financial Economics* 4 (March): 129–176.

Roll, R. 1978. "Ambiguity When Performance Is Measured by the Securities Market Line." *Journal of Finance* 33 (March): 129–176.

Sharpe, W. F. 1964. "Capital Asset Prices: A Theory of Market Equilibrium under Conditions of Risk." *Journal of Finance* 19 (September): 425–442.

Sharpe, W. F. 1988. *Investments.* Englewood Cliffs, NJ: Prentice Hall.

Chapter 12: Value at Risk

Beder, T. 1996. "VAR: Seductive but Dangerous." *Financial Analyst Journal,* September-October: 12–24.

Grundy, B. D., and Z. Wiener. 2000. "The Analysis of VAR, Deltas and State Prices: A New Approach." *European Finance Review.*

Hull, J. C. 2000. *Options, Futures, and Other Derivatives.* 4th ed. Prentice-Hall.

Jorion, P. 1997. *Value at Risk, the New Benchmark for Controlling Market Risk.* New York: McGraw-Hill.

Linsmeier, T., and N. Pearson. 1996. "Risk Measurement: An Introduction to Value at Risk." Working paper, University of Illinois.

Chapters 13–17: Options and Portfolio Insurance

Benninga, S., and M. Blume. 1985. "On the Optimality of Portfolio Insurance." *Journal of Finance* 40 (December): 1341–1352.

Benninga, S., R. Steinmetz, and J. Stroughair. 1993. "Implementing Numerical Option Pricing Models." *Mathematica Journal.*

Bhaghat, S., J. Brickley, and U. Loewenstein. 1987. "The Pricing Effects of Interim Cash Tender Offers." *Journal of Finance* 42 (September): 965–986.

Billingsley, P. 1968. *Convergence of Probability Measures.* New York: Wiley.

Black, F., and M. Scholes. 1973. "The Pricing of Options and Corporate Liabilities." *Journal of Political Economy* 81 (May-June): 637–654.

Bodie, Z., A. Kane, and A. J. Marcus. 1996. *Investments,* 3rd ed. Burr Ridge, IL: Irwin.

Brealey, R., and S. Myers. 1996. *Principles of Corporate Finance,* 5th ed. New York: McGraw-Hill.

Brennan, M. J., and E. S. Schwartz. 1976. "The Pricing of Equity-Linked Life Insurance Policies with an Asset Value Guarantee." *Journal of Financial Economics* 3 (June): 195–213.

Brennan, M. J., and E. S. Schwartz. 1979. "Alternative Investment Strategies for the Issuers of Equity-Linked Life Insurance Policies with an Asset Value Guarantee." *Journal of Business* 52 (January): 63–93.

Brennan, M. J., and R. Solanki. 1981. "Optimal Portfolio Insurance." *Journal of Financial and Quantitative Analysis* 16 (September): 279–300.

Chicago Board of Trade. 1985. *Commodity Trading Manual.*

Copeland, T. E., and J. F. Weston. 1983. *Financial Theory and Corporate Policy.* Reading, MA: Addison-Wesley.

Cox, J., and S. A. Ross. 1976. "The Valuation of Options for Alternative Stochastic Processes." *Journal of Financial Economics* 3: 145–166.

Cox, J., S. A. Ross, and M. Rubinstein. 1979. "Option Pricing: A Simplified Approach." *Journal of Financial Economics* 7:229–264.

Cox, J., and M. Rubinstein. 1985. *Options Markets.* Englewood Cliffs, NJ: Prentice Hall.

Franke, G. 1986. "Exchange Rate Volatility and International Trade: The Option Approach." Manuscript, University of Konstanz.

Gatto, M. A., R. Geske, R. Litzenberger, and H. Sosin. 1980. "Mutual Fund Insurance." *Journal of Financial Economics* 8 (September): 283–317.

Hull, John. 1989. *Options, Futures, and Other Derivative Securities.* Englewood Cliffs, NJ: Prentice Hall.

Jacobs, B. 1983. "The Portfolio Insurance Puzzle." *Pensions and Investment Age* (August 22): 26.

Jacques, W. E. 1987. "Portfolio Insurance or Job Insurance?" *Financial Analysts Journal* (January–February): 7.

Jarrow, R. A., and A. Rudd. 1983. *Option Pricing.* Homewood, IL: Irwin.

Knuth, D. E. 1981. *The Art of Computer Programming,* vol. 2: *Seminumerical Algorithms,* 2nd ed. Reading, MA: Addison-Wesley.

Leland, H. E. 1980. "Who Should Buy Portfolio Insurance?" *Journal of Finance* 35 (May): 581–594.

Leland, H. E. 1985. "Option Pricing and Replication with Transaction Costs." *Journal of Finance* 40 (December): 1283–1301.

Lessard, D. R., ed. 1979. *International Financial Management.* Boston: Warren, Gorham, Lamont.

Merton, R. 1973. "Theory of Rational Option Pricing." *Bell Journal of Economics and Management Science* 4 (Spring): 141–183.

Merton, R. 1976. "Option Pricing When Underlying Stock Returns Are Discontinuous." *Journal of Financial Economics* 3 (March): 125–144.

Omberg, E. 1987. "A Note on the Convergence of Binomial-Pricing and Compound-Option Models." *Journal of Finance* 42 (June): 463–469.

Pozen, R. C. 1978. "When to Purchase a Protective Put." *Financial Analysts Journal* (July-August): 47–60.

Press, W. H., B. P. Flannery, S. A. Teukolsky, and W. T. Vetterling. 1986. *Numerical Recipes: The Art of Scientific Computing*. Cambridge University Press.

Rubinstein, M. 1985. "Alternative Paths to Portfolio Insurance." *Financial Analysts Journal* (July-August): 42–52.

Rubinstein, M., and H. E. Leland. 1981. "Replicating Options with Positions in Stock and Cash." *Financial Analysts Journal* (July-August): 3–12.

Schwartz, E. S. 1986–87. "Options and Portfolio Insurance." *Finnanzmarkt und Portfolio Management* 1:9–17.

Somes, S. P., and M. A. Zurack. 1987. "Pension Plans, Portfolio Insurance, and FASB Statement No. 87: An Old Risk in a New Light." *Financial Analysts Journal* (January-February): 10–13.

Chapter 18: Real Options

Amram, M., and N. Kulatilaka. 1998. *Real Options: Managing Strategic Investment in an Uncertain World*. Boston: Harvard Business School Press.

Dixit, A. K., and R. S. Pindyck. 1995. "The Options Approach to Capital Investment." *Harvard Business Review,* May-June.

Luehrman, T. A. 1998. "Investment Opportunities as Real Options: Getting Started on the Numbers." *Harvard Business Review,* July-August.

Trigeorgis, L. 1993. "Real Options and Interactions with Financial Flexibility." *Financial Management,* Autumn.

Trigeorgis, L. 1995. *Real Options in Capital Investment: Models, Strategies, and Applications*. Westport, CT: Praeger.

Trigeorgis, L. 1996. *Real Options: Managerial Flexibility and Strategy in Resource Allocation*. Cambridge, MA: MIT Press.

Chapters 20–21: Duration and Immunization

Altman, E. 1989. "Measuring Corporate Bond Mortality and Performance." *Journal of Finance* 44 (September): 909–922.

Altman, E., and V. M. Kishore. 1996. "Almost Everything You Wanted to Know about Recoveries on Defaulted Bonds." *Financial Analysts Journal* (November/December): 57–64.

Babcock, G. 1985. "Duration as a Weighted Average of Two Factors." *Financial Analysts Journal* (March-April): 75–76.

Benninga, S., and A. Protopapadakis. 1986. "General Equilibrium Properties of the Term Structure of Interest Rates." *Journal of Financial Economics* 16 (July): 389–410.

Bierwag, G. O. 1977. "Immunization, Duration, and the Term Structure of Interest Rates." *Journal of Financial and Quantitative Analysis* (December): 725–741.

Bierwag, G. O. 1978. "Measures of Duration." *Economic Inquiry* 16 (October): 497–507.

Bierwag, G. O., G. G. Kaufman, and A. Toevs. 1983a. "Duration: Its Development and Use in Bond Portfolio Management." *Financial Analysts Journal* (July-August): 15–35.

Bierwag, G. O., G. G. Kaufman, and A. Toevs. 1983b. *Innovations in Bond Portfolio Management: Duration Analysis and Immunization*. Greenwich, CT: JAI Press.

Bierwag, G. O., G. G. Kaufman, R. Schweitzer, and A. Toevs. 1981. "The Art of Risk Management in Bond Portfolios." *Journal of Portfolio Management* (Spring): 27–36.

Billingham, C. J. 1983. "Strategies for Enhancing Bond Portfolio Returns." *Financial Analysts Journal* (May-June): 50–56.

Chance, D. M. 1983. "Floating Rate Notes and Immunization." *Journal of Financial and Quantitative Analysis* 18: 365–380.

Chance, D. M. 1996. "Duration Convexity, and Time as Components of Bond Returns. *Journal of Fixed Income* 6: pp. 88–95.

Chua, J. H. 1984. "A Closed-Form Formula for Calculating Bond Duration." *Financial Analysts Journal* (May-June): 76–78.

Cooper, I. A. 1977. "Asset Values, Interest Rate Changes, and Duration." *Journal of Financial and Quantitative Analysis* (December): 701–723.

Cox, J., J. Ingersoll, and S. Ross. 1979. "Duration and Measurement of Basis Risk." *Journal of Business* (January): 51–61.

Cox, J. C., J. E. Ingersoll, and S. A. Ross. 1985. "A Theory of the Term Structure of Interest Rates." *Econometrica* 53 (March): 385–402.

Fisher, L., and R. L. Weill. 1971. "Coping with the Risk of Market-Rate Fluctuatons: Returns to Bondholders from Naive and Optimal Strategies." *Journal of Business* (October): 408–431.

Gultekin, B., and R. J. Rogalski. 1984. "Alternative Duration Specifications and the Measurement of Basis Risk: Empirical Tests." *Journal of Business* (April): 241–264.

Gushee, C. H. 1981. "How to Immunize a Bond Investment." *Financial Analysts Journal* (March-April): 44–51.

Hicks, J. 1939. *Value and Capital.* Oxford: Clarendon Press.

Ingersoll, J. E., Jr., J. Skelton, and R. L. Weil. 1978. "Duration Forty Years Later." *Journal of Financial and Quantitative Analysis* (November): 627–650.

Joehnk, M. D., H. R. Fogler, and C. E. Bradley. 1978. "The Price Elasticity of Discounted Bonds: Some Empirical 'Evidence.' " *Journal of Financial and Quantitative Analysis* (September): 559–566.

Lanstein, R., and W. F. Sharpe. 1978. "Duration and Security Risk." *Journal of Financial and Quantitative Analysis* (November): 653–670.

Leibowitz, M. L., and A. Weinberger. 1981. "The Uses of Contingent Immunization." *Journal of Portfolio Management* (Fall): 51–55.

Macaulay, F. R. 1938. *Some Theoretical Problems Suggested by Movements of Interest Rates, Bond Yields and Stock Prices in the United States Since 1856.* New York: National Bureau of Economic Research.

Macaulay, F. R. 1983. *The Movement of Interest Rates, Bonds, Yields, and Stock Prices in the United States since 1865.* New York: Columbia University Press.

McCullogh, J. H. 1990. "U.S. Term Structure Data, 1946–1987." *Handbook of Monetary Economics,* vol. 1: 672–715. Amsterdam: North-Holland.

Morgan, G. E. 1986. "Floating Rate Securities and Immunization: Some Further Results." *Journal of Financial and Quantitative Analysis* 21: 87–94.

Ott, R. A., Jr. 1986. "The Duration of an Adjustable-Rate Mortgage and the Impact of the Index." *Journal of Finance* 41 (September): 923–934.

Redington, F. M. 1952. "Review of the Principle of Life-Office Valuations." *Journal of the Institute of Actuaries* 78:286–340. Reprinted in *Bond Duration and Immunization: Early Developments and Recent Contributions,* ed. G. A. Hawawini. New York: Garland, 1972.

Samuelson, P. A. 1945. "The Effects of Interest Rate Increases on the Banking System." *American Economic Review* 35 (March): 16–27.

Smith, Donald J. 1998. "A Note on the Derivation of Closed-Form Formulas for Duration and Convexity Statistics on and between Coupon Dates." *Journal of Financial Engineering* 7:177–193.

Standard & Poor's. 1996. *Standard & Poor's Corporate Ratings Criteria.* New York.

Standard & Poor's. 1997. *Standard & Poor's Ratings Performance 1996—Stability & Transition,* February. New York.

Vasicek, O. 1977. "An Equilibrium Characterization of the Term Structure." *Journal of Financial Economics* 5 (November): 177–188.

Weil, R. L. 1973. "Macauley's Duration: An Appreciation." *Journal of Business* (October): 589–592.

Chapter 22: Modeling the Term Structure

Adams, K. J., and D. R. Van Deventer. 1994. "Fitting Yield Curves and Forward Rate Curves with Maximum Smoothness." *Journal of Fixed Income* (June): 52–62.

Babbel, D. F., C. Merrill, and J. Zacharias. 1996. "Teaching Interest Rate Contigent Claims Pricing." *Journal of Financial Education* 22 (Fall): 41–59.

Bierwag, G. O. 1977. "Immunization, Duration, and the Term Structure of Interest Rates." *Journal of Financial and Quantitative Analysis* (December): 725–741.

Bierwag, G. O., G. G. Kaufman, and C. M. Latta. 1987. "Bond Portfolio Immunization: Tests of Maturity, One- and Two-Factor Duration Matching Strategies." *Financial Review* 22, no. 2 (May): 203–219.

Bierwag, G. O., G. G. Kaufman, and A. Toevs. 1983. "Duration: Its Development and Use in Bond Portfolio Management." *Financial Analysts Journal* (July-August): 15–35.

Chambers, D., W. Carleton, and D. Waldman. 1984. "A New Approach to Estimation of Term Structure of Interest Rates." *Journal of Financial and Quantitative Studies* 19 (3): 233–252.

Coleman, T. S., L. Fisher, and R. Ibbotson. 1992. "Estimating the Term Structure of Interest from Data That Include the Prices of Coupon Bonds." *Journal of Fixed Income* (September): 85–116.

Coleman, T., L. Fisher, and R. Ibbotson. *U.S. Treasury Yield Curves, 1926–1994.* New York: Moody's Investor Service.

de Boor, C. 1978. *A Practical Guide to Splines.* New York: Springer-Verlag.

Diament, Paul. 1993. "Semi-empirical Smooth Fit to the Treasury Yield Curve." *Journal of Fixed Income* 3 (June): 55–70.

Fabozzi, F. J. 1996. *Bond Markets, Analysis and Strategies,* 3rd ed. Upper Saddle River, NJ: Prentice Hall.

Fisher, M., and D. Zervos. 1996. "Yield Curve." In *Computational Economics and Finance: Modeling and Analysis with Mathematica,* ed. H. R. Varian, San Francisco: Telos-Springer. pp. 269–304.

Ho, T. S. Y. 1992. "Key Rate Durations: Measures of Interest Rate Risk." *Journal of Fixed Income* (September): 29–44.

Jarrow, R. A. 1996. *Modeling Fixed Income Securities and Interest Rate Options.* New York: McGraw-Hill.

Jones, F. J. 1991. "Yield Curve Strategies." *Journal of Fixed Income* (September): 43–51.

Jordan, J. V. 1984. "Tax Effects in Term Structure Estimation." *Journal of Finance* 39 (2): 393–406.

Litterman, R., and J. Scheinkman. 1991. "Common Factors Affecting Bond Returns." *Journal of Fixed Income* 2: 54–96.

Mann, S. V., and P. Ramanlal. 1997. "Relative Performance of Yield Curve Strategies." *Journal of Portfolio Management* 23, no. 4 (Summer).

Mann, S. V., and P. Ramanlal. 1998. "Duration and Convexity Measures When the Yield Curve Changes Shape." *Journal of Financial Engineering* 7:35–58.

McCulloch, J. F. 1971. "Measuring the Term Structure of Interest Rates." *Journal of Business* 44:19–31.

McCulloch, J. F. 1975. "The Tax-Adjusted Yield Curve." *Journal of Finance* 30:811–830.

McCullogh, J. H. "U.S. Term Structure Data, 1946–1987." *Handbook of Monetary Economics*, vol. 1: 672–715. Amsterdam: North-Holland.

Nelson, C., and A. Siegel. 1987. "Parsimonious Modeling of Yield Curves." *Journal of Business* 60 (4): 473–489.

Pascual, F. G., http://haribon.winona.msus.edu/mathematica/cubic_splines.html.

Reitano, R. R. 1990. "Non-parallel Yield Curve Shifts and Durational Leverage." *Journal of Portfolio Management* (Summer): 62–67.

Shea, G. 1984. "Pitfalls in Smoothing Interest Rate Term Structure Data: Equilibrium Models and Spline Approximations." *Journal of Financial and Quantitative Analysis,* 19, no. 3 (September): 253–269.

Shea, G. 1985. "Interest Rate Term Structure Estimation with Exponential Splines: A Note." *Journal of Finance* 40 (1): 319–325.

Stigum, M., and F. L. Robinson. 1996. *Money Market and Bond Calculations.* Chicago: Irwin Professional.

Suits, D. B., A. Mason, and L. Chan. 1978. "Spline Functions Fitted by Standard Regression Methods." *Review of Economics and Statistics* 60:132–139.

Sundaresan, S. 1997. *Fixed Income Markets and Their Derivatives.* Cincinnati: South-Western College Publishing.

Taggart, R. 1996. "Some Mathematical Notes on Bond Pricing, Duration and Convexity." Boston University Working Paper, March.

Taggart, R. A., Jr. 1996. *Quantitative Analysis for Investment Management.* Upper Saddle River, NJ: Prentice-Hall.

Tuckman, B., 1996. *Fixed-Income Securities.* New York: Wiley.

Tuckman, Bruce. 1995. *Fixed Income Securities.* New York: Wiley.

Vasicek, O. 1977. "An Equilibrium Characterization of the Term Structure." *Journal of Financial Economics* 5: 177–188.

Vasicek, O., and G. Fong. 1982. "Term Structure Estimation Using Exponential Splines." *Journal of Finance* 38:339–348.

Wahba, G. 1990. *Spline Models for Observational Data.* Philadelphia: SIAM.

Willner, R. 1996. "A New Tool for Portfolio Managers: Level, Slope and Curvature Durations." *Journal of Fixed Income* (June): 48–59.

Chapter 24: Cheapest to Deliver

Benninga, S., and A. Protopapadakis. 1983. "Real and Nominal Interest Rates under Uncertainty: The Fisher Theorem and the Term Structure." *Journal of Political Economy* 91 (October): 856–867.

Benninga, S., and A. Protopapadakis. 1994. "Forward and Future Prices with Markovian Interest Rate Processes." *Journal of Business* 67:401–421.

Benninga, S., and Z. Wiener. 1999."An Investigation of Cheapest to Deliver on Treasury Bond Futures Contracts." *Journal of Computational Finance* 2: 39–56.

Bierwag, G. O., G. G. Kaufman, and A. Toevs. 1983. "Duration: Its Development and Use in Bond Portfolio Management." *Financial Analysts Journal* (July-August): 15–35.

Boyle, P. 1989. "The Quality Option and the Timing Option in Futures Contracts." *Journal of Finance* 44:101–113.

Cox, J. C., J. E. Ingersoll, and S. A. Ross. 1981. "The Relation between Forward and Futures Prices." *Journal of Financial Economics* 9:321–346.

Cox, J. C., J. E. Ingersoll, and S. A. Ross. 1985. "A Theory of the Term Structure of Interest Rates." *Econometrica* 53:363–384.

Edwards, F. R., and C. W. Ma. 1992. *Futures & Options.* New York: McGraw-Hill.

Hanweck, G. A., Jr. 1995. "An Asset Pricing Formula for Interest-Rate Derivative Assets with'Application to Eurodollar Futures and Option." Unpublished working paper.

Hegde, S. 1988. "An Empirical Analysis of Implicit Delivery Options in the Treasury Bond Futures Contract." *Journal of Banking and Finance* 12:469–492.

Hemler, Michael L. 1990. "The Quality Delivery Option in Treasury Bond Futures Contracts." *Journal of Finance* 45 (December): 1565–1586.

Hull, John. 1991. *Introduction to Futures and Options Markets.* Englewood Cliffs, NJ: Prentice Hall.

Jarrow, R., and G. Oldfield. 1981. "Forward Contracts and Futures Contracts." *Journal of Financial Economics* 9:373–382.

Jones, R. A. 1985. "Conversion Factor Risk in Treasury Bond Futures: Comment." *Journal of Futures Markets* 5 (1): 115–119.

Kane, A., and A. J. Marcus. 1984. "Conversion Factor Risk and Hedging in the Treasury-Bond Futures Market." *Journal of Futures Markets* 4: 55–64.

Kilcollin, T. E. 1982. "Difference Systems in Financial Futures Markets." *Journal of Finance* 37 (December): 1183–1197.

Lucas, R. E., Jr. 1978. "Asset Prices in an Exchange Economy." *Econometrica* 46:1429–1445.

Richard, S., and M. Sundaresan. 1981. "A Continuous Time Equilibrium Model of Forward Prices and Futures Prices in a Multigood Economy." *Journal of Financial Economics* 9:321–371.

Ronn, E. I., and R. R. Bliss, Jr. 1994. "A Nonstationary Trinomial Model for the Valuation of Options on Treasury Bond Futures Contracts." *Journal of Futures Markets* 14:597–617.

Sundaresan, M. S. 1991. "Futures Prices on Yields, Forward Prices, and Implied Forward Prices from Term Structure." *Journal of Financial and Quantitative Analysis* 26 (3):409–424.

Vasicek, O. 1977. "An Equilibrium Characterization of the Term Structure." *Journal of Financial Economics* 5:177–188.

Chapter 25: Random Numbers

Abramowicz, M., and I. A. Stegun. 1972. *Handbook of Mathematical Functions.* New York: Dover Publications.

Knuth, D. E. 1981. *The Art of Computer Programming,* vol. 2: *Seminumerical Algorithms,* 2nd ed. Reading, MA: Addison-Wesley.

Index